A Practical Rhetoric of Expository Prose

A Practical Rhetoric of Expository Prose

THOMAS S. KANE
LEONARD J. PETERS

The University of Connecticut

New York OXFORD UNIVERSITY PRESS 1966

Library of Congress Catalogue Card Number: 66-14483
Printed in the United States of America

For H. S. K., N. P., and J. M. K.

ACKNOWLEDGMENTS

We wish to thank the following publishers and persons for allowing us to quote material from their publications:

University of Alabama Press: From William March, 99 *Fables*, University of Alabama Press, 1960.

E. P. Dutton & Co., Inc.: From H. M. Tomlinson, *The Sea and the Jungle*, New York, E. P. Dutton & Co., Everyman's Library, 1928; Gerald Duckworth & Co., Ltd., London.

Harcourt, Brace, & World, Inc.: From *The Modern Researcher* by Jacques Barzun and Henry F. Graff, copyright © 1957, by Jacques Barzun. Reprinted by permission of Harcourt, Brace & World, Inc. From *A Walker in the City*, copyright 1951, by Alfred Kazin. Reprinted by permission of Harcourt, Brace & World, Inc.

Harper & Row, Publishers: pp. 103–105, "A Cure for the Blues" from *The $30,000 Bequest and Other Stories* by Mark Twain (Harper & Brothers, 1917). Reprinted by permission of Harper & Row, Publishers.

Longmans, Green & Co., Ltd.: From G. M. Trevelyan, *History of England*, London, Longmans, Green & Co., 1929.

G. & C. Merriam Company: By permission. From *Webster's Seventh New Collegiate Dictionary*, copyright 1965 by G. & C. Merriam Company, Publishers of the Merriam-Webster Dictionaries.

Putnam's and Coward-McCann: From Richard E. (Admiral) Byrd, *Alone*, New York, G. P. Putnam's Sons, copyright 1938, by Richard E. Byrd.

Mrs. Helen Thurber: Copr. © 1948 James Thurber from "Ivorytown, Rinsoville, Anacinburg, and Crisco Corners" in *The Beast in Me and Other Animals*, published by Harcourt, Brace & World, Inc. Copr. © 1933, 1961 James Thurber. From "University Days" in *My Life and Hard Times*, published by Harper and Row. For permission to quote from these two works by James Thurber we are indebted to Hamish Hamilton, Ltd., London.

We should like also to thank the editorial staff of Oxford University Press, and all those who read our work in manuscript, for their valuable advice and generous assistance.

A PREFACE TO THE STUDENT

It is easy to be overwhelmed by the difficulty of writing, especially after one gets back his first paper and sees the teacher's marginal notations in glaring red ink, pointing out mistakes one hadn't even known existed. It takes a hardy soul not to feel discouragement at that point. Matters even grow a little worse when one begins to realize that learning to write is a constant, never-ending process. There are things one can learn to do in an absolute and final sense—learning to type for instance. There is a period of painful fumbling: one strikes a good many wrong keys, erases constantly, swears a bit. But ultimately there comes a moment of achievement; one has mastered the machine and types away confidently. The process of learning is over.

Unfortunately the process of learning to write is never over. For most of us writing is and remains hard work. William James, who wrote a great deal and who wrote very well, once remarked that "everything comes out wrong with me at first." But, he went on, once he had his composition in a crude shape he could "torture and poke and scrape and pat it until it offends me no more." It is hard for the beginner to accept the fact that "everything comes out wrong . . . at first," to realize that good writing usually starts out as bad writing and only slowly becomes good by painstaking work.

Yet if it is easy to feel discouraged about learning to write, there is no need for despair. Things are not all black. Writing can be taught and it can be learned. One must be willing to work and to take time, to study good prose systematically and thoroughly and to apply in his own writing what he has observed. Anyone who will do these things can learn to write clear, effective prose. This book tries to make the task of learning a little easier by setting out what a student needs to know about composition in order to write the kind of prose he is expected to write in college. It discusses specific problems of composition and shows how good writers have dealt with these problems.

If one applies himself, then, and if he respects but is not overwhelmed by the complexities of writing, he will learn to write exposition. Probably it will not be great exposition. But it will be clear, workmanlike prose. And this is no small achievement. It has important practical benefits. No matter what one's profession is to be, the ability to express his thoughts on paper will contribute to his success. Aside from these practical considerations, writing is in itself an endlessly fascinating and satisfying activity. As James implies, it is often frustrating; but when one has tortured and poked and scraped his work into shape and knows at last that he has succeeded in saying what he set out to say, then the satisfaction is very great.

A PREFACE TO THE TEACHER

Every English teacher has his own theory of how composition should be taught. This diversity of opinion derives, at least in part, from the very nature of the subject. Composition involves grammar, usage, style, and logic; it necessarily deals with ideas, feelings, and social, political, and ethical attitudes; and it requires knowledge, imagination, and sensibility. Any one of these can serve—and has served—as the foundation of a course in composition. Our own feeling is that one way to teach writing is to regard it as a rational, conscious activity and systematically to discuss the techniques of prose expression with a wealth of example and explanation. In this way the student will grow aware that good prose is not something that just happens, but is rather the result of an orderly process of mind.

So serious and detailed a study of prose is perhaps more than the average student bargains for. But it constitutes—or so it seems to us—the essential subject matter of a course in composition. If composition may claim any body of knowledge that is uniquely its own and that does not belong more properly to grammar or logic or literary criticism or sociology, that knowledge surely concerns how prose functions as a vehicle for the communication of thought. Too often this is exactly what freshman English is not about. The old tradition of rhetoric, which did pursue this end, remains tenuous despite attempts to revive it. As courses in composition have come to be less and less about the "art of composing," English teachers have cast in other seas for content for their lectures and discussions. This book attempts to reassert the primacy of writing as the legitimate subject matter of the class in composition. It tries to treat the art of expository prose systematically and thoroughly in order to provide a body of information complex and extensive enough to constitute a subject matter worthy of the name.

To treat all phases of prose composition in fine detail, however, would require not one book, but a dozen. We have restricted this text to expository writing, which we have tried to study more intensively than is usually done. Our justification for this narrow scope—if justification is needed—must be that exposition is what most college students are asked to write. If they are to learn how, they have got to be told as precisely as possible what exposition is.

Even restricted to expository writing, the book has proved difficult to organize. Probably there is no fully satisfactory way to arrange a course in composition. The subject separates into too many categories and these overlap one another too intricately. Our plan has been to move from the large unit to the small, beginning with the essay and ending with diction. This is not, certainly, the only possible scheme, but it does seem to fit the needs of the beginning writer. Students ought to be set to writing essays as quickly as possible, and we have found it more profitable to work from the larger unit of composition to the smaller than the other way round. Still, our organization is far from inflexible. We have tried to keep each section relatively self-contained so that any instructor who desires to follow some other sequence may easily do so.

In hopes of making the task of correcting papers easier for the teacher and more useful for the student, we have provided not only the conventional set of correction symbols, but also a supplementary list of abbreviations which may be used in conjunction with those symbols. These abbreviations allow the instructor to pinpoint the student's mistake without having to write a long explanation in a narrow margin. They seem to us to fill a very real need. It does not benefit a beginner very much to be told merely that a phrase is "DEAD." He is helped more if he is informed by means of a notation like "DEAD. (d.w.d.)" that the phrase is deadwood because it makes a "distinction without a difference." Consulting the page to which the abbreviation "(d.w.d.)" refers him, he can learn what a distinction without a difference is.

But of course to provide a set of abbreviations that would anticipate with absolute precision all the errors inexperienced writers make would tax the mind of an Aristotle. And it would try the patience of a Job to make practical use of such a compendium. We have arranged matters, therefore, so that no teacher need refer his students to these abbreviations unless he wants to. The conventional symbols printed on pages 577–9 are perfectly adequate for correcting themes. The list of abbreviations is no more than a supplement allowing for somewhat greater precision.

CONTENTS

INTRODUCTION

1
COMMUNICATION AND RHETORIC

Communication occurs when one successfully uses words (or some other set of signs) to reveal one's mind to other people, honestly and clearly. Communication must be distinguished from manipulation, which is using words in order to make people do what one wants without revealing what is really in one's mind. When words are employed either for communication or for manipulation, they become the special concern of the rhetorician. At various periods and in various hands rhetoric has sometimes been the art of communication, sometimes the art of manipulation, and sometimes a little of both. We shall restrict the term *rhetoric* to the study of how to employ words for communication, and primarily for the purpose of conveying information. This is a deliberately narrow sense of *rhetoric,* as the term may be, and often is, applied more broadly.

To understand what rhetoric entails, it is necessary to have some idea of what communication is. It is, for one thing, a complicated process, and it extends in many directions. Psychologists, sociologists, linguists, philosophers, mathematicians, and engineers (as well as English teachers) all have something to say about communication. Our discussion here cannot be very technical or very profound; we need simply to understand, in a rough way, what one is doing when he sits down to write an essay, that is, when he sits down to communicate himself to others.

Communication has four phases. It begins with what we shall call the *notion;* this is the original and generally ill-defined idea, mood, or feeling the would-be writer seeks to convey. The second step is *writing,* which is a rational activity of mind requiring forethought and conscious attention to what one is doing. The words that are written constitute the *expression,* the specific sentence or paragraph or essay as it exists on paper; the expression is what the reader sees. *Reading,* not simply the physical act of scanning the page, but the intellectual activity of understanding the expression, completes the process. If the writer has done his job, choosing his words wisely and arranging them clearly, and if the reader has contributed his part, thinking as well as seeing, one man's mind has been opened to another's. Communication has occurred. The process, of course, is much more complicated than all this suggests, and it will pay us to examine a little more closely each of the four aspects of communication, even though we do no more than scratch the surface of the complexities they involve.

The Elements of Communication

THE NOTION

"Notion" is not an entirely happy choice to designate the impulse that sets off the process of communication. Yet "notion" will do so long as it is understood in a very broad sense to include ideas, perceptions, information, emotions, desires, intentions — anything, in short, capable of being expressed, directly or indirectly, in words. Notion exists in the mind of the writer; it is what he *wants* to say. Notion comprises an enormously complicated mass of experience and knowledge, of hopes and fears, of beliefs and biases and principles. It should not be confused with either the content or the meaning of the expression.

Content is the information that is literally conveyed by the written sentence or paragraph. The information may be about the world outside the writer (as in the sentence "The moon is full tonight"); or about the world within ("I am sad today"). The information may be true in the sense that it agrees with the state of things it refers to (if the moon *is* full, the content of the sentence is true), or it may be false, whether jokingly, mistakenly, or mendaciously.

Meaning, on the other hand, is the full significance of the expression in relation to the occasion on which it was made, that is, with reference to the writer and the reader. When, for example, a young lady says to her escort, "The moon is full tonight," the chances are that she "means" something quite different than what an astronomer would mean when speaking the same words to his class. The content — in the narrow sense in which we have defined it — is the same in the two cases; the meaning is not. Meaning, then, includes content, but it includes as well another aspect of the expression called tone.

Tone is a function of style, and style amounts to the kinds of words and sentence patterns the writer has chosen as the vehicle of his content. It is obvious that by selecting different words people can convey the same content with different meanings: Juliet's "silver'd orb" does *not* mean what the astronomer's "moon" means, although it refers to the same heavenly body. The attitude toward his subject, his reader, and himself suggested by a writer's style is called tone. Just as a young lady can imply a variety of moods by the intonations with which she speaks the words "The moon is full tonight," so the writer, by diction, syntax, and rhythm, can create various tones to suggest different attitudes.

The "meaning" of a sentence or paragraph or essay, then, refers to the total significance, relevant to the context in which it was expressed, of its content and tone. In varying degrees both content and tone enter into everything people write. Even where content is plainly predominant, as in objective, scientific prose, some implications of tone will enter into meaning. Even in the most impassioned eloquence, where tone is exceedingly important, content helps to determine meaning; indeed, content cannot be excluded from words unless one speaks gibberish.

If a writer is competent, the meaning of his passage will correspond more or less closely to his original notion. Probably the meaning will be an improved version of notion — better organized, more clearly focused, more subtly qualified. Occasionally the meaning may be inferior to the notion, though only the writer could know that it was. One Romantic poet, for instance, claimed that the best poem was the one existing in the mind and that what the poet wrote down on paper was only a shadow of this inner poem. In any case, notion is not identical with meaning. Notion is the raw material of communication; meaning is what emerges when that material has been shaped and polished by the process of expressing it.

WRITING

A writer is not simply someone engaged in a physical activity — an eighth-grader, pencil clutched in hand; or a college freshman desperately hunched over his typewriter. Rather he is someone engaged in a rational exercise of mind. Admittedly, much that people do is not rational; still, writing, as a conscious art (and very little good writing is achieved unconsciously) is a reasoned activity requiring experience, knowledge, intelligence, and imagination.

There is no reason to suppose, however, that to write well one must have a special kind of intelligence, or even general intelligence of a markedly high order. No doubt the more intelligent the writer, the greater his ability to select what is important to his purpose and to organize his material effectively. But the idea that good writing requires extraordinary talent is nonsense. It is an idea that seems quite popular with students, who often believe that writing, like perfect pitch, is a genetic gift: either one has it or one does not, and in the first case there is no need of learning composition, while in the second there is no hope. Such a belief flatters the ancestry of those who write well and offers at the same time a convenient rationalization for those who do not. Still the theory is wrong. Good writing is an art that can be — and for 99 per cent of us must be — learned. Certainly to write great prose, as distinguished from the merely good or competent, does require an extraordinary ability — whether it be called talent, aptitude, verbal skill, or genius — though even here the genius must be sharpened by conscious practice and knowledge. But it is false and self-defeating to suppose that there is only great prose and bad prose. In between lies the vast range of good prose, and anyone of normal intelligence who is willing to take the pains may learn to write it.

With genius or without, there is no doubt that the intelligence, the knowledge, and the experience which the writer brings to bear upon the notion he starts with are vitally important if that notion is to be communicated. More often than not they creatively transform what they touch. One does not have to write very much before he realizes that writing is a kind of discovery. The very effort to express a notion leads the mind to new insights and new ideas and changes the essence of the old ones. We are not suggesting that a writer cannot know what he wants to say until he has written; but simply that, until one has written one cannot know what one *has* said, and that often what one does say is richer and fuller than the notion one started with.

Thus the writer transforms notion into expression. As he works he must keep one eye upon his reader, who stands, in a sense, between the writer and what he writes. The relationship between reader and writer is not direct, as it is for an audience and a speaker; yet it is very real. Or rather it is real for the good writer; poor or inexperienced writers all too often pay scant attention to their readers or, which is worse, never conceive that readers exist. "I know what I mean," these innocents answer to the complaint that their prose is not clear. One doubts that they really do, but in any case the point they forget is that writing is rarely self-expression — it is communication, and for communication to take place it is necessary that the reader know what they mean. Since different sorts of readers will require different degrees of help from the writer if they are to comprehend him, it follows that the reader does intrude in a way between the writer and his prose and so helps to shape that prose. A scholar, for instance, cannot use learned words as frequently or as easily for a general audience as he can for his fellow scholars, who share his special knowledge and interests. Nor is the reader's impact upon the expression merely the passive one of forcing minor changes in wording. Often the very effort to clarify ideas for particular readers leads to the substantial enlargement or qualification of the ideas themselves. Writing, we have said, is a kind of discovery. The discoveries are increased and deepened for the writer who is aware of his ultimate connection with a reader. For effective communication, a conscious, intelligent concern with his reader is as much a part of the writer's function as the analysis and organization of his thought.

THE VERBAL EXPRESSION

The verbal expression is the piece of prose that results from the writing activity. At its simplest the expression is a single word. But while words are the building blocks of prose, people do not often communicate in single words. The sentence is generally the minimum unit of expression in formal written prose. There are units, of course, that lie between the word and the sentence—phrases and clauses, for instance. These are important parts of sentences and occasionally stand in their place; even so, they are rarely employed as independent constructions in expository writing. Beyond the sentence lie such larger units of expression as the paragraph, the paragraph group, and the essay.

Whether it be a single sentence or an entire book, the form the expression takes is determined in part by the original notion; in part by the analysis and organization which the writer imposes upon that notion; and in part by the writer-reader relationship. The fact that all these things affect the expression complicates it enormously. But however complicated it may become, the purpose of any piece of prose is to communicate meaning. The process of communication begins in the writer. It ends when something happens in the reader. The hinge upon which it all turns is the expression. It is in the words written upon the page that the minds of writer and reader will meet, if they are to meet at all. It is here that the writer's task ends and the reader's begins. Because it is so central to communication — in a sense both its end and its beginning — the systematic study of all the various forms the expression may take is the heart of rhetoric. Most of this book will be concerned with those forms: the essay, the paragraph, the sentence, and ultimately the word, which underlies them all.

THE READER

For the moment we are surveying the total process of communication, the fourth and final element of which is the reader. The reader is a very important part of what goes on in communication. If he does not understand or respond, there is, in fact, no communication at all. Therefore the writer needs to know something about his reader. This is true even for the most objective, scientific prose, where concern for the reader is likely (and quite rightly) to be at a minimum, and it is all the more true for the more common kinds of expository writing. Of the numerous things that a writer ought to consider about his readers these are the most important: (1) Who are they? (2) What do I wish to do for them? (3) What sort of style will best do it? The second and third considerations we shall discuss in a later chapter. Here we shall concentrate upon the first question.

Determining who one's readers are is not so simple as might be supposed. Every audience will possess a set of characteristics which in effect defines them. These characteristics can be gathered under two considerations: (1) whether the audience is general or restricted; and (2) whether the writer regards them essentially as equal to himself or as unequal. "General" and "restricted," obviously, are relative terms. An absolutely restricted reader would be exemplified by a young lady reading a love letter (her own, we had better add), though even here it is likely, if it is a good love letter, that its writer had held in mind some general conception of young ladies as a class as well as a sharp image of the girl he addressed. Such one-reader audiences, however, do not concern us. With the multi-reader audiences in which we are interested it is never easy to draw the line between restricted and general; between writing for fifty or a hundred persons and writing for all adult twentieth-century Americans there is a wide range of potential audiences. But usually it is not difficult in the specific case to determine the range of readers a writer intends to reach. The author of a book entitled *English Pulpit Oratory from Andrewes to Tillotson,* for example, is plainly aiming at a much smaller and more specialized set of readers than the author of *Why Johnny Can't Read.*

Not only must he consider how wide or narrow his audience will be, the writer must also decide whether they stand in relative equality to himself, or above, or below him. Very roughly, reader and writer may be equal or unequal with respect to: (1) general intelligence, culture, and education; (2) special knowledge; (3) motivation and purpose; (4) ethical and political values; (5) social and economic position. The point is not that the reader and writer are or are not in fact equal, but rather that the writer regards or does not regard his readers as equals. Sometimes a writer will succeed better in communicating his ideas by treating readers who know much less than he does as if they were fully as knowledgeable. Sometimes he must recognize that a true equality does exist; and sometimes, though this is less common in a democratic society, he will find it best to write from a height of conscious superiority. In any event, some suggestion of equality or nonequality cannot be avoided when one writes. The careful writer will be aware of such suggestions and make them work for him, not against him. We have all been offended by those name-droppers and users of big words who assume a superiority we are unwilling to grant them. On the other hand, many of us have been made uncomfortable by people who assume an equality which our consciousness either of our own inferiority or of theirs will not allow us to accept.

But if a writer gauges correctly the nature of his audience, he will simplify his task considerably. With readers who know about his special subject the writer may be more concise, using technical terms, for example, without explanation; he may leave the processes of his thought implicit, or contrarily he may reveal them in great detail, knowing in either case that his readers have the information and the capacity to follow him. When he aims at general readers, the writer needs to remember that they require more help; technical terms do have to be defined on the first occasion of their use; the logical connection between sentences may have to be literally stated and not left to the reader to infer; and sentences may have to be kept simpler. With readers who are his social and cultural equals the writer may be more relaxed, able to assume a common ground of value and attitude; with readers who are not, he may have to be on his best behavior or work actively to arouse their sympathy and interest. In short, the writer must think, and think hard, about his readers — about their knowledge and intelligence and interests, about the values by which they live, about the needs and motives they bring to the act of reading. The more he considers these matters, the more it is likely that the writer will succeed in what he set out to do — communicate.

Rhetoric

A BRIEF HISTORY

Communication, then, is a complicated process that begins in the writer, is carried on by the verbal expression, and concludes in the reader. Rhetoric studies how communication may be best achieved. As a formal study, rhetoric began in the ancient world of the Greek city-states. It was brought into being by the very nature of that world, by the relatively high degree of legal and political freedom enjoyed by the citizen of the Grecian city. Originating as the art of legal pleading, rhetoric soon came to include what we should call political oratory; then, as now, it was a short step from the courtroom to the forum. Many of the ancient states were democracies, and in a more intimate and immediate sense than what we know today. Although the right to vote and so to influence policy and legislation was not so widely distributed as it is in a modern democracy, the much smaller size of the city-state meant that laws and judicial decisions could more easily be affected by the individual efforts of those of its citizens who did have the vote. Thus the citizen-voter of ancient Greece could directly stamp his own beliefs upon the law and the policy of the state. Or rather he could if other citizens would listen to him. And this was the function of rhetoric — to make others listen. In the ancient world, then, rhetoric was preeminently the art of using words to persuade, especially to persuade on questions of politics, law, and ethics.

These are questions that are not capable of being answered in clearly demonstrable ways. In this characteristic they differ from the problems with which science and logic typically deal. If one asks how grape juice becomes wine, science can make an indisputable answer. If one asks whether all X is Z when all X is Y and all Y is Z, logic can tell him. But when people ask, "Should the income tax be raised?" "Should universities be decentralized?" "Should the atom bomb have been dropped at Hiroshima?" they can expect no answers from science or logic, and scientists and logicians, to do them justice, make no pretence of offering any. It was with the art of debating questions like these that ancient rhetoric dealt. The rhetorician taught his student how to select the appropriate argument, how to apply logic in the situation of a debate, how to organize and mount a speech, what devices of style would be effective, what manner of delivery would best suit his purpose.

In a society where a man was his own advocate and where he could stand up and influence the course of political events by the words he spoke, the ability gained from the study of rhetoric was of immeasurable value. Rhetoric therefore played no small part in the education of the well-to-do, and it was especially cultivated by those who aspired to political or intellectual eminence. So great was its importance that teachers of rhetoric were notable, well paid men. A citizen who had special skill in using rhetoric, such as Demosthenes in Athens or Cicero in Rome, was sought out by his fellows to speak on matters of importance or to defend them before the law. Even philosophers concerned themselves with rhetoric. Indeed, the very distinction between philosopher and rhetorician was often not clear-cut; one faded into the other. Cicero, for instance, was both. Aristotle, the greatest thinker of antiquity, wrote a book on rhetoric, the best theoretical treatment of the subject in the ancient world, and perhaps in ours. Plato, less sympathetic to rhetoric and rhetoricians than Aristotle, none the less felt the subject and its professors worth discussion in several of his dialogues.

Rhetoric remained one of the essential elements of education during the entire period of Greco-Roman culture. If with the rise of the Roman Empire the democracy which had given rhetoric its early impetus died away, rhetoric itself remained. In part at least it was sustained by new or expanded areas of controversy, particularly the law and religion. St. Augustine, the most important spokesman of the early Church, began his professional career as a teacher of rhetoric. In *The City of God* and in his *Confessions* he practices the art with no little effectiveness. During the Middle Ages rhetoric maintained its central place in education. It was part of the trivium, the elementary course in the medieval school, consisting of grammar, rhetoric, and logic. And its importance continued through the Renaissance and the early modern period. In the sixteenth century numerous texts of rhetoric were produced, such as Thomas Wilson's *The Arte of Rhetorique,* a book that was studied by thousands of Elizabethan schoolboys, including quite probably William Shakespeare. The seventeenth, eighteenth, and nineteenth centuries continued to produce fine textbooks of rhetoric, their number no doubt a response to the spread of education through the middle class.

By the end of the nineteenth century, however, the luster of rhetoric had dimmed. This loss of prestige was due partly to the success of science, whose methods of investigation and proof had yielded spectacular results, alongside which the claims of rhetoric looked feeble indeed. Partly, too, the tarnish was due to the gross abuse of rhetoric by men of small minds and large ambitions. The spread-eagle oratory of the nineteenth-century politician rang less and less true as Americans grew more sophisticated and as the social and political realities of life grew more complex.

Yet the need for rhetoric remains, and today there are signs that men are beginning to realize that the old rhetorical tradition still has much to give. What lines the renewal of that tradition will take is uncertain. It seems plain that modern rhetoric cannot simply be the ancient *ars rhetorica* in twentieth-century dress. Our world is not the world of Aristotle; our rhetoric cannot be the rhetoric of Aristotle. It must be broader, including the informative as well as the persuasive use of language, the written as well as the spoken word. It must take into account what has been learned about the nature and the pyschology of language — and a great deal has been learned. We cannot pretend to supply this new conception of rhetoric. What we shall treat in this book will be deliberately limited to only one phase of prose composition. But it is worth remembering that this one phase is part of the broader area of rhetoric and that in studying rhetoric you stand in a tradition stretching back 2500 years.

A LIMITED DEFINITION

If rhetoric is restricted to the communicative use of language, it is necessary to see more exactly how it is concerned with that use. "Concerned with" is a hazy expression covering many possible relationships. So broad a phrase is required, however, because rhetoric is both a science and an art. On the one hand, rhetoric is the systematic, theoretical study of how language is employed for purposes of communication. On the other, rhetoric is the practical art of applying to any specific act of communication, the knowledge and the techniques acquired by that study. Because of this double nature, rhetoric is rather different from other subjects a student takes in college, being both an object of study, like physics, and an acquired skill, like drawing or playing the piano. It is possible to emphasize either aspect of rhetoric. Some rhetoricians — Aristotle, for instance, or in our own day I. A. Richards and Kenneth Burke — have been primarily scholars interested in developing a system or theory of rhetoric. Others, like the eighteenth-century rhetorician Hugh Blair, have been teachers concerned with instructing others in the art of using words. This latter emphasis, naturally enough, is the one we share. But theorists or teachers (ideally perhaps they should be both), rhetoricians have always recognized that the ultimate end of rhetoric is to teach the student how to use his language effectively, gracefully, precisely. It is well to remember that studying the technicalities of verbal communication is the means, and that acquiring the skill to communicate is the end.

It is now a little clearer what we mean when we say that rhetoric is "concerned with" language. But what do we mean by language? Very broadly, a language may be understood to be a system of signs shared by at least two (usually many more) persons; these signs, because they stand for other things and because they may be arranged in significant patterns according to formal rules, are capable of conveying information. In this sense, of course, there are many kinds of languages, depending upon the kinds of signs involved. Musical notes, the symbols of chemistry or physics or algebra, the hand signals of the American Indian have all been called languages, even though very specialized and in some ways very limited ones. There is even a "language of flowers." The least specialized kind of language — the one capable of conveying the widest variety of information — is that in which the signs are sounds of speech, or, from the special point of view of composition students, words written on paper. It is to the language of words that rhetoric traditionally confines itself, excluding all other types of language (though it is possible to apply rhetorical concepts even to these, as when mathematicians praise an "elegant" solution or when critics speak of an "eloquent and moving" piece of music).

Restricting rhetoric to verbal language still does not fully establish its subject matter. There are all sorts of words and all sorts of occasions for using them. Are poetry *and* prose, a written essay *and* an orally delivered speech, a love letter *and* a baccalaureate sermon all suitable occasions for the study and exercise of rhetoric? In one sense, yes. These are all instances of verbal communication and each will succeed or fail to the extent that its author understood (whether consciously or intuitively) the rhetoric appropriate to it. But in another sense — the narrower sense of rhetoric which we must follow — no.

In this book we cannot be concerned with poetry or with conversation or with speeches. We must confine our interest to written prose, and even more specifically to the relatively formal and public uses of written prose, ruling out all writing that is fictional, casual, or private in purpose. This is not the only proper area of rhetoric. Indeed, for most of the several thousand years during which it has existed as a formal study, rhetoric has been concerned primarily with oral communication and has interested itself in written composition only in so far as this was a preliminary step to speaking or a way of recording orations from the past. This oral traditon is maintained by teachers of speech in our high schools and universities, who certainly have as much right as English teachers to be dispensers of rhetoric, and possibly even more. It is, however, the nature of our culture that we place more emphasis upon the written word than upon the spoken as a vehicle of important, formal communication; and such is the nature of our schools and colleges that composition is taught by departments of English rather than by those of speech. If we here confine the subject matter of rhetoric to written prose, the restriction is not absolute but is merely a convenience which reflects a division of labor inherent in our educational system.

Another restriction we shall make is more arbitrary. Traditionally, rhetoric has been the study of persuasive prose, especially of that variety called argument. We shall change this emphasis and concentrate instead upon expository composition. At the borderline, persuasion and exposition are likely to merge. Generally, however, the distinction is reasonably clear: persuasion is writing that tries to get the reader to believe or to act in a certain way; exposition is writing that seeks simply to convey information to the reader. This information may be about the physical world, as in a guidebook; an explanation of some feature of that world, as in a book on physics; or a statement about the personal attitudes and feelings of the writer, as in a familiar essay. It may be about many things, but always in exposition the writer is chiefly concerned with telling his readers what he believes (or knows) to be true (or untrue) and why he believes (or knows) it. Of course, the writer of exposition usually hopes that his readers, after they have finished, will agree with him. But unlike the persuasive writer, he does not write primarily to convince them. His purpose, finally, comes down to revealing as clearly as he can what is in his mind.

Our concentration in this book upon exposition is not owing to any belief that it is the only proper area of rhetorical study. Argument, satire, eloquence, description, narration — all these must be analyzed and studied from the point of view of rhetoric by anyone who wishes to master them. But these are specialized instruments. Exposition is the prose of all work. It is the kind of writing that college students are expected to learn first, and it is a prerequisite to handling other kinds of prose. The fact that one has learned to write competent exposition is no guarantee that he will be able to compose, say, an effective argument. It does mean, however, that he will have acquired an ability fundamental to all kinds of writing and that he should not find it exceedingly difficult to learn the special techniques of argument or description or eloquence.

For our purposes, then, rhetoric is the systematic study of how one communicates in written expository prose, how he makes clear to readers what he thinks or feels or believes. Even when so restricted, rhetoric is a vast subject. In the pages that follow we shall touch upon a great many things — planning an essay, composing and revising it, constructing paragraphs and sentences, selecting words. There is no necessary sequence in how these matters must be learned. When one writes he does all of them more or less at once. Arbitrarily, we shall begin with the large unit of the essay and work down to the fundamental element of the word. This has the advantage of starting off with something large enough to give you practice in writing at length. That finally is what anyone must do in order to learn to write: he must write, just as often, as honestly, as self-critically as he can.

Summary

Communication is a complex activity. It originates in a *notion* which exists in the mind. Notion is derived both from one's experience of the many-faceted world about him and from his desire to report upon or to change that world. When one thinks about the notion, analyzing it, qualifying it, rearranging its parts, and finally expressing it in words, one becomes a *writer*. What one writes — the words, the sentences, the paragraphs, the total essay — constitutes the *verbal expression*. The expression is the heart of communication, the meeting ground between reader and writer. If we may borrow an analogy from neurophysiology, the expression is the synapse over which the communicative impulse must pass. The *reader*, finally, is not merely a passive element in communication. The good writer imagines his reader always before him. He chooses and arranges his words for readers of a particular sort. In doing so, he often discovers that what he writes is richer and clearer than it would have been had he written only for himself.

Rhetoric has been of central importance to Western education and culture for well over two thousand years. Despite the faltering of that tradition in the late nineteenth and early twentieth centuries, the importance of rhetoric is once more being acknowledged. But a modern rhetoric must include the written as well as the spoken word and the informative as well as the persuasive uses of language. In this book we shall restrict the term *rhetoric* to mean the systematic study of the qualities of good expository prose for the ultimate purpose of learning to write such prose. Good writing is effective writing, and effectiveness means achieving the end one intended to achieve when he began to write. Thus the purpose of rhetoric is to enable writers to attain effectiveness.

I

WRITING AS A PROCESS

We are ready, now, to begin our study of the practical art of exposition. In this section we shall try to give you an overview of the whole writing process, beginning, in the following chapter, with a brief survey of the various types of prose, the different purposes writers bring to their task, and how style and tone, in their general aspects, are related to purpose.

In the other three chapters of this section we shall discuss chiefly the preliminary steps of composition: discovering topics, outlining and organizing the essay, and writing the first draft. We shall conclude with a glance at revising, the final phase of the writing activity.

2

PURPOSE AND THE VARIETIES OF PROSE Style and Tone

Purpose

Even the simplest of writing situations involves many purposes, some conscious, others not, some immediate, others remote. More often than not these purposes work together, one implying others. When one considers this mixture of aims, it seems impossible to reduce purpose to any simple pattern. It can be done, however, if we accept certain limitations. First we shall ignore all nonconscious reasons that impel communication. Subconscious drives and impulses are real and they are important, but they are outside our subject, which is the *conscious* activity of writing. Second we shall exclude such specialized and unusual purposes as in classroom exercises, where there is an inevitable element of artificiality. If the exercise is to be helpful, however, you must at least pretend to have a genuine reason for writing. Finally, we shall not worry about the remote, ultimate goals a writer may have in view, but instead shall concentrate upon the immediate effect he wishes to have upon his reader.

This last is really the important thing. Writing is communication; an essay is written for particular people to read and respond to. The whole question of purpose may be handled quite simply by asking: What is this response supposed to be? How does the writer wish to affect his readers? There are three possible answers: (1) the writer may wish to inform his readers; (2) he may wish to persuade them of something; (3) he may wish to entertain them.

In practice none of these purposes exists by itself; usually all three are present in varying proportions. Indeed, one often requires the others. If people are to be persuaded they will probably first have to be informed, and they may be more susceptible to persuasion if the writer has entertained them a little. Even so, it is true that in most cases one purpose will clearly dominate the others. In the following passage, for example, the writer's purpose is obviously to inform:

> The uranium atom, to be sure, is a wobbly structure. Every now and then one ejects a cluster of protons and neutrons from the center, to leave a less crowded residue. This residue we call radium, and its nucleus in turn also explodes with a series of ejections, breaking down to form the simpler polonium. Finally polonium, after ridding itself of a cluster of 2 protons and 2 neutrons, settles into the stable structure we call lead.
>
> GEORGE W. GRAY, *The Advancing Frontier of Science*

On the other hand, in this passage from the *U.S. Coast Pilot* we see that in addition to informing his reader, the writer also hopes to persuade him to avoid doing something:

> The North Channel through Nantucket Sound has broken ground with depths of 16 to 17 feet in some places. Strangers should not attempt this channel at night. *U.S. Coast Pilot* 2, 6TH ED., 1960

The note of persuasion is clearly predominant in this paragraph:

> Democracy has another merit. It allows criticism, and if there isn't public criticism there are bound to be hushed-up scandals. That is why I believe in the press, despite all its lies and vulgarity, and why I believe in Parliament. The British Parliament is often sneered at because it's a talking shop. Well, I believe in it because it is a talking shop. I believe in the private member who makes himself a nuisance. He gets snubbed and is told that he is cranky or ill-informed, but he exposes abuses which would otherwise never have been mentioned, and very often an abuse gets put right just by being mentioned. E. M. FORSTER, *Two Cheers for Democracy*

And as a final example, we see that the following paragraphs by James Thurber have the immediate purpose of entertaining us:

> Another course that I didn't like, but somehow managed to pass, was economics. I went to that class straight from the botany class, which didn't help me in understanding either subject. I used to get them mixed up. But not as mixed up as another student in my economics class who came there direct from a physics laboratory. He was tackle on the football team, named Bolenciecwcz. At that time Ohio State University had one of the best football teams in the country, and Bolenciecwcz was one of its outstanding stars. In order to be eligible to play it was necessary for him to keep

up in his studies, a very difficult matter, for while he was not dumber than an ox he was not any smarter. Most of his professors were lenient and helped him along. None gave him more hints, in answering questions, or asked him simpler ones than the economics professor, a thin, timid man named Bassum. One day when we were on the subject of transportation and distribution, it came Bolenciecwcz's turn to answer a question. "Name one means of transportation," the professor said to him. No light came into the big tackle's eyes. "Just any means of transportation," said the professor. Bolenciecwcz sat staring at him. "That is," pursued the professor, "any medium, agency, or method of going from one place to another." Bolenciecwcz had the look of a man who is being led into a trap. "You may choose among steam, horse-drawn, or electrically propelled vehicles," said the instructor. "I might suggest the one which we commonly take in making long journeys across land." There was a profound silence in which everybody stirred uneasily, including Bolenciecwcz and Mr. Bassum. Mr. Bassum abruptly broke this silence in an amazing manner. "Choo-choo-choo," he said, in a low voice, and turned instantly scarlet. He glanced appealingly around the room. All of us, of course, shared Mr. Bassum's desire that Bolenciecwcz should stay abreast of the class in economics, for the Illinois game, one of the hardest and most important of the season, was only a week off. "Toot, toot, too-tooooooot!" some student with a deep voice moaned, and we all looked encouragingly at Bolenciecwcz. Somebody else gave a fine imitation of a locomotive letting off steam. Mr. Bassum himself rounded off the little show. "Ding, dong, ding, dong," he said, hopefully. Bolenciecwcz was staring at the floor now, trying to think, his great brow furrowed, his huge hands rubbing together, his face red.

"How did you come to college this year, Mr. Bolenciecwcz?" asked the professor. "*Chuffa*, chuffa, *chuffa*, chuffa."

"M'father sent me," said the football player.

"What on?" asked Bassum.

"I git an 'lowance," said the tackle, in a low, husky voice, obviously embarrassed.

"No, no," said Bassum. "Name a means of transportation. What did you *ride* here on?"

"Train," said Bolenciecwcz.

"Quite right," said the professor. "Now Mr. Nugent, will you tell us—" "UNIVERSITY DAYS," *My Life and Hard Times*

Except possibly for the first it is certainly true of these examples that their purposes are not simple. Below the surface of its humor Thurber's passage informs us of athleticism in college and subtly persuades us that such abuse of intellectual values is wrong. E. M. Forster, who wishes to persuade us of the virtues of democracy, is also informing us about his own beliefs and doing it so skillfully that we are entertained. But recognizing these complexities, we may still say that Thurber's immediate purpose is to entertain while Forster's is to persuade. It is fair to conclude that a writer's purpose — in the sense of the immediate effect he desires to have upon his reader — will come down to one or to some combination of these three: to inform, to persuade, to entertain.

Learning to recognize your purpose is an important preliminary to writing well. It is, indeed, the first important thing to consider. "How," you must say to yourself, "do I wish to affect my reader? Do I want to convey to him information which I know but he doesn't? Do I wish to tell him how to do something? Do I want to assure him that I know the material upon which he is testing me? Do I want to persuade him to believe as I do? Do I hope to change his behavior? Do I want to amuse him?" Without asking — and answering — such questions, you will find it difficult to write effectively. A clear sense of purpose is fundamental because it determines everything else that you do. Thus Mr. Forster's desire to persuade leads him to repeat "I believe," an iteration that is effective in persuasion but might very well prove irritating in exposition. And Thurber, trying to amuse us, introduces details of Bolenciecwcz's massiveness — "his great brow furrowed, his huge hands rubbing together" — which emphasize the comic disparity of all this physical might rendered impotent by a simple question in elementary economics. It is a good idea, then, to get into the habit of thinking about purpose before you begin to write — or even to plan — your essay. In fact, as a preliminary step to writing, jot down in a sentence or two what your purpose is. You may find as you go along that your aim will shift, but even so the initial step of writing a statement of purpose will have helped you discover what you really want to do, and it will certainly have kept you from forgetting purpose altogether.

The Varieties of Prose

From this simplified analysis of purpose are derived the basic kinds of writing which rhetoric traditionally studies: informative prose, persuasive prose, and entertaining prose. While we shall confine our interest in this book to only one variety of the first of these, it will help to understand both the aims and the limitations of exposition if we mention the chief subdivisions of each of the three primary types of prose.

Informative writing includes exposition, description, and simple narration. The term *exposition* is difficult to define. Often it is employed broadly to designate what we have called "informative writing." We are using the word in a narrower sense to signify the kind of informative writing that seeks to explain and analyze and explore. Exposition may be about many things, but whatever its subject, the essence of exposition is that it probes and expands. In this sense, a textbook on sociology, an article on French politics, an essay on the doubts and uncertainties of the new college student, an analysis of a poem, are all cases of exposition. Most of what you write in English compositions and in term papers for your other courses will be exposition. Exposition, in short, is the most important kind of writing for the college student, and what we shall say in this book about organizing the essay, developing paragraphs, handling sentences and words, will primarily concern expository writing.

Despite its importance, exposition is only one kind of informative writing. A second kind is description. In description the writer attempts to translate a perceptual experience into words. Usually that experience is visual and therefore the subject of most descriptive writing is something that can be seen — a city street, a house, the ocean building under a northeaster. But description can and does appeal to the other senses, and it is possible to describe how a tornado sounds or how velvet feels or what wine tastes like, though the problem of rendering these other perceptions into words is rather more difficult. Depending upon whether the writer confines himself to what his senses literally report or whether he includes his emotional responses to what he saw or heard, description falls into at least two subvarieties. These are distinctions, however, that need not concern us.

The last type of informative writing is simple narration. Where the subject of description is commonly a visual entity existing in space, the subject of narration is a series of events arranged in time. Usually these events involve human beings, but human actors are not inevitably necessary to narration; animals or machines or sometimes even abstractions like the Roman Empire may function as the dramatis personae in a piece of narrative writing. In distinguishing the kind of narration that is a subdivision of informative writing we used the qualifier "simple." This is because much narration is of a more complicated sort, as in the short story, the novel, and the play, and is properly a variety of creative writing and not generally included in the subject matter of rhetoric. In the sort of general informative writing you are expected to do in college, however, you will now and then find it necessary to tell a story, to tell, for example, in a simple and straightforward way what Cortez did in Mexico or how you spent last Thursday. On these occasions you will be writing simple narration.

The second major category of prose is persuasive writing, which was what the ancient rhetoricians were chiefly concerned with. Persuasion is equally important in our culture. One need only remember the part advertising plays in our lives or observe the streams of propaganda which run ceaselessly at all levels of politics. If anything, persuasive prose is less escapable in twentieth-century life than it was in ancient Athens, even though it occupies relatively less attention in our schools. Broadly, persuasion is writing that attempts to change the convictions, and frequently the activities, of the reader. Where the informative writer enlarges our experience, the persuasive writer tries to alter our values or attitudes. Whether he appeals to their good side or their bad, the writer of persuasion hopes to modify the allegiance of his audience — to turn atheists into Christians (or Christians into atheists), to make Democrats of Republicans, or enthusiastic customers out of an apathetic public. There are, of course, many kinds and shades of persuasion, ranging from purely theoretical conviction to incitements to riot, and there are many ways of persuading. Generally, however, persuasive prose will fall into one or another of four basic types: argument, eloquence, satire, and invective.

Argument makes its appeal to our reason, asking us to believe the writer's contention on the basis of evidence or because it has been demonstrated to be logically valid. While it is impossible completely to exclude emotionalism in any kind of persuasion that uses words, argument tries to restrict emotional appeal as rigorously as possible and never substitutes it for logic or evidence.

The other kinds of persuasive prose, however, do concentrate upon emotion. This does not mean that eloquence, satire, or invective are necessarily irrational and despicable. The reforms at which the satirist or the writer of eloquence aims may be fully as "reasonable" as those of argument (indeed they may be even more reasonable). The point is simply that in order to get us to accept those ends satire and eloquence appeal primarily to our emotions, even though in the end they may make us more reasonable men. In eloquence the appeal is to our nobler emotions, to our sense of obligation, our patriotism, our courage. Eloquence rings upon words like *duty, honor, country;* its sentence rhythms play upon our feelings; it avoids expressions which suggest the cynical world in which ideals cannot survive. Needless to say, our conception of eloquence is culturally and historically conditioned; the Churchillian prose of 1942 was hardly eloquent to Germans. But if a writer is seeking to move his audience by appealing to their ideals, it is fair to regard his prose as eloquent, even though we do not share his ideals.

Satire, on the other hand, aims at our sense of the ridiculous. By devices like exaggeration and irony the satirist tries to persuade us of the folly or the immorality of an action or belief. There is implied satire, for example, in the passage by James Thurber on page 20. While his immediate purpose is to amuse us, Thurber also desires that we recognize that an important value is being violated.

Invective — persuasion by insult — is less common than it used to be, at least in polite circles. It appears now and then. H. L. Mencken was very skillful at it. Here is his description of the politician William Jennings Bryan:

> He was the most sedulous flycatcher in American history, and by long odds the most successful. His quarry, of course, was not *Musca domestica* but *Homo neandertalensis*. For forty years he tracked it with snare and blunderbuss, up and down the backways of the Republic. Wherever the flambeaux of Chautauqua smoked and guttered, and the bilge of Idealism ran in the veins, and Baptist pastors dammed the brooks with the saved, and men gathered who were weary and heavy laden, and their wives who were unyieldingly multiparous and full of Peruna—there the indefatigable Jennings set up his traps and spread his bait.
>
> *The American Mercury*, OCTOBER 1925

The passage offers no evidence of Bryan's demagoguery; it does not satirize him; it simply bludgeons him with insult (along with the Chautauqua movement, backwoods idealism, and Baptist pastors).

In practice the writer of persuasion is likely to employ several or all of these ways of writing, but chances are that he will rely predominantly upon one, and that therefore his prose may be fairly described as argument or satire or eloquence or invective.

The last of the major categories of composition we called entertaining prose. The label is not really adequate. All good writing is capable of entertaining a responsive reader. Still it is obvious that Thurber's account of Bolenciecwcz and economics has as its immediate purpose to amuse, and that what you read in your history text entertains you only incidentally, its main purpose being to inform. Much entertaining writing succeeds by creating and releasing tension. A simple case is the arousal and satisfaction of curiosity in a detective story. In humor the release is achieved through laughter; in the thriller, by providentially rescuing the reader from fictional danger. The bulk of this kind of writing belongs to creative literature and is outside the limits of rhetoric. There is, however, a border area between creative literature of the more imaginative sort and informative writing, and here belongs what is known as the familiar essay. The entertainment value of the familiar (also called the personal) essay derives less from the release of fictionally created tension than from the revelation of personality. Most people are fascinated by personality, and the familiar essayist, by reacting to and commenting upon the world he and his readers share in common, satisfies that fascination. The satisfaction is all the stronger because usually his audience are in effect reading about themselves, or at least about what they dream themselves to be. The familiar essayist becomes a kind of second self who expresses attitudes and beliefs his readers also feel. (If they do not share his beliefs, people do not generally read a familiar essayist; he does not entertain them.) All this does not deny the persuasive or informative element in familiar writing; it is there — as we have seen in Thurber's case. It is merely to say that the immediate value to be found in familiar writing is entertainment.

We should not wish to leave you with the impression that "exposition," "description," "narration," "argument," "satire," "eloquence," are labels for clearly defined pigeon-holes to one or another of which any particular essay or paragraph must be assigned. Teachers, as we shall warn you from time to time, tend to chop up their subjects into bits and pieces; it is easier to handle them that way. But often such analyses, necessary as they are for teaching, ought not to be taken too literally. That is certainly the case here. The chances are that any composition of appreciable length will contain at least several of the varieties of prose we have mentioned. This paragraph will be expository, that descriptive, the next argumentative. Still it will prove useful to employ the terms we have mentioned. They enable one to label, even if only tentatively and too simply, the predominant mode of particular paragraphs and essays.

Style

We have seen that writers have different purposes which give rise to different kinds of prose. How these are handled results in what is called style. Style is a complicated matter, and if we pause here for a moment to consider it, it will prove helpful later on. All rhetorical teaching is finally an effort to awaken in the beginning writer an awareness of style. Most of what we discuss in the remainder of this book concerns style. What, then, is style?

The term has been so loosely applied that it has meant a great many quite different things. In some contexts it implies an elaborate beauty of language, vivid metaphors, fanciful similes, complex rhythms, and so on. We shall not mean this.

A second conception of style is an ideal of clarity or expressiveness, whether the ideal be peculiar to a specific writer or whether it be a cultural or even universal ideal to which any writer may aspire. It is in this sense that critics speak of "Hemingway's style," "the clear style of French prose," "the eighteenth-century style," or "the expository style." Finally, style is sometimes equated with the essential quality of the writer himself. Buffon put it well when he said that "the style is the man himself."

In a profound sense this is true, yet it is not very helpful to those who wish to study style in a specific way. A more technical description, not essentially different from Buffon's, does allow for a more specific analysis: Style is the sum total of all the grammatically nondetermined characteristics of an expression. It is necessary to specify "grammatically nondetermined" in order to exclude those characteristics that are demanded by the grammar of the language. To write "we saw the boy" rather than "we seed the boy," for example, is not a matter of style; after "we" the required form of the verb *to see* is "saw" — it is predetermined for the writer by the conventions of grammar. (Of course, one might write "we seed the boy" in, say, a hillbilly story and it would then be a matter of style; but this is a special case that does not invalidate the general point.) To write, on the other hand, "We spied the boy" instead of "We saw the boy" *is* a matter of style since the writer may choose the verb "spied" or the verb "saw" (or any one of many other generally similar words, such as "discerned," "observed," "looked at," "noticed"). Similarly to write "In the hall sat an old man" instead of "An old man sat in the hall" is a matter of style because the writer is free to choose.

To conceive of style as resulting from the choice of grammatically nondetermined forms permits us to understand the style of any particular writer as being like a series of strata in which we can discern the influences that circumscribed the writer's choice. The primary stratum is composed of the grammatical forms which all literate writers must accept. Next comes what we may call the cultural stratum. For example, a writer living in mid-twentieth-century America is likely to choose certain types of sentence patterns rather than others. If he wishes to, he can write in the elaborate and formal parallelism of the eighteenth century, but it is most unlikely that he will wish to. Thus we can distinguish on the one hand a twentieth-century style and on the other hand an eighteenth-century style. A third layer of style is that which reveals the influence of a particular profession, and in this sense we may speak of an academic style, a business style, a legal style, a journalistic style, and so on. A fourth stratum shows the effect of membership in a social class (or of aspirations to belong to a particular class). And so on we go through many strata until we come to the last, in which the only influence is that deriving from the writer and the notion he seeks to express.

On all levels, however, we are concerned with the same question of choice — why this word instead of another, why this sentence pattern rather than that. It is even arguable, paradoxically, that in "choosing" the style proper to his purpose the writer, if he succeeds, is simply realizing that he has no choice. Michelangelo once remarked that the statue was already there, in the rough block of marble, and that his task was merely to release it. In a similar sense it might be said that the style is there implicit in notion and purpose, and that the writer's function is to chip away the irrelevancies. But it is probably simpler, and certainly it is more consistent with the contention that writing is a conscious activity, to regard style as the total of the forms which the writer has been free, in varying degrees, to choose. What he chooses reveals what he says and is. In this sense, then, style is the man; in this sense style and content become one.

Before leaving the subject of style we should point out one or two implications of the conception we have advanced. Perhaps the most important is that style as we regard it is an inevitable quality of expression, neither necessarily good nor necessarily bad. To evaluate the style of any particular essay one must ask this: Is it appropriate to the writer's purpose? A student who writes about his future plans that he wants "to labor in the realms of science" is likely to strike his readers, especially if they happen to be scientists, as pretentious. If the student had wished to impress these readers with his sensitivity or modesty or the lucidity of his thought, the chances are that he failed. Hence we may fairly conclude that in so far as his style is inappropriate it is "bad." But notice that we judge this case on its own merits; before one can hazard a generalization about the stylistic effect of a phrase like "scientific realm" he must examine it in a great many contexts to see if it is always or even usually inappropriate. There are features of style so universally inept in a particular culture that they may be regarded, within the limits of that culture, as bad by definition. Yet here too we need to recognize that the badness is a result of inappropriateness and not a quality inherent in the stylistic feature itself. Even pretentiousness like "scientific realm" can be employed effectively in satire or humor. Similarly there are "good styles," but "good" here simply means that these ways of using words are generally appropriate, not that they conform to some absolute aesthetic law or that they are always, under all conditions, good.

Thus one implication of our conception of style is that it may be either good or bad depending upon how appropriate it is. A second implication is that when we think of style in the positive, or "good" sense, we must reject any doctrine of STYLE — any theory, that is, of a single absolute norm of writing at which all writers should aim. Instead we must accept that there are many good styles, each valuable for some purposes but ill-adapted to others. As a reader you may prefer James Thurber's way of writing to E. M. Forster's; but as a student of writing you need to remember that each of these men achieved a style peculiarly suited to what he had to say. It is less important to judge which style is "better" than to understand the particular merits and limitations of each. As you gain more experience in composition you will find that some kinds of sentences, certain types of words will seem natural to what you think and feel. You will, in short, begin to acquire a style. The acquisition will proceed more easily and more profitably if you keep an open mind about style and are willing to learn from many different writers.

Tone

The final point we wish to touch upon in this chapter is tone. Tone is closely related to style, but it is not the same thing. It may be thought of as the "voice" we hear in prose, the kind of person the author is or seems to be. Tone is determined in part by the writer's feelings about his subject — whether he is angry, sad, joyous, amused, serious, or objective and unemotional — and in part by his attitude toward his readers and toward himself — whether he regards them as friends or as foes or as impartial observers, whether he thinks them equal, superior, or inferior to himself. James Thurber, for instance, in the passage quoted on page 20, seems to be amused by the comedy of football versus economics, and his disapproval, while real enough, is tolerant and restrained, without the passion of personal involvement. He treats his readers as equals, almost as friends to whom he is telling a funny story of his college days. Thus his tone may be described as light, amused, informal. H. L. Mencken's tone is very different — angry, bitter, denunciatory. The tone of the *U.S. Coast Pilot* is, as we should expect it to be, soberly matter-of-fact.

Sometimes the three determinants of tone — attitude toward subject, attitude toward reader, and attitude toward self — are equally important. Sometimes they are not. In invective and satire, for instance, the principal aspect of tone is the emotional response of the writer to his subject. In other cases, the writer's attitude toward his reader is more important in creating tone. The familiar essayist, for example, is very conscious of his readers and strives for a tone that will charm them. But whichever of these aspects chiefly determines it, tone is important, and it resides in what the writer writes.

Like the style in which it is manifest, tone may be more, or less, appropriate. Usually, especially with experienced writers, it is fair to assume that the tone which is implicit in their style is truly rooted in their feelings and fairly reveals them. But this assumption is not always justified. Attitudes and feelings are built into words and expressions; few of us like to be addressed by "Hey you," for example. Since tone is often inherent in words, and even in the construction of sentences, it is always possible that a writer may make a mistake and choose a word or sentence pattern whose tonal implications are quite different from what he intended. In conversation we have all had the experience of offending a friend by using the wrong tone, not because we wished to hurt him, but because, momentarily abstracted and not fully aware of what we were saying, we chose the wrong form to express an innocuous point. Even when there is no question of hurting someone's feelings, one may suggest the wrong tone by using a type of sentence that is too formal (or too informal) for his subject, or by employing a word with unsuitable overtones. As we discuss types of sentences and paragraphs and problems of diction in later chapters, we shall often comment upon tonal implications. But even before you get that far along you should begin to think about tone. Learn to recognize the varieties of tone in the books and essays you read, and as you read ask whether the tone seems appropriate, and if not what the trouble is. An awareness of tone will help you in your own writing, for an inappropriate tone is an obstacle to effective communication. At best it delays understanding; at worst it is, like boorishness at a party, positively offensive.

Summary

While people may have many diverse ends in view when they sit down to write, their immediate purpose is to inform, persuade, or entertain their readers. Usually they will be concerned with two or with all three of these purposes; but usually, too, one will clearly predominate. From these three purposes derive the three basic types of prose: the informative, the persuasive, and the entertaining. Just as purpose is rarely simple, so any given essay will probably be a mixture of these kinds of prose, but here also one or another will generally be dominant. Style is the way in which a writer achieves his purpose. Style is, in effect, the sum of all the choices the writer has been free to make. Style may be good or bad depending upon whether it is conducive to the writer's purpose. There is no single best style, but rather there are many good styles, each more appropriate to some purposes, less appropriate to others. Tone, finally, is the writer's attitude toward his subject and toward his readers as that attitude is revealed in the words and sentence patterns he has chosen. Tone, like style, may be appropriate to one's purpose, or inappropriate. Since tone is an inevitable element in language, a skilled writer will select his words so that their tone works for him and not against him.

3
INVENTION

Introduction

Set the task of writing an essay, the composition student is likely to groan that he "just can't think of anything to say." Thinking of something to say often presents difficulties to the experienced writer as well as to the beginner, a fact of which ancient rhetoricians were well aware. Indeed, they developed a method of helping the writer to find something to say, a method which they called *invention*. In treating this subject we shall continue to employ the term *invention* in its old rhetorical sense because there is no exact modern equivalent. Teachers sometimes use the phrase "looking for material" to signify invention; but this is not quite adequate, for, while it is a fair description of what one does in most research papers, it becomes misleading when applied to the kind of essay that is written about one's own beliefs and opinions, where the material is in the writer himself. Even more to the point, an important aspect of invention precedes "looking for material." This aspect might be described as "looking at the subject," and invention in this sense is less being able to use the card catalogue in the library or knowing where to locate reference books than having the capacity to think about ideas from a compositional point of view. As a trained infantry officer "sees" terrain in terms of how best to attack or defend it, so the experienced writer acquires the knack of seeing an idea as the subject of an essay. He has learned to look for ways in which subjects may be opened up and developed.

It is this aspect of invention that will concern us here. Obviously there are sharp limitations to how helpful a sense of invention will be to writers. Invention is no substitute for sensitivity and experience and knowledge.

All the inventive cleverness in the world will be little help to a writer who has been too lazy to learn his subject or who has been asked to write about something he cannot reasonably be expected to have any knowledge of. The latter sometimes happens, for now and then English teachers make the mistake of assigning theme topics beyond the experience of their students, and in such cases the student's complaint that he can think of nothing to say is well founded. But most teachers do not make this mistake very often, and usually the student who cannot get going really does have something to say. He simply has not learned how to discover what he can say. And here invention will help, for invention is merely a systematic process for making such discoveries.

In showing how it will help, we shall confine ourselves in this chapter to a brief and general discussion. This is not the place to become involved with the details of how an essay is organized or a paragraph developed. Nor do we wish to study here such specialized problems of invention as mounting an argument or doing research for a term paper. We merely want to make clear what invention, in a general way, is, and how to apply it to the practical problem of the freshman theme.

At its simplest, invention may be regarded as a set of questions the prospective writer asks about his subject. Often the important question is implicit in the subject. Certain modes of discourse recur frequently in composition assignments — definition, for example, or comparison, or cause and effect. Someone defining "culture" is in effect asking, "What is 'culture'?" A history student discussing the political eclipse of ancient Athens in a final exam is answering the question: "What conditions caused the decline of Athens?" But often, too, a theme assignment or a question on a test will not be phrased so that it implies any specific plan of attack. Moreover, much writing is not in response to examination questions or theme assignments. When one is first struggling to hammer out his own ideas he is not able to formulate his subject so neatly that it suggests this method of development or that. The very problem he faces is to discover what methods are most fruitful. For these reasons one needs a set of general questions applicable to any of the subjects he is likely to deal with in exposition. These questions suggest ideas about the subject, or as we shall call them — topics of discourse. Not all the following questions are equally applicable on every occasion, but for any subject that you are asked to handle in a freshman composition course some of them will prove useful. For convenience we shall arrange them in several groups, though the arrangement is somewhat arbitrary.

Topics of Discourse

DEFINITION

The first group concerns the nature of the subject. The most obvious question here is:

1. What is it?

which might also be phrased:

What is the essence of the thing (or idea)? What is its definition?

For example, the historian Alan Simpson, writing about Puritanism, begins by asking simply and directly, "How does one define Puritanism?" What follows is an extended answer to that question. One need not make such a rhetorical question the literal starting point of an essay (though this is an easy way to generate a paragraph), but the question ought at least to exist in the writer's mind.

Other ways of approaching the nature of the subject are to ask such questions as these:

2. What have other people said about it?
3. What examples of it are there?
4. What are its parts or aspects?
5. Of these parts or aspects which are most significant for my purpose?
6. What is it similar to?
7. How is it different from something else?

and

8. What exceptions are there to it? What qualifications must be made?

When applied to a specific subject, these questions would, of course, be phrased more precisely. Suppose, for instance, that you have been asked to write a theme about your political beliefs. Applied to that problem, these questions might be put something like this:

1. What are my political beliefs?

2. What has been said by other men about their political beliefs that applies in my case?
3. Can I give an example of my beliefs in terms of a particular political problem (socialized medicine perhaps, or the issue of states' rights,) or in terms of specific politicians?
4. Can I analyze my beliefs into (for example) opinions about foreign affairs, about social legislation, about economic policy?
5. Should I concentrate upon one or two of these opinions, or discuss all of them?
6. Do my political beliefs resemble those of a particular group or individual?
7. Do they differ in a significant way from those of any other group or individual?
8. Are there any limits to what I believe, any qualifications to how far I carry my liberalism (or conservativism)?

One could apply the same questions if the subject of the composition was football or modern physics or a freshman's impressions of college. Not all the questions of this first set would be equally successful for all these various subjects, but enough would apply in each case to reveal material for a theme — that "something to say" which students complain is so elusive.

CAUSE AND EFFECT

Nor are these the only questions one may ask. A second set concerns the cause-effect relationship of the subject:

9. What caused it?
10. What purpose does it have?
11. What are its implications (or consequences)?
12. Is it logically related to anything else?

(We might note that the distinction between a cause and a purpose is not always clear-cut. Purpose is the end a thing is designed to serve. Of a chair we should say that its purpose — or in this case, function — is to enable someone to sit down. Purposes are often one of the causes that bring a thing into being, as the desire to sit down might be one of the causes of my building a chair. But in thinking about invention it is best to keep causes, in the sense of the immediate activities or forces that create something, distinct from purposes.)

Applied to the example of political beliefs, the four questions having to do with cause and effect might be phrased something like this:

9. Why am I a Democrat (or Republican or Socialist)? What factors in my background caused me to embrace this set of political beliefs rather than another?

10. Have I any purpose for my beliefs, any personal end that is best served by this set of opinions?

11. Have my beliefs had any effect upon my life? May I expect any future consequence?

12. Are my political attitudes consistent with, or contradicted by, my other beliefs, my way of life, my job?

Each phrasing of these questions for a particular topic suggests other, more precise, ways of putting them, and all these variations point to potential topics.

ADVANTAGES AND DISADVANTAGES

A third and final set of questions deals with what we shall term, somewhat inadequately, the vices and the virtues of the subject. It is not inevitably necessary in any writing assignment that one add up the advantages and disadvantages of his subject, but sometimes it is revealing to do so and sometimes it is required. Here the basic questions are obvious:

13. What advantages does it have?

14. What disadvantages?

Preparing the theme about political beliefs, one might ask:

13. What are the virtues of liberalism (or conservativism)? Or, putting the question in a more personal way: What are the advantages in being a liberal (or a conservative)? And putting it more argumentatively: Why is liberalism (or conservativism) more beneficial, realistic, viable, moral?

14. What are the vices of the liberal (conservative) position? Are there any hardships or personal disadvantages in believing one

way or the other? How may I attack this political philosophy? What charges must I anticipate against the beliefs I am defending?

Applying the Questions

The fourteen questions we have suggested do not exhaust the resources of invention. Other questions apply to such specific compositional problems as argument, description, narration, and so on. But for the needs of general exposition the questions we have enumerated will allow you to attack most writing problems. Not all the questions, it is worth repeating, are likely to prove useful on any given occasion. What you must do is to try them out, exploring those which seem to open up ideas and discarding those which do not. Think of these questions as so many doors that open onto a subject. In some cases a question will reveal only a blank wall, in others, a room fully furnished with topics.

Notice, too, that frequently these questions interconnect, so that one implies others. Any time one of the questions suggests a clear-cut topic, that topic itself becomes subject to investigation by the other questions of invention. If, for example, someone is planning a theme about college football and has listed several virtues and vices of the game, he might apply question 3, asking for specific examples of these virtues and vices, or questions 6 and 7 comparing them to the faults or virtues of some other sport. So numerous are such interconnections that, having mastered the technique of invention, you will find that far from having too little to say you will have too much. Your problem will become one of restriction.

The most practical way to proceed with invention is to work with a pencil and paper and to follow three steps. The first step is to jot down the questions we have listed (along with any others that occur to you), phrasing them, of course, with reference to your particular subject and leaving a blank space below each question in which to note any topics it suggests. Write down *all* the questions; don't decide beforehand that this one or that one cannot possibly have any bearing upon the subject. The supposition may be correct, but it is better to try the question before discarding it. In the blank spaces write any ideas that pop up. Work rapidly during this first stage. Try to get through the entire list quickly, noting the first ideas or impressions that the questions suggest. If for any question no ideas come, leave that space blank and move along to the next. During this stage of invention it is best not to get too deeply involved with any single topic, but briefly to survey all possible avenues of development.

This first step completed, however, you should go back over your jottings more carefully, starring or underlining those that seem especially promising and marking for discard those that do not. Now is the time to give further thought to those places that at first you left blank. If the thought discloses no significant topics, you can safely cross out these questions as having no value for your purpose.

Finally as a third step you should sort out the topics you marked as important and write down each at the top of a separate piece of paper. Then under each topic list all the ideas, examples, causes, effects, implications, contrasts, and comparisons that seem to support and develop it, as well as any qualifications that may have to be made about it. For example in planning the theme on political beliefs the writer might have listed as a topic of cause that his own conservatism was in part the result of following in the footsteps of his father, a life-long Republican. As a way of developing this topic the writer might think of a specific occasion when his father strongly expressed or acted upon his political convictions, an occasion that impressed him. When you have explored in similar manner each one of the potential topics you decided on at the end of step two, you will have amassed a good deal of material and thus completed the process of invention. Rather we should say that you will have completed the preliminary phase of invention. For invention never really ends until you have turned in the final copy of your paper. As you write you will constantly discover new ideas that must be joined with the old ones, and you may discover that some of your original ideas do not fit very well and must be discarded. But while invention goes continuously on, it will go on best if you have begun by asking some such questions as we suggested. These will get you started, and getting started is for many people the hardest part of the writing process.

We have seen how the method of invention worked with the subject of political beliefs. Before leaving invention altogether, let us look at another example in which we shall work through all the steps. We may take as our case that a freshman has been asked to write about his impressions of college; what follows is one way in which he might tackle the preliminary business of invention. (It is not, of course, the only way, or even necessarily the best. The topics we shall list are not the only ones possible. They are simply one method of developing this subject and other methods are not precluded.)

As a first step our student-writer ought to go through all fourteen of the questions of invention, noting briefly any ideas that occur to him:

1. What are my impressions of college?
   It might be wise to distinguish several different impressions:

   a. The initial conception of what college would be like. This is possibly a good way of beginning the essay.
   b. This conception could be refined, even radically changed, as I discover that college is not quite what I had anticipated.
   c. Finally as an effective closing I can return to my original impression, showing how it has been modified by actual experience.

2. What have other people said about college?
   Several topics are possible here:

   a. Advice given me by my father or older brother or friend.
   b. A relevant quotation from some famous person.
      (Someone once described college as "four years under the ether cone.")

3. What examples are there?
   The *general* subject "Impressions of College" is difficult to illustrate. However, examples would be useful in supporting specific aspects of that impression.

4. What are these aspects?
   Specific impressions must be classified in some way, for instance into those having to do with (a) homework, (b) teachers, (c) courses, (d) fellow students, (e) social activities, and so on.

5. Which of these aspects should I concentrate upon?
   Teachers and teaching methods (including homework), fellow students, and social activities.

6. What is college like?
   This question leads to two possible topics: (a) comparing my impressions of college with my impressions of something quite dissimilar (an analogy between college and a cafeteria, for instance), or (b) comparing college with something of the same nature (high school, say). The latter topic would probably be more useful; such a comparison would be an easy way of focusing particular impressions.

7. How is it different?
   This, of course, would be included as part of the comparison between college and high school.

8. What qualifications must be made?
   Rather than furnishing a main topic, qualifications, if necessary, should be worked in under specific impressions.

9. What are its causes?

   a. With regard to my initial idea about college — what I expected to find — *why* did I have this particular preconception? What factors in my schooling, family background, friends led me to conceive of college in just this way?
   b. A possible topic for the closing would be to discuss how this preconception was changed.

10. What purpose does it have?
    There seems to be no topic here.

11. What are its implications?
    There are some topics suggested by this question; on the whole, however, it does not appear to be very revealing for this essay.

12. How does the subject relate to anything else?
    Nor does this.

13. and 14. What are the advantages and disadvantages?
    Probably these questions will not provide much material, although I might consider the advantages or the detriment of arriving at college with a firm preconception of what it will be like.

Of the possible topics opened up by step one, not all are really usable. As the second step of invention our essayist must cull out those which hold no promise and make a second list containing only those which seem worthwhile. Let us go back over the questions, commenting upon their usefulness:

1. What are my impressions of college?
   This is the heart of the essay. Even the naïve idea with which I came to college (more a pre-impression) will be valuable as a way of beginning and leading naturally into the discussion.

2. What have other people said about college?
   These topics, too, are useful. My father's advice explains why I expected college to be harsh and difficult. The quotation mentioned might be a good opening line.

3. What examples are there?
   Examples should be used as subordinate topics to illustrate specific impressions.

4. What are these specific impressions?
   This topic is vital. The grouping of impressions around such centers as teachers and teaching methods, classmates, and social activities is the easiest way of organizing my material.

5. Which of these impressions should I concentrate upon?
   Restrict impressions to the three areas mentioned above and treat them in that order.

6. and 7. What is it like? and how is it different?
   The comparison of college and high school is worth developing, but it should remain a subordinate topic, pursued less for its own sake than to support the specific impressions listed in topics 4 and 5.

8. What qualifications must be made?
   This is a minor topic usable only where a specific impression needs to be hedged.

9. What are its causes?
   While it is relatively unimportant, I could discuss the reasons for my naïve ideas about college.

10. What purpose does it have?
    Discard.

11. What are its implications?
    Discard.

12. How does the subject relate to anything else?
    Discard.

13. and 14. What are the advantages and disadvantages?
    Discard.

At the end of step two, then, the writer is left with these topics:

1. Opening with the quotation about the ether cone, a beginning section in which he tells us what he expected college to be like, supporting and explaining his expectation by citing his father's advice.

2. A statement of what he actually found, which may have been much like or much different from what he expected. If this statement is kept brief it should form the last of the first paragraph. If it is more extended it ought to be cast as a second paragraph, and in this case the two paragraphs will serve to introduce the main body of the paper.

3. The main body will be a discussion of the writer's impressions of such phases of college life as teachers, classmates, and social activities, supported by specific examples and by comparison and contrast with high school.

4. A closing statement of how his impressions have changed and matured with his experience so far.

The third and last step of invention is to delve into each topic decided upon at the end of step two, seeking specific illustrations, causes, effects, implications, comparisons, qualifications, and so on. This step is exceedingly important; without it the resulting essay is likely to consist of a series of vague generalizations unanchored in firm detail. Failing to support the general with the particular is a widespread weakness in student writing. The simplest way to avoid that fault is to proceed with the third step of invention. List on separate sheets of paper each of the topics you have chosen. Upon each sheet jot down any ideas the topic suggests — *all* the ideas, however wild. Probably you won't use all of them; but it is easy enough to discard what you don't need, and the more material you have the more selective you can be. Here is a very brief exploration of the four topics of our example.

> TOPIC I. Opening with the quotation, a beginning paragraph in which the writer tells us what he expected college to be like, supporting and explaining his expectation by citing his father's advice.
>
> A. Conceived of college as a remote, businesslike place with little contact between teacher and student.

B. Why this conception?

1. Father, stressing the number of freshmen who had flunked out of his own university, had urged the writer to work hard and to expect little mercy from the instructors.
2. In general, parents had always emphasized the competitiveness of modern life and the necessity, together with the difficulty, of getting ahead in the world.
3. Of the writer's friends, the only one who had already begun college was attending a big-city university where the classes were relatively large and the instructors seemed remote. (If he has time and space the writer might provide an illustration of a specific friend at a specific university, taking this or that specific course.)

TOPIC II. A statement of what the writer actually found.

A. College proved to be very different. Teachers and other students were friendly and helpful. (An example or two from registration or from freshman week would help.)

B. Perhaps the difference resulted, at least in part, from the fact that the writer is attending a small college in a small town.

TOPIC III. Specific impressions of teachers, classmates, and social activities, supported by examples and by contrast and comparison with high school.

A. Teachers and teaching methods

1. Teachers are more businesslike than those in high school. (Example: math instructor who begins to lecture immediately and who never strays from the point.)
2. They are less concerned with discipline. (It might be worth mentioning why they can afford to be less concerned with it.)
3. They are more remote and formal. (For example, they address students as "Mr." and "Miss.")
4. They tend to lecture rather than ask questions of the class. (Example: a history professor who has carefully tailored his lecture to fit the fifty-minute period and allows no time for questions.)
5. They pay less attention to the textbook than do high school teachers. (Perhaps because they feel the student can

understand the text by himself and that their job is to supplement it.)

B. Classmates

1. Fellow students seem more serious than those in high school. (Probably college contains relatively few students who are merely "serving time.")
2. They are more mature. (For instance, they talk about politics and ideas as well as about girls and automobiles and sports.)
3. They are more interesting not only because they are older but also because they come from divergent backgrounds. In high school everyone was from the same town and more or less the same class. But in college there are people from remote states — even foreign countries — and with widely different social and family backgrounds. (Example of a classmate from Honolulu or Central America or France.)

C. Social activities

1. There are more activities in college than in high school: sports events; college-sponsored dances and teas; fraternity and sorority affairs; informal activities like the dormitory bull session; and such cultural events as special lectures, discussion panels, debates, orchestral and choral programs, plays, and so on.
2. In all these activities the students have greater freedom and a correspondingly greater responsibility.

TOPIC IV. A closing statement of how the writer's impressions of college have changed and matured.

Rather than being a cold education factory, college is a friendly and stimulating place with many exciting people and activities, both inside and outside the classroom.

By the end of step three our student has amassed a considerable amount of raw material. No doubt if you were to think about this subject you would unearth very different material. That fact, however, is not important. Obviously there is no one right way to develop an essay on a subject like this, which will give rise to as many different essays as there are different writers with varying experiences of college.

What is important is that the example demonstrates how invention may be used as a way of discovering "something to write about"; or better, of *uncovering* this something to write about. For our hypothetical student had it all along; it was a part of his experience. Invention, then, is merely a systematic way of examining a potential subject, of asking questions about it so that you will discover things to say. If for any subject within the range of your experience you honestly apply the process of invention, there should never be any reason for you to sit staring blankly at a sheet of paper, waiting for the inspirational lightning to strike. It is likely to be a long wait. Most of us have to think seriously about a subject in order to write about it — to think systematically. That, finally, is all invention comes to — thinking about a subject systematically.

Summary

Invention is a rational, orderly way of exploring a subject in order to discover topics of discourse. The exploration is carried on by asking a series of questions about the nature of the subject, about its causes and effects, and about its vices and virtues. Not all the questions will be useful for any particular subject, but in every case at least a few will reveal significant topics. These topics are the raw material of the essay.

Exercises

1. Listed below are several subjects suitable for development in an expository essay. Select one from each group and invent a series of topics for it, anticipating an essay of about 1000 words. Since the subjects are stated in the broadest possible terms, an important part of the problem is to arrange and restrict the topics of discourse so that they focus upon a particular aspect of the subject. In each of your four choices, carry the process of invention through the final step, so that you wind up with a series of specific topics comparable to those listed on pages 42–4.

1. Television
   Popular music
   Movies
   Modern art
2. Parents
   Teachers
   Aunts and uncles
   American teen-agers
   Frenchmen (or Spaniards, Italians, Englishmen, Germans—any nationality you know well)
3. The value of taking a course in history (or psychology, literature—any course will do)
   Freshman week
   English class
4. Shoes
   Hats
   Hobbies (a specific hobby or hobbies in general)

2. In the course of working out exercise 1 you may have thought of other questions that would be generally useful in expository invention. List any such questions and indicate whether they are essentially topics of definition, of cause and effect, or of advantage and disadvantage.

4
OUTLINING

Introduction

The ultimate result of invention will be a list of topics from which the essay will develop. These topics, however, still require to be organized and proportioned in the most effective way. To provide organization and proportion is the purpose of outlining. An outline is a plan view of an essay, which by a series of numbered headings indicates in a clearly perceivable way the major parts of the essay and the principal subdivisions of each, the subordinate headings being indented and contained under the major ones. The outline has value both for the writer and for the reader. It enables the writer to plan and organize his essay before he begins to write, thus permitting him to catch out and correct at least some errors of organization and emphasis in a preliminary stage and so making the task of actual writing easier. It is a convenience to the reader because, by offering him a bird's-eye view of the paper before he begins to read it, it allows him to follow the development of the essay more easily.

Depending upon whether it is designed to serve the convenience of the reader or only the needs of the writer, we can distinguish two types of outline. One is the scratch outline, intended solely for the writer's use. The scratch outline corresponds to the quick sketch a carpenter might make on the back of an old envelope to give himself a rough idea of what the finished work will look like. The scratch outline may be sloppily done with frequent deletions and additions, smudged and stained (although it will be more useful if it is kept neat and orderly). The only requirement is that it be clear to the person who drew it up; it may not be clear to anyone else, but then a scratch outline is not intended for anyone else.

The second type is the formal outline, which *is* designed for someone else, being a form of communication. This is more like the finished set of plans that an architect draws for a contractor who will erect a house. It must be neat, legible, and composed in accordance with conventional rules if it is to fulfill its purpose of indicating to the reader the general plan of the paper. While a scratch outline is used by the writer and then thrown away, a formal outline is turned in with the essay as introductory matter. It is in this respect like the table of contents of a book; in fact, tables of contents are a variety of formal outline. Both kinds of outline are alike in the essential feature that they analyze a subject into its parts and then synthesize these parts into a coherent and significant pattern. The only difference between them is that the scratch outline is a kind of talking to oneself and so can be — and usually is — fragmentary and private, like a page from a diary; while the formal outline is a communicative expression from writer to reader and so must observe rules understood and accepted by both.

The Formal Outline

RULES OF FORMAT

The rules of outlining vary somewhat from teacher to teacher and so we shall not lay down the fine points of the law about them, but simply note those generalizations about which most people agree. The most important rules governing the formal outline fall into two groups: (1) those concerned with the format of the outline, and (2) those concerned with the logic of analysis. To understand the rules of format you must remember that an outline is literally a plan and that like all plans it should have visual clarity. It is the virtue of a blueprint to be easily and immediately clear to anyone trained to read it; a blueprint whose lines are smudged and whose figures are blurred and shaky violates this virtue of clarity. Similarly a formal outline should be so arranged on the page that anyone familiar with the conventions of outlining can tell at a glance what the major divisions of the outline are, how many subdivisions there are in each, and so on.

To assure that your outline has visual clarity, observe the following rules. First adopt a conventional system of numbering and lettering the headings and maintain it consistently. There are several such systems. The one we use follows the pattern:

I.
  A.
    1.
      a.
        (1)
          (a)
            (I)
              (A)

Beginning with capital Roman numerals for the major headings, this system preserves a strict alternation between numerals and letters. Your teacher may prefer a different system. What is important is that you agree on which one to use and that you stick to it exactly, without adding a parenthesis here or a dash there, as fancy moves you.

The second rule of format is that subheadings be adequately indented under their primary headings in order to indicate that they are part of those headings. (The terms "primary heading" and "subheading" are, except for the initial Roman numerals, relative. Any heading "A" is a sub heading relative to "I" or "II," but a primary heading relative to the "1" under it; while "1," a subheading to "A," is a primary heading to "a.") When you indent do not go in so far that by the time you get down to step "(1)" you have only three-quarters of an inch against the right-hand margin into which to squeeze the topic. Keep the indentation to the minimum necessary for clarity, and indent the same distance in all cases.

The third rule of format is that equal headings should be vertically aligned; that is, all the Roman numerals should be one under another in a straight line parallel to the edge of the paper; all the "A's" and "B's" in a second vertical line a half-inch or so to the right; and similarly with the "1's" and "2's" and the "a's" and "b's."

If the two rules of indentation and vertical alignment are not observed, one gets something like this:

I.
A.
1.
 a.
  (1)
(2)
  b.
2.
    (and so on).

This is a blueprint so fuzzy as to be almost useless. Only a rare and tolerant reader would have the patience to work out such a Chinese puzzle. See how clear the outline becomes, however, when the headings are properly indented and aligned:

I.
  A.
    1.
      a.
        (1)
        (2)
      b.
    2.
      (and so on).

Two final rules of format are that the first word of each heading should be capitalized, and that headings in any outline are usually cast consistently all in the form of grammatically complete sentences or all in the form of fragments. About this second rule the point most teachers emphasize is consistency. In any particular outline they prefer that all headings are the same: either sentences or non-sentences. On the basis of this distinction two varieties of the formal outline are sometimes differentiated: the sentence outline and the topic outline. In the first, every heading, from the major divisions right down to the smallest subdivision, is cast in the form of a complete sentence. In the second, every heading is a fragment. For most purposes the so-called topic outline is preferable because it is more succinct. In this matter, however, you should be guided by your teacher's preference.

RULES OF ANALYSIS

The second set of rules that govern the formal outline are rules of logic. Outlining is essentially a technique of analysis, of breaking down a series of topics, step by step, into their immediate constituents. Thus an outline works from the general to the particular, the degree of generality or of particularity being indicated by the letter or number assigned to the heading and by its indentation. The first logical rule is simple: There can never be *only one* subdivision under any heading. Put another way, the rule states that every "I" demands at least a "II," every "A" at least a "B." The rule holds, of course, not merely for the Roman numerals and the capital letters, but for all "one's" and all degrees of "A-ness." But notice that the rule does *not* mean that you may have only two subdivisions under any heading; you may have three or four or as many as you think necessary. Nor does it mean that you must have two subdivisions under every heading; to attempt this would make the outline endless. What the rule boils down to is that if you *do* make one subdivision, you must make at least one more. Thus in the following outline the analysis under "A. 2" is at fault because there is an "a" but no "b":

I.
  A.
    1.
    2.
      a.
    3.
      (and so on).

The rule of at least two subdivisions or none at all is not arbitrary. It is logically necessary. The indentation of "a" under "2" in our example means that "a" is part of "2." If it is part, it is less than "2," and "2" must therefore include something else. This something else has to be expressed by at least a "b," though there may be, as we have said, a "c" or "d" or even further steps. It may happen when you make a formal outline that you cannot think of a second subdivision after you have made a first. If this should happen you certainly ought not to make up a meaningless topic just to have something to label "2" or "b." Instead, combine the topic you listed as "1" (or as "a") with the major heading above it, placing a colon or a dash between them. You may even wish to go further and remove the original primary heading altogether, replacing it with what had been the solitary subheading. In either case you will wind up with no subdivision at all and so will have preserved the rule of no "1" without at least a "2," no "a" without at least a "b."

The second logical rule is that topics of equal weight must be placed in equal headings and, conversely, that unequal topics belong in appropriately unequal headings. Suppose, for example, that someone were making an outline of the various types of vessels in the U.S. Navy during World War II. Under the general heading "Ships of the Line" he might list the classes of fighting ships something like this:

I. Ships of the line
  A. Battleships
  B. Aircraft carriers
  C. Cruisers
  D. *U.S.S. Morgan*

In that outline, heading "D" violates the second logical rule. Headings "A," "B," and "C" all signify classes of ships, but in "D" the writer has shifted to a particular vessel. "D" should read, of course, "Destroyers." It would be equally illogical to include "Destroyers" as heading "1" under "Cruisers."

Stretching the meaning of "logical" a little we may consider a third rule: Headings should be meaningful — that is, they should convey something specific to the reader. Whether or not a heading is meaningful must be determined not simply by the heading itself, but by the heading plus everything that is subsumed under it, since this material is logically a part of the heading. As a case in point consider this very brief outline:

Books

I. Books I like
II. Books I don't like

This sort of thing is all too often what is submitted in lieu of an outline. The headings are meaningless. They tell the reader nothing precise, only that in the first part of his essay the writer will talk about books he likes while in the second part he will discuss those he doesn't like. But what kinds of books these are, what reasons the writer has for preferring this variety to that — of all this the reader learns nothing. The objection that the essay itself will inform the reader of these matters is not valid. For one thing, part of the function of a formal outline is itself to be informative. Obviously the outline cannot and should not say everything the essay will say, but it should be more meaningful than this. For a second thing, so brief and superficial an outline is, more often than not, an omen that the theme which follows is similarly thin and insubstantial. The way to give meaning to these headings is to analyze them further:

Books

I. Books I like
  A. Travel books
    1. Especially those about remote and unusual places

a. *Hashish,* by Henry de Monfreid
b. *Travels in Arabia Deserta,* by Charles M. Doughty
2. Also travel books about Europe
a. *The Path to Rome,* by Hilaire Belloc
b. *Travels with a Donkey,* by R. L. Stevenson
B. Biographies
1. Prefer those which are historical and scholarly
a. *Hitler,* by Alan Bullock
b. *Thomas Jefferson,* by Dumas Malone

This is enough to show that the heading "Books I like" has begun to take on meaning. The outline now tells the reader something precise and gives him reason to expect that the theme will be detailed and specific.

Finally, under the category of logical rules we should include this: The headings of a formal outline ought to be analyzed to roughly the same degree. There is, for instance, a disparity in an outline that breaks down major headings "I" and "II" into the fourth subdivision but merely lists heading "III" — presumably comparable in importance — with no analysis at all. There is a rule of thumb that will keep you from making such gross errors in proportion: Try to carry the analysis of any heading to within one step of the analysis of parallel headings. If topics "I" and "II" have been analyzed to subdivision "(1)," topic "III" ought to be carried to at least subdivision "a," "a" coming to within one step of "(1)." Or topic "III" could be carried one step further than the other major headings to "(a)." Equality of analysis obviously cannot be applied too rigidly. In any outline some headings will be more important than others of equal rank and will require more analysis. Usually, however, the rule of one-step equality is enough to allow for such differences in emphasis. Anytime you find that you have violated this rule consider whether you have neglected something important or whether the topic you have slighted is less important than you first thought and might better be placed in a more subordinate position or perhaps dropped altogether.

The Scratch Outline

The general rules governing the formal outline do not apply, in any legal sense, to the scratch outline. Since a scratch outline is for the writer's eyes alone, he is under no compulsion to obey the law. But if they are not legally binding, these rules still retain a validity for scratch outlining. The more carefully you observe them, the more useful your rough outline is likely to prove and the easier will be the task of making a formal outline from your scratch work.

One or two tips on scratch outlining are worth notice. If you have carried invention through the third stage as we suggested, you have arrived, in effect, at a crude outline in the list of topics you have drawn up. In working up a scratch outline from that list, try to keep the whole essay always in mind. As you fit the topics into outline form, proceed with the analysis one step at a time. Decide first upon the several major divisions of your essay; then upon the primary subdivisions of each of these; then upon the secondary subdivisions; and so on. There are several advantages to proceeding in this way. You are less likely to lose sight of your whole plan and become embroiled in irrelevant details. You will find it easier to maintain the relative equality of analysis we spoke of earlier. And you will be able to cut off your analysis at any step and still have a complete outline suitable for a theme of specific length.

This last point brings us to another question—how far to carry the rough outline. For most students the answer is "Further than you do." The majority of beginning writers tend to slight the outline, and the failure to carry analysis far enough usually reveals itself in the thinness of the essay. For the sort of brief compositions you write in English class you ought to take the outline through at least the second subdivision; that is, through:

I.
  A.
    1.

Often you will find it necessary to work into the third subdivision ("a," "b," "c," and so on). Whether you will need to go further into "(1)" and "(a)" or even "(I)" and "(A)" will depend upon subject and occasion. For long term papers you should get down into these finer stages; but for the average English theme they would hardly be necessary since you have too little space to convey all this information. It is, however, less a fault in outlining to do too much than to do too little.

Summary

Outlining is the process of organizing the topics uncovered by invention into a coherent and well proportioned plan. Outlines may be either scratch work or a kind of formal communication. A scratch outline is a rough sketch which the writer uses and then discards. A formal outline is turned in with the essay. It must be composed according to conventional rules of format and analysis, and it must be a full and honest plan of the essay it introduces.

Exercises

1. Choosing any two of the sets of topics you invented in the exercise following Chapter 3, work them into formal outlines, being careful to observe all the rules, both of format and of logic.

2. Trade these outlines with a classmate and see if you can find places where he has broken any rules. Look especially for vague, meaningless headings and for "1's" without "2's" and "a's" without "b's."

3. Make a formal outline of this chapter (or a chapter from some other book or essay, if your teacher prefers). Carry the analysis to the fourth subdivision, that is to "(1)," "(2)," and so on.

5
DRAFTING AND REVISING

Introduction

Considered as a physical activity, writing has two phases: (1) working up the outline into a full length theme, and (2) correcting and improving the theme so developed. The first phase is called drafting; the second, revising. Both are essential. Indeed, a writer may go through this twofold process several times before he achieves what he considers to be his final composition. He will compose a first draft; then — perhaps immediately, perhaps not until some time has passed — he will completely rewrite his essay, incorporating the revisions of the first version into the second draft, which in turn he will read over and revise.

Some people feel it is a mistake to work over a composition through three or four versions; and occasionally one does come upon a writer whose first effort is usually his best, whose prose gets worse the more he "improves" it. But as a general rule the more one writes and rewrites, the better his work will become. In this respect a well written essay is like a finely finished piece of mahogany, which has had to be sanded many times with paper of increasing fineness, then carefully varnished with five or six coats, being assiduously rubbed between each. Few people, however, have the patience to finish wood in this fashion, and fewer still have the patience to handrub so meticulously upon an essay. Even if they have the patience, they seldom have the time. This is especially true of the composition student, who must sandwich his English essay between his calculus problems and a review of the Assyrian Empire. But if impatience and time conspire to defeat us, we ought not to rationalize the defeat by trying to convince ourselves that second and third drafts are wasteful and unnecessary. They are not wasteful and they are necessary; and most people who write well have learned to accept this weary work, which the poet Horace compared to the "labor of the file."

A little of the weariness may be avoided by going about drafting and revising in a methodical and intelligent manner. That is what we should like to discuss in this chapter. We cannot delve into matters of style at this point; such problems as choosing words, constructing sentences, developing paragraphs will not concern us here. Obviously these are vital matters, for what you draft will be words and sentences and paragraphs, and these are the things you must attempt to improve when you revise. But precisely because they are vital we must study these details of style through many chapters. All we can attempt at the moment is to talk about the general problems of drafting and revising in the hope that you will acquire a technique of handling these activities. If you master the "mechanics" of drafting and revising, you will be able to apply more profitably what you learn about paragraphs, sentences, and diction in the chapters to come. The place to begin is with drafting.

Drafting

WORKING FROM THE OUTLINE

Although there are people who prefer to plunge directly into their first draft without wading through the preliminaries of invention and outlining, it is not a practice we recommend. On rare occasions, when the usual techniques of invention seem to lead nowhere, you might try simply beginning to write, in hopes that the physical action of pushing pencil across paper will arouse mental activity, thus reversing the usual flow of thought. But nine cases in ten it will be best to think first, asking questions, selecting topics, and arranging them into a plan before you begin the first draft. Assuming that you have done so, our primary question here is: How does one move from the outline to the essay?

The first thing is to decide upon the length of your paper, which in most college work — whether freshman theme or senior honors thesis — will be determined, at least within limits, by the teacher who made the assignment. The length may be stipulated by a particular number of pages or by so many words; in either case the next step is to translate this length into a prospective number of paragraphs. It is impossible to formulate any firm arithmetic rule for doing this. Paragraph length is exceedingly variable, changing from generation to generation, from writer to writer within the same generation, and even from essay to essay with the same writer depending upon his subject and purpose. The best thing to do is to determine the average length of your own paragraphs (but not until you have learned the art of developing expository paragraphs) and to use this figure as a rough guide in planning your work. If you wish some number to cling to in the meantime, let us say arbitrarily that 150 to 200 words is a fair average for an adequately developed expository paragraph. Accepting this figure — and it is arbitrary — a 1000-word essay means about six paragraphs. (We stress the word *about.*) In projecting the number of paragraphs in a theme, give yourself latitude; even in a short paper you should allow for a difference of one paragraph either way.

Once you have determined roughly how many paragraphs your paper will have, you are in a position to examine your outline to decide the most likely places for paragraph breaks. Count all the headings of each order — all the Roman numerals, all the capital letters, all the Arabic numerals, and so on — tentatively locating your paragraph breaks at the level where the count corresponds most closely to the estimated number of paragraphs. In a very short paper of 500 words, for instance, developed from an outline having three major headings, the paragraph breaks would probably come at "I," "II," and "III"; in a slightly longer version of the same paper, the new paragraphs might begin at the "A's" and "B's" and "C's" under the Roman numerals; and in a still longer theme with the "1's" and "2's" and "3's."

It might be helpful to see how this process works with an actual outline. We shall suppose that the imaginary student who in a previous chapter endured the task of inventing topics for a theme on his impressions of college has now gathered and organized his topics into the following outline:

First Impressions

I. Beginning: Preconceptions about college life
  A. Supposed that college would be cold and businesslike, with little contact between teacher and student
    1. Due in part to the attitude of my parents, who emphasized
      a. The competitiveness of college
      b. The necessity of getting ahead in the world
    2. And in part to the opinion of a close friend who was attending a large university in a great city
      a. His classes crowded
      b. His instructors remote

B. Actually college very different
  1. People helpful and kind
    a. Instructor who spent an hour helping me fill out my schedule
    b. Upperclassmen who showed us around the campus, identifying the buildings
    c. Housemother who explained the rules and privileges of the dormitory
  2. Several reasons for this difference between what I had expected and what I found
    a. This a small college in a small town
    b. A self-contained community in which people are friendly and polite because they must live together

II. Specific impressions of college life
  A. Teachers and teaching methods
    1. Teachers more businesslike than in high school
      a. Keep to the point — my math professor a good example
      b. Different from high school, where the teachers sometimes talked about current affairs not related to their subject
    2. Tend to lecture rather than to ask questions — my history instructor a case in point
    3. Do not pay much attention to the textbook
      a. Take for granted that the students can understand the text
      b. Unlike high school, where the teachers carefully explained the material in the text
    4. Somewhat remote
      a. Address students as "Mr." and "Miss"
      b. Do not joke with individual students
    5. Less concerned with discipline
  B. Classmates
    1. More serious than those in high school
      a. Not many time-servers
      b. Have specific ambitions
    2. Seem more mature
      a. Talk about politics and ideas
      b. In high school, bull sessions about girls and cars and sports exclusively

3. More interesting
    a. Partly because of this greater maturity
    b. But partly because of greater diversity of background
        (1) My roommate a native of Honduras
        (2) The son of a U.S. Senator in one of my classes

C. Social activities
1. More frequent and more diverse than in high school
    a. Sports events
    b. Dances and teas
        (1) College-sponsored
        (2) Fraternity and sorority affairs
    c. Cultural activities
        (1) Orchestral programs
        (2) Plays
        (3) Special lectures and discussions
        (4) Debates
    d. Dormitory bull sessions
2. Students allowed more freedom at these social activities than in high school, but also expected to be more responsible

III. Conclusion
A. College not a cold education-factory
B. An exciting place where people are warm and friendly

If this outline were to be adapted to a short theme of 500 words, the place to make the paragraph breaks — on the estimate of 150–200 words per paragraph — would seem to be at the major headings "I," "II," and "III." In this instance, however, the outline cannot be followed rigidly in determining the paragraph structure of the essay; otherwise topics "I" and "III" would issue in quite brief paragraphs, while if all the material under "II" were lumped into a single paragraph it would be bulky and unwieldy. Therefore "II" would be better divided into two paragraphs, and "III," rather than being treated separately, could be included as the last several sentences of the final paragraph. Such an essay would be better proportioned than one composed of the one very long and the two quite short paragraphs which would result if the paragraph breaks were fixed inflexibly at the major headings.

Now suppose that the length of the assignment was 1000 words. Still figuring 150–200 words to a paragraph, we would tentatively select the initial subdivisions ("A," "B," and so on), of which there are seven, as marking the boundaries of the paragraphs. Here again we cannot be inflexible. There does not seem to be enough material in topic "III," for example, to warrant two paragraphs, and even though it contains an "A" and a "B" these probably ought to be combined into a single closing paragraph. On the other hand, either "A" or "B" under topic "II" might be handled more effectively in two paragraphs. But even allowing for these exceptions, we would still be justified in thinking of the potential paragraphs in terms of the "A," "B," "C" headings. If, finally, the length of the paper were to be 2500 words, we would plan paragraph divisions at the "1's," "2's," "3's," and so on, again allowing for adjustments.

You may begin to see the advantage of developing a good outline before you begin to write. Not only have you amassed and arranged a substantial body of material, but you have in effect a rough paragraph plan. It is, moreover, a very flexible plan, capable of being compressed to fit a paper of two or three pages or expanded to fill one of ten or twelve. Notice, too, that if you have taken care to compose meaningful headings, you also have the germ of your topic sentences and much of the detail that will support and develop them. If, to continue from our example, the student is writing a 1000-word theme and beginning a new paragraph at "II. A," the heading "Teachers and teaching methods" might be expanded into a topic sentence and support paragraph like this:

> I think that what struck me most was how different the teachers are from what I had been used to in high school. Their methods at first seemed strange. For one thing, they are much more businesslike. They keep to the point; my math professor, for example, begins to talk about trigonometry immediately, without even bothering to say, "Good morning." This is different from high school, where teachers sometimes discussed current affairs not related to their subjects or talked about their army experiences. Another thing is that college instructors tend to lecture rather than ask questions. It's even difficult for us to ask them a question. In my history class I couldn't ask one even if I wanted to, since my instructor plans his lectures to fill every second of the fifty minutes. He does not pay much attention to the text either, which is also typical of college teaching and unlike that of high school, where the teacher carefully explained the book. Apparently a college professor assumes that his students can read the text for themselves. Finally, college teachers are more formal; they call students "Mr." and "Miss" instead of by their first names, and they seldom relax and joke with the class.

You will notice that the paragraph does not follow the outline exactly. The most notable difference is that subheading "5" (the topic of discipline) has been omitted. It was dropped both because the paragraph had already grown rather long and because it proved difficult to relate to the other topics. Since the matter was hardly essential, the easiest solution was to delete it. Such slight changes are inevitable when turning an outline into an essay. No matter how carefully you have thought about an outline you will forget something, or you will find that in the context of the essay some topics turn out to be less important than you thought, while others require more treatment than the outline provided.

You should not feel, therefore, that you are bound to your outline, slavishly committed to elaborating its every twist and turn. If you have drawn up a good outline, certainly you ought to follow its general plan, but you ought also to make those adjustments inevitably demanded by the essay itself. Naturally this will mean that your draft will be slightly different from the outline you began with. If you have been asked to turn in a formal outline as part of the assignment it becomes necessary to incorporate these differences into the final copy of the outline. A formal outline submitted to your teacher along with a theme assignment must be an honest preview of that theme, promising nothing that the essay does not in fact develop and omitting no significant topic that the essay does treat.

This method of working from the outline to the essay is sometimes objected to. One complaint is that it is cumbersome. To draw up a plan, to calculate where the paragraphs will fall, to block them out, and finally to string them together with adequate transitions, seems to some people to be an unnecessarily awkward and complicated way of writing a theme. Probably to the experienced writer it would be. Yet the experienced writer himself works in essentially this way; only he works more quickly and intuitively. He does not lay out his paragraph plan so explicitly as we have suggested, but that is because he has developed a sense of paragraphing which he applies automatically when he thinks about the essay he will write. What an experienced writer can do quickly and half-consciously, the beginner must achieve more painstakingly. When you have acquired experience, you too will be able to move rapidly from the outline into the essay without counting headings and calculating where the paragraphs will fall. In the meantime, this method, cumbersome though it is, will serve in the stead of such experience and enable you to acquire it with a minimum of painful effort.

A second complaint, more serious, is that this method of drafting a composition from the outline results in themes that are mechanically cut and dried, an offense to the spirit of originality and imagination. Worked up like this, an essay seems little different from a pair of shoes cobbled out of bits and pieces of leather stamped out by a machine. There is an element of truth in the criticism. Essays planned and developed in the manner we have suggested will be, at their worst, mechanically stitched together. But for the beginning writer even mechanical organization is likely to be a step forward. Moreover, there is no reason why essays written this way have got to be at their worst. Even when he plans his draft carefully from an outline, a writer has had ample opportunity for originality of invention, and as he writes he still may express his uniqueness in his style. What we have suggested here is really nothing more than a method of working. What results from that work may be brilliantly original, if the writer has the talent and the training to make it so, or, for that matter, miserably dull, if he does not.

MECHANICS

We have seen how one goes about turning an outline into an essay. We need next to consider the activity of drafting itself, what we may call the "mechanics" of writing a draft. Knowing a few do's and don't's will not make the procedure easy — writing is seldom "easy" — but it will decrease the difficulties. The first bit of advice is this: when you compose a draft, work rapidly and force yourself to keep going right to the end. Do not get bogged down in details. If the exact word or example eludes you, write down the best substitute that comes to mind and place a question mark after it to remind you of your dissatisfaction when you revise. Even leave the space completely blank, to be filled in later — but keep going! Do not stop because you are unsure whether a sentence requires a comma or a semicolon, or whether a word is spelled "ie" or "ei" — keep going! To hesitate over such uncertainties is likely to cost you momentum. Writing is not unlike pedaling a bicycle uphill: it is easier to keep on pumping no matter how hard the effort than to stop and hope to pick up speed again. Certainly there will be times when the hill is too steep and you cannot go on. On such occasions you will have to do more than stop; you will find it necessary to go back to the beginning and start anew. But these, we hope, will be rare occasions, and most often you can keep on if you make yourself.

Do not be paralyzed by an unreasonable desire for perfection or by the wrongheaded notion that a theme should emerge in its finished form by the end of the first draft. Some students do attempt to write a perfectly finished essay the first time round by laboriously adding one finely wrought sentence to another. It is as if a sculptor tried to work by starting at the top of his block and finishing the hair of his subject to the finest detail before he had even cracked the rest of the marble; then moving down several inches to the forehead, bringing that to a fine polish; then successively completing the eyes, the nose, and on down to the feet, seeking to perfect his figure inch by meticulous inch. In like manner some people attempt to chisel out an essay a word at a time. No wonder they find writing an impossible task. In any work of art it is necessary to block out the entire form roughly before elaborating the details. Obviously you cannot slam-bang your way through an essay without thought or plan. But if you have taken the trouble to invent topics, to outline them, and to plan your essay from the outline, a certain amount of dash and verve unimpeded by a compulsion to perfection is all to the good. Your work will be rough and spotty, but a first draft is expected to be rough and spotty. It is not the finished essay.

Working rapidly, then, and getting down a complete version of the essay — no matter how crude — is more important in the first draft than going slowly and meticulously and trying to achieve perfection a line at a time. There are one or two other tips we can suggest, simple matters and obvious enough, yet able to save you unnecessary labor. Do not hesitate to use abbreviations ("&" instead of "and," for instance) or even a private shorthand, especially if doing so will help you to keep going. Remember, however, that such abbreviations, both public and private, must be replaced in the final copy turned in to your instructor by the conventional words and spellings proper to formal composition.

Write your draft on every other line. The blanks in between will provide space for additions and alterations. Keep adequate margins on both left- and right-hand sides, wide enough to allow you to make notes suggesting improvements to be incorporated in future drafts. Some people prefer to use only one side of a sheet of paper when they write a draft, reserving the obverse for extended revisions and comments. Whether you type your first draft or write it in longhand, do not be overly nice about correcting errors. Feel free to cross out mistakes or to overtype them rather than carefully erasing. Sloppiness like this is unforgivable in final copy, but it may be advantageous in a first draft since it helps maintain pace.

Revising

If the first draft attempts to get down on paper a version of the essay in its entirety, revising that draft begins the process of polishing. Revising, an activity too often neglected by rushed and impatient students, is an exceedingly important part of composition. We cannot hope to tell you here what specifically you ought to correct. What lapses in diction, sentence structure, and paragraphing to look for when you revise, you will have to learn from the chapters that follow. As you begin to judge your writing in terms of the principles of style these chapters explain, you would be wise to compile a list of errors you frequently make. Some of these mistakes will concern such mechanical matters as spelling and punctuation; others will be questions of grammar and usage; and probably more will involve points of style — the tendency to write too many sentences of the same pattern, perhaps, or to use too few examples. But whatever you find them to be — and none of us is without faults when he writes — making a list of such weaknesses will not only keep you more conscious of them as you draft but will also give you something very precise to look for when you revise.

If we cannot be more specific at this point about what to look for, we can offer you some bits of advice about how to look. The first advice is this: Think consciously and constantly of your reader. Ideally you should put yourself in the reader's position and look at your sentences as though you were coming upon them for the first time. When you write you see your words from the inside, aware to begin with of all the thoughts and feelings those words have been chosen to convey. Knowing so much, you may easily overlook ambiguities. You will spot them more easily by cultivating a detachment from your own work and by asking as you read: "Is the reader for whom I'm writing likely to misunderstand this sentence? What can I do to make sure that he does not?" For example, back on page 26 of this book you will find the sentence:

> The familiar essayist becomes a kind of second self who expresses attitudes and beliefs his readers also feel.

As it was first written the sentence used the phrase "alter ego" instead of "second self." On revision "alter ego" seemed potentially misleading. The exact meaning of the Latinate phrase is probably not immediately clear to a modern student, and since the term "ego" often suggests "conceit" to twentieth-century Americans, the possibility is high that some readers would have taken "alter ego" to mean something quite different from "second self," and that consequently their conception of the familiar essayist would have been badly askew. Why not, then, avoid this difficulty by employing the much clearer English phrase to begin with?

To all this it can be objected that readers might be expected to know about dictionaries. But in this case at least, some students who would have misread "alter ego" would have thought that they *did* know what it means, and most of us do not look up words we think we understand. Moreover, even when we know that we have failed to understand a word, we may lazily go on reading in the hope that the context will clarify matters and not stir ourselves to scramble through the dictionary. Certainly a reader has part of the responsibility for the success of the communicative act; a writer cannot be expected to explain everything. But a writer ought not to tax his readers unnecessarily. It is part of revision to search out unnecessary difficulties and resolve them. In this instance "second self" is just as precise as "alter ego" and less likely to lead to misunderstanding.

Thinking as the reader will think and anticipating his questions and uncertainties, that is the first principle of revision. A second is to read your work several times. In order to catch the ambiguities we have been speaking of, go through the essay first at normal speed, just as a reader will do. After you have corrected potentially misleading passages, read your paper a second time, much more slowly, in order to uncover grammatical and mechanical errors and infelicities of style. Deliberate slowness is essential to this kind of proofing, and since college students have long since mastered the art of silent, rapid reading, it is usually necessary that they employ some artifice to slow themselves down. One method is to force yourself to read a line at a time by covering the remainder of the page with a card or a sheet of paper. A second method — and to us a better one — is to read out loud. Reading aloud not only is slower, but also brings into play a second sense and so increases the chances of perceiving errors. When you are reading silently it is easy to skip right over a mistake like "The man, along with the boys, are going to town." Listening to yourself say the sentence, you may *hear* that something is wrong, even if you do not immediately see what it is.

Revising by reading your work out loud has one further advantage: in addition to discovering grammatical errors you will be more likely to hear awkward turns of phrase, discordant combinations of sounds, monotonous or jarring rhythms. Good prose is good to the ear. Most people have ears capable of intuiting the difference between prose that is harmonious and prose that is flat or ugly in sound, even though they may not be able to explain where the difference lies. Since your car is a more knowing guide to good style than you may suspect, learn to trust it. Listen to your sentences and when they sound flat or dull or cumbersome, work on them till they sound better. Later on in the chapters on sentence style we shall try to give you a more precise idea of what mistakes to look for and of how to correct them. In the meantime, play it by ear.

Finally, we suggest that as you read through your work, placing yourself in the role of your own audience, you read actively with a pencil or a pen in hand. (It is a good idea, incidentally, to revise with a writing instrument different from that with which you wrote the draft.) Whatever kind of writing tool you hold, *use* it. Mark up your paper, crossing out the inexact word, pruning the verbose phrase. In the blank line you left above, set down the more precise term, the more economical phrase. "Think" with your pencil. Place a question mark in the margin opposite any passage that seems murky or misleading. Make marginal notes of any doubts you feel about a sentence or a paragraph and jot down ideas for improving it. Thus you might write notes like these: "Strengthen the transition between these paragraphs"; "This paragraph needs more examples"; "Use an analogy to clarify this point"; "This sentence is ambiguous — rework it." To write well you must, in effect, play two roles — that of writer and that of critical reader. In these two capacities you have to maintain an inner dialogue, a dialogue revealed in the marginal notes you scribble as you revise.

After you have read through the first version of your essay several times and have made all the corrections it requires and noted all the places where meaning must be clarified or expanded, it is time to think about a second draft. Whether you proceed with a second draft immediately or wait a few days or even weeks will depend upon the assignment you face and upon your approach to composition. If there is no need to rush an assignment, however, you ought to consider setting aside the first draft with its revisions for a certain waiting period. The psychology of writing is subject to so many individual variations that one must hesitate to be dogmatic about it. Still, many people find that a period of quiescence between drafts is beneficial. When they return to their first draft after a week or so, they discover that the interval has given them a new angle of vision, enabling them to see new ideas and to detect weaknesses they had been unaware of in their organization or style. Contrarily, you may find that waiting between drafts costs more than it pays, causing you to forget the main lines of your thought or even to lose interest in the whole business.

But whether you start immediately on a second draft or wait a week, you should rewrite the essay from beginning to end on fresh paper. If the second draft is to be the final copy, write it neatly in accordance with the conventions of formal composition and in the format your teacher desires. If the second draft is not final, you need observe only your own standards of neatness. You should revise it as you did the first draft. Presumably you will find far fewer mechanical and grammatical errors and lapses of style. But you will discover some, and these must be marked so that corrections may be incorporated into the third draft.

The third draft may be followed by a fourth, the fourth by still another. The business of drafting and revising, like polishing wood, can go on forever. But somewhere you must stop. Where depends upon the time you have and the motives that drive you. To the perfectionist, one more draft will always seem desirable; to the unambitious or easily satisfied writer, one more draft will always seem unnecessary. You know best the extent of your own ambitions.

Summary

Drafting is the process of getting the essay down on paper. The first draft is usually developed from an outline or at least from a list of topics. As a beginner you would be wise to plot the paragraph structure of your essay from the outline, though without confining yourself rigidly to a predetermined plan. Drafting should proceed at a fairly rapid and uninterrupted pace; it is a mistake to fret about details of style or correctness during a first draft. These are matters to be picked up and corrected on revision. Revision means reading over and improving the draft. When you revise, study your prose critically, trying to anticipate the reader's reactions so that you can be sure he will react as you wish him to. Revise with a pen or pencil in hand, editing your own work — crossing out, correcting, questioning. If possible, read aloud and *listen* to what you have said. Carry on with the process of drafting and revising until you are satisfied that you have written as good an essay as your talents and the time available to you permit.

Exercises

1. From one of the outlines you developed in the last chapter compose the first draft of an essay of about 1000 words. Write on every other line and, since your teacher may want to check your work, write neatly and avoid personal abbreviations (though usually in first drafts, which are normally for your eyes alone, such abbreviations are all right). After you have completed the draft, revise it. Using a different colored pen or pencil, note in the margin any large changes or additions or deletions you wish to incorporate into the second draft, and in the blank lines above write in revisions of specific words or sentences. If you wish to cross out any part of the draft, do it with a single line so drawn through the word or passage that it can still be read. Try to work neatly so that if your teacher wishes

to inspect your work he will be able (1) easily to read everything you wrote in the first draft, (2) to understand every change you have made in revision, and (3) to distinguish draft from revision in all cases. Be able to justify any changes that your instructor may challenge. After he has returned your paper he may ask you to write a second draft. In that event incorporate all changes you think worthwhile as well as any others that may occur to you in the process of composing the second draft.

2. Write the draft of another essay from the second of the two outlines you did in the preceding exercise. In this instance, however, do not make any revisions. Instead, exchange papers with a classmate. Using a different colored pen or pencil, revise his draft as if it were your own; he will do the same for yours. When you have both finished, get together and discuss all the revisions you have each suggested, but do not come to blows.

II
THE ESSAY

We have seen that writing an essay is not a simple task, to be dashed off fifteen minutes before class. A well-written essay requires thinking and planning and polishing. But while we have said a good deal about how to invent topics and to plan and draft and polish, we have said nothing about the essay itself as a unit of composition. It is time that we did.

Essay is a difficult word to define. It came into English from French and originally meant — and in some contexts still does mean — an initial, uncertain attempt to do something. In this sense of being a tentative effort, a "try" as we might say today, the word was extended in the seventeenth century to designate prose compositions that discussed a general question from a limited and often personal point of view with no pretension to being exhaustive and final. Such writings were "essays" at treating their subjects, and they made no claim to thoroughness and authority. Since its first use in this sense, the word *essay* has been applied rather indiscriminately to a wide variety of compositions, some of them no more than fifty or a hundred words, others learned volumes of many hundreds of pages.

Most of what you will write in college is still conventionally designated as essays: freshman themes, critical studies in literature courses, term papers for history or sociology. In all these cases it is important to understand that the essay, like the sentence and the paragraph, is a unit of composition. It must have a beginning, a middle, and an end, and the paragraphs or paragraph groups that compose these parts must be tied together so that the essay is a unified whole and not simply a collection of aphorisms of varying length. Of course, it is easy to say that an essay must be unified and must have a beginning, a middle, and an end. It is more difficult to show how these parts are to be written and how that unity achieved. However, in the remainder of this chapter and in the next two we shall make a try, discussing (1) how to begin an essay, (2) how to reveal the organization and establish the unity of the body (or middle) of the essay, and (3) how to bring it to an end.

6
BEGINNING THE ESSAY

Introduction

When a reader sits down to an essay, he brings with him a set of questions: What is this about? What does the writer plan to do (and not to do) with his subject? How will he go about it? Will it interest me? To begin properly the writer must, one way or another, answer these questions. Thus from the writer's point of view beginning is a fourfold process of (1) announcing the subject, (2) limiting that subject, (3) indicating the plan of the paper, and (4) engaging the reader's interest or attention. To be more precise we should say that beginning *can* be a fourfold process, for only the first two steps are essential. Supplying the reader with the plan of an essay in the opening paragraph and deliberately angling for his interest may or may not be necessary, depending — as we shall see a little later — upon subject and purpose. Even when a beginning does all four things, it does not necessarily do them in the order we have listed. Most often, for instance, any effort to catch the reader's eye will come before the announcement of subject. But it doesn't have to; sometimes it comes toward the end of the beginning, and sometimes the effort is so pervasive that it exists all through the entire beginning rather than belonging to this part or that. A final qualification is that, while all good beginnings will do much the same thing, there is no rule about how long a beginning must be. It is conceivable that it may be no more than a sentence or two. In a book the beginning might be a full chapter. For most freshman themes a short paragraph usually suffices.

Announcing the Subject

Of the four beginning functions, the announcement is certainly the most important. There are two aspects of the announcement that we must consider. The first is whether it should be made explicitly or only by implication. In an explicit announcement the writer actually says (in the following words or in others equally precise), "My subject will be . . ." For example, the philosopher Alfred North Whitehead begins *Religion in the Making* like this:

> It is my purpose to consider the type of justification which is available for belief in the doctrines of religion.

The words "It is my purpose" make this an *explicit* announcement of topic. The chief virtue of this kind of beginning is its clarity. No intelligent and tractable reader can fail to understand what Whitehead is going to write about. But misunderstanding would have been more possible (although hardly likely) had he begun implicitly:

> Belief in doctrines of religion may be justified in various ways.

Here there is no literal statement that this *is* the subject. We might think only a witless reader could fail to infer that it was the subject; still the reader might not infer it.

Because of its clarity the explicit opening is sometimes used by scholars and scientists, especially when they are writing for their fellows. It is likely to seem dull, but a scholar writing for other scholars does not worry overmuch about catching their attention. In fact, he may feel it is professional good manners to tell his readers very explicitly what he is writing about so that they can easily decide for themselves whether the subject interests them enough to continue.

Thus explicit announcements are useful in academic writing (although even here some teachers and scholars object to them as being stiff and old-fashioned), and you might find it advisable to begin this way in a term paper. For the less formal writing you do in English composition class, however, a literal statement of purpose is very likely to seem heavy-handed. To begin an English theme: "The purpose of this paper is to contrast high school and college," for instance, is long-winded and pretentious. It is much better to announce such a subject implicitly, that is, simply to make a generalization about the subject without actually saying, "This is what I intend to write about." Thus one might begin: "High school and college are different in several ways," leaving to the reader the obvious inference that the theme which follows is about high school and college.

Sometimes writers attempt to make the inference more obvious by framing an implicit announcement in the form of a rhetorical question. Hilaire Belloc, for example, starts an essay on "The Historian" like this:

> What is the historian?
> The historian is he who tells a true story in writing.
> Consider the members of that definition. . .

Answering his beginning question with a definition, Belloc makes clear what he takes the historian to be and so is well launched into his discussion. Similarly, Professor Whitehead might have written:

> How may belief in the doctrines of religion be justified?

Or the theme on high school and college might have stated its subject like this:

> In what ways are high school and college different?

In the last example, however, the rhetorical question begins to sound painfully mechanical. Such obviousness is the danger of using rhetorical questions to identify the subject. Good writers can now and then get away with announcing their subjects this way (Belloc does), but announcement by rhetorical question is likely to prove a poor expedient. Using a rhetorical question to announce the subject of a freshman theme is better than no announcement at all; it is even better than the elephantine clumsiness of, "The purpose of this theme is . . ."; but it is not very original. State your subject in a rhetorical question only when you feel you can do it with originality or when all other ways seem even less attractive.

The same restriction holds for beginning with a dictionary definition, another way of announcing the subject in a clear but implicit manner. There is nothing inherently wrong in beginning an essay by quoting the Merriam-Webster *International* or the *New English Dictionary;* but it has been done so often that it has become trite. The student who starts off:

> The Merriam-Webster *Collegiate Dictionary* defines "college" as "an independent institution of higher learning offering a course of general studies leading to a bachelor's degree . . ."

has made it clear that he is going to write about college, but he may very well have annoyed his teacher, who has been exposed to this sort of beginning too often. Of course, if the definition is somehow clever or unusual it may make an effective beginning. The earlier definition of college as "four years under the ether cone" is certainly more novel and interesting (though, let us hope, less accurate) than the dictionary definition, and it might make a good opening indeed. Again, when the purpose of the entire essay is to define something, it is legitimate to start with the dictionary. But having admitted these qualifications, we may repeat that dictionary definitions, like rhetorical questions, have been overworked as ways of announcing the subject.

In addition to being expressed explicitly or implicitly, the announcement of subject may be made immediately or it may be delayed. The American poet and critic John Peale Bishop begins an appreciation of Pablo Picasso with the following sentence:

> There is no painter who has so spontaneously and so profoundly reflected his age as Pablo Picasso.

This is a good example of immediate announcement; the very first sentence tells us the subject of the essay. Similarly Aldous Huxley opens his essay "Selected Snobberies":

> All men are snobs about something.

And Jonathan Swift begins "A Treatise on Good Manners and Good Breeding" like this:

> Good manners is the art of making those people easy with whom we converse.

There are several advantages to letting the reader know at once what the subject is. It is a no-nonsense, businesslike way of proceeding. It shows a care for the reader's energy and time; the reader knows right away what he is getting into and he can back off if he wishes. On the other hand, an immediate announcement is not very seductive. Bishop's opening, for instance, will attract people who are interested in Picasso to begin with, but it is less likely to attract those who need to be persuaded that they ought to be interested in the painter. If there is interest inherent in the subject itself, an immediate announcement will catch the reader's eye. This is true of Huxley's sentence "All men are snobs about something," where the idea is sufficiently strange to arouse our curiosity. Generally, however, immediate announcement, like explicit announcement, is long on clarity and short on interest.

Delayed announcement is perhaps more common in essays. Usually the delay is achieved by beginning quite broadly and gradually narrowing the topic down, a process exemplified in miniature in this sentence that opens the chapter on Samuel Johnson in F. L. Lucas's book, *The Search for Good Sense:*

> Among all English writers, or in all English history and biography, or in all English fiction and drama, it may be doubted if there is any character that has more stamped itself on English memories than Johnson.

Such "focusing down," as we may call it, more frequently proceeds through several sentences, so that the specific subject is not announced until the very end of the beginning paragraph or section. The opening of A. J. Liebling's essay "A Talkative Jerk" is a good example:

> The traditional Englishman of Gallic fiction is a naïve chap who speaks bad French, eats tasteless food, and is only accidentally and episodically heterosexual. The sole tolerable qualities ever allowed him are to be earnest, in an obtuse way, and physically brave, through lack of imagination.
>
> When I began reading *The Quiet American,* in its British edition, on a plane between London and New York last December (Viking has just now brought it out in this country), I discovered that Mr. Graham Greene, who is British, had contrived to make his Quiet American, Pyle, a perfect specimen of a French author's idea of an Englishman. I had bought *The Quiet American* at the waiting-room newsstand, on the assurance of the young lady attendant that it was good light reading. *The Most of A. J. Liebling*

Less commonly, the announcement of the subject may be delayed by the opposite process, that is, by beginning very specifically and focusing up until the subject is reached. E. M. Forster opens an essay on Sinclair Lewis with this paragraph:

> "I would like to see Gopher Prairie," says the heroine of Mr. Sinclair Lewis's *Main Street,* and her husband promptly replies: "Trust me. Here she is. Brought some snapshots down to show you." That, in substance, is what Mr. Lewis has done himself. He has brought down some snapshots to show us and posterity. The collection is as vivid and stimulating as any writer who adopts this particular method can offer. Let us examine it; let us consider the method in general. And let us at once dismiss the notion that any fool can use a camera. Photography is a great gift, whether or no we rank it as an art. If we have not been to Gopher Prairie we cry: "So that's it!" on seeing the snap. If we have been we either cry: "How like it!" or "How perfectly disgraceful, not the least like it!" and in all these cases our vehemence shows that we are in the presence of something alive. *Abinger Harvest*

A slightly more extended example of announcement delayed by focusing up are the paragraphs that begin Aldous Huxley's essay on "Tragedy and the Whole Truth":

> There were six of them, the best and bravest of the hero's companions. Turning back from his post in the bows, Odysseus was in time to see them lifted, struggling, into the air, to hear their screams, the desperate repetition of his own name. The survivors could only look on, helplessly, while Scylla "at the mouth of her cave devoured them, still screaming, still stretching out their hands to me in the frightful struggle." And Odysseus adds that it was the most dreadful and lamentable sight he ever saw in all his "explorings of the passes of the sea." We can believe it; Homer's brief description (the too-poetical simile is a later interpolation) convinces us.
>
> Later, the danger passed, Odysseus and his men went ashore for the night, and, on the Sicilian beach, prepared their supper — prepared it, says Homer, "expertly." The Twelfth Book of the *Odyssey* concludes with these words: "When they had satisfied their thirst and hunger, they thought of their dear companions and wept, and in the midst of their tears sleep came gently upon them."
>
> The truth, the whole truth and nothing but the truth — how rarely the older literatures ever told it! Bits of the truth, yes; every good book gives us bits of the truth, would not be a good book if it did not. But the whole truth, no. Of the great writers of the past incredibly few have given us that. Homer — the Homer of the *Odyssey* — is one of those few.

In both these cases the essayists begin with a specific incident and rather than narrowing into their subjects move from the particular to the general.

Whether the delay be achieved by focusing down or focusing up, the effect is much the same. The chief advantage is that in either case the reader suspects that the generalization or the specific incident is not exactly the subject, and curious to find out what is, he is pulled along into the essay. To be more exact we should say that he is willing to be pulled along a little way; curiosity is not the strongest of drives and in most people does not survive much frustration. Consequently, a writer can afford to delay the announcement only so long as his readers will not desert him. A less obvious advantage of delayed announcement is that the skill with which the writer manages the performance can be interesting in itself. There is a pleasure, akin to that of watching a high-wire performer or listening to a fine pianist, in observing an accomplished writer close in upon his subject through indirection. The skill ought not, of course, to become mere virtuosity — the subject is the essential thing, not the cleverness with which the writer announces it. Still we can admire cleverness in writing so long as it is restrained to being a means to the end of communication and not allowed to become the end itself. Finally, the delayed announcement can help to clarify the subject by setting it within a meaningful framework or by offering a specific instance of what it entails. Liebling's remarks on the Englishman in French fiction, for example, suggest a fault of many novelists to rely upon national types rather than to create believable Frenchmen or Britons or Americans; and this generalization enables us to understand Liebling's reaction to Graham Greene's novel. Similarly Huxley's recounting the episode from the *Odyssey* reveals what Homer knew: that men die and their friends grieve for them, but the living must eat and sleep, and their grief is no less genuine because they cook their meal well and then rest — that this is the "whole truth" about human existence.

The delayed announcement, then, has the advantages of arousing curiosity, of being clever, and of clarifying the subject. For these reasons delayed announcement is valuable in writing that seeks to entertain as well as to inform. But in writing, as in life, every virtue has its vice, and the disadvantages of delaying the statement of the subject are several. First, as we have already noticed, it will lose more readers than it attracts if it is overdone. Second, it is likely to irritate those readers who expect a writer to get to the point. In situations where getting to the point is more important than awakening the reader's curiosity or entertaining him, delayed announcement is likely to be a fault. Most readers of scholarly and technical articles, for instance, rightfully expect the subject to be stated as quickly as possible; most teachers reading term papers prefer the businesslike efficiency of immediate announcement to the cleverness of delay. We may conclude, then, that whether you tell your reader at once what your subject is or whether you delay the announcement to the end of the opening paragraph will depend upon your subject, your reader, and your purpose in addressing him.

Limiting the Subject

If the announcement of subject is the most essential function of a beginning paragraph, the announcement must in most cases be followed by a limiting sentence or clause. Few essays discuss *all* there is to be said about their subjects; rather they treat this aspect but not that. It is important that the writer clearly define the boundaries of his essay. As with the announcement, the limitation may be made explicitly — the writer literally saying, "I will do such and so" — or implicitly. Explicit limitation is usually confined to technical and scholarly writing, where, as we have seen, clarity is the chief consideration. The following paragraph is a case in point; it begins an essay by Benjamin Farrington entitled "The Hand in Healing: A Study in Greek Medicine from Hippocrates to Ramazzini":

> My purpose in this essay is not to discuss the details of Greek surgical practice, a subject with which I am not competent to deal. I wish rather to speak of Greek medicine as a whole and to examine the effect upon it of the Greek prejudice against manual labour. It would still more accurately define my purpose if I spoke not simply of the prejudice against manual labour, but of the decline in social status of the manual labourer which accompanied the growth of civilization. My subject lies, therefore, not within the domain of pure science, but within that of the social relations of science, and may accordingly claim to be topical.
>
> *Head and Hand in Ancient Greece*

In English compositions, however, it is usually preferable to limit the subject less obviously, implying the boundaries of the paper rather than literally drawing them. Joseph Wood Krutch, for example, begins his essay "Is Reading Here To Stay?" with this brief paragraph:

> Publishers, I am told, are worried about their business, and I, as a writer, am therefore worried too. But I am not sure that the actual state of their affairs disturbs me quite so much as some of the analyses of it and some of the proposals for remedying what is admittedly an unsatisfactory situation. *The Nation*, 26 FEB. 1949

Mr. Krutch makes it clear that his interest in the problems of publishing will be confined to criticizing some of the attempts that have been made to analyze and solve those problems. Yet he does not literally state this limitation; it is merely implied by the second sentence.

Limitation, in addition to being explicit or implicit, may also be both positive and negative. That is, the writer may indicate what he *will* do, or what he *will not* do, or he may indicate both. Thus, Mr. Farrington tells us in the first sentence what he does not intend to cover and in the second and third what he does. The following opening paragraph by John Buchan even more plainly illustrates both negative and positive limitation:

> The title of this chapter ["My America"] exactly defines its contents. It presents the American scene as it appears to one observer — a point of view which does not claim to be that mysterious thing, objective truth. There will be no attempt to portray the "typical" American, for I have never known one. I have met a multitude of

> individuals, but I should not dare to take any one of them as representing his country — as being that other mysterious thing, the average man. You can point to certain qualities which are more widely distributed in America than elsewhere, but you will scarcely find human beings who possess all these qualities. One good American will have most of them; another, equally good and not less representative, may have few or none. So I shall eschew generalities. If you cannot indict a nation, no more can you label it like a museum piece.
> *Pilgrim's Way*

Some limitation — explicit or implicit, positive or negative — is necessary at the beginning of most essays. Term papers, formal essays whose purpose is to inform, technical and scholarly articles may all have to engage in a substantial amount of boundary fixing in the beginning section to ensure that the reader will not be misled or disappointed. The usual freshman theme, however, does not require extensive limitation of subject. We are told all we really need to know about the subject, for example, by an opening sentence like this:

> College is different from high school in several ways.

Here the limitation is contained in the final prepositional phrase and is coupled in the same sentence with the announcement. We know that the subject is a contrast between college and high school and that it will be limited to two or three specific points of difference. This is limitation enough for a brief, informal essay, and the student can get on with his discussion without the heavy addition of a sentence like:

> I shall limit this comparison to teaching methods, homework, and tests.

No one can give you a rule by which to test whether you have limited a subject sufficiently. All you can do is to put yourself in the reader's place and ask if it is clear (whether by implication or by direct statement) what the essay will do and what it will not do.

Another sort of limitation that must be established in the opening paragraph is point of view. *Point of view* means how the writer presents his material, whether he literally reveals himself by using "I," "me," "my"; or avoids all explicit reference to himself. In the first case the point of view is called "personal"; in the second, "impersonal." While it might seem to be so, the difference between the personal and the impersonal points of view is *not* that in the first the subject is the writer and in the second it is something else. Actually every subject anyone writes about involves himself. A physicist discussing the structure of atoms is (to be precise about it) discussing his own understanding of that structure.

Many subjects can be presented from either side, though adopting a personal point of view or an impersonal one will result in considerably different treatments. Other subjects plainly involve the personality of the writer and hence require a first-person presentation. It would be ridiculous, for example, for someone to be completely impersonal in describing a trip he took to Sweden; he would be forced into circumlocutory passive constructions and in general would sound pompously artificial. On the other hand, there are subjects in which a personal point of view would be inappropriate. For instance, a scientist, when he writes professionally, usually tries to keep his personality in the background, and properly so: his subject is best handled impersonally.

Whichever point of view a writer chooses, it is important that he establish it in his beginning paragraph, for a point of view constitutes a limitation a writer imposes upon himself. If he writes from a personal point of view, he says, in effect, "This is how it seems to me"; if he writes impersonally, he says, "This is how it is." In establishing a point of view it is not necessary to say, "My point of view will be such and such"; one merely needs to use "I" in the course of his opening to make clear that his point of view is personal, or avoid the first-person pronoun to indicate that it is not. Do not be afraid, incidentally, to use "I" if it fits your subject. Some students seem to have been conditioned to regard "I" as a taboo word in English class. When handling a subject that requires personal comment, they hide behind such false beards as "this observer," "your reporter," "the writer," the editorial "we," and so on. If what you are writing about requires personal comment, say "I."

Once established, point of view should be kept the same throughout the essay, that is, the writer should not jump back and forth between personal and impersonal treatments. This does not deny that within the personal point of view it is allowable — and sometimes even desirable — to make slight adjustments. A writer may legitimately expand "I" to "we" when he wishes to say "I the writer and you the reader." And whether writing personally or impersonally, he may address his readers as individuals by employing "you," and shift to "one," "anyone," "people," and so on when he intends no particular individual. But such shifts in point of view must be compatible with the emphasis the writer desires, and they should be slight. Radical changes in point of view, nine times in ten, are awkward. It is good practice, then, (1) to select a point of view appropriate to the subject;

(2) to establish that point of view, implicitly but clearly, in the beginning; and (3) not basically to change it during the course of the essay.

Indicating the Plan of the Essay

All essays follow a plan and this plan will be present in the writer's mind when he composes his beginning paragraph (or at any rate when he revises it). The question that must be asked here is: Should the plan be revealed to the reader?

Writers often do consider it necessary. The historian Harold Mattingly, for instance, begins his book *Roman Imperial Civilization* with this paragraph:

> The object of this first chapter is to give a sketch of the Empire which may supply a background to all that follows: to explain what the position of Emperor from time to time was, how it was defined in law, how it was interpreted by the subjects; then, around the Emperor, to show the different parts of the State in relation to one another and to him. Later chapters will develop particular themes. We shall have to consider at the close how far the constitution of the Empire was satisfactory for its main purposes, how much truth there is in the contention that imperfections in the constitution were a main cause of Decline and Fall.

This paragraph skillfully indicates not only the plan of the first chapter and that of the whole book, but also how the first chapter fits into that larger plan.

Even with subjects less complex and grand than the Roman Empire, a writer may wish to tell us his plan. Read this opening paragraph of a biographical sketch by Kenneth Andler:

> I want to tell you about a woodsman, what he was like, what his work was, and what it meant. His name was Alfred D. Teare and he came originally from Nova Scotia, but all the time I knew him his home was in Berlin, New Hampshire. Probably the best surveyor of old lines in New England, he was — in his way — a genius. "SURVEYOR IN THE WOODS," *Harper's Magazine*, JULY 1947

This straightforward, businesslike paragraph achieves more than you may think. It not only clearly announces and limits the subject, but also reveals the organization of the essay to follow. The sensitive reader is prepared for a three-part structure, and he expects the first part to describe Mr. Teare as a person, the second to discuss the nature of his work, and the third to evaluate that work. Naturally, these expectations are based on the assumption that the writer knows his craft — as in this case he does — and that he would not have mentioned these aspects of his subject in the particular order he does unless the order reflected the organization of the essay. Here, then, the writer has conveyed his plan quite subtly, but none the less effectively.

Whether the writer does it subtly or obviously, revealing the plan has several advantages. One, of course, is that it makes the reader's task easier. Knowing where he is going, the reader is better able to see the significance of the writer's ideas as they present themselves in the body of the essay, and he is more prepared for twists of thought and movement from one section to another. A second advantage is that an initial indication of plan also simplifies the task of the writer. If he can assume that his readers know the general organizational scheme of his essay, the writer will find it easier to move from point to point. Readers who have been briefed beforehand do not need elaborate transitions (assuming, of course, that the writer himself is following a clear plan; it won't help a writer to brief his readers if his own ideas are confused).

As with the matter of limiting the subject, we cannot set down clear-cut rules about revealing your plan. On the whole, it is wise to indicate a plan in papers that are relatively long and which divide into several parts — term papers, for example. The briefer, less formal, simpler English essay is not as likely to require an indication of plan in its beginning paragraph, though here you must be guided by your subject, purpose, and reader. When it is necessary to indicate a plan, do it as implicitly as you can. The imaginary theme about high school and college, for example, might be expanded like this to indicate plan:

> College is different from high school in several ways — especially in teaching methods, homework, and tests.

As with the paragraph by Mr. Andler, this clearly implies the divisions of the essay and their order. Occasionally, especially in longer, more scholarly work, you may feel you have to indicate your plan explicitly; do so if clarity demands it. But when you do, be sure that your subject is substantial and your purpose serious enough to support a ponderous beginning.

Interesting the Reader

The last of the principal functions of the opening paragraph is to engage the reader's attention. This is not an inevitable function of beginning an essay. A scholar or scientist or engineer writing for his colleagues can afford to take their interest for granted. More often, however, the writer's potential audience will include at least some people whose interest must be deliberately sought. There are many ways of seeking it. Indeed, there are far more than we can discuss here; in what follows we shall indicate merely a few of the devices good writers have used.

Before we do, however, two precautions need to be made. The first concerns the term "device," which is, perhaps, a little misleading. Do not equate it with the attention-getting gimmicks of advertisers and pitchmen. Faced with the problem of engaging his reader's mind, the good writer finds a solution that is legitimately a part of, or related to, his subject. He cannot start with any anecdote that happens to be funny or with any quotation that is clever. The anecdote or quotation must lead him naturally into what he wants to discuss. Because they are part and parcel of the writer's topic, then, devices of engaging the reader are more than tricks. They are compositional techniques that every effective writer needs to know.

The second point is that to understand how the writer attracts his reader's interest, we must distinguish two different things. There is on the one hand, the psychological aspect of the appeal — whether it arouses curiosity or amuses or shocks and so on. On the other hand, there are the specific compositional devices the writer employs — an anecdote, for instance, or an allusion, a rhetorical question, a paradox, a *non sequitur*, a metaphor, a definition, or some odd word or syntactical pattern. These two things tend to cut across one another. Anecdotes, for example, may shock, amuse, or surprise; curiosity may be aroused by quotations, rhetorical questions, or paradoxes, as well as by anecdotes. It is a complicated business systematically to relate all the various compositional techniques we mentioned above to all the psychologically different kinds of appeal — too complicated for our purposes. Here, we shall simply ask rather generally: What is the psychology of interesting a reader, and how may specific compositional devices be used to engage this interest?

One type of appeal is to assume the reader to be a reasonable, intelligent man and to suggest to him, "Here is something that you ought to know or that probably will interest you." In effect, the writer engages the reader by justifying his essay as being about something important. There was something of this in the sentence by John Peale Bishop quoted on page 76; Picasso, he implied, is worth our attention. A more extended instance is the following passage by J. E. Neale, introducing an essay on Elizabethan politics:

> We are living in an age of ideological conflict and are troubled by the strains it imposes on society. The totalitarian state spreads alarm; we fear doctrinaires with their subversive organizations; we suspect fellow-travellers; we endure the Cold War; we think of quislings and the fifth column as instruments of foreign conquest. The fanatic's way of life we know to be dynamic; and though we say "It shall not happen here," we are not inclined, after our experience of the last twenty years, to boast that it cannot happen here. We are at odds about the policy we should pursue. Passion breeds passion; and unless we feel deeply about our own ideals, inevitably we are at a disadvantage against the enemies of society. Moderation, which is a liberal virtue, takes on a watery appearance. It seems uninspired and inglorious, prone to defeat.
>
> In such a dilemma it may be useful to turn to history, which is the treasury of recorded experience. History never repeats itself, but it offers analogies. Just as the historian, consciously or unconsciously, uses the present to understand the past, so there is a reverse process. It is the most weighty of the justifications for the writing and the study of history; and a nation which is historically minded is more likely to be fortunate in its affairs than one which is not.
>
> For an analogy with our own times we cannot do better than turn to the Elizabethan period in English history . . .
>
> "THE VIA MEDIA IN POLITICS: A HISTORICAL PARALLEL,"
> *Essays in Elizabethan History*

So restrained and rational an appeal, however, is likely to be of limited effectiveness, and more often a writer will aim at his reader's curiosity. He may begin, for instance, with a short statement which is apparently factual, yet which raises more questions than it answers. W. Somerset Maugham starts a short biographical sketch by writing: "I knew he was drunk." "Who," we ask, "is 'he'? How did you know he was drunk?" The fact may be even more obviously question-provoking. The astronomer Sir Arthur Eddington begins a chapter in his book *The Philosophy of Physical Science* with this sentence:

> I believe there are 15,747,724,136,275,002,577,605,653,691,181, 555,468,044,717,914,527,116,709,366,231,425,076,185,631,031,296 protons in the universe, and the same number of electrons.

It would be a curiously incurious reader who would not boggle at this and read on to find out how the writer arrived at so precise a figure.

Again a writer may arouse curiosity by beginning with a paradox — not a logical paradox involving self-contradiction, but simply a statement that seems to contradict reality as we know it. Hilaire Belloc starts off his essay "The Barbarians" by asserting:

> It is a pity that true history is not taught in schools.
>
> *One Thing and Another*

"This is strange," the reader thinks; "I had supposed that it *was* taught in the schools. What can the fellow mean?" And he reads on to find out. Sometimes the surprise will take the form of a *non sequitur*, as in this sentence with which an enterprising student began a theme: "I hate botany, which is why I went to New York." As the rest of her essay revealed, there was in fact a logical connection here, but the seeming illogicality pulled the reader in.

A similar device is to begin with a cryptic statement, a remark that is mysterious or not exactly clear. Arthur H. Little, for example, opens an essay entitled "The King's English: An Appreciation" with the following sentence:

> This is a second attempt.
>
> I had heard him over the air. I had heard an English King explain to his people his renunciation of the British throne.
>
> *Printer's Ink*, DEC. 17, 1936

And Kenneth Grahame begins an essay with: "It was the day I was promoted to a toothbrush" ("The Finding of the Princess" in *The Golden Age*). In both these cases we are puzzled. How is one "promoted to a toothbrush"? "The second attempt" at what? It is important to observe that cryptic openings like these cannot simply be murky. At their best they combine clarity of statement with mystery of intent. It is plain enough what "This is a second attempt" literally says, the mystery results from the fact that "attempt" has not been specified. When we realize, as we quickly do, that the writer means his second attempt to convey how deeply he was affected by the abdication speech of Edward VIII, the mystery disappears. Just as it does when we come to see that Grahame means "the day I was allowed to use a toothbrush by myself." Notice, moreover, that the mystery must be cleared up rather soon if the reader's interest is to be retained. For most of us, curiosity, like love, does not linger long without satisfaction; it goes elsewhere.

In all these examples, the curiosity-rousing passage has been in the form of a statement. It doesn't have to be; often a writer can as easily express it as a rhetorical question. Hilaire Belloc, for instance, might have written:

> I wonder why true history is not taught in schools?

Even without a cryptic or a paradoxical implication, rhetorical questions are likely to arouse our curiosity simply by being questions and making us wonder about their answer. Thus Francis Bacon began a famous essay "On Truth" like this:

> "*What is truth?*" said jesting Pilate and would not stay for an answer.

And F. L. Lucas opens an essay on James Boswell:

> The central dissension over James Boswell turns on the question —ass or genius? *The Search for Good Sense*

Whether or not these are fair questions, we are likely to be curious about what the answers will be.

Aside from arousing their curiosity, the writer may try to engage his readers by amusing them. One device is to open with a witty remark, often involving an allusion to some historical figure or a quotation or paraphrase of a remark attributed to such a figure. Professor Colin Cherry, for example, starts his book *On Human Communication* by noting:

> Leibnitz, it has sometimes been said, was the last man to know everything.

George Santayana begins his essay "Heathenism" with this allusion:

> Schopenhauer somewhere observes that the word heathen, no longer in reputable use elsewhere, had found a last asylum in Oxford, the paradise of dead philosophies. Even Oxford, I believe, has now abandoned it; yet it is a good word.

The readers at whom Santayana aimed would have smiled at hearing Oxford described as the "last asylum" for heathenism and a "paradise of dead philosophies," and at the subtle implication of "Even." A beginning allusion may be even more subtle and still be entertaining. Katherine Fullerton Gerould starts an essay entitled "What, Then, Is Culture?" by alluding implicitly to the beginning of Bacon's essay "On Truth":

> "*What is truth?*" said jesting Pilate, and would not stay for an answer.

> "*What is culture?*" said an enlightened man to me not long since; and though he stayed for an answer, he did not get one.

Anecdotes are still another way of amusing the reader. They can have a double value, attracting us twice over — once by their own wittiness and again by the skill with which the writer applies them to his subject. A good example is the following opening by Nancy Mitford:

> "What became of that man I used to see sitting at the end of your table?" somebody asked the famous eighteenth-century Paris hostess, Mme. Geoffrin.
>
> "He was my husband. He is dead." It is the epitaph of all such husbands. The hostess of a salon (the useful word salonnière, unfortunately, is an Anglo-Saxon invention) must not be encumbered by family life, and her husband, if he exists, must know his place.
>
> The salon was invented by the Marquise de Rambouillet at the beginning of the seventeenth century . . .
>
> "SOME ROOMS FOR IMPROVEMENT," *The Water Beetle*

A second instance is this paragraph by Professor J. G. Randall, which opens his discussion of the Emancipation Proclamation in his study *Lincoln and the South*:

> A suitable text for this lecture might be the statement of an old Alabama Negro a few years ago. When questioned about Lincoln, he said: "I don't know nothin' 'bout Abe Lincoln 'ceptin' dey say he sot us free, an' I don't know nothin' 'bout dat neither." The old darky's saying might apply to many among our worthy citizens, though perhaps few of us could match him in the wisdom of admitted ignorance.
>
> To say that a thing is "well known," as is the emancipation proclamation . . .

Both these stories are amusing (in a cynical fashion) and each is integrally a part of the writer's subject; neither anecdote is forced upon the material from the outside.

Another opening device that is often entertaining is the clever or appropriate comparison. It may be an analogy, as in the following passage by Virginia Woolf, the first part of the opening paragraph of her essay "Reviewing":

> In London there are certain shop windows that always attract a crowd. The attraction is not in the finished article but in the worn-out garments that are having patches inserted in them. The crowd is watching the women at work. There they sit in the shop window putting invisible stitches into moth-eaten trousers. And this familiar

> sight may serve as illustration to the following paper. So our poets, playwrights, and novelists sit in the shop window, doing their work under the eyes of reviewers.
>
> *The Captain's Death Bed and Other Essays*

Less commonly the comparison calculated to arouse our interest is a simile or a metaphor. G. K. Chesterton wittily begins an essay "On Monsters" with this metaphorical comparison:

> I saw in an illustrated paper — which sparkles with scientific news — that a green-blooded fish had been found in the sea; indeed, a creature that was completely green, down to this uncanny ichor in its veins, and very big and venomous at that. Somehow I could not get it out of my head, because the caption suggested a perfect refrain for a Ballade: A green-blooded fish has been found in the sea. It has so wide a critical and philosophical application. I have known so many green-blooded fish on the land, walking about the streets and sitting in the clubs, and especially the committees. So many green-blooded fish have written books and criticisms of books, have taught in academies of learning and founded schools of philosophy that they have almost made themselves the typical biological product of the present stage of evolution. *Selected Essays*

This is not all of the first paragraph, but it is enough to show that Chesterton is using "green-blooded fish" as a metaphor for all the fools and men of ill-will with which the world abounds. Even those who do not think the metaphor especially appropriate might be engaged by its originality.

Finally, here is a clever opening that depends upon a definition:

> "Foreigner, differing from speaker in language and customs, outside the Roman Empire; rude, wild, or uncultured person." The Barbarian of yesterday is the Tourist of today and he still preys on the rich old cities where our civilization began.
>
> NANCY MITFORD, "THE TOURIST," *The Water Beetle*

We have seen (page 75) that opening with a dictionary definition can be trite. Here, however, it works because it neatly forces us to see the connection between the ideas "tourist" and "barbarian."

Thus by using such devices as allusion, quotation, anecdote, rhetorical question, metaphor, analogy, paradox, and *non sequitur,* the writer attempts to engage our interest. He may try to amuse us, to arouse our curiosity, to shock, or simply appeal to our desire to be well-informed, reasonable human beings; but somehow he must make an effort to pull us into his essay. All this is preliminary to the writer's main business; yet it is important. The writer with something worth saying needs first to attract his reader's attention; if he cannot, he is little better off than the man with nothing to say. The composition student may feel that in his case interesting the reader is academic — the teacher must read the themes. But even (perhaps, especially) for the composition student there is a practical advantage in interesting his reader; and practicalities aside, it is something you should learn, for the ability to engage a reader is part of being a good writer.

Summary

The chief functions of the beginning are to announce and limit the subject, to indicate a plan (if the writer thinks the reader requires one), and to attract the reader's eye (if he is not committed to the subject to begin with). When these functions have been fulfilled, the beginning is usually over and the writer is in a position to embark upon a discussion of his subject. In this respect the beginning is like the remarks by which a master of ceremonies at a banquet introduces the main speaker. Certainly that introduction ought to make clear who the speaker is and in a general way what he will do, and it ought to persuade the diners to listen. But it ought not, we would think, to summarize the speech. This is a common fault of inexperienced writers. They sometimes suppose that a beginning should contain a synopsis of the essay, and in their effort to supply such a summary they find themselves saying the same thing twice over — once in the beginning, again in the body of the essay.

There are exceptions, of course. Now and then a writer may anticipate his main thesis in order to stress its importance, or to make sure that the readers understand how he feels about a controversial issue. In the final sentence of the following opening paragraph, for instance, Professor Samuel R. Levin anticipates one of his conclusions, in order to make his own position clear and to enable the reader better to follow his argument:

> In the last few decades, a significant change has developed in the attitudes of people interested in the study of language. This change results from a different way of looking at language—the structural way. In this paper, I should like to discuss what a comparison of traditional and structural grammar reveals about their respective adequacies, specifically as each is applied to a description of English. I may say, at the outset, that in my opinion the traditional grammar often fails to satisfactorily explain the linguistic facts, whereas structural grammar does not fail in this way—precisely because it deals with them.
>
> "COMPARING TRADITIONAL AND STRUCTURAL GRAMMAR,"
> *College English*, FEB. 1960

Even less commonly a writer may carry anticipation to the extreme by starting at the very end of his account. In *The Long Death* (a history of the defeat of the Plains Indians) Mr. Ralph K. Andrist begins with the last scene of that defeat:

> The last gunfire on the Great Plains between Indians and soldiers of the United States was exchanged on a bitterly cold day in 1890, the next to the last day of the year. On that day, on Wounded Knee Creek in South Dakota, a forlorn and hungry band of Sioux, including women and children, was goaded and frightened into making a gesture of resistance to Army authority. When it was over, the Indian wars of the plains were ended, and with them the long struggle of all American Indians, from the Atlantic to the Pacific, to preserve some portion of their ancestral lands and tribal ways.
>
> When the Civil War ended, a Union band played "Auld Lang Syne" at Appomattox, and many magnanimous words were spoken ("The men who own a horse or mule can take them home, General. They will need them to work their little farms.") But no band blared "Auld Lang Syne" into the frigid air at Wounded Knee Creek and there was no one who offered kind or noble words; when the frozen bodies were thrown into a common grave, not one of the ministers or priests who was in the area to lead the Sioux into the gentle religion considered it worth his trouble to bring God's presence to the bleak burial.
>
> The condition of the Sioux, or of the other tribes of the plains had not always been so low. Half a century earlier, the Indians had been almost sole possessors of the Great Plains.

By giving this glimpse of the end, Mr. Andrist has effectively drawn us into his book. Moreover, by the very terms in which he describes that end he has enlisted our sympathy with the Indians and made us take a stand on the moral issue implicit in this bit of American history.

Successful anticipations like these, however, are difficult to do well. The inexperienced writer is wise to avoid attempting them and running the risk of making his beginning seem like a capsule version of the entire essay. Remember: The beginning *introduces* the topic; it does not discuss it.

The opposite fault — having too brief a beginning, or even none at all — is just as common. It is especially likely under the artificial conditions of a freshman theme assignment, when the student is writing for the teacher, who, after all, gave the assignment and hardly needs to be told what the subject is. But often a teacher will have allowed you some latitude and may not know exactly what you have chosen to do. Even when he does know, you ought to assume that he does not and so give yourself practice in the art of opening an essay. Try not to throw your discussion at the reader before he has had a chance to settle down and learn what all this is about. You may prefer the quick, down-to-business opening like that of Mr. Andler ("I want to tell you about a woodsman . . ."), or you may prefer a more discursive start. Quite apart from your own preferences, your subject or your purpose may require this method of beginning or another. But in any case, introduce your essay; do not simply dump it down before the reader.

Exercises

1. Study the following passages, each the beginning of an essay or book. In the light of the principles and techniques discussed in this chapter be able to discuss why each is an effective opening, the sort of reader at whom the writers seem to be aiming, and what each writer intends to achieve with this reader.

> 1. I hope the two ladies from the country who have been writing to the newspapers to know what sights they ought to see in London during their Easter holiday will have a nice time. I hope they will enjoy the tube, and have fine weather for the Monument, and whisper to each other successfully in the whispering gallery of St. Paul's, and see the dungeons at the Tower and the seats of the mighty at Westminister, and return home with a harvest of joyful memories. But I can promise them that there is one sight they will not see. They will not see me. Their idea of a holiday is London. My idea of a holiday is forgetting there is such a place as London.
>
> A. G. GARDINER, "ON TAKING A HOLIDAY"

> 2. Anybody who dares to discuss the making of tragedy lays himself open to critical assault and general barrage, for the theorists have been hunting for the essence of tragedy since Aristotle without entire success. There is no doubt that Aristotle came very close to a definition of what tragedy is in his famous passage on catharsis. But why the performance of tragedy should have a cleansing effect on the audience, why an audience is willing to listen to tragedy, why tragedy has a place in the education of men, has never, to my knowledge, been convincingly stated. I must begin by saying that I have not solved the Sphinx's riddle which fifty generations of skillful brains have left in shadow. But I have one suggestion which I think might lead to a solution if it were put to laboratory tests by those who know something about philosophical analysis and dialectic.
>
> MAXWELL ANDERSON, "THE ESSENCE OF TRAGEDY"

> 3. The title of this paper is too brief to be quite accurate. Perhaps with the following subtitle it does not promise too much: A partial account

of the origin and development of the attitudes which commonly pass for grammar in Western culture and particularly in English-speaking societies.

KARL W. DYKEMA, "WHERE OUR GRAMMAR CAME FROM," *College English*, VOL. 22, NO. 7, APRIL 1961

4. In the preceding lecture we were concerned with the ideal form of democracy. It is obvious that the reality does not strictly conform to this ideal. There is nothing remarkable in that. The ideal is always better than the real — otherwise there would be no need for ideals. We have been told, as if it were a surprising thing, that in Russia the Revolution has been betrayed. But it was bound to be betrayed. It is in the nature of revolutions to be betrayed, since life and history have an inveterate habit of betraying the ideal aspirations of men. In this sense the liberal-democratic revolution was likewise bound to be betrayed — men were sure to be neither so rational nor so well-intentioned as the ideology conceived them to be. But while a little betrayal is a normal thing, too much is something that calls for explanation. The liberal-democratic revolution has been so far betrayed, the ideal so imperfectly portrayed in the course of events, that its characteristic features cannot easily be recognized in any democratic society today. In this lecture I shall attempt to disclose some of the essential reasons for the profound discord between democracy as it was ideally projected and democracy as a going concern.

CARL BECKER, "THE REALITY," *Modern Democracy*

5. There is a pleasant story of an itinerant sign-painter who in going his rounds came to a village inn upon whose sign-board he had had his eye for some months and had watched with increasing hope and delight its rapid progress to blurred and faded dimness. To his horror he found a brand-new varnished sign. He surveyed it with disgust, and said to the inn-keeper, who stood nervously by hoping for a professional compliment, "This looks as if someone had been doing it himself."

That sentence holds within it the key to the whole mystery of essay-writing. [The essay goes on.]

ARTHUR C. BENSON, "THE ART OF THE ESSAYIST"

6. This paper is about the phrase "the meaning of a word." It is divided into three parts, of which the first is the most trite and the second the most muddled: all are too long. In the first I try to make it clear that the phrase "the meaning of a word" is, in general, if not always, a dangerous nonsense-phrase. In the other two parts I consider in turn two questions, often asked in philosophy, which clearly need new and careful scrutiny if that facile phrase "the meaning of a word" is no longer to be permitted to impose upon us.

J. L. AUSTIN, "THE MEANING OF A WORD"

2. The two following beginning paragraphs are not skillfully done. Revise each one to make it a more effective opening and be able to explain your revisions.

1. The purpose of this theme is to discuss college football. College football has even been criticized, but I shall argue that it is on the whole worthwhile. I shall suggest three reasons why this is so. The first reason is that football builds character. The second is that it provides entertainment for many people, and the third that it gives many athletes a chance to go to college which otherwise they might not have had. Let us turn to the first of these reasons.

2. College is very different from high school. Perhaps the most obvious of these differences is that the student is made responsible for his own education. Teachers do not fuss at him to do his work. If he misses exams they leave to him the responsibility of arranging a make-up. There are a number of consequences that come from this greater freedom given the college student. However, these will concern us later. First we need to list a few of the other differences: college is much bigger and more diverse than high school; the students are more mature and vary more widely in their backgrounds; and the social life is more sophisticated. I shall treat each one of these points briefly and then return to the matter of responsibility, which, as I said, is really the most important difference.

3. Find in a magazine or book one or two opening paragraphs that seem well done and one or two that are ineffective. Be able to explain in every case why the opening worked or why it failed.

4. Imagine that you have been asked to write a formal, academic essay on one of the subjects listed below. Compose a beginning paragraph of about 150 words appropriate to such a paper. Consider carefully how best to announce and limit your subject. Indicate the plan clearly and decide whether you need deliberately to cast for the reader's attention:

1. The rights of college undergraduates
2. Drinking in college
3. The theater of the absurd
4. The advantages and disadvantages of a college student's having his own car
5. Living at home while attending the university
6. The decay of modern cities
7. Communication (or the lack of it) between parents and children (or, if you prefer, between teachers and students)
8. A short history of the Korean War
9. The poetry of Dylan Thomas
10. The effects of air pollution
11. The dangers of expanding population

5. Compose a second beginning paragraph on the same subject you chose in exercise 4, this time to introduce an essay informal in tone and aimed at a more general reader. Make appropriate changes in your opening to adapt it to the occasion and reader.

6. Practice both focusing down and using anecdotes by composing an opening paragraph on one of the subjects listed below. Do not announce the subject until the end of the paragraph, and be sure that the anecdote is apposite to the subject.

1. Cousins
2. Vacations
3. Poverty in America
4. Cats
5. Learning a foreign language
6. Faculty advisers
7. Foreign films
8. Listening to classical music
9. Restaurants
10. Propaganda in everyday life
11. Hi-fi enthusiasts
12. Cocktail parties
13. Freshmen convocations
14. Older sisters
15. Younger brothers
16. A definition of science

7
ORGANIZING THE MIDDLE OF THE ESSAY

Introduction

In the last chapter we remarked that an essay has a beginning, a middle, and an end, and we discussed generally what the beginning must do. We cannot deal here with the middle in quite the same way; for while the opening paragraphs of all essays will fulfill more or less the same functions, the body (or middle portion) of any essay will be unique, its structure and content depending upon the interaction of writer, subject, purpose, and reader. The problem of organizing this middle portion must be solved in the outline. No doubt the process of drafting an essay will modify the original plan here and there, but the essential organization should have been arrived at in the outline. That, indeed, is what an outline is: a plan of an essay.

Yet even assuming that the writer has established his organization during the outlining stage, he still needs to make that organization clear to his reader. If the writer has skillfully analyzed his subject and clearly followed that analysis in his draft, the unity and organization of his essay ought to be, we suppose, plain enough. Most of the time, however, a reader will require some overt help to follow the flow of the writer's thought. How much help will vary with the reader's intelligence and education, with the writer's reasons for addressing him, and with the complexity of the subject. But usually it is part of the writer's job to give the reader a hand. Broadly, there are three ways of helping the reader follow the organization and so of giving an essay a sense of unity: (1) leitmotifs, (2) signposts, (3) interparagraph transitions.

Leitmotifs

Of the three, the first is the least important. A leitmotif (the term is borrowed from music) is a recurrent word or phrase, clause or sentence carrying a meaning that is important to the subject. The simple repetition of this key expression binds together the parts of the essay. You may remember that in the preceding chapter we mentioned as a device of opening, G. K. Chesterton's clever metaphor of "the green-blooded fish." Three or four times in his brief essay "On Monsters" Chesterton repeats the refrain "a green-blooded fish has been found in the sea" as a sardonic commentary upon the various foibles he castigates. It becomes a unifying theme, reminding us of the monstrous form human folly can assume.

Employed as cleverly as Chesterton employs "green-blooded fish," leitmotifs can be wonderfully effective unifying devices. Their usefulness is limited, however. While they unify, they do not usually reveal very much about the organization of the essay, about the turns and developments of the writer's thought. Moreover, even as unifying devices their effectiveness diminishes as an essay increases in length. Finally, their very cleverness can become a disadvantage in the kind of formal prose whose chief purpose is to inform. Leitmotifs, then, are most efficient in the brief, simple, personal essay, where the writer intends not only to inform but to amuse or persuade as well. You ought to know about leitmotifs and you ought to feel free to experiment with them. But generally you will find that signposts and transitions are more effective ways of unifying compositions and of helping readers to follow you.

Signposts

EXTRINSIC

While a writer may suggest the main divisions of his essay in the opening paragraph, he still needs to include in the body of his paper words and phrases that point out its structure. These pointers are called "signposts"; they include any word, phrase, or sentence (even occasionally an entire paragraph), or any extraneous device that tells the reader what the writer has just done, is about to do next, or will do later on. Signposts are to be distinguished from topical development. Topical development asserts something about the subject; signposts reveal something about how the discussion of the subject has been organized. For example, the second sentence in the following passage is clearly a signpost (the sentences ended the first paragraph of our introduction to this section of the book):

> But while we have said a good deal about how to invent topics and to plan and draft and polish, we have said nothing about the essay itself as a unit of composition. It is time that we did.

Sometimes the same sentence may contain both topical development and a signpost; that is true of the first of the two sentences just quoted. But even when signpost and topic are intimately related, they are still distinguishable.

There are two kinds of signpost: extrinsic and intrinsic. The first are not, properly speaking, a part of the actual prose text. A preliminary outline is a case in point. Most textbooks have a table of contents, which precedes the actual composition and which constitutes a signpost indicating in broad terms the plan of the entire work. Some books even place a briefer outline before each chapter. Less commonly a writer may preface a chapter or section with a brief statement of the main points he plans to cover. (Such prefaces are called "arguments" in literary works; Milton uses them, for example, before each book of *Paradise Lost.*)

In addition to such preliminary pointers as outlines, a writer may also set up extrinsic signposts as he goes. An obvious one is the visual signal implicit in the indention of new paragraphs. This is not the place, however, to discuss the difficult question of when to begin a new paragraph. Here we need only observe that when the writer does begin one, he automatically tells his reader something about his organization.

He doesn't tell him much, however. A clearer extrinsic signal is to place numbers before the groups of paragraphs that make up major sections of the essay. A writer may indicate the three-part structure of his essay by placing the Roman numerals I, II, III before the appropriate sections. Sometimes a title is combined with such a number, the title often being set in a different type face from that of the text.

In much philosophical and scientific writing the technique of numbering is carried even further by assigning a two-part number to each paragraph, the first number designating the chapter, the second the paragraph. The numerals 3.7 set before a paragraph mean the seventh paragraph in the third chapter. A two-part number like this is very useful for referring the reader back to earlier material (the writer need only say "See 3.7"); but it does not really help the reader to follow the organization of what he is currently reading. It informs him only that this is chapter three, paragraph seven, a fact he hardly needs to be told.

There are, however, several variations of this numbering technique that are more helpful to cluing the reader. One is to place three numbers before each paragraph, the new one (in the second position) designating the section (that is, the paragraph group) within the chapter; 3.2.7, for example, means chapter three, section two, paragraph seven. Every time this second number changes, the reader knows that the writer is beginning a new section. Another variation keeps the two-part number, but uses the second one to designate not a separate paragraph but rather a paragraph group; 3.2, for instance, might include four or five paragraphs. When the reader saw 3.3 he would know that he had come to the third section of chapter three.

A more subtle extrinsic signpost is to vary the spacing between paragraphs. Between major sections of an essay a space may be left three or four times that ordinarily separating paragraphs. Occasionally the first letter (or even the first word or entire first line) of the new section is typographically emphasized, being set in italic, boldface, or capital letters.

All these various signposts are extrinsic in the sense that they are not part of a writer's actual prose. Most of them are typographical devices. Because they are not integrally a part of the text some people object to them. It is true that section and paragraph numbers and overfrequent changes of type face are unaesthetic, tending to destroy the harmony of the page. More importantly, by offering the inexperienced writer a convenient crutch, they may keep him from learning to use signposts actually embedded in his prose. Like a pony in a foreign language course, they can prevent development in the long run despite their short-term advantages.

But granting these objections, we may still say that extrinsic signposts are useful. Properly applied they are a very real help to the reader. Probably they are best restricted to purely informative writing or to closely reasoned argument, where clarity is the overriding consideration. You are unlikely to need them in a freshman theme. But you ought to remember the existence of these devices when in the next few years you face the compositional problems of the term paper or the graduate thesis.

INTRINSIC

The second kind of signposts — which are of more immediate value to you — we call intrinsic. Unlike paragraph numbers and so on, these are actual words that are incorporated into the text of an essay or book. The beginning paragraph, in so far as it identifies and limits the subject and suggests a plan of treatment, is such an intrinsic signpost. However, one can never take for granted that his reader will remember the plan suggested in the beginning or that the suggestion itself was sufficiently detailed. Therefore a writer must weave into his essay words and phrases and sentences that remind the reader of the general plan or reveal its details more closely.

Of the many kinds of intrinsic signposts, the most frequent are those which set up an immediately following section: "Let us begin by examining the causes of the depression"; "First we need to consider the meaning of the word *science*"; "Next we must ask why the mutiny occurred at all." Such sentences are in effect explicit topic statements. They are like the topic sentence of a paragraph except that (1) they usually set up more than a single paragraph; and (2) they are explicit — that is, the writer literally *says*, "My topic is the depression" (or "the meaning of *science*" or "the mutiny"), rather than simply writing "The depression was caused by several things" or "The word *science* is not easy to define." To be precise we might say about such sentences that they are topic statements containing signposts, the signposts being the clauses, "Let us begin by examining," "First we need to consider," and "Next we must ask." But however we analyze them, it is clear that these sentences literally *tell* the reader what the writer is about to do.

In addition to setting up what immediately follows, signposts may also anticipate later portions of an essay. In composition it is often difficult to analyze a subject into completely separate, watertight compartments. As he develops one section a writer frequently must touch upon a problem that he does not plan to treat fully until later, or even that he does not plan to treat at all. When this happens it may be advisable to post a warning. You have probably noticed a considerable number of these warnings in the course of this book. Such signposts serve one (or both) of two functions: they may be essentially negative, merely warning the reader not to expect a particular problem to be discussed at this point; or, more positively, they may be "postponing expressions," putting off full discussion of a topic until later and thus giving the reader a clue about the plan of the remainder of the essay. Several pages back, for example, you will find the sentence:

> This is not the place, however, to discuss the difficult question of when to begin a new paragraph . . .

which serves the negative function of warning the reader what not to expect. Had we added the clause "which will concern us in Chapter 9," the signpost would also have pointed to future organization. Signposts may also point backwards, telling the reader what the writer has already done, which is sometimes necessary when one must remind the reader of a point treated earlier that bears upon the current topic. Thus the writer may say, "(see page 8)"; or he may integrate his reminder more neatly into his text by using a signpost like "As we have seen . . ."

There is, finally, a special kind of signpost that consists of a group topic statement plus subsequent framing words. A paragraph group is a unit of thought comprising two or more paragraphs. Often (though not necessarily) a writer may begin such a unit with a sentence that functions as a topic statement covering all the paragraphs in the group. Here, for example, is the organizational scheme of a five-paragraph group from an essay by the scientist J. B. S. Haldane (we have taken the liberty of numbering the paragraphs):

> ¶ 1. Science impinges upon ethics in at least five different ways. In the first place . . .
> ¶ 2. Secondly . . .
> ¶ 3. Thirdly . . .
> ¶ 4. Fourthly . . .
> ¶ 5. Fifthly . . .

The opening sentence of paragraph 1 is the group topic statement, setting up all five paragraphs in the unit. This sentence does two things: first, it indicates the general subject (the impingement of science upon ethics), and second, it reveals that this subject will be analyzed into five parts. The phrase that reveals the five-part analysis is what we call the "organizing element." The function of an organizing element, while obvious, is important: it prepares the reader to look for a particular pattern in the material that follows. As Professor Haldane begins each paragraph in the group he needs only to introduce it with the appropriate expression ("In the first place," "Secondly") to fit it into the plan predicted by the organizing element. Such expressions are called "framing devices" because they remind us of the plan (or framework) of the essay.

The commonest kind are those, like Professor Haldane's, that indicate mere sequence of ideas. Sometimes sequence is signaled by numbers or letters — usually enclosed within parentheses — rather than by words or phrases like "first" or "in the second place." A brief example is the following sentence in which Professor A. P. Hudson sets out the essential characteristics of a folk song:

> . . . a song that, from the point of view of the author using it, and of mine observing it, seems to be marked by (1) anonymity of origin (unconsciousness, on the part of singer and audience, of authorship and provenience amounting to the same thing); (2) textual fluidity; (3) vitality through a fair period of time.
>
> "THE SINGING SOUTH," *The Sewanee Review*, JULY–SEPT. 1936

Numbers may even be used to introduce whole paragraphs which, like those by Haldane, have been set up by an organizing statement. Numbers (and letters) like these constitute an actual part of the writer's thought and therefore are different from the numerals we mentioned earlier as one kind of extraneous signpost. They share, however, the disadvantage of being unattractive to the eye, especially if they are employed very often, when they make the page look like an accountant's notebook.

Numbers have an even more serious disadvantage when they are overused, for they lose their primary purpose of helping the reader to follow the plan of the essay, and may, indeed, confuse him. A text in which numerous (1)'s and (2)'s introduce ideas which in turn are broken into (a)'s and (b)'s is likely to leave the reader feeling he has entered a labyrinth. The danger, of course, applies not only to numerals but also to framing words like "first" and "second." These words are fine to introduce main points, but if they are repeated to indicate the divisions of these main points, the reader will be lost. Even when it is not confusing, the overuse of numerals and of framing words is an awkward stylistic mannerism. Formulas like these are so convenient that some writers tend to fall back upon them too often, without even realizing that they are doing so. Learn how to set up a three- or four-part analysis and how to introduce each part with the appropriate word of sequence. You will help your reader a great deal. But learn also not to overdo it.

Instead of merely indicating sequence, framing words sometimes suggest relative importance: "Most important . . . ," "Hardly less important . . . ," and so on. Framing expressions like these are not as likely to prove confusing as "first" and "second," but they are even more obviously formulas incapable of much variation in form. In a sense this is an advantage since they exist ready made for the writer. It also means, however, that they may seem mechanical and may easily become repetitious. In a short essay framing words denoting relative importance cannot be used more than once or twice without awkwardness.

It is possible to employ framing words that are less mechanical and more integrally a part of the subject. But the writer must be careful to prepare for such words in his general topic statement. Here, for example, is the structural skeleton of part of a student theme:

> ¶ 1. The causes of the American Civil War fall into three broad categories: economic, political, and cultural. Economically . . .
> ¶ 2. Politically . . .
> ¶ 3. Culturally . . .

In the group topic sentence the student has set up his three-part organization and has given implicit titles to the three sections. To introduce each part he has only to repeat its title (or some variation): "Economially . . . Politically . . . Culturally . . ."

Whatever kind of framing words are used, it is important that framing words and an organizing element both be present. An organizing statement not followed up by appropriate framing expressions is inadequate; framing expressions for which the reader has not been prepared by an organizing element will probably puzzle him. Moreover, this is a technique that once begun has to be carried through to completion. Sometimes writers start off with something like this:

> There are three reasons why the treaty was unsatisfactory. First . . .

but then make the mistake of failing to introduce the next two reasons with the demanded terms "second" and "third" (or some variation of those terms such as "secondly" and "finally"). The reader is bewildered when the other shoe fails to drop and may not recognize when the writer passes from reason one to reason two or from two to three.

These, then, are a few of the signposts, both extrinsic and intrinsic, that make the organization of an essay clear to readers. They are only a few. There are many more; if you wish to improve your writing observe how experienced authors employ signposts. But with all this a word of warning, or rather, two words of warning. First remember that signposts *reveal* organization; they do not *create* it. Signposts cannot bring order from chaos, and they will not redeem a badly planned essay.

Second, remember that the effectiveness of signposts varies a good deal with purpose and occasion. For example, when you write a paper you intend to read aloud to an audience, you must include more signposts and make them more obvious than if the audience were going to read it. Listeners require more help than readers because they apprehend words in time rather than in space and so cannot easily pause and puzzle out what they fail to follow. To take another example, the writer aiming at an audience unfamiliar with his subject has to lead them carefully. Thus in textbooks signposts need to be more frequent and more obvious than in scholarly works, where the writer can assume his readers know enough to follow him with little help.

If the need for signposts varies with purpose and reader, it follows that a writer may err in either of two directions: he may employ too few signposts, or he may employ too many. The first is the more serious error. Failing to indicate your plan clearly will confuse the reader, preventing or seriously distorting communication. Having too many signposts, or making those you have too manifest will render your work unnecessarily wordy and it may irritate the reader. To tell a reader what you are going to do next when he can plainly see it for himself may strike him as insulting, as if you had no faith in his capacity of mind. But while overposting an essay may be annoying, it is less likely to be confusing and therefore will interfere less fundamentally with communication. The ideal writer, of course, will not err in either direction. But most of us are not ideal writers. If you are uncertain about the necessity of a particular signpost, the wiser course is to put it in. Knowing how to use signposts requires a great deal of experience; be prepared to make mistakes while you learn.

Transitions

The third way of clarifying organization for the reader is by linking successive paragraphs. Such links or transitions are made necessary by the fact that a new paragraph represents a change of thought. Having been traveling over one track, the reader is asked to change direction — sometimes slightly, sometimes sharply — and move on a new track. The words, phrases, or clauses linking paragraphs act like a switch and make the transfer from track to track smooth and even. Without such a switch the reader may be able to follow the change of thought, but he will have to bump along for himself.

Most interparagraph transitions are placed at the beginning of the new paragraph (though occasionally, as we shall see, a writer may set up a transition at the end of the old paragraph). We may distinguish two kinds of interparagraph transitions: full and partial. The first has three elements:

(1) a summary of the old topic, (2) an introductory statement of the new one, and (3) an indication of the relationship between the two topics. Each of these three elements may be a word, a phrase, a clause, or even a complete sentence. Partial links usually dispense with the summary and contain only the new topic plus a word or phrase showing how it is related to what has gone before. In some cases partial transitions consist merely of repeating a key term. Let us look more closely at each type of transition.

Full transitions are best understood if we ask first what relations are likely to occur between the kinds of topics treated in exposition. These relationships may be chronological (for example, event B may occur before, after, or simultaneously with event A); they may be spatial (one object may be positioned in front of, behind, or above another); or they may be notional (that is, relationships purely of idea). Here we shall be concerned only with the last, temporal and spatial linkage being more properly aspects of narrative and descriptive writing. Many different relationships in thought are possible, but for the writer three kinds are by far the most common: adversative, causal, and additive.

An adversative relationship occurs whenever a following paragraph in some way contradicts or qualifies the topic or the emphasis of the preceding paragraph. Suppose, for instance, that in an American history course you are writing a term paper about the failure of the United States to join the League of Nations after the First World War. You have been arguing that most of the blame must be placed on the United States Senate, and next you wish to say that President Wilson was also responsible. Now if you begin your paragraph with a simple statement like "President Wilson was also to blame," your reader may well be puzzled by the apparent contradiction between this new topic and the previous one. You require in this case a transition that will prepare the reader for the particular kind of ideational shift you are making. Thus you might say:

> But if the Senate was chiefly responsible, President Wilson was also partly to blame.

By adding such qualifiers as "chiefly" and "partly" you have muted the contradiction; but even more importantly the "But if . . ." construction has clarified the adversative relationship between the two ideas. Notice that in this sentence the summarizing statement is subordinated and placed first, while the introduction of the new topic comes last. This is the best order for a full interparagraph transition and should be followed whenever possible. The fact that at the beginning of a transitional sentence one is still talking about the old topic reduces to a minimum the gap between paragraphs; while the fact that at its end he has switched to the new topic means that he is able to step directly into developing that topic in the following sentence. Inexperienced writers often reverse this order in their transitions. Beginning with the new topic and winding up on the old one, they create an awkward bump at either end of the sentence. Now and then a question of idiom may make the order "new topic . . . summary" unavoidable, but such occasions will be rare.

As you can see, the "But if X, Y" transition is a formula, applicable to a great many relationships of contradiction. The "X" is filled in with the summarizing clause, the "Y" with the main clause stating the new topic. Thus as well as our earlier example, we could write

> But if the Senate was shortsighted, there was some excuse for the fault,

which is more a qualification of idea than a shift of topic. Formulas, as we have already noted, are useful to the writer. But we also noticed that they easily become repetitive, and that certainly is the case here. In a short essay one "But if X, Y" transition is usually enough; two become a mannerism.

Of course the formula can be varied. Transitional words like *however, yet, still* can be substituted for *but,* and these, being adverbs, are more variable in their positioning. We could write, for example, "If X, however, Y." (The pattern "If X, Y, however," while possible, is less effective because it postpones the signal of contradiction too long.) Another variation is to substitute a single subordinating conjunction for *but if:*

> Although the Senate was shortsighted, the President must bear some share of the responsibility.

Moreover, completely different formulas for showing full adversative transition are possible. One is to reduce the summary to an initial prepositional phrase, selecting a preposition that shows the proper degree of qualification or contradiction. For example, our transition might be rendered:

> Despite the Senate's primary responsibility, President Wilson was not without blame.

Or the transitional sentence may be constructed so that its subject summarizes the old topic, its object introduces the new, while the verb carries the idea of contradiction:

> The fact that the Senate was primarily at fault does not altogether remove responsibility from the President.

In this last pattern the summary may be reduced drastically to one or two words (the resulting transitions would often be reinforced by some contradictory connector like *but* or *however*):

> (But) The Senate's primary responsibility does not altogether excuse the President.
>
> This does not mean (however) that President Wilson was completely guiltless.

In short, there are many ways of handling a full adversative transition, and the various patterns we have suggested are no more than a sample. While these sentences have all shown the general relationship of contradiction or qualification, they are not, of course, identical. The "But if X, Y" pattern, for instance, emphasizes the idea of contradiction more strongly than the "Despite X, Y" construction. For any particular occasion you must select the adversative transition that is most appropriate. Rather than resting content with one or two ways of showing contradiction, the beginner needs to watch how experienced writers handle this problem and to try out in his own writing the patterns he observes.

He must do the same for the transitional consructions that signal the other kinds of logical relationship we mentioned. Cause and effect, for example, may be handled in various ways. One is to use two independent clauses, the first summing up, and the second, introduced by some such adverb as *consequently, thus, hence,* or *therefore,* stating the new topic. If (to continue with our imaginary history paper) you have finished discussing President Wilson's responsibility and wish next to treat the consequences of the failure of the United States to join the League, you might proceed like this:

> Between them, then, the Senate and the President assured the defeat of the Treaty; thus the ultimate failure of the League was preordained.

The transition can be made tighter by subordinating the first clause behind some such conjunction as *because, as,* or *since:*

> Because the Senate and the President had failed, the League of Nations was doomed.

The subordination of the summarizing idea may be carried still further by employing a prepositional construction:

> As a result of the failure of the Senate and the President, the League's chances for success were seriously diminished.

Or the logical relationship of cause and effect may be signaled by the verb while the subject summarizes the old topic and the object introduces the new one:

> The twin failure of Senate and of President assured the fatal ineffectiveness of the League of Nations.

In the foregoing cases the cause preceded the effect; however, the relationship may be reversed. For instance, you might have preferred to regard the policy of the Senate as an effect and wished to move to a discussion of the causes of that effect. Here are several full transitions you could have used, ranged roughly from a strong emphasis upon the idea of causality to a relatively weak one:

> The Senate, then, refused to ratify the Treaty; the causes of this curious attitude were several.

> The Senate refused to ratify the Treaty, for it believed, honestly if mistakenly, that ratification was against the best interests of the country.

> If the Senate refused there were several reasons why.

> The Senate's refusal was the result of several factors.

> The Senate refused to ratify the Treaty for three reasons.

> The Senate's refusal to ratify the Treaty can only be explained by the mood of the American people.

As with adversion, there are many patterns of cause-effect transition, each with overtones that make it more appropriate to some situations than to others.

Finally the relationship between paragraphs may be additive — that is, the new topic may be similar to or parallel with the old. For instance, having developed one cause for the Senate's failure you wish to go on to a second. The two causes are logically parallel in the sense that they both contribute to the same consequence; the relationship between them is in composition called additive. The second paragraph might begin with a "Not only X, but (also) Y" construction; or with "In addition to X, Y"; or with "Besides X, Y," to cite only three of many possible patterns:

> Not only were Americans traditionally afraid of what had come to be called "foreign entanglements," but many were so busy making money that they had little time for "politics" and "treaties."

> In addition to their traditional fear of international entanglements, many Americans, absorbed in making a living, simply did not care about politics.

> Besides their traditional fear of Europe, few Americans had any interest in what went on in Washington.

The full transitions we have looked at thus far have all dealt with specific types of logical relationship. Sometimes, however, the topics of successive paragraphs are not related in a way that is clearly adversative, causal, or additive. On these occasions the writer must cast about for some other common ground on which the topics may meet. They may be similar in some respect, or dissimilar; they may share some degree of importance or truth; they may be related as a particular to a general. In the theme about the League of Nations we can imagine paragraphs that might be linked by such transitions as:

> Unlike the Senate, who were parochial in their point of view, the President had a larger vision.

> Just as the Senate was tradition-bound in its attitude toward Europe, so the people generally could not see that isolationism, honored by a century of success, was no longer possible.

> Even more important than the Senate's attitude was the feeling of the American people.

> The general feeling of the Senate was particularly strong in a few individual Senators.

On rare occasions it may prove impossible to reduce the relationship between successive paragraphs even to such generalized grounds as these. In that case the writer may have to make a more explicit transition, as in:

> From the Senate we must turn next to a consideration of the President.

Explicit transitions, however, often sound awkward. It is, indeed, a common fault of inexperienced writers to make their transitions overobvious. Too often they write something like the sentence just quoted, or something even worse:

> Now that I have shown you the extent of the Senate's responsibility, I will pass on to a discussion of President Wilson's share of the blame.

This is explicit because the writer actually says, "I have finished doing that; now I will do this." In effect such a sentence combines a double signpost with a transition. Rarely do two paragraphs require linkage that strong. Ninety-five per cent of the time transitions like this are embarrassingly heavy-handed. If the topics cannot be related in one of the more precise logical ways we have mentioned (and it is surprising how often seemingly disparate topics can be hooked together by contradiction, cause-effect, or addition), one can usually fall back upon the rhetorical *if* (which is not to be confused with the *if* of logic):

> If the Senate was to blame, so was the President.

So far we have looked at a few of the varieties of full interparagraph transitions. Even more often transitions will be much briefer. In one type of partial transition the writer dispenses with the summary of the old topic and simply introduces the new subject with the word or phrase indicating its relationship to the idea of the preceding paragraph. Thus the adversative relationship might be reduced to:

> But President Wilson was not entirely without responsibility.

The cause-effect transition might become:

> Thus America was confirmed in isolationism.

The additive:

> Moreover, Americans were simply not interested in politics.

A slightly different kind of partial transition works by picking up a key term at the end of the preceding paragraph and repeating it at the beginning of the new one. As a case in point we may imagine that the paragraph begun by the sentence just quoted ended:

> Most people, wrapped up in their own work, had little conception of, or interest in, what was going on in Washington.

In the next paragraph the point is that the federal government was becoming more remote to many Americans. The transition can be made easily by repeating "Washington" and buttressing it with a strong additive connector like *indeed:*

> Washington, indeed, was growing increasingly remote to many Americans.

It is fair to note, however, that this type of transition is risky. It works well when the key term (that is, the term which, like "Washington," leads into the new topic) occurs naturally toward the end of the preceding paragraph. But to force such a term into the last sentence of a paragraph merely to set up a transition is likely both to spoil the focus of that paragraph and to make the transition awkward and artificial. Beginners sometimes fall into this error. In effect they place their transition at the end of the preceding paragraph instead of at the beginning of the following one, a practice that leaves their reader feeling they have made the paragraph break one sentence late. But when the key term does occur naturally at the close of a paragraph and can easily be picked up at the start of the next one, the transition is neat and efficient.

If partial transitions are more common than full transitions, they are not necessarily better. As with so much in composition, it all depends. Full transitions are usually clearer and more formal. For these reasons they are more at home in academic writing than in the personal essay, where they seem rather heavy and even condescending. How full your transitions ought to be on any occasion will be contingent upon how much help your readers require and upon the tone you wish to maintain. Transitions, indeed, are important determinants of tone. A "But if X, Y" construction is relatively stiff and would likely ring false in relaxed, informal prose. On the other hand a quick transition like "This was due to several causes" might seem a little breezy for a scholarly article.

It has been said that style is the art of "making transitions." This is oversimple; good prose is a great deal more than good transitions. Yet without effective links between paragraphs no essay can be really well written, no matter how skillfully its paragraphs are developed or its sentences constructed. Both as you read and as you write cultivate an eye for transitions. You may at times overdo them, but too strong a transition is preferable to one that is too weak, or to no transition at all.

Summary

In most essays the writer must help his readers follow the flow of his thought and thereby give a sense of unity to his composition. Leitmotifs — key words or phrases repeated throughout an essay — serve to unify it and to keep an essential idea before the reader. Signposts, which may be either typographical devices extraneous to the composition or words actually a part of the text, tell the reader what the writer is about to do next, what he will postpone, or what he will not do at all; and occasionally they remind him of something the writer has already done. Transitions, or links, are words and phrases that tie a paragraph to what has preceded it. They may be relatively long or quite brief. Their length and degree of formality help to define tone.

Exercises

1. The following passage is the beginning of Chapter 14 ("The Arts of Quoting and Translating") of *The Modern Researcher* by Jacques Barzun and Henry F. Graff. Identify all the signposts in these paragraphs and analyze the transitions that link each paragraph to what has preceded it:

Three Recurrent Tasks

Whether a researcher writes well or ill, he finds himself repeatedly quoting and citing. This is true regardless of his subject. And unless that subject is purely local, he also finds himself using sources in a foreign language, which perforce makes him a translator.

Quoting other writers and citing the places where their words are to be found are by now such common practices that it is pardonable to look upon the habit as natural, not to say instinctive. It is of course nothing of the kind, but a very sophisticated act, peculiar to a civilization that uses printed books, believes in evidence, and makes a point of assigning credit or blame in a detailed verifiable way.

Accordingly, the conventions of quoting and citing should be mastered by anyone whose work makes him a steady user of these devices. Citing is in fact so stylized and yet so adaptable to varying needs that we shall devote to it most of the next chapter. The present one will deal with the two forms of quoting — in the original and in translation. They are capable of more intelligent handling than is sometimes suspected, and a study of the technique will contribute to ease and efficiency if not to art.

The Philosophy of Quoting

The habit of quoting in nearly every kind of printed and spoken matter and the rules for doing it are quite recent developments in Western culture. Formerly, the practice was limited to scholars, and was taken as a sign of the unoriginal, timid, pedantic mind. Although Montaigne's *Essays* and Burton's *Anatomy of Melancholy* were admired for their abundance of quaint quotations, most writers preferred to appropriate the knowledge of others and to give it out again in their own words. Emerson, by no means an unscholarly man, expressed a common feeling when he said: "I hate quotations. Tell me what you know." And another scholarly New Englander, of our century, John Jay Chapman, pointed out that what they seize upon, the great quoters alter as they repeat it.[1]

The views of these two American writers should be kept in mind, not as a

[1] *Lucian, Plato, and Greek Morals*, Boston, 1931, pp. 3–4.

bar to quotation or as a license to quote inaccurately,[2] but as a reminder that *your* paper, *your* essay, *your* book should be primarily *your* work and *your* words. What was said in Chapter 2 about taking notes through immediate assimilation and rewording holds good on the larger scale of the finished work. If you have not made other people's knowledge your own by mixing it with your thoughts and your labor of recomposition, you are not a writer but a compiler; you have not written a report but done a scissors-and-paste job.

And the chief defect of such an evasion of responsibility is that the piece will probably be tedious to read and lacking in force and light. Many writers of master's essays and doctoral dissertations think that what is expected of them is a string of passages from other authors, tied together with "on this point he said: . . ." and "in reply, he stated: . . ." These are varied with: "Six months later, Thomason declared: . . ." and "Jennings thereupon differed as follows: . . ." The effect is of an unbearable monotony. Every page looks like a bad club sandwich — thin layers of dry bread barely enclosing large chunks of some heavy solid.

Unfit for handling, the sandwich falls apart, and the reason is easy to see: unless your words and your thought predominate in your work, you lose control of your "story." The six or eight people whom you quote in any given section had different purposes from yours when they wrote, and you cannot make a forward-moving whole out of their disjointed fragments. This fact of experience gives rise to the first principle of the art of quoting: *Quotations are illustrations, not proofs.* The proof of what you say is the whole body of facts and ideas to which you refer, that is, to which you *point.* From time to time you give a *sample* of this evidence to clinch your argument or to avail yourself of a characteristic or felicitous utterance. But it is not the length, depth, or weight of your quotations that convinces your reader.[3]

Two rules of thumb follow from the principle just enunciated: (1) Quotations must be kept short, and (2) they must as far as possible be merged into the text. The form of quoting that we have just used in introducing these two rules — stopping dead, a colon, and a new sentence — is convenient in books of instruction; it is awkward in writing which describes, argues, or narrates. Far better is the form which we are about to use and which incorporates into your sentence "that portion of the author's original words which [you] could not have put more concisely" without losing accuracy.

Longer quotations than this cannot, of course, be inserted entire into your own sentence, but your words can lead to the brink of the other author's remarks and, *with or without an ushering verb, can make the two speakers produce one effect,* like singers in a duet. Consider a passage from the biography

[2] H. W. Fowler in his *Modern English Usage* says, under "Misquotation": "The misquoting of phrases that have survived on their own merits out of little-read authors . . . is a very venial offense; and indeed it is almost pedantry to use the true form instead of so established a wrong one; it would be absurd to demand that no one should ever use a trite quotation without testing its verbal accuracy."

[3] An apparent exception to this rule occurs when you try to prove a point by reproducing documents. The exception is only apparent, because documents that are longer than a couple of pages should be relegated to an appendix and only discussed or quoted from in the text.

of a famous English trial lawyer, in which the author wants to make use of an important letter:

> He was bitterly disappointed when his old friend Clavell Salter was given the first vacancy. "I am told that S. is to be recommended," he wrote to Lord Edmund Talbot. "Well, he is a splendid chap and a great friend of mine of thirty years standing. I think he will tell you he owes much to me in the early days . . ." The letter is that of a bitterly disappointed man, and ends with a prophecy about his future, which came almost exactly true. "Well, I am fifty-nine; if my health lasts, I suppose I can enjoy another ten years hard work at the Bar." Within a few months of ten years after the date of the letter he died, almost in harness. Shortly after this disappointment he was approached as to the writing of his memoirs and he discussed the project and even wrote a few pages. "What will you call the book?" he was asked. "Better call it *The Story of a Failure*," he said sadly, and laid aside his pen.[4]

If instead of this running narrative and commentary, the biographer had used the lazy way of heralding each quoted remark with "he said" or one of its variants, we should have halted and started and halted and started at least four times.

Notice also that the method of Merged Quotation here recommended has the advantage of preventing the kind of repetition that *Punch* picked up recently from the London *Times:*

> Land at Freshwater, Isle of Wight, is being prepared as a rocket-motor testing sight, the Ministry of Supply said yesterday. "This land is being prepared for the ground testing of rocket motors," a Ministry official explained.
>
> "Clear now?" asks *Punch.*

Whole books have been composed on this system, especially in graduate schools. When the candidate has collected his material, he "writes it up" by the simple process of (1) announcing what the quotation implies, (2) giving the quotation, and (3) rehashing what has just been said. To the reader this is death in triplicate. To the author, who has to pay for the typing and possibly the printing, it is a great waste. Knowing how to quote might have reduced the bulk of the paper and wordage by more than a third; for what we have called the merged quotation is usually docked of head and tail — only the body of it plays its part in *your* presentation.

2. In a theme comparing men and women drivers you have been arguing that men have more manual skill in handling a car. In the next paragraph you wish to make the point that women are more prudent. Between these paragraphs an

[4] Edward Marjoribanks, *The Life of Sir Edward Marshall Hall*, with an Introduction by the Earl of Birkenhead, London, 1929, p. 377.

adversative relationship will exist. Devise six full and six partial transitions with which to begin the new paragraph. Make these transitions as different as you can in order to explore various possibilities of linkage that are available in this situation.

3. Imagine that in a third paragraph of the same theme you wish to add as another aspect of their superiority the fact that women are more courteous. Construct six full and six partial transitions (again as different as possible) to show this additive relationship.

4. Finally, in a fourth paragraph your point is that women have fewer accidents. The relationship between this paragraph and the preceding two is that of an effect to a cause. Compose six full and six partial transitions to establish that relationship.

8
CLOSING THE ESSAY

Introduction

> I see there is little, or no, time to continue my instructional essay on "How To Begin a Story." "How To End a Story" is, of course, a different matter . . . *One* way of ending a story is . . .

It is also one way of ending an essay — simply to stop as Dylan Thomas wittily does in this final paragraph. It is not, however, a very good way, unless one is among those rare people blessed, like Thomas, with wit and grace. For most of us simply ceasing to write will not do. Instead of merely stopping, the able writer must know how to close his essay, how to bring it neatly and unmistakably to an end. Although this is much easier to say than to accomplish, it is possible to learn how. To help you we shall look in this chapter at a few of the ways in which good writers manage closing paragraphs. (We are using the term *paragraph* rather loosely here, just as we did in the phrase *opening paragraph*. In a short theme the closing may comprise only the last sentence or two; in a longer one it may involve the final three or four paragraphs. For convenience we shall continue to speak of the "closing paragraph," whether it be a single sentence or several paragraphs. In any case, all good closings will do much the same things.)

One is to make a summary. Another is to set out a final conclusion — that is, draw a logical inference or pronounce a judgment of some sort. Again, the closing paragraph may ask the reader to do something (or not to do something) — that is, it may make an imperative. But most important of all the closing paragraph must draw the curtain; it must say, in effect, "The End." It has got to say this so clearly that if the last word of the essay chanced to fall at the extreme right-hand side of the very bottom line, the reader would not turn the page.

Subsidiary Functions of Closing

SUMMARY, JUDGMENT, AND GUIDE TO ACTION

Of these various functions only drawing the curtain is always necessary in a final paragraph. Before discussing how a writer signals finality to his readers, however, it will pay us to look at the other functions. To say that they are not always necessary is not to imply that they are unimportant or that one may include them or omit them as he pleases. The importance — even the necessity — of summaries, judgments, and imperatives depends upon subject and purpose. In some cases they are irrelevant; in others, optional. But there are also cases in which they are as necessary an element of closing as the signal of finality itself. Someone comparing two candidates for political office, for instance, ought certainly in his final paragraph to decide which is the better choice (or, if no choice is possible, to point out this fact). If his essay has been long and the evidence complicated, he may well feel the need of preparing for his final judgment by summarizing the main points on either side. And having decided in favor of Candidate X or Candidate Y, he may feel impelled to ask the reader to do something — to get out and work or at least vote for the better man.

On such an occasion, then, all three of these functions of closing are required by subject and purpose. It is easy to find other cases demanding simply one or another of them. Technical articles often close with a summary. Scholarly works and textbooks frequently place a summary at the end of each chapter to help the reader remember what is important. The British philosopher G. E. Moore concludes every chapter of his *Principia Ethica* with a summary; the final paragraph of the third chapter ("Hedonism") starts off:

> The most important points which I have endeavoured to establish in this chapter are as follows. (1) Hedonism must be strictly defined as the doctrine that "Pleasure is the only thing which is good in itself". . .

In similar fashion Moore goes on to summarize the other main points of his chapter, but there is no need to quote the rest.

Summaries are usually explicitly introduced. Moore, as you can see, clearly labels his summary in the first sentence. More commonly the label will be a mere phrase: "In summary," "To sum up," "To recapitulate," "To repeat," "To review," "In review," "In short," "Summing up," and so on. The label may be subtler: "We have seen, then, that . . ." or "We need hardly repeat that . . ." (though the writer does, of course, repeat "that"). In essays that attempt to be relaxed and informal, summaries — if they are needed in the closing section — should be labeled as unobtrusively as possible. It is likely, however, to prove oversubtle to slip a summary in without introducing it at all. The purpose of summaries is to clinch a point in the reader's mind, and they will do it best if the reader is aware that he is reading a summary.

Just as one subject requires a closing summary, so another demands a judgment or a conclusion in the logical sense. Mark Twain ends his essay "Saint Joan of Arc" with this clear, considered opinion:

> Taking into account, as I have suggested before, all the circumstances — her origin, youth, sex, illiteracy, early environment, and the obstructing conditions under which she exploited her high gifts and made her conquests in the field and before the courts that tried her for her life — she is easily and by far the most extraordinary person the human race has ever produced.
>
> *In Defense of Harriet Shelley and Other Essays*

Any essay on Saint Joan would have to pass judgment. Saint or fool? traitor or patriot? dupe or heroine? divinely inspired or victim of hallucinations? — these questions inhere in the very subject of Joan of Arc. When any subject implies a question, the writer must answer it (even if his answer amounts to an admission that he cannot answer). In one sense, of course, his whole composition (essay, article, book, whatever) constitutes an answer. Even so, most readers feel the need for a sharply focused and succinctly stated judgment in the closing.

The judgment does not have to be expressed in a declarative sentence. It may be phrased as a rhetorical question. Hilaire Belloc, for instance, ends his essay "On Megalomania" like this:

> But all that is no one else's business, so I will put it aside, but in closing, ask you this: Have you ever found in history or experience an ambitious man who found happiness or a megalomaniac who missed it? *One Thing and Another*

Another technique is to support the judgment with a quotation, which is placed at the very end of the closing paragraph. F. L. Lucas concludes an essay on Oliver Goldsmith:

> To-day, as one drives through industrial cities, on every side rise forests of television masts — as if in our new termitaries the very houses, like ants, had grown antennae. I doubt if they find much time for Goldsmith. He was no aristocrat; but, champion of the poor though he was, the taste that came to value him was not un-

> touched by aristocratic standards. But now it is that odd, somewhat pathetic being, the commonplace man, the "*pauvre Pecus*" of Anatole France, who most pays our pipers and most calls our tunes. And *Pecus* likes cruder fare than Goldsmith offered. And yet —
>
> The heart distrusting asks, if this be joy.
>
> Had Goldsmith lived to-day, he might have changed one word in his *Deserted Village* —
>
> Ill fares the land, to hastening ills a prey,
> Where *Science* accumulates, and men decay.
>
> I have no wish to gird indiscriminately at science. Without science our civilization could no longer even eat; yet one may be allowed at times to wonder what sort of civilization the scientific future holds in store. And the ghost of Johnson answers: "Sir, you *may* wonder." *The Search for Good Sense*

On occasion a writer may feel that it would not be wise (or even possible) to round off his essay with a neat and final judgment. Joseph Conrad once remarked that it is the business of the novelist to ask questions, not to answer them, and the same point sometimes applies to the essayist, who may wish to suggest a judgment rather than formulate it. This technique may be called the implicative ending. The writer stops short and allows the reader to infer the conclusion. Instead of shutting a door, the final paragraph opens one. Here, for example, is the end of a student theme describing a teen-age hangout:

> The old lady who lives across the street from the place says that the most striking thing is the momentary silence that, now and then, breaks up the loud, loud laughter.

The implicative ending is sometimes deliberately trailed off, as in the final sentence of a Belloc essay, "On Cooking":

> If I ever write a cookery book I shall begin by telling my readers that the best meal in the world is bread, salt, wine, and an onion (which needs no cooking), and I shall go on to talk of other things than cooking, for I confess to irrelevance. And, after all, what does it matter? Writing is a poor trade, but cooking is sacred. Any fool can write, but to cook . . . *One Thing and Another*

There are judgments implied in these cases, but the reader must draw them out for himself. This has the advantage of involving the reader with the essay and so of increasing the chance of communication on the principle that what we see for ourselves (or think we have seen for ourselves) we are more likely to believe than what we have merely been told.

Now and then a judgment, whether suggested or stated, is not enough, for the judgment may imply action and the subject requires that the writer tell the reader what to do. In the case of Saint Joan, Twain is not really concerned with persuading us to do this or that (though no doubt he hopes to deepen our respect for Jeanne d'Arc). But in the following paragraph Eric Partridge not only expresses an opinion about clichés; he also issues a bit of advice:

> Perhaps we might summarize the pros and cons for and against clichés in some such way as this. In the interplay of conversation, a cliché is often redeemed by a *moue* or a shrug or an accomplice-smile: "There! I've used a cliché. Very careless and humdrum of me, I suppose. But at least you know what I mean." Intonation, pauses, emphasis, these and other means can invest a cliché-ridden sentence, or set of sentences, with humour and wit, and with realism and trenchancy. In writing, we lack these dramatic, these theatrical, these extraneous aids: we *stand or fall alone*. In writing, the battered simile and the forgotten metaphor may well be ludicrous or inept or repellent; the hackneyed phrase so commonplace that it offends, the idiom so weak that it enfeebles the argument or dulls the description or obscures the statement; the foreign phrase either so inadequate or so out of place that it sets up a misgiving, a doubt, a dissent; the quotation so mauled by the maudlin, so coy in the mouths of the prim, so bombastic in the speech of the pompous, as to be risible, so very common as to lose all distinction, so inept as to fail.
>
> "If in doubt, don't!"
>
> "CLICHÉS," *A Charm of Words*

The Main Function of Closing

"DRAWING THE CURTAIN"

Thus a closing paragraph often involves a summary, a judgment, a guide to action. When these elements occur in a final paragraph (even when only one of them occurs) they are in themselves signals of closing, for it is at the end of a composition that a conclusion is drawn or a summary made. Often, however, the sense of closing they convey will be weak, and, as we have seen, not all subjects demand a final summing up or a logical inference or a suggestion to the reader about what he should do. The writer therefore must know other ways of marking the finish. Four are especially effective: (1) terminal words, (2) cyclic return, (3) rhythmic variation, and (4) the built-in closing.

Terminal words (that is, signal words of closing) are very frequent. The most obvious case is when the writer simply says "This is the end," as Ernest Hemingway does, for instance, in the last paragraphs of *A Moveable Feast:*

> That was the end of the first part of Paris. Paris was never to be the same again although it was always Paris and you changed as it changed. We never went back to the Vorarlberg and neither did the rich.
>
> There is never any ending to Paris and the memory of each person who has lived in it differs from that of any other. We always returned to it no matter who we were or how it was changed or with what difficulties, or ease, it could be reached. Paris was always worth it and you received return for whatever you brought to it. But this is how Paris was in the early days when we were very poor and very happy.

Hardly less obvious — though more mechanical — are such signposts as "In conclusion," "Finally," "Lastly," "In the last [final] analysis," "Concluding," "To conclude," "To close," "In closing," and so on. There are others that are less transparent. Adverbs that show a loose kind of consequential relationship, for instance, can also serve as signals of finality: "Then," "And so," "Thus." All these words and expressions are like the flag flying on the eighteenth green. How obvious they should be depends, as with signposts in general, upon the sophistication of the reader. It is well to keep signal terms subtle and unobtrusive if possible. In writing the best technique hides itself.

For that reason the second closing signal is often preferable. This is what we have called the cyclic return, or "completing the circle." It is simple enough, working on the analogy of a circle, which ends where it began. The writer repeats in his closing an important word or phrase first mentioned in the opening paragraphs. The word or expression may involve an image or metaphor, a quotation, allusion, or rhetorical question. The only necessity is that it be important to the subject and that the writer have been careful to stress its importance at the beginning so that the readers will remember it. Of course, he must stress it subtly; he cannot say: "Reader, remember this, for I shall return to it at closing." But if the device is to work he must be sure that the reader will recall that the word or phrase occurred in the beginning paragraph. In an essay of more than several pages it may be necessary to mention the key term (again as unostentatiously as possible) once or twice in the middle to keep it before the reader's eye, and in his closing the writer may wish to make the fact of completion very explicit by saying something like "We return, then, to . . ."

An example or two will make clear how the cyclic return works. The British poet Robert Graves has an essay entitled "It Was a Stable World"; he begins it with the sentence "The world was stable," and starts the last paragraph with the echo sentence "It was a stable world." In this case, as you see, the title plays a part. In the example quoted below, Lytton Strachey relies only upon stressing the key expression in the opening paragraph. Here is the first paragraph and the final several sentences from Strachey's essay "Lady Hester Stanhope":

> [*The opening paragraph*] The Pitt nose has a curious history. One can watch its transmigrations through three lives. The tremendous hook of old Lord Chatham, under whose curve Empires came to birth, was succeeded by the bleak upward-pointing nose of William Pitt the younger — the rigid symbol of an indomitable *hauteur*. With Lady Hester Stanhope came the final stage. The nose, still with an upward tilt in it, had lost its masculinity; the hard bones of the uncle and the grandfather had disappeared. Lady Hester's was a nose of wild ambitions, of pride grown fantastical, a nose that scorned the earth, shooting off, one fancies, towards some eternally eccentric heaven. It was a nose, in fact, altogether in the air.
>
> . . .
>
> [*The final three sentences*] The end came in June, 1839. Her servants immediately possessed themselves of every moveable object in the house. But Lady Hester cared no longer: she was lying back in her bed — inexplicable, grand, preposterous, with her nose in the air.
>
> *Books and Characters*

The return to the key phrase "nose in the air" is not the only reason this is a good closing, but it is an important one. Notice that in both examples the repeated expression not only latches the end of the essay to the beginning, but also conveys an idea that is important — even vital — to the writer's thesis. The fact is worth remembering, for the term that completes the circle will necessarily loom large in the reader's attention and it must be important or the emphasis it receives by being repeated will mislead him.

An even better signal of closing is rhythmic variation. Exactly how prose rhythm works is not a settled question. For the moment we need only remark that however it works, rhythm is a real and an inevitable aspect of prose. Since it is, a writer can often indicate closing by inducing a variation in the movement of his final sentence. The technique is very similar to what a composer does. One does not have to know a great deal about the technicalities of music to recognize the approach of the end of a song or symphony. A change in tempo or loudness or a variation in the melodic line signals the fact.

In writing, such a variation often takes the form of a slowing down and regularizing of the rhythm of the last sentence. The closing sentence is likely to contain interrupting constructions; its stressed syllables will be somewhat more regularly spaced; and the five or six last syllables may fall into one of the rhythmic patterns called "cursus," used in Latin prose as conventional indicators of closing and adapted by many writers of English. As an example of all this, consider the end of Thackeray's essay on Jonathan Swift:

> He was always alone — alone and gnashing in the darkness, except when Stella's sweet smile came and shone upon him. When that went, silence and utter night closed over him. An immense genius: an awful downfall and ruin. So great a man he seems to me, that thinking of him is like thinking of an empire falling. We have other great names to mention — none, I think, however, so great or so gloomy.
>
> *English Humorists*

The final sentence is slowed by the pause in the middle and the second half is broken by the interrupters "I think" and "however." Much of the effectiveness of the rhythm comes from the phrase "so great and so gloomy," in which the stresses upon "great" and "gloom-" are preceded by comparable numbers of non-stressed syllables. The final five syllables of this phrase, moreover, are an instance of the *cursus planus*, a variety of cursus in which the stresses fall on the second syllable from the end (here "gloom-") and on the fifth ("great"), while the last syllable ("-y") and the third and fourth from the end ("so" and "and") are unstressed.

The other kinds of Latin cursus were similarly adapted to English prose, and English writers have, in addition, developed comparable patterns of stressed and non-stressed syllables called cadences. These are too complicated and too numerous for our attention, and their importance as devices of closing is debatable. It does seem true, however, that when one finds an ending whose rhythm seems especially effective, the final syllables, more often than not, *do* fall into one or another of the patterns of cursus or cadence.

It is true, for instance, in the following paragraph, which closes a eulogy by Adlai Stevenson of Eleanor Roosevelt:

> We pray that she has found peace, and a glimpse of sunset. But today we weep for ourselves. We are lonelier; someone has gone from one's own life — who was like the certainty of refuge; and someone has gone from the world — who was like a certainty of honor.
> *Progressive*, JAN. 1963

The final six syllables show the stress "certainty of honor," an extension of the *cursus planus* in which the first stress falls upon the sixth rather than upon the fifth syllable from the end. Perhaps even more important here to the effectiveness of the rhythm is the repetition in the final sentence both of words and of syntactic patterns: "someone has gone from one's own life . . . someone has gone from the world"; "who was like the certainty of refuge . . . who was like a certainty of honor." Iteration has a regularizing effect. Repeating syntactic patterns is especially important in this regard, for rhythms are built, so to speak, into the various phrases and clauses of English. To repeat the same pattern of clause or phrase is to repeat the same rhythm.

Repetition is also advantageous in another way. By restating words which are not essential to the meaning and which in a more rapid style would be omitted, a writer can slow down and regularize his last sentence. Thackeray, for instance, repeated *so*: "so great and so gloomy," and there is similar repetition in the following sentence, which closes G. K. Chesterton's book on George Bernard Shaw:

> But this shall be written of our time: that when the spirit who denies besieged the last citadel, blaspheming life itself, there were some, there was one especially, whose voice was heard and whose spear was never broken.

Chesterton writes "there were some, there was one especially," rather than the more economical "there were some, especially one." He writes "whose voice was heard and whose spear was never broken," not "whose voice was heard and spear never broken." It is worth noticing also that "spear was never broken" is another instance of the extended *cursus planus*.

Thus by repeating connectives and modifiers, by using the same syntactic patterns, employing cursus, spacing stressed syllables more regularly, and inserting interrupters, a writer can slow down and regularize the movement of his final sentence and so say to the reader: "This is all." Less commonly he may take the opposite tack and signal closing by making the final sentence relatively quick and straightforward. Kenneth Grahame, for example, closes an essay describing a small boy's meeting with an itinerant artist who had talked with him of Rome and of an imaginary city where everyone was beautiful and happy:

> Upon this compact we parted, and I went down-heartedly from the man who understood me, back to the house where I never could do anything right. How was it that everything seemed natural and sensible to him, which these uncles, vicars, and other grown-up men took for the merest tomfoolery? Well, he would explain this, and many another thing, when we met again. The Knights' Road! How it always brought consolation! Was he possibly one of those vanished knights I had been looking for so long? Perhaps he would be in armour next time; why not? He would look well in armour I thought. And I would take care to get there first, and see the sunlight flash and play on his helmet and shield, as he rode up the High Street of the Golden City.
>
> Meantime, there only remained the finding it. An easy matter.
>
> "THE ROMAN ROAD," *The Golden Age*

A final short, quick sentence is neatly played against a longer, more complicated one in the closing of Hilaire Belloc's essay "On the Selection of Books":

> For of its [the Bible's] many rhetorical optative phrases (which long for the wings of a dove, for peace, for justice and, in exile, for the native land), none strikes a stronger chord in the human heart than that profound, that major cry, "Oh, that mine enemy had written a book!" I am glad to say he sometimes has.
>
> *One Thing and Another*

Brief final sentences like these differ in tone from the slow, rhythmically regular finales. They are less solemn, more lighthearted. Kenneth Grahame's reminiscence of childhood is gay rather than somber, and there is more wit than malice in Belloc's closing.

But in spite of the effectiveness of the brief final sentence, inexperienced writers frequently fail to make use of it when they could do so. Here, for example, is the last sentence of a student paper:

> Thus after many hard-fought battles General Cornwallis and England ended the American War of Independence by surrendering on October 19, 1781.

Potentially, there is a good closing here, but it is thrown away. The passage can be improved by being broken into two sentences, the first slowed by interruption, the second rapid and straightforward:

> Thus, on October 19, 1781, General Cornwallis, after many hard-fought battles, surrendered. The American War of Independence was over.

And so is the theme — much more effectively "over" than in the original closing sentence.

The last way of drawing the curtain is to end the essay at a natural place of closing, one that is built right into the subject. For example in a biographical sketch of someone whose life is over, the natural point of closing is the death-scene, as in the passage by Lytton Strachey quoted a little earlier. Another example is this paragraph, the end of Llewelyn Powys's essay "Michel de Montaigne":

> On 13 September, 1592, Michel de Montaigne, having distributed certain legacies to his servants, summoned his parish priest to his bedside, and there in his curious room with the swallows already gathering on the leaden gutters outside, he heard Mass said for the last time in the company of certain of his neighbors. With due solemnity the blessed sacrament was elevated, and at the very moment that this good heretical Catholic and Catholic heretic (unmindful for once of his nine learned virgins) was raising his arms in seemly devotion toward the sacred morsel which in its essence — *que sçais-je* — might, or might not, contain a subtle and crafty secret, he fell back dead. *Thirteen Worthies*

Here the inherent effectiveness of a death-scene as a point of closing is reinforced by the careful construction of the last sentence, which does not complete its main thought until the end. (Such sentences are called "periodic.") "Dead" falls into place like the last piece of a picture puzzle and so ends the essay.

"Natural points of closing" are not restricted to the death-scenes of biographies. In an essay describing one's daily routine, for instance, the natural way to end is with some variation of the phrase Samuel Pepys made famous: "And so to bed." Even when a subject does not have a built-in closing, it is possible to introduce one by a comparison or figure of some sort. Thus W. H. Prescott concludes *The Conquest of Peru* like this:

> With the benevolent mission of Gasca, then, the historian of the Conquest may be permitted to terminate his labors, — with feelings not unlike those of the traveller, who, having long journeyed among the dreary forests and dangerous defiles of the mountains, at length emerges on some pleasant landscape smiling in tranquillity and peace.

The simile of the traveler emerging from the hardships of his journey is a terminal signal. It is important when you use them to make such figures of closing appropriate to the subject; otherwise they will seem forced and artificial.

The various devices of closing we have looked at are not mutually exclusive. A good writer will usually rely upon some combination of them rather than upon any one alone. The devices are, moreover, perfectly compatible with such other closing functions as making summaries or pronouncing judgments or issuing imperatives; indeed, these other functions are not in themselves adequate curtain indicators and must be reinforced. Nor, finally, are these the only things a writer can do to end his essay. They are simply the most common. Good writers devise additional means of closing. We have seen how Dylan Thomas stopped abruptly and made it work. Here is one last example, extremely effective yet so subtle that it is not easy to analyze; it closes an essay by Virginia Woolf entitled "Reading":

> Some offering we must make; some act we must dedicate, if only to move across the room and turn the rose in the jar, which, by the way, has dropped its petals.
>
> *The Captain's Death Bed and Other Essays*

It is difficult to say why this works. The flower that has dropped its petals is a kind of figure of closing. Perhaps too the irrelevancy of the final clause is a signal, a peculiarly feminine graciousness that closes a conversation by lightly changing the subject. In any case it works. It ends the essay neatly and unmistakably. And that is the important thing — not only here, but in every essay.

Summary

The essential function of a final paragraph is to make clear that the writer has completed his essay. Subject and purpose may require the closing to include a summary, a final inference or judgment, or a guide to action. In addition, all closing paragraphs must contain clear cut signals of ending. These may be (1) terminal words, (2) cyclic return, (3) rhythmic variation, and (4) a natural climax. Most often a writer will depend upon several of these signals in order to bring his essay to a close.

Exercises

1. While it is obviously difficult to gauge accurately the effectiveness of a closing paragraph without seeing it in its context, the following passages are all

clear-cut examples of good closings. What techniques of closing does each passage illustrate?

1. The grammarian does not see it as his function to "raise the standards" set by Franklin, Lincoln, Melville, Mark Twain, and hundreds of millions of other Americans. He is content to record what they said and say.

   Insofar as he serves as a teacher, it is his business to point out the limits of the permissible, to indicate the confines within which the writer may exercise his choice, to report that which custom and practice have made acceptable. It is certainly not the business of the grammarian to impose his personal taste as the only norm of good English, to set forth his prejudices as the ideal standard which everyone should copy. That would be fatal. No one person's standards are broad enough for that.

   BERGEN EVANS, "GRAMMAR FOR TODAY," *The Atlantic Monthly*, MARCH 1960.

2. To sum up: my thesis has been that in most modern educational schemes the training of character, if not neglected, has been given a subordinate place; that we have very little, if anything, like the concentration on it in Plato's thought and in Arnold's practice; that nowhere have the tactics of attack been methodically thought out, though it is the crucial point, and should therefore be the centre of our system; that it needs exact and thorough study; and that we ought to undertake this study without delay, for time presses. When the atomic bombs fell on Japan, we had a glimpse of the precipice on whose edge we stand.

   Our task in character training falls under two heads. We have to develop the qualities necessary for life in a community. But, by itself, such training has two dangers: it might produce either a world of human bees or ants, efficient but limited and static, or a highly disciplined mass like the Nazi youth, whose social virtues were directed to disastrous ends. Hence the importance of knowing the right end; and the right end is the first-rate in every province of life. This is the greatest of all branches of knowledge, and it should be the centre, though it is not the whole, of education.

   May not the desire to make first-rate human beings and a first-rate society replace, or rather carry on, the spirit which united and inspired us in the war and be a master whom all would accept? Is not that in itself a sufficient motive for life? To see the vision of excellence, so far as our limitations allow; to get at least a glimpse of the unchanging values of the eternal world as they are revealed in whatever is beautiful and good in the material world of earth; to attempt to make one's infinitesimal contribution towards a society which will embody them more fully than does our own — to do that is to take seriously the tremendous words of Christ: "Be ye therefore perfect, as your Father in Heaven is perfect."

SIR RICHARD LIVINGSTONE, "EDUCATION AND THE TRAINING OF CHARACTER," *Some Tasks for Education*

3. To remember Lincoln is to remember his ideals. Sometimes we tend to dismiss a leader's ideals too cavalierly. Or sometimes we pin the wrong labels on people and call the wrong ones "realists." It has not been in pursuing ideals that this nation has gone wrong. It has been in following the lead, or the drift, of negative men that we have fallen into disaster. We do not have to be perfectionists either. It has been said that ideals are like stars: we do not reach them, but we do steer by them. The study of history will be of some use if it enables us to remember that our true leaders are not the obstructionists, not those who negatively exploit every disagreement or difficulty. Leaders in a challenging emergency should not set their sights too low. They will do well to remember with Herbert Agar that there is "a time for greatness." Rightly considered, history is no merely academic subject. Historical insight can become the truest foresight. On the broader world stage which the present era demands it is well to recapture the significance of Woodrow Wilson's "organized opinion of mankind" and of Abraham Lincoln's "just and lasting peace among ourselves and with all nations."

J. G. RANDALL, *Lincoln and the South*

4. No great thing is achieved without a price, and on the Somme fell the very flower of our race, the straightest of limb, the keenest of brain, the most eager of spirit. In such a mourning each man thinks first of his friends. Each of us has seen his crowded circle become like the stalls of a theatre at an unpopular play. Each has suddenly found the world of time strangely empty and eternity strangely thronged. To look back upon the gallant procession of those who offered their all and had their gift accepted, is to know exaltation as well as sorrow. The young men who died almost before they had gazed on the world, the makers and the doers who left their tasks unfinished, were greater in their deaths than in their lives. They builded better than they knew, for the sum of their imperfections was made perfect, and out of loss they won for their country and mankind an enduring gain. Their memory will abide so long as men are found to set honour before ease, and a nation lives not for its ledgers alone but for some purpose of virtue. They have become, in the fancy of Henry Vaughan, the shining spires of that City to which we travel.

JOHN BUCHAN, *The Battle of the Somme*

5. All that we can say of the composition of Shakespeare's audience, other than that it was a cross section of the London population of his day, is that youth may have predominated somewhat over age,

male over female, the worldly over the pious, and, of course without the "perhaps," the receptive over the unreceptive. Although the more leisured classes would have been better represented than by their pro rata of the population, it was predominately a working class audience because of the greater numerical superiority of the working classes in the London area and because theatrical tariffs had been designed largely for them. It was not much different from the assemblage which gathered to hear the sermons at Paul's Cross. Stephen Gosson, the one really likable antagonist of the Elizabethan stage, says with a kind of weary resignation: "Indeede I must confesse there comes to Playes of all sortes, old and young; it is hard to say that all offend" — then his higher nature triumphs — "yet I promise you, I wil sweare for none." ALFRED HARBAGE, *Shakespeare's Audience*

6. In short ladies, I may be found in many places. But I shall not tell you where. I am not quite sure that I could tell you where at this moment, for I am like a fellow who has come into great riches and is doubtful how he can squander them most gloriously. But, I repeat, ladies, that you will not find me in London. I leave London to you. May you enjoy it. [This is the final paragraph of the essay whose beginning was quoted on page 93.]
A. G. GARDINER, "ON TAKING A HOLIDAY"

2. The two paragraphs following are instances of unsuccessful closings. What is wrong with them? Revise each to make it a better ending. Stay as close as possible to the original wording, but where necessary you may add or delete, rearrange the order of phrases and sentences, or break a sentence into two or three separate statements.

1. At last the hard-working housewife is ready to watch her favorite television program but before fifteen minutes are up she is sound asleep in her chair and before she realizes it the 6:30 alarm is going off and it is time to start another day.
2. In conclusion, then, let me finally say that I feel that students should be allowed to cut class if they want to. We are mature enough to decide whether we need to attend a lecture or not and the administration should not treat us as children by compelling us to go to class. Someone has said that "ultimately all education is self-education," and this is a truth that the administration forgets when it forces us to obey silly rules and go to class whether we really need and want to or not.

3. Imagine that you must write a closing paragraph for the theme on men and women drivers for which you worked out transitions in the exercises at the end of the preceding chapter. First compose a one-sentence closing such as might do for a theme about 300 words long. Next, write a more expansive closing of about 150 words, appropriate for a theme some 800 words in length. Finally,

expand the closing to three paragraphs totaling 400–450 words, such as would be suitable for an essay of 3000–4000 words. In each case remember that your primary purpose is to make clear to the reader that your paper is drawing to a close. As the closings grow longer, you will want to include more extensive summaries and conclusions.

4. Listed below are several titles for possible themes. Along with each is suggested a key phrase which might serve the purpose of establishing a cyclic return to close the essay. Select any two and for each compose (1) an opening paragraph incorporating the key phrase in a position of some prominence, and (2) a brief closing paragraph which picks up the key expression and uses it as a device of closing.

1. Title: "Dieting"; key phrase: "peanut butter sandwich"
2. Title: "Blind Dates"; key phrase: "five-dollar corsage"
3. Title: "Christmas Vacation"; key phrase: "no money"
4. Title: "Term Papers"; key phrase: "hopeless"
5. Title: "Movies"; key phrase: "popcorn"

III
THE PARAGRAPH

After the essay the next compositional unit is the paragraph, the subject of the next six chapters. Perhaps the most difficult thing for inexperienced writers to grasp about the paragraph is that it is more than a series of sentences. It has a unity unto itself, being a compositional whole made up of sentences which have been fitted together to form a design. The general principles of constructing and unifying expository paragraphs will occupy us in the first chapter of this section. In the following four chapters we are going to study in detail the various methods by which expository paragraphs are developed. It is especially important here that you write out the exercises. You cannot learn to write paragraphs merely by reading a book. In the final chapter we shall shift our attention momentarily from exposition in order to glance at a few of the rudimentary kinds of descriptive and narrative paragraphs.

9
THE STRUCTURE OF THE EXPOSITORY PARAGRAPH

Introduction

THE NATURE OF THE PARAGRAPH

Beginning writers are frequently bewildered by the paragraph. Their confusion is understandable. The paragraph is not, like the sentence, a more or less natural unit of speech, learned in childhood. It is not, properly speaking, even a unit of speech at all (unless one talks like a book), but rather a unit of writing. Moreover, it is developed in so many different ways that often it seems to follow no laws of any sort, but simply to begin and end at the whim of the writer. Admittedly, there is much variety in how writers — and good writers — develop paragraphs. There is hardly less variety in how they handle sentences, yet we do agree that the sentence obeys, if not laws, at least conventions of syntax. Paragraphs, too, despite their seeming diversity, follow conventions, not of syntax, but of rhetoric. These cannot be formulated as hard and fast rules, for, although rhetoricians sometimes attempt such formulations, paragraphs will not stand still for rhetoricians. If these conventions may be expressed only as generalizations, however, they are none the less valid and helpful.

The chief one is this: The paragraph is an integral unit of composition. It is not simply an occasional indention by which the writer breaks up the monotony of the page. Rather it is a structure of sentences unified by their common relation to a general conception — whether this be a feeling, an idea, an opinion — which we call the topic of the paragraph. It must be granted that this description of the paragraph applies equally well to the entire essay; an essay, or even a whole book, is, or ought to be, a series of unified sentences all about the same general subject. All of Hemingway's *Death in the Afternoon* is about bullfighting; all of Professor Toynbee's multi-volume study is about history. But the paragraph differs from these larger units in treating its subject less extensively. Either it confines itself to a rather narrow subject to begin with, or, if it develops a broader one, it treats it much more generally. What it comes down to, of course, is that the distinction between the paragraph and the essay or even the book is a difference of degree. No one can draw the line between where the paragraph ends and the larger unit begins. This fact need not disturb us, however; in practice we are not likely to grow confused about what is a book and what is a paragraph.

The paragraph, then, is an integral unit of composition. We can most easily understand the nature of this unit by comparing it with the sentence. Like the sentence it has two parts, corresponding to the subject and predicate (understanding the terms *subject* and *predicate* in their broad rather than in their narrow sense). The subject of a paragraph, usually more complicated than that of a sentence, generally requires a whole sentence for its full statement, although sometimes it may be expressed in something less than a sentence, while occasionally it will need two or even three. The remainder of the paragraph, which develops or supports that subject, corresponds to the predicate. In practice the paragraph often grows quite complicated in how it varies this subject-predicate pattern. Sometimes the subject may not be stated in so many words, but merely be implied by the entire paragraph; sometimes the paragraph, like the sentence, may be compounded and have not one but two or even three topics. Such complications we shall observe more closely a little later. Here we need only to understand that, however complex they may become, all paragraphs are really only variations of the subject-predicate pattern and that this pattern is the essence of their structure.

In terms of the difference in the nature of their subjects, the paragraphs of informative writing may be divided into three general types — narrative, descriptive, and expository. Expository paragraphs are our immediate concern. Like most vast and inclusive terms, *exposition* is not easy to define. Essentially it is writing that explains, whether in a very specific sense (how a boat sails) or in a more general way (how one feels about ballet). To put this another way, we might say that exposition is writing that is about what the writer thinks, as distinguished from narration and description, which, at their simplest, are about what the writer sees. Although no hard line separates exposition from description and narration (a character sketch, for instance, may involve all three), it is generally true that in exposition the writer's purpose is to communicate and develop an idea, a feeling, or what he considers a matter of fact — to say in effect, here is what I think and here is why I think it, or what I mean, or what my thought implies. The expository writer, then, is a man thinking rather than a man seeing, and this fact conditions the structure of the paragraph he writes. He will formulate his thought — whether idea or feeling or fact — and then support and develop it by employing such specific techniques as illustration, analogy, contrast, or any of the others that we shall shortly examine.

Expository paragraphs differ in the precision with which they formulate their subjects. This important difference determines the relative rigidity or looseness of the organization. Broadly we can distinguish three degrees of such organization — tight, loose, and discursive (but, of course, these represent points on a scale, not absolutely distinct types). In the tight, or, as we shall also call it, the propositional, paragraph the topic is expressed as a full proposition, for example: "It was inevitable that Spain should lose the war." In the paragraph that develops such a topic every sentence must be concerned not simply with Spain, not simply with the war, but with the inevitability of Spain's losing the war. In other words the relevance of each sentence is to be determined by referring it to the total proposition that comprises the topic. Such a conception of the paragraph obviously implies a rigid principle of selectivity. The writer chooses his material rigorously, excluding what is not strictly relevant, permitting himself no rambles in green fields along the way. Carefully he links each sentence to those preceding it, and his paragraph moves straight ahead, the thoughts in perfect file and no nonsense. Such tightness is well illustrated in this paragraph by Bertrand Russell:

> The intellectual life of the nineteenth century was more complex than that of any previous age. This was due to several causes. First: the area concerned was larger than ever before; America and Russia made important contributions, and Europe became more aware than formerly of Indian philosophies, both ancient and modern. Second: science, which had been a chief source of novelty since the seventeenth century, made new conquests, especially in geology, biology, and organic chemistry. Third: machine production profoundly altered the social structure, and gave men a new conception of their powers in relation to the physical environment. Fourth: a profound revolt, both philosophical and political, against traditional systems in thought, in politics, and in economics, gave rise to attacks upon many beliefs and institutions that had hitherto been regarded as unassailable. This revolt had two very different forms, one romantic, the other rationalistic. (I am using these words in a liberal sense.) The romantic revolt passes from Byron, Schopenhauer,

> and Nietzsche to Mussolini and Hitler; the rationalistic revolt begins with the French philosophers of the Revolution, passes on, somewhat softened, to the philosophical radicals in England, then acquires a deeper form in Marx and issues in Soviet Russia.
>
> *A History of Western Philosophy*

Here the sentence unit analyzes the paragraph into its parts. The first sentence states the topic, the second establishes the plan of the paragraph to follow. Sentences three, four, five, and six develop the separate reasons that support the topic, each introduced by the appropriate framing word (*First, Second, Third, Fourth*) setting it into the plan indicated by sentence two. The final two sentences, expanding the idea introduced in sentence six, also work analytically, the first distinguishing the two forms taken by the revolution, and the second tracing the history of each. Mr. Russell's paragraph is a workmanlike example of tight expository development; it begins with a well-defined topic idea and it keeps strictly within the limits of that idea.

The loosely developed expository paragraph differs essentially in the nature of its topic, which is more diffuse, less sharply defined. In the tight paragraph the topic sentence states a full proposition, containing both a logical subject and a logical predicate, and the predicate delimits precisely the extent of the paragraph. The loose paragraph, on the other hand, develops out of a subject that is not limited by any general predicate determining the length and structure of the paragraph. The subject thus becomes a center about which the paragraph revolves. The loose paragraph offers the writer more scope, more freedom to wander — provided he does not stray too far — from the center of his subject. Consider this paragraph by G. M. Trevelyan:

> The importance of the Roman roads after their makers had gone, lay in this: no one made any more hard roads in the island until the turnpike movement of the Eighteenth Century. Throughout the Dark Ages and in early medieval times, these stone highways still traversed an island otherwise relapsed to disunion and barbarism. The Roman roads greatly increased the speed of the Saxon, Danish and Norman Conquests, and aided, both in peace and in war, the slow work of Saxon and Norman Kings in uniting England as one State, and making the English nation. Thanks to the Roman legacy, Britain had better national highways under the Saxon heptarchy than in Stuart times, though in the later period there were more by-roads. The imperial stone causeways, often elevated some feet above the ground, ran from sea to sea, generally keeping the higher land, but where needful marching majestically over bog and through forest. If the bridges soon fell in from neglect, the paved

> fords remained. For centuries wild tribes who only knew the name of Caesar as a myth, trod his gigantic highways and gave them the fantastic names of Watling Street, Ermine Street, and the Foss Way. Gradually the stones subsided and men were too careless and ignorant to replace them. Next, the road was used as a quarry, when the medieval Englishman, having somewhat exhausted his timber, began to build for himself dwelling-houses of stone. From driving roads they declined into pack-horse tracks, finally disappearing for the most part in moor or plough-land. Stretches of them have been repaired and modernized, and the motor car now shoots along the path of the legions. But other stretches — and those the best beloved, — are reserved for the Briton or Saxon who still fares on foot; they are to be traced as green lanes, starting up out of nowhere and ending in nothing, going for miles straight as a die through the magical old English countryside. *History of England*

Here the topic is, quite simply, the Roman roads, not this or that *about* them. At various places in the paragraph the writer asserts particular predications about these roads — for example, that they were important — but there is no predication about them which unifies and organizes the entire paragraph. Instead the paragraph develops by moving easily from one aspect of its topic to another. The roads, it states, were important, and it tells why. But shortly we notice that their importance has been forgotten and that the paragraph has slid into a description of the roads and from that into the history of their gradual decay.

Even looser is this paragraph by James Thurber:

> I left the University in June, 1918, but I couldn't get into the army on account of my sight, just as grandfather couldn't get in on account of his age. He applied several times and each time he took off his coat and threatened to whip the men who said he was too old. The disappointment of not getting to Germany (he saw no sense in everybody going to France) and the strain of running around town seeing influential officials finally got him down in bed. He had wanted to lead a division and his chagrin at not even being able to enlist as a private was too much for him. His brother Jake, some fifteen years younger than he was, sat up at night with him after he took to bed, because we were afraid he might leave the house without even putting on his clothes. Grandfather was against the idea of Jake watching over him — he thought it was a lot of tomfoolery — but Jake hadn't been able to sleep at night for twenty-eight years, so he was the perfect person for such a vigil.
> "DRAFT BOARD NIGHTS," *My Life and Hard Times*

Here the paragraph is so loose that it may be called discursive. Its structure is associative. Lacking even a central subject like Trevelyan's, this paragraph develops by the deceptively simple technique of linking together casually associated incidents. Simple and casual as it seems, however, the paragraph is as carefully unified as the more rigorously controlled passage by Bertrand Russell.

It would be foolish to attempt to judge between these styles of paragraphing. Each has its virtues and its vices. If Russell's paragraph is lucid, it is also relatively formal and perhaps a trifle mechanical; if Trevelyan's is more pleasing in the subtlety of its control, it is also more diffuse; and if Thurber's entertains us by the colloquial looseness appropriate to the informal essay, the same looseness in an historical study or philosophical treatise would be irritating. Given a writer's subject and purpose, his tone and his audience, probably one or another type of paragraph structure will be best. The important point is not that one type is better than another, but that all are possible, that the expository paragraph may range so widely between the poles of rigidity and looseness and still remain a unit of developed thought.

How thoroughly to develop the topic of a paragraph is a question no one can answer very precisely. Unfortunately this matter of development is hopelessly relative. It is true that for a paragraph to be a true paragraph its topic must be extended; it cannot simply be stated and then dropped. It is also true that this development must be held within certain limits; otherwise the paragraph swells into an essay. Still the problem remains — how long must one develop an idea before it becomes a paragraph, and after what length in its exposition will even a slight shift in idea warrant a new paragraph? The answers are not easy. Consider again Bertrand Russell's paragraph. He offers here four points to support his contention that the intellectual life of the nineteenth century was more complex than that of the seventeenth or eighteenth. Excepting the last, which requires three, each of these points is expressed in a single sentence. Suppose, however, that Mr. Russell had amplified each of these reasons with a brief example stated in a following sentence. Would the shift to reason number two have required a second paragraph and that to number three still a third? Probably not. But suppose still further that each example had been more involved, its full development demanding not one but six sentences. Then probably we should say yes, that at the shift to each successive reason a new paragraph would be in order. Thus what is now a single paragraph would have become four, yet the shift in idea — usually assigned as the reason for beginning a new paragraph — would not be essentially different in these four paragraphs than it now is in one. Plainly, we must consider length of development as well as change of subject in deciding when to begin a new paragraph. The answer to the question: "When does one begin a new paragraph?" is less simple than the query itself.

It is not very helpful to say that the writer begins a new paragraph when, after having developed his topic for a sufficient length, he switches to a new subject (or a new aspect of the old). We still must decide what "sufficient length" means. For the inexperienced writer it usually means a paragraph longer than he is used to writing. More often than not beginners have a foreshortened view of paragraph length. For one thing they are most used to the abbreviated unit of journalism and do not realize that the newspaper paragraph is quite different from that of literary and scholarly exposition. For another, the very nature of assignments in high school and college composition courses tends to confirm the short paragraph as the norm. Given a four or five page essay to write, the student, fresh from having read an essay of ten or twelve printed pages, reduces everything in his assignment to scale. An essay, he reasons, should have at least six or eight paragraphs, and six or eight paragraphs squeezed into five handwritten pages cannot be anything but underdeveloped. Remembering, then, that you are more likely to write too many and too short paragraphs, take the phrase "sufficient length" to signify a paragraph somewhat longer than you are used to writing. A rule of thumb of one to two pages of handscript or one-third to one-half a page of typescript per paragraph is reasonable. But such figures are only very approximate and must not be taken too literally. Many writers will drastically shorten paragraphs for emphasis, and many will be forced to extend them because of the complexity of their subjects. The important thing is to cultivate a feeling for the paragraph, to begin, as it were, to think in paragraphs, and always to remember that a paragraph must develop an idea in depth.

Paragraph Unity

COHERENCE

"Developed" was only one of two key terms in our definition of the paragraph; the other was "unity," and it is equally important. Paragraph unity involves two different problems — unity of thought and unity of form. Although these are necessarily closely related, they are still separable, for it is possible for a paragraph to have one without the other. The first, which we shall call coherence, concerns the content of the paragraph as distinguished from its form, that is, the ideas, considered apart from the sentences in which they are expressed. To be coherent a paragraph must satisfy several criteria: (1) relevance — every idea must relate to the topic of the paragraph; (2) proper order — these ideas must be arranged in the correct logical, or most effective rhetorical, order; (3) inclusiveness — nothing vital to the topic must be omitted.

As an instance of the violation of the first of these rules consider this brief paragraph:

> College is very different from high school. The professors talk a great deal more and give much longer homework assignments. This tends to interfere with a student's social life. It may even cost him his girlfriend. Girls don't like to be told that you have to stay home and study when they want you to take them to a show or out dancing, and so they find some boy who doesn't have to study all the time. Another way in which college is different is the examinations . . .

This is not all of it, but we needn't go on. The paragraph, after a capable enough beginning, slides into irrelevancy. The first sentence establishes the topic and the second supports it. In sentences three and four the writer is starting to drift, though we might allow him even these were they properly subordinated. But in the fifth and sixth sentences the student has lost any real contact with his subject. No doubt it is very true that young ladies do not like to take second place to textbooks (although one suspects that in real life they are very seldom asked to), but it is not pertinent information in a paragraph attempting to contrast high school and college. The writer himself tacitly acknowledges this irrelevancy, feeling it necessary to throw us a long transitional lifeline ("Another way in which college is different") to pull us back to shore. Rid of its irrelevancy the paragraph might read:

> College is very different from high school. The professors talk a great deal more and give much longer homework assignments, which interfere with a student's social life, sometimes even costing him his girlfriend. College examinations, too, are different . . .

This is better, though even here some people might still object that the loss of a girlfriend remains irrelevant, and probably, measured by the standard of tight organization, it is.

Relevancy alone, however, is not enough to establish coherence. It is possible for all the ideas in a paragraph to relate to the topic, yet for them to be badly arranged. Here is an example:

> The South had little hope of winning the war. For one thing, its supply of manpower was not sufficient. Although it was large in area,

> the South was thinly populated and most of its people lived on farms, not in cities. In fact, the South had little of the urbanized industry necessary to fight a modern war. It did not have enough iron and coal mines or enough foundaries to make cannons. Toward the end of the war the Confederate generals were terribly short of artillery. And even if they had had the guns they did not have enough troops to man them. Boys of fourteen and fifteen were fighting in the field, and companies that should have had a hundred men or more numbered thirty or forty.

Except possibly for the remark about most Southerners living on farms, one could not say that any of this is beside the point; it all has to do with why the South lost the war. But the paragraph is not as coherent as it might be because it fails to place its ideas in a significant order. The writer advances two reasons to support his contention that the defeat of the Confederacy was inevitable: that the South had (1) insufficient manpower and (2) not enough industry. But instead of handling each of these points in turn, finishing with one before going on to the other, he drifts uncertainly back and forth between them, from manpower to industry back to manpower. Study this revision; it is not brilliant prose, but at least it makes the paragraph reasonably coherent:

> The South had little hope of winning the war. For one thing Southern industry was not equal to modern war. The South did not have enough iron and coal mines. Nor did it have enough foundries to make cannon; by 1864 the Confederate army was terribly short of artillery. For another, the South, although it was large in area, was thinly populated, a fact which constantly plagued its military leaders. Toward the end of the war boys of fourteen and fifteen were fighting in the field, and companies that should have had a hundred men or more numbered thirty or forty.

Sometimes the failure of order is more subtle. In the following paragraph we feel that something is not quite right, although it may take us a moment or two to detect exactly what is wrong.

> New York fascinated me. There were so many things to do that I had never done before. My hometown has no ferryboats or subways to ride on, no Fifth Avenue to walk down. It has no museums to visit like the Cloisters or the Guggenheim. Nor is my hometown filled with excitement like New York. In Manhattan everyone seems to rush about his business as if it were the most important thing in the world. That's why New York seems so very much alive. Besides, this was my first visit and everything was new. I had looked forward to coming to New York for a long time, and I was already excited even before I got there.

The difficulty lies in the last portion of the paragraph; up to that point it is all relevant and well-ordered. But the final sentences subtly contradict what has gone before. Although the writer does not say so, he seems to imply that the excitement was not really in New York at all but in his own anticipation. An even more serious fault is that these final sentences are anticlimactic. Of all the reasons brought forward to show us why the topic idea is true, that contained in the final sentence is the least imposing. This does not mean that it is irrelevant, simply that it would be better placed early in the paragraph, as in this revision:

> New York fascinated me. This was my first visit and everything was new. There was so much to do that I had never done before. My hometown has no ferryboats or subways to ride on, no Fifth Avenue to walk down. It has no museums to visit like the Cloisters or the Guggenheim. Nor is my hometown filled with excitement like New York. In Manhattan everyone seems to rush about his business as if it were the most important thing in the world. That's why New York seems so very much alive.

Dropping the idea contained in the final sentence of the original version strengthens the paragraph, for that idea was not strictly relevant and was even, perhaps, subtly contradictory. And moving what had been the next to last sentence to a position immediately following the topic statement avoids the feeling of anticlimax. Moreover the sentence works well in its new place; the phrase "everything was new" helps to set up the series of particulars that follows.

Paragraph coherence, then, has to do with what we may call the logic of the paragraph (using that troublesome term *logic* in a rather loose sense). As we can see from even these few examples, coherence is not easy to achieve, although it is always easy to lose. The best advice on this matter for the beginning writer is this: always ask about each idea in the paragraph, is it (1) relevant and (2) placed in the best position? If he keeps these criteria consciously in mind, he will find that the problem of coherence will loom less large in his future work.

FLOW

Coherence is only half the problem of paragraph unity. A so-called paragraph may consist of sentences that all contain relevant ideas arranged in the best possible order and still not have become a real paragraph at all, remaining simply a series of sentences, no more intimately connected than beads on a string. For a paragraph to emerge, the sentences must be bound together so that the thought flows smoothly and steadily from the first sentence to the last. Most commonly this flow is achieved by transitional links, of which there are four principal sorts: repetitions, connectors, pronouns and demonstratives, and syntactic patterning.

Repetitions are by far the most common and the most natural, consisting merely of key terms repeated from one sentence to another and thus serving to hold the sentences together. If one is writing coherently such repetitions take care of themselves. Still it is worth becoming aware of a few of the ways in which repetitions may be used, for a skilled writer can often attain a very high degree of paragraph unity by carefully reiterating important words. When the same word is repeated in the same form it is called "tautotes." (Classical rhetoric distinguishes many varieties of repetition and gives to each an imposing technical label; here we shall mention only three or four of the most common.) For example, G. K. Chesterton writes of Bernard Shaw:

> Bernard Shaw is a Puritan and his work is Puritan work. He has all the essentials of the old, virile and extinct Protestant type. In his work he is as ugly as a Puritan. He is as indecent as a Puritan.
>
> *George Bernard Shaw*

Chesterton shifts once to the synonym "Protestant type," but basically his repetition is of the key term "Puritan." Dickens, too, is fond of tautotes, beginning the second chapter of *Our Mutual Friend* with this paragraph:

> Mr. and Mrs. Veneering were bran-new people in a bran-new house in a bran-new quarter of London. Everything about the Veneerings was spick and span new. All their furniture was new, all their friends were new, all their servants were new, their plate was new, their carriage was new, their harness was new, their horses were new, their pictures were new, they themselves were new, they were as newly married as was lawfully compatible with their having a bran new baby, and if they had set up a great-grandfather, he would have come home in matting from the Pantechnicon, without a scratch upon him, French polished to the crown of his head.

Dickens generally arranges the term "new" so that it falls toward the end of the sentence or clause, a device that is called "epistrophe." It is even more common to place the repeated word at the beginning of the sentence, which is called "anaphora." A little later in the same chapter, for instance, Dickens describes a dinner party at the Veneering's "bran-new" house like this:

> The great looking-glass above the sideboard reflects the table and the company. Reflects the new Veneering crest, in gold and eke in silver, frosted and also thawed, a camel of all work. The Herald's College found out a Crusading ancestor for Veneering who bore a camel on his shield (or might have done it if he had thought of it), and a caravan of camels take charge of the fruits and flowers and candles, and kneel down to be loaded with the salt. Reflects Veneering; forty, wavy-haired, dark, tending to corpulence, sly, mysterious, filmy — a kind of sufficiently well-looking veiled-prophet, not prophesying. Reflects Mrs. Veneering; fair, aquiline-nosed and fingered, not so much light hair as she might have, gorgeous in raiment and jewels, enthusiastic, propitiatory, conscious that a corner of her husband's veil is over herself. Reflects Podsnap; prosperously feeding, two little light-coloured wiry wings, one on either side of his else bald head, looking as like his hair-brushes as his hair, dissolving view of red beads on his forehead, large allowance of crumpled shirt-collar up behind.

The paragraph goes on for seven more sentences, all (except the last) beginning with "Reflects."

Another effective way of using repetition is to begin a following sentence with the same word or phrase that closed the preceding one. (This device, if you care to know, is called "anadiplosis.") Virginia Woolf, for example, has this passage in her essay "All About Books":

> That is what he writes about, and, of course, about the habits of the natives. The habits of the natives are disgusting . . .
>
> *The Captain's Death Bed and Other Essays*

And Hilaire Belloc writes this in his essay "The Spaniard":

> Glorious or tragic, each national experience gives a new impetus to the historic memory of the French people. Not so the Spaniard. All Spain is bound together by the enormous recollection of the *Reconquista.* Here is a province in which the Faith and the Roman Order were not recovered by persuasion (as was the case with Britain) nor were utterly lost (as was the case with Africa for so long) but were got back mile by mile as the prize of hard fighting. That fighting was, so to speak, the very trade of the Spaniards.
>
> *Selected Essays*

Repetition need not be of the same identical term, as for instance "fighting . . . fighting" here. A writer may repeat variant forms of the same word, shifting, say, from "Senate" to "Senator" or, as Belloc does, from "Spaniard" to "Spain." Again he may employ synonyms, which is what Charles Lamb does in this paragraph from his essay "The Convalescent":

> Household rumours touch him not. Some faint murmur, indicative of life going on within the house, soothes him, while he knows not distinctly what it is. He is not to know anything, not to think of anything. Servants gliding up and down the distant staircase, treading as upon velvet, gently keep his ear awake, so long as he troubles not himself further than with some feeble guess at their errands. Exacter knowledge would be a burthen to him; he can just endure the pressure of conjecture. He opens his eye faintly at the dull stroke of the muffled knocker, and closes it again without asking "Who was it?" He is flattered by a general notion that inquiries are making after him, but he cares not to know the name of the inquirer. In the general stillness, and awful hush of the house, he lies in state, and feels his sovereignty. "LAST ESSAYS OF ELIA"

The idea conveyed in the opening sentence by "rumour" is repeated in such terms as "faint murmur," "conjecture," and "general notion."

As you see, repetition takes many forms; these are only a few. Usually repetition is primarily a device of emphasis and probably in the examples we have looked at, the writers were more concerned with stressing important ideas than with unifying their paragraphs. Still unity is one of the effects of repetition, which is the point that interests us here.

Unity may also be achieved by the use of connective words and phrases, called conjunctive adverbs by some grammarians and transitional adverbs by others. These connectors establish a relation between the ideas expressed by successive sentences. The relationship may be one of time (*presently, meanwhile*), of space (*above, below, next*), or of logic (*therefore, consequently, however*). Rhetoricians are inclined to disagree about the value of such words. Some feel that they are of essential importance to good writing; another school argues that it is a fault to rely very much on connectors, that the able writer implies rather than states the relationship between his sentences. Probably there is room for both styles. It is certain that some good writers employ many connectors and that others, equally skilled, use them rarely; and it is also true that poor writers sometimes overuse connectors and other times obscure meaning by neglecting them. But it is safe to say that most students do not have enough connectors in their working vocabulary to make a wise decision about whether to use them or not.

Acquiring a collection of these words and phrases is not very difficult. English is exceedingly rich in them. Just to show some variation of contradiction, for example, we have available *but, however, still, yet, none the less, nevertheless, though, instead, on the other hand, on the contrary, not-*

withstanding; and this is a far from complete list. These words are not simple equivalents. They convey subtly different nuances of meaning and tone. *However,* in "It was late. However, we didn't go home" is more formal than *though* — "We didn't go home though." It is precisely because of tiny distinctions in meaning and tone that a good writer will have at hand a large number of transitional adverbs so that he can choose the one closest to the meaning he wishes to convey. If he can call upon only *but* or *however,* he will be unable to communicate the nuance carried by *yet* or *still* or *though.* And whether or not it is true that writing is the art of transitions, it is certainly true that it is the art of making subtle distinctions.

Like the logical connectors, pronouns and demonstratives also bind sentences into paragraphs. The personal pronouns and such words as *one, another, some, the former, the latter, the first, the second, the third,* and so on all link sentences by acting as substitutes in a later sentence for a word or phrase expressed in an earlier. Especially useful in this way are *this* and *that* (along with their plurals *these* and *those*). They may be employed either as true pronouns or as demonstratives, both of which uses are illustrated in this passage by E. V. Lucas:

> The blind in particular seem to become indifferent to climatic extremes; and there must be in everyone's cognizance two or three immovable sightless mendicants defying rain and chill . . .
>
> This insensitiveness to January blasts and February drenchings may be one of the compensations that the blind enjoy. Whatever else happens to them they never, perhaps, catch cold. And that is more than something. "MY FRIEND FLORA," *Selected Essays*

"This" functions as a demonstrative, modifying "insensitiveness," while "that" acts as a pronoun. But in both cases the effect of the word is to throw us back to the preceding material, thus establishing the link.

There is a danger, however, in using *this* and *that* too loosely as the subjects of sentences, for, though it is usually plain enough to the writer, it may not always be clear to the reader exactly what they refer to. The danger is especially great when the antecedent of *this* or *that* is not a single word, or even a phrase, but rather the total idea expressed by an entire sentence or paragraph. In this case the writer must be very sure that there can be no doubt about the referents of these pronouns. "That" in the example from E. V. Lucas, for instance, refers not to any specific word in the first sentence but rather to the idea conveyed by "they never . . . catch cold." Here the reference is clear enough. The less experienced writer should be sure of equal clarity when he employs *this* or *that* as the subject of a sentence.

Moreover, he should use them in this way only when his tone is relatively informal (as is Lucas's). In more formal writing it is wise to use *this* and *that* demonstratively (that is, as modifiers), attaching them to a noun that sums up or repeats the preceding point, as "insensitiveness" repeats for Lucas the indifference he speaks of in the first sentence. Used as demonstratives, *this* and *that* still fulfill their transitional purpose, linking their sentence to the preceding portion of the paragraph, but they run no risk of creating confusion by vague reference.

Aside from repetitions, connectors, and pronominal and demonstrative linkage, paragraph unity may be achieved by a fourth device, a more subtle one. This is syntactic patterning: that is, unifying the sentences of the paragraph by casting them in the same syntactic mold. The technique is exemplified in these pairs of sentences:

> Above floats the god with his staff and his winged cap and sandals. Below him stretches the immeasurable stream of ocean.
>
> LUDWIG LEWISOHN, *Upstream*

> In the dead stillness a child started crying suddenly and incoherently. In a city far to the north a French diplomatist and a German aristocrat were talking.
>
> G. K. CHESTERTON, "THE CONSCRIPT AND THE CRISIS," *Selected Essays*

In neither pair is the repetition of the syntactic pattern exact; probably it would be less effective if it were. But in both passages we can recognize that each of the two sentences is a variation of the same pattern—in Lewisohn's: adverbial prepositional phrase-verb-subject; in Chesterton's: adverbial prepositional phrase-subject-verb. And in both cases the similarity is enough to unify the passage. The same technique is worked even more extensively in this portion of a paragraph from an essay by Virginia Woolf on Turgenev's novels:

> But when we have finished *Rudin, Fathers and Children, Smoke, On the Eve* and the others many questions suggest themselves to which it is not so easy to find an answer. They are so short and yet they hold so much. The emotion is so intense and yet so calm. The form is in one sense so perfect, in another so broken. They are about Russia in the fifties and sixties of the last century, and yet they are about ourselves at the present moment.
>
> *The Captain's Death Bed and Other Essays*

Often syntactic patterning is combined with repetition. Virginia Woolf uses the phrase "and yet" three times. Anaphora is especially frequent in conjunction with sentence patterning, the writer using the same words to begin a series of similar sentences. Chesterton, for example, begins three sentences in his study of Bernard Shaw this way:

> That idolatry was bad for England. . .
> It was bad for literature. . .
> It was bad for religion . . .

Landor in his imaginary dialogue between Diogenes and Plato has Diogenes say:

> The great man is he who hath nothing to fear and nothing to hope from another. It is he who, while he demonstrates the iniquity of the laws, and is able to correct them, obeys them peaceably. It is he who looks on the ambitious both as weak and fraudulent. It is he who hath no disposition or occasion for any kind of deceit, no reason for being or for appearing different from what he is. It is he who can call together the most select company when it pleases him.
> *Imaginary Conversations*

And finally, perhaps an even better instance is this paragraph by F. L. Lucas:

> "Everyone," says Professor Abbott, "liked Boswell." I doubt if such a claim was ever true of any man since Adam. It is certainly not true of Boswell. And even if it *were* true? Are men's merits to be judged by Gallup polls? Not everyone liked Johnson — far from it; does that make Boswell his superior? Not everyone liked Socrates — he was given hemlock. Not everyone liked Joan of Arc — she was burnt. Not everyone liked Abraham Lincoln — he was shot.
> *The Search for Good Sense*

In practice, as you might suspect, the writer will rely upon all of these transitional devices to unify his paragraph, repeating key words, employing transitional adverbs and pronouns, and modeling his thought to a basic sentence pattern. It can happen, of course, that one may *overuse* these devices, boring or even insulting the reader by pointing out relations obvious to the meanest intelligence. It is not necessary to tie up a rowboat with a six-inch hawser. Still a boat so secured is not likely to drift away, and if one must make a fault with transitions, it is better to err on the side of too much than of too little. Too much may be bad style; too little is plain bad writing. When, however, these transitions have been skillfully applied, the paragraph, assuming it is coherent to begin with, will be an organized, unified statement of a complex thought.

There is one other way besides transitions in which the rhetorical unity of the paragraph can be achieved. This is by the use of an organizing element and framing words, which you may recall as a unifying device in the larger unit of the essay. We have already seen an example in the paragraph by Bertrand Russell on page 137. Organizing elements and framing words unify a paragraph in a rather different way than transitions do. Transitions link up successive sentences, hooking sentence two to sentence one, three to two, and so on. The linkage may be more complex than this: the fourth sentence may be tied to the second rather than to the third, or the fifth to both the third and the fourth; but still the principle remains the same: each sentence is attached to one or more of those preceding it. With the organizing element and framing words, however, the principle of unification is a little different. In the first or second sentence of his paragraph the writer sets out its plan; then as he comes to the various parts indicated by that plan, he introduces each with an appropriate word or phrase fitting it into its place. Consider this paragraph by Lafcadio Hearn:

> The second half of the sixteenth century is the most interesting period in Japanese history — for three reasons. First, because it witnessed the apparition of those mighty captains, Nobunaga, Hidéyoshi, and Iyéyasu, — types of men that a race seems to evolve for supreme emergencies only, — types requiring for their production not merely the highest aptitudes of numberless generations, but likewise an extraordinary combination of circumstances. Secondly, this period is all-important because it saw the first complete integration of the ancient social system, — the definitive union of all the clan-lordships under a central military government. And lastly, the period is of special interest because the incident of the first attempt to christianize Japan — the story of the rise and fall of the Jesuit power — properly belongs to it.
>
> *Japan: An Attempt at Interpretation*

The first sentence tells us that the plan of the paragraph is to develop "three reasons"; this is the organizing element. As each reason is introduced, it is fitted into the triadic scheme by the framing words "First," "Secondly," and "lastly." Notice that the writer makes no effort to link the second reason to the first or the third to the second, as he would have done had he been relying upon transitions. Here no such links are needed because we begin with the plan in our minds and can follow the fulfillment of that plan as the paragraph develops.

This method of unifying a paragraph is rather more mechanical — and for that reason less preferable — than the use of transitions. Still, it has its virtues. It is quick and easy, a fact that makes it especially suitable for discussion questions on examinations. Most teachers will agree that students do not unify discussion answers very well; and while the unity achieved by the organizing element-framing word technique may be mechanical, mechanical order is better than chaos. Quite apart from this practical application, the use of organizing elements and framing words is almost demanded in paragraphs whose ideas are connected only in their common relation to the topic. Such is the case in the example from Hearn. The attempts of the Jesuits have no causal connection with the attainment of a strong central military government; these things share only the fact that they both contribute to the interest of Japanese history in the sixteenth century. It is wiser to admit this lack of interconnection than to attempt to unify the paragraph by forcing artificial links between its sentences. It remains true, however, that of the two ways of giving rhetorical unity to the paragraph, transitions are generally better than framing words.

Coherence and flow — these are the requirements of paragraph unity. Either one without the other is insufficient. A paragraph may be coherent, its ideas relevant and in order; but if they do not flow together, the paragraph is not unified and thus not a paragraph at all. It is less common that one finds rhetorical unity without coherence, but now and then a glib writer without much to say succeeds in hiding, at least for a moment, the incoherence of his thought beneath the skill of his transitions. Such a paragraph, while it may impose upon us more easily, is still a failure. It will not fool the careful reader.

Summary

The expository paragraph is like a sentence in having a subject (the topic sentence) about which a predicate is made (the remainder of the paragraph). The paragraph may be tightly organized, in which case its topic is not simply a general subject but one specific proposition about that subject. It may be organized more loosely, centering about one subject but developing several assertions about it rather than being confined to a single proposition. Finally, the expository paragraph may be quite loosely organized by the simple association of ideas, though such associational development is most appropriate to familiar writing and ought usually to be avoided in formal composition.

However tightly or loosely they are organized, all expository paragraphs must be unified. This means first that they must be coherent in thought: the ideas composing the paragraph have all got to be relevant to the topic and they must be arranged in a significant order. Secondly, the paragraph must have unity of form. Its sentences must be tied together so that thought flows uninterruptedly from the beginning of the paragraph to the end. Flow is achieved (1) by transitions (which include repeating key words, using transitional adverbs, and cutting successive sentences to the same pattern); and (2) by an organizing element followed by appropriate framing words.

Exercises

1. List all the transitional devices that link together the sentences in each of the two following paragraphs. Look for repetitions of key words, conjunctive adverbs, and sentences of similar construction.

1. Above the beginner's level, the important fact is that writing cannot be taught exclusively in a course called English Composition. Writing can only be taught by the united efforts of the entire teaching staff. This holds good of any school, college, or university. Joint effort is needed, not merely to "enforce the rules"; it is needed to insure accuracy in every subject. How can an answer in physics or a translation from the French or an historical statement be called correct if the phrasing is loose or the key word wrong? Students argue that the reader of the paper knows perfectly well what is meant. Probably so, but a written exercise is designed to be read; it is not supposed to be a challenge to clairvoyance. My Italian-born tailor periodically sends me a postcard which runs: 'Your clothes is ready and should come down for a fitting.' I understand him, but the art I honor him for is cutting cloth, not precision of utterance. Now a student in college must be inspired to achieve in all subjects the utmost accuracy of perception combined with the utmost artistry of expression. The two merge and develop the sense of good workmanship, of preference for quality and truth, which is the chief mark of the genuinely educated man.

JACQUES BARZUN, "HOW TO WRITE AND BE READ," *Teacher in America*

2. The program of studies in a comprehensive high school is made up of general subjects, required of all, and of electives. The general subjects usually are, and I think they should be (including the ninth grade), four years of English; three or four years of the social studies; one year of science; and one year of mathematics, usually either general mathematics or algebra. In those general classes, enrolling all students, there will be a wide diversity of ability, a diversity so wide as to make it impossible for a teacher to adapt his teaching to the whole range in the class. Therefore students should be grouped in separate classes by ability, but the grouping should be subject by

subject. Thus a student might be in a top-level class in English but in an average one in mathematics. Three levels of grouping are probably enough — one for the more able in the subject, another for the middle group, and a third for the slow readers, who need teachers especially qualified to teach them. However, grouping is not recommended in the twelfth-grade course dealing with problems in American democracy. Here great value can accrue from the discussion of problems by students of all levels of ability and of diverse interests and backgrounds.

JAMES B. CONANT, "DIVERSIFIED STUDIES FOR DIVERSIFIED STUDENTS," *The PTA Magazine* (*National Parent-Teacher*)

2. The following paragraphs all lack unity. The problem may be merely inadequate links between sentences, or it may go deeper, involving incoherence of thought. Rewrite each paragraph, staying as close as you can to the original wording but making whatever changes are required to unify the passages.

1. There are several kinds of test. Quizzes deal with only a small amount of material, usually that covered in the preceding week or so. Pop quizzes are given without any announcement. Students often miss them and have to arrange make-ups. Examinations are longer and cover more ground. The mid-term comes about the sixth week and in some courses is the only grade the teacher has for the mid-semester mark. It is important. The final comes at the end of the course and is a large part of one's grade. Students work hard preparing for finals.

2. Hats have served a number of different functions. One is comfort. People living in the hot areas of the Southwest like the ten-gallon hat because its wide brim shelters them from the sun and the large air space insulates the head and keeps it cool. Ten-gallon hats come in a smaller size (called the five-gallon); both kinds are made of felt, and both have spread to other sections of the country because of the popularity of the cowboy in American culture. (Americans are cowboy-conscious; they see cowboys on television and in the movies from early childhood on.) Hats also offer protection. Football players and racing car drivers wear helmets made of a hard plastic that completely encircles the head, which is cradled inside in a kind of webbing (which reduces the shock of impact). Construction workers wear helmets of steel or plastic in case tools or bolts are dropped on them. Hats are also decorative. Many people, especially women, wear hats simply to increase their attractiveness (they hope). Frequently, women's hats are merely silly, and sometimes they are annoying, especially if you get stuck behind one in a movie.

3. Colleges are becoming increasingly crowded. Many parents today have more money and can afford to send their children to college. The war babies are now reaching college age. As more people

graduate from college, employers are able to demand college degrees where they were once happy to accept a high school diploma. To meet this competition for jobs more and more young men and women are realizing they need an education beyond high school and so are flocking to universities. The crowded college is here to stay.

It has its drawbacks. There are not enough teachers to provide individual attention for the students. Some sections of freshman and sophomore subjects have three and four hundred students. The libraries are inadequate; one book may be placed on reserve for fifty students, and there are not enough tables and chairs available even if one gets a book. Scheduling is done impersonally, and the student feels that no one really cares what he takes, so long as he doesn't waste time in making up his mind. Many undergraduates are frustrated and angry. Student rebellions, like the one at Berkeley, are likely to grow more frequent. Despite these growing pains, the American university will survive.

3. Selecting any one of the following subjects, develop it three ways in three separate paragraphs. Organize the first paragraph tightly around one specific assertion about the topic. In the second, loosen the organization, making everything relevant to the subject but feeling free to range through three or four assertions concerning it. In the third, attempt a discursive, associational paragraph; you may wander completely away from the initial topic, but you should do it cleverly so that one idea leads naturally into another. In each of the three paragraphs underline or encircle your transitional words and phrases with a different colored pen or pencil.

1. Sandwiches
2. Sailing
3. Kindergarten
4. Opera
5. Folk music
6. Political liberalism (or conservatism)
7. Civil rights
8. Religion
9. Art
10. New York (or any other city)
11. Plato
12. The new mathematics

10

DEVELOPING THE PARAGRAPH
I. Techniques of Amplification

Introduction

The subject-predicate structure of expository paragraphs can become exceedingly complicated, but until we have looked over all the different techniques of development we shall stick to fairly simple varieties. In such simple paragraphs the topic sentence, which ought to be as concise as the complexity of its idea permits, will generally be found toward the beginning of the paragraph, often being the very first sentence. Occasionally it is cast as a rhetorical question, a device that is effective now and then, although it easily becomes a mannerism. The topic is supported by such techniques as illustration, analysis, restatement, comparison or contrast, analogy, cause and effect, definition, and qualification. In this chapter and the next two we shall survey these ways of building paragraphs, observing examples of each and trying to learn what rules govern them.

Roughly, they fall into three groups. Those in the first tend to remain within the topic idea. They repeat it, they exemplify it, they break it down into its parts; but they do not move from it into other, related ideas. These may be called techniques of amplification. Those in the second group — the techniques of comparison — introduce a second topic into the paragraph. Usually (not invariably, however) the new topic is subordinate, serving to clarify or emphasize some aspect of the original topic idea. The third class of developing techniques is concerned with investigating the meaning or the ramifications of the topic idea; they seek its causes or follow out its effects. These we shall label the discursive techniques. The three categories are not hard and fast, but if the distinctions are not taken too literally they are a useful way of studying expository paragraphs. We shall begin with the techniques of amplification.

Illustration

One of the simplest of these is illustration, which is supporting a generalization by citing one or more particular instances of its truth or reality. Professor Brand Blanshard, for example, in the following paragraph criticizes the tendency of academic writers to overuse abstract nouns:

> I am not sure that philosophers are worse sinners in this respect than sociologists; indeed I suspect the reverse. Here, at any rate, is an example of what a sociologist can achieve when warmed to his theme in an article judged worthy of reprinting in a source-book of sociology: "Social and political organizations tend to become accommodated to spatial distribution or ecological organization resulting from the prevailing forms of transportation. The introduction of new forms of communication such as the railway, automobile, telegraph, radio, necessitates a reaccommodation of social organization to the new interpretation of spatial distance." Of the thirteen different nouns in those two sentences, seven of them are *-tion* nouns, and of these one, "organization," appears three times over. What is it that makes civilized men do these things? Often, I am sure, a sense that what they have to say is so commonplace that it must be dressed up for dignity's sake, the sort of feeling that led the American Collectors' Association, meeting recently in Detroit, to announce that henceforth bill collectors preferred to be known as "adjusters of delinquent obligations." *On Philosophical Style*

This uncomplicated paragraph has four parts: the topic statement, which is the first sentence; the introduction of the illustration, which is the first part of the second; the illustration itself, which occupies the last part of the second and all of the third sentence; and Mr. Blanshard's commentary upon his example, sentences four, five, and six. The pattern is typical of a simple illustration paragraph, except that often the commentary will not be necessary. If an example can stand alone, it is foolish to labor it.

Regardless of whether it needs to be explained, an illustration must generally be introduced. To leap from a generalization immediately into an example without telling the reader that it is an example, is very likely to bewilder him. The writer of the following passage committed exactly this fault:

> The modern private-eye operates on radically different principles than did the purely rational creatures of Poe and Conan Doyle. Sam Spade jumps feet first into a case . . .

This brings the reader up very short indeed: Who or what is a Sam Spade? The context has not made it clear, and consequently the illustration, thrown down with no introduction at all, succeeds only in puzzling the reader. Had the example been prefaced there would have been no confusion:

> The modern private-eye operates on radically different principles than did the purely rational creatures of Poe and Conan Doyle. Dashiell Hammet's private detective Sam Spade is a good example of the type. Sam jumps feet first into a case . . .

The introduction does not have to be an entire sentence as it is here, or even a full clause, as it is in Professor Blanshard's paragraph. In fact, it should be kept as brief as possible. The illustration is the important thing, and the sooner one gets to it the better. Often a short phrase (*for example, for instance*), or even a single word (*take, consider, say, suppose*) will suffice. And occasionally, when the context has made it very clear that the example is an example, no introduction at all is required.

The illustration itself, to be effective, must be detailed. Examine this paragraph by E. B. White:

> There is always the miracle of the by-products. Plane a board, the shavings accumulate around your toes ready to be chucked into the stove to kindle your fires (to warm your toes so you can plane a board). Draw some milk from a creature to relieve her fullness, the milk goes to the little pig to relieve his emptiness. Drain some oil from a crankcase, and you smear it on the roots to control the mites. The worm fattens on the apple, the young goose fattens on the wormy fruit, the man fattens on the young goose, the worm awaits the man. Clean up the barnyard, the pulverized dung from the sheep goes to improve the lawn (before a rain in autumn); mow the lawn next spring, the clippings go to the compost pile, with a few thrown to the baby chickens on the way; spread the compost on the garden and in the fall the original dung, after many vicissitudes, returns to the sheep in the form of an old squash. From the fireplace, at the end of a November afternoon, the ashes are carried to the feet of the lilac bush, guaranteeing the excellence of a June morning.
>
> "COLD WEATHER," *One Man's Meat*

Where a lesser writer would fob us off with a generality, saying merely that waste products have their uses, Mr. White is precise. His paragraph is about a worm and a young goose, about a barnyard and an old squash and a lilac bush; and it convinces us as no generalization would ever do.

Mr. White's illustrations are not only specific; they are also numerous.

Professor Blanshard, on the other hand, worked with a single example, although he does introduce as a kind of final sting, a brief second instance in the last sentence. Hilaire Belloc works out a single example in even greater detail in these paragraphs from his essay "On Boycotts":

> . . . All mad people like to break one or more of the conventions (which, let me tell those who despise formal logic, is not equivalent to saying that all those who break one or more conventions are mad). What I mean is that there is an insane pleasure in shocking people, and one can surely tell by one's common sense when that pleasure is insane and when it is of a sane and merely impertinent sort. Well, so much has the taboo got into the income-boycott that a certain class of people love to break it.
>
> I knew a don of Oxford in my youth whose nervous disease took this particular form: he invariably opened conversation with the lady next whom he might happen to be sitting at dinner with this phrase pronounced in a low voice: "*What is your precise income?*" It was calculated to startle, and it did. Having delivered that shell the worthy man would put on a very interested expression, not unlike that which we should see, I think, on the face of a spider when he is watching for flies; for he well knew that his victim was cut off, with only three avenues of escape open to her. If, as was usually the case, she answered by the feminine habit of ignoring the question he would chuckle gently and say: "Ha! ha! I see you don't like to admit it!" If she got angry and said it was none of his business, his pleasure was so indecently obvious that he scored. If (as was the case with some witty women, who had strayed into the university from outside) she answered with an exact figure (a wrong one of course), he would arch his eyebrows in surprise and say: "Oh, surely more than *that!*" Such was the simple pleasure of his old age. After all, every man must have his hobby. *Selected Essays*

Whether the writer uses only a single example, which he works out in detail, or calls upon three or four, which he treats more briefly, the technique of supporting the topic idea by illustration is essentially the same. The illustration must be relevant to the topic. It (or they) must usually be introduced. And always it must be developed with enough detail to offer a specific instance of the truth stated generally in the topic sentence.

Analysis

Another simple way of amplifying an idea is to analyze it into its components. Samuel Taylor Coleridge, for instance, once remarked that

Readers may be divided into four classes:

1. Sponges, who absorb all they read and return it nearly in the same state, only a little dirtied.

2. Sand-glasses, who retain nothing and are content to get through a book for the sake of getting through the time.

3. Strain-bags, who retain merely the dregs of what they read.

4. Mogul diamonds, equally rare and valuable, who profit by what they read, and enable others to profit by it also. *Notebooks*

The whole passage is merely a working out in specific terms of what is meant by the generalization that "readers may be divided into four classes." This way of developing a paragraph is given many names: analysis, general to particular, classification, all meaning much the same thing. Coleridge utilized paragraphs to separate the classes into which he divided readers. But the technique is often worked out within a single paragraph; in fact, most modern writers would probably prefer one paragraph in a treatment so brief as Coleridge's. G. K. Chesterton, for example, uses only one paragraph to classify all the people in the world into three groups:

> Roughly speaking, there are three kinds of people in this world. The first kind of people are People; they are the largest and probably the most valuable class. We owe to this class the chairs we sit down on, the clothes we wear, the houses we live in; and, indeed (when we come to think of it), we probably belong to this class ourselves. The second class may be called for convenience the Poets; they are often a nuisance to their families, but, generally speaking, a blessing to mankind. The third class is that of the Professors or Intellectuals, sometimes described as the thoughtful people; and these are a blight and a desolation both to their families and also to mankind. Of course, the classification sometimes overlaps, like all classification. Some good people are almost poets and some bad poets are almost professors. But the division follows lines of real pyschological cleavage. I do not offer it lightly. It has been the fruit of more than eighteen minutes of earnest reflection and research.
>
> "ON RUNNING AFTER ONE'S HAT"

This follows much the pattern of the passage by Coleridge, except that Chesterton does in one paragraph what he did in four brief ones. Generally, as it does in both these cases, the topic sentence, the generalization, will come first, to be followed by the specific components into which it is analyzed. Occasionally this order is reversed (in a later chapter we shall see instances of such variants), but not very often. The analysis paragraph is easily unified by an organizing element and framing words, which are, as it were, built into this method of paragraph development. But frequently a writer will supplement these with links of various kinds. Chesterton, in addition to the framing words "first," "second," "third," uses all the transitional devices: syntactic patterning ("The first kind of people are . . ." "The second class may be called . . ." "The third class is . . ."); pronominal reference ("It"); connectors ("But"); and even alliteration (the names of his three classes all begin with *p*). As a result his paragraph is very tightly knit.

Fully as unified is this analysis paragraph by Robert L. Heilbroner, describing the eccentricities of the great economist Thorstein Veblen:

> As might be expected, he was a mass of eccentricities. He refused to have a telephone, kept his books stacked along the wall in their original packing cases, and saw no sense in daily making up the beds; they were thrown back in the morning and pulled up again at night. Lazy, he allowed the dishes to accumulate until the cupboard was bare and then washed the whole messy heap by turning the hose on them. Taciturn, he would sit for hours in silence when all his visitors were eager to hear his pronouncements. A flouter of convention, he gave all his students the same grade, regardless of their work, but when one student needed a higher mark to qualify for a scholarship, Veblen gladly changed a C into an A. . . . And perhaps strangest of all, this sardonic and unprepossessing man had that indefinable quality of being attractive to women. He was always engaged in one liaison or another, and not always of his own doing. "What are you to do if the woman moves in on you?" he once inquired of a friend.
>
> *The Worldly Philosophers*

Notice how Mr. Heilbroner uses syntactic patterning to unify the middle portions of his paragraph: "Lazy, he allowed . . ."; "Taciturn, he would sit . . ."; "A flouter of convention, he gave . . ."

Restatement

Restatement is at once the simplest and one of the most difficult techniques of amplification. It is simple because the writer hardly moves at all from his topic idea. He does not have to cast about for an example, or explain reasons, or struggle with a definition; he merely repeats his topic sentence in various ways. But finding ways various enough is what creates the difficulty. It is easy to repeat onself; but it is not easy to repeat oneself without boring the reader. Study this brief paragraph from a student paper:

> Henry was greedy. He was avaricious in the fullest sense of that term. He squeezed every penny; he clutched every possession. A veritable magpie, he hoarded worthless bits of old string as scrupulously as bright new dollars, no longer capable of distinguishing any difference in value between them.

From beginning to end this paragraph says nothing more (at least explicitly) than that Henry was greedy, but it says it so often that we are convinced of the fact.

As we have seen — in the Dickens paragraphs, for instance — a writer can achieve effective emphasis by hammering away at the same word, though it is difficult to get away with. In this case the writer, by not using the same key word more than once, avoids the danger of monotony. Moreover the key terms take different grammatical forms: "greedy" and "avaricious" are adjectives; "clutched," "squeezed," and "hoarded," participles; and "magpie" is a noun. Here again syntactic patterning unifies the paragraph; all the sentences follow the same basic scheme of subject followed by verb followed by object. Such syntactic regularity is quite common, although certainly not necessary, in development by restatement, for it is always a good idea to allow form to mirror sense, in this instance stressing the similarity of idea by similarity of sentence pattern. But even more than repetitious diction, syntactic regularity can become monotonous if pursued too rigidly. Listen to the same paragraph when handled like this:

> Henry was greedy. He was very avaricious. He squeezed every penny. He clutched every possession. He was a veritable magpie. He hoarded worthless bits of string as scrupulously as bright new dollars. He was no longer capable of distinguishing any difference in value between them.

The original paragraph is saved from such bone-crushing regularity by the introduction of a little variation into every sentence after the first. The second has two prepositional phrases tacked on its end; in the third the pattern is simply doubled; the fourth begins with an elliptical participial construction. In this way the writer varies his syntax just enough to avoid boring us.

One more point is worth remarking. We said that nowhere does this paragraph say anything but that Henry was greedy. In a subtler sense of "say," however, this is not quite true. The paragraph *suggests* something about the nature and the effect of greed. "Squeezed" and "clutched" imply the subhuman, animal-like quality of avarice, a note that becomes more open in "magpie." And the final sentence makes it quite clear that the ultimate consequence of greed is the corrosion of all ability to differentiate values. Thus the paragraph really does more than merely repeat itself. The fact is important, for it applies to all good restatement. The writer using restatement is like the art critic holding up for the inspection of his audience a small piece of sculpture. He does not hold it steadily in one position but rather revolves it slowly so that they can study it from all angles. All the time they see the same thing, yet they see it differently; only in this way can they see it whole. Similarly the writer. One can never say the same thing twice. The very fact of phrasing the "same" idea in a different way alters it, and thus slightly develops it.

Developing a topic idea while one seems to be only repeating it, is well illustrated in this paragraph by F. L. Lucas:

> No doubt memory is important; it may have been, in part, man's better memory that enabled him to rise above the chimpanzee; but one can easily remember far too much. The past may all be recorded in our Unconscious; but a good deal of it had better stay there. Excessive retrospection, like excessive introspection, can become perilous. The healthy mind looks a little ahead, and not too much behind — there is the present to be used, the future to be prepared, without playing Lot's wife towards the past.
>
> *The Search for Good Sense*

The topic is stated in the final clause of the opening sentence, the first two clauses being qualifications of the topic. The second sentence repeats the main idea; but the third not only restates the point, it also warns of the dangers of excessive dwelling in memory. The final sentence develops even further the idea of peril by alluding to Lot's wife, who was turned into a pillar of salt because she could not resist looking back at the past from which she was fleeing.

The progression of thought is even clearer in this brief restatement paragraph from *The Education of Henry Adams*:

> America has always taken tragedy lightly. Too busy to stop the activity of their twenty-million-horse-power society, Americans ignore tragic motives that would have overshadowed the Middle Ages; and the world learns to regard assassination as a form of hysteria, and death as neurosis, to be treated by a rest-cure. Three hideous political murders, that would have fattened the Eumenides with horror, have thrown scarcely a shadow on the White House.

Adams not only states his topic three times, but in the first part of the second sentence he suggests a reason why it is so, and in the last part he touches upon one or two of its consequences.

The examples of restatement we have looked at so far have been complete, though brief, paragraphs. Because restatement is difficult to sustain for great length, it is more likely to occur as a technique to develop a portion of a paragraph rather than the paragraph in its entirety. Professor George Saintsbury, for example, uses restatement very effectively in the passage printed below. It is the final portion of a paragraph in which he defends the fourth book of Swift's *Gulliver*, the section in which Swift satirizes the brutishness of mankind in the figures of the apelike Yahoos:

> . . . will anybody who chooses to contemplate man as he is, put hand on heart and say that the picture — though one-sided, exaggerated, painted with foul colours, and so on — is *false?* If he does, cynicism and Christianity will for once unite in a mocking or grave, "Thou fool!" The Yahoo lurks in the Greek, behind and under his culture and his art and his philosophy; the Yahoo shows himself almost unabashed and unconcealed in the brutal tyranny, the vulgar ostentation, and the graceless vice of Rome. He is to no small extent let loose in the chaos of the Dark Ages; and, though somewhat tamed by Christianity and Chivalry, not absent from the Middle. He triumphs alike, though masked and muffled, in the frank paganism of the Renaissance and about the stakes and scaffolds and battle-fields of the Reformation. Although still further changed and clothed and made outwardly decent, he is seldom more loathsome than in the tamed mercantile ages that follow. Frederic the Great was a crowned and cultured Yahoo; there have been others crowned likewise before and after him. The French Revolution was the Yahooism of the Demos broken loose: and at the present day it is difficult to say whether this Yahooism is most apparently concentrated in a Trade Union agitator or in a millionaire who gives "freak" suppers. No! the Yahoo man pure and simple, man as he is, has always not far from him; something of the Yahoo, it may almost be said, he has always actually latent in him.
>
> *The Peace of the Augustans*

Saintsbury uses syntactic patterning and anaphora to unify these sentences and to emphasize the iteration of idea. He neatly gives point to the universality of Yahooism by organizing his material historically, ranging over Yahooism from Classic Greece to the twentieth century.

In progressing from antiquity to the modern world, Saintsbury's paragraph (or at least this portion of it) also moves from the particular to the general. The final sentence acts as a topic statement. (We shall see more examples later on of delaying the topic sentence to the end of the paragraph.) Even more often restatement will progress from the general to the particular. Beginning with a broad formulation of his idea, the writer repeats it in more specific ways, as in this paragraph from an essay by John Masefield on the famous pirate John Ward:

> It is difficult for one accustomed to the law and order of the present day to understand the dangers which threatened the Jacobean traveller. The seas swarmed with pirates; so that few merchantmen dared to put to sea without arms; while very few came home without some tale of an encounter. There were pirates in the Atlantic, to intercept the ships coming home from the Newfoundland fisheries. There were pirates in the West Indies, roving for Spanish treasure-ships. There were pirates in the Orkneys, preying upon the Iceland trades. There were pirates near Ireland, especially in the south and west, ranging over the Channel, and round these coasts. But there were, perhaps, more pirates in the Mediterranean than in all the other waters put together . . .
>
> "CAPTAIN JOHN WARD," *A Mainsail Haul*

The generalization, of course, is the clause: "The seas swarmed with pirates"; this is repeated more specifically in each of the following five sentences. Like Saintsbury, Masefield unifies his paragraph by syntactic patterning and anaphora; and, also like Saintsbury, he organizes his material to emphasize the universal truth of his topic idea, ranging through geographical area as Saintsbury had ranged through time. The sentences, moreover, are arranged climactically. As the strong "But" beginning the seventh sentence implies, the writer is leading up to the Mediterranean, which was, as you can guess, the area in which Captain Ward operated. It is, indeed, with this very gentleman that Masefield's long paragraph concludes, thus fulfilling the movement from the general — pirates — to the particular — Captain John Ward.

The value of restatement as an expository technique is obvious. It may or may not be that "what I tell you three times is true"; but certainly one of the oldest ways of convincing others of the rightness of one's ideas is to repeat them. The most effective form of restatement is a kind of theme and variations. The writer states his basic idea in a particular sentence pattern. This idea and this pattern he repeats, but always with enough variety to sustain his reader's attention. Though some development of the topic necessarily occurs in restatement (and may even be skillfully utilized by the writer), the restatement technique is concerned more with establishing the idea than with exploring it.

Summary

A simple expository paragraph consists of a topic sentence which is supported by such techniques as illustration, analysis, restatement, cause and effect, comparison or contrast, analogy, definition, and qualification. The first three of these are called techniques of amplification; they stay within the topic and try simply to clarify it in detail. The other techniques are more discursive, tending to move from the topic into other ideas significantly related to it. A writer may use only one extended illustration in a paragraph or he may employ several. In either case the illustrations must be relevant and specific, and they usually require to be explicitly introduced, though the label should be as brief as possible. Analysis development consists of opening out the components of the topic idea; often, though not necessarily, the analysis paragraph is unified by an organizing element and framing words. Restatement development, finally, simply repeats the topic idea. The repetition must exhibit enough variety to avoid seeming monotonous. In restatement there is frequently a movement from an initial general formulation of the idea to more specific repetitions.

Exercises

1. Loosely modeling your work upon Professor Blanshard's paragraph on page 157, write an illustration paragraph to support one of the following topic sentences. Copy down the sentence to start the paragraph and then work out your illustration as specifically as possible, prefacing it with a brief but clear introduction.

    1. The fact is that some teachers talk too fast and use too many big words.
    2. A college catalogue is not easy to understand.
    3. I don't know who writes the directions that come with do-it-yourself Christmas toys, but I suspect he hates his fellow man.
    4. Some people will suffer torture just to be fashionable.

2. Beginning with one of the topic sentences listed below, compose an illustration paragraph after the fashion of that by E. B. White on page 158. Use numerous brief illustrations and try to make them clear enough so that you can dispense with an introduction.

    1. One function of teen-age slang is to serve as a secret language which adults cannot understand.
    2. Every national group has its favorite foods.
    3. Courtship practices vary widely from culture to culture.
    4. People make hobbies out of collecting the most peculiar things.
    5. I have known a few Yahoos in my time.

3. Develop a single illustration in detail (comparable to what Belloc does in the paragraph on page 159) to support one of these topic sentences.

1. The typical TV family situation comedy is ridiculous.
2. All parents have peculiarities.
3. At times my uncle acts very strange.
4. College is a completely new world.
5. It is surprising how many adults continue to play with toys.

4. Choosing any two of the following topics, compose two separate analysis paragraphs. Begin each with a topic sentence like Chesterton's (see page 160) and unify the paragraph with appropriate framing words.

1. Types of students (or professors)
2. Kinds of dancing
3. The basic varieties of detective fiction
4. The major kinds of narrative literature
5. Small sailboat rigs
6. Kinds of used-car salesmen
7. The various "lines" employed by romantically inclined young men
8. The basic types of hammer (or of any other tool)

5. Begin with one of the following topic sentences and write a brief restatement paragraph. Follow the general lines of the student passage on page 162, and try to construct your sentences to resemble one another, though with enough variety to avoid seeming monotonous.

1. There was no doubt about it — Harry was ugly.
2. I think it was the dullest party I have ever been to.
3. She was beautiful.
4. I studied very hard for the exam.

6. General to particular restatement, as in the passage by John Masefield, begins with a broad topic and then repeats it more specifically. Develop one of these topic sentences along lines similar to Masefield's.

1. If a native of the African jungle were magically transported to Manhattan, he would think it the most dangerous spot on earth.
2. Every summer Sunday afternoon highways all over America swarm with maniacs.
3. College is sometimes called formal education; there are certainly plenty of forms.
4. Blind-dating has many perils.

11

DEVELOPING THE PARAGRAPH
II. Techniques of Comparison

Comparison

The second general way of developing a topic idea is to compare it with something else. The specific techniques are called comparison (which includes contrast) and analogy. There are several special problems connected with comparison. The first concerns the "focus" of the paragraph and results from the fact that in a comparison not one but two topics are involved. There may even be three or four, in which case focus becomes more difficult; but most of the time it will be necessary to handle only two topics. Now this means that the writer faces at least three possibilities. If he is comparing high school and college, say, he may be primarily interested in the first or in the second, or he may be interested equally in both. But whatever the focus of his interest, it is important that he establish it clearly at the beginning and maintain it consistently. With this point in mind study the following paragraph:

> In many ways the England about which Shakespeare wrote was like the Athens of Aeschylus and Pericles. The Elizabethans, like the Athenians, had just overcome a great threat to their national identity. Moreover, the great victory over the Armada, no less than the victories of Salamis and Marathon, let loose a wave of confidence in the future. The average Athenian felt that the victory had been, at least in part, his doing, and he claimed his share in the dreams which that victory begot, and so did the average Englishman.

This starts well enough. From the first sentence or two we infer that the center of attention is England, which, in fact, is exactly what it ought to be since the paragraph was taken from a theme about Elizabethan England.

The writer establishes this focus by making "England" the subject of the first sentence, "Elizabethans" the subject of the second, and "the great victory over the Armada" the subject of the third. But in its final sentence the paragraph begins to slip. The subject changes. Now it is the Athenians who engage our attention, and the remark about the similar case of the Englishman is tacked on almost as an afterthought. The paragraph blurs the focus it had itself established. That focus could have been different, of course. The paragraph could have begun: "In many ways the Athens of Pericles and Aeschylus was like Shakespearean England," or, had the writer wished to suggest equal interest in both periods: "The England of Shakespeare and the Athens of Aeschylus and Pericles were much alike." But had the focus been either of these, it would still have been incumbent upon the writer to keep it that.

The second problem that confronts the writer of comparison is to decide exactly how he will compare his subjects. Here again three possibilities exist: he may restrict himelf to showing the similarities between them; he may, on the other hand, limit himself to their differences; or he may cover both. (Usually the term "contrast" is reserved for comparison dealing only with differences, while "comparison" means either discussing only likenesses or showing both similarities and dissimilarities.) Of these three varieties of comparative writing, the paragraph on Greece and England illustrates the first. A good example of the second is this passage (only the latter part of a paragraph) by the nineteenth-century historian James Anthony Froude:

> . . . the distinctions between the Reformers were after all, but insignificant shades of variety, compared with the principle which parted all of them from the orthodox Catholic. The Catholic believed in the authority of the Church; the Reformers in the authority of reason. Where the Church had spoken, the Catholic obeyed. His duty was to accept without question the laws which councils had decreed, which popes and bishops administered, and so far as in him lay to enforce in others the same submission to an outward rule which he regarded as divine. All shades of Protestants on the other hand agreed that authority might err; that Christ had left no visible representative, whom individually they were bound to obey; that religion was the operation of the Spirit on the mind and conscience; that the Bible was God's word, which each Christian was to read, and which with God's help and his natural intelligence he could not fail to understand. The Catholic left his Bible to the learned. The Protestant translated the Bible, and brought it to the door of every Christian family. The Catholic prayed in Latin, and

> whether he understood his words or repeated them as a form the effect was the same; for it was magical. The Protestant prayed with his mind as an act of faith in a language intelligible to him, or he could not pray at all. The Catholic bowed in awe before his wonder-working image, adored his relics, and gave his life into the guidance of his spiritual director. The Protestant tore open the machinery of the miracles, flung the bones and ragged garments into the fire, and treated priests as men like himself. The Catholic was intolerant upon principle; persecution was the corollary of his creed. The intolerance of the Protestant was in spite of his creed. In denying the right of the Church to define his own belief, he had forfeited the privilege of punishing the errors of those who chose to differ with him. *The Reign of Elizabeth*

Froude is concerned here only with how the Protestant and the Catholic of the sixteenth century differed; he discusses no similarities at all, except to imply that both were intolerant. The paragraph is also a good example of balanced focus. While Froude's sympathies are plainly with the Protestant, his subject involves Protestant *and* Catholic and his focus is wide enough to include both.

Finally a comparison may treat likenesses and differences at the same time, as the following paragraphs by F. L. Lucas demonstrate:

> Chesterfield and Johnson form a pair as antithetical as a sentence of Johnson's own. One can picture them as two figures symmetrically opposed on some mantelpiece of the period. On one side stands the rich Whig peer, typical of that confident aristocracy which dominated the course of the whole age; sceptical and irreligious (except for a tenuous theism, and his far more fervent worship of the Graces); strict in manners, but often loose in morals; light in style, yet never laughing, never losing his temper, never except in closest intimacy (if even then) giving away his private thoughts. And opposite him rises that needy, uncouth son of a provincial bookseller, who remained in his politics a fanatical Tory, and whose class in the coming century was to wrest supremacy from the heirs of Chesterfield; a man imbued with violent prejudices and and gloomy piety; rigid in morals, yet reckless at moments of every canon of courtesy; often elephantine in style, yet a rhinoceros in laughter; with a temper perpetually exploding, and an outspokenness that thundered forth its views on almost any topic before a world partly awed, partly outraged, partly fascinated.
>
> And yet Chesterfield and Johnson had also qualities in common. Both were ugly and grew infirm, yet triumphed over physical defects by force of mind and brilliance of tongue; both were impassioned educators; both were intensely, often bleakly, rational and realist; both were disillusioned, sombre, and haunted by the same

> melancholy lines on human life from Dryden's *Aurengzebe.** Both were, in essence, lonely figures; and each found that the person on whom he had long centered his affection, had preferred, in secret, a marriage most unwelcome. Yet both, as life darkened over them, faced its deepening shadows, to the end, with stoic fortitude.
>
> *The Search for Good Sense*

Mr. Lucas uses his paragraphs to separate the similarities of the two men from their differences, but in a shorter comparison these could be handled as two portions of a single paragraph. The contrast between Johnson and Chesterfield is emphasized by the organization of the first paragraph, which has two balanced parts, the first focusing upon Chesterfield, the second upon Johnson. In the second paragraph, however, where he is concerned with what these men had in common, Mr. Lucas always focuses on the two simultaneously: "*Both* were ugly . . . *both* were disillusioned . . . *Both* were, in essence, lonely figures . . ."

In addition to establishing his focus and deciding whether to contrast or compare, the writer of comparison faces still a third problem, perhaps the most difficult of all. It concerns organization, and it derives from the fact that in any comparison the writer has available two sets of variables to organize his material: the things being compared and the specific ways in which they are alike or different. To clarify the point let us consider one more time the comparison between high school and college, assuming that the writer has decided to contrast them and that he will focus upon college. The problem is whether to organize the paragraph around "high school" and "college" (the things being compared) or around such things as teaching, homework, examinations, and so on (the specific points of contrast). If the writer chooses the first alternative he will devote a section of his paragraph (or in a longer composition an entire paragraph or group of paragraphs) to discussing teaching, homework, and examinations *in college*; and then a comparable section to discussing the same topics, preferably in the same order, *as they relate to high school*. In other words, he will say everything he has to say about college in one section, everything he has

* Those lines are:

> When I consider life, 'tis all a cheat;
> Yet, fool'd with hope, men favour the deceit;
> Trust on, and think to-morrow will repay;
> To-morrow's falser than the former day;
> Lies worse, and, while it says, we shall be blest
> With some new joys, cuts off what we possest.
> Strange cozenage! None would live past years again,
> Yet all hope pleasure in what yet remain!

to say about high school in another. If, on the other hand, the writer chooses to organize his composition by the points of comparison, he will talk about teaching, both in high school and in college, in one section; move on to discuss homework in a comparable section; and conclude in a third by contrasting examinations. Here too the size of the sections will be determined by the length and complexity of the composition; it could all be done in a single paragraph, or in three, or in sixty.

Whether one organizes a comparison primarily around the two things being compared or around their points of difference or similarity depends upon exactly what one wants to say. If the writer of our example were more interested in the total experience of college as distinguished from the total experience of high school, the first would be the better scheme. If he were more concerned with the specific ways in which they differ (or in another case resemble one another), the second.

A further look at Mr. F. L. Lucas's paragraphs will prove instructive in this matter. We have already noted that in the first paragraph he opposes Chesterfield and Johnson in two sections, fully discussing the first man before moving on to the second. Mr. Lucas organizes the paragraph in this way because he is most concerned to reveal the distinctions between the total characters of the two men. He wants us to observe each man whole and to see the startling differences between them. Mr. Lucas emphasizes those differences by following the same progression in his treatment of each. Although there are minor variations, the plans of the two sections are essentially the same, so that point by point the characteristics of the one are played against those of the other. We see the wealth of Chesterfield — the need of Johnson; we see their antithetical political loyalties — Whig and Tory; the worldly skepticism of the lord — the piety of the provincial bookseller's son; the polish, the loose morality, the urbane reticence of Chesterfield — the uncouthness, the unyielding morality, the outspokenness of Johnson. In short the organization of the paragraph beautifully shows us the full figure of each man yet forces us to realize the very real differences between them. The second paragraph, on the other hand, is organized by points of comparison, but it is no less adapted to its quite different purpose. Here Mr. Lucas is interested less in contrasting the total characters of the two men than in listing the particular ways in which they were alike. The arrangement is subtly climactic. Although he does not label it such, it is plain that for Mr. Lucas the most significant characteristic of each man, one that goes deeper than the differences noted in the first paragraph, is the stoicism with which each endured the tragedies of life.

Mr. Lucas's paragraphs, then, demonstrate the two basic ways in which a comparison may be organized. They also reveal something about the fourth and last of the special difficulties of comparison development. Perhaps this is not so much a completely new problem as it is a consequence of how the comparison is organized. In any case, it is important. The problem is this: In what units shall the comparison be developed? In the passage by Mr. Lucas the contrast in the first paragraph is developed in two sections of that paragraph, actually two single, though long and complicated, sentences. The second paragraph, however, develops in a series of miniature comparisons, each complete within a sentence. Always, of course, it takes two units to make a comparison, but the units may be of any syntactic size: two clauses within the same sentence ("John was tired, but Sam seemed wide awake"); two sentences ("New Orleans is often warm in January. Boston, on the other hand, is invariably cold"); two groups of sentences within the same paragraph; and in longer themes two paragraphs or even groups of paragraphs.

An instance of a comparison developed in sentence groups within the paragraph is this passage by Joseph Addison from *The Spectator:*

> True happiness is of a retired nature, and an enemy to pomp and noise; it arises, in the first place, from the enjoyment of one's self; and, in the next, from the friendship and conversation of a few select companions. It loves shade and solitude, and naturally haunts groves and fountains, fields and meadows: in short, it feels everything it wants within itself, and receives no addition from multitudes of witnesses and spectators. On the contrary, false happiness loves to be in a crowd, and to draw the eyes of the world upon her. She does not receive any satisfaction from the applause which she gives herself, but from the admiration which she raises in others. She flourishes in courts and palaces, theaters and assemblies, and has no existence but when she is looked upon.

The same source supplies an instance of the type of comparison development in which the contrast is built up by clauses within individual sentences:

> . . . This gives a different turn to the reflections of the wise man and the fool. The first endeavors to shine in himself and the last to outshine others. The first is humbled by the sense of his own infirmities, the last is lifted up by the discovery of those which he observes in other men. The wise man considers what he wants and the fool what he abounds in. The wise man is happy when he gains his own approbation and the fool when he recommends himself to the applause of those about him.

These two techniques may be combined as the writer builds his comparison both within the sentence and between separate sentences, as in this paragraph:

> The quartets were perfectly clear and easy to understand. One was by Mozart and the other by Beethoven, so that I could compare the two masters. Their individuality seemed to become plain to me: Mozart — grace, liberty, certainty, freedom, and precision of style, — the health and talent of the master, both on a level with his genius: Beethoven — more pathetic, more passionate, more torn with feeling, more intricate, more profound, less perfect, more the slave of his genius, more carried away by his fancy or his passion, more moving and more sublime than Mozart. Mozart refreshes you like the dialogues of Plato: he respects you, reveals to you your strength, gives you freedom and balance. Beethoven seizes upon you: he is more tragic and oratorical, while Mozart is more disinterested and poetical. Mozart is more Greek, and Beethoven more Christian. One is serene, the other serious. The first is stronger than destiny, because he takes life less profoundly: the second is less strong, because he has dared to measure himself against deeper sorrows. His talent is not always equal to his genius, and pathos is his dominant feature, as perfection is that of Mozart. In Mozart the balance of the whole is perfect, and art triumphs: in Beethoven feeling governs everything, and emotion troubles his art in proportion as it deepens it. A. HYATT KING, *Mozart in Retrospect*

Which of these various ways of building a comparison is best depends upon one's purpose in making the comparison in the first place. Most commonly a writer employs comparison because the method is implicit in his subject. Froude, for example, was writing about the Christian religion in the sixteenth century and such a discussion will somewhere require a comparison of Catholic and Protestant. Similarly, Mr. Lucas was writing about *two* famous eighteenth century Englishmen, and Mr. King about *two* composers. Sometimes it is necessary to contrast two ideas or terms as a way of defining them or of making clear how one is using them. This is what Addison intends in the passage about true and false happiness. An even clearer case is the following paragraph by Professor Louis Gottschalk, distinguishing the two kinds of sources with which the historian must deal:

> Written and oral sources are divided into two kinds: primary and secondary. A *primary source* is the testimony of an eyewitness, or of a witness by any other of the senses, or of a mechanical device like the dictaphone — that is, of one who or that which was present at the events of which he or it tells (hereafter called simply *eyewitness*). A *secondary source* is the testimony of anyone who is not

> an eyewitness — that is, of one who was not present at the events of which he tells. A primary source must thus have been produced by a contemporary of the events it narrates. It does not, however, need to be original in the legal sense of the word original — that is, the very document (usually the first written draft) whose contents are the subject of discussion — for quite often a later copy or a printed edition will do just as well; and in the case of the Greek and Roman classics seldom are any but later copies available.
>
> *Understanding History*

Often a writer is interested not in both parts of his comparison but only in one. The other he has introduced only to explain something about the main subject. The simplest instance is the brief comparisons called similes and metaphors, as when Virginia Woolf speaks of "a plot as complicated as a medieval mouse-trap," or when Hilaire Belloc, describing a valley in Italy, remarks that "it has a splendid name, like the clashing of cymbals — Garafagnano." A simile or metaphor may be extended to greater length and used to develop an entire paragraph or the major section of one. Thoreau, for example, describes the geography of Cape Cod like this:

> Cape Cod is the bared and bended arm of Massachusetts; the shoulder is at Buzzard's Bay; the elbow, or crazy-bone, at Cape Mallebarre; the wrist at Truro; and the sandy fist at Provincetown, — behind which the State stands on her guard, with her back to the Green Mountains, and her feet planted on the floor of the ocean, like an athlete protecting her Bay, — boxing with northeast storms, and, ever and anon, heaving up her Atlantic adversary from the lap of the earth, — ready to thrust forward her other fist, which keeps guard the while upon her breast at Cape Ann. *Cape Cod*

Analogy

When similes are extended, like the one by Thoreau, they are often called analogies, which are detailed comparisons between two things for the purpose of explaining, emphasizing, or drawing conclusions about one in terms of the other. Often, though not necessarily, the two subjects in an analogical comparison are of very different orders of being. It would be perfectly natural, for example, to compare the movies to stage drama, and we would hardly call such a comparison an analogy. But to liken the movies to a savage tribe pounding on symphonic musical instruments, as Virginia Woolf does in the paragraph quoted below, draws attention to a similarity between things we would not think comparable, and so is an analogy. However similar or dissimilar they may be, one of the two subjects in an analogy is always primary, and the comparison serves a very specific purpose. Macaulay, for instance, heaps ridicule upon the foolish "niceness" of prudish readers who would censor classic literature:

> . . . a man, who, exposed to all the influences of such a state of society as that in which we live, is yet afraid of exposing himself to the influence of a few Greek or Latin verses, acts, we think, much like the felon who begged the sheriff to let him have an umbrella held over his head from the door of Newgate to the gallows, because it was a drizzling morning and he was apt to take cold.

Virginia Woolf, on the other hand, employs analogy for clarification:

> For a strange thing has happened — while all the other arts were born naked, this [the movies], the youngest, has been born fully-clothed. It can say everything before it has anything to say. It is as if the savage tribe, instead of finding two bars of iron to play with, had found scattering the seashore, fiddles, flutes, saxophones, trumpets, grand pianos by Erard and Bechstein, and had begun with incredible energy, but without knowing a note of music, to hammer and thump upon them all at the same time.
>
> "THE CINEMA," *The Captain's Death Bed and Other Essays*

Where Macaulay's analogy is an instrument of ridicule, Mrs. Woolf's transposes an abstraction into concrete reality.

The passage by Mrs. Woolf comes close to exemplifying still another use of the analogy — to state the unfamiliar in familiar terms. Mark Twain develops the following analogy in order to communicate to his readers the wonders of the memory of a Mississippi River pilot:

> One cannot easily realize what a tremendous thing it is to know every trivial detail of twelve hundred miles of river and know it with absolute exactness. If you will take the longest street in New York, and travel up and down it, conning its features patiently until you know every house and window and door and lamppost and big and little sign by heart, and know them so accurately that you can instantly name the one you are abreast of when you are set down at random in that street in the middle of an inky black night, you will then have a tolerable notion of the amount and exactness of a pilot's knowledge who carries the Mississippi River in his head. And then, if you will go on until you know every street-crossing, the character, size, and position of the crossing-stones, and the varying depth of mud in each of those numberless places, you will have some idea of what the pilot must know in order to keep a Mississippi steamer out of trouble. Next, if you will take half of the signs in that long street, and *change their places* once a month, and still manage to know their new positions accurately on

> dark nights, and keep up with these repeated changes without making any mistakes, you will understand what is required of a pilot's peerless memory by the fickle Mississippi.
>
> *Life on the Mississippi*

Twain could not assume that very many of his readers had had any experiencing of piloting river boats. To tell them, then, merely that a pilot must have a remarkable memory would convey only the haziest of ideas. To communicate his point, Twain must translate it into terms with which his readers are familiar. Few of us have steered a riverboat, but even fewer of us have not walked the streets of a large city, and we know that to remember what we are told we should have to remember about the street signs and crossings and houses would indeed be a notable feat.

Scientists often find analogy a useful way of explaining technicalities to lay readers, especially in our day when the mathematical languages of the physical and even of the biological and social sciences are making them less and less intelligible to the nontechnical reader. For instance Sir William Bragg explains how atoms link together by the following comparison:

> We have seen how it can happen that when two atoms approach each other at great speeds they go through one another, while at moderate speeds they bound off each other like two billiard balls. We have to go a step further, and see how, at very slow speeds of approach, they may actually stick together. We have all seen those swinging gates which, when their swing is considerable, go to and fro without locking. When the swing has declined, however, the latch suddenly drops into its place, the gate is held and after a short rattle the motion is over. We have to explain an effect something like that. When the two atoms meet, the repulsions of their electron shells usually cause them to recoil; but if the motion is small, and the atoms spend a longer time in each other's neighbourhood, there is time for something to happen in the internal arrangements of both atoms, like the drop of the latch-gate into its socket, and the atoms are held. *Concerning the Nature of Things*

For a similar purpose Sir Arthur Eddington compares the physical scientist casting about for his facts to a man netting fish:

> Let us suppose that an ichthyologist is exploring the life of the ocean. He casts a net into the water and brings up a fishy assortment. Surveying his catch, he proceeds in the usual manner of a scientist to systematize what it reveals. He arrives at two generalisations:
>
> 1. No sea-creature is less than two inches long.
> 2. All sea-creatures have gills.

> These are both true of his catch, and he assumes tentatively that they will remain true however often he repeats it.
>
> In applying this analogy, the catch stands for the body of knowledge which constitutes physical science, and the net for the sensory and intellectual equipment which we use in obtaining it. The casting of the net corresponds to observation; for knowledge which has not been or could not be obtained by observation is not admitted into physical science.
>
> An onlooker may object that the first generalisation is wrong. "There are plenty of sea-creatures under two inches long, only your net is not adapted to catch them." The ichthyologist dismisses this objection contemptuously. "Anything uncatchable by my net is *ipso facto* outside the scope of ichthyological knowledge, and is not part of the kingdom of fishes which has been defined as the theme of ichthyological knowledge. In short, what my net can't catch isn't fish." Or — to translate the analogy — "If you are not simply guessing, you are claiming a knowledge of the physical universe discovered in some other way than by the methods of physical science, and admittedly unverifiable by such methods. You are a metaphysician. Bah!" *The Philosophy of Physical Science*

There is a danger in analogies like these. The careless reader may take them literally, forgetting that an analogy reveals similarities between things that are not the same. Sir William Bragg's comparison, for example, is a very good simile; but a reader should not conclude that atoms come equipped with tiny latch-pins. Yet used with proper caution, as these certainly are, analogies can make clear a concept that we lack the experience to comprehend directly.

Summary

In comparison a writer must deal with two subjects and reveal their similarities, their dissimilarities (which is called "contrast"), or in some cases both. Comparison involves several special problems. The first is establishing and maintaining the focus upon the more important subject, or equally upon both if both are equally important. The second is making clear whether the comparison will treat likenesses or differences, or will say something about each. The third is determining the best way of organizing the comparison. The main division may be according to the two subjects being compared, or according to their specific points of difference or of similarity. Finally is the problem of what compositional units are best suited to developing the comparison. The paragraph may be built out of two or more groups of sentences, each group contributing part of the comparison. Or it may be built in a series of paired sentences or even in a series of sentences each one of which is itself a miniature comparison. Analogy is a special kind of comparison — often between things of unlike nature — in which the analogical subject is used to explain or clarify something about the main subject. Analogies are often employed to render abstract ideas concretely or to translate the unfamiliar into familiar terms.

Exercises

1. Write a one-paragraph contrast on any of the subjects listed below. Build the paragraph out of a series of specific contrasts, each complete within a single sentence, after the fashion of the second passage by Joseph Addison, on page 173.

    1. The good-natured man and the grouch
    2. Psychology and sociology
    3. The Yankees and the Mets
    4. L'il Abner and Dick Tracy (either the comic strips in general or the two characters)
    5. A jazz musician and Lawrence Welk
    6. Impressionism and cubism

2. Develop in two paragraphs a composition modeled roughly upon F. L. Lucas's comparison of Johnson and Chesterfield. Select any of the following topics and in one of the paragraphs (it may be either the first or the second) discuss the chief differences between the items, allocating the first part of the paragraph to one item, the second part to the other. In the remaining paragraph deal with the similarities, developing these in a series of sentences which, like those by Mr. Lucas, apply to both subjects. Begin the second paragraph with an adequate transition.

    1. Two actors alike in some ways, different in others
    2. New York and Chicago (or any two cities you know well)
    3. A sports car and the family sedan
    4. Theater in the round and the conventional stage
    5. Snow skiing and water skiing
    6. The English language and the French (or German, Spanish, Italian, Latin)

3. On one of the following topics write a short comparison essay of about 600 words. Include an outline (the outline does not count toward the 600 words) and be sure that you have a good beginning, a clear closing, and adequate transitions between all paragraphs. You may confine your discussion to either similarities or differences or you may treat both. But try to employ as many of the ways of developing comparison as you can.

1. Men and women drivers
2. Sailing and motorboating
3. Studying alone or studying with one or two friends
4. History and literature
5. Living at home or living away
6. Modern furniture and traditional styles
7. Country life and city life

4. Because they are personal things that must grow out of one's own experience, it is difficult to suggest analogies. Still, we have listed a few that occur to us. Develop one of them in a single paragraph, arranging the paragraph so that it treats the analogy first and winds up on the main topic, which is listed first in the suggestions below. (If none of these analogies appeals to you, devise one of your own.)

1. A tragic hero and a man who leaps off the Empire State Building, confident of his ability to fly to Hoboken by flapping his arms
2. Reading a good book and climbing a mountain
3. A library and a cemetery
4. The New York subway and Dante's Inferno
5. College and a horse race

12

DEVELOPING THE PARAGRAPH

III. Logical Techniques

Cause and Effect

The last of the three broad methods of developing expository paragraphs is, like comparison and analogy, discursive in the sense that it explores and moves out from the topic idea. Unlike comparison, however, it concentrates upon what we shall call, a little inaccurately, the "logic" of the topic. The specific techniques include cause and effect, definition, and qualification. The most prevalent of these is development by cause and effect, of which the following paragraph by Robert Louis Stevenson is a simple example:

> Now, to be properly enjoyed, a walking tour should be gone upon alone. If you go in a company, or even in pairs, it is no longer a walking tour in anything but name; it is something else, and more in the nature of a picnic. A walking tour should be gone upon alone, because freedom is of the essence; because you should be able to stop and go on, and follow this way or that, as the freak takes you; and because you must have your own pace, and neither trot alongside a champion walker, nor mince in time with a girl. And then you must be open to all impressions and let your thoughts take colour from what you see. You should be as a pipe for any wind to play upon. "I cannot see the wit," says Hazlitt, "of walking and talking at the same time. When I am in the country, I wish to vegetate like the country," — which is the gist of all that can be said upon the matter. There should be no cackle of voices at your elbow, to jar on the meditative silence of the morning. And so long as a man is reasoning he cannot surrender himself to that fine intoxication that comes of much motion in the open air, that begins in a sort of dazzle and sluggishness of the brain, and ends in a peace that passes comprehension. "WALKING TOURS"

Stevenson begins with a flat assertion of opinion, that a walking tour ought to be a solitary affair. But instead of bringing forward an instance of such a tour, or, contrarily, the disastrous case of one that was taken in company, or simply of repeating his opinion three or four times, Stevenson tells us *why* he thinks as he does. In short, he develops his paragraph by explaining the reasons or causes that lie behind his topic.

Development by reasons is very frequent in expository writing, as we might expect when we remember how much exposition is concerned with the why of things. In "reasons development" the writer regards his topic idea as a consequence, and he devotes the paragraph to setting forth the reasons that account for it. He may develop several reasons, treating each quickly, as did Stevenson, or he may work out a single reason in greater detail, as in this paragraph from Carl Becker's *The Declaration of Independence:*

> If the classic philosophy of the American Declaration of Independence and the French Declaration of Rights proved unacceptable to the nineteenth century, it was thus not because it could be easily made the basis of democratic government, but because it had been, and could again be, so effectively used as a justification of revolutionary movements. The nineteenth century, while progressively democratic, was on the whole anti-revolutionary. In the United States, from the Revolution to the Civil War, the strongest political prepossession of the mass of men was founded in the desire to preserve the independence they had won, the institutions they had established, the "more perfect Union" they had created. The European world, for half a century after the French Revolution, lived in perpetual apprehension of a new Reign of Terror, and not the least of its difficulties was that of making terms with political democracy without opening the door to social upheaval and international conflict. The classical political philosophy of the eighteenth century therefore survived, in so far as it did survive, chiefly as an aftermath of the great revolutions. It maintained at best a precarious existence among the obscure and outcast parties that were frankly revolutionary, and flourished unashamed only in the full light of brilliant but brief revolutionary days.

To support his point that the liberalism of the great revolutionary documents of the eighteenth century was unacceptable to the nineteenth, Mr. Becker brings forward only one reason: the anti-revolutionary conservatism of the later era. This reason he establishes in the last part of the first sentence, restates generally in the second, and repeats specifically for the United States in the third sentence and for Europe in the fourth.

When a writer works with several reasons he faces the problem of arranging them in a significant order. If his reasons are serially related — that is, if the topic idea is the result of A, and A in turn the effect of B, which was brought about by C — the organization of the paragraph is, for all practical purposes, predetermined. It would be awkward to handle such a chain of cause and effect in any but the natural order of topic idea — A-B-C. But when, as is more likely, the various reasons stand in parallel — that is, when they have no causal connection among themselves, but are related only in being common contributors to the same result — the writer will have more latitude. His material may fall into some natural chronological pattern, and if it does he would be wise to adhere to it. Failing that, he will probably have to rank his reasons according to their relative importance.

Occasionally it will happen that their importance will not differ in any way, as in this paragraph from Lewis Mumford's *Sticks and Stones* (he is criticizing the use of the Greek temple as a model for domestic architecture in the nineteenth century):

> On the whole, however, the Greek temple precedent was a bad one. For one thing, since the Greek *cella* had no source of light except the doorway, it was necessary to introduce modifications in the elevation, and to break up the interior; and it was only in the South that the vast shadowed retreats formed by porches and second-story balconies proved a happy adaptation to the climate. Again: Greek architecture was an architecture of exteriors, designed for people who spent the greater part of the year out of doors. With no temple ritual comparable to the services of the church or cathedral, the Greeks lavished their attention upon externals, and as a great admirer of the Greeks, Sir Reginald Blomfield, well says, "may have been more successful with the outside of their buildings than with the inside." To fail with the interior in a northern climate is to fail with the essentials of a habitation; and these vast rooms, for all their ornament, too often remained bleak.

It would make no real difference here if, properly adjusting the framing words "For one thing" and "Again," we moved the second sentence to follow the fourth. The paragraph would remain just as unified, for the two reasons are of equal significance.

More commonly, however, there will be a difference in weight, and the writer will have to arrange his paragraph either climactically or anticlimactically. In the first case he will begin with the least important reason and work his way up to the most important; in the second he will begin with the principal reason and work down. Of the two patterns the climactic is more common. This is the way in which Stevenson arranged the paragraph quoted on page 181, as it is the way A. C. Benson orders the reasons in this paragraph:

> I doubt if the English temperament is wholly favourable to the development of the essayist. In the first place, an Anglo-Saxon likes doing things better than thinking about them; and in his memories, he is apt to recall how a thing was done rather than why it was done. In the next place, we are naturally rather prudent and secretive; we say that a man must not wear his heart upon his sleeve, and that is just what the essayist must do. We have a horror of giving ourselves away, and we like to keep ourselves to ourselves. "The Englishman's home is his castle," says another proverb. But the essayist must not have a castle, or if he does, both the grounds and the living-rooms must be open to the inspection of the public.
>
> "THE ART OF THE ESSAYIST"

In developing his topic by effects the writer works in the same way as when he uses reasons. He simply reverses the logical relationship between his topic and the supporting sentences. In reasons development the topic is regarded as a result and the rest of the paragraph develops the cause or causes accounting for that result. In the effects paragraph it is the other way around: the topic becomes the cause, and the remainder of the paragraph develops the consequences that derive from it. Consider this paragraph from Vernon L. Parrington's *Main Currents in American Thought:*

> The change of temper that came over American society with the loss of the Loyalists, was immense and far-reaching. For the first time the middle class was free to create a civilization after its own ideals. In rising to leadership it brought another spirit into every phase of life. Dignity and culture henceforth were to count for less and assertiveness for more. Ways became less leisurely, the social temper less urbane. The charm of the older aristocracy disappeared along with its indisputable evils. Although a few of the older wits like Mather Byles lingered on bitterly, and others like Gouverneur Morris accepted the situation philosophically, they belonged to the past. A franker evaluation of success in terms of money began to obscure the older personal and family distinction. New men brought new ways and a vulgar clamor of politics went hand in hand with business expansion. The demagogue and the speculator discovered a fruitful field for their activities. The new capitalism lay on the horizon of republican America, and the middle class was eager to hasten its development. But a new economic order required a new political state, and as a necessary preliminary, the spirit of national-

> ism began that slow encroachment upon local frontiers which was to modify profoundly the common psychology. Americanism superseded colonialism, and with the new loyalty there developed a conception of federal sovereignty, overriding all local authorities, checking the movement of particularism, binding the separate commonwealths in a consolidating union. This marked the turning point in American development; the checking of the long movement of decentralization and the beginning of a counter movement of centralization — the most revolutionary change in three hundred years of American experience. The history of the rise of the coercive state in America, with the ultimate arrest of all centrifugal tendencies, was implicit in that momentous counter movement.

In tracing the consequences for the new American state of the emigration of the Tories, Mr. Parrington brings forward one chief effect — the rise of the middle class to sovereign power — from which he then deduces a series of more specific effects. These consequences are serially related. They are not all immediate results of the departure of the Loyalists; rather they are generated in turn, one from another. The rise of the middle class brings with it the new, economic evaluation of success; and this, in its turn, encourages a fresh and different conception of politics, which leads to the strengthening of the federal theory of the state. These multiple effects are held together by various linking devices: repetitions ("new"-"new," "Americanism"-"America," "capitalism"-"economic order," "movement"-"movement"); connectors ("henceforth," "but"); and pronominal links ("this"). Like A. C. Benson, Mr. Parrington arranges his paragraph climactically, leading up to the most important consequence.

Just as a paragraph may develop a single reason rather than several, so may it develop a single effect:

> If the moon were suddenly struck out of existence, we should be immediately apprised of the fact by a wail from every seaport in the kingdom. From London and from Liverpool we should hear the same story — the rise and fall of the tide had almost ceased. The ships in dock could not get out; the ships outside could not get in; and the maritime commerce of the world would be thrown into dire confusion. ROBERT BALL, *The Story of the Heavens*

In this case the consequence is imaginary; this is what would happen *were* the moon to disappear. The development of such conjectural or potential effects is a frequent device of rhetoric. The politician asks the voters to imagine the disastrous consequences of electing his opponent; the preacher reminds his congregation of the results of continued immersion in sin. But whether the effects he derives from his topic are imaginary, as in this example, or real, as in the paragraph by Mr. Parrington, the writer's problem is the same. He must make clear what consequences issue from the topic idea; if there are more than one of these, he must order them — logically when a causal or other logical relationship is implicit in them, chronologically or rhetorically otherwise.

Thus far we have considered paragraphs which dealt either with reasons or with effects, but not with both at once. So complex — at times so inextricable — is the logic of cause and effect, however, that often one cannot separate them. And often one may not wish to. When the writer must treat both together, he faces greater problems of organization. Not only must he arrange the causes and the effects each in some meaningful order (assuming, as is usually the case, that he has several of each to deal with), but also he must decide how to handle the relationship between these two parts of his total thought. Shall he discuss all the causes and then all the effects; or shall he move more subtly back and forth between them, perhaps gaining complexity of thought but risking clarity? The first is the simpler solution. The writer develops the paragraph in two parts (or possibly employs two paragraphs), discussing the reasons in one, the consequences in the other. Of course, the order may be reversed. Sometimes in real life we grow aware of effects before we understand what has created them, and for this reason, or perhaps simply because he wishes to lead up to the cause, the writer will arrange these parts or paragraphs in the order effect-cause. But more commonly the sequence will run cause-effect, as in this passage from *The Education of Henry Adams:*

> Outside of occult or fetish-power, the Roman world was incredibly poor. It knew but one productive energy resembling a modern machine—the slave. No artificial force of serious value was applied to production or transportation, and when society developed itself so rapidly in political and social lines, it had no other means of keeping its economy on the same level than to extend its slave-system and its fetish-system to the utmost.
>
> The result might have been stated in a mathematical formula as early as the time of Archimedes, six hundred years before Rome fell. The economic needs of a violently centralizing society forced the empire to enlarge its slave-system until the slave-system consumed itself and the empire too, leaving society no resource but further enlargement of its religious system in order to compensate for the losses and horrors of the failure. For a vicious circle, its mathematical completeness approached perfection. The dynamic law of attraction and reaction needed only a Newton to fix it in algebraic form.

Though he does not blaze the trail of his thought with logical connectors like *therefore* and *consequently,* Adams's logic is easy to follow. He uses the paragraph break to analyze the cause-effect relationship. In the first paragraph he establishes the reason — the failure of the Roman state to utilize any other form of productive power than slavery — and in the second he deduces the ultimate effect of that failure — the never-ending spread of slavery.

The paragraph by Adams is a fairly simple instance of development by both cause and effect. The next is more complicated. Discussing the problems that beset modern boxing, A. J. Liebling writes:

> The immediate crisis in the United States, forestalling the one high living standards might bring on, has been caused by the popularization of a ridiculous gadget called television. This is utilized in the sale of beer and razor blades. The clients of the television companies, by putting on a free boxing show almost every night of the week, have knocked out of business the hundreds of small-city and neighborhood boxing clubs where youngsters had a chance to learn their trade and journeymen to mature their skill. Consequently the number of good new prospects diminishes with every year, and the peddlers' public is already being asked to believe that a boy with perhaps ten or fifteen fights behind him is a topnotch performer. Neither advertising agencies nor brewers, and least of all the networks, give a hoot if they push the Sweet Science back into a period of genre painting. When it is in coma they will find some other way to peddle their peanuts. *The Sweet Science*

Liebling brings cause and effect closely together by treating both in the same paragraph. Still his technique is not essentially different from that of Adams. He handles each part of his idea in turn, disposing of the cause — television — before moving on to the effect — the low quality of modern boxing. Conceptually, however, the paragraph is more complicated than it seems. With a neat simplicity Liebling works out a rather complex chain of cause and effect, one that runs something like this: the use of television to sell beer —(causes)— too many free fights —(which causes)— the disappearance of the small fight club —(which causes)— the inadequate training of young fighters —(which causes)— the crisis in boxing. All this is clearly conveyed with only one transitional adverb ("consequently"), which the writer uses to signal the result he is chiefly concerned with.

From these several examples we may conclude not only that cause and effect is a frequent mode of developing expository paragraphs, but that it may take a variety of forms. Always, however, the writer must analyze his topic, distinguishing its various causes or consequences, or both, and then synthesize them into a significant pattern.

Definition

In order to develop an idea it is frequently necessary to establish the meaning of a particular word or expression. This process is known as definition. It is, as any textbook of logic will make clear, beset with difficulties. Most of these, however, are logical or metaphysical, and need not detain us. Our concern necessarily must be superficial, confined, more or less, to the question of the specific compositional methods of handling definitions. The quickest way to define anything is, of course, simply to point to it. One can make clear what the word *apple* means merely by pointing to a specific apple or even better picking it up. This is the most fundamental way of defining; technically it is called ostensive definition, and it is the way we learn most of our first words as small children. The writer, however, cannot point. He can draw a picture or a diagram (notice how many pictures there are in your dictionary), but then he ceases to be a writer. And, in any case, drawing pictures is seldom convenient or even possible, for many things exist that cannot be depicted or, for that matter, pointed to.

Generally, then, a writer will have to depend upon techniques of definition which employ words. The simplest of these methods is synonymous definition. In the sentence "Blank verse, that is, unrhymed iambic pentameter, is the most important form of English dramatic poetry," the writer has defined "blank verse" by the equivalent verbal expression "unrhymed iambic pentameter." The synonymous definition is usually quite brief (though it can be more detailed than this) and it has rather a limited range of usefulness. This definition, for instance, assumes that a reader will understand the terms "unrhymed," "iambic," and "pentameter"; one cannot help supposing that the reader who understood them would also understand "blank verse." Still it sometimes happens that a writer can make clear the meaning of a word his reader does not know by equating it with one he does, and when it is feasible this is a simple and easy method of defining.

Sometimes rather than strict synonyms a writer will use figurative equivalents. Jeremy Taylor, a famous seventeenth-century English divine, explained the meaning of prayer by a series of metaphors in this celebrated passage:

> Prayer is the peace of our spirit, the stillness of our thoughts, the evenness of recollection, the seat of meditation, the rest of our cares, and the calm of our tempest; prayer is the issue of a quiet mind, of untroubled thoughts, it is the daughter of charity and the sister of meekness; and he that prays to God with an angry, that is, with a troubled and discomposed spirit, is like him that retires into a battle to meditate, and sets up his closet in the outquarters of an army, and chooses a frontier-garrison to be wise in. Anger is a perfect alienation of the mind from prayer, and therefore is contrary to that attention which presents our prayers in a right line to God. For so have I seen a lark rising from his bed of grass, and soaring upwards, singing as he rises, and hopes to get to heaven, and climb above the clouds; but the poor bird was beaten back with the loud sighings of an eastern wind, and his motion made irregular and unconstant, descending more at every breath of the tempest than it could recover by the libration and frequent weighing of his wings; till the little creature was forced to sit down and pant, and stay till the storm was over; and then it made a prosperous flight, and did rise and sing, as if it had learned music and motion from an angel as he passed sometimes through the air about his ministries here below. SERMON: "THE RETURN OF PRAYERS"

Taylor, striving to define a reality that transcends reason, is forced into figurative language, but some writers will use this method of defining even when it is not really necessary, hoping by their metaphors and similes to heighten the significance of the term. As a rule the effort costs more than it earns. The essence of a definition is that it be clear; and figurative language, though it is highly expressive, is frequently imprecise in conveying concepts. The beauty and undeniable effectiveness of Jeremy Taylor's passage notwithstanding, it is wise to avoid figurative language in definitions if you can.

A method closely related to defining by synonyms, although less common, is negative definition, which is to define something by showing what it is not. G. K. Chesterton, for example, defines miserliness in terms of thrift:

> Thrift by derivation means thriving; and the miser is the man who does not thrive. The whole meaning of thrift is making the most of everything; and the miser does not make anything of anything. He is the man in whom the process, from the seed to the crop, stops at the intermediate mechanical stage of the money. He does not grow things to feed men; not even to feed one man; not even to feed himself. The miser is the man who starves himself, and everybody else, in order to worship wealth in its dead form, as distinct from its living form. "ABOUT BAD COMPARISONS"

Such negative definition is of limited use, but now and then, as in this case, it is neatly appropriate. Chesterton is defining something he regards as a minus quality; miserliness he takes to be that which negates the positive virtue of thrift.

Still a third technique of definition is exemplification, which is simply to bring forward specific instances of the thing being defined. "Miserliness," we might say, "is behaving like Silas Marner, or M. Grandet, or the Collier brothers." Like synonymous definition, this has limitations. For one thing it assumes that the reader already knows the reality, for which it merely attempts to tell him the name. Here, for instance, it is assumed not only that the reader will recognize the Collier brothers and the characters of the two novels but also that he has realized that in their refusal to spend money these figures behave abnormally. Presumably all the reader does not know is what this abnormality is called. For another thing, the definition we arrive at through exemplification is likely to be limited by the examples we have chosen. Very rarely, if ever, can we examine all the members of a class. We could not cite every miser in the world. Instead we must select a sample (usually a very small sample from a very large class) and consequently it is always possible that our examples may miss an important characteristic of miserliness, or contrarily that by the accidental fact of our examples having it in common we may be led to exaggerate the significance of a characteristic that is not really essential to the definition. In practice these dangers are not so severe as they sound. A little common sense in choosing illustrations will ensure a sound enough working definition. Nonetheless, it is well to remember that exemplificatory definitions are tentative rather than final.

A fourth way of defining is classification and differentiation, or, as it is also called, the method of analysis. This is the so-called genus-species definition, and it is the one most commonly discussed by traditional logicians and rhetoricians. It consists of setting the thing to be defined into the class (or genus) to which it belongs and then of differentiating it from the other members of that class. Thus we might define miserliness by saying that "it is a vice [classification] which consists of devoting oneself to acquiring money and of refusing to spend it [differentiation]." Or, to take another example, we might define football like this:

> Football is a game played on a rectangular field 120 yards long by 55 yards wide between two teams of eleven men each, who, in accordance with certain rules, alternate possession of an ovoid ball,

> which they attempt to carry or pass to that end of the field which is defended by the team not having possession of the ball.

This analytic definition begins by placing football into its genus ("game") and then immediately distinguishing it from other games: it is played on a rectangular field (not an ice rink or a clay court); the teams have eleven men (not nine or five); the ball is ovoid (not spherical).

You can see that in defining by analysis most of one's time must be spent in differentiation. Differentiation may proceed by describing the features of the thing being defined without actually contrasting it with other members of the class. Thus our definition of football simply sets forth the characteristic features of the game; it does not literally compare it with baseball or basketball or hockey. But of course the definition does *implicitly* distinguish football from these other sports, and we may call this method implicit differentiation.

Sometimes, however, it is necessary to contrast explicitly the thing being defined with other members of its genus. Voltaire, for instance, says of history that it is "the recital of facts given as true, in contradistinction to the fable, which is the recital of facts given as false." Voltaire introduces the other member ("fable") of the genus "recital of facts" in order clearly to distinguish history from it, the difference being that in the case of history these facts are accepted as true (which does not mean, of course, that they necessarily are true), while in the case of fable the facts are accepted as false (which does not mean they may not be true). In a more complicated example, the English novelist John Galsworthy defines sentiment like this:

> Sentiment (so for as literature is concerned) may be defined, I suppose, as the just verbal expression of genuine feeling; it becomes sentimentalism when the feeling is not genuine, or when the expression strikes the reader as laid on with too thick a pen . . .
>
> *Candelabra: Selected Essays and Addresses*

Here the explicit contrast is between "sentiment" and "sentimentalism," both members of the class "verbal expression of feeling." Notice, however, that in the very phrase by which he classifies sentiment ("the just verbal expression of genuine feeling") Galsworthy is really already beginning to differentiate it. The adjectives "just" and "genuine" actually distinguish sentiment from sentimentalism, which is not a "just" expression because its feelings are not "genuine." Such intermixture of classification and differentiation is not illegitimate, but it often can be misleading. In this case, for instance, a careless reader might suppose that there are other members than sentiment belonging to the class "just verbal expression of genuine feeling"; but plainly Galsworthy means that all "just verbal expression of genuine feeling" is sentiment, that sentiment is the sole member of this class. Generally it is wise, then, in developing an analytic definition to begin with classification, to proceed to differentiation, and to make sure that the reader understands where one begins and the other ends. How far the process of differentiation must be taken cannot be settled by rule. Circumstances alter cases, and about all that can safely be said is that when the differentiation has made clear the unique signification of the term, it need be pursued no further.

Closely related to analytic definition is what Professor Richard Robinson calls the synthetic method, which defines words by "indicating the relation of the thing they mean to other things." If, for instance, we say that "football is the game played on autumn Saturday afternoons in open-air stadiums holding thousands of people," we have defined football by relating it to the context in which it usually occurs. Obviously in establishing these relations we have effectively distinguished football from other sports (which are not played in the autumn or not in the open air); but this differentiation is the consequence rather than the method of definition. The method itself is simply to say, in effect, "football has these relations; it exists in these circumstances."

Still another way of developing a definition is the etymological and historical method, in which the writer establishes the meaning of a word by investigating its original sense and tracing the changes this root meaning has undergone, frequently citing authority to fix the meaning of the word at various phases of its career. Professor Louis Gottschalk, for example, defines *history* in this way:

> The English word *history* is derived from the Greek noun *ἱστορία*, meaning *learning*. As used by the Greek philosopher Aristotle, *history* meant a systematic account of a set of natural phenomena, whether or not chronological ordering was a factor in the account; and that usage, though rare, still prevails in English in the phrase *natural history*. In the course of time, however, the equivalent Latin word *scientia* (English, *science*) came to be used more regularly to designate non-chronological systematic accounts of natural phenomena; and the word *history* was reserved usually for accounts of phenomena (especially human affairs) in chronological order.
>
> By its most common definition, the word *history* now means "the past of mankind." Compare the German word for *history*—*Geschichte*, which is derived from *geschehen*, meaning to happen. *Geschichte* is *that which has happened*. This meaning of the word

> *history* is often encountered in such overworked phrases as "all history teaches" or "the lessons of history." *Understanding History*

These, then, while they are by no means all, are the common methods of defining: synonyms, opposites, examples, analysis (with implicit or with explicit differentiation), and etymology and semantic history. The techniques are not mutually exclusive, and in practice a writer may work with two or three of them at once.

However it proceeds, definition serves several purposes in expository writing. To understand these purposes we must pause for a moment or two over a question that is more a matter of philosophy than of rhetoric: what exactly is it that is being defined in a definition? Two answers are possible: that the thing being defined is a word, or that it is the reality signified by the word. (The first is sometimes called nominal definition, the second real definition, and great disputes have raged among philosophers about whether both are equally valid.)

Nominal definition, then, seeks to define how a word or an expression is used. Nominal definitions may be made for various reasons. Most commonly they indicate the contemporary public meaning of a term, that is, with what meaning it is actually employed by the people of a particular time or place. Usually the time and place are those in which the writer himself lives. But sometimes the purpose of a nominal definition may be to fix an older meaning of a word. In the following passage, for instance, Professor Arthur O. Lovejoy is not attempting to define "pride" as we use it today but rather as it was applied in the eighteenth century:

> In its most significant aspect, then, "pride" gets its meaning for eighteenth-century thought from this group of conceptions. It is, in Pope's words, the "sin against the laws of order," *i.e.*, of gradation; it is the vice which causes man to set pretensions to a higher place in the Scale of Being than belongs to him.
>
> Pride still is aiming at the blest abodes,
> Men would be angels, angels would be gods.
>
> The virtue which is its opposite lies in a contented recognition of the limitations of the human lot and the littleness of man's powers;
>
> The bliss of man (could pride that blessing find)
> Is not to act or think beyond mankind.
>
> "'PRIDE' IN EIGHTEENTH-CENTURY THOUGHT," *Essays in the History of Ideas*

Or the purpose of a nominal definition may be to establish not the general sense of a word but the special sense in which a writer intends to use it in the context of his book or essay. Professor Robinson calls this "stipulative definition," and a passage from his book will serve as an example:

> The phrase "word-thing definition," then, means in this book any process, whether verbal or otherwise, by which any individual, whether God or angel or man or beast, brings any individual, whether himself or another, to know the meaning of any elementary symbol, whether a word or other, and if a word whether a noun or an adjective or a preposition or any other sort of word. *Definition*

Finally, the purpose of nominal definition may be normative or, to use a term often applied, legislative, that is, to establish what the writer thinks a word *should* mean as opposed to what it generally is used to mean. Professor Gottschalk, for example, argues for a more precise application of the word *document* in historical writing:

> The word *document* (from *docere*, to teach) has also been used by historians in several senses. On the one hand, it is sometimes used to mean a written source of historical information as contrasted with oral testimony or with artifacts, pictorial survivals, and archeological remains. On the other, it is sometimes reserved for only official and state papers such as treaties, laws, grants, deeds, etc. Still another sense is contained in the word *documentation*, which, as used by the historian among others, signifies any process of proof based upon any kind of source whether written, oral, pictorial, or archeological. For the sake of clarity, it seems best to employ the word *document* in the last, the most comprehensive meaning, which is etymologically correct, using *written document* and *official document* to designate the less comprehensive categories. Thus *document* becomes synonymous with source, whether written or not, official or not, primary or not. *Understanding History*

In all these cases the writers, despite the differences of their immediate reasons for defining, have been concerned with the meaning of a word. But the second type of definition — real definition, which is of things — assumes that we already know, more or less, how the word is used. Its purpose is rather to define the essential nature of the reality signified by the word. When in *The Republic* Socrates says that the just man is he who

> does not allow the several elements in his soul to usurp one another's functions; he is indeed one who sets his house in order, by self-mastery and discipline coming to be at peace with himself, and bringing into tune three parts like the terms in the proportion of a musical scale . . .

he is defining the reality of justice rather than the verbal label. When Matthew Arnold remarked that "poetry is at bottom a criticism of life," it was, in so far as it constitutes a definition, a definition not of the word *poetry*, but of the art itself. Or when G. K. Chesterton writes that

> Marriage is not a mere chain upon love as the anarchists say; nor is it a mere crown upon love as the sentimentalists say. Marriage is a fact, an actual human relation like that of motherhood, which has certain human habits and loyalties, except in a few monstrous cases where it is turned to a torture by special insanity and sin. A marriage is neither an ecstasy nor a slavery; it is a commonwealth; it is a separate working and fighting thing like a nation.
>
> *George Bernard Shaw*

he is telling us what marriage is, not defining *marriage*.

It is not always easy to distinguish between these two kinds of definition. When, for example, someone writes that "democracy means the greatest good for the greatest number," does he mean (1) that "the word *democracy* commonly signifies that form of government which achieves the greatest good for the greatest number"; or (2) that "the essential feature of democratic government is that it always achieves the greatest good for the greatest number"? Either way it is a poor definition; but the point to notice is that it is far from clear exactly what sort of definition this is. Probably the confusion does no real harm in this case, but the damage can be more serious. When you define, make clear whether you are talking about the word itself or about the reality to which the word refers. If, for instance, you are defining the term "democracy" as it is generally employed today, you might begin: "*Democracy* is usually understood to mean . . ."; if stipulating a special meaning: "By *democracy* I shall mean here . . ."; if attempting to legislate the "proper" meaning of the word: "The term *democracy* we should reserve to signify . . ." (in all these cases underlining *democracy*, or placing it in quotes, to make clear that your concern is with the word itself). If, on the other hand, you are framing a definition of the kind of government called democracy, you might start off: "The essential feature of democractic government is that . . ."

To establish real definitions is usually the purpose of works dealing with such topics as the nature of beauty or of art, truth, democracy, virtue, and so on. In such cases the definition often comprises the entire book or essay, its most succinct formulation being reserved for the closing paragraphs or chapter. The writer builds toward that final statement, sometimes, as Socrates often does, by trying on and discarding a number of erroneous or incomplete definitions, sometimes by the more positive method — which Socrates also uses — of analyzing specific examples and abstracting the essential feature they share.

On the other hand, nominal definition, while it can be an end in itself (as it was the ultimate purpose of Mr. Lovejoy's essay to define the meaning of the word *pride* for the eighteenth century), is more likely to occur in an essay whose purpose is something other than definition. A writer contrasting democracy and fascism, say, must first make very clear what he means by those terms. But his purpose is to compare political systems, not to define words; definition is merely a necessary preliminary. Since it is usually a means rather than itself an end, nominal definition is likely to be relatively brief. Generally, too, such definition will be found toward the beginning either of the essay or of the section in the essay where the defined term first occurs. Obviously it is foolish to use a possibly ambiguous word for ten pages of discussion and define it only in the last paragraph.

Of the two kinds of definition, nominal definition is more immediately important for the expository writer. This is not to imply that it is absolutely more important. The formulation of real definitions is one of the most fundamental concerns of science and scholarship. But one may write a good deal of exposition without probing to fundamental levels. One cannot write very much exposition without having to define an important word in order to clarify what he means. In fact, it is with definition as with using cause and effect — if one cannot define his terms he cannot really write exposition at all.

Qualification

However well he may have defined his terms, the writer will find that in developing them it is frequently necessary to admit some limitation to their truth or applicability. This process is called qualification. It is necessary because the ideas and opinions and feelings with which exposition deals are seldom absolutely true or absolutely false. Rather than black or white, truth often wears a shade of gray. To write honestly, one cannot drastically oversimplify the delicate complexity of the truth he wants to express; he must accept the fact of this grayness, that is, he must qualify. But qualification poses a very real problem in composition — the danger of blurring the focus of the paragraph. Suppose, for example, that one is writing an essay about college football. If he began with the flat statement "College football is a semi-professional sport," his point would be clear and emphatic enough, but it would not be true. The question is just not this simple. Now suppose that, recognizing the complexity of his topic, our writer adds a second sentence so that the passage reads:

> College football is a semi-professional sport. Some universities do play a purely amateur game.

He would no longer be open to the charge that his statement is grossly oversimple, but he would have gained this protection at the cost of confusing his reader, who no longer knows quite what to expect. Is the theme going to be about those universities which subsidize football, or about those which do not? Has the writer contradicted himself, or are both of these assertions — each in a limited way — true? As the example shows, qualification involves what at least seems to be a contradiction. The trick is to qualify without allowing this contradiction to become apparent, to qualify without confusing the reader about what one's point really is.

Actually it is not difficult to do, once you have mastered a few simple principles. The first is this: Whenever possible subordinate the qualification:

> College football is a semi-professional sport, although a few universities do play a purely amateur game.

This is better, but still the progression of thought is awkward. By placing the qualification last the sentence leaves in our minds the fact that some universities do not support their athletes, which, considering the writer's purpose, is not the main point. This brings us to the second principle: When you can, place the qualification first:

> Although some universities do play a purely amateur game, college football is a semi-professional sport.

There is still a third principle: Use qualifying words and phrases (*most, many, a few, some, generally, occasionally, usually,* and so on) to establish the limits of the idea:

> Although a few universities do play a purely amateur game, big-time college football is, in general, a semi-professional sport.

The addition of such qualifiers as "a few," "big-time," "in general" helps to make clear the limitations of the writer's opinion. So phrased the sentence is clear yet sufficiently complex not to be easily challenged, even by those who would not admit its complete truth.

In this example it was possible to work the qualification into the sentence containing the main point. While it is desirable, such compression is not always easy to achieve. Sometimes the qualification must be phrased in a separate sentence. It is wise to begin that sentence with a word or phrase stressing the obviousness of the concession; such a beginning tends to remove some of the force of the contradiction. "Of course," (or "certainly," "surely," "obviously," "plainly," "doubtlessly," "no doubt," "to be sure") one writes, "such and such is true"; and the reader is half convinced that its truth really doesn't matter very much. Then, when the qualification has been completed, the writer returns to his main point with a strong signal of contradiction ("but," "yet," "still," "nevertheless," "however"), and restates that point, either in a new sentence or in a clause co-ordinated with the qualification. Thus he concludes with the idea with which he began, making clear to his reader that this, and not the qualification, is what is important. The pattern may be seen in this adaptation of our earlier example:

> Big-time college football is essentially a semi-professional sport. Certainly, there are a few universities that play a purely amateur game. But these are only a few; on the whole the game is subsidized.

The technique is even more clearly revealed in these sentences from Professor Brand Blanshard's essay *On Philosophical Style:*

> Does it follow from all this that philosophers and their readers are doomed to roam a stylistic desert, and munch cactus as the sole article of their diet? Happily the situation is not so desperate as that. It is true that the philosopher must live in a drier climate than most men would find habitable, and be content with what Bacon called the *lumen siccum* or dry light as distinct from the *lumen humidum*, or light drenched in the affections. But that is not necessarily fatal to the life of feeling; even a rigorous austerity does not require that one's heart stop beating altogether.

Professor Blanshard's argument is that philosophical writing does not have to be as difficult and as arid as it often is; this is the point he asserts in the second sentence. But he is forced to admit that the subject matter of philosophy is drier than what most men are used to. That qualification he introduces by a phrase of concession ("It is true"). The qualification made, he returns in the final sentence to his main point, signaling the return by the strong "But."

At times the complexity of the subject and of the exception that must be granted to it, requires more extended treatment of the qualification, so that it must be stated in several sentences or even in an entire paragraph. For example, Professor George R. Stewart, arguing for the essential homogeneity of the early settlers of the American colonies, writes:

> With few exceptions the colonists of European stock were of northwestern European origins, and there can have been, racially, only negligible differences among them. Even in their cultural back-

> grounds they differed little. They were heirs of the European Middle Ages, of the Renaissance, and of the Reformation. They were Christians by tradition, and nearly all were Protestants.
>
> Naturally the groups differed somewhat, one from another, and displayed some clannishness. They were conscious of their differences, often more conscious of differences than of resemblances. Thus a Pennsylvania governor of 1718 was already voicing the cry that the American conservative has echoed ever since. "We are being overwhelmed by the immigrants!" he said in effect. "Will our country not become German instead of English?"
>
> Nevertheless, from the perspective of two centuries and from the point of view of the modern world with its critical problems of nationality and race, the differences existing among the various colonial groups fade into insignificance. We sense, comparatively speaking, a unified population. In the political realm, indeed, there were divergences that might lead even to tarrings and featherings, but racially and socially and religiously the superficial differences were much less important than the basic unity. *American Ways of Life*

The second paragraph is an elaborate qualification upon the point made in the first, admitting that despite their sameness the colonists did differ. But its greater length does not change the technique of qualification. The second paragraph begins with the concessive term "Naturally," stressing the truth of the qualification and thus removing its sting. In the third paragraph Professor Stewart swings back to his main point, signaling the return with the emphatic connective "Nevertheless." And throughout he uses such qualifying modifiers as "few," "only negligible," "nearly all," "somewhat," "some," and "comparatively speaking." (The final sentence, incidentally, contains a minor qualification which, as a close reading will show, illustrates again the principles we have been discussing.)

The ability to handle qualification is essential to a good expository style. It is certainly true that poor writers often overqualify. There are people who cannot bring themselves to state as a fact what plainly is a fact, and such unnecessary qualification is irritating and often misleading. But this does not mean that qualification is a weakness to be avoided. It means rather that the writer must know when he should not qualify as well as when he should. Reality being what it is, he will find that the occasions when he must make a qualification are not infrequent.

Negative Development

Before we leave altogether the logical techniques of building paragraphs, there is one more we should consider, even though it is not, perhaps, strictly "logical." This is the negative or antithetical method of paragraph development. It is perhaps less a particular means of support than a way of applying those we have already studied. In any event, it is not uncommon. Antithetical support means extending the topic by explaining what it is not, or why it has not come about, or what effects have not followed from it. A good example is this passage by Professor A. E. Taylor:

> What is the real significance of Socrates in the history of European thought? We may at once dismiss two views which have sometimes been held on this question as incapable of explaining the facts which need to be accounted for. Socrates was not a mere preacher of a commonplace morality of acting like an *homme de bien* for the utilitarian reason that bad ways "do not pay"—a view of him suggested by undue attention to certain parts of Xenophon's *Memorabilia*. Such a man would hardly have been put to death as a public danger; he would not have won the devotion of Plato, nor the general admiration of all the outstanding men of his age, or been caricatured as he was actually caricatured by Aristophanes. You may say Anytus misunderstood his man, Plato "idealized" him, Aristophanes distorted his features. But there must have been something to prompt the misunderstanding, the idealization, the distortion. The subject of them must have been in some way an extraordinary, in fact a *singular* character, an "original," and we have to discover in what his singularity consisted. Nor can Socrates have been what he has sometimes been taken to be by superficial readers of Plato, a mere sceptic, quick at disturbing the convictions of others by ingenious questions, but without convictions, and intense convictions, of his own. Mere clever scepticism is as ephemeral in its results as it is temporarily dazzling; Socrates created the intellectual and moral tradition by which Europe has ever since lived. *How* this could be is what has to be explained.
>
> At bottom the answer seems to be a very simple one, and may best be given in the elementary way in which it has been stated by Burnet. It was Socrates who, so far as can be seen, created the conception of the *soul* which has ever since dominated European thinking.

The passage is the beginning of the final chapter of Professor Taylor's *Socrates*, and the rhetorical question with which it opens is less the topic sentence for its paragraph than for the entire chapter. But the paragraph is related to the question, to which it stands as a negative reply. The real significance of Socrates, says Professor Taylor, does *not* lie in these aspects of him. We have included enough of the next paragraph to make clear that the writer does answer the question positively, and that, indeed, the negative statement in the opening paragraph is merely a way of leading up to that answer. This is usually the function of antithetical development — to prepare for or lead into positive statement.

Professor Taylor is quite definite in his rejection of these other explanations of Socrates. Sometimes, however, a writer may employ negative development more tentatively, suggesting not so much that the alternate explanations are wrong as that they are partial or unimportant. Consider, for instance, this paragraph in which Harold Nicolson discusses America's treatment of the elderly Tom Paine:

> It is not easy to explain why American opinion should, after his return to his adopted country, have treated him as a pariah. It may well have been that they were shocked by his drunken habits, by his freethinking on religious matters, by his cohabitation with Madame Bonneville, and by his attacks on Washington. Mr. Woodward, one of his most ardent defenders, suggests even that America in those days was in fact an aristocracy and that Americans were alienated by Paine's low origin and filthy ways. It may be even that they were unwilling to acclaim as their godfather a man who was English born and bred. He was certainly not an engaging companion, having acquired a blend of arrogance and self-pity, a displeasing mixture in which alcoholics frequently indulge. Yet I cannot but derive the impression that there was some other reason that explains the coldness with which Washington, and even Jefferson, regarded him. They must have suspected Paine of some act of treachery or disloyalty far worse than any that has yet been disclosed. But it is sad that the author of *Common Sense* and the *Crisis* should have been ostracized by his adopted country and allowed to die in penury and squalor. He was without any money and lived in utter destitution in lodgings in Partition Street, New York. He was able to sell his farm at New Rochelle and moved into slightly better rooms at No. 59 Grove Street. He had already in 1806 had one stroke and was affectionately nursed by Madame Bonneville. He died on June 8, 1809, and was buried at New Rochelle.
>
> *The Age of Reason*

Here too the negative leads into the positive, the shift coming in the sentence beginning: "Yet I cannot but derive the impression . . ." Still there is a difference in the way the two writers employ the antithetical technique. Professor Taylor says, in effect, "Socrates was not the sort of man that Xenophon suggests; therefore we must look elsewhere to discover his real significance." Mr. Nicolson, on the other hand, says, "Granted that Paine was a drunkard, that he was a freethinker, that he lived disreputably — still these are not enough to explain why America treated him as it did."

But the difference is slight, and both paragraphs demonstrate that one way to develop a topic is to approach it from the rear.

Summary

The "logical" techniques of paragraph development include working out the causes and effects of the topic idea, defining the topic, qualifying it, and approaching it negatively. In cause (or reasons) development the topic is regarded as a consequence and the paragraph discusses the cause (or causes) that brought it about. In effects development that relationship is reversed. In the cause-effect paragraph, both are treated. Causes (and/or effects) must be arranged in a significant order in the paragraph. In some cases that order will reflect their inherent logic, in others their temporal sequence, and in still others their relative importance.

Definition is important to good expository writing. It usually consists of making clear exactly what a word means. This may be done by citing synonyms or antonyms, by offering specific examples, by classification and differentiation, or by exploring the etymology and semantic history of the word.

Qualification means indicating the limits of an idea, conceding that beyond a certain point it is no longer applicable or valid. Qualification is likely to appear to be a contradiction of the main point and thus to distort the focus of the paragraph. But by applying certain techniques it is possible to qualify without confusing the reader.

Negative development simply means discussing the topic in terms of what it does not mean, does not give rise to, was not caused by, and so on. It is useful for emphasis and for building up to an important positive assertion.

Exercises

1. Compose a single paragraph developing three or four reasons to support one of the topic sentences listed below. Consider carefully the order of the reasons and provide the paragraph with adequate links. Feel free to employ an illustration, a comparison, a restatement, and so on; but give the bulk of the paragraph to the reasons.

    1. Folk music has become very popular with young people.
    2. It is not easy to become a physician.
    3. I prefer living at home [or away from home] while going to college.
    4. To be properly enjoyed a hike should always be taken in company.

5. A gulf seems to have opened up between the artist and the average man.
6. Professional football has grown enormously popular during the last ten years.

2. Work out one reason in some detail to support a topic sentence dealing with one of these subjects.

1. The harsh treatment of the Indians by the American settlers
2. The Second World War
3. Violence among young people
4. Poor driving
5. Failing out of college
6. The change in American sexual mores in the last forty years

3. Selecting any one of the topics that follow, write a single paragraph developing several effects. Here, also, consider the problem of arranging the effects in the best sequence and be sure to tie them together to make a unified paragraph and not simply a list of consequences.

1. Final examinations
2. Television and the family
3. Owning a car
4. Dropping out of high school
5. Drug addiction
6. Taking a course in sociology (or psychology, economics, and so on)
7. Getting a ticket for speeding

4. Compose a brief essay treating both the causes and the effects of any topic listed in exercises 1–3 that you have not already written a paragraph on. The essay should be about 700 words long (excluding any words in an outline if your teacher requests one), and it should have a short beginning paragraph and a clear closing.

5. Using as many of the methods of definition as the problem requires, formulate a one-paragraph definition of one of the following subjects. Your task is to make clear the nature of the thing or idea designated by the word.

1. Scholarship
2. Honor
3. Courage
4. Patriotism
5. Evil

6. Modeling your work upon Professor Gottschalk's definition of the term *history* (see page 192), define one of the following words in a paragraph or two. You may consult a dictionary, but ultimately your paragraph should be your work and not a rehash of assorted dictionary definitions; it should be a miniature essay which makes clear what the word means to contemporary users.

1. Philosophy
2. Science
3. Teen-ager
4. Communist
5. Radical
6. Poetry
7. Christian

7. Consult the *Oxford English Dictionary* and compose a brief definition of one of the following words as it was used in the eighteenth century, comparable to what Professor Lovejoy does with the term *pride.*

1. Enthusiasm
2. Science
3. Undertaker
4. Epic

8. Listed below are five pairs of sentences, all examples of poor qualification. Revise each pair twice to make a proper qualification contained in a single sentence. In the first revision take idea (a) as the main point and (b) as the qualification; in the second reverse the relationship of (a) and (b). Keep generally to the wording as it is given, but you may change the order of the clauses and add whatever qualifying words and connectives the task requires.

1. (a) College is difficult.
   (b) Some aspects of college are easy.
2. (a) Baseball is the great American game.
   (b) Its claim to supremacy is being challenged by professional football.
3. (a) The Romans are regarded as culturally inferior to the Greeks.
   (b) They created a great, and on the whole a just, Empire.
4. (a) Exercise is necessary to health.
   (b) Too much exercise or the wrong kind can kill a man.
5. (a) The "absent-minded professor" is a myth.
   (b) Some professors are forgetful.

9. Attempt a paragraph of essentially negative development modeled on the passages by Professor Taylor (page 200) and Harold Nicolson (page 201). Select any one of the following subjects and frame your topic statement any way you wish, to deal with the cause, the effect, the definition, or the components of the subject. The important thing is to work negatively, that is, to show what the cause, effect, definition, and so on, is *not*.

1. Love
2. Friendship
3. Happiness
4. Maturity
5. The American Civil War
6. Prejudice

13

DEVELOPING THE PARAGRAPH
IV. Complex Patterns

Introduction

In the preceding chapters we surveyed the means by which the writer may develop expository paragraphs. Throughout we held to the simple notion that a paragraph begins with a relatively brief topic sentence which it then supports by one of the various techniques we examined. Essentially, no doubt, this is the structure of the expository paragraph, and such simple cases of development do occur, a fact demonstrated by the examples we have seen. But without being really changed, the pattern of topic statement and support sentences may be developed — indeed, often is developed — far more complexly than these examples suggest. It will be worth while to consider a few of these complexities. For here, too, the similarity between paragraph and sentence holds true. The simple sentence has many virtues, but no good writer employs it exclusively. Just so, the skilled writer must learn to handle complicated patterns of paragraph development. These complications involve (1) the form, the placement, and the range of the topic sentence; (2) the use, within a single paragraph, of two, three, or even more of the various developing techniques; and (3) a compounding of subject so that the same paragraph may actually develop two or more topics. Necessarily we shall treat these matters one at a time, but in practice they are not mutually exclusive: a paragraph may exhibit all of them at once.

The Topic Sentence

VARIATIONS IN FORM

So far we have regarded the topic statement as being a single sentence; we have, in fact, described it as the "topic sentence." Actually this is something of a misnomer (which we shall, however, continue to use), for although the topic very frequently is contained in a single sentence, it does not have to be. Sometimes it may be only a clause, being combined in the opening sentence with a transitional element that hooks the paragraph onto the preceding one. James Thurber begins a paragraph: "If the towns in Soapland are not developed as realistic communities [transition], neither are the characters — except in rare instances — developed as authentic human beings [topic]." On the other hand, the topic statement may require more than a single sentence, as it does in this paragraph:

> There are in the English vocabulary, as everybody knows, two chief elements — the one native, the other complexly foreign. And it is the fusion of these two which constitutes the unrivalled flexibility and variety of our speech. To its native, Saxon element it owes a homely vigour, a forthrightness and vividness and concreteness, an emotional appeal, in which it matches the Hebrew itself. To its foreign element — chiefly the Latin component, which will concern us in a moment — is due, among other things, a sonorousness, a stateliness, a richness of music, a capacity for delicate discrimination which makes it an instrument of almost endlessly varied stops. Now one element is predominant, now the other; more frequently there is an intimate fusion of the two. Every page of English literature, whether prose or poetry, illustrates the possibilities of infinite variety inherent in this fundamental character of English diction; but it is its bearing on the translation of the Bible which concerns us now, and to that I pass at once.
>
> JOHN LIVINGSTON LOWES, "THE NOBLEST MONUMENT OF ENGLISH PROSE," *Essays in Appreciation*

Here the topic statement moves from the general premise contained in the first sentence to the particular implication in the second; but fully to comprehend the subject of the paragraph we require both sentences.

The topic statement may also be varied by being cast as a rhetorical question rather than as a declarative sentence. A rhetorical question is a question asked not by genuine ignorance seeking knowledge, but by knowledge forcing a predetermined answer. Sometimes this answer is so obvious that it is left implicit, as when a patriot asks: "Are we to desert our nation in time of trouble?" But often the answer is actually stated, the question serving merely to introduce or occasion the answer; it is this sort of rhetorical question that may serve as a topic sentence. Thus Justice Louis Brandeis writes:

> What is Americanization? It manifests itself, in a superficial way, when the immigrant adopts the clothes, the manners, and the

customs generally prevailing here. Far more important is the manifestation presented when he substitutes for his mother tongue the English language as the common medium of speech. But the adoption of our language, manners and customs is only a small part of the process. To become Americanized the change wrought must be fundamental. However great his outward conformity, the immigrant is not Americanized unless his interests and affections have become deeply rooted here. And we properly demand of the immigrant even more than this, — he must be brought into complete harmony with our ideals and aspirations and coöperate with us for their attainment. Only when this has been done will he possess the national consciousness of an American.

"TRUE AMERICANISM," *Business — A Profession*

This is a simple way to generate a paragraph: the topic sentence asks a question which the remainder of the paragraph answers. It is a technique especially useful for what we called in Chapter 9 the topical paragraph, that is the paragraph whose subject is a general topic rather than a specific proposition about that topic. It would be difficult, for instance, to phrase Justice Brandeis's topic statement in declarative form: "Americanization is . . ." Is what? The topic sentence contains no specific predication. It is the function of what follows to complete the proposition, to tell us what "Americanization is." Similarly William James, in *Pragmatism*, begins a paragraph: "But what do the words verification and validation themselves pragmatically mean?"; and the rest of the paragraph, by answering the question, completes the proposition.

Even where the topic statement does assert a full proposition, it may still be phrased as a rhetorical question. John Milton, for example, doubting the validity of certain writings attributed to the early Church Fathers, argues:

Now besides all this, who knows not how many surreptitious works are ingraffed into the legitimate writings of the Fathers? And of those Books that pass for authentic, who knows what hath been tampered withal, what hath been razed out, what hath been inserted? Besides the late legerdemain of the Papists, that which Sulpitius writes concerning Origen's books gives us cause vehemently to suspect there hath been poaching of old. In the third chapter of his 1st Dialogue we may read what wrangling the bishops and monks had about the reading or not reading of Origen; some objecting that he was corrupted by heretics; others answering that all such books had been so dealt with. How then shall I trust these times to lead me, that testify so ill of leading themselves? Certainly of their defects their own witness may be best received, but of the rectitude of their life and doctrine, to judge rightly we must judge by that which was to be their rule. *Of the Reformation in England*

Milton's initial questions are really thinly veiled assertions. They say, in effect, "Many surreptitious works are ingraffed into the legitimate writings of the Fathers. Of those Books that pass for authentic, some have been tampered with, some material has been razed out, some material inserted." John Donne used much the same technique when he began a sermon by asking "Doth not man die even in his birth?", which is another way of saying "Man dies even in his birth." Thus both Milton and Donne state the full propositions of their paragraphs in their topical rhetorical questions. This is slightly different from using a rhetorical question, as does Justice Brandeis, simply to state the first part of the proposition, which the remainder of the paragraph is to complete.

Occasionally the rhetorical question, rather than standing alone as the topic statement, functions in conjunction with a declarative sentence. For example, I. A. Richards answers a criticism of modern scientific terminology like this:

> To pass to another type of complaint — that these words are cumbrous and ugly in themselves. I have seen it urged — and by no slight authority — that whereas good old words like *mind* and *thought* are neat, concise and beautiful, a word like *psychology* is cumbrous and disagreeable. How sound a complaint is that? And is it really a complaint against the form of the word or against some of its uses? Let us grant that some of the derivative uses of psychology are objectionable — because inconveniently and unnecessarily ambiguous — as when someone persists in talking and writing of *Shakespeare's psychology* without letting us see whether he means (1) Shakespeare's theories, if any, about the mind, (2) the assumptions Shakespeare unconsciously made about mental processes, (3) the inference as to mental processes we might arrive at from Shakespeare's work, or (4) (to go no further into these possibilities) just the way Shakespeare's own mind worked. These vagaries of the word are typical and unfortunate. They endanger discourse, and much use of that sort of language rightly discredits a speaker or writer. But such uses of *psychology* are no ground for complaint against the word in its use for the theoretical study of how the mind works, or in derivative uses where the context takes care of them. The complaint against *Shakespeare's psychology* is really against the inadequate contextual control. And for controlled uses of the word — seeing what a cumbrous subject psychology is — a cumbrous word may have therein its recommendation. *The Philosophy of Rhetoric*

Here the topic comprises not one but three sentences, the first of which ("I have seen it urged . . .") is declarative. Of course, all this could have been asked as one question. But long, involved questions are frequently awkward and confusing, and Mr. Richards has been wise to split his topic statement into a declaration and a pair of questions about that declaration.

In all these cases the rhetorical questions have functioned as genuine topic sentences. So employed, the rhetorical question is easily adapted to any of the techniques of development — reasons, effects, comparison, definition, and so on — that we discussed in the preceding chapters. By being repeated throughout a paragraph the rhetorical question can even function as a variety of restatement development, as in the following paragraph by Professor Gilbert Highet:

> Another unique attribute characterizes the American student: his huge numbers. Can four real universities exist in one city? Can it be possible that in one state fifty or sixty thousand youths and maidens are capable of the activity required to absorb a university education? Are the inhabitants of California (whose very name derives from a romance describing the Earthly Paradise) so talented that they can every year produce a myriad of university graduates? And what educators could be at once so inspiring and so industrious as to teach, effectively, this enormous horde? Or, finally, can the vast multitudes of adolescents in the United States all be so much more talented than their coevals in Canada, in France, in Sweden?
>
> "THE AMERICAN STUDENT AS I SEE HIM"

But despite the ease with which it may be adapted to different patterns of development — perhaps, in fact, because of this very ease — the rhetorical question can easily become a mannerism of style. It is a good way to begin a paragraph now and then, but if one begins every second or third paragraph with a rhetorical question, he has overworked the device and spoiled it. Rhetorical questions certainly are a legitimate form of topic statement; still they should not be used too often.

VARIATIONS IN POSITION

The topic sentence may also be varied by its position. In the examples we have seen so far its place has always been at, or very near, the beginning of the paragraph. Now and again, however, the topic statement will be delayed until later in the paragraph. Sometimes it will be pushed down toward the middle, most often because the writer had to devote the first sentence or two to connecting the paragraph with the preceding material. Though in this section we have been considering the paragraph in isolation, it should be remembered that commonly it will be a part of an essay, functioning in conjunction with other paragraphs to which it will be linked by the devices we studied in Chapter 9. Occasionally such links, by requiring appreciable space will delay the topic statement. A simple instance is the following paragraph from Alan Simpson's study of Puritanism:

> So the first response to frustration is the fragmentation of the movement, and another is the decision to migrate. But what of those who remained? Ought they to rebel? Puritans had never thought so. When an Elizabethan Puritan had his right hand cut off by the executioner for writing a pamphlet which the government had found seditious, he raised his hat with his left hand to cry, "God save the Queen!" When Charles I suspended parliamentary government in 1629, it was still far from clear that God ever intended his saints to take up arms against constituted authority. Even in 1642, when king and Parliament faced each other in civil war, there were still some Puritans who would have held aloof if they had not been harried into parliamentary garrisons by a royalist rabble. But by that time the bulk of them had been converted to the duty of resistance, and the neutrals could hardly be surprised if they found themselves hustled on the streets because their dress and deportment marked them out as fellow-travelers of the Puritans in arms.
>
> *Puritanism in Old and New England*

In the sections preceding this paragraph, the writer discussed two of the effects upon seventeenth-century English Puritanism of the policies and doctrines of the Anglican church. The first was to cause the Puritans to split into smaller sects, the second to force the migration of some of these sects. In this paragraph the writer treats the problem of loyalty faced by those who chose not to leave England. Needing, however, to link this paragraph to its context, he spends the first sentence summarizing the preceding material. In sentences two, three, and four Mr. Simpson establishes his topic, using two rhetorical questions, which focus down from the general to the particular, and a declarative sentence, which states briefly the answer that is exemplified and developed in the remainder of the paragraph. Another instance is this paragraph by George R. Stewart:

> On the whole, neither the influence of later immigration, nor native developments, nor international ideas seem greatly to have affected our meat-eating habits. The early northwestern European hereditary traits are evident and important in setting the taboo against horse meat, and probably in establishing a preference for

> the more popular meats. But the land itself has exerted an even stronger influence. This has been important in taking away any chance there was that we should be eaters of fish, mutton, or goat flesh. It has made turkey one of our national dishes. By enabling us to have an abundance of beef it has made us beef-eaters. Most striking of all, by receiving hospitably the fast-breeding and omnivorous chicken and pig, the land assured that these two meats should be perhaps even more characteristic of our food than is beef. "A chicken in every pot" can become a political symbol, and *Chicken Every Sunday* the title of a popular book. "Pork chops" has become a phrase by which the labor unions symbolize economic advantage. The two meet even in alliance, and one of the most typical of our dishes is ham and eggs. *American Ways of Life*

The topic sentence ("But the land itself has exerted an even stronger influence") is delayed even longer than in Mr. Simpson's paragraph, but here too the delay is the result of having to establish a connection with what has gone before, in this case the discussion of other influences that have acted upon the American diet.

Even where transitions are not necessary or can be dispensed with in a word or phrase, the topic statement may be delayed as a consequence of approaching it negatively or through a comparison. For example, George Santayana puts off the topic sentence almost to the middle of this paragraph:

> Judaism and Christianity, like Greek philosophy, were singly inspired by the pursuit of happiness, in whatever form it might be really attainable: now on earth if possible, or in the millennium, or in some abstracted and inward life, like that of the Stoics, or in the last resort, in a different life altogether beyond the grave. But heathenism ignores happiness, despises it, or thinks it impossible. The regimen and philosophy of Germany are inspired by this contempt for happiness, for one's own happiness as well as for other people's. Happiness seems to the German moralists something unheroic, an abdication before external things, a victory of the senses over the will. They think the pursuit of happiness low, materialistic, and selfish. They wish everybody to sacrifice or rather to forget happiness, and to do "deeds." "HEATHENISM"

Santayana builds up to his topic statement ("But heathenism ignores happiness, despises it, or thinks it impossible") by the initial comparison to the Judaic-Christian tradition, and the postponement here is the result of developing the topic in contradistinction to its antithesis.

When the topic statement is delayed it is probably even more common that it be pushed all the way to the end of the paragraph. Voltaire, for instance, begins the entry "Laws" in his *Philosophical Dictionary* with this paragraph:

> Sheep live very placidly in community; they are considered very easy-going, because we do not see the prodigious quantity of animals they devour. It is even to be believed that they eat them innocently and without knowing it, like us when we eat a Sassenage cheese. The republic of the sheep is a faithful representation of the golden age.

The usual pattern is here reversed. It is the last sentence that functions as the topic statement and the first portion of the paragraph that supports it. Again, consider this paragraph from Carlyle's *The French Revolution:*

> Raging multitudes surround the Hôtel-de-Ville, crying: Arms! Orders! The Six-and-twenty Town-Councillors, with their long gowns, have ducked under (into the raging chaos); — shall never emerge more. Besenval is painfully wriggling himself out, to the Champ-de-Mars; he must sit there "in the cruelest uncertainty": courier after courier may dash off for Versailles; but will bring back no answer, can hardly bring himself back. For the roads are all blocked with batteries and pickets, with floods of carriages arrested for examination: such was Broglie's one sole order; the Œil-de-Bœuf, hearing in the distance such mad din, which sounded almost like invasion, will before all things keep its own head whole. A new Ministry, with, as it were, but one foot in the stirrup, cannot take leaps. Mad Paris is abandoned altogether to itself.

Delaying the topic sentence until the end of the paragraph has several advantages. For one thing it may pique the reader's curiosity — which is especially important toward the beginning of an essay, or even of a section — by presenting him with a series of particulars that are not drawn together until the end. For another, placing the topic statement finally instead of initially is emphatic. Like a periodic sentence, such a paragraph stresses its main point by reserving it for last.

But in composition advantages must be paid for, and setting the topic sentence at the end causes several difficulties. Obviously it can bewilder the reader. In effect the writer is developing his predication before he has really established his subject. This is to reverse the usual order, and the reversal may sacrifice in clarity whatever it gains in emphasis. To some degree this danger can be avoided by beginning with a generalization which the paragraph particularizes before making the final statement of the topic at the end. Voltaire's paragraph does something like this. Its actual topic is at the end, yet its first clause ("Sheep live very placidly in community") functions as a kind of substitute topic sentence that sets up the details that follow. But this device results, in effect, in having two statements of topic, one at the beginning, another at the close, and thus is likely to lose whatever advantage there may have been in delaying the topic in the first place.

A second disadvantage of the closing topic sentence is that it tends to shut the paragraph off tightly, making it difficult for the writer to move on. In a concluding paragraph this is a virtue, and closing paragraphs often do build up to a final generalization. Elsewhere in the essay, however, it creates a problem in transition. If he has saved his topic statement for the end, a writer may find he has painted himself into a corner. Granted, neither of these disadvantages is insuperable; a good writer can delay his main point without confusing his readers and, most of the time at least, he can extricate himself from corners. Even so, the topic ought to be placed at the end of the paragraph only when the advantages of putting it there are greater than the problems it will create.

Very occasionally a writer will solve the problem of where to put the topic sentence by simply dispensing with it altogether. Here is an example:

> The Massachusetts farmer who witnessed the revolution ploughed his land with the wooden bull-plough, sowed his grain broadcast, and when it was ripe cut it with a scythe and threshed it on his barn floor with a flail. His house was without paint; his floors were without carpet. When darkness came on, his light was derived from a few candles of home manufacture. The place of furnaces and stoves was supplied by huge cavernous fireplaces which took up one side of the room and, sending half the smoke into the apartment, sent half the heat up the chimney. His food was of the simplest kind, was served in the coarsest of dishes, and was eaten with the coarsest of implements. Beef and pork, salt fish, dried apples, and vegetables made up the daily fare from one year's end to another.
>
> JOHN BACH MCMASTER, *A History of the People of the United States*

The paragraph has no topic sentence. But it is clear what that topic would be were it necessary to formulate it; it would run something like "The colonial farmer in Massachusetts lived under very primitive conditions." The fact that the topic is so clear is important, for it reveals that one cannot really dispense, in any final sense, with the topic idea. Now and then it may be left implicit, as it is here, but always it must be clear that the paragraph has a topic — that it is about something, even if that something is nowhere stated.

There is no great advantage to leaving the topic implicit. It is possible that the unsaid topic (always assuming it is clear enough) may communicate itself more forcefully on the principle that what we discover for ourselves we are more likely to accept. But at best this is an occasional advantage of the implicit topic. Nor is the argument that it varies the pattern of the paragraph any stronger. Admittedly this is a variation, but there are many ways to vary paragraphs without leaving out the topic sentence. And certainly the dangers of doing it are very great. It can be successful only in relatively brief paragraphs which are so tightly structured, their matter so rigidly selected, that there can be no doubt of their topics. To control such paragraphs takes a skilled and disciplined writer. The beginner would be wise to state his topic sentence, no matter where he places it, clearly and explicitly.

VARIATIONS IN RANGE

In our examples thus far the topic sentence, while varied in form and position, has at least been restricted to a single paragraph. Even this characteristic, however, may be modified, for as we saw in Chapter 7, a topic sentence may set up more than one paragraph. Here is another case in which a topic statement reaches beyond the single paragraph. A. G. Gardiner asks about Rudyard Kipling:

> What was the secret of the hypnotism he exercised? It was partly the magic of an appeal perfectly attuned to the temper of the time. Israel [that is, England] had waxed fat, and had turned to the worship of the golden calf. It was the emergence of the baser passions, the lust of power without a purpose, of wealth without industry. The gold of South Africa had set up a fever in the blood. It was as though the nation had left the temples of its ancient worship to fall down before the Baal of the Stock Exchange. And in its haste to grow rich it turned passionately upon the stupid little pastoral people that stood insolently in its path, and
>
> Drunk with sight of power, we loosed
> Wild tongues that had not Thee in awe.
>
> In that momentary flash of the "Recessional," Mr. Kipling pierced to the heart of the disease, and delivered his own merciless sentence.
>
> And partly it was due to the astonishing intensity of his vision. Coleridge said of Kean that to see him act was like reading Shakespeare by flashes of lightning. It is a world filled with sudden and sinister shapes — not men, but the caricatures of men; not women, but Maenad sisters, with wild and bloodshot eyes and fearful disheveled locks; with boys that drink and smoke and swear like dragoons; animals that talk and machinery that reasons like a Yellow journalist. It is all a disordered, frenzied motion, soulless and cruel

— a world seen in a nightmare, with all the intensity and literalness of a nightmare and all its essential truth. It is

> Fantastic mockery, such as lurks
> In some wild poet when he works
> Without a conscience or an aim.

The initial question sets up not simply the paragraph it introduces, but the entire passage. Actually there are three topic statements here: "What was the secret of the hypnotism he exercised?" — the topic sentence of the entire passage; "It was partly the magic of an appeal attuned to the temper of the time" — topic of the first paragraph; "And partly it was due to the astonishing intensity of his vision" — topic of the second.

Complex Patterns of Development

Aside from what may be done with its topic sentence, the expository paragraph may be complicated by employing more than a single method of development. Indeed, it is probably true that complex paragraphs are more common than the simple paragraphs we have studied in the preceding chapters. Usually, however, a paragraph that utilizes two or more techniques of support will still be primarily structured by only one of those techniques; it will be essentially a "reasons" paragraph or an "illustration" paragraph or what have you. Here is an instance:

> No one can tell the whole truth about himself. It is not only vanity that has prevented those who have tried to reveal themselves to the world from telling the whole truth; it is direction of interest; their disappointment with themselves, their surprise that they can do things that seem to them abnormal, make them place too great an emphasis on occurrences that are more common than they suppose. Rousseau in the course of his "Confessions" narrates incidents that have profoundly shocked the sensibility of mankind. By describing them so frankly he falsified his values and so gave them in his book a greater importance than they had in his life. There were events among a multitude of others, virtuous or at least neutral, that he omitted because they were too ordinary to seem worth recording. There is a sort of man who pays no attention to his good actions, but is tormented by his bad ones. This is the type that most often writes about himself. He leaves out his redeeming qualities and so appears only weak, unprincipled, and vicious.
>
> W. SOMERSET MAUGHAM, *The Summing Up*

The paragraph contains both an illustration and a reason (and even, in its final three sentences, a particular restatement of the point made in the second sentence). Yet it remains basically a reasons paragraph; the illustration is subordinate to the purpose of explaining why it is that "no one can tell the whole truth about himself." It is, in fact, an example brought forward to substantiate the second sentence, which states the reason supporting the topic. Thus the pattern of the paragraph is:

TOPIC —(supported by)→ REASON —(supported by)→ ILLUSTRATION

F. L. Lucas handles a similar idea rather more complexly in this paragraph:

> Even autobiography, however frank and full, remains at best a mere sketch of life's infinite complexity. We forget; we distort — if not consciously, then unconsciously. It is sometimes possible to tell nothing but the truth; but the whole truth — never. Even Montaigne sometimes misleads; even Rousseau, though unblushing in his exhibitionism, is quite untrustworthy. Pepys, indeed, and Boswell, journalizing for themselves alone, do convince us; but they remain almost unique. *The Search for Good Sense*

The first sentence establishes the topic; the second states a reason for it, which the third repeats; the fourth brings forward two examples in support of this reason; and the fifth offers an instance that qualifies it. But despite this complexity the paragraph is a variety of illustration paragraph, for if it is not organized around its examples, these examples clearly are its climax.

Here is one final instance of a complex paragraph in which the basic structure is still relatively simple:

> The first and most obvious result of the technological revolution has been to increase the amount of wealth in the form of material things which can be produced in a given time by a given population. For example, in 1913 there was produced in Great Britain seven billion yards of cotton cloth for export alone. In 1750 the total population of Great Britain, working with the mechanical appliances then available, could have produced only a small fraction of that amount. A second result of the technological revolution is that, as machines are perfected and become more automatic, man power plays a relatively less important part in the production of a given amount of wealth in a given time. Fifty years ago, when all type was set by hand, the labor of several men was required to print, fold, and arrange in piles the signatures of a book. Today machines can do it all, and far more rapidly; little man power is required, except that a mechanic, who may pass the time sitting in a chair, must be present in case anything goes worng with the machine. And finally, a third result of the technological revolution is that, under the system of private property in the means of production and the price system as a method of distributing wealth, the greater part of the wealth pro-

duced, since it is produced by the machines, goes to those who own or control the machines, while those who work the machines receive that part only which can be exacted by selling their services in a market where wages are impersonally adjusted to the necessities of the machine process. CARL BECKER, *Modern Democracy*

This paragraph contains three effects, and of these the first two are supported by illustrations that involve contrasts. Yet the paragraph as a whole is an analysis of the effects of the technological revolution, which it unifies by the use of framing words ("first," "second," "third"). Within itself the paragraph has no topic statement, but its general subject is implicitly clear (it might be phrased: "There have been three important results of the technological revolution"); and, in any case, the paragraph was adequately set up in its original context. Its structure, then, is:

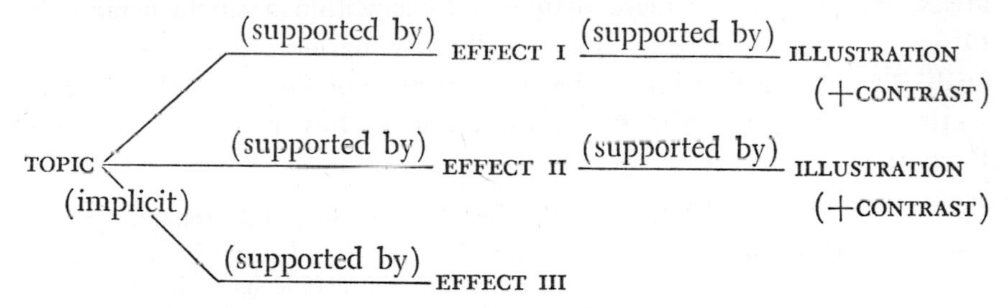

As these examples show, illustration and comparison are easily blended with other techniques. So is restatement; for anything, of course, may be repeated. In the following paragraph, for instance, the writer is explaining why war inculcates patience. But first he asserts several times that it does, and then, having indicated the reason, he restates that reason in a series of particulars:

> War, without virtue in itself, breeds virtue. It breeds patience in the impatient and heroism in the cowardly. But mostly it breeds patience. For war is a dull business, the dullest business on earth. War is a period of waiting. Each day of it crammed with the little hesitations of men uncertain of themselves and awed by the ghastly responsibilities — responsibilities of life and death, the responsibilities of gods — that have been thrust into their hands. The soldier waits for food, for clothing, for a letter, for a battle to begin. And often the food is never served, the clothing is never issued, the letter never arrives, and the battle never begins. The soldier learns to wait meekly, hoping that something will happen. And when the period of waiting is at an end the something that does happen isn't what he expected. So in the end he learns to wait and expect nothing.
>
> HARRY BROWN, *A Walk in the Sun*

Even these few instances make plain how numerous are the possible combinations of the various techniques of paragraph development. The tendency of modern writing, however, is toward simplicity, and the paragraph is no exception. Contemporary writers are less likely than most nineteenth-century writers to elaborate long, highly complex paragraphs. None the less they do weave paragraphs out of more than a single strand, and this ability has to be acquired in some degree by anyone who wishes to write exposition well.

The Compound Paragraph

In addition to those complications of paragraph form that involve either the topic sentence or the methods of supporting it, there is a third sort that arises from developing more than one topic within a single paragraph. Often the compound paragraph is really nothing more than a species of analysis paragraph that breaks down a general topic into several units and works out each in turn. Study, for example, this passage by Jacques Barzun:

> Unfortunately, with the vast increase in public schooling since 1870, an entirely new notion of what is good English has come to prevail. Awakened by free schooling, the people have shown worthy intentions. They want to be right and even elegant, and so become at once suspicious of plainness and pedantic. They purchase all sorts of handbooks that make a fetish of spelling, of avoiding split infinitives, of saying "It is I" (with the common result of "between you and I") — in short, dwell on trivialities or vulgarisms which do not affect style or thought in the slightest. But with this intolerance toward crude and plain error goes a remarkable insensitivity to inflated nonsense. Most bad journalism is only highbrow verbosity, yet the popular mind continues to believe that the pedantry which it likes is simple and the simplicity which it finds hard is complex. Here is the opening of a serial thriller in a Boston paper: —
>
> > Strange things happen in Chinatown. But even that exotic and perverse district seldom presented drama as fantastic as the secret that hid among the silk and jade and porcelain splendors of the famous House of the Mandarin on Mulberry Lane.
>
> *Teacher in America*

The phrase "new notion of what is good English" establishes the general topic of the paragraph. But that "notion," we learn, has two facets: on the one hand the "worthy intention" to correctness, on the other "a remarkable insensitivity to inflated nonsense." Thus the second sentence and the fifth function as what we may call subtopic statements, each setting up a portion of the paragraph. Like a full topic statement, each is supported by the sentences that follow it, the first by both a reason (the desire for correctness) and an effect (the concern with trivialities), the second by the illustration taken from a newspaper story.

In other cases the compound paragraph is a variety of the topical paragraph, that is, a paragraph in which the topic consists only of a general subject rather than of a full proposition about that subject. The following passage from Tom Paine's *The Crisis* illustrates the type:

> 'Tis surprising to see how rapidly a panic will sometimes run through a country. All nations and ages have been subject to them: Britain has trembled like an ague at the report of a French fleet of flat bottomed boats; and in the fourteenth century the whole English army, after ravaging the kingdom of France, was driven back like men petrified with fear; and this brave exploit was performed by a few broken forces collected and headed by a woman, Joan of Arc. Would that heaven might inspire some Jersey maid to spirit up her countrymen, and save her fair fellow sufferers from ravage and ravishment! Yet panics, in some cases, have their uses; they produce as much good as hurt. Their duration is always short; the mind soon grows through them, and acquires a firmer habit than before. But their peculiar advantage is, that they are the touchstones of sincerity and hypocrisy, and bring things and men to light, which might otherwise have lain forever undiscovered. In fact, they have the same effect on secret traitors, which an imaginary apparition would have upon a private murderer. They sift out the hidden thoughts of man and hold them up in public to the world. Many a disguised tory has lately shown his head, that shall penitentially solemnize with curses the day on which Howe arrived upon the Delaware.

Paine's paragraph does not have a topic statement that embraces all of it. Rather it divides into halves, each introduced by a subtopic sentence: the first — " 'Tis surprising to see how rapidly a panic will sometimes run through a country"; the second — "Yet panics, in some cases, have their uses; they produce as much good as hurt." Perhaps a modern writer would break this into two paragraphs, although as it stands it does not mislead or confuse us. It is easily grasped as one paragraph, for it is certainly coherent; all of it is about panic.

The compound paragraph may be even more subtle. There are paragraphs that begin conventionally enough with a single topic, but which use that topic as a stepping off place. As they develop their subjects these paragraphs range rather widely, traveling, by their conclusions, some little way from the point at which they began. Such is the case with this paragraph from W. Somerset Maugham's *The Summing Up:*

> I have never had much patience with the writers who claim from the reader an effort to understand their meaning. You have only to go to the great philosophers to see that it is possible to express with lucidity the most subtle reflections. You may find it difficult to understand the thought of Hume, and if you have no philosophical training its implications will doubtless escape you; but no one with any education at all can fail to understand exactly what the meaning of each sentence is. Few people have written English with more grace than Berkeley. There are two sorts of obscurity you find in writers. One is due to negligence and the other to wilfulness. People often write obscurely because they have never taken the trouble to learn to write clearly. This sort of obscurity you find too often in modern philosophers, in men of science, and even in literary critics. Here it is indeed strange. You would have thought that men who passed their lives in the study of the great masters of literature would be sufficiently sensitive to the beauty of language to write if not beautifully at least with perspicuity. Yet you will find in their works sentence after sentence that you must read twice to discover the sense. Often you can only guess at it, for the writers have evidently not said what they intended.

Mr. Maugham begins by asserting his impatience with obscure writers. He goes on to justify that impatience by the *a fortiori* argument that if philosophers can write clearly so can any man, citing in support two illustrations. His impatience justified, he shifts to an analysis of the varieties of obscurity, of which he isolates two. The first of these he discusses in the remainder of the paragraph, concluding by belaboring literary critics, who, he complains, are often guilty of it. The progression of thought is more discursive than in most of the expository paragraphs we have seen, moving toward the rambling, associative paragraph typical of the familiar essayist, which is less a unit of thought than a vehicle for the development of thought.

An even clearer case is this paragraph by James Thurber; it is taken from an essay satirizing radio soap-opera, which Thurber refers to as "Soapland":

> The people of Soapland are subject to a set of special ills. Temporary blindness, preceded by dizzy spells and headaches, is a common affliction of Soapland people. The condition usually clears up in six or eight weeks, but once in a while it develops into brain tumor and the patient dies. One script writer, apparently forgetting

that General Mills was the sponsor of his serial, had one of his women characters go temporarily blind because of an allergy to chocolate cake. There was hell to pay, and the writer had to make the doctor in charge of the patient hastily change his diagnosis. Amnesia strikes almost as often in Soapland as the common cold in our world. There have been as many as eight or nine amnesia cases on the air at one time. The hero of "Rosemary" stumbled around in a daze for months last year. When he regained his memory, he found that in his wanderings he had been lucky enough to marry a true-blue sweetie. The third major disease is paralysis of the legs. This scourge usually attacks the good males. Like mysterious blindness, loss of the use of the legs may be either temporary or permanent. The hero of "Life Can Be Beautiful" was confined to a wheel chair until his death last March, but young Doctor Malone, who was stricken with paralysis a year ago, is up and around again. I came upon only one crippled villain in 1947: Spencer Hart rolled through a three-month sequence of "Just Plain Bill" in a wheel chair. When their men are stricken, the good women become nobler than ever. A disabled hero is likely to lament his fate and indulge in self-pity now and then, but his wife or sweetheart never complains. She is capable of twice as much work, sacrifice, fortitude, endurance, ingenuity, and love as before. Joyce Jordan, M.D., had no interest in a certain male until he lost the use of both legs and took to a wheel chair. Then love began to bloom in her heart. The man in the wheel chair has come to be the standard Soapland symbol of the American male's subordination to the female and his dependence on her greater strength of heart and soul.

"IVORYTOWN, RINSOVILLE, ANACINBURG, AND CRISCO CORNERS"

Unlike the propositional paragraph or even the topical paragraph, this one does not stay within the limits set by the topic sentence. Beginning with an analysis of the "set of special ills" to which the citizens of Soapland are subject, Thurber concludes by pointing out the matriarchal nature of Soapland culture. But the progression of thought is plainly marked. Paralysis of the legs is the switching topic, for it is, on the one hand, a common affliction in Soapland, and, on the other, it brings out the best (or, if you prefer, the worst) in the women, and thus leads Thurber quite naturally into the topic of the dominance of the male by the female in the towns and villages of the world of soap-opera.

Summary

The expository paragraph, basically constructed on the simple pattern of topic-support, can vary and complicate that pattern by changing the form and the position of the topic statement, by combining several techniques of development, and by working with more than one topic. The topic statement may be cast as a rhetorical question; it may be placed in the middle of the paragraph or at its end, as well as in its more usual position at the beginning. It may even be omitted, implied rather than actually stated. Any combination of the various developing techniques — illustration, restatement, analysis, comparison, analogy, cause and effect, definition, qualification — is possible, and some combination of them is typical of most expository paragraphs. The basic structure of such a paragraph, however, will usually make it a "variety of reasons" paragraph, or of illustration, restatement, and so on. Paragraphs, especially in the looser, less formal kind of exposition, often become more discursive, encompassing two or more topics, setting up each with an appropriate subtopic sentence.

Exercises

1. Each of the following paragraphs is complexly developed, employing two or three of the techniques we have studied in preceding chapters. Identify all the means of support (reason, effect, restatement, comparison, and so on) each paragraph exhibits.

> 1. But the chief cause of our natural unwillingness to admit that one species has given birth to clear and distinct species, is that we are always slow in admitting great changes of which we do not see the steps. The difficulty is the same as that felt by so many geologists, when Lyell first insisted that long lines of inland cliffs had been formed, and the great vallies excavated, by the agencies we see still at work. The mind cannot possibly grasp the full meaning of the term of even a million years; it cannot add up and perceive the full effects of many slight variations, accumulated during an almost infinite number of generations.
>
> CHARLES DARWIN, *On the Origin of Species*
>
> 2. At least four-fifths of the American people — Adams among the rest — had united in the election of General Grant to the Presidency, and probably had been more or less affected in their choice by the parallel they felt between Grant and Washington. Nothing could be more obvious. Grant represented order. He was a great soldier, and the soldier always represented order. He might be as partisan as he pleased, but a general who had organized and commanded half a million or a million men in the field, must know how to administer. Even Washington, who was, in education and experience, a mere cave-dweller, had known how to organize a government, and had found Jeffersons and Hamiltons to organize his departments. The task of bringing the Government back to regular practices, and of

restoring moral and mechanical order to administration, was not very difficult; it was ready to do itself, with a little encouragement. No doubt the confusion, especially in the old slave States and in the currency, was considerable, but the general disposition was good, and every one had echoed the famous phrase: "Let us have peace."

The Education of Henry Adams

3. It is an oversimplification to say that Lincoln was antislavery and leave it there. Relativity was a big factor. There were degrees, orders, and grades among antislavery men. Leaving John Brown aside as eccentric, criminal, and untypical, we may note in extreme antislavery ranks such uncompromising souls as Garrison, Weld, Phillips, Gerrit Smith, T. W. Higginson, and Theodore Parker; but Garrison's following was negligible and the whole combined Northern support given to abolitionists was exceedingly small. Though this may be hard to realize, the word "abolitionist" in the antebellum North was comparable to the present word "communist" as a hate-word — a term of scorn, derision, and devastating disrepute. One who doubts this assertion may take the episode of the abolitionist debate among students at Lane Seminary in Cincinnati in 1834, resulting in a mass departure of students after their abolition society had been abolished by Seminary authorities. Gilbert Hobbs Barnes, authority in this field, quotes a contemporary Northern comment that "abolitionism was regarded as the climax of absurdity, fanaticism and blood." To be an abolitionist in antebellum days was to be without political influence and to be widely despised in the North.

J. G. RANDALL, *Lincoln and the South*

2. Show that the two following paragraphs are compound in the sense that each develops two topic ideas. Indicate the subtopic sentences.

1. Though Ford never contributes to charity and has been outspoken and even violent in his disapproval of it, he sometimes performs erratic acts of kindness. He is said to have given a stove to an old hermit whom he found living in the woods near Dearborn and to have celebrated the birthday of another old man whose threshing machine he had fixed in his youth by sending one of his trimoto-airplanes to take him out for a ride. And he has protected the birds on his place with a tenderness almost excessive, providing them with food in winter, building thousands of birdhouses for them and even on one occasion nailing his front door up so as not to disturb a robin that had nested over it. In his malevolent moods, on the other hand, he is capable of overturning his whole organization as if it were a house of blocks which a child pushes down in a rage because he thinks that the children with whom he is playing have taken the project out of his hands; and he is ready, on occasion, to dismiss his oldest and closest associates without a word of explanation or

warning. People innocently come back to their offices to discover that their departments have been abolished and that they themselves are no longer supposed to exist; they have found, in certain cases, their desks smashed to bits with an axe.

EDMUND WILSON, "DETROIT MOTORS," *The American Earthquake*

2. What is gamesmanship? Most difficult of questions to answer briefly. "The Art of Winning Games Without Actually Cheating" — that is my personal "working definition." What is its object? There have been five hundred books written on the subject of games. Five hundred books on play and the tactics of play. Not one on the art of winning. STEPHEN POTTER, *Gamesmanship*

3. Does the following paragraph have a topic sentence? If you think it does, indicate that sentence. If you think it does not, decide whether the absence of a topic statement is a fault and supply what you think would be a reasonable topic sentence.

Ask a toad what beauty is, the supreme beauty, the *to kalon*. He will tell you it is his lady toad with her two big round eyes coming out of her little head, her large flat snout, yellow belly, brown back. Interrogate a Negro from Guinea; for him beauty is a black, oily skin, sunken eyes, and flat nose.

VOLTAIRE, "BEAUTY," *The Philosophical Dictionary*

4. Choosing a topic connected with your school work, write a single paragraph, using several techniques of development, in which the topic statement is framed as a rhetorical question placed at or near the beginning of the paragraph.

5. Rewrite the paragraph you composed in exercise 4, this time without expressing the topic statement at all. Construct the paragraph so clearly that the reader will have no doubt of what the topic idea is. To check how well you have done ask a classmate to read the paper and, without your giving him any other clue, to compose a topic sentence for it.

6. Listed below are several topic sentences suitable for placing at the end of a paragraph. Compose a paragraph that leads naturally to one of them.

1. Chicago is a wonderful city.
2. I was now a full-fledged college student.
3. I hate dances.
4. The war was over.

7. Compose a paragraph using reasons, illustration, and restatement to support a topic of your own choice. Write a second paragraph on the same general subject, this time employing effects, comparison, and qualification.

14

DESCRIPTIVE AND NARRATIVE PARAGRAPHS

Introduction

According to the classification adopted in this book, description and narration are not varieties of expository writing. Rather they are first cousins, parallel to exposition in being kinds of informative writing. By any classification it must be acknowledged that description and narration deal with topics other than ideas and feelings. Descriptive and narrative writing, in short, present different problems than exposition, problems that are complicated and numerous enough to warrant a book devoted to them alone. But even though description and narration are technically outside the limits of this text, it is necessary to consider them, for the college writer must occasionally tell how something looks or narrate a simple story. Here, then, we shall discuss elementary techniques of descriptive and narrative composition, though what we shall say will be a short and sketchy introduction to an enormously complicated and endlessly fascinating aspect of the art of writing.

For the college student description is a more common writing problem than narration and consequently deserves most of our attention in this chapter. As a general term "description" means writing that attempts to convey a perceptual experience, that is, to translate into words an experience of the senses. Most often the sense involved will be sight, and probably 90 per cent of description deals with how things look to the eye. For convenience, therefore, we shall refer to the subject of description as being an object or scene existing in space. But it is possible to render other perceptions in words, and description may be of sounds (the next most common kind) or of taste, smell, and so on.

Whatever sense it deals with, descriptive writing is of two broad kinds, depending upon whether it is primarily about the object or about the writer's private awareness of that object and his response to it. In an immediate sense, of course, the subject of all description is not really the object (or whatever) as it actually exists in space, but rather the image of that object in the mind of the observer. We shall suppose, however, that this mental image corresponds more or less exactly with the reality. (The supposition is naïve, but the many problems that inhere in this matter belong to metaphysics and may safely be ignored by rhetoric.) Now, a writer may set aside all aspects of his perception that are peculiar to himself and concentrate simply on describing the object as it exists independent of his vision of it. This we shall call "objective" description. At the other extreme is "subjective" description, which occurs when a writer deliberately allows his own feelings and reactions to the object to enter into and color his language. In the first case the writer says, in effect, "This is how the thing really is"; in the second he says, "This is how it seems to me; this is my private vision of it, my feelings about it." Rather than being two separate categories, objective and subjective description represent two extremes on a continuum. Most actual descriptive writing reveals both types, but generally one or the other will dominate. In scientific and legal prose, for instance, objectivity is the great desideratum; in highly personal writing description is likely to be more subjective. What follows will clarify some of the differences between them.

Description

OBJECTIVE

Objective description often starts with a brief overview of the object. It then analyzes the object into its significant parts and discusses each in turn, following an order that reflects a principle of organization inherent in the object itself. While it is neither necessary nor universal, this method of developing an objective description is workable and usually efficient; the beginner would do well to follow it. A good example is this short student paragraph describing a lake in northern New England:

> In shape the lake resembles a gently curving S, its long axis lying almost duc north-south. The shoreline is ringed with rocks, rocks of all sizes from huge boulders to tiny pebbles — the detritus of the ice-age. Beyond the rocks the forest comes almost to the water's edge. Mostly pine and hemlock, it contains a few hardwoods

> — maple, oak, and birch. Here and there an old pine, its roots washed nearly clean of support, leans crazily over the water, seeming about to topple any instant. But it never does; trees fall this way for years.

Generally in objective description the point of view is impersonal, the writer avoiding any "I," "me," "my." The point of view, moreover, is likely to be of that special variety which in fiction is called "omniscient," allowing the writer to range about the object with complete freedom. In the preceding paragraph, for instance, we are not confined to any one angle of vision but move freely about the lake so as to comprehend it totally. In the first sentence we are above, seeing the lake as a bird might. In the following sentences we seem to be on the lake itself, looking shoreward. To effect these changes of vision the writer does not waste his time and ours explicitly directing us about. He does not say "As we leave the bird's-eye view and come down for a closer look, we observe that the shoreline is ringed with rocks . . ." Inexperienced writers are often overly explicit about changes in the angle of vision, a fault that leads to awkwardness and deadwood. In objective description an implicit use of the omniscient point of view is perfectly acceptable. Unless there is a particular reason for being obvious about it, you should feel free to move about the object without dragging your readers by the hand.

The movement, however, ought not to be at random. It should proceed according to a principle, preferably, as we have said, a principle inherent in the object itself, or at least one that seems natural under the circumstances. In the student paragraph, for example, we seem, once on the lake, to move progressively closer to shore. We see first the rocks, then the forest, then the various kinds of trees, and finally the old pine leaning over the water. The movement roughly follows a plan, and the plan roughly analyzes the visual experience of the lake into three parts: the lake as a whole, its shoreline, and the forest beyond.

The same technique of organizing the visual experience can be seen in the following sentence by Joseph Conrad. Here the angle of vision does not change, but the principle of organization is perfectly clear; the scene is organized from the near to the distant:

> Beyond the sea-wall there curves for miles in a vast and regular sweep the barren beach of shingle, with the village of Brenzett standing out darkly across the water, a spire in a clump of trees; and still further out the perpendicular column of a lighthouse, looking in the distance no bigger than a lead pencil, marks the vanishing point of the land. *Amy Foster*

The eye is taken successively outward through a series of receding planes: first the sea wall; then the beach (here we are allowed a lateral sweep before returning to the distant perspective); next a leap across water to the village, its spire, and trees; and finally the pencil of a lighthouse that marks the offing.

A more extended example of how objective description organizes vision is the following passage from Admiral Richard E. Byrd's account of his sojourn at the South Pole; he is describing the hut in which he spent several months:

> The day's work done, I took the luxury of a meditative inventory; and what I saw was good. The means of a secure and profound existence were all handy, in a world I could span in four strides going one way and in three strides going the other. It was not a bright world. The storm lantern hanging from a nail over my bunk burned dimly; and the gasoline pressure lamp, suspended from the ceiling, seemed to concentrate its brilliance all in one patch, making the shadows seem all the darker. But the dimness was rather to my liking. It gave depth to the room, and, somehow, made my possessions seem bigger.
>
> My bunk, fastened to the north wall, was about three feet off the floor, with the head flush against the eastern wall. At the foot of the bunk, on a small table, was the register, a glass-enclosed mechanism of revolving drum and pens which automatically recorded wind direction and velocity as reported by the wind vane and anemometer cups to which it was electrically connected. The dry cells powering the pens and driving the drum were racked underneath. Across the room, in the southeast corner, was a triangular shelf holding the main combination radio transmitter and receiver, with a key fastened near the edge. The transmitter was a neatly constructed, 50-watt, self-excited oscillator which Dyer had assembled himself, and which was powered by a 350-watt, gasoline-driven generator weighing only 35 pounds. The receiver was a superheterodyne of standard make. Above this shelf was a smaller one holding the emergency radio equipment, consisting of two 10-watt transmitters powered by hand-cranked generators, plus two small battery receivers, each good for about a hundred hours. These were stand-by equipment. And above this shelf was a still smaller shelf holding spare parts for the radio.
>
> The east wall, between the head of the bunk and the radio corner, was all shelves — six, to be exact. The lower ones were stocked with food, tools, books, and other odds and ends. On the top shelves were instruments and chronometers, all placed high and some wrapped in cotton. On the south wall my windproofs, fur

mukluks, parka, and pants hung drying from tenpenny nails. Pushed against the middle of the same wall was a food box on which was a portable victrola in a battered green case. The table was also the family board. On the floor in the southwest corner was a box which I called the ice box, since anything put into it would stay frozen. Among other things it then contained were two Virginia hams which my mother had sent me.

The stove was a foot or so out from the west wall, about midway between the door and the triple register. It was an ordinary two-lid, coal-burning caboose stove, except that this one had been converted into an oil-burner by fitting a round burner over the grate and rigging a three-gallon gravity tank to feed it. It burned Stoddard solvent, ranking midway between kerosene and gasoline among the petroleum distillates. A liquid fuel was chosen instead of coal because coal was too bulky to haul. From the stove the stack went straight up to within two feet of the ceiling, where it bent and ran along the wall before passing through a vent above the foot of the bunk. By carrying the pipe across the room in this way, we thought we were providing the equivalent of a radiator; but the scheme was a clumsy makeshift. Two or three pipe sections were lost on the trail, somewhere between Little America and Advance Base; and, the only reserve sections being of a different size, we had used empty five-gallon tins as joints, cut open at the ends to fit. Ingenious as they were, the connections were scarcely air tight. This crude, inoffensive-looking heating plant held for me the power of life and death. Innocent in every rude line, it would nearly kill me a few months hence. And the time would come when I should wonder how I could have been such a fool as not to see what was in plain sight for me to see.

Alone

In the first paragraph Admiral Byrd gives us a general view of a small, dimly lighted world. In the remainder of the passage he analyzes this world into its four walls (an analysis that is implicit in the subject). We stand in the middle of the room as he treats each wall in turn, moving from north to east to south to west, a progression that would seem natural to a sailor. His description is objective in the sense that he wishes to give us an accurate picture of the place where he lived. Assuming Admiral Byrd's readers were all competent draftsmen and had read the passage with equal care, it would be fair to suppose, in theory, that they would all draw much the same sketch of the shack at Antarctica, just as they would draw much the same picture of Conrad's sea view or the student's lake.

This kind of accuracy is especially important in scientific and legal writing. It is vital that a patent attorney, for instance, describe an invention precisely and objectively. For a scientist the ability to write clear objective description is equally necessary. A case in point is the following passage by Gilbert White, in which he describes a fresh water fish:

> The loach, in its general aspect, has a pellucid appearance: its back is mottled with irregular collections of small black dots, not reaching much below the *linea lateralis,* as are the back and tail fins: a black line runs from each eye down to the nose; its belly is of a silvery white; the upper jaw projects beyond the lower, and is surrounded with six feelers, three on each side; its pectoral fins are large, its ventral much smaller; the fin behind its anus small; its dorsal fin large, containing eight spines; its tail, where it joins to the tail-fin, remarkably broad, without any taperness, so as to be characteristic of this genus: the tail-fin is broad, and square at the end. From the breadth and muscular strength of the tail, it appears to be an active nimble fish.
>
> *The Natural History of Selborne,* "LETTER XVIII"

Precision is vital to this sort of scientific reporting. White, for example, says "six feelers, three on each side," not simply "a number of feelers"; he is careful to differentiate the fins by the proper technical terms: "pectoral," "ventral," "dorsal." He has the advantage, of course, of writing for a trained reader and, by using technical language, can achieve precision without sacrificing economy. Scientific description is easy to write, but exceedingly difficult to write well. Give enough time to observe it and sufficient training in biology to know what to observe, almost anyone can compose a reasonably accurate description of a fish. But it requires a special (and a very rare) talent to write a description that is both scientifically accurate and rhetorically effective. It is worth studying White's passage to see how he organizes it and how he gives a sense of vitality and movement to his prose by using short, direct clauses, with just enough variation in their syntax to avoid monotony.

SUBJECTIVE

In objective description the observer is a camera recording images precisely and impersonally. In subjective writing he becomes a participant in what he describes, not merely its recorder. He allows his own attitudes and values to color the scene and he projects back into it the feelings it has aroused in him. The subject is no longer a thing as it exists in space; it is this thing as it exists for the particular mind perceiving it at a particular time and from a particular angle.

Always in this kind of description the object creates an impression upon the viewer, and this impression is as much a part of the topic as the object itself. Sometimes the writer tells us explicitly what his feelings are. For example, the English poet Rupert Brooke, describing the skyline of lower Manhattan, says of the great buildings:

> Their strength, almost severity, of line and the lightness of their colour gave a kind of classical feeling, classical, and yet not of Europe. It had the air, this block of masonry, of edifices built to satisfy some faith, for more than immediate ends. Only, the faith was unfamiliar. But if these buildings embodied its nature, it is cold and hard and light, like the steel that is their heart. The first sight of these strange fanes has queer resemblances to the first sight of that lonely and secret group by Pisa's walls. It came upon me, at that moment, that they could not have been dreamed and made without some nobility. Perhaps the hour lent them sanctity. For I often have noticed since that in the early morning, and again for a little after sunset, the sky-scrapers are no longer merely the means and local convenience for men to pursue their purposes, but acquire that characteristic of the great buildings of the world, an existence and meaning of their own. *Letters from America*

Brooke tells us directly the impression made upon him by the massiveness of Manhattan, and his point of view is necessarily personal. Similarly, Nancy Mitford writes in the first person in reporting her reactions to the citizens of Moscow:

> I wandered about in the morning and looked at the streets and the people. All my visit I looked and looked at the people. They seem neither happier nor sadder than in the West, and neither more nor less worried than any town dweller. (People in towns are always preoccupied. "Have I missed the bus? Have I forgotten the potatoes? Can I get across the road?") But they appear stupid, what the French call *abruti*. What do they think? Perhaps they don't think very much, and yet they read enormously. I never saw such a country of readers — people sitting on benches, in the metro, etc., all read books (magazines seem not to exist); on the trains they have lending libraries. They are hideously ugly. Except for a few young officers, I never saw a handsome man; there seem to be no beautiful women. They have putty faces, like Malenkov. It is nonsense to speak of Asiatics, Mongol Hordes and so on — the pretty little Tartar guards at Lenin's tomb were the only people I saw with non-European cast of features. *The Water Beetle*

But while subjective description often states impression directly, it cannot rely upon such statement exclusively. The writer must anchor his description in the careful use of detail. The explicit statement of feeling merely directs and orders these details, telling us what to see in them. This reliance upon detail is important, for the purpose of subjective description is different from that of objective. The latter wants to make us see the object, accurately and dispassionately, as it is; the former wants to make us see in a personal way and ultimately to feel. The writer of subjective description attempts to arouse in us a feeling comparable to his own. To do it he has got to re-create the scene, not as it literally is but in a deliberately altered manner. He must select some details, ignore others; distort or exaggerate this image, underplay another; introduce comparisons and similes from outside the scene. In short, the visual image he creates is filtered through his own consciousness and by the process changed. It may be idealized, like a landscape by a romantic painter; it may be distorted into ugliness, like the reflection in a funhouse mirror. But as it is described, it is not quite what it would be to the eye. Such idealization or distortion is perfectly legitimate. The writer of subjective description signs no contract to deliver the literal truth. "Here," he says, "is how it seems to me." What he feels about the scene may reveal a higher truth than literal fidelity — as an artist's caricature often reveals an essential truth about his sitter — but his description makes no claim to scientific accuracy.

Now in order to convey that truth the writer must rely upon the details of the scene. He may tell us his feelings, as do Brooke and Miss Mitford, but this alone will not convince us. He must project these feelings back into the scene. Often, in fact, a writer will rely exclusively upon such projection, making no extended statement of feeling, but forcing the scene to speak for itself. Perhaps the simplest case is the catalogue description, in which the writer simply lists detail after detail. The following paragraph by John Peale Bishop is a good example. (He is describing Decatur Street in New Orleans.)

> The booths are Sicilian, hung with red peppers, draped with garlic, piled with fruit, trayed with vegetables, fresh and dried herbs. A huge man, fat as Silenus, daintily binds bunches for soup, while his wife quarters cabbages, ties smaller bundles of thyme, parsley, green onions, small hot peppers and sweet pimientos to season gumbos. Another Italian with white mustache, smiling fiercely from a tanned face, offers jars of green filé powder, unground allspice, pickled onions in vinegar. Carts and trucks flank the sidewalk; one walks through crates of curled parsley, scallions piled with ice, wagonloads of spinach with tender mauve stalks, moist baskets of crisp kale; sacks of white onions in oyster-white fishnet, pink onions in sacks of old rose; piles of eggplant with purple reflections,

> white garlic and long sea-green leeks with shredded roots, grey-white like witches' hair. Boxes of artichokes fit their leaves into a complicated pattern. Trucks from Happy Jack, Boothville and Buras have unloaded their oranges; a long red truck is selling cabbages, green peppers, squashes long and curled like the trumpets of Jericho. There is a more than Jordaens profusion, an abundance more glittering in color than Pourbus. A blue truck stands in sunlight, Negroes clambering over its sides, seven men in faded jeans, washing-blue overalls; the last over is a mulatto in a sweater of pure sapphire. A mangy cat steps across a roadway of crushed oranges and powdered oyster-shells. "NEW ORLEANS: DECATUR STREET"

Bishop piles up details in a rich profusion, overwhelming us with a sense of vitality and abundance. In writing of this sort it is impossible to overestimate the importance of specificity. The reader must be made to *see*, and the more precise the image the more likely it will prove an adequate stimulus. Notice how careful Bishop is to name colors: the "pink onions" in their sacks of "old rose," the spinach with its "mauve stalks," the "washing-blue overalls" of the men — all this makes the scene colorful in the literal sense of that overworked word.

There would seem to be little of the principle of selectivity we mentioned in Bishop's prose. But Bishop exercised selectivity in picking the scene. Like a skillful photographer, rather than retouch the photograph he chose his composition to reflect an impression. More often the writer of subjective description will re-create the scene so that only details conducive to his impression are included. Samuel Eliot Morison, for instance, draws a picture of idealized beauty in this imaginative re-creation of a clipper's return to Boston Harbor:

> A summer day with a sea-turn in the wind. The Grand Banks fog, rolling in wave after wave, is dissolved by the perfumed breath of New England hayfields into a gentle haze, that turns the State House dome to old gold, films brick walls with a soft patina, and sifts blue shadows among the foliage of the Common elms. Out of the mist in Massachusetts Bay comes riding a clipper ship, with the effortless speed of an albatross. Her proud commander keeps skysails and studdingsails set past Boston light. After the long voyage she is in the pink of condition. Paintwork is spotless, decks holystoned cream-white, shrouds freshly tarred, ratlines square. Viewed through a powerful glass, her seizings, flemish-eyes, splices, and pointings are the perfection of the old-time art of rigging. The chafing-gear has just been removed, leaving spars and shrouds immaculate. The boys touched up her skysail poles with white paint, as she crossed the Bay. Boom-ending her studdingsails and hauling

> a few points on the wind to shoot the Narrows, between Georges and Gallups and Lovells Islands, she pays off again through President Road, and comes booming up the stream, a sight so beautiful that even the lounging soldiers at the Castle, persistent baiters of passing crews, are dumb with wonder and admiration.
>
> *The Maritime History of Massachusetts, 1783–1860*

Professor Morison carefully controls his details. Everything suggests beauty and perfection: the air is "perfumed" and the haze "gentle," the State House dome gleams like "old gold" and the ship herself is "spotless," her deck "cream-white." Nothing ugly is allowed to intrude; there is no unsightly flotsam, no evil smell of rotting fish.

In both the foregoing cases the impressions carried by the details are generalized and not easily defined in a very precise way. More often the feelings conveyed in subjective description are relatively precise, in which event the selection of detail is even more important. Thomas Wolfe, for example, describes a modest home like this:

> On the outskirts of a little town upon a rise of land that swept back from the railway there was a tidy little cottage of white boards, trimmed vividly with green blinds. To one side of the house there was a garden neatly patterned with plots of growing vegetables, and an arbor for the grapes which ripened late in August. Before the house there were three mighty oaks which sheltered it in their clean and massive shade in summer, and to the other side there was a border of gay flowers. The whole place had an air of tidiness, thrift, and modest comfort. "THE FAR AND THE NEAR"

The last sentence sums up the scene and constitutes a kind of direct statement of feeling, as do such modifiers as "neatly," "clean," and "gay." But on the whole it is the details that count here in communicating a sense of middle-class fulfillment. As in Professor Morison's passage, nothing ugly is allowed to enter. If the lawn was disfigured here and there by crabgrass or a bit of litter, the fact is discreetly hidden.

Very different are the details (and the impression) in this description of another home by George Orwell; he is writing about the dwelling places of British miners:

> I found great variation in the houses I visited. Some were as decent as one could possibly expect in the circumstances, some were so appalling that I have no hope of describing them adequately. To begin with, the smell, the dominant and essential thing, is indescribable. But the squalor and the confusion! A tub full of filthy water here, a basin full of unwashed crocks there, more crocks piled

in any odd corner, torn newspaper littered everywhere, and in the middle always the same dreadful table covered with sticky oilcloth and crowded with cooking pots and irons and half-darned stockings and pieces of stale bread and bits of cheese wrapped round with greasy newspaper! And the congestion in a tiny room where getting from one side to the other is a complicated voyage between pieces of furniture, with a line of damp washing getting you in the face every time you move and the children as thick underfoot as toadstools! *The Road to Wigan Pier*

Sometimes a writer concentrates upon one or two details, which stand as symbols of the emotion he seeks to convey. In the following graphic description Alfred Kazin, for instance, projects his childhood despair at stuttering and being forced to attend a special school once a week:

It troubled me that I could speak in the fullness of my own voice only when I was alone on the streets, walking about. There was something unnatural about it; unbearably isolated. I was not like the others! At midday, every freshly shocking Monday noon, they sent me away to a speech clinic in a school in East New York, where I sat in a circle of lispers and cleft palates and foreign accents holding a mirror before my lips and rolling difficult sounds over and over. To be sent there in the full light of the opening week, when everyone else was at school or going about his business, made me feel as if I had been expelled from the great normal body of humanity. I would gobble down my lunch on my way to the speech clinic and rush back to the school in time to make up for the classes I had lost. One day, one unforgettable dread day, I stopped to catch my breath on a corner of Sutter Avenue, near the wholesale fruit markets, where an old drugstore rose up over a great flight of steps. In the window were dusty urns of colored water floating off iron chains; cardboard placards advertising hairnets, EX-LAX; a great illustrated medical chart headed THE HUMAN FACTORY, which showed the exact course a mouthful of food follows as it falls from chamber to chamber of the body. I hadn't meant to stop there at all, only to catch my breath; but I so hated the speech clinic that I thought I would delay my arrival for a few minutes by eating my lunch on the steps. When I took the sandwich out of my bag, two bitterly hard pieces of hard salami slipped out of my hand and fell through a grate onto a hill of dust below the steps. I remember how sickeningly vivid an odd thread of hair looked on the salami, as if my lunch were turning stiff with death. The factory whistles called their short, sharp blasts stark through the middle of noon, beating at me where I sat outside the city's magnetic circle. I had never known, I knew instantly I would never in my heart again submit to, such wild passive despair as I felt at that moment, sitting on the steps

> before THE HUMAN FACTORY, where little robots gathered and shoveled the food from chamber to chamber of the body. They had put me out into the streets, I thought to myself; with their mirrors and their everlasting pulling at me to imitate their effortless bright speech and their stupefaction that a boy could stammer and stumble on every other English word he carried in his head, they had put me out into the streets, had left me high and dry on the steps of that drugstore staring at the remains of my lunch turning black and grimy in the dust. *A Walker in the City*

In Kazin's description selection of detail is extremely important. The passage focuses down and down to sharpen finally on the two images of THE HUMAN FACTORY and the pieces of salami. Certainly Kazin tells us what his feelings were (he is even more explicit in this respect than Rupert Brooke). But he succeeds in communicating the despair of an alienated child because he projects and concentrates this feeling in the images of the salami with its "odd thread of hair . . . turning black and grimy in the dust," and the utter inhumanity of the little robots endlessly shoveling food from chamber to chamber of a body that has become a mere machine. In this world there seems little room for human values, for love or compassion or tender understanding.

In such passages as Kazin's we begin to transcend the limits of informative description and approach the imaginative re-creation of reality that is the special province of the creative writer. But Kazin's paragraph does demonstrate what rigid selection of detail can achieve. Especially it reveals the importance in all description of the "crystallizing image." The writer of description, we have said, must make his readers see. He cannot achieve this by mechanically listing every detail that falls within the visual field. He must seize upon relatively few. (Even in catalogue descriptions like that by Bishop, which seem to include everything, we are allowed to see only a small proportion of what actually exists to be seen.) These few details, however, must be rendered with such precision that the reader can see them vividly in his mind's eye. Since they are essential details, they will crystallize the scene, making it solid and real. To vary the analogy, we may say that writing description is something like developing a photograph. The writer, carefully choosing his images and transcribing them vividly, begins the process; the reader develops the rest in the fluid of his own experience. The point, then, to remember about using details is this: select only those which are essential to the impression you want to convey, but describe these precisely and concretely so that your reader can *see* them.

In addition to the selection and control of detail, subjective description also is likely to introduce comparisons, often in the form of metaphors and similes. In Bishop's paragraph about Decatur Street, for example, the proprietor is "fat as Silenus," the leeks "sea-green" with shredded roots "like witches' hair," and the squashes "long and curled like the trumpets of Jericho." In Professor Morison's passage, the clipper ship rides out of the mist "with the effortless speed of an albatross." W. Somerset Maugham makes metaphor an even more central device in the following paragraph. The Great Wall of China assumes a monstrous inhuman humanity, marching over and dominating the land:

> There in the mist, enormous, majestic, silent, and terrible, stood the Great Wall of China. Solitarily, with the indifference of nature herself, it crept up the mountain side and slipped down to the depth of the valley. Menacingly, the grim watch towers, stark and four-square, at due intervals stood at their posts. Ruthlessly, for it was built at the cost of a million lives and each one of those great grey stones has been stained with the bloody tears of the captive and the outcast, it forged its dark way through a sea of rugged mountains. Fearlessly, it went on its endless journey, league upon league to the furthermost regions of Asia, in utter solitude, mysterious like the great empire it guarded. There in the mist, enormous, majestic, silent, and terrible, stood the Great Wall of China.
>
> *On a Chinese Screen*

Still another example is this paragraph by H. M. Tomlinson describing an army of ants in the Amazonian jungle; Mr. Tomlinson sees in the ants something like a flowing stream:

> There were the sauba ants; they might engross all a man's hours, for in watching them he could easily forget there were other things in the world. They would move over the ground in an interminable procession. Looked at quickly, that column of fluid life seemed a narrow brook, its surface smothered with green leaves, which it carried, not round or under obstructions, but upwards and over them. Nearly every tiny creature in that stream of life held upright in its jaws a banner, much larger than itself, cut from a fresh leaf. It bore its banner along hurriedly and resolutely. All the ants carrying leaves moved in one direction. The flickering and forward movement of so many leaves gave the procession of ants the wavering appearance of shallow water running unevenly. On both sides of the column other ants hurried in the reverse direction, often stopping to communicate something with their antennae, to their burdened fellows. Two ants would stop momentarily, and there would be a swift intimation, and then away they would go again on their urgent affairs. We would see rapid conversations of that kind everywhere in the

> host. Other ants, with larger heads, kept moving hither and thither about the main body; having an eye on matters generally, I suppose, policing or superintending them. There was no doubt all those little fellows had a common purpose. There was no doubt they had made up their minds about it long since, had come to a decision communally, and that each of them knew his job and meant to get it done. There did not appear to be any ant favoured by the god of the ants. You have to cut your own leaf and get along with it, if you are a sauba. *The Sea and the Jungle*

Finally, the writer of subjective description may feed his reaction back into the scene by the distortion or exaggeration of specific details. Mark Twain was wonderfully adept at this sort of writing. In *Roughing It,* for example, he tells about a trip on an overland stage. The passengers have spent the night at a way station and Twain is describing the arrangements for cleaning up the next morning:

> By the door, inside, was fastened a small old-fashioned looking-glass frame, with two little fragments of the original mirror lodged down in one corner of it. This arrangement afforded a pleasant double-barreled portrait of you when you looked into it, with one half of your head set up a couple of inches above the other half. From the glass frame hung the half of a comb by a string — but if I had to describe that patriarch or die, I believe I would order some sample coffins. It had come down from Esau and Samson, and been accumulating hair ever since — along with certain impurities.

Then there is breakfast:

> There was only one cruet left, and that was a stopperless, fly-specked, broken-necked thing, with two inches of vinegar in it, and a dozen preserved flies with their heels up and looking sorry they had invested there.
>
> The station-keeper up-ended a disk of last week's bread, of the shape and size of an old-time cheese, and carved some slabs from it which were as good as Nicholson pavement, and tenderer.
>
> He sliced off a piece of bacon for each man, but only the experienced old hands made out to eat it, for it was condemned army bacon which the United States would not feed to its soldiers in the forts, and the stage company had bought it cheap for the sustenance of their passengers and employes. We may have found this condemned army bacon further out on the plains than the section I am locating it in, but we *found* it — there is no gainsaying that.
>
> Then he poured for us a beverage which he called "*Slumgullion,*" and it is hard to think he was not inspired when he named it. It really pretended to be tea, but there was too much dish-rag, and

> sand, and old bacon-rind in it to deceive the intelligent traveler. He had no sugar and no milk — not even a spoon to stir the ingredients with.

We are not supposed, of course, to take all this literally. Twain must be allowed the satirist's right to exaggerate, but his exaggeration is legitimate, for it leads us to see the essential truth about this Western hostel.

Thus in subjective description the writer tries, not simply to make us see, but to make us see in a certain way and thereby to react to the object or scene. He seeks to communicate to us (which in this case means arouse in us) much the same response that he himself experienced. He may do this by telling us directly what that response was. To assure effective communication, however, he must project his feelings into the scene. By carefully selecting, and even now and then exaggerating, the significant details and introducing appropriate comparisons, he re-creates the scene in such a way that it will necessarily evoke the proper response in a sensitive reader.

Narration

Narration is a more complex and subtle art than description, a fact which any representative collection of modern short stories demonstrates. We cannot be concerned here, however, with the subtleties of creating character and building a plot. Our interest is in only the most elementary type of narration. At this level the essential thing to realize is that a story consists of a series of episodes arranged in an order that reveals both their temporal and logical relationships. The writer of narration must first analyze his story into its parts and then in the actual telling organize these parts so as to open up what is significant in them. In this respect the writer of simple narrative is like the writer of subjective description, who first analyzes the scene and then presents it in a manner calculated to reveal its essential truth.

As with any analysis paragraph, the first step in writing narration is to organize. We can see how this has been done in the following modern fable by William March:

> *Aesop's Last Fable*
>
> Aesop, the messenger of King Croesus, finished his business with the Delphians and went back to the tavern where he had taken lodgings. Later, he came into the taproom where a group of Delphians were drinking. When they realized who he was, they crowded about him. "Tell us," they began, "is Croesus as rich as people say?"

Aesop, since the habit of speaking in fables was so strongly fixed in him, said, "I can best answer your question with a parable, and it is this: The animals gathered together to crown their richest member king. Each animal in turn stated what he possessed, and it was soon apparent that the lion had the largest hunting preserves, the bee the most honey, the squirrel the largest supply of acorns, and so on; but when the voting began, the difficulty of arriving at a decision was plain to all, for to the bee, the nuts that represented the wealth of the squirrel were of no consequence; to the lion, the hay that the zebra and the buffalo owned was worthless; and the panther and the tiger set no value at all on the river that the crane and crocodile prized so highly."

Then Aesop called for his drink, looking into the faces of the Delphians with good-natured amusement. He said, "The moral of the fable is this: Wealth is an intangible thing, and its meaning is not the same to all alike."

The stolid Delphians looked at one another, and when the silence was becoming noticeable, one of them tried again: "How was the weather in Lydia when you left home?"

"I can best answer that question with another fable," said Aesop, "and it is this: During a rain storm, when the ditches were flooded and the ponds had overflowed their banks, a cat and a duck met on the road, and, wanting to make conversation they spoke at the same instant. 'What a beautiful day this is,' said the delighted duck. 'What terrible weather we're having,' said the disgusted cat."

Again the Delphians looked at one another, and again there was silence. "The moral of that tale," said Aesop, "is this: What pleases a duck distresses a cat." He poured wine into his glass and leaned against the wall, well satisfied with the start he had made in instructing the barbarous Delphians.

The Delphians moved uneasily in their seats, and after a long time, one of them said, "How long are you going to be here?"

"That," said Aesop, "can best be answered in the Fable of the Tortoise, the Pelican, and the Wolf. You see, the pelican went to visit his friend the tortoise and promised to remain as long as the latter was building his new house. Then one day as they were working together, with the tortoise burrowing and the pelican carrying away the dirt in his pouch, the wolf came on them unexpectedly, and —"

But Aesop got no farther, for the Delphians had surrounded him and were, an instant later, carrying him toward the edge of the cliff on which the tavern was built. When they reached it, they swung him outward and turned him loose, and Aesop was hurled to the rocks below, where he died. "The moral of what we have done," they explained later, "is so obvious that it needs no elaboration."

Ninety-nine Fables

These nine paragraphs are put together like a three-act play. The first act comprises the first three paragraphs; the second act, paragraphs four through six; and the third, paragraphs seven through nine. Each act follows the same pattern of question, fable, and moral application. The second act is tied to the first by its initial clause, which tells the reaction of the Delphians to the first fable; and the third act is linked to the second by beginning with a similar statement of reaction: "The Delphians moved uneasily in their seats."

But the acts do more than repeat a pattern; they vary it slightly and thereby thrust forward the action to its climax. The reactions of the Delphians, for example, are not quite identical. After the first fable they merely look at one another; after the second they stir uneasily; and during the third — ! Similarly, the silences grow longer and, by implication, more ominous, though the smug Aesop is oblivious to the warning. And even the questions change in a significant direction; the first two are mere polite conversation-makers, but the third is pregnant with possibilities. By showing us these changes Mr. March implies the meaning of his story. He wittily twists the moral tag that was traditional at the end of the ancient fable and, using it to announce that he will not announce the moral, he pokes sophisticated fun at the sententiousness of the Aesopian tale.

Most inexperienced tellers of stories have trouble with this matter of meaning. Either, like poor Aesop, they labor the obvious, or else they fail to reveal any meaning at all. In the latter event the narrative degenerates into a dreary recital of facts having no more point than a series of numbers randomly set down upon a page. Meaning does not have to consist of a specific philosophical or ethical truth as in the theme of a literary work. In simple narrative it may be only a generalized attitude or feeling. But meaning of some sort there must be. "What I Did Last Tuesday" is an empty catalogue of trivialities unless it adds up to something like "I had a wonderful, exciting day" or "I had a terrible day when everything went wrong" or "I had a dull and uneventful day."

The meaning of his story ought to be clear to a writer before he starts to tell it. He needs always to ask himself as a preliminary step to writing: "What is it that I want to make clear?" Only then can he analyze his story into its significant parts and arrange these into a pattern that will lead the reader to the proper interpretation. With narration as with subjective description, it is ultimately the details that must carry the point. It is all right to tell your readers "this is what I mean," but telling them is not an adequate substitute for *showing* them.

Summary

Description is translating a perceptual experience (usually but not necessarily visual) into words. In objective description the writer uses words impersonally to denote how the scene or object exists in space, and he excludes any purely private attitudes. Subjective description endows the visual experience with an emotional charge, and arouses in the reader an affective state comparable to what the writer experienced. The writer of subjective description allows his personal feelings to enter in, either by directly stating them or by projecting them back into the scene through selecting, idealizing, or distorting details and through introducing comparisons, especially in the form of metaphors and similes. Narration means telling a story. At an elementary level good narrative writing requires (1) knowing what the meaning of the story is before you start to tell it, (2) analyzing the story into its episodes according to that meaning, and (3) presenting the episodes to the reader in a way that will enable him to discern the meaning for himself.

Exercises

1. As Joseph Conrad did in the sentence quoted on page 227, describe a panoramic view in a single sentence. You may organize the view from the near to the far or the other way round, from right to left or from left to right. The important thing is to compose the sentence so that the view *is* organized and to do it implicitly without such heavy-handed obviousness as "Moving our eyes a few feet to the right, we are able to make out . . ."

2. Describe your classroom, or your room at home, much as Admiral Byrd did with his shack at Antarctica. Try to make the reader see the room so clearly that he could draw an accurate plan. Despite its apparent simplicity, this assignment is not easy to write. Unless you vary sentence style a little and prune all deadwood, it will be dull, dull to write and dull to read.

3. Describe with as much literal accuracy as you can a plant, flower, insect, or fish. Even though your teacher may not be familiar with them, you should feel free to employ appropriate scientific terms. If you are not knowledgeable enough about any science to handle one of the topics suggested above, attempt an equally objective and precise description of a piece of furniture, a tool, an item of sports equipment, a dress or other article of clothing.

4. Catalogue description like that by John Peale Bishop on page 232 is fun to write if you enter into the spirit of the thing. Go to a department of your supermarket, or to a hardware store, a bakery, or a toy shop and describe what

you see. Learn the names of things. Do not say simply "cheeses," but "Edam and Camembert and Gorgonzola"; tell the colors and shapes and sizes. Behind all of this there should be a general implicit impression, even if nothing more than a sense of the beauty or variety or profusion of the articles on display.

5. This exercise requires two separate paragraphs (each complete in itself) describing similar objects or scenes. The first, like the paragraphs by Thomas Wolfe or Professor Morison, is to idealize the object; the second, like Orwell's description of the miner's house, to show an ugly or dilapidated version of something comparable. A number of topics are possible — two neighborhoods in the same city, or two towns of the same size but very different atmospheres, two automobiles, two different cellars, playrooms, bars, or restaurants. Attempt in both paragraphs to introduce metaphors and similes that help you to convey your impression.

6. Mark Twain is a discouraging writer to imitate. If you feel daring, try your hand at an exaggerated description of a hotel you have stayed in, a tourist attraction you have visited, a boarding house you have eaten in. You are free to exaggerate and distort, but the distortions must reveal an essential truth.

7. Quoted below is part of a paragraph by Virginia Woolf describing a painting by the English artist Walter Sickert. Study it and write a similar description of one of these paintings (or any other your teacher may suggest): *Pope Leo X* by Velázquez, *The Card Players* by Cézanne, *Gulf Stream* by Winslow Homer, *Guernica* by Picasso, *Gin Lane* by Hogarth. (If your library has copies of Sickert's work, try to find the painting Mrs. Woolf describes. Comparing her description with the actual painting will enable you to see what she has done.) Use any of the techniques of subjective description we have discussed:

> You remember the picture of the old publican, with his glass on the table before him and a cigar gone cold at his lips, looking out of his shrewd little pig's eyes at the intolerable wastes of desolation in front of him? A fat woman lounges, her arm on a cheap yellow chest of drawers, behind him. It is all over with them, one feels. The accumulated weariness of innumerable days has discharged its burden on them. They are buried under an avalanche of rubbish. In the street beneath, the trams are squeaking, children are shrieking. Even now somebody is tapping his glass impatiently on the bar counter. She will have to bestir herself; to pull her heavy, indolent body together and go and serve him. The grimness of that situation lies in the fact that there is no crisis; dull minutes are mounting, old matches are accumulating and dirty glasses and dead cigars; still on they must go, up they must get.
>
> "WALTER SICKERT," *The Captain's Death Bed and Other Essays*

8. What *did* you do last Tuesday? Write a narrative essay explaining your activities. Give it a point and make it interesting, neither of which is easy to do.

IV
THE SENTENCE

"A sentence and a worm," wrote the English critic T. E. Hulme, "are the most stupid of animals and the most difficult to teach tricks." At times sentences do seem to oppose the writer's will with an almost human obstinancy. To change the metaphor we may say that sentences are the channels in which our thought must run. While there are many, many channels (English syntax is complex and varied), one channel or another the writer must choose; for our thought can travel only in the lines which the conventions of syntax have dug out. The trick is to learn the system of these trenches so as to avoid the dead ends and the meandering twisting loops that carry one round and round and finally deposit him where he came in. To return to Hulme's metaphor, the problem is to learn which tricks the sentence can be taught and which it cannot.

That, broadly, is what we shall attempt in this section. Beginning with a general discussion of the types of sentences available to the expository writer, we shall turn to examine the four cardinal virtues of the sentence: concision, emphasis, clarity, and shape. We shall conclude the section with three chapters that deal with more mundane matters: grammar and punctuation.

15
TYPES OF SENTENCES

Grammatical Types

It is possible to classify sentences in different ways depending upon what characteristics are selected as important. For our purposes in this chapter, however, it will be enough if we distinguish two ways of classifying sentences — the first on the basis of the number and type of clauses the sentence contains; the second on the basis of whether sentences have one idea or several and, if they have several, of what means they employ to hold these different ideas together.

The first method of classification gives three basic types of sentence: the simple, the compound, and the complex. (A fourth variety, the compound-complex, is not a basic type, but rather an amalgam of the latter two.) While it is elementary and probably already familiar to you, this classification of sentences is still important. Much of what we shall say in this and the following chapters about the rhetoric of sentences will assume that you know what simple and compound and complex sentences are. For that reason we need briefly to define these terms.

A simple sentence is one that contains one subject-finite verb connection. (For convenience we shall call such a connection by its technical name of "nexus.") Thus "The boy went home" is a simple sentence. A sentence may have several subjects and several verbs and yet remain simple so long as these subjects and verbs constitute only one nexus. This sentence, for instance, is simple: "The books, papers, and cards were scattered about the desk and seemed to be in no order at all." It has three subjects ("books, papers, and cards") and two verbs ("were scattered . . . and seemed"), but these six words form only one connection:

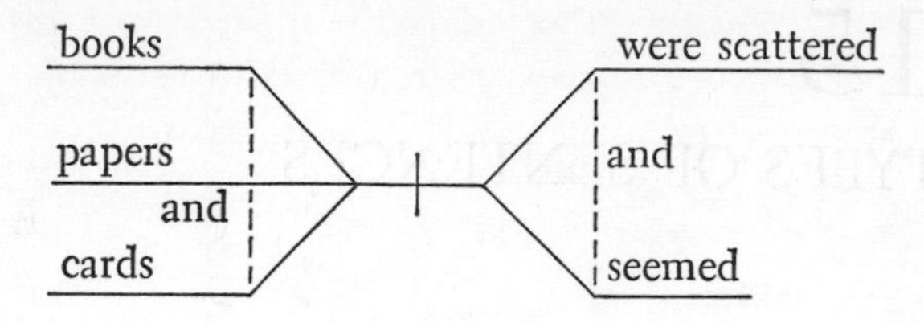

As this example suggests, grammatically simple sentences may become stylistically complicated, especially when the writer uses parallelism to pile up several subjects and predicates. As a rule, however, sentences that are simple in the grammatical sense are also simple in the stylistic sense. Usually they are short emphatic sentences, moving straight forward with few pauses or interruptions. They have very real virtues for the writer as well as severe limitations. But these stylistic applications we shall discuss later in the chapter.

The second basic type of sentence is the compound. Compound sentences have at least two nexus, both independent. (An independent nexus is a subject-finite verb connection that does not form part of a subordinate clause, that is, of a clause acting as an adjective, adverb, or noun.) The sentence "Harry has already left school, and he took the books with him," is compound because it contains two subject-verb relationships—"Harry has left" and "he took"—and both are independent. Similarly "John went to town and his sister went with him" is compound. The verbs in this case are both "went," but they are two different statements of the same word and hence from a grammatical point of view are two verbs, each with its own subject. "John and his sister went to town," however, is a simple sentence because now one verb is made to serve both subjects.

While our examples of compound sentences have shown only two nexus, there is no theoretical limit to how many independent nexus a compound sentence may contain. But in practice three independent subject-verb relationships are likely to be as many as one can conveniently handle without overloading the sentence. This, too, is a matter of style, better postponed for a few pages.

Whether the compound sentence consists of two or of several nexus, it is possible to join them in two different ways. The first is to use co-ordinating conjunctions, such as *and, but, for, or, nor, yet,* and the correlatives *either . . . or, neither . . . nor, both . . . and, not only . . . but* (*also*). Compound sentences employing these words are called co-ordinated sentences, as in "The party was very nice, but we were tired and we decided to leave a little early." On the other hand, the independent clauses comprising a compound sentence may be butted together with no co-ordinating word between them, a technique that is called parataxis. Accordingly, such a construction is called a paratactic compound sentence. An example is: "The sky was rapidly darkening; the wind was rising; a heavy sea appeared to be making up." Independent clauses joined paratactically are conventionally punctuated by placing a stop of some sort between them. Usually the stop is a semicolon, although under special circumstances it may be a colon or a dash or a comma. Later on we shall examine the punctuation of paratactic clauses; for the moment it is probably best if you simply remember to place a semicolon between independent clauses that are not joined by a co-ordinating conjunction.

The third basic type of sentence is the complex sentence, which contains one independent nexus and at least one dependent nexus. (A dependent nexus is a connection between a subject and a finite verb that is part of an adjective, adverbial, or noun clause.) "John lost the book simply because he was careless," for example, is a complex sentence. The independent nexus is "John lost"; the dependent, "he was." Usually the dependent clause in a complex sentence will be joined to the main clause by some sort of relative word or subordinating conjunction (*that, which, who, when, where, how, why, if, whether, than, as, since, because, although, though,* and so on). However, a dependent nexus may be in the form of a contact clause with no conjunctive word, as in "He said he would go," where "he would go" constitutes a noun clause acting as the direct object of "said." Such constructions are just as much complex sentences as "Although it was late, he decided to stay" or "I'll ask whomever I please."

Complex sentences are capable of a high degree of refinement. Skilled writers can weave seven, eight, or more dependent clauses around one main clause, thus creating a tightly structured and richly meaningful sentence. For the kind of writing you are expected to do in college, the complex sentence is the most important of the three basic types. In a very real sense, learning to write good expository prose is learning to write complex sentences.

There is one last type of sentence — the compound-complex. This is not a basic type, but, as its name implies, a combination of the compound and complex varieties. It must have at least two independent nexus and at least one dependent, as in "It was early evening but although the moon was already out the sky was still light." The independent nexus are "It was" and "the sky was"; the dependent is "the moon was." These are, of course, minimum requirements, and in theory the compound-complex sentence can have an infinite number of each type of clause. But in practice there is always a sharp limitation to how many of either it may contain without growing so complicated and formless that it ceases to communicate.

Grammatically classified, then, sentences are simple, compound, complex, and compound-complex. The first contains one independent clause and is usually stylistically as well as grammatically simple. The second has at least two independent clauses, which may be joined either by coordination or by parataxis. A complex sentence contains one independent and at least one dependent clause, while a compound-complex has a minimum of two independent clauses and one dependent.

Segregating and Aggregating Sentences

A second way of classifying sentences is in terms of the number of ideas they contain. Very broadly, we can distinguish between sentences that contain only one "idea," which are called segregating sentences, and those that bring together several "ideas," which are called aggregating. Thus the sentences in the following passage are segregating because each states one and only one of the basic ideas in the description:

> The night was dark. The moon slipped in and out of the clouds. In the woods an owl hooted softly.

In an aggregating style, on the other hand, these separate sentences would be combined into one more complicated construction, for instance:

> The night was dark and the moon slipped in and out of the clouds, while in the woods an owl hooted softly.

Although it is quite old and still useful, the classification of sentences into segregating and aggregating types is not very scientific, because it is exceedingly difficult to decide what an "idea" is and where to draw the line between one idea and two. But even if the distinction is not very clear philosophically and even if it is oversimple, it works well enough from the point of view of rhetoric, enabling us to differentiate and to study important differences in sentence style.

In pursuing that study we shall make two important assumptions. The first is easily stated: we take for granted that none of the kinds of sentence we shall discuss is inherently better than any other. Each has advantages and limitations. Our purpose is not to praise one above another, but to show what functions each is suited to. The second assumption requires a little more explanation. Briefly put it is this: sentence style has a communicative effect of its own, an effect that, while it is closely related to the meanings of the words in the sentence, is none the less distinct from those meanings. To put the point another way: the total meaning of a sentence is more than the sum of the meanings of the individual words composing it. The same words arranged in a different sentence style would not say exactly the same thing. We have in mind here more than the obvious differences that result from changing the subject from one word to another, or from making a clause the main element in this sentence and a subordinate construction in that. Such changes in syntax obviously alter meaning. What we are concerned with are more subtle differences of style. The sentence:

> The night was dark and the moon slipped in and out of the clouds, while in the woods an owl hooted softly

is *not* merely another way of saying what was said by the same words arranged in three sentences. Its meaning is different. The difference is subtle, but such subtleties are important. Indeed, nuances are vital to good prose. As we talk more specifically and practically about the various sentence styles, you will see more clearly how style enters into meaning. For the moment, take our word that it does — that the exact same thing cannot be said in different types of sentences even though the words are identical.

The Segregating Sentence

The segregating sentence, we have said, contains one "idea" and is usually short and simple, in both the grammatical and the stylistic sense of that term. It may be used in the company of other segregating sentences — which constitutes a segregating style — or it may be used singly in the context of longer, more complicated constructions. Let us look first at the segregating style.

Such a style is commonly associated with childish writing or with writing for children: "John has the ball. John throws the ball. See John run." So common, in fact, is the association between children and the segregating style that it is sometimes referred to as the "primer style," and college students are warned against falling into this kind of juvenile, unvaried sentence pattern. However, in the hands of an experienced writer the segregating style may be employed for serious purposes with great effect.

For example, the British essayist Beverly Nichols once interviewed the novelist Philip Guedalla and described Guedalla's method of writing like this:

> He writes, at most, 750 words a day. He writes and re-writes. He polishes and re-polishes. He works in solitude. He works with agony. He works with sweat. And that is the only way to work at all.
>
> "PHILIP GUEDALLA," *Are They the Same at Home?*

These short, repetitive sentences are as strong and as monotonous as a hammer on an anvil. The monotony is perhaps more to the point than the strength. Mr. Nichols suggests that writing is often a dull, weary business. In part, of course, the monotony is conveyed by the repetition of words — "writes" is repeated three times, "works" four times, "he" six, and "polishes" twice. But fully as important as the repetition of words is the iteration of the short, simple sentence pattern. If anything, it contributes even more to the feeling of monotony. It is a dangerous business to suggest dullness in one's sentence style; but Mr. Nichols gets away with it. The very skill with which he implies monotony makes his own sentences interesting. The passage is a good example of how the segregating style may be used to reflect and reinforce an idea.

Another example of the effective use of the segregating style is the following passage by the historian Thomas Babington Macaulay. Macaulay is describing the schemes of unscrupulous politicians to manipulate the dying Spanish king, Charles II, and to seize control of the unstable government:

> The next object was to get rid of the ministers. Madrid was supplied with provisions by a monopoly. The Government looked after this most delicate concern as it looked after everything else. The partisans of the House of Bourbon took advantage of the negligence of the administration. On a sudden the supply of food failed. Exorbitant prices were demanded. The people rose. The royal residence was surrounded by an immense multitude. The Queen harangued them. The priests exhibited the host. All was in vain. It was necessary to awaken the King from his uneasy sleep, and to carry him to the balcony. There a solemn promise was given that the unpopular advisers of the Crown should be forthwith dismissed. The mob left the palace and proceeded to pull down the houses of the ministers. The adherents of the Austrian line were thus driven from power, and the government was intrusted to the creatures of Porto Carrero [the Archbishop of Toledo, who had inspired the uprising as a way of forcing his enemies out of office].
>
> "THE WAR OF THE SUCCESSION IN SPAIN,"
> *Critical and Historical Essays*

Macaulay employs the segregating style for narration, where it is not uncommon. His short sentences neatly analyze a complex action into its separate episodes: the failure of the food supply, the rise in prices, the popular rebellion, the descent upon the palace, the vain haranguing by the Queen and the priests. Not only do they analyze the event; the staccato sentences also create a sense of the rush and violence of this manufactured crisis and so enable Macaulay to build to a climax. With that climax — the King's being carried to the balcony — the sentences grow a little longer and somewhat less breathless, and the change indicates that the conflict has been resolved. The drama is over and the pace abates.

A final example of the segregating style, again used for narration, shows what a modern writer can do with it. W. Somerset Maugham is describing a criminal in China being marched to his place of execution:

> The judge and the vice-consul rose and walked to the gateway, where their chairs awaited them. Here stood the criminal with his guard. Notwithstanding his tied hands he smoked a cigarette. A squad of little soldiers had been sheltering themselves under the overhanging roof, and on the appearance of the judge the officer in charge made them form up. The judge and the vice-consul settled themselves in their chairs. The officer gave an order and the squad stepped out. A couple of yards behind them walked the criminal. Then came the judge in his chair and finally the vice-consul.
>
> "THE VICE-CONSUL," *On a Chinese Screen*

This is not so pure an instance of the segregating style as the passages by Nichols and Macaulay. Of its eight sentences, one is complex, three are compound, and only half are simple; and of these four at least two contain two "ideas." Even so, the sentences *are* relatively short and uncomplicated; four of them *are* grammatically simple, and none of the others is a really long, intricate sentence. It is justifiable to treat this as a case of the segregating style. Because of his greater variation, Mr. Maugham's sentences suggest none of the urgency or excitement of Macaulay's or the monotony of Mr. Nichols's. Rather their impression is of a conscious, controlled objectivity, as if the writer were a scientist or a careful, conscientious reporter. Mr. Maugham has used the segregating style to make us see as clearly as possible. The sentences break the scene into a series of still-lifes perfectly arranged. Thus the sentence style enables us to view the scene as Mr. Maugham sees it — from a detached and critical angle. This does not mean that Mr. Maugham is callous; simply that he allows the scene to speak for itself.

In these examples we have seen at least a few of the effects which the segregating style can achieve. Obviously it is a difficult style to maintain for any length of time. Even the examples we have shown are not typical of the sentence patterns in the works in which they occur. They do demonstrate, however, that the segregating sentence may be more than the primer style. It is effective in telling stories, especially when the emphasis is upon the raw facts of action and the writer wishes to suggest speed and violence. It is effective in description, when the writer wants to dissect a scene or an object into its parts and present them serially. It is certainly not the only way in which stories may be told or scenes described. But the segregating style is one way, and, given the purposes of Macaulay or Somerset Maugham, it is the best way.

For the sort of writing you are likely to be doing in a composition course, however, the segregating style is less useful. You are more likely to be treating ideas than describing riots, and the segregating style is not a good style for handling ideas. It does not allow the writer to convey complex relationships of cause and effect, or to suggest subtleties of qualification and contradiction. Its very strength and emphasis make it unsuitable for establishing the nuances of tone that are so important in exposition.

But if the segregating style is not so useful for the expository writer, the isolated segregating sentence may be very useful indeed. Set in the context of longer, more complicated constructions, a single brief sentence can prove extremely effective. G. K. Chesterton, for instance, gets more out of the final three words of this passage by treating them as a separate sentence:

> I placed myself comfortably in the London cab and told the London driver to drive me to the other end of Hertfordshire. And he did. "A CAB RIDE ACROSS COUNTRY," *Tremendous Trifles*

Dylan Thomas uses the isolated segregating sentence with equal effect at the end of the following paragraph, the opening of an essay called "Welsh Poets":

> The position — if poets must have positions, other than upright — of the poet born in Wales or of Welsh parentage and writing his poems in English is today made by many people unnecessarily, and trivially, difficult. There are a number of young Welshmen writing poems in English who, insisting passionately that they are Welshmen, should by rights be writing in Welsh, but who, unable to write in Welsh or reluctant to do so because of the uncommercial nature of the language, often give the impression that their writing

> in English is only condescension to the influence and ubiquity of a tyrannous foreign tongue. I do not belong to that number.
>
> "WELSH POETS," *Quite Early One Morning*

The real point of Thomas's paragraph is not revealed until we come to the very end, and of course the point gains a good deal of emphasis from being so unnaturally delayed. But part of its strength is also due to its being expressed in the only simple sentence in the paragraph and in much the briefest (the sentence before it contains 69 words).

It is interesting to compare with Thomas's paragraph this passage from a freshman composition:

> Some of us make a real chore of studying for examinations. The last night before the exam we sit down and cram for ten or twelve hours and probably we learn nothing.

The contrast that is so strong in the final sentence of Thomas's paragraph, is here obscured because of the writer's failure to use sentence structure to reinforce the difference between the effort and the result. Had the "and" been dropped and the last clause treated as a separate sentence, the futility of cramming — which is the point of the passage — would have been more effectively conveyed: "Probably we learn nothing." As it is, the writer almost throws his point away.

The segregating sentence is not only strong; it is also clear, always a virtue in a topic sentence, whether it comes at the end of the paragraph as in Thomas's or more conventionally at the beginning. E. B. White, for example, opens a paragraph with this simple statement: "There are three New Yorks," thus setting up an analysis paragraph. An initial segregating sentence is also used effectively to state the topic in this brief paragraph by the American historian Bruce Catton:

> We Americans are a very fortunate people. Nothing really bad has ever happened to us. Our remote ancestors braved the cold gray Atlantic, got to these shores, and found that life could begin anew. They shot a number of Indians, cut down a great many trees, and then began to build for themselves a new world, in which the ancient ideal of human brotherhood actually was something visible, something attainable, something that one's own children could inhabit if everything went well.
>
> "THE TRAGIC STRUCTURE OF THE CIVIL WAR," *Thought*, XXXV, SPRING 1960

The opening segregating sentences that state and restate the topic are so clear that even the dullest reader can be in no doubt of Mr. Catton's topic.

It is worth noticing, too, that the short statements at the beginning of this paragraph start a progression from a simple sentence structure to a more complicated, a progression that reaches its climax in the relatively long complex sentence that completes the paragraph.

Just as it is well suited to stating the topic, so the initial segregating sentence may be used to make a transition. In his essay "Highbrow, Lowbrow, Middlebrow," for instance, Russel Lynes links the section on lowbrows to the preceding section on the highbrow with this brief sentence: "The highbrow's friend is the lowbrow."

The isolated segregating sentence, then, if not the segregating style, is valuable to the expository writer when forcefulness and lucidity are cardinal considerations. It is especially useful in topic sentences and in transitions, in emphatic restatements within the paragraph, and, less commonly, in closing sentences. It is exceedingly difficult to write exposition effectively in segregating sentences for any length of time. But it is equally true that it is difficult to write well for any length of time without using a segregating sentence now and then. If for no other reason, short sentences should be called upon to break up the monotony of longer constructions. The able writer, however, will employ them for more than this. He will make the segregating sentence do double duty, using it not only to vary the rhythm and movement of his style but at the same time to emphasize an important point.

Aggregating Sentences

Unlike the segregating sentence, which places one idea in one sentence, the aggregating sentence brings several ideas together within the same unit. At its simplest the aggregating sentence contains two separate statements; in its most developed form it can combine twenty or thirty. Depending upon how they hold these ideas together, aggregating sentences may be classified into three basic types: the first is the freight-train sentence, which utilizes the technique of co-ordination or of parataxis; the second is the parallel sentence, which uses syntactic parallelism; and the third is the subordinate sentence, which relies upon grammatical subordination. There is another variety of aggregating sentence sometimes called the encapsulating, or (our preference) the convoluted sentence; we shall list this as a fourth type, though in fact it is really a variation of the subordinate sentence. No one of these varieties is inherently better than the others; each will prove to have advantages and limitations. Our task is to understand what each can do.

THE FREIGHT-TRAIN SENTENCE

The simplest type of aggregating sentence is the multiple co-ordinate, or as it is known in its longer varieties, the freight-train sentence. Of all the aggregating sentences, it is closest in syntax and in spirit to the segregating construction. It consists of at least two, and often of many more, independent clauses. These clauses may be linked by co-ordinating conjunctions like *but, for, or, nor, yet* — and most frequently — *and;* or they may be arranged paratactically, separated simply by stops — usually semicolons, though sometimes colons, dashes, or commas.

The freight-train sentence has several virtues. For one thing, it is useful when the writer wishes to suggest a sense of equal multiplicity, that is, to convey a series of events, ideas, impressions, or perceptions without making any judgment of their relative value. This kind of uncritical, immediate acceptance of the world is often how children see reality, and authors writing for children or trying to re-create the vision of childhood not infrequently use the freight-train style. Kenneth Grahame, for instance, tries to suggest the child's world in sentences like these:

> And I'll look out for you, and you'll sing out as soon as you see me. And we'll go down the street arm in arm, and into all the shops, and then I'll choose my house, and you'll choose your house, and we'll live there like princes and good fellows. *The Golden Age*

Not only in childlike literature, but sometimes in more adult prose the same desire to convey reality as immediately and as uncritically as possible leads a writer to select the freight-train style, as in the following passage by Ernest Hemingway, in which the hero of *A Farewell to Arms* escapes from the dull business of war by dreaming of a romantic adventure with the heroine, Catherine Barkley:

> Maybe she would pretend that I was her boy that was killed and we would go in the front door and the porter would take off his cap and I would stop at the concierge's desk and ask for the key and she would stand by the elevator and then we would get in the elevator and it would go up very slowly clicking at all the floors and then our floor and the boy would open the door and stand there and she would step out and I would step out and we would walk down the hall and I would put the key in the door and open it and go in

> and then take down the telephone and ask them to send a bottle of capri bianca in a silver bucket full of ice and you would hear the ice against the pail coming down the corridor and the boy would knock and I would say leave it outside the door please.

An even more striking case of how the freight-train style can suggest the immediacy of experience is the following sentence, taken from an interview with a British seaman, a survivor of a dive-bombing attack that sank his freighter in the early days of World War II. The sailor is describing the onrush of the German plane:

> . . . you're standing there, and you can feel the sweat running down the back of your knees, and he gets closer and closer and you can see those horrible splashes of the bullets as they come across the water and go whipping across the deck . . .
>
> "DIVE BOMBER," *The Oxford Book of English Talk*

There is a good deal in the diction of this passage to suggest fear — the word "horrible," for instance, or the image "sweat running down the back of your knees." But quite apart from words, the sentence structure also contributes to the feeling of terror. The simple repetitive addition of "and . . . and . . . and" implies a mind that, like a camera, can do nothing but record images; fear has made it incapable of imposing any kind of order upon experience, it can only register raw perception. Thus the very style suggests a kind of paralysis. The speaker is too terrified to move, and there is, in any case, no place to move to. If a rabbit, immobilized by the onrushing lights and roar of a massive truck, were gifted with speech and able to describe his reaction, we feel it would be some such sentence pattern as this he would choose.

The refusal, or the inability, to distinguish degrees of importance are essential to what Hemingway and the British sailor want to say. Virginia Woolf, on the other hand, employs a similar style ironically, as a way of criticizing an eighteenth-century diarist who was incapable of recording anything more about the Paris of 1765 than the routine impressions of a provincial British tourist:

> That is what he writes about, and, of course, about the habits of the natives. The habits of the natives are disgusting; the women hawk on the floor; the forks are dirty; the trees are poor, the Pont Neuf is not a patch on London Bridge; the cows are skinny; morals are licentious; polish is good; cabbages cost so much; bread is made of coarse flour . . .
>
> "ALL ABOUT BOOKS," *The Captain's Death Bed and Other Essays*

The freight-train style, which is a positive element in Hemingway, here serves the negative purpose of satire. By hooking detail onto detail with no suggestion of order or significance, Mrs. Woolf is ridiculing the insensitivity of the diarist.

The freight-train sentence is also useful when the writer wants to analyze his topic but wishes to suggest a closer relationship between its parts than is possible in a segregating style. Consider, for example, this sentence by Hemingway:

> It was a hot day and the sky was very bright and blue and the road was white and dusty. *A Farewell to Arms*

The first clause makes us feel the heat, the second shows us the sky, the third moves our eyes downward to the road. But while we are made conscious of the parts of the experience, the sentence structure brings the parts together so that they compose one complex experience, not three separate ones.

To look at the same point from another side, we may imagine that the last three of the segregating sentences in the passage quoted earlier by Somerset Maugham, were put together in a freight-train style:

> The officer gave an order and the squad stepped out, and a couple of yards behind them walked the criminal, and then came the judge in his chair and finally the vice-consul.

What was a series of snapshots has become more like a motion picture. The scene is more fluid, and the separate images, while still discernible, flow into one another to make a unified experience. All this is not to suggest that the revision improves what Mr. Maugham wrote; it is, in fact, inferior, given Mr. Maugham's purpose. Rather the point is that the slight adjustment of the sentence structure slightly changes the meaning.

As this last example indicates, the freight-train style is nicely suited to telling stories, especially when, as with the segregating style, the writer desires to focus upon the action itself. More than the segregating style, however, the multiple co-ordinate sentence has the effect of suggesting continuity of action, as in this passage from Malory's description of the death of King Arthur:

> Then Sir Bedivere departed, and went to the sword, and lightly took it up, and went to the water side; and there he bound the girdle about the hilts, and then he threw the sword as far into the water as he might; and there came an arm and an hand above the water and met it, and caught it, and so shook it thrice and brandished, and then vanished away the hand with the sword in the water.

That much the same narrative style is still useful in modern prose is illustrated by this sentence from Hilaire Belloc's *The Path to Rome:*

> We passed a fountain at which oxen drank, and there I supped up cool water from the spout, but he [Belloc's guide] wagged his finger before his face to tell me that this was an error under a hot sun.

When the clauses are kept very short and joined paratactically, the freight-train sentence can convey the same sort of rush and excitement we noticed in Macaulay's segregating style. An instance is the following sentence by Mark Twain describing the effect upon a sleepy river town of the arrival of a steamboat:

> The town drunkard stirs, the clerks wake up, a furious clatter of drays follows, every house and store pours out a human contribution, and all in a twinkling the dead town is alive and moving.
>
> *Life on the Mississippi*

One advantage of the freight-train sentence, then, is to suggest equal multiplicity, whether of ideas, sense impressions, or the events of a story; a second advantage is to imply a tone of informality, even of relaxed intimacy. A tendency to string statements together with *and* is common in everyday speech, and a writer who desires a colloquial flavor can use the freight-train sentence to advantage. Thus A. J. Liebling in a very fine book about prizefighting called *The Sweet Science,* writes about Joe Louis:

> He had fought often since then, and I had seen his two bouts with Jersey Joe Walcott on television, but there hadn't been any fun in it.

The colloquial tone suggested by these short, straightforward clauses is reinforced by the multiple co-ordination; and, of course, a relaxed, informal tone is appropriate to Liebling's subject.

A final advantage of the multiple co-ordinate sentence is that it is easily adapted to a regular rhythm. In a later chapter we shall say more about sentence rhythm, observing here only that an increase in the regularity of rhythm, while it is dangerous to the integrity of prose, can be effectively used to heighten emotion. Part of the intensity we feel in the passage by Malory or in the following paragraph from *A Farewell to Arms* arises from the relatively high degree of regularity in the rhythm:

> The wind rose in the night and at three o'clock in the morning with the rain coming in sheets there was a bombardment and the Croatians came over across the mountain meadows and through patches of woods and into the front line. They fought in the dark in the rain and a counter-attack of scared men from the second line

> drove them back. There was much shelling and many rockets in the rain and machine-gun and rifle fire all along the line. They did not come again and it was quieter and between the gusts of wind and rain we could hear the sound of a great bombardment far to the north.

In such passages the multiple co-ordination is not the only device of syntax that determines rhythm — prepositional phrases, for instance, are also important. All the same, the multiple co-ordinate style is an important condition of the rhythm here, as it is in the Biblical prose of the King James version:

> For, lo, the winter is past, the rain is over and gone; the flowers appear on the earth, the time of the singing of birds is come; and the voice of the turtle is heard in our land.

That a rhythmic effect very like that of this seventeenth-century prose is still possible is demonstrated by such freight-train sentences as these:

> There was a magic, and a spell, and a curse; but the magic has been waved away, and the spell broken, and the curse was a curse of sleep and not of pain. R. L. DUFFUS, *Williamstown Branch*

> The soul of the man in Islington is certainly a soul. He also has been bewildered and broadened by youth; he also has been tortured and intoxicated by love; he also is sublimely doubtful about death.
> G. K. CHESTERTON, "THE IRISHMAN," *Selected Essays*

> We hear the hum of life in the fields; a horse champs his bit; a butterfly circles and settles.
> VIRGINIA WOOLF, "THE NOVELS OF TURGENEV," *The Captain's Death Bed and Other Essays*

In summary, the advantages of the freight-train sentence are several: it allows the writer (1) to show equal multiplicity; (2) to convey a sense of flow and continuity in describing a scene or telling a story without at the same time subordinating any part of the scene or the story to any other; (3) to create a relaxed, informal tone; and (4) to attain a high degree of rhythmic regularity if this suits his purpose. But even with all these virtues, the freight-train style is limited in its usefulness for exposition. Like the segregating style — to which it is so close — it is not well adapted to handling ideas. Ideas tend to form in ordered hierarchies of thought, and to link them together with the democratic equality of *and* is usually to oversimplify and distort them. Consider, for example, this brief statement about the Peloponnesian War:

> The Athenians grew very prosperous and they became greedy and arrogant and so they angered their neighbors and the Peloponnesian War resulted.

The historical accuracy of this is debatable, but even if we grant that the causes of this ancient war were what the writer has suggested, we must still note that his use of the freight-train sentence has obscured the essential cause-effect relationship between Athenian prosperity and the war. A clearer statement of the idea would be something like this:

> The very prosperity of Athens caused the Peloponnesian War since, by making the Athenians arrogant and greedy, this prosperity turned their neighbors against them.

This is not the only way — or even the best way — in which the passage could be revised, but it does have the virtue of making clear the essential idea — that the prosperity caused the war. The point of the example is not that the freight-train sentence has no place in college composition. It has — in description, in narration, even on occasion in exposition. But for workaday college writing it is not a good basic style. College writing requires the subordinate style.

THE PARALLEL SENTENCE

Before turning to the subordinate style, however, we must say a word about the parallel sentence, which is distinguished by the fact that it casts its major ideas in syntactically parallel constructions. A parallel construction is one in which two or more words, phrases, or clauses are syntactically related in the same way to the same thing. "Jack" and "Jill" in the sentence "Jack and Jill went up the hill" are parallel because they are both subjects of "went." In "Jack went up the hill and Jill went with him," on the other hand, "Jack" and "Jill" are not parallel since they are subjects of different verbs; in both cases the verb is the word "went," but that does not alter the fact that these are two different statements of "went." A sentence like "Jack and Jill went up the hill" we would not call a parallel sentence, for, while it contains parallelism, the constructions so treated do not dominate the sentence. In the following sentence by Edmund Burke, however, we are justified in speaking of a parallel style:

> To complain of the age we live in, to murmur at the present possessors of power, to lament the past, to conceive extravagant hopes of the future, are the common dispositions of the greatest part of mankind. . . . *Thoughts on the Present Discontent*

Of the thirty-seven words in this passage, twenty-seven are contained in the four parallel infinitive phrases which make up the compound subject and contain the key ideas of the sentence.

The parallel style was used with great effect in the eighteenth century by men like Burke, who were orators trained in the rhetorical tradition deriving from Cicero, the greatest of the Roman orators, and even further back from Isocrates, one of the greatest teachers of oratory in ancient Greece. This association of the parallel style with oratory is no accident; it is, for several reasons, a style well suited to the needs of the speaker. For one thing, it is impressive; it allows the public speaker to build climaxes, to engage his reader's attention by the expectation of a pattern to be fulfilled. For another, it enables the speaker to pack his sentences with ideas without unduly straining their syntax. Despite its length, Burke's sentence would be grammatically simple except for the three words "we live in," a contact adjective clause that makes the sentence complex. The ability to contain several ideas within a basically uncomplicated sentence pattern is an important advantage to the speaker. Listeners confronted with intricate and difficult sentence structure are likely to lose the thread of discourse. Consequently the speaker must keep his sentences relatively easy. Yet, if he is addressing mature men and dealing with important problems he must be able to handle ideas in the aggregate. The parallel style, then, is one compromise between simplicity of syntax and complexity of thought.

The parallel style has other advantages. A parallel sentence is economic. It makes one element do double, triple, or even quadruple duty. This is a distinct advantage when one wants to assert the same predication for several different subjects, as did Burke. All these things, he says, "are the common dispositions of the greatest part of mankind"; but he needs to say it only once, not four times. It is even more usual to make several predications about the same subject, and here, too, the parallel style is thrifty. The writer need state the subject only once and then parallel his verbs, as in this sentence describing the early converts to Christianity among the American Indians:

> The Indian convert, in short, "wore a crucifix, hung wampum on the shrine of the Virgin, told his beads, prayed three times a day, knelt for hours before the Host, invoked the saints, confessed to the priests; but, with rare exceptions, he murdered, scalped, and tortured like his heathen countrymen."
>
> DAVID LEVIN, *History as Romantic Art.*
> Inner quotation is from FRANCIS PARKMAN, *Frontenac.*

Not only is paralleling verbs a matter of economy; it is also a device of emphasis. In the sentences just quoted the parallelism of the verbs forces us to realize just how deep and meaningful was the conversion of a woodland savage to Christianity. There is a similar irony implicit in the parallel predicates of the following sentence. The writer is speaking of the fate of the young ladies of nineteenth-century Athens:

> He assured me that beauty there was in bud at thirteen, in full blossom at fifteen, losing a leaf or two every day at seventeen, trembling on the thorn at nineteen, and under the tree at twenty.
>
> W. S. LANDOR, "SOUTHEY AND PORSON," *Imaginary Conversations*

In the next example the parallelism of the verbs, leading to an unexpected and disappointing conclusion, is slyly amusing:

> She laid two fingers on my shoulder, cast another look into my face under her candle, turned the key in the lock, gently thrust me beyond the door, shut it; and left me to my own devices.
>
> WALTER DE LA MARE, *Come Hither*

In narrative writing the emphasis attaching to parallel verbs may easily be utilized to give pace and excitement to the story. Ralph Roeder describes the invasion of Italy in 1494 by Charles VIII of France like this:

> Charles borrowed his way through Savoy, disappeared into the Alps, and emerged, early in September, at Asti, where his ally met him and escorted him to the suburbs of Milan.
>
> *The Man of the Renaissance*

Capable of economy and a concentrated emphasis, the parallel style is also highly formal, even artificial, and so lends itself to dignity and gravity. In its fullest development it has something of the grandeur of a great building, and, properly used, this architectural impressiveness gives weight and richness to what the sentence says. One feels this in Samuel Johnson, for instance, in sentences like these from his "Preface to the Dictionary":

> That it [the Dictionary] will immediately become popular I have not promised to myself: a few wild blunders, and risible absurdities, from which no work of such multiplicity was ever free, may for a time furnish folly with laughter, and harden ignorance in contempt; but useful diligence will at last prevail, and there can never be wanting some who distinguish desert; who will consider that no dictionary of a living tongue ever can be perfect, since while it is hastening to publication, some words are budding, and some falling away; that a whole life cannot be spent upon syntax and etymology, and that even a whole life would not be sufficient; that he, whose design includes whatever language can express, must often speak of

> what he does not understand; that a writer will sometimes be hurried by eagerness to the end, and sometimes faint with weariness under a task, which *Scaliger* compares to the labours of the anvil and the mine; that what is obvious is not always known, and what is known is not always present; that sudden fits of inadvertency will surprize vigilance, slight avocations will seduce attention, and casual eclipses of the mind will darken learning; and that a writer shall often in vain trace his memory at the moment of need, for that which yesterday he knew with intuitive readiness, and which will come uncalled into his thoughts to-morrow.

> I have protracted my work till most of those whom I wished to please have sunk into the grave, and success and miscarriage are empty sounds: I therefore dismiss it with frigid tranquillity, having little to fear or hope from censure or from praise.

The first of these sentences is a good example of just how complicated the parallel style can become. The sentence piles up eight "that" clauses as objects of the nexus "who will consider," and each of these clauses, with but one exception, contains parallelism within itself. So elaborate a sentence pattern is artificial in the sense that it is the result of conscious art and so removed from the spontaneous naturalness of everyday speech. But artificiality as we are using the term here does not imply phoniness or coldness. The second of Johnson's sentences indicates that the parallel style is capable of conveying, and even of intensifying, deep and genuine emotion. Like many men, Johnson felt the emptiness of success long delayed. But instead of directly crying out these feelings, Johnson expressed them in a parallel sentence, which requires self-control, a discipline that gives the emotion — and the writer — greater dignity and greater significance.

The sense of dignity implicit in the parallel style may also be placed in the service of irony, the dignity of the sentence form increasing our sense of the ridiculous folly of the subjects being described. Thornton Wilder, for instance, uses parallelism very effectively in this mildly satiric character sketch:

> Don Andrés de Ribera, the Viceroy of Peru, was the remnant of a delightful man, broken by the table, the alcove, a grandeeship and ten years of exile. As a youth he had accompanied embassies to Versailles and Rome; he had fought in the wars in Austria; he had been in Jerusalem. He was a widower and childless of an enormous and wealthy woman; he had collected coins a little, wines, actresses, orders and maps. From the table he had received the gout; from the alcove a tendency to convulsions; from the grandeeship a pride so vast and puerile that he seldom heard anything that was said to him and talked to the ceiling in a perpetual monologue; from the exile,

> oceans of boredom, a boredom so pervasive that it was like pain, — he woke with it and spent the day with it, and it sat by his bed all night watching his sleep. *The Bridge of San Luis Rey*

The very virtues of the parallel style, however, limit its effectiveness. Its formality is largely out of place today; for we have generally discarded artificiality and formality — whether in speech, in manners, or in dress. The parallel style, moreover, tends to wordiness. In the sentence we quoted on page 262 by Edmund Burke, for example, the final six words are a kind of makeweight against the front end of the sentence, made heavier by the paralleling of the subjects. "Of the greatest part of mankind" is merely a wordy way of saying "of most men." But if the briefer phrase is substituted for the longer the sentence seems to fall flat. A tendency to pad the sentence in order to maintain some semblance of equality between the parallel elements and the rest of the sentence is one of the pitfalls of the parallel style. Its final, and perhaps its most severe, limitation is that it is a style suited only to ideas and feelings that are truly parallel. Three causes of the same thing can easily be handled in a parallel sentence, or three effects of the same cause. But when the ideas themselves are not parallel — when one must explain the cause of a cause or the consequence of an effect — then to jam ideas into a parallel sentence can only distort them and confuse the reader. Some of the worst eighteenth-century writing comes from just this attempt.

Yet if our age, less formal and less inclined to reduce experience and thought to parallel patterns, no longer finds the parallel style suited to its needs, the modern writer none the less can learn a great deal from that style. Even so contemporary and informal a writer as A. J. Liebling demonstrates the value of parallelism:

> Instead of flicking, moving around, and so piling up enough unhurting points to goad Johnson into some possible late activity, he was reconnoitering in close, looking the challenger over as if he had never seen him before. *The Sweet Science*

The contemporary writer does not want to construct elaborate sentences like those of Burke or Dr. Johnson, but he can learn to use occasional parallelism as a means of attaining economy, emphasis, and pace in his sentences.

THE SUBORDINATING SENTENCE

Like the freight-train and the parallel sentences, the subordinating sentence also brings together several ideas in one construction. It differs, however, in an important respect. It introduces a principle of rank, of relative importance, into the ideas it combines. Neither the multiple coordinate nor the parallel sentence differentiates in any clear and certain way between ideas that are more important and ideas that are less. In Hemingway's sentence on page 259, for instance, the heat, the sky, and the road are equally significant; in the parallel sentence by Burke on page 262, each of the discontents is of much the same magnitude. But in expository prose, inequality of idea is more likely than equality. Thus the writer of exposition requires the subordinate sentence, for it enables him to select one idea as most important and to order his others around it, using the various phrases and dependent clauses of English grammar. A simple instance of the subordinate sentence is this: "When the sun had set, the men returned to camp, the search abandoned until morning." Of the three ideas, it is the men's returning to camp that is paramount, and the others are subordinated to it, one in the form of an adverbial clause, the other in that of a nominative absolute.

A more complicated example is the following sentence by Jonathan Swift, one of the greatest masters the English sentence has ever known:

> After ten years' fighting to little purpose, after the loss of above a hundred thousand men, and a debt remaining of twenty millions, we at length hearkened to the terms of peace, which was concluded with great advantages to the empire and Holland, but none at all to us, and clogged soon after with the famous treaty of partition.
>
> "THE CONDUCT OF THE ALLIES"

Swift is criticizing the English participation in the War of the Spanish Succession. Granted a broad and uncritical notion of "idea," we can say that the sentence contains eight ideas: (1) the "ten years' fighting," (2) the "loss" of men, (3) the "debt remaining," (4) the "hearkening" to peace, (5) the "conclusion" of peace, (6) the "advantages" that followed for England's allies, (7) the absence of such advantages for England herself, and (8) the "clogging" of the peace. Eight ideas make rather a full sentence, yet this is not really difficult to read. There are several reasons why it is not. One is that Swift has neatly subordinated all other points to the "hearkening to peace," the main clause of this complex sentence. Second, he has avoided monotony by employing several kinds of subordinating constructions — gerundive phrases, prepositional phrases, and an adjective clause. Third, he has treated each idea as a unit before moving on to the next; there is no interruption in the flow of thought.

Finally, he has arranged the elements that compose his sentence in a natural order so that the pattern of syntax reflects the pattern of events. In the sentence, as in history, the fighting comes first, then the loss of life and the debt, then the hearkening to peace, and so on. Effecting a workable compromise between the natural order of thought or reality on the one hand, and the conventional order of sentence elements on the other, is one of the most difficult tasks a writer faces. In logic, for example, causes come before effects; in time, yesterday precedes today. But the English sentence must move to its own tempo, and often it is difficult to adapt the flow of thought to the requirements of sentence order. Swift usually succeeded better than most writers of English. His success is worth studying.

It is worth noticing, too, that Swift's sentence contains several parallel constructions. It is not a "parallel sentence," for the parallelism is not the major principle of its construction. But the parallelism is important. It enables Swift to economize a little and to keep his syntax somewhat simpler. As an exercise jot down all the parallel words and phrases you can find in this sentence by Swift. All in all, it is a fine illustration of the subordinate style. It is syntactically complex, yet easy to read; complicated in thought, yet proceeding in easy, self-contained stages; extensive and wide-ranging, yet sharply focused.

Swift placed his key idea in the middle of the sentence, where it is a kind of peak to which the first part builds and from which the last part falls away. This is a variety of sentence form that we shall discuss more fully in the chapter on sentence movement and rhythm. For now we need only observe that placing the important idea in the middle is one way of shaping the subordinate sentence. Another way is illustrated in the following sentence by Thomas Carlyle describing a Welsh town:

> Llanblethian hangs pleasantly, with its white cottages, and orchard and other trees, on the western slope of a green hill; looking far and wide over green meadows and little or bigger hills, in the pleasant plain of Glamorgan; a short mile to the south of Cowbridge, to which smart little town it is properly a kind of suburb.
>
> *Life of John Sterling*

Carlyle's sentence is more like a kite than a mountain surrounded by foothills. The main idea comes first; then dangling from it, a series of tails, are the dependent constructions. The result is a relaxed and discursive sentence; like the scene it describes, it is natural rather than artificial and unfolds slowly and leisurely. Noticc the effective use Carlyle makes of the participle "looking." Participles are one of the easiest subordinating devices in English, but one which many people, for some reason, seem leery of using. And notice, finally, how neatly and conversationally the final construction is slipped in; "a short mile to the south," Carlyle writes, not bothering to supply the participle "being." Sentences like this, which make their point first and then seemingly ramble on are called "loose" sentences.

Another variety of subordinate construction reverses the order of the loose sentence and places the main clause at the end, building up to it with initial subordinated phrases and clauses. Such sentences, which do not complete their thought until the end, are often called "periodic." The periodic sentence is more formal and generally more emphatic than the loose; consequently subordinate sentences of this sort, especially if they contain two or three subordinated constructions rather than just one, are usually suited to rather formal occasions. A not very complicated example is this sentence by the American writer Logan Pearsall Smith:

> Finally, one Sunday afternoon in June, when I was up in a cherry tree picking cherries, the whole supernatural scheme of things seemed to fade away into the blue sky, never to return. *Unforgotten Years*

You can hear the tone of this sentence change in the direction of informality if it is recast with the main clause first:

> Finally, the whole supernatural scheme of things seemed to fade away into the blue sky, never to return, one Sunday afternoon in June, when I was up in a cherry tree picking cherries.

Precisely because it offers the writer so many patterns of structure and so many different kinds of phrases and clauses to draw upon, the subordinate sentence is not easy to write. There are several kinds of AWKWARD SUBORDINATION. One of the commonest is mistaking the important idea and subordinating the wrong thing. The following passage is an example:

> Ralph is a young lad of about eighteen, well built and with dark curly hair, who is an honor student in high school.

Since the point which the writer goes on to develop is Ralph's aptitude as a student, he has, in this sentence, subordinated the wrong idea. The sentence would have been better constructed like this:

> Ralph, a well built lad of about eighteen with dark curly hair, is an honor student in high school.

Very similar to subordinating the wrong idea is the failure to subordinate any idea at all. In the following passage, for instance, we feel a lack of focus:

> Frederick the Great was a brilliant reader. He opened libraries and museums and patronized the arts.

Although the relation between the ideas contained in these two sentences is implicitly clear, we still wonder which idea is more important. Did the writer mean:

> Frederick the Great, a brilliant reader, opened libraries and museums and patronized the arts;

or

> Frederick the Great, who opened libraries and patronized the arts, was a brilliant reader?

In other words, was Frederick's "brilliant reading" the cause of his patronizing the arts, or was his patronage of the arts a sign of his brilliant reading? Perhaps it is not important. But if it were, we shall never know which alternate the writer intended.

The blurring of idea is even more pronounced in this example:

> He is a professor of phonetics. He is tall and lean and is about thirty-five years old. He is almost totally devoid of manners.

In this case, too, an annoying range of possibilities is open to the reader:

> A professor of phonetics, tall, lean, about thirty-five, he is almost totally devoid of manners.
>
> A professor of phonetics and almost totally devoid of manners, he is tall and lean and about thirty-five.
>
> Tall and lean and about thirty-five, almost totally devoid of manners, he is a professor of phonetics.

By varying the positions of the subordinated constructions we could arrive at further possibilities of emphasis and meaning. But the point is clear. As the sentences originally stand, the writer's meaning is fuzzy. It is fuzzy either because the writer was not sure about what his point was, or because, if he was sure, he failed to subordinate his other ideas to it.

Subordinating the wrong idea, then, or failing to subordinate any idea at all are common faults in expository writing. One can commit other mistakes as well in using the subordinate style — fail to place a modifying construction clearly next to the word it modifies, for example, or so position the main clause that most of its importance is lost. These, however, are matters we shall examine in closer detail in the chapters on sentence clarity and sentence emphasis. Here we shall conclude our review of the subordinate sentence by repeating that it is the basic style which all writers of exposition should acquire. You will need all the kinds of sentences we have talked about so far in this chapter, even the convoluted sentence, which we shall look at in a moment. But in the composition you are expected to do in college, the style you must chiefly rely upon is the subordinate sentence.

THE CONVOLUTED SENTENCE

Though we are treating it separately, the convoluted sentence is really a special variety of the subordinate sentence. It is a complex sentence in which the subordinated constructions, instead of preceding, following, or surrounding the main clause, are inserted into the middle of that clause. In its extreme form this type of sentence is like a nest of Chinese boxes, one construction nestling within another. The writer begins his main point, but before he completes it he interrupts it to introduce a subordinated construction. This construction, in turn, may be interrupted by a second, the second by a third, and so on. Such sentences are not easy to read; they can become tortuous. A simple example of the convoluted sentence is this one by G. K. Chesterton about Charles Dickens:

> In spite of all the silly talk about his vulgarity, he really had, in the strict and serious sense, good taste.

But the refinements of which the convoluted sentence is capable are better illustrated in this long construction by George Saintsbury, who is writing about the last words spoken by Jonathan Swift on his death bed — "only a woman's hair":

> But if any person — no matter how little of a fool at other times or in other ways, no matter how rare his sojurn in the House of Folly may be — if any person has seen, sees, or till the Day of Judgment shall see in those four words cynicism, brutality, anything but the expression of the riddle of the painful earth in one of its forms expressed more poignantly and finally than it has ever been expressed by any uninspired human being excepting Shakespeare — then it is safe, with no flippancy or triumph, but with all the gravity and sadness that the thoughts of Life and Death can inspire, to pronounce that person — at the point of time and in the actual expression of his thought — not a brute, not a cynic, not anything — but an utter and hopeless fool. *The Peace of the Augustans*

This is a long way to go to argue that any man who misunderstands Swift's dying words is a fool. A reader sympathetic to Saintsbury may claim that his sentence, admitting all possible qualifications and pushing its main point to the end, carries a note of conviction it might otherwise lack. Still, this kind of prose seems inspired virtuosity, like a high-wire performer doing triple somersaults blindfolded: we admire a man who chooses to live so dangerously, but we wonder what is to be gained by such risks. Most of us would not care to imitate him; it is a long way down. Interrupted movement, the principle upon which the convoluted sentence is built, is a valuable device of emphasis and variety, as we shall shortly see. But so extreme an application of the principle is rarely warranted in expository writing. Brilliant as it is, most readers have to go over Saintsbury's sentence several times — and closely too — to grasp its point. And the point is not really worth so much trouble. It is true that novelists have sometimes employed a convoluted style as a way of suggesting subtle complexities. Henry James is a notable case. But for conveying information or communicating the simpler attitudes and feelings with which exposition deals, the convoluted sentence in its extreme form is to be avoided.

Summary

Considered simply as to the type and the number of its clauses, the sentence may be simple, compound, complex, or compound-complex. Considered as to whether it expresses one idea or several, the sentence may be segregating or aggregating. Aggregating sentences, in turn, may be further differentiated on the basis of what device of style they employ to hold their several ideas together. The simplest aggregating sentence is the freight-train construction, which links a succession of independent clauses, either by using co-ordinating conjunctions like *and*, or by paratactically butting the clauses together. The parallel sentence arranges its several ideas as syntactically parallel constructions, often as subjects of the same verb, objects of the same verb, or predicates of the same subject. The subordinate sentence selects one idea as important and, placing it first or last or in the middle of the sentence, organizes the other ideas about it in subordinated clauses and phrases. The convoluted sentence is a variety of the subordinate, its special feature being that the subordinated constructions are intruded into the main clause. In practice writers often construct sentences combining elements of these various styles.

Each style is more valuable for some purposes, less valuable for others. The college writer ought to know them all. The simple, segregating sentence is useful for topic statements, for emphatic restatement, and often for description or narration. The freight-train sentence is also well adapted for the simpler kinds of description and narration, and it is informal and capable of establishing relatively regular rhythms. Parallelism, if not the parallel style, is economic and emphatic. The convoluted sentence is useful for variation and for special stress.

But the best modern expository style is that built upon the subordinate sentence. Such a style may make use of parallelism and interrupted movement as minor devices of economy, emphasis, or variety; but its essence is the complex sentence. Because it is able to suggest relative degrees of importance and to establish subtle and complicated connections of logic and feeling, the subordinate style allows the writer the greatest flexibility in handling thought. And handling thought, finally, is the job of exposition.

Exercises

1. In the following list identify which sentences are gramatically simple and which are compound, complex, or compound-complex. In the case of compound sentences be able to explain whether the clauses are joined by co-ordination or by parataxis; and in the case of complex and compound-complex indicate the main clause (or clauses) and the subordinate one(s).

1. Till he had a wife he could do nothing; and when he had a wife he did whatever she chose. THOMAS BABINGTON MACAULAY
2. Bats drink on the wing, like swallows, by sipping the surface, as they play over pools and streams. GILBERT WHITE
3. But at last the first shadow fell across this unity and the shadow was cast by the love of women. THORNTON WILDER
4. And thus he rode home, meditating many things in his mind. ANTHONY TROLLOPE
5. Generally, the old-fashioned and unpainted houses on the Cape looked more comfortable, as well as picturesque, than the modern and more pretending ones, which were less in harmony with the scenery, and less firmly planted. HENRY THOREAU
6. There is no weather so good as English weather. G. K. CHESTERTON
7. One day when we were on the subject of transportation and distribution, it came Bolenciecwcz's turn to answer a question. JAMES THURBER
8. He had never felt like that himself toward any woman, but he knew that such a feeling must be love. JAMES JOYCE
9. I am going to read what I have written to read, because in a general way it is easier even if it is not better and in a general way it is

better even if it is not easier to read what has been written than to say what has not been written. GERTRUDE STEIN

10. My clothes felt wet and clammy and I slapped my arms to keep the circulation going. ERNEST HEMINGWAY

11. Ten minutes later the steamer is under way again, with no flag on the jack-staff and no black smoke issuing from the chimneys. MARK TWAIN

12. Power is measured by the amount of resistance which it overcomes, and, in the last resort, the moral power of men was greater than any purely material force, which could be brought to bear upon it. FREDERIC MANNING

13. I am not one of those who cannot enjoy the feeling of salt water without knowing that, if I sink, I shall go down thirty or forty feet. ROBERT LYND

14. Sabotage and murder as a cure for political abuses have never proved permanent and have often aggravated the disease. GEORGE BERNARD SHAW

15. At this late season there were not many boarders; and yet I was not alone in the public part of the monastery. ROBERT LOUIS STEVENSON

16. Rome loses one man; she hath lost many such, and she still has many left. W. S. LANDOR

2. In this list identify which sentences are examples of the segregating style and which are instances of the freight-train, parallel, subordinate, and convoluted styles. In each case be able to justify your decision by pointing out the main clause and the subordinate, identifying the parallel elements or the interrupting constructions, or showing whether several independent clauses are joined by co-ordination or by parataxis.

1. We arrived at Odiham about half after eleven, at the end of a beautiful ride of about seventeen miles, in a very fine and pleasant day. WILLIAM COBBETT

2. We came up on the railway beyond the canal. It went straight toward the town across the low fields. We could see the line of the other railway ahead of us. ERNEST HEMINGWAY

3. In hope of giving longevity to that which its own nature forbids to be immortal, I have devoted this book, the labor of years, to the honor of my country, that we may no longer yield the palm of philology, without a contest, to the nations of the continent. SAMUEL JOHNSON

4. The men we met walked past, slow, unsmiling, with downcast eyes, as if the melancholy of an overburdened earth had weighted their feet, bowed their shoulders, borne down their glances.
JOSEPH CONRAD

5. Boats without awnings were too hot to touch; ships blistered at their moorings; the stones of the quays had not cooled, night or day, for months. CHARLES DICKENS

6. And finally, stammering a crude farewell, he departed.
THOMAS WOLFE

7. Looking out from the bushes, I saw her trotting towards an open space of lawn the other side the pond, chattering to herself in her accustomed fashion, a doll tucked under either arm, and her brow knit with care. KENNETH GRAHAME

8. To suffer, to labor, to toil and force your way through the spikes of life, to crawl through its darkest caverns, to push through the worst, to struggle under the weight of economy, to make money — only to become the father of a fourth-rate man of the world like this, so flat-looking, with his ordinary, clean, rosy, uninteresting, self-satisfied, fundamentally bourgeois face. SAUL BELLOW

9. Bullies jostled him into the kennel. Hackney coachmen splashed him from head to foot. THOMAS BABINGTON MACAULAY

10. The thought was yet in his mind, when, first one then another, with every variety of pace and voice — one deep as the bell from a cathedral turret, another ringing on its treble notes the prelude of a waltz — the clocks began to strike the hour of three in the afternoon. ROBERT LOUIS STEVENSON

11. To make men perfect was no part of Bacon's plan. His humble aim was to make imperfect men comfortable.
THOMAS BABINGTON MACAULAY

12. The walls of his great hall are covered with the horns of the several kinds of deer that he has killed in the chase, which he thinks the most valuable furniture of his house, as they afford him frequent topics of discourse, and show that he has not been idle.
JOSEPH ADDISON

13. Fortune cares little about philosophers; but she remembers where she hath set a rich man, and she laughs to see the Destinies at his door. W. S. LANDOR

14. The station-keeper lights his lamps, kindles a fire of twigs, prepares our beds. LAFCADIO HEARN

15. A spot for the fire was found with some difficulty, for the earth was moist, and the grass high and rank. A. W. KINGLAKE

16. If we start, as we should, from a consideration of ignorance, we shall be struck first of all, I think, by its passivity and inertness, and this raises a presumption that knowledge is above all, as Plato held it to be, an activity of the soul. JOHN BURNETT

3. Identify the parallel constructions in the following sentences.

1. The men dozed, waked, sighed, groaned. JOSEPH CONRAD

2. Before me lies a bundle of these sermons, rescued from six-score years of dust, scrawled on their title-pages with names of owners dead long ago, worm-eaten, dingy, stained with the damps of time, and uttering in quaint old letter-press the emotions of a buried and forgotten past. FRANCIS PARKMAN

3. He ground the powders, mixed the pills, rode with the doctor on his rounds, held the basin when the patient was bled, helped to adjust plasters and to sew wounds, and ran with vials of medicine from one end of the town to the other. JOHN BACH MCMASTER

4. The godly community of Philadelphia Quakers, going their ways and attending to their affairs in peace and quietness, would, to an observer from outside, have seemed a uniform community of pious people, all dressed in the same garb, all speaking the same language, all living in the same houses, all sitting in the same meditative silence, or listening to the same doctrines in the same square, unadorned meetinghouses. LOGAN PEARSALL SMITH

5. The motives that may engage a wise prince or state in a war I take to be one or more of these: either to check the overgrown power of some ambitious neighbor; to recover what has been unjustly taken from them; to revenge some injury they have received, which all political casuists allow; to assist some ally in a just quarrel; or, lastly, to defend themselves when they are invaded. JONATHAN SWIFT

6. [Of Garibaldi] Sore at heart, and preoccupied by bitter thoughts, he galloped up to the Capitol, dismounted, and entered the Assembly as he was, his red shirt covered with dust and blood, his face still moist with the sweat of battle, his sword so bent that it stuck half-way out of the scabbard. GEORGE MACAULAY TREVELYAN

7. They who maintain the opposite opinion, display the happiness and innocence of those uncultivated nations who live without learning; urge the numerous vices which are to be found only in polished society, enlarge upon the oppression, the cruelty, and the blood which must necessarily be shed, in order to cement civil society, and

insist upon the happy equality of conditions in a barbarous state preferable to the unnatural subordination of a more refined constitution. OLIVER GOLDSMITH

8. Hill and valley followed valley and hill; the little green and stony cattletracks wandered in and out of one another, split into three or four, died away in marshy hollows, and began again sporadically on hillsides or at the borders of a wood. ROBERT LOUIS STEVENSON

9. [Of the dying Queen Victoria] Perhaps her fading mind called up once more the shadows of the past to float before it, and retraced, for the last time, the vanished visions of that long history — passing back and back, through the cloud of years, to older and ever older memories — to the spring woods at Osborne, so full of primroses for Lord Beaconsfield — to Lord Palmerston's queer clothes and high demeanour, and Albert's face under the green lamp, and Albert's first stag at Balmoral, and Albert in his blue and silver uniform, and the Baron coming in through a doorway, and Lord M. dreaming at Windsor with the rooks cawing in the elm-trees, and the Archbishop of Canterbury on his knees in the dawn, and the old King's turkey-cock ejaculations, and Uncle Leopold's soft voice at Claremont, and Lehzen with the globes, and her mother's feathers sweeping down towards her, and a great old repeater-watch of her father's in its tortoise-shell case, and a yellow rug, and some friendly flounces of sprigged muslin, and the trees and the grass at Kensington.
LYTTON STRACHEY

10. It was a big, squarish frame house that had once been white, decorated with cupolas and spires and scrolled balconies in the heavily lightsome style of the seventies, set on what had once been our most select street. WILLIAM FAULKNER

11. There never did, there never will, and there never can, exist a Parliament, or any description of men, or any generation of men, in any country, possessed of the right or the power of binding and controlling posterity to the "*end of time*," or of commanding for ever how the world shall be governed, or who shall govern it; and, therefore, all such clauses, acts, or declarations by which the makers of them attempt to do what they have neither the right nor the power to do, nor the power to execute, are in themselves null and void.
THOMAS PAINE

12. When in the Course of human events, it becomes necessary for one people to dissolve the political bands which have connected them with another, and to assume, among the powers of the earth, the separate and equal station, to which the Laws of Nature and of Nature's God entitle them, a decent respect to the opinions of man-

kind requires that they should declare the causes which impel them to the separation. We hold these truths to be self-evident, that all men are created equal, that they are endowed by their creator with certain unalienable Rights, that among these are Life, Liberty and the Pursuit of Happiness. THOMAS JEFFERSON

4. The following sentences are all examples of the subordinate style. Keeping as close as you can to the original diction, recast each sentence in the segregating style, using two or three or four sentences. Even though you may not be able to improve the original, write as good a passage as you can, and study what you have written to see how you have changed the tone and meaning.

1. In the holy of holies three magnificent old men were chanting ecstatically to the accompaniment of a small portable harmonium, which was being played with one finger by a fourth, yet more superbly patriarchal. ALDOUS HUXLEY

2. Being unable to remove the chain, I jumped over, and, running up the flagged causeway bordered with straggling gooseberry bushes, knocked vainly for admittance, till my knuckles tingled and the dogs howled. EMILY BRONTË

3. Youth is a kind of delirium, which can only be cured, if it is ever to be cured at all, by years of painful treatment. LOGAN PEARSALL SMITH

4. In the center of the great city of London lies a small neighborhood, consisting of a cluster of narrow streets and courts, of very venerable and debilitated houses, which goes by the name of Little Britain. WASHINGTON IRVING

5. The mountain paths stoop to these glens in forky zigzags, leading to some grey and narrow arch, all fringed under its shuddering curve with the ferns that fear the light; a cross of rough-hewn pine, iron-bound to its parapet, standing dark against the lurid fury of the foam. JOHN RUSKIN

5. Turn the following freight-train sentences into the subordinate style. Again, stick as closely as you can to the original diction, and be able to discuss how you think the change of style has affected tone and meaning.

1. Then he stood up, and he was very straight and tall, and the sunset was in his hair and beard as he stood there, high over me. KENNETH GRAHAME

2. Presently the arm that embraced the Bible began slowly, slowly to close it, and the exposition was at an end, and we knelt; and then there was nothing to do but wait, helping oneself out with a little rhythmical fidgeting. PERCY LUBBOCK

3. The sails blew away, she lay broadside on under a weather-cloth, the ocean poured over her, and we did not care. JOSEPH CONRAD

4. The carter has tied his horse to a tree; the soldiers stroll in barefoot in their shoes; the many fez shine vividly against the straight white wall. ARTHUR SYMONS

5. They jabber over cheese, they chatter over wine, they gabble at the corners in the bright sunshine. AMY LOWELL

6. The Burong Islands may be boldly approached from the westward; large sailing vessels had better pass outside them, but smaller craft and steam vessels may often with advantage, pass between them, taking care to avoid the charted reefs. *China Sea Pilot, 1st edition*

6. Below are listed five nouns. Write a complex sentence in which the first noun functions as the main subject while each of the other four is set into a subordinate clause or a phrase. Then repeat the process four times, in sentence two making the second noun the main subject, in sentence three the third, and so on.

1. Elephant
2. Tree
3. Rifle
4. Truck
5. Grass

7. Following the pattern set by Edmund Burke (see page 262), construct a parallel sentence on one of these topics.

1. The duties of a housewife
2. The complaints of a college student
3. The mistakes you make in composition class

8. Compose a convoluted sentence describing someone getting up in the morning, a student preparing to study, or a teacher getting ready to lecture. Follow the sentence below very carefully, beginning with some such adverbial word as *then* (*but, thus, finally,* for example), following this with a participial construction, the main subject and the first of its two verbs, a second interrupting participial phrase, and finally the second predicate.

> Then, tucking his paper under his pillow, he popped out the guttering candle, and turning around upon his side with a smile of exceeding sweetness, settled himself to sleep. AUSTIN DOBSON

9. Write a brief paragraph in the segregating style loosely modeled upon the passage by W. Somerset Maugham on page 253. Select a comparable topic, a family departing on a trip, for instance. Rewrite the paragraph in freight-train sentences as Hemingway might do it.

16
CONCISION

Introduction

Different as they are in their structure and in their range of effectiveness, all the various kinds of sentences we surveyed in the last chapter, if they are to function effectively, must possess certain qualities. These qualities — or "virtues" as we shall name them — are what we shall discuss in this chapter and in the several that follow. There are four sentence virtues. The first three are easily labeled by single words: concision, clarity, and emphasis. The fourth cannot be designated by a simple term. Essentially it has to do with the sentence as an aural unit, that is, as a unit of sound, as something that is heard; we shall treat it under the main headings of sentence shape, movement, and rhythm.

Before we begin to talk about these matters a double warning is necessary. First, breaking down the quality of a good sentence into these four virtues is oversimple and, if taken too literally, misleading. Elsewhere in this book we have alerted you to the tendency of teachers to make pigeonholes, even though the problems with which they deal are often so intricate that they cannot easily be separated. The warning is worth repeating. Concision, clarity, emphasis, and shape-movement-rhythm are not really as distinct as you might suppose. Possibly they are not distinct at all, being less separate qualities of the sentence than various ways of viewing the same thing. In any case, each of these virtues implies the others. A sentence that is properly "shaped" will be, almost by definition, concise and emphatic and clear; a sentence that is concise is very likely to be emphatic and clear and well shaped; and so on.

The fact that these aspects of the sentence are so interdependent means that treating them one at a time will occasionally prove repetitious, though what we repeat will be important enough to hear twice. But if we be allowed some repetition and if you do not lose sight of the fact that the virtues of the sentence generally imply one another, treating them separately will be advantageous, permitting us to concentrate upon one thing at a time and ultimately to understand better the interdependence we have spoken of.

The second warning is this: some of what we shall say in this and in the immediately following chapters will have as much to do with diction as with sentence style, especially in regard to concision and emphasis. Some deadwood, for example, has its source in faults of sentence structure, while some arises from mistakes in word choice. However, even though we may now and then move from the sentence into the area of diction, it seems best to concentrate discussions of concision and of emphasis in one place. We shall begin, then, with concision.

Concision

Concision does not mean exactly the same thing as brevity. Brevity is absolute; concision is relative. A sentence that has five words is brief; a sentence that has fifty is not. But the five-word sentence might not be concise, while the fifty-word one might be. Concision is *brevity relative to purpose.* If there is no way of saying what the writer wanted to say in less than fifty words, then that sentence, long as it is, is still concise; if the five-word sentence could be reduced to four, then it is not concise. No matter how many words a sentence contains, its concision can be determined only in terms of whether or not its word count could be reduced without changing the substance of its meaning.

We have asserted that concision is a virtue; but it is not a virtue in and of itself. Rather it is a virtue because it is a means to effective communication. The purpose of a sentence is to affect a reader in a certain way. Concision — like the other qualities we have mentioned — is a virtue because it increases the probability that this purpose will be realized. Consider, for instance, the sentence:

> She dresses in a beautiful manner,

and suppose that the point the writer wished to emphasize was that conveyed by the word "beautiful." The chances are that some readers will pay less attention to "beautiful" than to "manner," an empty word that really doesn't say anything here but serves merely as a hook upon which to hang the adjective "beautiful." Now if the writer had used an adverb he could have dispensed with the noun "manner" and attached the modifier directly to "dresses." His sentence would read:

> She dresses beautifully.

Six words have been reduced to three — a major gain in concision. The important point, however, is not saving three words — words are not gold pieces that we must hoard — but rather that the sentence has been made more effective. Even a dull reader will now realize that the key term is "beautifully," for by removing the deadwood we have given the modifier prominence at the end of the sentence, where it stands by itself, no longer under the shadow of "manner." In other words, we have increased the chances that a reader will understand the writer's point. The example is, of course, a simple and obvious one. But the principle it illustrates applies to all sentences: failure to be concise interferes with communication.

Deadwood

In practice, concision is best studied and achieved negatively, by learning to recognize deadwood. Deadwood is what results when a writer fails to be concise; it is a word, a phrase, a clause — even an entire sentence — that is not essential to the writer's meaning.

To understand the nature of deadwood you need to remember that meaning is frequently a more complex matter than it seems to be on the surface. Sentences may imply a good deal more than they seem at first reading to say. Let us look again at the sentence by Jonathan Swift which earlier we said was a fine example of the subordinate style:

> After ten years' fighting to little purpose, after the loss of above a hundred thousand men, and a debt remaining of twenty millions, we at length hearkened to the terms of peace, which was concluded with great advantages to the empire and Holland, but none at all to us, and clogged soon after with the famous treaty of partition.

It could be argued that two "after's" are one too many, that the two initial prepositional phrases could be combined into a single phrase having one preposition and three objects:

> After ten years' fighting to little purpose, the loss of above a hundred thousand men, and a debt remaining of twenty millions, we at length hearkened . . .

But the revision loses a nuance of meaning. By repeating "after" Swift hints at the irrationality of men who must endure so much before they give up war.

Often such nuances are questions of tone, and it may very well be that a word or phrase that is not needed to convey any referential meaning *is* needed to establish tone. A writer sometimes employs formulas like "I am sure you all know" or "As you are well aware," expressions whose function is essentially to establish rapport between himself and the people he addresses, in other words, to create tone. It would be wrong to judge such constructions as deadwood; they may be very necessary to the writer's purpose.

With regard to tone it is important to recognize that a word is a unit of sound as well as a unit of meaning. It is possible, even if it is not likely, that a writer may employ a word as much for its rhythm and sound as for its sense. Admittedly, words are usually selected primarily because of what they refer to (on a conscious level, indeed, that is all many people ever consider). But now and then a word that is not strictly necessary for meaning may be required by the demands of sound or rhythm. As a case in point study this sentence by the British politician Stanley Baldwin:

> We turn aside today for a moment from controversy and from business, and, as we leave this Chamber, we shall leave it for this afternoon to darkness and to silence.

The passage is from a eulogy to Lord Oxford, delivered by Baldwin before the British House of Commons. One's first reaction might be that the sentence contains a good deal of deadwood. Are both "from's" necessary, and both "to's"? Does Baldwin really have to say "for this afternoon," having already specified "today"? Would it not have been thriftier to reduce the full adverbial clause "as we leave this Chamber" to a participial phrase "leaving this Chamber"? In fact, is even the participial phrase necessary, since the writer says "we shall leave it"? And why not simply replace "it" with "Chamber"? Suppose we revise the sentence in these ways:

> We turn aside today for a moment from controversy and business and leave this Chamber to darkness and silence.

The revision is certainly briefer; the original has been cut by more than a third. And so far as factual information is concerned, the substance is the same: we know that the House will recess for the remainder of the day. To insist here upon brevity, however, is to miss the whole point. The purpose of this sentence is not to convey factual information; it is to arouse a mood of sadness. To achieve that purpose Baldwin depended upon the eloquent rhythm sustained by the repetitions of "from" and "to," of "as we leave" and "we shall leave." These words, then, are not dead, because they help to create tone, and in this passage tone is the most important aspect of meaning.

As these examples make clear, we must conceive "meaning" in the broadest possible sense before deciding that a word or phrase is truly dead. Even when we apply our conception of meaning so carefully, however, we shall still find that deadwood is a recurring misfortune in the prose of most inexperienced writers. It is, indeed, one of their fundamental faults. Deadwood is probably a symptom rather than a cause of bad prose; but the case is one in which removing the symptoms would cure the disease. If teachers could wave a wand and magically remove all the deadwood from the compositions of student writers there would be little need of teaching anything more about sentences. They would have become, in that miraculous instant, clear, concise, effective. Teachers, unhappily, have no magic wands. All we can do is to discuss deadwood, first looking very briefly at a few of the motives that lead to it, and then examining in more detail some of the specific faults of thinking, of sentence construction, and of word choice that result in deadwood. At the end of the discussion you will still be writing deadwood — it is, to be honest, a constant, continuing problem for everyone who writes — but at least you will have a better idea of what it is, where it comes from, and what to do about it.

The Psychology of Deadwood

The most important part of our study of deadwood will be with how it manifests itself in actual writing. It will help us understand these manifestations, however, if we consider for a moment the states of mind that render a writer especially prone to deadwood. One is certainly the "fallacy of verbal profundity," the notion that just because a word or phrase looks profound and sounds profound it *has* to say something. The person, for example, who exclaimed of a painting that it "exhibited orderly and harmonious juxtapositions of color patternings" seems to be saying a great deal. But if the phrase means anything more than "color harmony," it is difficult to see what.

Closely related to verbal profundity is the desire to endow a mundane subject with a heightened dignity or elegance. Someone who writes

A worker checks the watch's time-keeping performance

is trying to cast a verbal spell over the job of quality control in a watch factory. It would be better simply to say ". . . the watch's accuracy." To describe chemistry as

> that branch of physical science that is deeply involved with the study of matter

is to suggest a false aura of impressiveness that this simpler statement avoids:

> Chemistry is that branch of physical science that studies matter.

(It is beside the point that neither version is a particularly enlightening definition of chemistry.) The trouble with phrases like "time-keeping performance" and "deeply involved with the study of" is that they are inherently false. Anyone who has worked in a factory or a chemistry laboratory recognizes the falseness. The point is not that quality control and chemistry are unimportant. Rather it is that their importance is not honestly conveyed by such pretentious phrases.

Confusion and ignorance are less reprehensible than verbal profundity and false elegance. Yet these, too, are part of the psychology of deadwood. Confusion about what one's point really is, results in a great deal of wordiness. Here is a case:

> Music is similar to dress fads in that its style changes from time to time. Perhaps the change is subtle, but no one style of music will remain on top for a very long time. I am not talking about classical music, but rather about popular music that appeals to the majority of young people.

As soon as we read the last sentence we realize that when he began this paragraph the writer was not sure of his point. His confusion led him to choose far too big a topic ("music"), which he later realized had to be restricted ("popular music"). Had he been sure from the beginning of what he wanted to say, he could have started off:

> Popular music is similar to dress fads . . .

and have dispensed altogether with the twenty-one-word third sentence.

Probably in the preceding case the confusion was simply the result of the writer's not taking the trouble to think out what he wanted to say. Sometimes, however, the reason for deadwood is less a confusion about what one wants to say than a simple ignorance of the words needed to say it, a limitation of one's working vocabulary. That was certainly the problem for the writer of this sentence:

> In this novel part of the theme is stated directly in so many words and part is not so much said in specific words but is more or less hinted at.

Had he known the terms *explicit* and *implicit* he could have stated his point much more succinctly:

> In this novel part of the theme is explicit and part is implicit.

Vocabulary limitations of this sort are no disgrace. In varying degrees we all suffer from them, and education, in part, is the process of removing them. But pardonable or not, ignorance of words often results in deadwood and obscurity. It is helpful to beginners to make a list of words which, like *implicit* and *explicit*, enable one to make distinctions quickly and neatly (*extrinsic-intrinsic, concrete-abstract, actual-ideal, absolute-relative* are other examples).

Finally, excessive caution is another psychological cause of deadwood. Some people are afraid of expressing anything as being certain. They will say, "It seems as if it were in the vicinity of twelve o'clock" instead of "It is noon." There is certainly a time to be cautious, and no one can lay down a blanket rule about when a qualification is necessary and when it is so much deadwood. We shall look at over-qualification in more detail a few pages further on; here let us merely note that in composition extreme caution is more likely to be a vice than a virtue.

A false sense of what is significant, confusion about one's ideas, ignorance of words, failing to think out a writing problem, and an overdeveloped sense of caution are some of the main psychological factors involved in deadwood. It remains to examine deadwood more closely as it reveals itself in the writer's ideas, sentences, and diction.

The Sources of Deadwood

DEADWOOD IN IDEA

It is arbitrary to assign some cases of deadwood to confusion of idea and others to errors in sentence structure or diction. Any error in word choice or syntax that results in wordiness is evidence of confused or mistaken thinking. Still, even if it does not reflect any absolute distinction, it is convenient for purposes of learning to distinguish these three sources of deadwood. The first is confusion of idea, which reveals itself in two ways: (1) uncertainty about what the point is, and (2) failure to exclude irrelevancies.

Uncertainty of the main point often results in selecting the WRONG SUBJECT. The sentence gets off on the wrong foot and then labors to its end like a man plodding through thick mud. Here is an example from a theme about baseball; in the paragraph the writer has been discussing the players' equipment:

> The first baseman wears a special leather glove that is designed especially for easy scooping and for long-range catching. The catcher wears a large glove that is heavily padded in order to protect him from fast pitches.

The subject of the first sentence is "the first baseman," of the second "the catcher"; but the things really being compared here are the gloves, not the players. Consequently, both sentences require unnecessary verbs ("wears") to get from the grammatical subject to the real topic. If we revise the passage, making "glove" the subject, several economies are possible, the "that is's" can be dropped; one of the "for's" in the first sentence can be excised; and "in order" can be omitted from the second. The two sentences, moreover, could easily be co-ordinated so that one use of "glove" serves both statements:

> The first baseman's glove is specially designed for easy scooping and long-range catching, and the catcher's is large and heavily padded to protect him from fast pitches.

So pruned the sentence is improved. It begins with the proper subject and moves along smartly.

Even when a writer knows what his principal topic is, he may still be confused about what is relevant to it and what is not. Irrelevancies, indeed, are a major source of deadwood. Sometimes they take the form of UNDEVELOPED IDEAS. Consider this sentence:

> The people had come here for freedom of different sorts, and had found injustice instead.

The trouble is in the phrase "of different sorts." Since the writer nowhere discusses the "different sorts" of freedom he here mentions, mentioning it at all is deadwood. It is certainly true that there are various kinds of freedom, but here, since it is not an idea the writer intends to develop, it is irrelevant and thus dead.

A special type of undeveloped idea is making a DISTINCTION WITHOUT A DIFFERENCE, as in this sentence:

> Under the honor system, teachers would not have to stand guard during exams, tests, or quizzes.

There are legitimate distinctions to be made between examinations, tests, and quizzes; and had this theme been about the various kinds of testing students must endure, the distinctions might have been vital. In the context in which this sentence did occur, however, the topic was the honor system, not examinations, and only one word, probably "tests" as being the most general, was needed.

Another kind of irrelevancy is the UNNECESSARY DEFINITION, as in this example:

> Accountants sometimes function as auditors (men from outside a company who check the books kept by the company's accountants).

The writer did not need to define "auditor"; he could have assumed an understanding of this term to be within the general knowledge of his reader. We grant that it is not easy to decide when one needs to define a term. One must always decide this question on the basis of his reader's needs. Whenever you define a word, ask yourself if the definition is necessary *for the reader for whom you are writing.* Not only does unnecessary definition result in deadwood; it can interfere with communication in a more important way — irritating the reader by seeming to insult his intelligence. Few people enjoy being taught what they already know.

Closely related to unnecessary definition is the irrelevancy called OVER-EXPLICITNESS, which is stating what is already clear by implication. Some over-explicitness is the result of not understanding the implicit aspect of word meaning, as when someone says that a book is "blue in color," not realizing that the idea "color" is already part of the meaning of "blue." Words such as *involved, looking, needed, particular, employed,* are often guilty of being deadwood in this way:

> Usually this pitch is thrown only by the expert because of the danger *involved.*
>
> It was a comical *looking* sight.
>
> In order to play billiards, the equipment *needed* has to be of high quality.
>
> A coach may spend an hour with a *particular* player, teaching him fundamentals.
>
> We may question the value of the methods *employed.*

Over-explicitness may take more subtle form; for example:

> Most countries of the world have their own system of coinage.

When men get to other worlds they may discover other countries, but, so far at least, the term "countries" implies "the world." Or again:

> These are matters that must be met and dealt with.

To deal with anything implies that it has first been "met with."

Now and then over-explicitness is the result of saying something that is implicitly clear — not in the meaning of a specific word, but rather in the total context. Consider the phrase "metal nuts and bolts" in this sentence:

> Since the gasoline engine is small, metal nuts and bolts tend to work loose.

Now it is not necessary that nuts and bolts be made of metal; they are sometimes made of plastic or of wood, for instance — but not for gasoline engines. Because the context here makes abundantly clear that the material must be metal, the word itself is unnecessary. Another example is the following passage:

> Skiing is limited to the northern and mountainous regions of the United States because of the geographic and weather conditions necessary for satisfactory skiing.

What is dead here?

A rather special, but very frequent, form of contextual over-explicitness is the unnecessary connective, a fault especially frequent with conjunctive adverbs. For example, the following sentence does not really need "however":

> People think that stamp collecting requires money. However, it doesn't.

The negative verb is enough to establish the contradiction; "however" merely labors the obvious. Note, too, that in this case stating the contradiction by the adverb "however" has the paradoxical effect of muting the contradiction and so of de-emphasizing what should be a strong assertion. This is more emphatic:

> People think that stamp collecting requires money. It doesn't.

On the whole, student writers are more likely to use too few conjunctive adverbs than too many, and certainly it is better to annoy a reader by being over-explicit in indicating logical relationships, than to confuse him by taking too much for granted. Even so, it would pay you to check connectives like *however, thus, therefore, consequently, then, still,* and so on to be sure that you really need them, or, to be more precise, that your reader needs them.

Finally, over-explicitness may result in making STATEMENTS OF STATEMENTS. Here is an example:

> Let me state the fact that the robin's migration is not sudden.

This sentence contains two statements, which — if we may reverse their order — are: (1) that the robin's migration is not sudden, and (2) that the writer is going to state this fact. Now the act of writing is itself an implicit statement that one is stating something. Occasionally emphasis or clarity requires one to say in effect, "I am now going to say something," but not very often. In the case of the robin's migration there is certainly no need of it; all the writer has to say is:

> The robin's migration is not sudden.

Perhaps the most common instance of "stating statements" is being too explicit about the plan of a paragraph or essay. Here, for example, are two sentences from the beginning paragraph of a theme:

> The two major divisions of modern pharmacy are drug store pharmacy and research pharmacy, the latter being the more difficult and the higher paying. I will concentrate my efforts on analyzing each and its importance to the community.

The chief problem is the second sentence. We have seen that in beginning paragraphs and in signposts there is sometimes a virtue in indicating organization very explicitly, especially in legal, scholarly, or scientific writing. In student themes, however, such literal statement of intent is rarely necessary. In this case the second sentence can easily be reduced to: "Both are important."

Still another kind of irrelevancy is REDUNDANCY (also called TAUTOLOGY), which means needlessly saying the same thing more than once. It is possible to repeat a key idea as a way of stressing it, but such legitimate repetition is called "restatement" and is distinguished from redundancy, which is a functionless and wasteful repetition. Examples are easy to come by:

> bisect in half
> sufficiently satisfied
> vital essentials
> It is clearly evident that . . .

While they are very similar, these cases of redundancy are not quite the same thing as making implicit ideas explicit. "Blue" implies "color"; but "bisect" means the same thing as "cut in half," and "essentials" means that which is "vital."

These are all obvious instances. Tautology can be more subtle, hidden by an apparent difference in the meanings of the words in which it is expressed, as in these two sentences:

> It has many parts, each with its own function to perform.
>
> New England weather has been going through a process of changing from hot to cold.

To have a "function" is to have something "to perform"; "going through a process" is "changing." It is to this variety of deadwood that the constructions "reason is because" and "the reason why" belong:

> This is the reason why many people enjoy the hobby of stamp collecting.

Now and then it may be arguable that emphasis requires a writer to state the idea of cause twice. But usually "reason" (or "why") by itself is enough:

> This is the reason many people enjoy the hobby of stamp collecting.

(Might it be argued, incidentally, that the phrase "the hobby of" is not needed here?)

A final variety of irrelevancy is OVER-QUALIFICATION. We have already mentioned that excessive caution is one of the psychological aspects of deadwood; over-qualification is the expression of that caution. The person who wrote:

> Theater in the round somewhat resembles an arena

was being much too timid. "Resembles" does not mean "is identical with"; it is in itself a cautious word and hardly requires the extra protection of "somewhat." Writing of this sort is comparable to a man's holding up his pants with a belt, suspenders, and two or three huge safety pins for good measure.

Verbs like *tend, seem, would,* and the prolix phrase *can be said to be* (in place of the simpler *is*) are often instances of over-qualification:

> This play *tends to be* a tragedy.
>
> After a square dance the people are pretty tired, but *it seems that* when they have tried it once, they can't stop asking for more.
>
> Scarcity *can be said to be* a major cause of inflation.

Seems is an especially common offender. Some writers are afraid to say anything without the cautionary preface of "it seems that."

In all this talk about over-qualification we do not want to leave you thinking that any qualification is a sign of weak-mindedness or timidity. The writer who puts his head down and plunges straight ahead, ignoring the limitations of his ideas, is likely to plunge headfirst into a brick wall. But there is a danger in unnecessary caution. Qualify, but qualify only when you must.

SYNTACTIC SOURCES

So far we have considered those kinds of deadwood that result from uncertainty of what the main point is or of what is important to that point. Let us turn next to deadwood that comes from handling sentence structure inefficiently. One fault is NOT USING THE MAIN ELEMENTS PROPERLY. The main elements of a sentence — its subject, verb, and object — ought to convey the heart of the idea, so that if we abstract these elements and string them together we have the essence of the statement or as close to it as we can get. Consider this sentence: "The war caused many changes." Applying the test of abstraction, we have: "war caused changes," certainly the nub of the idea. Applying the same test to the sentence "The fact of the war had an effect of bringing about many changes," we have "fact had effect" — hardly a meaningful phrase. The second sentence is much longer than the first. It is longer because the writer did not use his main elements effectively. Here is another example:

> Golf is a means of support for professional golfers, who play in tournaments throughout the world to support themselves by earning prize-money.

The main elements are "golf is means," which do not convey what the writer wanted to say. His point was this:

> Professional golfers support themselves by playing in tournaments throughout the world.

Often the failure to use the main elements efficiently is the result of AWKWARD ANTICIPATORY CONSTRUCTIONS. (An anticipatory construction is a sentence in which the subject is introduced by a word like *it, this, there,* and so on, as in "There are people who like Chicago" or "It is truc that we objected to him at first.") Though it is usually wordier than a direct statement, an anticipatory construction is not necessarily awkward or dead. To revise "there are many kinds of wine" into "many kinds of wine exist," for example, would prune one word but would result in a stiff, unidiomatic sentence much less effective than the "there are" construction. But a sentence like the following is less easy to justify:

> These are the golfers that are known as "hackers."

Here the important subject ("golfers") is followed by an adjective clause containing the essential predicate ("are known as 'hackers' "). It would be briefer and clearer to write:

> These golfers are known as "hackers."

When you use anticipatory constructions be sure that idiom or emphasis justify them.

Much like failing to use main elements effectively is using ADVERBIAL CLAUSES TO CONTAIN IDEAS THAT BELONG TO THE SUBJECT, as in:

> If a student wishes to change his course, he must see his adviser.

The logical subject is "student," but notice that the writer is referring only to a particular kind of student — one wishing to change his course — and that therefore he must add modifiers to narrow down the idea "student." Instead of employing an adjective construction, which would seem the natural choice to restrict a noun, he chose the adverbial clause "if a student wishes to change his course." Thus an idea that logically belongs to the subject has been transferred grammatically to the predicate, and the sentence has been made longer than it need be. More form words are required (the conjunction "if," for example) and the subject must be stated twice ("student" and "he"). It would be more concise to write:

> A student wishing to change his course must see his adviser.

The gain in economy is slight. What is more important is that the revision is clearer and stronger. It is clearer because the subject-predicate structure of the sentence corresponds to the subject-predicate structure of the proposition the sentence states. The writer's proposition is about the student who wishes to change his course, and "a student wishing to change his course" is the subject of the sentence (we are using the term "subject" here in its broad sense to mean the actual subject word plus all its modifiers). Similarly, the predicate of the proposition — that this student "must see his adviser" — is the same as the predicate of the sentence.

Adverbial *when* and *if* clauses are often misused to convey information that would be expressed more efficiently and more logically in adjective constructions modifying the subject word:

> When a student goes to college for the first time he must learn new habits of study.

Another syntactic source of deadwood is INDIRECT MODIFICATION, that is, not linking modifiers as immediately as possible to the words they modify. The sentence we quoted on page 281 is a good example. The trouble with "She dresses in a beautiful manner" is that the adjective does not modify grammatically the same word that it relates to notionally. Notionally it describes how she "dresses"; but grammatically it is tied to "manner," through which it connects to the verb only indirectly. This tendency to apply essentially adverbial ideas indirectly by expressing them as adjectives is very frequent:

> The organization of a small business can be described in a short time. (Better: ". . . can be briefly described.")

> She conducted herself with irrational behavior. (Better: "She behaved irrationally.")

Equally wordy is attaching adjectives to dead nouns, that is, to words which simply repeat or stand for a noun that was expressed earlier in the same sentence and which the adjective logically modifies. The following construction is typical:

> Riots became frequent affairs.

"Affairs" is a dead noun merely standing for the idea already expressed by "riots" and serving as a peg upon which to hang the attributive adjective "frequent." But "frequent" can be used more directly as a predicative:

> Riots became frequent.

This is a better sentence, not only because it is more concise but because it ends strongly on a key term. Here are other examples:

> Mr. Martin is a quiet, patient, and cautious person. (Better: "Mr. Martin is quiet, patient, and cautious.")

> The day was a perfect one. (Better: "The day was perfect.")

> Each player on the offensive team . . . (Better: "Each offensive player . . .")

Notice that while the effect is the same the last sentence differs from the others in that the dead word ("team") is not predicate noun like "affairs" or "person" but the object of a preposition. A more general way of describing the fault in this case is to say that the writer has used a phrase where a single word would do. The same flaw is evident in these sentences:

> He prefers wine having a French origin.
>
> The weapon best manipulated by them is the boomerang.

In the first, the phrase "having a French origin" is easily replaced by the single word "French." In the second, "the weapon best manipulated by them" reduces to "their best weapon."

There are several special varieties of using phrases in place of words. One is the habit of needlessly putting complements into periphrastic form, as in:

> The counter is of mahogany. (Better: "The counter is mahogany.")

Another is using a prepositional construction instead of the genitive form of a noun or pronoun. Sometimes one cannot employ the *'s* genitive, but where one can it is more concise. Thus the sentence:

> He didn't take the advice given to him by his doctor

might be better expressed:

> He didn't take his doctor's advice.

And similarly it would be wise to tighten this sentence:

> The nurse's first year in training teaches her the causes of many diseases and the cures for them. (Better: ". . . and their cures." Notice again how the emphasis is improved.)

On a slightly larger scale the same habit is revealed in using full clauses as modifiers when a briefer phrase will serve as well:

> American exploration was rapid considering the means by which the pioneers had to go about it. (Better: ". . . was rapid considering the means available to the pioneers.")

Sometimes an entire clause may be boiled down to a single word. Thus the sentence:

> The targets that are supplied in skeet shooting are discs made of clay

can be pruned to:

> Skeet targets are clay discs.

A final instance of non-direct modification is using words like *most, some, many, a few, both, several,* and so on, as headwords when they would function better as modifiers. The following sentences illustrate the point:

> Most of the Connecticut farmhouses are of the saltbox type. (Better: "Most Connecticut farmhouses are . . .")
>
> In both of these cases . . . (Better: "In both cases . . .")

A special kind of non-direct modification is so widespread that we shall treat it separately. This is the FAILURE TO USE PARTICIPLES. An inexperienced writer will employ a full adjective or adverbial clause (or even an independent clause) to express an idea that could be conveyed just as clearly by a participle. Study, for example, the relative clause in this sentence:

> This is the idea that was suggested last week.

The clause consists of a relative word (here "that"; in other cases *which* or *who*) immediately followed by "was" (or *is, are,* and so on) and then by the past participle "suggested" (sometimes a present participle or a predicate adjective or predicate noun follows the linking verb). Relative adjective clauses often follow this pattern. In some instances it is better to dispense with the relative word and the linking verb and move directly from the noun being modified to the participle (or predicate adjective or noun), as in this revision of the example:

> This is the idea suggested last week.

Occasionally such a revision, while briefer, will sacrifice emphasis or move so rapidly that the reader may be confused. Then, of course, the full relative clause should be kept. When they prevent misunderstanding or establish important stress, the words *that is* are certainly not deadwood. But if no shading of emphasis has been lost and if no confusion is likely, then using the participle directly to modify the noun will improve the sentence. In the same way abstract nouns in prepositional phrases can often be replaced by participles:

> It leaves us with the thought that . . . (Better: "It leave us thinking that . . .")

Full adverbial clauses are sometimes as unnecessary as full relative clauses. For instance, the sentence:

> Because they were tired, the men returned to camp

can be shortened to:

> Tired, the men returned to camp.

Occasionally even an independent clause can be reduced to a participial construction. In the sentence:

> These football plays are very effective, and they often prove to be long gainers

the finite verb "prove" may be turned into the non-finite form, "proving":

> These football plays are very effective, often proving to be long gainers.

In the same way an entire second sentence may be better handled as a participial construction. Thus the sentences:

> The women of the settlement would gather at one home and work together on the quilt. They brought their children with them and spent the entire day there, and chattered gaily as they worked,

become:

> The women of the settlement would gather at one home and work together on the quilt, bringing their children and spending the entire day, chattering gaily as they worked.

The saving in words has not been great here; only two terms were lopped off by using the participle: the subject did not have to be repeated by "they," and "there" was no longer needed as an adverb of place (the phrase "with them," unnecessary in the context, could have been dropped in any case). But the tightening of the passage improves its clarity. The original two sentences forced an awkward analysis of the writer's idea, dividing into two parts what was essentially the single, unified experience of the quilting bee. The second sentence, moreover, placed too much stress upon the women's bringing their children, which was not important. Using a participle to subordinate the second statement not only serves the virtue of concision but also focuses the sentence more sharply and preserves the unity of the topic.

Even in cases that do not involve participles the FAILURE TO SUBORDINATE is productive of much deadwood. Here is an example:

> Pocket billiards is a very old game that originated in Europe. The game is a variation of billiards.

These two sentences can be reduced to a single construction by subordinating one or the other in the form of a non-restrictive modifier:

> Pocket billiards, a variation of billiards, is quite an old game that originated in Europe.

or

> Pocket billiards, quite an old game that originated in Europe, is a variation of billiards.

In either version the focus is clearer.

Still another syntactic source of deadwood is NOT USING PARALLELISM. We saw in discussing the various kinds of sentences that parallelism is thrifty. The following passages illustrate the deadwood that results from not employing parallelism. The first repeats a verb unnecessarily:

> These plays are not used primarily to gain yardage, but are used to set up other plays. (Better: "These plays are used primarily not to gain yardage but to set up other plays.")

The second repeats both the verb and the subject word:

> The beginner must work more slowly and he must work more consciously. (Better: "The beginner must work more slowly and more consciously.")

The concision gained by parallelism may at times sacrifice emphasis or rhythm. Then it is better to repeat the subject or the verb or whatever words require stress. Where such emphasis is not a consideration, parallelism will avoid deadwood.

Parallelism can be regarded as a special case of ELLIPSIS, that is, omitting from a sentence words that the reader can supply for himself. Ellipsis is quite common in sophisticated writing; in addition to parallelism, some of the techniques we mentioned under "non-direct modification" might be viewed as matters of ellipsis. There are other situations involving neither parallelism nor direct modification in which the omission of words secures concision with no cost in clarity or emphasis, and may in fact even enhance these qualities. A simple instance is the adverbial clause of comparison:

> He is taller than his brother is.

The meaning does not require the second "is"; notice that removing it allows the sentence to end on "brother," a key term. Another instance is omitting the subject and verb in certain adverbial clauses, using only the conjunction and the participle (or object or adverb) of the clause. Thus the sentence:

> When you are late, you must sign yourself in

can be treated elliptically:

> When late, you must sign yourself in.

A third, less common, use of ellipsis is omitting the linking participle in nominative absolutes. In this way the sentence:

The party being over, we decided to leave

may be rendered:

The party over, we decided to leave.

A final case of ellipsis is dropping the verb in the second of two independent clauses when it repeats the verb of the first. For example:

He lost his wallet; she lost her pocketbook

can be reduced to:

He lost his wallet; she, her pocketbook.

A reader may be expected to supply the second verb by analogy with the first, though often a writer will place a comma between the subject and the object to signal that the verb needs to be supplied. Ellipses such as this involving the omission of a repeated verb are rather artificial (in a neutral, not derogatory sense of that term), but used on appropriate occasions they are concise and effective.

Another source of deadwood that is in essence a matter of syntax is FAILURE TO USE THE COLON OR DASH. In expository writing it is often necessary to introduce a list or series. The work of setting up the list can usually be done by a colon or a dash, thus making unnecessary a phrase or clause of introduction. (Either the colon or the dash may be employed for this purpose. The only difference between them is a matter of tone — the colon being more formal. In other functions, however, the colon and the dash are *not* interchangeable; but this we shall discuss in the chapter on punctuation.) The following sentence is an example of how a colon may be used for economy:

> There were many reasons for the Civil War, which include slavery, economic expansion, the issue of state's rights, cultural differences, and sectional jealousies.

It is more effective and concise like this:

> There were many reasons for the Civil War: slavery, economic expansion, the issue of state's rights, cultural differences, and sectional jealousies.

Sometimes two sentences can be more economically combined into one by using a colon or dash:

> Their pitchers are divided into two classes. These classes are the starting pitchers and the relieving pitchers. (Better: "Their pitchers

> are divided into two classes — starting pitchers and relieving pitchers.")

(Is it necessary to have so many "pitcher's"? Why not: "Their pitchers are divided into two classes — starters and relievers"?)

The conciseness of the colon and the dash is useful not only in introducing lists and series but also in setting up a key term that has been delayed for emphasis. Consider these sentences:

> But a counterforce has been established within the weapons platoon. This counterforce is the anti-tank squad.

The key phrase is "anti-tank squad." The writer, correctly wishing to stress it, has delayed the phrase until the very end. But by placing his phrase in an unnecessary second sentence he has forced himself to repeat the subject ("counterforce") and to supply a linking verb ("is"). He would have been better off using a dash (or colon):

> But a counterforce has been established within the weapons platoon — the anti-tank squad.

So expressed, the passage is not only more concise, but the phrase "anti-tank squad" has more stress than it had before.

A final syntactic source of deadwood involves SOLECISMS, or grammatical mistakes in sentence structure. Many such mistakes are possible in English (and ingenious people now and then discover new varieties), but two are especially common in composition and both result in deadwood. The first is unnecessary repetition of the subject, as in:

> The man who went to Chicago, he was very foolish.

This device of stating the subject twice is not a technique of English syntax. Although occasionally it may be a useful means of emphasis, it ought to be avoided in the crude form of our example. The second common solecism that produces deadwood is repeating the preposition in certain types of *which* clauses, as in:

> The idea of which you spoke of is very good.

Beginning writers are sometimes uncertain about the syntax of adjective clauses of this kind and resolve their uncertainty by covering both ends of the clause with a preposition (and not always the same preposition — which makes matters worse).

DICTIONAL SOURCES

So far we have been concerned with deadwood that results either from confusion of idea or from failure to handle sentence structure efficiently. A third source remains — not using words effectively. Some of what we have already said about deadwood of idea and deadwood of syntax has overlapped the area of diction (in discussing concision it is not really possible to separate thoughts, sentences, and words except arbitrarily); but it is only in this section that we leave completely the precincts of sentence style and enter those of diction.

One important dictional source of deadwood — failure to understand the nature of implicit meaning — we have already touched upon. Here we need only remind you that expressions like "young in age" and "expensive in cost" will prove, ninety times out of a hundred, to contain deadwood. A source of wordiness that we shall discuss here is BEGINNING WITH TOO BIG A WORD, an error especially prevalent with nouns. Here is a good example:

> Most people today consider golf a recreational activity.

The problem is that "activity" is far too inclusive a word for what the writer wants to say; there are all kinds of activities — business activity, educational activity, manufacturing activity, and so on. Having begun with so inclusive a noun, the writer is forced to add modifiers (in this case "recreational") to indicate which of these many activities he means. Why not use a precise noun? The problem is easily solved:

> Most people today consider golf a recreation.

The following sentence is a more extreme illustration:

> When a boy enters college he has his ideas of what he would like to do with his life.

"Ideas" is a vast word; the writer must follow it with a string of modifiers totaling ten words to narrow it down, and even then it is not clear what he means. What he means, we think, is:

> When a boy enters college he has his ambitions (or possibly "dreams").

In these two examples the too-big noun and its modifier could be replaced with a single noun precise enough to require no modification. In other cases it is impossible to find a noun so precise that it needs no adjective to clarify it, but even then unnecessary modification will be avoided by beginning with as exact a noun as possible. Thus in revising the sentence:

> People who enter college for the first time find it difficult to adjust to new routines,

it is not easy to find a single word that means "people who enter college for the first time." ("Matriculants" might do, but it is a learned and forbidding word.) The closest one can get in common language is this:

> Beginning college students must adjust to new routines.

Even so, the sentence has been cut from sixteen words to eight and made clearer in the bargain. Over-big nouns, then, are a common source of deadwood. By "over-big nouns" we mean over-big for their context. Do not suppose that general, inclusive nouns are always bad. Sometimes you *do* mean activity in general or people of all varieties. But when you wish to designate a special activity or a particular group of people, begin if you can with a more precise noun.

The too-big word is also a problem with verbs. For example, in the sentence:

> The sudden change motivated him into a rage,

"motivate" is too large. To specify it the writer must add the phrase "into a rage." Why not use "enrage"?

> The sudden change enraged him.

Here are two more examples:

> The thermostats are adjusted so as to keep the heat higher. (Better: "The thermostats are raised.")

> Meteorology is that branch of science which deals with the prediction of weather. (Better: "Meteorology is that branch of science which predicts weather.")

Using too-big a verb is merely one aspect of an even more general source of deadwood — FAILURE TO USE VERBS COMMUNICATIVELY. Too many inexperienced writers tend to convey their ideas almost exclusively in nouns, employing verbs simply as empty words to hook up subjects and objects. A typical example is:

> The depression had an effect upon world trade.

The key words here — "depression," "effect," "world trade" — are all nouns. The verb "had" simply links "depression" and "effect"; it is not essentially different in function from the preposition "upon," which similarly links "effect" and "world trade." But if "effect" were to be expressed as a verb, the word would do double duty, not only linking subject and object but also communicating part of the idea:

> The depression affected the economy.

This habit of employing verbs only as form words to connect nouns is very common. As a consequence there are such wordy sentences as these:

> These are the men who do the actual work involved in the manufacture of the product. (Better: "These are the men who actually manufacture the product.")

> The head of the business is the president, who is the overseer of the rest of the executives. (Better: "The head of the business is the president, who oversees the rest of the executives.")

> A teacher has to have a knowledge of his students. (Better: "A teacher has to know his students.")

In your own writing try to use precise verbs that communicate part of your key idea, instead of conveying the point exclusively in nouns and trotting out the same old linking verbs — *is, has, does, makes, seems,* and so on.

Another variety of deadwood connected with verbs is the AWKWARD AND UNNECESSARY USE OF THE PASSIVE VOICE. The passive voice has legitimate functions in English. One case is when the active subject is not known or cannot easily be stated, as in "He was hurt in an accident." To express this in an active construction we must know what hurt him. It would be unidiomatic to write "The accident hurt him." Unless we do know what inflicted the damage — the other car, his own windshield or steering wheel — it is much more convenient to use the passive voice. Another case is when the passive subject is more important. Someone watching an electrical storm and more interested in the lightning than in what it strikes, would find it natural to use the active voice and say, "Lightning struck the tree." But if the tree is the center of his attention, the passive affords the more appropriate emphasis: "The tree was struck by lightning." Still a third case is that in which tact, delicacy, or modesty makes the active voice seem conceited or impolite. "It has been decided that no raises will be given this year," for example, is a tactful way of saying, "We will not raise your salary."

It is perhaps an over-sensitive concern with this kind of delicacy that has helped to spread the passive construction. Too many people seem to have been taught that it is bad manners to write "I." Seeking to avoid reference to themselves, they have fallen, quite naturally, into an habitual use of the passive — and the passive *is* habit-forming. When the passive is not called for, the extra words it requires become so much deadwood, as in this sentence:

> The writer's point must be clearly stated by the writer at the beginning of the paragraph.

The context in which this passage occurred was about "the writer," a focus that this sentence blurs (the student's repetition of "writer's . . . by the writer" suggests that he is uneasily aware of the shifting focus). The sentence is better this way:

> The writer must state his point at the beginning of the paragraph.

Do not conclude that the passive voice is always wrong in composition — it is not. But use it only when the focus or emphasis of the sentence requires it.

Finally in connection with verbs we may remark upon the habit of PILING UP VERBS AND VERBIDS. Some writers delight in heaping gerund upon verb, infinitive upon gerund, as in this sentence:

> The four infielders have the job of building a barrier to stop any ball hit to them.

"*Have* the job of *building* . . . *to stop*" — one wonders if the verbs and metaphors will ever end. This is simpler, more direct, and much clearer:

> The four infielders must stop any ball hit to them.

Piling up verbs is a common mistake, and examples abound:

> The current Berlin situation *should serve to start* many Americans thinking.
>
> Nucleonics investigates the smaller particles that *go to make up* the nucleus of the atom.
>
> He used his fine intelligence *to keep from having to get* a job.

Like verbs, pronouns are often employed inefficiently. The FAILURE TO USE PRONOUNS SUBSTANTIVELY is another source of deadwood. Instead of allowing it to stand for a noun already stated, a prolix writer will use a pronoun as an adjective modifying an unnecessary repetition of that noun, as in the sentence:

> When assembled, a rifle is a perfect functioning unit, each part relying on the other parts. (Better: ". . . each part relying on the others.")

The same habit is often revealed with framing words (see page 151) used to unify the sentences within a paragraph:

> One way to read a poem is . . . Another way is . . . (Better: "One way to read a poem is . . . Another is . . .")

Very similar to not using pronouns in place of nouns is the FAILURE TO USE ADJECTIVES SUBSTANTIVELY. When an adjective modifies a noun or pronoun whose meaning is clearly implied by the context, it is possible to substitute the adjective for the noun. Thus the sentence:

> On quilts, silk patches replaced the earlier homespun ones

can be expressed:

> On quilts, silk patches replaced the earlier homespun.

Here again the revision is not simply more concise; it heightens the important contrast between "silk" and "homespun." Since the point is that the use of silk patches was a sign of the increasing prosperity of colonial America, the revision, by sharpening the contrast, communicates that point more effectively.

Finally in connection with adjectives, deadwood may result from USING THE DEFINITE ARTICLE UNNECESSARILY. For example, in the sentence:

> Great players cannot win the games by themselves,

"the" implies not games in general but certain specific games. Sometimes specification is exactly what the writer intends. Here it was not; the writer meant games in general. Consequently the definite article is not only dead, but subtly misleading; and the sentence would be both more concise and clearer like this:

> Great players cannot win games by themselves.

In the same way the first three "the's" are dead in the following sentence describing the routine duties of a housewife:

> For two hours she makes the beds, washes the dirty dishes, dusts the furniture, and mops the bathroom and kitchen floors.

Why, incidentally, isn't the last "the" deadwood? And might "dirty" be pruned?

We saw a few pages back that inexperienced writers pile up verbs; some also have a habit of using OVERLONG CONNECTIVES. Here is a case:

> More than one game has been decided on the basis of a fumble.

The windy phrase "on the basis of" can be replaced by the preposition "by." Wordy equivalents for *because* are especially common:

> Great Britain is losing her industrial position *through the fact that* the authorities do not value or promote intelligence.
>
> His success was probably *due to the fact that* all his problems were easily solved.
>
> The bill failed *as a result of the fact that* the Senate was misinformed.

So are wordy equivalents for *how:*

> He will show us *the way in which* to do it.
>
> He can be classified more specifically depending upon *the manner in which* we interpret his character.

And so, finally, are three or four word connectives that are simply awkward ways of saying *so . . . that:*

> He becomes self-conscious *to the extent that* he withdraws into himself. (Better: "He becomes so self-conscious that he withdraws into himself.")
>
> Some men are brave and courageous *to the point where* they overstep their limitations. (Better: "Some men are so brave and courageous that they overstep their limitations." Are both "brave" and "courageous" necessary here, by the way?)

There are many more instances of overlong connectives — *off of, outside of* (as in "outside of the house"), *at about,* to cite only a few. Perhaps originally these extra prepositions were thought to add forcefulness. If so, they have lost that capacity and now are merely deadwood. In all these cases a fundamental principle of good writing is being violated: connecting words should be kept to a minimum.

Another dictional source of deadwood is USING GERUNDS INEFFICIENTLY. In the evolution of English the gerund and the present participle, once pronounced and spelled in different ways, chanced to fall together in the same form. Consequently the gerund, in origin simply a noun made from a verb, has acquired some of the verb-like characteristics of the participle. Of these the ability to take an object is especially conducive to efficiency. But sometimes writers, rather than stating the object of a gerund directly, will express it periphrastically like this:

> She worried about the cooking of the dinner.

If the writer meant that "she" was worried about someone else's cooking the dinner, this construction makes sense. As it happens, however, "she" was her own cook, and consequently the meaning could be more succinctly expressed:

> She worried about cooking the dinner.

Here is another example:

> Basketball guards must be skilled in the dribbling and the handling of the ball. (Better: "Basketball guards must be skilled in dribbling and handling the ball.")

Using the verbal qualities of the gerund also allows the writer to dispense with the definite article.

So far we have seen how misusing the various parts of speech — nouns, verbs, pronouns, connectives — results in deadwood. We come, finally, to several varieties of dictional deadwood that derive from lapses of taste and simpe ignorance of idiom. A frequent instance of the first is TRITENESS. The trite phrase is one in which an originally effective meaning has been rubbed thin by long use. Not all trite expressions contain deadwood; but many do, since they are likely to involve similes or metaphors which, once their freshness has passed, are simply wordy. Thus the sentence:

> His money was all gone, and his friends had departed to the promised land

is not only shorter but more dignified expressed this way:

> His money was all gone, and his friends had died.

Similarly "Mother Nature" is usually better simply as "nature," and "state of affairs" as "state" or "affairs" or "business."

Another lapse in taste is PRETENTIOUS DICTION, that is, saying something simple in several difficult words instead of in one or two easy ones. This is a good example:

> Someone once formulated the saying that united we stand and divided we fall.

If the maxim is worth repeating at all there is no excuse for introducing it with so magniloquent an expression as "formulated the saying." It is much better like this:

> Someone once said that united we stand, divided we fall.

Not only does the revision shorten the original, but it also improves it — playing down the verb of introduction, which is not important, and stressing the saying, which is.

A special case of wordy pretentiousness is the AWKWARD FIGURE. Properly used, figures of speech are, as we shall see in the chapters on diction, an important way of gaining concision and expressiveness by compressing many meanings into few words. But improperly used, metaphors and similes become mere deadwood, as in this sentence:

> The arsenal of a baseball manager includes weapons designed to produce tie-breaking runs in the final innings.

The sentence is better, because it is clearer, when the metaphor has been cut away:

> A baseball manager must know how to produce tie-breaking runs in the final innings.

Finally, dictional deadwood may be due to NOT KNOWING THE PROPER WORD. The foreign student who wrote about a football halfback that "He is the holder of the ball," didn't know the idiomatic phrase "ball-carrier." Native speakers are less likely to make such errors in idiom, though they do crop up ("It is of no wonder," for instance, instead of "it is no wonder"). But even among native speakers, more than a little deadwood is due to sheer ignorance of words. While such ignorance is understandable, there is no reason to rest in it, happily content that what you don't know won't hurt you. Work consciously at increasing your writing vocabularly. The more words you know, the better become your chances of writing clearly and concisely.

Summary

Though we have by no means exhausted it, we have explored the subject of deadwood in some detail because it is important. Deadwood is a symptom rather than a cause of poor writing, but symptom and cause are here so intimately related that to treat one is to remove the other. No one ever learns to avoid deadwood altogether. It would probably be bad if one did. Effective communication depends upon a certain amount of repetition. Moreover, there are times when the need to achieve other virtues in a sentence overrides the demands of concision. Even some of the examples we have cited might be justified for special reasons.

Granting these qualifications, it remains true that a good writer needs constantly to be alert to deadwood. Such vigilance can be wearying. It is disheartening to go over a paragraph for the fourth or fifth time and still find crabgrass among the clover. But even though it is discouraging, systematic weeding is as necessary to writing well as it is to growing a fine lawn.

You ought to know by now a little more about where to look for deadwood in your own writing. If we were to boil down everything we have said about concision into a few principles, they would be these:

1. Think before you write about what you want to say and about whom you are saying it to.
2. Express your ideas in as precise nouns and verbs as you know.
3. Use the main elements of the sentence — the subject, the verb, the object — to carry the essence of your statement; try especially to use the verb communicatively.
4. Keep connecting words to a minimum.
5. Avoid trite expressions, fanciful figures of speech, and big impressive words.

Following these principles will not remove all the wordiness from your writing, but it will get rid of enough deadwood so that you will be composing clearer, more emphatic, and hence much more effective sentences.

Exercises

1. It is not easy to judge deadwood out of context; even so, study the following sentences for examples of this fault. Staying as close as possible to the original syntax and diction, revise the sentences to make them more concise; in each case be prepared to justify your revision.

1. He handled the story very well as to presentation.
2. I dislike television. Most programs on television have a tendency to be directed specifically either toward the young child or toward the adult instead of toward the family as a whole.
3. I find it somewhat enjoyable to be able to accomplish and discover the things that math uncovers for me.
4. They refuse to pay attention or take notice of him.
5. The medical profession is indeed a worthwhile one.
6. He must take courses that will help him to become a well-educated man.
7. The rifle must be lightly oiled in the sense that it can be worked freely without jamming.

8. The Civil War showed that a victory could be possible only if the troops were well supplied. They had to be supplied with food, water, and clothing.
9. This is a gibberish type statement.
10. This exercise serves to help each player to loosen up.
11. Submarines contribute to naval defense by giving protection to the transport ships.
12. He differs in the respect that he values freedom.
13. The do-it-yourself undertakings are fast becoming the most favorite American pastime.
14. One must remember the fact that these people did not have our advantages.
15. They are still subject to obeying the law.
16. We must be on the alert at all times.
17. The people were under the pressure of great conflict and strife at home.
18. As certain situations arise in a football game, there are some plays that are more effective than others.
19. If a person lives in India he would reflect the culture of that country.
20. The operation having been concluded, the patient was wheeled out of the operating room.
21. A good personality will help anyone, no matter what profession he chooses in life.
22. There are many aspects that make up civilization.
23. We must take into consideration the other side of the question.
24. For instance, the sociologist may try to determine why a person who lives in the slums might tend to become an alcoholic.
25. Under these conditions there is usually a flowing stream of knowledge leaving the book and traveling to our brains.
26. This law was designed solely for the purpose of appeasing the conscience of the rich.
27. The repeating of words with the same meaning is a source of deadwood.
28. Thus we shall say that this type of woman may be described as being the ideal customer.
29. This problem has two sides to it.
30. Let us look at the basic fundamentals.
31. There were many reasons for the depression. These reasons include credit buying, widespread speculation in stock, and over-optimism among businessmen.
32. Productivity exceeding the consumer's demands, technological improvement reducing the need for manpower, excessive cost of commodities, and high taxation are some of the economic problems that we must face up to and deal with and solve.
33. With a knowledge of why he is reacting in such a fashion, the neurotic individual may be able to overcome his or her problems.

34. This is done by executing a climbing turn. A climbing turn is a maneuver in which the nose of the plane is held up to gain altitude and the plane is banked just enough to counter the centrifugal force encountered in the turn.
35. Such a display of confidence has a relaxing effect upon the patient.
36. These are the people directly in connection with the automobile industry.
37. The paper must be written by him by tomorrow.
38. Therefore the Navy is organized in such a manner that these aims may be carried out.
39. Our team has emerged victorious.
40. An army, which is a body of men organized and trained to fight, is necessary to every state.
41. No matter what subject was approached, Alice would go into lengthy explanations of the situation. Alice, who had the thought that she was eloquent, in actuality was just plain talkative.
42. The campus contains many new and modern buildings.
43. In platoon headquarters there is a first, or sometimes a second, lieutenant acting as commanding officer of the platoon.
44. This is the biggest factor in determining the success of anyone.
45. When he is at a party, he thinks first of himself.
46. In many European countries a game exists which is similar to football. This game is played on a field and a spherical ball is used in the game. Two teams play the game and the object is to kick the ball into the other opponent's goal.
47. Blood samples were collected from certain ones among the patients.
48. One would be led to believe that people had never heard of a balanced diet.
49. There are many new terms which must be committed to memory.
50. The main advantage of a play like the end run is that the play goes around the defense instead of through it.
51. Probably they were irritated due to the fact that we were late in arriving.

2. Examine a current magazine or look through one of your textbooks (perhaps this one) for half a dozen passages containing deadwood. Be fair in applying the standard of necessity, considering tone as well as content. Be prepared to explain why specific words or phrases or sentences are not necessary, and to demonstrate how the passages could be improved.

3. Using a red pencil, go over the last theme you wrote and see how much deadwood you can remove.

4. If your teacher is willing, exchange themes with a classmate and see how much deadwood you can take out of his paper. He will do the same with your paper.

17
EMPHASIS IN THE SENTENCE

Introduction

Emphasis means strong statement, and it is an important aspect of both spoken and written communication. In speech we have various ways of stressing certain words, or even whole sentences. We may use a special intonation, speak key words more loudly, or more slowly, carefully separate words that ordinarily we run together, or, like a drill sergeant, change the timbre of our voices. There are, moreover, non-vocal means of emphasis in conversation: a rigid, uncompromising posture, a clenched fist, a pointing finger, or any of many other gestures — varying from culture to culture — which signal special degrees and kinds of significance. In short, the speaker has ready at hand many devices of emphasis, both vocal and non-vocal.

The writer can depend upon none of these. Yet he, too, requires emphasis for effective communication. What he must do is translate intonation, loudness, and speed of speech into graphic (that is, written) terms, and even try to devise written equivalents for such things as gesture and bodily attitude. In this chapter we shall survey briefly the important techniques of emphasis available to a writer. Some are simply graphic equivalents to things we do in speech; much punctuation, for example, indicates pauses one would normally make in speaking. Other techniques, while not unknown in speech, are primarily techniques of composition.

Before beginning the survey we should distinguish two kinds of emphasis — general and specific. The first is stress that applies to an entire sentence; the second, stress that applies only to a word or word-group within the sentence. General emphasis is much less common. By the very nature of things, generally emphatic sentences must be relatively rare. They work because they stand out from their contexts, and therefore their effectiveness depends upon their occurring only now and then. Writing in which every sentence is emphatic — or even every other sentence — is like having someone shouting in your ear.

Specific emphasis, on the other hand, is quite common. In fact, every well-written sentence exhibits special emphasis in the sense that it makes one word or phrase or clause the most important. The problem for the writer is to ensure that the reader understands correctly which word or phrase *is* the most important. Communication is easily impeded by mistakes concerning emphasis, and such misunderstandings are not always the reader's fault. It is part of the writer's business so to construct his sentences that they reveal the emphasis he desires.

How he does it is what we are about to study. We shall divide the chapter into two parts, corresponding to the two types of emphasis we have distinguished. The distinction is not perfect; in rhetoric very few distinctions are. Some sentences exhibit both kinds of emphasis, while in others it is difficult to decide where specific emphasis leaves off and general emphasis begins. But if we do not insist upon applying it too literally, the distinction is useful. Let us begin with general emphasis.

General Emphasis

THE IMPERATIVE SENTENCE

General emphasis involves the total statement, and it is thus a function of how the entire sentence is constructed. Certain types of sentence structure are inherently emphatic. The most obvious case is the imperative sentence, which may take several forms:

> Listen to me!
> You listen to me!
> John, listen to me!
> John, you listen to me!

In speech these forms would have the same intonation, a fact we cannot show in writing without getting involved with a special set of signs to indicate how intonation works. If you will speak aloud each of these sentences as you would use it in speech to give an order, you will hear the similarity of intonation clearly enough.

In addition to sharing the same intonation, these sentences have other similarities. They are all brief. Each completes its predicate as quickly as possible, moving immediately from the verb to the prepositional phrase. (In other imperatives the movement may be from the verb to a direct object, as in "Shut the door!") Finally, all are closed by the exclamation point, which is the common closing punctuation of the imperative sentence. (Sometimes when the sentence contains a noun of address, as in examples (3) and (4), the exclamation mark is placed after that noun: "John! come here.")

Imperative sentences, then, are one example of emphatic sentence structure. They are severely limited, however, in their usefulness. They are emphatic commands, but commands are rare in expository writing, which is chiefly concerned with making statements. It is more to the point for us to ask what other kinds of sentence patterns make strong statements.

THE SHORT SENTENCE

One is the short, simple, segregating sentence, which is constructed much like the second variety of imperative (though in speech its intonation is different). Here is a good example; the writer is discussing whether the madness of William Cowper, the English poet, was caused by his deep religious feelings:

> Cowper's madness finds its origin far deeper in the sufferings of childhood, it may be in inherent physical defect. All his life it was hung over him. And religion, so far from being the cause, was the most considerable of the remedies by which he tried to get rid of it. It failed. And once he realised that it had failed, it is true that the emotional tension encouraged by Evangelicalism, and the personal responsibility for its own state which it placed on the individual soul, did increase Cowper's nervous agitation and so accelerate the advent of his madness. But though it accelerated it, it did not make that advent more sure.
>
> LORD DAVID CECIL, *The Stricken Deer*

We have quoted the passage at some length to show that the effectiveness of the brief statement "It failed" depends upon its being set in the context of longer sentences. Notice, too, that while it is much the shortest, "It failed" is not the only sentence that achieves emphasis by brevity and directness. The second sentence is also emphatic and, to a lesser degree, so is the last.

Here is another example, a short paragraph. In this case the emphatic construction comes at the end, where it functions as a summarizing statement for the whole paragraph; the writer is describing a bust by the sculptor Jacob Epstein:

> But as I stared at that bust, hypnotized, it seemed to fill the room with savage beauty. The atmosphere became troubled. It was as though there were some virtue escaping from the cold bronze which charged the ether with its own spirit, entering one's veins, stirring one's brains. The metal sang.
>
> BEVERLEY NICHOLS, *Are They the Same at Home?*

Much of the effectiveness of that last sentence certainly comes from the vivid metaphor. But the brevity of the sentence also contributes. If you read aloud the final two sentences, revising them like this:

> It was as though there were some virtue escaping from the cold bronze which charged the ether with its own spirit, entering one's veins, stirring one's brains, as though the metal sang,

you will realize how much emphasis Mr. Nichols gains by treating the last statement as a separate sentence.

The effectiveness of short, direct statements may be increased by using rhythm and rhyme to separate and emphasize the words that compose them. An instance is the following sentence by Frederick Lewis Allen describing the collapse of the stock market, which preceded and portended the great depression of the 1930's:

> The Big Bull Market was dead.

Read aloud, the sentence sounds as if it were written, "The BIG BULL MARKET was DEAD." Several factors help to create this effect. One, of course, is the shortness and directness of the statement. Of more special interest is the use of monosyllabic words ("big," "bull," and "dead") and the alliteration in "*B*ig *B*ull." Moreover in the first four words there are three successive stresses ("the Bíg Búll Márket"), which slow down the sentence and, in a subtle way, disarticulate it, forcing slight pauses between key words. These pauses are reinforced by the fact that in each case the closing sound of the preceding word is sufficiently unlike the opening sound of the following word to require an instant's pause in order to rearrange the lips and tongue. Even when reading silently, most people have enough "speech memory" to respond to such audible devices of emphasis. In this case they make the sentence "The Big Bull Market was dead" an exceptionally strong statement; it conveys a sense of unalterable finality, which is as much a part of the meaning as is the simple fact of the market's collapse.

THE INVERTED SENTENCE

Another type of sentence that carries general emphasis is that having inverted structure. There are two kinds of inversion: primary, in which the main elements of subject-verb-object are rearranged; and secondary, in which an adverbial modifier is moved to the beginning of the sentence from its more usual place after the verb. Some sentences exhibit both. In fact, under certain conditions secondary inversion causes primary. If, for example, an adverbial phrase is moved to the initial position in a construction which otherwise contains only a subject and a form of the verb *to be*, the resulting sentence is likely to seem awkward unless the subject and verb have been inverted. Consider the sentence "A book was on the table." If the phrase is transposed, the pattern "On the table a book was" is unidiomatic. Idiom is restored by switching the positions of the subject and verb: "On the table was a book." Even when the verb is more than a pure linking verb like *to be*, it may sound awkward to begin with the phrase without inverting the subject and verb. Thus if we transpose the phrase in "An old man sat in the hall," the first of these two alternates seems the more conventional:

> In the hall sat an old man.
> In the hall an old man sat.

Often, however, a sentence will exhibit only one of the two types of emphatic inversion. Of the two, primary inversion is more important for general emphasis. Here are several examples:

> Wrangles he avoided, and disagreeable persons he usually treated with a cold and freezing courtesy. DOUGLAS SOUTHALL FREEMAN

> So coo and snivel the sweet ones; so wags the national tongue.
> H. L. MENCKEN

The first follows the pattern of object (or complement)-subject-verb, which is the most frequent kind of emphatic inversion. In the first clause of this example, the inversion stresses two key terms: "wrangles" and "avoided." The second sentence has the pattern: verb-subject, which is less common. Here, too, the inversion results in general emphasis; both the inverted verb and the subject gain stress.

But such differences in order are superficial; both these inverted sentences are emphatic. Statements like "Wrangles he avoided" or "In the hall sat an old man" are stronger than the same words arranged in normal order. "An old man sat in the hall" states a fact; "In the hall sat an old man" attaches special significance to that fact. This does not mean, of course, that the inverted sentence is inherently superior. It all depends upon what one wants to say. There are times when general emphasis is vital to effective communication; there are times when such stress would be awkward, jarring a relaxed or objective tone. Inversions, moreover, are tricky things. They do not all work, a fact we shall observe in more detail in the chapter on sentence clarity.

THE CONVOLUTED SENTENCE

The same restrictions apply to a fourth type of sentence that is sometimes employed for general emphasis. This is the convoluted sentence, which intrudes a subordinate construction into the middle of the main clause. Such interrupted movement may have the effect of stressing the whole statement, as in this sentence by Thomas Wolfe:

> And finally, stammering a crude farewell, he departed.

There are in this sentence five important words: "finally," "stammering," "crude," "farewell," and "departed." Three of them occur before stops (a stop is a punctuation mark signaling a pause); a fourth is placed after such a stop. Now pauses in a sentence generally increase the stress upon the word immediately preceding them, and, to a lesser degree, upon the word following them. Thus the total effect of the interrupted movement here is to emphasize the entire statement, an emphasis you may hear by contrasting this revision with the sentence Wolfe wrote:

> And stammering a crude farewell, he finally departed.

A more complicated instance of how interrupted movement may achieve general emphasis is the first clause of this sentence by Ralph Roeder describing Pope Alexander VI:

> The lax mouth, the veiled, weary, wistfully cynical eyes, betrayed, through the slackening flesh, the softening brain; and the reform of the church began.

Mr. Roeder employs simple, straightforward movement in his second clause, the effectiveness of which is increased by contrast with the convoluted structure of the first part of the sentence. The contrast in length and style between the two clauses reinforces the cynical comparison of the reform movement and the Pope.

An emphatic sentence may sometimes combine convoluted and inverted structure:

> And in one corner, book piled like the rest of the furniture, stood a piano.
> KENNETH GRAHAME

Grahame's sentence uses secondary inversion, primary inversion, and interrupted movement. A more complicated, and a more famous, instance of the same combination of interruption and inversion is the second clause of this sentence from Edmund Burke's *Reflections on the Revolution in France:*

> It is now sixteen or seventeen years since I saw the Queen of France, then the dauphiness, at Versailles; and surely never lighted on this orb, which she hardly seemed to touch, a more delightful vision.

ANTICIPATORY CONSTRUCTION

A fifth type of emphatic sentence pattern is the anticipatory construction. Such a sentence begins with a pronoun (or sometimes the adverb *there*) that anticipates the real subject, which is pushed to the end, as in:

> It pleased his parents — his going to college.

Very often the postponed subject is completed by an adjective clause:

> It was this consequence that we feared.

Anticipatory constructions, whether employed for emphasis or for some other reason, require more words than direct statement. It would be a mistake, however, to insist that "His going to college pleased his parents" or "We feared this consequence" are better sentences simply because they are briefer. Brevity is not concision. Concision, you recall, can be estimated only relative to purpose, and if purpose requires emphasis an anticipatory construction may be exactly right.

THE PERIODIC SENTENCE

The periodic sentence — of which anticipatory constructions are a special variety — is a sixth kind of emphatic construction. A periodic sentence is one in which the thought is not completed until the end. Not only those having anticipatory subjects but most of the emphatic patterns we have looked at so far have been periodic. Syntactic devices like interruption and inversion often suspend completion of the thought until the very end, as in this passage by Thomas Babington Macaulay:

> On the greatest and most useful of all human inventions, the invention of alphabetical writing, Plato did not look with much complacency.

Periodic structure, however, does not demand inversion, interruption, or anticipation. The following sentence by George Bernard Shaw is cut to the conventional subject-object-verb pattern. The subject, which consists of two parallel noun clauses, is quite long, but there is no interruption:

> That the author of Everyman was no mere artist, but an artist-philosopher, and that the artist-philosophers are the only sort of artists I take quite seriously, will be no news to you.

The very length of the subject postpones the completion of the idea and makes the sentence periodic and emphatic.

THE FRAGMENT

A fragment is a construction that in writing begins with a capital letter and ends with full stop punctuation, but which does not satisfy the conventional definition of a sentence. For purposes of composition a sentence is defined as a syntactically independent group of words built around a nexus between a properly related subject and finite verb. "Syntactically independent" means that the construction is not acting as a noun or a modifier in any larger construction. "When John goes," for instance, is not a sentence by this definition since the "when" turns it into an adverbial clause. A "finite verb" is one that shows by virtue of its form some limitation of person or number. English possesses two kinds of non-finite verb forms, the participle and the infinitive. If one of these constitutes the verb in a construction, it is not a sentence. Thus "John going home" would be, standing by itself, a fragment.

This definition applies to sentences as they are conventionally structured in formal English, especially in formal written English. In conversation and in informal writing most of us use many fragments. But in college compositions a fragment should be employed rarely and only under the conditions that we shall treat in the chapter on sentence clarity. One legitimate purpose of the fragment that does concern us here is emphasis. An instance of how effective it may be is the last sentence in the following passage (the writer is talking about the difficulty of writing drama):

> For every capable play I saw — not great, but well constructed and interesting — I must have seen, at a very charitable estimate, twenty bad ones. A mysterious thing the theatre. Entirely incalculable one would imagine, for the average run of men.
>
> BEVERLEY NICHOLS, *Twenty-Five*

The final two sentences are not merely fragments, but inverted fragments. In addition to being strong statements, they are important in determining tone. The ease with which Mr. Nichols dispenses with verbs suggests the relaxed tone of sophisticated conversation. Another example of the emphatic fragment is the second sentence of this passage from *Lincoln and the South* by Professor J. G. Randall, who is discussing the events leading up to the Civil War:

> Neutrality for Kentucky did not mean retreat into a bomb-proof cellar because of unreadiness to fight for a cause. Not at all. It did mean that in mid-April 1861 a prolonged four-year horror could not be prospectively envisaged. If war was started, perhaps it was a false start.

THE RHETORICAL QUESTION

One of several functions to which rhetorical questions may be put is emphasis. The same passage by Professor Randall provides an example. The paragraph goes on:

> If war was started, perhaps it was a false start. Who could know? Why should the fifteenth of April be so devastatingly different from the fourteenth or the eleventh? Why, merely because of Sumter, should the hand of war control the whole nation's coming destiny instead of the hand of peace? Had measures of adjustment been in fact exhausted? Did the country intend to drop so unpremeditatedly into fraternal strife? Why should an incident produce a war? Why should a step, or misstep, toward human slaughter be the irrevocable thing and peace the unrecoverable thing?

Much of the emphasis here comes from the sheer repetition; but it is not insignificant that the repeated sentence pattern is the rhetorical question. Here is one more example, a brief passage from Lytton Strachey's *Eminent Victorians:*

> A desirable young man? Dust and ashes! What was there desirable in such a thing as that?

The first sentence is both a fragment and a rhetorical question; the second a fragment only; and the third only a rhetorical question. But all are emphatic.

SYNTACTIC REPETITION

Another way of achieving general emphasis is by repeating the same pattern of sentence or clausal construction. A simple case is:

> The book is clear and it is concise.

Each clause is short and straightforward, and each is constructed so that the key word comes last. In this final position the important terms are balanced against each other, and the emphasis they thus gain is reinforced by the alliteration of the *c*-sounds. In the following example the clauses are similarly short, though the key words come first:

> Astronomy can regularly predict; astrology cannot. F. L. LUCAS

Emphasis gained by repeating the same syntactic pattern may involve several sentences. We have seen an instance of this device in the reiterated rhetorical questions of Professor Randall's paragraph. Here is another example, several sentences by G. K. Chesterton:

> Bernard Shaw is a Puritan and his work is a Puritan work. He has all the essentials of the old, virile and extinct Protestant type. In his work he is as ugly as a Puritan. He is as indecent as a Puritan.
> *George Bernard Shaw*

A good deal of the stress comes from hammering away at the word "Puritan," which is usually placed at, or near, the end of the sentence or clause. But the emphasis is also partly the result of the reiterated "he has . . . he is" sentence pattern.

NEGATIVE-POSITIVE RESTATEMENT

Negative-positive restatement is saying that something "is not this but rather is that," as in the sentence "It is not that we were tired but rather that we were worried." A more extended instance is this passage from Michael Harrington's *The Other America:*

> The poor are not like everyone else. They are a different kind of people. They think and feel differently; they look upon a different America than the middle class looks upon.

Another example comes from G. K. Chesterton, who was fond of developing an important point by stating it both negatively and positively in similar clausal patterns. In the following case (in which the progression is more positive to negative) he is writing about social conventions:

> Conventions may be cruel, they may be unsuitable, they may even be grossly superstitious or obscene; but there is one thing that they never are. Conventions are never dead.

All this could be said much more briefly:

> Although conventions may be cruel, unsuitable, or even grossly superstitious or obscene, they are never dead.

But it would not be said so strongly.

PARATAXIS

A final device of general emphasis is parataxis, the butting together of words or constructions instead of joining them with a conjunction. Omitting co-ordinate conjunctions between independent clauses is risky; when the sense requires an *and* or a *but* usually one ought to be supplied. Now and again, however, parataxis results in a stronger, more effective statement. For example, this sentence:

> At first gardening seems simple enough, but the real chore comes later on

is improved when it is revised this way:

> At first gardening seems simple enough; the real chore comes later on.

Similarly one feels that an *and* would dull the effectiveness of this description of Miami Beach by Edmund Wilson:

> You have acres of nougat-like shops, mountain ranges of vanilla ice-cream hotels.

Or of this sentence by James Anthony Froude telling of Drake's capture of a Spanish treasure ship:

> They took the kernel; they left the shell.

The question in such cases is whether the relationship between the clauses or phrases is strengthened or weakened by omitting the conjunction. There is no clear-cut rule. You must consider each case on its merits. Occasionally there will be an advantage in dropping the connective.

Special Emphasis

So far we have discussed the more common means by which emphasis is given to entire sentences. It is more likely, however, that a writer will wish to stress only part of a sentence. Often this is done by syntactic subordination, which is an important way of establishing relative degrees of importance. But we have already seen that the subordinate sentence is essentially a way of emphasizing one idea over another, and we shall put off until the chapter on clarity the special problems that subordination entails. Here we need to examine some of the other means by which one can stress a particular idea within the sentence. There are quite a few; some are more precise applications of techniques we have already mentioned, others devices we have not yet discussed.

POSITIONING

One of the easiest ways of stressing a word or phrase is to place it in a prominent position in the sentence. The most prominent place, generally, is the end. The following sentence seems weak and flaccid because the writer did not use the final position effectively; he is speaking of Daniel Dravot, the hero of Kipling's story "The Man Who Would Be King":

> As the military power of Kafiristan increases, so, too, does the pride that Dravot has.

Instead of wasting the emphatic final position on the form word "has," the student would have been wiser to construct his sentence in either of these ways, depending upon the shade of meaning he desired:

> As the military power of Kafiristan increases, so, too, does Dravot's pride.

> As the military power of Kafiristan increases, so, too, does the pride of Dravot.

It is because they waste the final position that prepositions are often regarded as being awkward at the end of the sentence. The old dictum "Never end a sentence with a preposition" is not taken so literally today as it once was; there are times when ease and naturalness make such endings a virtue. When emphasis is required, however, a closing preposition is likely to be ineffectual, as it is in this case:

> Kings, like other men, have rules which they must live by.

Here, too, alternative revisions are possible, according to whether the writer wishes to stress "live" or "rules":

> Kings, like other men, have rules by which they must live.
> Kings, like other men, must live by rules.

Although it is less inherently strong than the final position, the initial spot is also emphatic, especially when it is occupied by a word that does not customarily come at the beginning of a sentence. Of the following sentences, for instance, the second places more stress on "suddenly":

> It suddenly began to rain.
> Suddenly it began to rain.

Part of the effectiveness of all inverted sentences derives from the fact that they begin with something unusual — the direct object or complement, a prepositional phrase, or an adverb.

ISOLATION

The emphasis gained by placing a key term at either the beginning or the end of a sentence is increased if the term is isolated. Isolation, in this special sense, means being cut off from the movement of the sentence. In speech, isolated elements are set between pauses; in writing, between stops of some sort. If, for instance, a comma had been placed after the initial adverb in the last example, the adverb would have been isolated and its emphasis strengthened:

> Suddenly, it began to rain.

Although it does not have to be, isolation is often the result of interrupted movement, as it is in the first clause of this passage:

> The castle, uninhabited now but by jackdaws and starlings, is old; the chapel which adorns it is older still; and the lake behind both, and in which their shadows sleep, is, I suppose, as old as Adam.
>
> ALEXANDER SMITH

(What other devices of emphasis do you find in this sentence?)

Isolation may occur in the middle of the sentence:

> They even sell water, clear, crystal water, for a paul or two.
>
> AMY LOWELL

But it is most common at the end of the sentence. Here is a good example:

> Under the lights of the corner crossing of the great avenue, a huge closed vehicle whizzed past, screaming. KATHERINE ANNE PORTER

In the following more complicated sentence, the isolated adjectives at the end are played off against those at the beginning in order to underscore the contrast between American culture and the great economist Thorstein Veblen (the "he" of the sentence):

> In the bustling, boosting, gregarious community in which he lived, he stood apart; uninvolved, unentangled, remote, aloof, disinterested, a stranger. ROBERT HEILBRONER

The emphasis gained from isolation (as, indeed, from all the various techniques we are discussing) is not simply a clever manner of saying something that could be said as easily in other ways; rather it is a way — the only way — of saying precisely what the writer wants to say. To understand that fact, study this sentence from Macaulay's *History* (the "King" is Charles II of England):

> If the King notified his pleasure that a briefless lawyer should be made a judge or that a libertine baronet should be made a peer, the gravest counsellors, after a little murmuring, submitted.

By placing "submitted" at the end and isolating it, Macaulay implies the subservience of the counsellors. Had he ended his sentence like this: ". . . the gravest counsellors, although eventually submitting, murmured," he would have stressed their discontent and changed the meaning of his sentence, changed it in rather an important way. Of course, the emphasis in Macaulay's sentence is established by more than the isolation — the lesser idea is subordinated, for instance, and "little" serves to de-emphasize the "murmuring." Even so, the final position of the key term and its isolation are an important reason why the revision is not simply another way of saying the same thing. The difference in meaning between the original and the revision is subtle. But it is no less real and no less important for that. Good writing consists of the sum total of just such subtleties.

REPETITION

In addition to being the effect of positioning and of isolation, special stress is also achieved by repeating the important idea, either in the same words or in synonyms. The sentence by Amy Lowell on page 324 is a case in point. Repetition is so common a device of emphasis that the ancient rhetoricians carefully differentiated many varieties of it, each with its own imposing name. Of these we shall mention only a few. *Tautotes* is the frequent iteration of a key term, as in this passage by Charles Dickens quoted earlier:

> Mr. and Mrs. Veneering were bran-new people in a bran-new house in a bran-new quarter of London. Everything about the Veneerings was spick and span new.

The repetition may be less extensive, involving only one iteration of the term:

> She left the village running, she entered the wood running, looking at nothing, hearing nothing. VICTOR HUGO

Depending upon where the key words are placed in their clauses, it is possible to distinguish many patterns of emphatic repetition. Sometimes the repeated terms come close together (which, if you care to know, is called *epizeuxis*):

> I hold, and hold fast, to a different philosophy.
> J. MIDDLETON MURRY

> The baby had been dropped, her frail, frail skull striking the table edge, so that a thread of blood was soaking into the gossamer hair.
> CARSON MCCULLERS

Or they may be placed at opposite ends of the sentence or clause (a technique called *symploche*), as in these examples by Virginia Woolf:

> Emotion is our material; but what value do we place on the emotion?

> Royalty is no longer royal.

Sometimes the repeated words come at the beginnings of successive sentences or of clauses within the same sentence (*anaphora*):

> I wanted to go to Austria without war. I wanted to go to the Black Forest. I wanted to go to the Harz Mountains.
> ERNEST HEMINGWAY

Sometimes at the end:

> Yes, father. That is true, father. No, father. Well maybe yes, father. You know more about it than I do, father. ERNEST HEMINGWAY

And sometimes the repetition occurs at the end of one clause or sentence and the beginning of the next (*epanadiplosis*), as in this sentence by Max Beerbohm:

> Lovely and excessive monster! Monster immeasurable!

Occasionally a repeated word may even be placed at the beginning, middle, and end of a sentence:

> Of all wastes the greatest waste that you can commit is the waste of labor.
> JOHN RUSKIN

By changing not only the positions but the forms of the repeated words (a technique called *polyopton*), further variations of emphatic repetition are possible. For example, a word that acts as a transitive verb may be repeated as the cognate object to that verb:

> She smiled a little smile and bowed a little bow.
> ANTHONY TROLLOPE

In the following sentence the key term "blind" is used first as a past participle and then as an adjective:

> Visitors whom he desired to impress were invariably ushered into the Sala del Tesoro; they rubbed their eyes, he rubbed his hands, they returned home blinded, he remained at home, blind.
> RALPH ROEDER

(Can you find other examples of emphasis in this sentence?)

As even this brief survey makes abundantly clear, repetition comes in many, many forms. While we no longer use — or even know — the technical terms by which the classical rhetoricians classified the varieties of repetition, good writers still employ the techniques themselves. Students are sometimes bewildered about repetition, and not without reason. On the one hand they are told that it is a fault leading to deadwood and monotony; on the other that it is a valued device of emphasis. Both counsels are true. There is repetition and there is repetition, and it is not always easy to distinguish the good from the bad. As a general rule, repetition is a fault when it involves relatively unimportant ideas, or when it fails clearly to stress an important idea in spite of repeating it. For instance, the sentence: "The modern student of today is different," is awkward, not simply because it is unnecessary to specify the "student of today" as being "modern," but also because it is not clearly emphatic. By repeating "student," however, the writer would make his intention plain:

> The modern student, the student of today, is different.

Whether such emphasis would be appropriate would depend, of course, upon the context in which it was placed; but one can imagine situations in which it would be effective.

BALANCE AND ANTITHESIS

Closely related to repetition as a device of emphasis is balance and antithesis. The balanced sentence, which we shall treat in more detail a little later, is a sentence that splits into two roughly equal halves; "It was now nine o'clock, and he still hadn't come" is a simple example. In such constructions key words are often played off against one another, as in this sentence:

> It is no wonder that their hearts distended with pride, and, hardening in their strength, gloried. WALTER RALEIGH

The balance between "pride" and "gloried" emphasizes each and makes us see the close relationship between the ideas they signify. Similarly Thomas Paine stresses the connection between free choice and moral right by balancing key phrases in this sentence:

> That which a whole nation chooses to do, it has a right to do.

When the balanced terms form a sharp contrast, we speak of it as antithesis. Thus Charles Lamb contrasts "dream" and "unattainable substance" in this sentence:

> We have let go a dream in quest of an unattainable substance.

What words are antithetically balanced in the following sentence by Washington Irving?

> As London increased, however, rank and fashion rolled off to the west; and trade, creeping on at their heels, took possession of their deserted abodes.

Balanced terms, while still forming an antithesis, may be repetitions of the same word. In the following sentence, for example, Professor Richard Hofstadter repeats "great," "created-creates," and "fortunes-fortunate" in order to reveal the difference between the America of the twentieth century and the America of the nineteenth:

> Once great men created fortunes; today a great system creates fortunate men.

Notice also that the sentence sets "today" against "once" and "system" against "men," and, by the difference in its beginning and its end, suggests a contrast between "great men" and "fortunate men."

A more complicated kind of balance, called chiasmus, involves repeating a pair of key terms. The two words are placed in the order X-Y in one phrase, clause, or sentence and then repeated in the order Y-X in the next. A well-known instance is President Kennedy's "Let us never negotiate out of fear; but let us never fear to negotiate." Another is this passage from the Gospel of Matthew:

> He that findeth his life shall lose it: and he that loseth his life for my sake shall find it.

While it is somewhat formal, chiasmus is more common than is often supposed. It can be a very effective way of making a reader see an important contrast or grasp a significant relationship of cause and effect, as these examples further demonstrate:

> Goodness does not more certainly make men happy than happiness makes them good. W. S. LANDOR

> If the Superman may possibly be a thief, you can bet your boots that the next thief will be a Superman. G. K. CHESTERTON

> You say a good cause justifies any war; but I say a good war justifies any cause.
> NIETZSCHE, paraphrased, not approvingly, by CHESTERTON

THE USE OF MODIFIERS

In addition to such things as repetition and balance, modifiers are often used for special stress. There is, in fact, an entire class of modifiers called intensives, whose function is simply emphasis. Intensives include such words as *great, much, very, extremely, terribly, greatly, so,* and many more. On the whole such words are not a very satisfactory source of emphasis. They are used too often and too indiscriminately and so lose their force and become devalued, a process that results in a never-ending search for fresh and expressive intensives. We do not urge you to avoid intensives altogether; rather we suggest that you do not rely upon them exclusively, or even primarily.

There is, incidentally, a special problem with *so*. This adverb is so commonly employed to set up a *that* clause, that it often sounds awkward when it is used solely as an intensive, confusing readers because they have been conditioned to look for a following *that* construction. Anyone reading the sentence "It was so cold," is likely to think " 'So cold' that what?" Probably it is better not to use *so* as a simple intensive without a following clause of consequence.

Besides acting as intensives, modifiers may contribute to specific emphasis by how they are employed within the sentence. Adverbs, as we have already seen, are frequently given extra strength by being isolated or by being placed at the beginning of the sentence. The same techniques apply to adjectives. There are, moreover, other ways of using adjectives that give them special stress. For one thing, they may be paired:

> And as a war should be undertaken upon a *just* and *prudent* motive . . . SWIFT

> . . . this *artful* and *pathetic* composition. MACAULAY

> They are his for a *brief* and *passing* season . . . MARGARET MEAD

> The Knight stands *dark* and *lonely*. MARY ELIZABETH COLERIDGE

Now and then the pairing is reinforced by alliteration:

> He carries his English weather in his heart wherever he goes, and it becomes a cool spot in the desert, and a *steady* and *sane* oracle amongst all the deliriums of mankind. GEORGE SANTAYANA

Adjectives may be piled up as well as paired, the writer achieving his effect by an avalanche of modification. An extreme instance is this sentence by Macaulay damning the French revolutionist Barrère:

> Renegade, traitor, slave, coward, liar, slanderer, murderer, hack-writer, police-spy — the one small service he could render to England was to hate her; and such as he was, may all who hate her be.

Finally, adjectives may be given special stress by being unusually positioned. There is something of this in the sentence by Macaulay, where the adjectives are simply thrown out in an initial elliptical construction. More often, the unusual placement of adjectives consists of putting them after their nouns. Thus in these sentences the participial modifiers are set in postposition in order to emphasize them:

> The man, tired, sat down.
> The family, heartbroken, gave up the search.

The emphasis is increased if the adjectives are pushed to the end of the sentence:

The man sat down, tired.
The family gave up the search, heartbroken.

Paired adjectives are occasionally split for emphasis, one preceding the noun, the other following:

A great man and a mighty . . .
But a republican is a rare bird, and a noble one. G. K. CHESTERTON

In the second of these sentences the postpositive adjective actually modifies the pronoun "one," but rhetorically the effect is the same.

POLYSYNDETON AND ASYNDETON

How words are handled in a list or series is also susceptible of special emphasis. The conventional way of treating a series is exemplified in this sentence: "He bought bread, cheese, eggs, and milk." The last and the next-to-last items are joined by "and," while the other items are merely separated by commas (a comma before the "and" is optional). There are, however, two other ways in which this series might be treated:

He bought bread and cheese and eggs and milk.
He bought bread, cheese, eggs, milk.

The first separates each item by "and" (sometimes a comma is placed before each "and" to increase the separation; more often there is no punctuation), this technique is called *polysyndeton.* The second uses no coordinating word between any items, separating them only by a stop (usually a comma); this is called *asyndeton.* In the conventional treatment of a series none of the items is especially emphatic, although the last item generally seems a little more important than the others. In polysyndeton the emphasis falls not only more equally upon each member of the list, but also more heavily. Each item receives greater stress and the entire series is more important. In asyndeton, too, the series as a whole is given more significance than it is in the usual arrangement of "bread, cheese, eggs, and milk." But the stress on each item is lighter than in polysyndeton and the sentence moves less ponderously. Lists and series are not necessarily improved by polysyndeton and asyndeton. Most of the time the conventional treatment will be the most appropriate. When, however, you desire to give more emphasis to a series than the usual method permits, remember that these devices exist. Sentences like the following show how effective they can be:

> But her face was harsh and pinched and meager; the flesh sagged wearily in sallow folds, and the small eyes peered at him with timid suspicion and uneasy doubt. THOMAS WOLFE

> It was bright and clean and polished . . . ALFRED KAZIN

> His care, his food, his shelter, his education — all of these were by-products of his parents' position. MARGARET MEAD

> Instinctively the Englishman is no missionary, no conqueror.
> GEORGE SANTAYANA

ELLIPSIS

We have seen that ellipsis — the omission of form words — is a way of achieving concision; usually it also strengthens the statement, or at least a part of the statement. For example, omitting "were" in the second clause of the following sentence conveys more emphatically the blackness and the stickiness of the children's fingers:

> Their hair was full of dust and their fingers black and sticky.
> SHERWOOD ANDERSON

And in this sentence Macaulay strengthens his point by a combination of ellipsis and polysyndeton:

> Holland was gone, and Portugal, and Artois, and Roussillon, and French Conté.

RHYME AND RHYTHM

Most people do not think of rhyme and rhythm as being elements in prose, but they are not uncommon (though they have their dangers). We shall discuss rhythm and rhyme a little more fully in a later chapter; here we need only observe that they are a legitimate and an important means of emphasis. In prose, emphatic rhyme often takes the form of alliteration, that is, employing the same sound to begin two or more words that are close together. In the following passage, for instance, the key terms are underscored by the initial *s* sounds:

> Caesar flies to his hunting lodge pursued by ennui; in the faubourgs of the Capital, Society grows savage, corrupted by silks and scents, softened by sugar and hot water, made insolent by theaters and attractive slaves; and everywhere, including this province, new prophets spring up every day to sound the old barbaric note.
> W. H. AUDEN

Sometimes alliteration is used to point up an antithesis or to tie together the beginning, middle, and end of a sentence. In another sentence by Auden it does both:

> Reason will be replaced by Revelation.

Types of rhyme other than alliteration are also useful for emphasis. The following sentence by John Ruskin contains both consonance (the repetition of consonants, as in the *l* sounds) and assonance (the repetition of vowels, as in the long *e* sounds):

> What else there is of light is from torches, or silver lamps, burning ceaselessly in the recesses of the chapels; the roof sheeted with gold, and the polished walls covered with alabaster, give back at every curve and angle some feeble gleaming to the flames; and the glories round the heads of the sculptured saints flash out upon us as we pass them, and sink again into the gloom. *Stones of Venice*

Rhythm is even more important than rhyme as a means of emphasis. Two devices of rhythm are especially useful. The first is the clustering of stressed syllables, which we noticed in connection with Frederick Lewis Allen's sentence "The Big Bull Market was dead" (page 315). Here is another instance (stressed syllables are indicated by ′, the unstressed by x):

> x ′ x ′ ′ ′ ′ x ′ x
> He speaks and thinks plain, broad, downright English.
> WILLIAM HAZLITT

The forcing together of four stressed syllables gives to this sentence a tone of extraordinary conviction.

The second device of rhythm useful for emphasis is the metrical run, that is, a more or less regular sequence consisting of a stressed syllable followed (or preceded) by one, two, or three unstressed ones; then another stress followed (or preceded) by a similar number of weak syllables; and so on through three or four stresses. Key terms are set in stressed positions and thus given added importance by the impetus of the beat. In the following passage, for instance, the important words ("itched," "squirmed," "life," "night," and so on) are emphasized by the generally regular rising rhythm:

> x x ′ x ′ x ′ x ′ x x ′ x x ′
> It has itched and squirmed with life and now it is night and the life
> x ′ x x ′
> has all gone away. SHERWOOD ANDERSON

In this sentence the writer combines a metrical run with alliteration:

> For one brief moment the world was nothing but sea — the sight, the sound, the smell, the touch, the taste, of sea.
>
> SHEILA KAYE-SMITH

(Do you notice any other devices of emphasis in that last sentence?)

Occasionally a writer will get stress by establishing and then disrupting a metrical run. In the following sentence by Amy Lowell, much of the stress that falls upon "nipped" derives from the fact that it breaks the metrical run in the first clause.

> The roses have faded at Malmaison, nipped by the frost.

MECHANICAL DEVICES

The techniques of emphasis discussed so far have been essentially matters of syntax, resulting from the way in which the sentence is constructed or arranged. Other devices of emphasis are essentially mechanical, depending upon how the sentence is printed (or, of course, written). These include capitalization, italic and bold-faced type, other changes in the style or size of the type, underlining, the use of colored inks, spacing of words or letters, and the exclamation mark.

Individual writers now and then devise special kinds of mechanical emphasis. Bernard Shaw, for instance, favored spacing out the letters of emphatic words. A more extreme case is the paragraphing of this passage by John Dos Passos describing the passing of John Pierpont Morgan:

> *I commit my soul into the hands of my savior,* wrote John Pierpont Morgan in his will, *in full confidence that having redeemed it and washed it in His most precious blood, He will present it faultless before my heavenly father, and I entreat my children to maintain and defend at all hazard and at any cost of personal sacrifice the blessed doctrine of complete atonement for sin through the blood of Jesus Christ once offered and through that alone,*
>
> and into the hands of the House of Morgan represented by his son,
>
> he committed,
>
> when he died in Rome in 1913,
>
> the control of the Morgan interests in New York, Paris and London, four national banks, three trust companies, three life insurance companies, ten railroad systems, three street railway companies, an express company, the International Mercantile Marine,
>
> power,

on the cantilever principle, through interlocking directorates

over eighteen other railroads, U.S. Steel, General Electric, American Tel and Tel, five major industries;

the interwoven cables of the Morgan Stillman Baker combination held credit up like a suspension bridge, thirteen percent of the banking resources of the world. *Nineteen-nineteen*

The way in which this long sentence is arranged into printed lines emphasizes the magnitude of the Morgan empire; and it throws tremendous weight upon the word "power," placing it, no doubt suggestively, naked and alone.

Such experimental techniques, however, are not for the beginner. He ought, in fact, to use even the conventional devices of mechanical emphasis with some restraint. Tricks like underlining, exclamation points, and capital letters are, by themselves, likely to prove inadequate. Generally they are too obvious. Telling the reader that the writer wants emphasis, they also reveal that he is not sure how to go about it and so, in effect, has shouted.

Summary

There are two kinds of emphasis: general, which involves the entire sentence; and special, which involves only a word or a word group within the sentence. General emphasis is achieved by the imperative construction, and, more usefully for purposes of exposition, by the short, direct sentence; by inversion and convolution; by anticipatory construction and the periodic sentence generally; by the fragment and the rhetorical question; and by syntactic repetition, negative-positive restatement, and parataxis. Special emphasis is the result of positioning key words at the beginning or the end of the sentence; of isolating such words, repeating them, or placing them in balance or antithesis; of using intensives; of pairing and piling up adjectives, and of placing adjectives in postposition; of treating series in polysyndeton and asyndeton; of using ellipsis; of employing special devices of rhyme and rhythm; and, least effectively, of using various mechanical devices. Emphasis, finally, is not something that the writer is called upon to achieve now and then. General emphasis is relatively uncommon, but special emphasis is so essential a virtue of good prose that it is, by definition, a property of every well-written sentence.

Exercises

1. Below are listed a number of sentences, all clear instances of effective emphasis. Study them to determine what devices of stress their writers employed.

1. They don't build their houses to last in Belgrade because they know that in ten years or so there will be another war, and the whole thing will be blown to pieces again. That is the sort of spirit one met the whole time. Nothing permanent. No trust. No faith. I looked into a photographer's shop and saw a photograph of the Parliament in session. So pompous, so threadbare, so utterly, damnably sad. BEVERLEY NICHOLS

2. Out rushes the husband.

3. Any fool, any savage can make love — of a kind. But it needs a *viveur* of genius to think of combining amorous dalliance — on carpets, be it added, of the most exquisite Persian design — with the leisured smoking of a silver and crystal hookah. That, surely, is true art. ALDOUS HUXLEY

4. He is a dapper little fellow, with bandy legs and pot belly, a red face, with a moist merry eye, and a little shock of gray hair behind. WASHINGTON IRVING

5. But in that scene between the Sphinx and Caesar, Caesar is as cold and as lonely and as dead as the Sphinx. G. K. CHESTERTON

6. If we had lived from childhood with a boa constrictor, we should think it no more a monster than a canary-bird. W. S. LANDOR

7. The endless sands yielded nothing but small stunted shrubs; — even these fail after the first two or three days, and from that time you pass over broad plains, you pass over newly reared hills, — you pass through valleys that the storm of the last week has dug, and the hills and the valleys are sand, sand, sand, still sand, and only sand, and sand, and sand again. A. W. KINGLAKE

8. But it was not so: "the elements" were "so mixed" in Mr. Gladstone that his bitterest enemies (and his enemies were never mild) and his warmest friends (and his friends were never tepid) could justify, with equal plausibility, their denunciations or their praises. LYTTON STRACHEY

9. I didn't like the swimming pool, I didn't like swimming, and I didn't like the swimming instructor, and after all these years I still don't. JAMES THURBER

10. What he [Robert E. Lee] seemed, he was — a wholly human gentleman, the essential elements of whose positive character were two and only two, simplicity and spirituality. DOUGLASS SOUTHALL FREEMAN

11. And often, when the word did come from my mouth in its great and terrible birth, quailing and bleeding as if forced through a thorn-bush, I would not be able to look others in the face, and would walk out in the silence, the infinitely echoing silence behind my back, to say it all cleanly back to myself as I walked in the streets.
ALFRED KAZIN

12. It is nonsense, and costly nonsense none the less.
BRAND BLANSHARD

13. Some of these hopes and visions were, indeed, realized; but, in the end, the career of Sidney Herbert seemed to show that, with all their generosity, there was some gift or other — what was it? — some essential gift — which the good fairies had withheld, and that even the qualities of a perfect English Gentleman may be no safeguard against anguish, humiliation, and defeat. LYTTON STRACHEY

14. For the true rationale of humanistic study is now what it has always been, even though now it is not only in decay, but dead. I allude to the arts of rhetoric. ALLEN TATE

15. It is Ethan who must suffer; it is Ethan who must watch his dream die away. STUDENT

16. There is a tendency which, being human, is like most human things not unpardonable, but like many human things rather irritating — to try to make out that everything is something else.
GEORGE SAINTSBURY

17. Idealism will be replaced by Materialism. W. H. AUDEN

18. A horse is galloping, galloping up from Sutton. AMY LOWELL

19. Yet this need not be. The means are at hand to fulfill the age-old dream: poverty can now be abolished. How long shall we ignore this underdeveloped nation in our midst? How long shall we look the other way while our fellow human beings suffer? How long?
MICHAEL HARRINGTON

20. I am not thinking of philosophy as courses in philosophy or even as a subject exclusive of other subjects. I am thinking of it in its old Greek sense, the sense in which Socrates thought of it, as the love and search for wisdom, the habit of pursuing an argument where it leads, the delight in understanding for its own sake, the passionate pursuit of dispassionate reasonableness, the will to see things steadily and to see them whole. BRAND BLANSHARD

21. A middle-aged lady, frail, very frail; exceedingly pale from long ill-health, prematurely white haired, with beautiful grey eyes, gentle but wonderfully bright. W. H. HUDSON

22. Honest the man might be, and ingenuous, but nothing was so mischievous as misguided virtue . . . RALPH ROEDER

23. Many laws as certainly make men bad, as bad men make many laws. W. S. LANDOR

24. But a lighter, livelier, more deftly thrown off piece of writing, literature has seldom had to boast of. GEORGE SAINTSBURY

25. Of remote countries and past times he talked with wild and ignorant presumption. THOMAS BABINGTON MACAULAY

26. And then, you will recall, he told of being present at the auction of the deacon's effects and of noticing, among the innumerable odds and ends representing the accumulation of a lifetime of endeavor, a dried tapeworm. E. B. WHITE

27. For a moment — if only for a moment — we are utterly estranged. F. L. LUCAS

28. He gives one a sense, in his writings, of a little group of intelligentsia clinging unhappily together in a grossly hostile world. Not merely unsympathetic, or lacking in understanding, but grossly, actively hostile. BEVERLEY NICHOLS

29. The hills grew brighter and brighter — the brightness for which there is no name among colours. GEORGE GISSING

30. The English lake country has, of course, its grandeurs. WALTER PATER

31. The word was my agony. The word that for others was so effortless and so neutral, so unburdened, so simple, so exact, I had first to meditate in advance to see if I could make it, like a plumber fitting together odd lengths and shapes of pipe. ALFRED KAZIN

32. No garden, no fruit trees, no ties to the earth, often no ties to the neighbors, just a number on a street, just a number of a house for which the rent is $10 more than the rent in the old foreign district from which they moved — how can it mean anything? But it does. MARGARET MEAD

33. The offensive was going to start again I heard. ERNEST HEMINGWAY

34. Alexander she neither loved nor respected. ANTHONY HOPE

35. Unsatisfying, unpleasing to the ear, it is not — in its place; but its place is not in oratory, which demands definite measures to mark definite stages of thought. C. S. BALDWIN

36. At fourteen, when he emerged from the valley of the shadow of education, there survived something, indeed it survived still, obscured and thwarted, at five and thirty, that pointed — not with a visible

and prevailing finger like the finger of that beautiful woman in the picture, but pointed nevertheless — to the idea that there was interest and happiness in the world. H. G. WELLS

37. Living things have no inertia, and tend to no equilibrium.
T. H. HUXLEY

2. Revise each of the following sentences so that the italicized word, phrase, or clause receives stronger stress. Use any of the devices of emphasis we have discussed (except for underlining, capitalization, and other mechanical devices, which offer too easy a solution). You may break any of the longer passages into two sentences if you feel that a clause requires separate statement for proper emphasis.

1. *An old boot* lay in the corner.
2. The *leaderless* mob rioted down the street.
3. School work is very difficult for many students, though *it doesn't have to be.*
4. He was a strange man who always seemed to be a *brooding, withdrawn,* and *silent* one.
5. If the *day* had been nicer, the men would have gone, even though reluctantly.
6. The day was gray and rainy and when we got there we found the store closed and *all in all the trip was wasted.*
7. He was a very *strong* man and a very *generous* one.
8. Dancing seems exceedingly hard, but *actually it is quite easy.*
9. The day was *clear, sunny,* and *cold.*
10. I never cared for *tapioca pudding.*

3. Rewrite each of the following sentences three times, so that in each revision a different one of the italicized words or phrases receives maximum stress.

1. The sloop was *clawing* her way from *a lee shore* with her *sails close hauled.*
2. The achievement of *Athens* is all the *greater* when we consider how *relatively brief* was the period of her political supremacy.
3. *Chaucer's* characters in *The Canterberry Tales* are so *lifelike* that it is difficult to realize they never existed.
4. The *brilliant* scheme *slowly* took shape *in his mind.*

4. In the following cases the stress on the italicized expressions is muted by awkward construction. Revise each sentence so that it clearly balances the key terms and so emphasizes them properly.

1. The novelist creates *a purely imaginary world;* but we can see *the dramatist's world* right before our eyes.
2. Sailors are generally *cheerful* fellows, while *sombreness and sobriety* are the chief characteristics of members of the legal profession.

3. *Geography* is the science of the earth, while the nature of animals is what *biologists* study.
4. College is more *interesting* than high school, but college is less *fun* than high school.
5. He likes *chocolate* ice cream, but has never cared for *strawberry* very much.

5. Improve the emphasis of each of the following sentences by rewriting it in periodic structure.

1. The large red house was silent and uninhabited, apparently abandoned like all the others.
2. War ought to be the last method of settling disputes, though many people seem to think it the first.
3. Teachers look with disfavor on students who are habitually late with their homework.

6. Modeling your work upon passages like those by Charles Dickens and G. K. Chesterton on pages 326 and 321, expand each of the sentences listed below so as to repeat the italicized term three or four times.

1. College is *difficult.*
2. The firm was *old* and *conservative.*
3. He looked *tired.*
4. The day was *lovely.*

7. Develop any one of the topics in exercise 6 in several sentences of negative-positive restraint. It would be best to begin negatively and lead up to the positive assertion.

18
CLARITY IN THE SENTENCE

Introduction

In this chapter we consider the third of the sentence virtues — clarity. Clarity implies two things: (1) that the sentence make good sense to the reader in the context in which it occurs; and (2) that the sense it makes is what its writer intended. It is possible for a sentence to be clear in the first way and yet to say something quite different from what the writer desired, although generally the chances are high that if the first condition is satisfied, the second will be also.

The reasons for lack of clarity are numerous. One is simple carelessness, which is sometimes the result of laziness, sometimes of haste. Another is inexperience. A writer who has not yet mastered the art of parallel subordination, for instance, or who has not learned the restrictions about double negation will entangle himself and his reader in a confusing, circumlocutory syntax.

Perhaps even more important sources of confusion are two basic misconceptions which inexperienced writers bring to the task of composition. One is failing to grasp the essential difference between writing and speaking. The high school or college student, like all of us, talks a great deal more than he writes, and when he sits down to compose an essay he is likely to forget that he can no longer depend upon the non-verbal elements that are so intimately a part of speech communication — gesture, facial expression, bodily movement, intonation. Moreover, he is accustomed in conversation to sharing with his friends a common ground of communication, a commonly held body of experience, beliefs, and attitudes. But a writer cannot presume so complete a sharing with his readers, whose knowledge and opinions are more likely to be different. In writing everything depends upon words; there is nothing else.

The second misconception is failing to understand the full nature of the communicative process. As we said in our introduction, communication is not complete until the reader has been informed or persuaded. Writers sometimes forget the reader. When they check over their sentences they see them merely as expressions of their own ideas, not as stimuli to which particular readers will react in particular ways. These writers evaluate a sentence by asking, "Is that what I meant?" when they should ask, "Will my reader understand from this what I meant?" Seeing their prose exclusively from the viewpoint of the writer, they fail to detect areas of possible misunderstanding, and they are surprised when their readers "get the wrong idea." It is not enough to be clear to yourself; you must also be clear to your reader.

These, then, are some of the psychological components of confused writing. The clarity which these bad habits and misconceptions obscures is not confined to sentences. Clarity — or the lack of it — is an aspect of all forms of prose. An essay may be more, or less, clearly organized; a paragraph more, or less, clearly developed; a word more, or less, clear in its meaning. At the moment our interest is in clarity as a function of syntax, and we shall study lapses in clarity that derive from not handling sentences effectively.

As with concision, we shall find that the most practical way to proceed is negatively, that is, to study what causes sentences to be unclear. To identify this fault teachers use the symbol CL, standing for CLARITY, as a blanket designation for any failure of meaning. It is convenient to distinguish two degrees of non-clarity, represented by the symbols AMBIG and MEAN. The first stands for AMBIGUOUS, and it designates either of two possibilities: (1) that the sentence is capable of two interpretations; or (2) that while the sentence seems clear enough there is an apparent contradiction or divergence between its meaning and the meaning its context suggests it should have. A student who wrote about an examination that "my grade was surprising" without explaining why it was surprising, composed an ambiguous sentence in the first sense. His statement could be interpreted as "surprising because it was low" or "surprising because it was high" (there is even a third possibility — that he was surprised because his grade was neither low nor high). On the other hand, a writer who says:

> The party was dull and it was very late and we were exhausted; however, we went home.

has written an ambiguous sentence in the second sense. In the context the use of "however" suggests that he meant to say "we didn't go home."

In both varieties the ambiguous sentence makes surface sense in itself; it is either its interpretation or its fit with the context that is doubtful. The MEANINGLESS sentence, however, is technically nonsensical, making no sense whatever, even of the most superficial sort. While they are less common among native speakers, meaningless sentences are a more serious fault than ambiguous ones. In the case of ambiguity a certain amount of static has interfered with the writer's voice so that we hear him incompletely and must guess at what he is saying. But there is still a chance that we may guess correctly. In the meaningless sentence there is so much noise that communication is no longer possible at all.

These, then, are the general symbols we shall employ to indicate problems in meaning. Often, just because they are so general and include so much, symbols like CL, AMBIG, and MEAN are very little help to the puzzled student. They tell him that the teacher has not understood him, but they do not tell him why. To give you a more precise indication of what went wrong, we shall set in capital letters some of the more specific errors that interfere with clarity. Your teacher my choose to refer to these by using the more precise symbols printed at the end of this book.

Much of what we said in a preceding chapter about deadwood has application also to problems of clarity. Not utilizing the main elements of the sentence to carry the essence of the idea, failing to make modification as direct as possible, and using anticipatory constructions unnecessarily — are all syntactic faults that may disturb clarity fully as much as they hinder concision. It would seem needlessly repetitious, however, to go over these matters a second time. Here we shall concentrate upon mistakes in sentence structure that we have not yet examined in any detail.

Poor Sentence Order

It is helpful, though it is in no sense necessary, to gather these mistakes into several broad categories, the first of which comprises those errors that derive from not arranging the parts of the sentence effectively. Any English sentence involves order on two different, but related, levels. There is, on the one hand, order of thought or of experience; there is, on the other, order of sentence elements, or, as we shall call it, syntactic order. A general correspondence exists between these two kinds of order. In thinking we usually cast our ideas into some sort of propositional form, first identifying what we are thinking about (that is, fix the subject) and then establishing whatever we are supposing to be true or not true of that subject (that is, fix the predicate). In other words, we think in sentences of a rough sort, "saying" to ourselves: "The exam will be easy" or "Today is Thursday and I'd better get a date if I want one for Saturday."

But while the correspondence between order of thought and syntactic order is close, it is far from perfect, as we constantly rediscover whenever we begin to render thought into written sentences. In some ways syntactic order tends to restrict the relative fluidity of our minds, confining thought to the pre-established patterns of sentence structure. For example, while we may think "It's getting dark now," or "Now it's getting dark," or even "It's now getting dark," we probably would not think the idea in the following form because it would violate idiom to write it that way: "It's getting now dark." There are thousands of such restrictions about the word order of English, and a good writer must learn to stay within them.

Yet in another way syntactic order can work toward freedom rather than restraint. The very fact that he has so many patterns to choose from may open up for the writer possibilities of expression that perhaps he was not aware of when the idea he seeks to convey first came into his mind. Consider once again the thought "Today is Thursday and I'd better get a date if I want one for Saturday." The conventions of syntax allow many other possibilities:

1. Today is Thursday, and, if I want one for Saturday, I'd better get a date.
2. Today is Thursday, and I'd better — if I want one for Saturday — get a date.
3. If I want a date for Saturday, I'd better get one since today is Thursday.
4. I'd better get a date if I want one for Saturday since today is Thursday.

It would be easy to offer more versions by changing the connective word, but these are enough to illustrate the point. No two mean exactly the same thing, and the construction of some may seem a little forced. Still, all are possible ways of conveying the same basic idea.

Probably the original sentence — "Today is Thursday and I'd better get a date if I want one for Saturday" — is closest in its arrangement to the notion the writer began with. Its order might therefore be called the most "natural." Probably the second of the revisions is the least natural in its order, or, to put it another way, the most "artificial." We shall use these two terms, solely in reference to syntactic order, to distinguish two extremes of the sentence. A "natural order" is one in which the arrangement of the sentence elements reflects as closely as possible the order of the thought or perception that the sentence conveys. An "artificial order" is one in which the logic of thought or the order of perception has been significantly rearranged, either because the writer was awkward or because he desired to achieve some special purpose.

As a very general rule surface clarity is best served by a natural order in the sentence and tends to be disrupted by artificial order. By "surface clarity" we mean an obvious, easily grasped sense. It might be presumed that surface clarity is what any writer ought always to aim at; and in most exposition the presumption is reasonable. There are, however, times when immediate meaningfulness is either not possible or even not primarily important. Sometimes the writer's idea is in itself so intricate and subtle that it can be conveyed clearly only in a relatively artificial sentence pattern; sometimes the writer is not really concerned with lucidity of thought but rather with intensity of feeling and therefore will arrange his sentence in complicated rhythms to arouse or to increase an emotional response in his readers. But in most exposition such situations are exceptions. It is certainly true that one of the chief obstacles to clarity in expository writing is arranging the sentence in an awkwardly artificial manner. The fault most commonly reveals itself in four ways: (1) not positioning modifiers effectively, (2) making non-functional interruptions, (3) employing awkward inversions, and (4) allowing ambiguous parallelism.

AWKWARD PLACEMENT OF MODIFIERS

One of the most obvious mistakes in using modifiers is the so-called DANGLING PARTICIPLE, as in:

> Walking to school, my books were dropped and my papers blew away.

The difficulty is plain: the participle must be construed as modifying syntactically a term it cannot modify logically. If this sentence were parsed the participial phrase "walking to school" would have to be treated as an adjective modifying the subject "books." But books cannot walk to school. Dangling constructions can be fixed in two ways. One is to keep the participial construction and to change the main clause so as to supply a subject that the participle may legitimately modify. Sometimes that subject idea is already in the sentence acting in another capacity, as it is in this case in the genitive pronoun "my"; sometimes the subject idea is merely implied. In either event, the main clause must be recast so that the subject idea becomes the grammatical subject. So corrected our example would read:

> Walking to school, I dropped my books and my papers blew away.

The second way of correcting the dangling modifier is to keep the main clause and to change the participial construction, perhaps making it into a prepositional phrase or an adverbial clause:

> As I walked to school, my books were dropped and my papers blew away.

(Even here, however, it would probably still be better to shift the main subject to "I" and to do away with the awkward passive "books were dropped.")

Although the difference is sometimes hard to define, dangling participles should not be confused with legitimate absolute participles. Absolute participles are useful devices of transition. They differ from "danglers" in that they involve so complete and so intentional a shift of idea that no reasonable reader would be misled by them. An example is this sentence:

> Speaking of books, that new novel by Jones has had good reviews.

Absolute participles have an informal, even colloquial, tone, which of course limits their applicability. The line that divides a dangling construction from an allowable absolute participle is not always clear. If ever you find yourself puzzled by a borderline case, it would be best to assume the construction to be dangerous and avoid it.

A second misuse of modifiers is the MISPLACED MODIFIER. Here the problem is not that the modifier is attached syntactically to something it cannot logically modify, but rather that it is so positioned in the sentence that the reader may be confused about what it does modify. The fault can occur with both adverbial and adjectival constructions.

A common case is when a writer must arrange a series of adverbial constructions in the clearest sequence, as is often a problem with several adverbial phrases set in a row. Thus in the sentence "I didn't speak to you about the conference over the phone," the final phrase is ambiguous. If the writer means that the conference was held over the phone, he will probably have to expand the phrase to a full clause to make the point clear: "I didn't speak to you about the conference we held over the phone." If, on the other hand, he means he didn't speak to "you" on the telephone concerning the conference, he must rearrange the order of his phrases: "I didn't speak to you over the phone about the conference." It is possible to formulate rules that govern the sequence patterns of prepositional adverbial phrases; however, the rules would be enormously complicated. It is simpler to remember that when several adverbial prepositional phrases are put in sequence, the possibility always exists that their order may not be clear. You should read such a sentence carefully when you revise.

Another case in which an adverbial modifier may be misplaced occurs when a clause of cause or of consequence or of qualification must be applied to only one part of a compound or complex sentence. For instance, in the following sentence the middle clause is slightly ambiguous:

> Although it was a very complicated lecture because it was interesting we stayed.

Does the writer mean that the lecture was complicated because it was interesting, or that "we" stayed because it was interesting? Probably the latter. A comma after "lecture" would help, but it would help even more to arrange the sentence like this:

> Although it was a very complicated lecture, we stayed because it was interesting.

Because clauses create a special problem when they follow a negated main clause. For instance, the sentence:

> I didn't go to the party because I was tired,

may be read in two ways: (1) as a simple statement of why the writer did not attend the party, or (2) as an emphatic and colloquial way of saying that he did go and that he was far from tired. In speech these alternative meanings would be distinguished by intonation. But in writing the order of the clauses has to be changed to prevent ambiguity, the *because* construction being placed first to convey the first alternate. There is a similar ambiguity in this sentence:

> The war was not won because the generals were poor.

(How else, besides rearranging the clauses, may the ambiguity of this sentence be removed?) In handling *because* clauses after a negative statement it is a good idea to place yourself in your reader's place and listen consciously for any ambiguity.

Misplaced modifiers are more likely with adjectives, especially with relative clauses. Single word adjectives do not occasion much difficulty. These are generally restricted in their positions. Sometimes several adjectives in succession may present a minor problem of order. Whether to say "the weary, hungry men" or "the hungry, weary men" can be, depending upon the context, a subtle matter of clarity. But usually a writer does not have much latitude in choosing where to put single adjectives. Nor is the choice much wider with phrases. Nonrestrictive participial phrases may come either before or after their nouns, and one can write: "Waiting anxiously for news, the families stood silently at the pithead" or "The families, waiting anxiously for news, stood silently at the pithead." But the difference is more a matter of emphasis than of surface clarity. When several prepositional phrases follow a noun, problems may arise similar to those we observed with adverbial prepositional phrases. Here, too, the writer must select the order that best reflects his idea. "The book by the window on the chair," for example, exhibits a misplaced modifier that interferes with clarity; "the book on the chair by the window" is what the writer meant.

With relative clauses, however, misplacement is more possible. The general rule is that a relative clause, whether restrictive or nonrestrictive, should immediately follow the noun it modifies. Thus the adjective clause in a sentence like "The man sat down who arrived late" is misplaced and would be better positioned: "The man who arrived late sat down." There is an exception, however. For strong emphasis a restrictive *who* or *that* clause is sometimes pushed away from its noun to the end of the sentence, as in: "He laughs best who laughs last." This pattern, while old-fashioned, is still alive in English, and one now and then hears such sentences as:

> He writes best who thinks first.
> He talks wisely who listens well.

But in the great majority of cases the best place for a relative clause is immediately after its noun if it is possible to put it there.

Unfortunately it is not always possible. Not infrequently a noun will be followed by two different adjective constructions, two relative clauses, say, or a prepositional phrase and a relative construction:

> I am submitting the report of our meeting which you asked me to draw up.

> I went to see the movie at the Mecca Theater that you raved about.

In such sentences there is usually a trace of ambiguity; "which you asked me to draw up" modifies "report," yet a careless reader might attach it to "meeting." And it is at least possible that someone reading the second sentence might conclude that it was the theater that was being "raved about." Some grammarians have said about such constructions that the phrase ought always to precede the clause, but others have maintained just the opposite. If it is not possible to lay down the law about the sequence of adjective phrase and adjective clause, there are one or two ways in which a writer can improve clarity in particular cases. Occasionally such sentences may be clarified by reducing the prepositional phrase to a single adjective, which is then placed before the noun, leaving the relative clause in sole possession of the space after the noun. For instance in this sentence:

> We spoke about the meeting of the committee he had missed,

any ambiguity is removed by making "committee" a preposed adjective:

> We spoke about the committee meeting he had missed.

The revision is also more concise, another example of how the removal of deadwood sharpens meaning.

If several adjective phrases intrude between a noun and its relative clause and if these phrases cannot be reduced and placed before the noun, an easy solution is to use an appositive before the clause. Thus the sentence:

> It was a hard voyage of many months, through many storms, which seemed at times doomed to failure,

can be treated:

> It was a hard voyage of many months, through many storms, a voyage that seemed at times doomed to failure.

The second "voyage" serves as a hook upon which to hang the relative construction, which, without the appositive, seems only loosely articulated to the sentence. Instead of repeating the same word, the writer may use a synonymous term — in this case "trip" or "journey" would do — or an appropriate pronoun. Syntactically the effect is the same; the appositive ties the relative clause down, keeping it from floating along after the main clause. This device draws attention, of course, to the repeated word. When such attention would distort emphasis the modification will have to be tightened in some other way. Generally, however, nouns that are so extensively modified are important enough to warrant restatement.

Appositives may be used in essentially the same way to hold down the type of relative clause which modifies the whole of a preceding construction rather than any single noun within it. Here is a case in point:

> We suspected that he had lied to us before, which made us distrust him now.

The clause "which made us distrust him now" loosely modifies the entire main clause. Some rhetoricians feel that constructions like this are inevitably sloppy and ought to be avoided. That goes too far, but such clauses should be checked carefully. If ambiguity seems possible an appositive can be added after the main clause and the relative construction attached to it:

> We suspected that he had lied to us before, a suspicion which made us distrust him now.

Using an appositive is awkward, however, when the relative clause is separated from its noun by only a single brief phrase, in which case an appositive seems repetitious.

NONFUNCTIONAL INTERRUPTION

As we saw in the last chapter, interrupting constructions are valuable devices of emphasis. Even when properly used, however, they ripple the surface clarity of the sentence. When they have the virtue neither of emphasis nor of rhythmic variety, they will seriously disturb that clarity. Theoretically a sentence may be interrupted at many points, but there are five places where loss of clarity is especially likely as a result of AWKWARD INTERRUPTION: (1) between the subject and the verb, (2) between the verb and the object, (3) between a direct object and an objective complement, (4) within the verb phrase, and (5) between the *to* and the verb of the periphrastic infinitive.

As a rule surface clarity is served by keeping the subject and verb as close together as possible. Not everything that may come between the subject word and the verb is an interrupter, however. Restrictive modifiers placed between the subject and the verb are not regarded as interrupting constructions. They are felt to be part of the subject idea. In the sentence "The book on the table is mine" we conceive of the notional subject as being "the book on the table," and so do not really treat the prepositional phrase as an interrupter, a fact confirmed by our tendency to read the sentence straight through with neither of the pauses that signal an interrupting construction. Nonrestrictive modifiers, however, are genuine interrupters, as in:

> The green and blue book, which is lying on the table, is mine.

When the modification is as short as this the chance of any serious loss of clarity is very slight. But as nonrestrictive phrases and clauses increase in length and complexity the chance of confusion rapidly increases; loss of clarity has become a very real possibility in a sentence like this:

> The South, which was ill-prepared for the struggle, which had neither the men, the equipment, nor the money to wage modern war, which was united only in the negative determination to resist the North, had little hope of winning.

A writer may sometimes gain emphasis by using nonrestrictive modifiers to postpone his predication, but as you can see from this example he risks the reader's failing to connect the subject and verb correctly. One may have his cake and eat it too in such cases by restating the subject in an appositive, employing either the same word or a synonym:

> The South, which was ill-prepared for the struggle, which had neither the men, the equipment, nor the money to wage modern war, which was united only in the negative determination to resist the North — the South had little hope of winning.

(The dash is useful here because after the preceding commas a stronger mark is needed to signal the completion of the modification.)

If repetition of the subject seems inappropriate, sentences like this which intrude several nonrestrictive adjective clauses between subject and verb can be clarified by reducing the relative clauses to participial constructions, which are placed before the subject, thus allowing it immediately to precede the verb:

> Ill-prepared for the struggle, having neither the men, the equipment, nor the money to wage modern war, united only in its negative determination to resist the North, the South had little hope of winning.

Not only nonrestrictive adjective constructions but also adverbial modifiers may interrupt the subject and verb. Conjunctive adverbs like *therefore, however, none the less,* and *consequently* are frequently placed here in order to make transitions seem less obvious. Single word adverbs do not seriously interrupt the clarity of the subject-verb nexus. As the interrupting adverbial construction grows longer, however, the danger to clarity becomes more immediate. In the following sentence the intrusive adverbial clause forces the reader to pay close attention:

> The men, when the sun had finally sunk below the horizon, returned to camp.

If such a clause gets much longer the hasty reader is likely to be thoroughly confused:

> The men, when the sun had finally sunk below the horizon, making the search impossible and forcing them to postpone it until the morning, returned to camp.

We noticed in a preceding chapter that the convoluted style, which is based upon this kind of interruption, has its uses; but it is not a style notable for surface clarity.

There is one case in which it is difficult to split the subject and verb in any way, even by a brief phrase. This is when the subject is a personal pronoun. While it is perfectly idiomatic to write "He suddenly sat down," it is difficult to get much more than a single adverb between a subjective personal pronoun and its verb. Perhaps this is because we have been conditioned to think of the subjective forms of personal pronouns in immediate relation to verbs. In any case, most readers would feel that the sentence "He, when it was late, went out" sounds much more awkward than it would if the subject were "the boy" or "John."

A second place in which interrupters may disturb clarity is between the verb and the object. Here, the problem is less severe because interrupting adverbs and nonrestrictive adjective constructions are rarely set between verb and object. Sentences like "The man saw immediately the point" and "The class understood, when the teacher had explained the problem, the answer" violate English idiom. When the object is composed of more than a single word, however, it is more easily separated. Thus a noun clause acting as direct object may be split from its verb, as it is in the following sentence:

> We acknowledged, however, that the charge was true.

In fact, though it is less likely than a single word, a full adverbial clause may intrude between a noun clause object and the verb:

> We acknowledged, when we had understood all the facts, that the charge was true.

Similarly, when a single word object is followed by restrictive modifiers, it is, like a noun clause, more easily separated from its verb than is a single unmodified object:

> We acknowledged, when we had understood all the facts, the truth of the charge brought against him.

Despite these exceptions, interrupters are much less often set between verb and object than between subject and verb. One is well advised not to split his verb and object by intrusive constructions unless he can be very sure that what he gains in emphasis and rhythm will not be paid for by clarity.

Interrupters may also be confusing when they split the direct object from an objective complement. ("Objective complement" is the traditional term to designate a second object that is required to complete the meaning of certain transitive verbs. For example, if someone were to say, "They made Sam," the sentence would seem incomplete. We naturally ask, " 'Made Sam' what?" The "what" is the objective complement; in the following case it is "fire chief": "They made Sam fire chief.") Objective complements usually follow the direct object quite closely, and consequently nonrestrictive relative clauses and adverbial constructions seem awkward when placed between these two objects. The awkwardness is apparent in the following sentences:

> They elected the new man, even though he seems inexperienced, shop-steward.
>
> They decided to make John, who has worked very hard, assistant manager.

The first sentence is easily revised by placing the "though" clause either first or last. But there is no way of revising the second so as to keep the relative clause. The simplest solution is to recast the adjective construction as an adverbial clause of cause:

> Since he has worked very hard, they decided to make John assistant manager.

The fourth type of interruption that may confuse the reader occurs within the verb phrase. Except for the present and the past in the simple conjugation all tense forms in English are phrasal, that is they consist of at least two words, as in "I *am going*" or "he *will go*" or "they *have been going*." As a rule surface clarity is served by keeping the elements of the verb phrase together. It is possible, however, to split them for brief adverbial modifiers, as in "I have often gone to concerts." In fact adverbs like *often, frequently, occasionally* are completely at home within the verb phrase, and a writer wishing a relaxed informal tone ought to put them there. A more formal tone is better maintained by keeping the adverb outside the phrase:

> I have gone often to concerts.
> I often have gone to concerts.
> I have gone to concerts often.
> Often have I gone to concerts.

It is difficult to generalize about such patterns. English has so many single word adverbs, these are subject to so many subtle variations in idiom, that what is true in one case may be wholly false in another. Perhaps the best advice about placing single adverbs within the sentence is this: read the sentence aloud and if the adverb sounds awkward try it in other positions until it sounds right.

When the adverbial construction intruding into the verb phrase is itself a phrase or a clause, it very probably will prove awkward. Sentences like the following are strained and confusing:

> I have, on the other hand, gone to concerts that I liked better.

> I have, although I can't recall one at the moment, gone to concerts that I liked better.

> Ethan will, regarding Mr. Hale, later on in the chapter, in his desperation to get money, attempt to get an advance of fifty dollars.

If in the first of these the writer desires interrupted movement, he can get it by placing the phrase after the verb. He gains little by inserting it into the middle of the verb. In the third example the verb phrase is so riven that a reader is likely to lose any sense of connection between "will" and "attempt." The sentence is much clearer like this:

> Regarding Mr. Hale, Ethan, in his desperation to get money, will attempt to get an advance of fifty dollars later on in the chapter.

Closely related to interrupting the verb phrase is the fault known as splitting the infinitive. This means inserting a modifier between the *to* and the verb form of the periphrastic infinitive, as in "to suddenly go." Once a shibboleth of style, split infinitives are no longer corrected so rigorously and so uncompromisingly. There are cases in which idiom, if it does not demand them, permits split infinitives as the most efficient way of saying something. And there are times when a colloquial tone justifies splitting an infinitive. Even so, good writers avoid constructions like "to quickly sum up," "to finally comc to thc point," "to briefly answer the question," and "to once again acknowledge." How awkward a split infinitive can be is revealed in this passage:

The ends have to on certain key plays in important situations run downfield.

AWKWARD INVERSIONS

A third case in which poor arrangement of the sentence elements is likely to result in a loss of clarity is the AWKWARD INVERSION. This is especially likely to be a problem with primary inversions, that is, arranging the main elements of the sentence in an order other than their natural sequence of subject-verb-object. When the object is placed before the subject and verb, as it sometimes is for emphasis, it may cause confusion. Patterns such as object-subject-verb or object-verb-subject are artificial and formal, and ought to be relatively rare if they are to prove fully effective when they are used. That they can be effective, these examples show:

> Resentments he never cherished. DOUGLAS SOUTHALL FREEMAN
>
> Alexander she neither loved nor respected. ANTHONY HOPE
>
> Him the Almighty Power Hurl'd . . . MILTON

It is easy, however, to misuse inversions of this sort. Probably the commonest mistake is in failing to distinguish a complement (complements follow linking verbs; "weary" is one in "He was weary") from a direct object. Complements, especially if they are adjectives, are much less easily inverted than true objects, as these cases attest:

> The house was out of the question; mere plasterboard it was.
> Twenty-six years old, quite handsome, and well-built was he.
> Dimly lit, smelling of dust was the deserted house.

Even fine writers are sometimes betrayed by the inverted complement. The beginning of this sentence by Thomas Carlyle (who had a weakness for inversion) is likely to seem strained to most readers:

> Remarkable it is truly, how everywhere the eternal fact begins again to be recognized . . .

And the following sentence by W. S. Landor, while less extreme than Carlyle's, is certainly debatable:

> Fortunate we may call ourselves to have been born in an age so productive of eloquence, so rich in erudition.

Occasionally a writer does succeed in inverting a predicate adjective:

> Honest the man might be, and ingenuous, but nothing was so mischievous as misguided virtue . . . RALPH ROEDER

Even here only one of the complements is inverted; the other — "ingenuous" — comes in the usual place. Success with inversions, for the beginner at least, is less likely than failure. Do not be so afraid of inversions that you never attempt any, but test those you try by reading them aloud. Your ear is the best judge.

AMBIGUOUS PARALLELISM

The last of the problems of clarity that results from misarranging the sentence elements is AMBIGUOUS PARALLELISM, a situation in which a sentence element can be read as parallel to either one of two different constructions. This sentence is an instance:

> He saw the woman who sat on the couch and smiled.

Is "smiled" parallel to "saw" or to "sat"? In other words, who was smiling — "he" or "the woman"? There is no sure answer; the sentence is ambiguous. In such cases punctuation sometimes helps; a comma before "and smiled" would make it more likely that it was "he" who smiled. But even punctuation may leave a trace of ambiguity; it does here. Such sentences can only be properly fixed by altering their syntax. It may be possible, for example, to change the form of one of the verbs. Putting the verb of the relative clause into the progressive form straightens out this example:

> He saw the woman who was sitting on the couch and smiled.

Or, if she were the one who smiled:

> He saw the woman who was sitting on the couch and smiling.

Another method of correction would be to expand the second verb into a complete clause:

> He saw the woman who sat on the couch and he smiled.

Conversely, the adjective clause might be reduced to a participial construction:

> He saw the woman sitting on the couch and smiled.

Less commonly ambiguous parallelism may involve objects and subjects, as in "We asked him to go and John also." Most of us would take this to mean "We asked him to go and we also asked John." As it happened, the writer meant that "John also asked him." In the following sentence the ambiguity involves a noun that can be construed as paralleling either the subject of the sentence or the object of the preposition:

> Ethan's helplessness against Zeena and his fate must be understood in this way.

If "fate" is supposed to be a second object of "against," the sentence can be clarified by repeating the preposition:

> Ethan's helplessness against Zeena and against his fate must be understood . . .

or by using "both":

> Ethan's helplessness against both his fate and Zeena must be understood . . .

If, on the other hand, "fate" is intended to be a second subject, it should be placed first to avoid ambiguity:

> Ethan's fate and his helplessness against Zeena must be understood . . .

Often, too, such ambiguous parallelism can be cleared away by the judicious use of correlatives such as *both . . . and* or *not only . . . but also.*

The Sentence as Analytic/Synthetic Unit

A sentence is both a unit of analysis and a unit of synthesis. As a synthetic unit it puts together, or synthesizes, the more basic elements of word, phrase, and clause in order to communicate an idea that cannot be conveyed by any of these elements acting alone. But while it is an obvious truth, it is sometimes a neglected one that the sentence is also a unit of analysis. In fact, relative to such larger constructions as the paragraph, sentences are essentially analytic; they must reflect the orderly process of mind as it breaks down a complex perception or concept into its parts. In a simple expository style this function of the sentence can be seen quite easily:

> (1) Northwest Africa lies between the sea and the desert. (2) Its climate is the driest form of the Mediterranean. (3) Rains come only in the winter, and amounts are small except high in the Atlas Mountains. (4) The landscape is similar to that of southern Spain or Italy, but is drier and browner. (5) Agriculture is less

extensive; the green patches of irrigation are fewer, and most of the hills are covered only with a thin brush. (6) There are few rivers. (7) Some, rising in the Coast Range, make their way to the sea. (8) But in the interior the rivers are too feeble to do this; they dry out on the Tell, between the Atlas ranges, or on the margins of the Sahara Desert as the water gradually evaporates; the rivers thicken, turn to mud, and then cease to flow. (9) This dry country is scarred by the deep, canyon-like wadis, excavated by violent storms of the past, but most of these are now dry and have no certain prospect of ever having flowing water in them again.

NORMAN J. G. POUNDS, *The Earth and You*

This paragraph (we have taken the liberty of numbering its sentences) develops a general description of the geography of North Africa. The first sentence establishes the location of the area, the second the general nature of its climate. In the remainder of the paragraph pertinent geographical features are listed, one to a sentence — rainfall, landscape, agriculture, canyons. The only exception is the rivers, to which three sentences are given. But this is because the writer must distinguish two kinds of river, those of the coast and those of the interior, a contrast that requires two sentences, which are set up by the brief preliminary statement: "There are few rivers." All in all, the paragraph is a good example of the analytic use of sentences.

In expository paragraphs generally this is how the sentence should be used, to enclose a conception which in relation to other ideas in the paragraph is felt to be a unit. It is never easy to say what constitutes such a unit. It will vary from age to age, from writer to writer, and from subject to subject. The ideas in a paragraph may often be grouped in several ways, in six or seven sentences or in three or four, depending upon precisely what shadings the writer desires. So subtle and so numerous are the variables that affect the decision of when to begin a new sentence that no one can lay down hard and fast rules. The experienced writer begins to develop a "feel" for sentences; and even he will find when revising that ideas he first treated in separate sentences should be combined or that something else he first combined should be separated.

But if the variety of expository prose does not allow rigid generalization about when to begin a new sentence and when not to — that is, when to be analytic and when synthetic — it is possible at least to suggest a few of the faults that arise from not using the sentence unit wisely, faults that interfere with clarity. There are four: (1) the overloaded sentence,

(2) forced co-ordination, (3) improper subordination, and (4) the illogical fragment.

OVERLOADING

The OVERLOADED SENTENCE is one that contains too much; it results from failing to use the sentence effectively as an analytic unit. The following passage is a good example:

> On a Monday, which is always a busy day, the housewife washes and hangs out her clothes, after which she must get lunch for the children, who always seem hungrier than usual on a Monday, and then she can relax for an hour or two before she goes to the store, and when she returns she must make dinner for her family, the last job she has to do except wash the dishes, after which she can watch TV for a few hours before going to bed.

Such a sentence is a mere heap of ideas. Had he used his sentences analytically, the writer might have composed something like this (we shall prune a little deadwood in the revision):

> (1) For the housewife Monday is always a busy day. (2) First she washes and hangs out her clothes. (3) Then she must get lunch for the children, who always seem to be hungrier on a Monday. (4) Lunch over, the housewife is free to relax for an hour or two before going to the store. (5) Finally she must prepare dinner and then wash the dishes, her last task. (6) After dinner she watches TV for an hour or two. (7) And then to bed.

The sentences have now been used to sort out the several duties of the housewife. The first sentence sets the topic; the others distinguish the various aspects of her routine — washing clothes, making lunch, relaxing in the afternoon, going to the store, preparing dinner, watching TV, and finally retiring. That routine has been analyzed.

Sometimes overloading is the result of packing too many modifiers into the sentence, as in this example:

> Near the old-fashioned sewing machine stood an elderly, gray-haired woman with a long, dirty-white tape measure around her neck and large pinking shears in her hand, bending over a huge, deeply scarred cutting table on which was spread out a roll of heavy crimson velour, to which was pinned an intricate pattern ready to be cut.

Like wallpaper with too many lines, this sentence is so "busy" that it fails to bring the scene to focus. We are distracted by being shown too much, and paradoxically the effect of all this detail is to make the scene fuzzy.

The writer's intentions were good; he wanted to be accurate and precise. But he has loaded his sentence too heavily, and it sinks beneath the weight.

Overloading may also be the result of co-ordinating too much. We have seen the virtues of the multiple co-ordinate style, but multiple co-ordination has dangers. It is awkward in this sentence:

> English is not my favorite subject and I never did well in it in high school, but I realize that it is important and I would like to improve my writing and I want to learn more about literature.

This needs to be broken in half, with the second sentence being pruned by a little judicious parallelism:

> English is not my favorite subject and I never did well in it in high school. But I realize that it is important and I would like to improve my writing and to learn more about literature.

It is a good idea to study very carefully any sentence in which you have co-ordinated three or more independent clauses. It may very well be overloaded, and if it is, it will not be clear.

AWKWARD CO-ORDINATION

Clarity may be disturbed even when only two clauses are co-ordinated if the ideas expressed in the clauses are so different that they do not belong in the same unit of thought. This mistake is called AWKWARD (or FORCED) CO-ORDINATION; the following brief paragraph offers an example:

> History is my favorite subject. I enjoy reading about the past and learning how it has helped to shape the modern world. For example, much that puzzled me about the beginning of the Second World War became clearer when I studied the history of World War I and the Treaty of Versailles, and I find, in short, that I cannot understand what is happening today without knowing something about yesterday.

For most of the paragraph the writer has used sentences effectively to analyze his idea. The first sentence states the topic; the second repeats it in more specific form and suggests a reason in support; the third begins by offering a brief illustration to amplify the reason. But in the middle of this third sentence the paragraph stumbles. A summarizing statement, which should be a fourth sentence, has been forced into co-ordination with the illustration. That the writer intends his final statement to be a summary is indicated by the phrase "in short." As a summary, however, it is sufficiently different from the example of Versailles to deserve separate statement. If it had been given such statement, the sentence analysis of the paragraph would be perfect:

sentence 1 . . . . topic
sentence 2 . . . . restatement plus reason
sentence 3 . . . . illustration
sentence 4 . . . . summary.

No rule is available that will enable a writer to detect forced co-ordination with absolute certainty. What may seem awkward in one context will appear natural enough in another; and sometimes writers deliberately use forced co-ordination for shock effect. It is wise, however, to check any co-ordinate sentence in which the subjects of the clauses are different. It is possible to have forced co-ordination even when the subjects are the same ("The man seemed very tired, and he had gone to Harvard College as a youth," for example); but the chances increase when the clauses contain different subjects, and as these different subjects move apart from one another in similarity, the chances become greater.

A special kind of awkward co-ordination involves two constructions that appear to contradict one another. Although this is more likely to be a fault of diction than of sentence structure, we shall consider it here. The following sentence is an instance:

> The composition of a baseball team is very complicated and it may be described in a few words.

The difficulty is obvious. If a baseball team is "very complicated," how may it be described in a "few words"? By using "and" the writer has implied, if not a cause-effect relationship, at least a greater compatibility between these ideas than they have. The error may be corrected by substituting "but" for "and," or even better by removing "and" and subordinating the first clause to the second:

> Although the composition of a baseball team is very complicated, it may be described in a few words.

Critical readers may still feel a trace of the contradiction, but it is much less glaring.

The connective *and*, widely used to cover a great variety of relationships, is not infrequently involved in awkward constructions like this. Even more precise conjunctions may be misused, however, as is "but" in this sentence:

> He was not very bright, but he didn't impress anyone with his ideas.

Unless the writer is being cynical, "and" would be preferable here to "but."

A final problem of co-ordination involves AWKWARD CORRELATIVES. Correlative constructions are those using such paired connectives as *both . . . and, not only . . . but (also), either . . . or,* and *neither . . . nor.* The rule for formal composition is quite simple: units of the same syntactic order should follow each conjunction of any of these pairs. Thus we say:

> He is not only tired but discouraged.
> Not only is he tired, but he is also discouraged.

In the first sentence "not only" is followed by a single participle and therefore "but" must be completed by a single modifier (in this case also a participle). In the second sentence the same principle holds; since "not only" is now completed by an entire clause, "but" must be similarly followed. The following sentence violates the rule because the correlated constructions are of different syntactic orders, the first being an independent clause, the second a single word:

> Not only is he tired, but discouraged.

IMPROPER SUBORDINATION

Awkward co-ordination, then, may muddle the writer's ideas and confuse the reader in several ways. Perhaps errors in subordination are even more common. One mistake is OVERSUBORDINATION, which is really a special variety of the overloaded sentence. The fault consists of packing too many subordinate constructions into a single sentence, as in this case:

> Although riding a horse is not really a difficult thing to do, since one need master only a few techniques such as mounting properly, holding the reins, sitting in a certain way, and adjusting to the rhythm of the horse, many people are afraid of riding, supposing it to be an art that one must acquire in childhood and that no grown-up person can learn it, even though this simply is not true.

Everything in this sentence relates to riding horses, but so many subordinate constructions are packed in here that the reader has difficulty sorting them out. As with the overloaded sentence generally, the remedy is to be more analytical, breaking this up into four or five separate statements:

> Riding a horse is not really difficult. One need master only a few techniques such as mounting properly, holding the reins, sitting in a certain way, and adjusting to the rhythm of the horse. Even so,

> many people are afraid of riding. They suppose it to be an art that one must acquire in childhood and which no grown-up can learn. This simply is not true.

Another mistake is FAILING TO SUBORDINATE IDEAS OF LESSER IMPORTANCE. For example, the paragraph we quoted earlier about the duties of a housewife might have been developed like this:

> (1) For the housewife Monday is always a busy day. (2) First she washes and hangs out her clothes. (3) Then she must get lunch for the children. (4) The children always seem hungrier on Monday. (5) Lunch is finally over. (6) The housewife is free to relax for an hour or two. (7) Then she has to go to the store. (8) Finally she must prepare dinner and wash the dishes. (9) This is her last job. (10) After dinner she watches TV for an hour or two. (11) And then to bed.

The seven sentences in the revised paragraph on page 359 have become eleven, and the paragraph is the poorer for it. The extra sentences all contain relatively unimportant ideas, and expressing them separately blurs the focus of the paragraph. The topic here is the housewife, and in one term or another this topic is the subject of all the sentences in the earlier revision except the first. Here, however, the subject has been shifted in three of the four additional sentences: it is "children" in sentence (4), "lunch" in (5), and "this . . . job" in (9). Certainly the ideas expressed in these sentences are relevant. But their relevancy is minor, and there is no need to give them independent statement.

Awkward subordination may take the opposite form when the writer SUBORDINATES A KEY IDEA, as in the final sentence of this brief paragraph:

> In spite of some similarities, the tragic drama of fifth-century Athens is quite different from that of Elizabethan England. The plays are shorter and have much less physical action. The plots are simpler and have little melodrama and no comedy at all. Although there are these differences, the similarities are real but superficial.

The last sentence subordinates the wrong clause; it is the differences that are important, not the similarities. The confusion engendered by this shift of emphasis is clarified by recasting the sentence:

> Although there are similarities, they are superficial compared to these differences.

Even though it is not strictly a question of subordination, we might notice in the final sentence of that paragraph another source of confusion.

This is the AWKWARD CONTRADICTION in the "although . . . but" construction. Clarity is usually strained when a writer begins to contradict his contradictions. Even an alert reader feels puzzled by sentences like the following with its successive contradictions in "But . . . although . . . However":

> But the depression had a great effect upon American politics, although many of the reforms of the 'thirties would have occurred if there had been no depression. However, the failure of the economy quickened the process.

It is a good rule not to have two or more successive contradictions in the same sentence, and not to begin successive sentences with adverbs of contradiction. (There are exceptions to this generalization. Sometimes a writer will have parallel clauses of contradiction in a single sentence which are perfectly clear: "Although there were many who resisted and although a few threatened violence, the measure was passed," for example. And sometimes for emphasis a writer may begin several sentences in a row with "but" or "however.") Still, these are special cases and not what we are talking about here. *Parallel* contradictions do not contradict one another; the problem is contradicting a contradiction — it is this which disrupts surface clarity.

Very similar to the confusion caused by successive contradiction is that resulting from AWKWARD TREATMENT OF CAUSE AND EFFECT. Writers now and then get tangled up in trying to explain that one effect has several different causes. Often the confusion stems from expressing logically parallel causes in non-parallel constructions, as in this sentence:

> Since the day was cloudy the party was held indoors because there was not much of a crowd.

All that needs to be done here is to express the two reasons in parallel clauses:

> Since the day was cloudy and since there was not much of a crowd, the party was held indoors.

Or, more concisely:

> Because of the cloudiness and the smallness of the crowd, the party was held indoors.

The confusion resulting from having two causal statements in the same sentence cannot always be removed by making the statements parallel. It may be that the causes are not logically parallel, but rather are serial, one growing out of the other. That condition is true of this sentence:

> Since the South had limited industry it fought under a great handicap as it was unable to supply its armies with the cannons they needed.

The logic is something like this:

ULTIMATE CAUSE		IMMEDIATE CAUSE		RESULT
The South's limited industry	⟶	Too few cannons	⟶	Fighting under a handicap

This logic, however, is obscured by the manner in which the writer has handled his subordinate constructions. He must do two things in order to improve clarity: (1) rearrange the order of the sentence so that it reflects the natural logical progression of ultimate cause, immediate cause, effect; and (2) distinguish the relative importance of the two causes he mentions. In connection with (2) it is worth remembering that not all subordinate constructions are of equal weight, that there are relative degrees of subordination. Roughly, a full adverbial or adjectival clause or a nominative absolute are subordination of the first order; an elliptical clause, a participial or gerundive or infinitive phrase, and a prepositional phrase represent subordination of the second order; while a single word is subordination of the third order. In the sentence we are considering clarity would be served if the writer expressed one cause (perhaps the immediate) in a first order clause and reduced the other to a second order construction, a participial phrase, for instance. Thus improved the sentence would read:

> Since the South, limited in industry, was unable to supply its armies with the cannon they needed, it fought under a great handicap.

The logic is now clearer and the sentence is more sharply focused. It is also slightly more concise, further affirmation — if further were needed — of the close relationship between the virtues of concision and clarity.

The several cases we have examined by no means exhaust the kinds of confusion that can result from handling multiple causes in the same sentence. And, of course, essentially the same problems occur when one must deal with several effects of the same cause. The examples, however, do demonstrate the dangers inherent in having two *since, because, as* constructions in one sentence. When you write a sentence of this sort be sure

(1) that you have placed logically pararallel causes (or effects) in syntactically parallel constructions and, if possible, have kept them side by side; and (2) that if the causes (or effects) are not parallel, you have arranged them in the clearest and most natural order and, if clarity requires, have expressed them in different degrees of subordination so that the reader knows which you consider primarily important.

A final instance of awkward subordination is FALSE COMPARISON, that is comparing two things that are not comparable. Usually it is the result of carelessly omitting a vital term from the second half of the comparison, as in:

> Homework in college is very different from high school.

Literally read, this sentence contrasts "homework in college" with "high school"; what the writer intended obviously was to contrast "homework in college" to "homework in high school." To be clear the sentence should read:

> Homework in college is very different from homework in high school.

If in such comparisons repeating the same word seems monotonous, a synonym may be used (here "assignments" might do) or a relative pronoun ("that" or "those," for example). But whatever terms are used, remember that a sentence making a comparison ought explicitly to compare items or ideas of equal order.

FRAGMENTS

Earlier (see page 319) we defined a FRAGMENT as a unit of written expression beginning with a capital letter and ending with full stop punctuation which does not satisfy the formal requirements of a sentence, that is, which does not contain an independent nexus between a subject and a finite verb form. Teachers differ a great deal in their attitudes toward the fragment. Some are quite liberal, permitting a student to use fragments at his own discretion; others are stricter, allowing only fragments that are clearly functional, or even outlawing them altogether. Our own feeling is that students ought not to use fragments very often and that when they do they should identify them in a marginal note so that their teacher realizes they have not made an error in grammar. However, you will have to adapt your practice in this matter to your teacher's requirements.

We wish only to make it clear that there are fragments and there are fragments — that some work while others do not. Let us look first at one or two positive examples. Here is a passage by F. L. Lucas:

> Sweeping criticism of this type — like much other criticism — throws less light on the subject than on the critic. A light not always impressive. *The Search for Good Sense*

The final sentence, a fragment, is simply an appositive construction that has been detached from the first sentence. By stating it separately, Mr. Lucas has both gained emphasis and contributed to an urbane, informal tone. Below is another example, this from an essay by Beverley Nichols. Mr. Nichols is describing a luncheon with the novelist George Moore, who kept the maid waiting in the background with an omelette while he told stories. Mr. Nichols's mind was more on the omelette than on the stories:

> I saw that the omelette was already feeling the strain. It had a sullen look. Its fine careless rapture was evaporating. It was settling down for the night. And when an omelette settles down for the night . . .
> *Are They the Same at Home?*

The ellipsis in the final sentence (which is in Mr. Nichols's text) is an example of what the Greek rhetoricians called aposiopesis, the technique of breaking off in the middle of a sentence, of "falling silent." Here the fragment is not only emphatic but richly implicative. Falling silent, Mr. Nichols suggests a great deal, and the reader, assuming he knows about omelettes, can bring his own imagination into play.

But for every successful use of fragments comparable to these, an inexperienced writer is likely to compose ten bad ones. A common type of awkward fragment is the DETACHED ADVERBIAL CLAUSE. Sometimes such "sentences" are plainly ambiguous, as in this case:

> The test was not difficult. Although I didn't do well. I hope to do better next time.

This floating adverbial clause is ambiguous because the reader does not know whether it qualifies the first statement or the third, a plain instance of how a fragment may interfere with clarity. Even when such a construction is not ambiguous, it may not achieve anything positive. One feels about the following passage, for example, that the final fragment is not justified by emphasis and would be better attached to the second sentence, which it logically completes:

> There are many interesting sections in New York. But I prefer Times Square. Because it is the most crowded and exciting.

A second type of fragment is the DETACHED PARTICIPIAL CONSTRUCTION. Sometimes this is a nominative absolute, as in:

> Sam returned home. The others staying behind.

More often it is a participial modifier:

> The plane twisted through the sky. Trailing clouds of smoke.

In neither case is the fragment justified. The concepts expressed in these fragments are too intimately a part of the preceding statements to allow their being treated as separate sentences, no matter how much the writers desired emphasis.

Still a third variety of fragment common in student writing is the DETACHED MODIFIED NOUN, which is what Mr. Lucas used so successfully. These are less happy instances:

> He saw several people. The man who had written him. The boy who had returned the lost letter. The woman who had called him last week.

> He was very impressive. The man doing the trapeze act.

> That is my home. The house on the hill.

Each of these fragments differs from those of Mr. Lucas and Mr. Nichols. Theirs were logically complete; these are not. To be sure, the completeness of the statements by Mr. Lucas and Mr. Nichols was implied rather than literally realized, but it is none the less real for that. Mr. Lucas used a fragment to add a second predication that was in itself logically complete, that is, his fragment is essentially a full proposition with subject and predicate — he has simply omitted the connecting link. Similarly Mr. Nichols's adverbial clause implies its own completion. Each of the three examples above, however, contains an idea which is not in itself a logical whole, which instead depends upon the preceding sentence for something essential to its completion. Logically incomplete fragments are usually awkward and are better attached to the sentence before or after. If a writer desires to emphasize an idea, he can attach the noun-modifier construction by a comma or a dash to the appropriate contiguous sentence. Thus the first example might be rendered:

> He saw several people — the man who had written him, the boy who had returned the lost letter, the woman who had called him last week.

About fragments, then, we may conclude that while they are not necessarily awkward or confusing, they very often are. If your teacher permits you to use fragments at all, you may apply these tests to determine their usefulness: (1) is the idea expressed in the fragment a self-contained logical unit (that is, a clear, even if implicit, proposition) or does it depend upon its context for its logical completion? If the latter is the case, the fragment probably should be attached to the appropriate sentence. If the former is true, two further questions must be answered before you can be sure that the fragment is warranted: (2) does the emphasis justify separate statement? (3) Have you been using too many fragments? Remember that whatever effectiveness the fragment may have as a device of emphasis depends upon its being used only occasionally. Applying these tests will not ensure that you never write an awkward fragment, but it will keep you from writing a great many.

Awkward Negation

We have surveyed the most important of the essentially syntactic causes of confusion. One relatively minor point remains — awkward negation. Negation means asserting the non-truth or non-reality of a positive concept. To say "I am not tired" is, in effect, to assert, "That I am tired is not true." Philosophically considered, negation is a complicated process, which has long intrigued logicians. Our interest in it will be much more superficial, being confined to two questions of style: (1) where ought the negative element be placed in the sentence? and (2) what rules govern the use of the "double negative"?

The first question can be asked another way: what element in a sentence should be negated? Consider, for example, these sentences:

> Nobody wants pineapples.
> People do not want pineapples.
> People want no pineapples.

Any purely logical differences between these sentences are so subtle that we need not consider them. But if we study the meanings of these sentences in a broader sense, we become aware of differences in emphasis and tone. The first sentence stresses the absence of any buyers; the second stresses more the absence of desire in potential buyers; while the third implies an almost positive, willful rejection of pineapples. In tone the first and second are relatively conversational; the third is rather more formal.

As a further illustration, study this pair of sentences:

He hasn't any poise.
He has no poise.

Here, too, the difference is a matter of emphasis and tone. The second sentence is a stronger negative statement than the first; and the second is also more formal. (Sometimes people argue that sentences of the type "He has no poise" are illogical because the nexus "he has" implies a positive possession and one cannot "have" a negative. Such an argument forces upon language, which is, after all, not logic, an oversubtle distinction. Most speakers would not see anything illogical in their saying, "I have no money" and would be irritated by a listener who insisted that this was a paradox.)

As these examples make clear, negation may be made in the subject, the verb, or the object (with which the complement may be included). When a sentence offers a choice between these possibilities — and such a choice does not always exist — the writer must place his negative particle where emphasis and tone demand. As a very general rule, negation in the object is likely to be concise and emphatic and also quite formal in tone, relatively far removed from the patterns of ordinary speech. Negation in the verb, especially when the negative particle is contracted with the verb (*isn't, doesn't, hasn't,* and so on) is the most conventional. It is usually used informally and is not particularly strong. (Lack of emphasis, incidentally, is not necessarily a fault in negative statement; sometimes unemphatic negation is what the writer wants.) If you are uncertain of where to negate a sentence, try various alternatives, reading each aloud in its context to determine which is clearest.

The second problem involving negation is the so-called DOUBLE NEGATIVE. Some double negation is allowable, and some is not. The latter case is exemplified by sentences like these:

I'm not going nowhere.
He hasn't got no money.
Nobody doesn't know nothing.

All of these sentences negate one basic proposition at two different points (in the last case at three). In earlier stages of its history, English style made full use of such double, triple, and even quadruple negation. In the eighteenth century, however, grammarians, forcing upon language rules derived from Latin and from an overstrict analogy between language and logic, concluded that two negatives made a positive and so outlawed constructions like "He hasn't got no place to go." In this effort, at least, grammarians have succeeded, and educated persons today shun constructions of this sort both in writing and in conversation. Socially, such patterns are today "unallowable." Logic really has nothing to do with it. Nobody would seriously take the sentence "He hasn't got no money" to mean that he does have money. It is worth noticing, too, that if two negatives make a positive, three ought to restore the negative; yet while grammarians were quick to point out the illogic of "He doesn't have no money," they rarely acknowledged the "logic" of "Nobody doesn't have no money."

But if the modern writer is no longer permitted to negate the same proposition at several points, he is allowed another kind of double negative. This is the negation of a negative term within the proposition, as in:

> He was not unafraid.

A statement like this is legitimate because the writer is using the double negative to make a positive. To be more exact, he is asserting a qualified positive, for "He was not unafraid" is not really equivalent to "He was afraid." Rather it says something like this: "He was afraid in a limited and special sort of way."

Because they are rich in implication, double negatives of this kind are often concise. In their very subtlety and suggestiveness, however, they risk confusing the reader, who, by a sort of mental algebra, must supply the equation that "not not-x=a kind of x." When the negative particle is separated from the negative term, the confusion is likely to increase geometrically. The following sentence, for example, requires more thought than the point is worth:

> In a not very uncertain way, he knows what he wants.

And when the double negation is combined with further negation in the sentence, the difficulties become too heavy for many readers. This passage almost needs to be translated before it can be understood:

> It was not that we were not unafraid, but rather that we were not certain about the best course of action.

On the whole, double negatives of this second, "allowable," variety ought to be indulged in rarely and only when the writer can control the confusion implicit in them. It is self-defeating to employ such constructions very much. They are dangerously habit-forming. One easily becomes addicted to these "not un-" constructions. They have an aura of impressiveness (though frequently it is specious), and they are especially appealing to the timid writer inclined to overqualification and always ready to hedge his bet. Certainly there are times when "He was not unafraid" is exactly what one wants to say. But on many occasions when you are tempted to use such a double negative, the positive assertion "He was afraid" will convey your meaning just as accurately and much more clearly and forcefully.

Summary

Confusion is often the result of poor sentence structure, especially of not ordering the elements of the sentence efficiently, of using loose and dangling modifiers, awkward interrupters, confusing inversions, and ambiguous parallelism. Secondly, confusion may result from not using sentences properly as units of analysis and of synthesis: overloading them, forcing awkward co-ordination, subordinating improperly, and employing nonfunctional fragments. Negation, specifically the problems of where to place the negative term and of double negation, is also a source of confusion.

All this hardly exhausts the question of clarity. Many failures of meaning derive from mistakes in choosing words — writing "but," for instance, when the context demands "and," or relying upon a vague "this" as the subject of a sentence, or employing a word with too little attention to its connotations. Indeed, failures in diction are an even more frequent and more serious threat to clarity than faults of syntax. But their discussion belongs to the later section on diction.

Exercises

1. In each of the following sentences there is a lapse of clarity. Study them and be prepared to explain what the trouble is and to show how it can be corrected. Keep your revisions as close as possible to the original.

1. Running down the street, the church appeared to be on fire.
2. I tried the new sails on my boat that you recommended.
3. Most college freshmen, entering the university directly from high school, unsure of their teachers and subjects, though determined to work hard and get good grades, are a little frightened by the new world they have entered.
4. Few people have, when all is said and done, really taken the trouble to master a second language.
5. Doing homework is usually difficult in my home because my younger brother has the television on while my sister is playing records, and there is just too much confusion.
6. Driving is not easy. Some people think it is.
7. He didn't want to seem unappreciative; otherwise he would not have shown so much interest.

8. Even though there have been few periods of great tragedy there have been many times when genuine tragic literature has been written, although it wasn't of the very finest sort.
9. I'll do better next time. Because I have learned from my mistakes. I won't flunk again.
10. Sam was not only asked to attend but he was made chairman.
11. His fall off the ladder and injury were most unfortunate.
12. The people remembered the empty promises he had made them in other years, which made them wary of his presnt assurances.
13. We want to make everyone, even the newest man in the organization, happy.
14. It was not a good game because the field was wet.
15. Requiring a good deal of reading, most students find history a difficult course.
16. The committee hope to pass on the report of the meeting that was drawn up.
17. The class, when the laughter, which had erupted suddenly, died down, turned their attention back to the teacher.
18. I want to thoroughly and completely finish the job.
19. Summer is the best season of the year, and school is out then.
20. We saw neither Harry nor Sam did.
21. Since the exam was on Tuesday I didn't go out on Sunday because I was behind in my reading.
22. Nobody goes nowhere till I say so.
23. Life in the army is not at all like summer camp.
24. We saw our cousins not the Sullivans.
25. The ship slowly settled lower in the water. Dense clouds of smoke billowing from the forward hatch.
26. The car was out of the question; rusted and badly dented was the body.
27. English is my poorest subject and I like it best of all.
28. He grasped the rope that had been thrown to him and pulled.
29. We had a very hard passage with almost continuous headwinds and heavy seas which seemed as if it would never end.
30. Although the film was rather long because it was entertaining we stayed.

2. The following paragraph is poorly written, less because of failures in its organization (though even this could stand tightening) than because of faults of sentence structure that lead to loss of clarity. Rewrite the paragraph, staying as close to its wording and order as you can. Add whatever marks of punctuation or words are required to remove ambiguities. Where necessary, you may add a word or phrase, combine sentences, or break a single sentence into two.

> A volunteer fire department is all most towns can afford. Although some people object to them because of their inefficiency and cost, they are very common. Their equipment is usually somewhat old,

and this varies with the community. Some towns having quite modern pumpers and ladder trucks. Though these are the exception. Usually the chief and the other officers are elected at a general meeting of all the volunteers, which is a not undemocratic way of doing it. Their terms are for one year and many are re-elected. Volunteers do not make any real salaries though some towns pay a small sum for each fire attended, which may be about two or three dollars. However, being without large tax revenues, the volunteers are all most small towns can afford.

3. With your teacher's permission, exchange themes with a classmate and check his work for lapses of clarity. Using a different colored writing instrument, correct any mistakes that you find. Be ready to justify your revisions.

19

THE AUDIBLE SENTENCE

Introduction

The final virtue of the sentence is one which, you may recall, we said could not be labeled by a single word. Essentially it has to do with the sentence as an audible unit, that is, as something perceived by the ear and possessing certain qualities of sound and rhythm. These are qualities often neglected. So much communication in our culture depends upon the written word that it is easy to forget that language, both in its historical development and in its acquisition by individuals, is speech long before it is writing. We hear language before we see it, and while people who have learned to read differ a great deal in how much they tend to hear the words they are reading, some traces of our early, exclusively auditory experience of language remain with most of us. Good writers realize this fact, and they construct their sentences — sometimes intuitively, sometimes with a high degree of consciousness — for the ear as well as for the eye.

Much of what goes on in a sentence to create its movement and rhythm is still mysterious. It is certainly safe to say that in well-written prose many things are going on, that the total auditory effect is complicated and that it includes the sounds of the words, the stresses upon their syllables, the grouping of words into larger sound units, and the intonation of the entire sentence. Probably it is also safe to say that in a good sentence all these things are so integrated that we hear them as a single harmonious effect, even though it is necessary to separate them in order to talk about rhythm. When one attempts to get beyond such generalizations, however, and discover in a specific way what is happening, he is likely to get into difficulty. In this case, at least, it is much easier to see the forest than the trees, to hear and respond to the rhythm of a sentence than to explain exactly how that rhythm is achieved.

But if the "audible sentence" (we shall use this term to designate the sentence as it exists for our ears) is too complicated to understand completely, a writer cannot afford to ignore it. We would urge that it is almost axiomatic that good writing must be "good" to the ear. At the very least, the sound and rhythm of the sentence should not interfere with what the writer wants to say. We have all had the experience of reading a book that seems to lull us into semi-consciousness; we read on and on, until after some pages we are startled to realize that we cannot remember a single word. Sometimes we even fall asleep. When this happens, it is very often because the rhythms of the sentences are flat and monotonous. But sound and rhythm have an even more important function than keeping us awake. More positively, they become integral elements of communication, reinforcing what the writer says in his words. Listen, for example, to this sentence by Rachel Carson:

> The tide reaches flood stage, slackens, hesitates, and begins to ebb.

Even without quite understanding how it happens you can hear in the movement a suggestion of the tidal flow the sentence describes.

The ability to create the "audible sentence," then, to make it contribute to his meaning, is important to the writer's art. It is probably true that in the act of composing most people do not think consciously of how sentences sound. But the more one understands about prose rhythm, the more it will influence, presumably for the better, the words he selects and the patterns into which he groups them. Moreover, a knowledge of how rhythm and sound and intonation work will be helpful when a writer revises, for it is especially in revision that those adjustments in structure are made which render the audible sentence effective.

Prose Rhythm

There is no universally accepted way of analyzing prose rhythm. Such systems as do exist are too complicated for our purposes. However, we shall try to suggest a little of what happens in the sentence to create a sense of rhythm. To begin with, we had better define rhythm. In language, rhythm is the more or less regular alternation of sounds that are more emphatic with sounds that are less emphatic. In English the basic rhythmic units of sound are the syllables of words. There are, however, several kinds of patterns into which syllables may be arranged: (1) the simple groupings of stressed and unstressed syllables — which are the basic units of syllabic rhythm; (2) groups of words which form minimal syntactic units within the sentence — called here stress groups; and (3) entire clauses, which are bound together by intonation. We shall look briefly at each of these, always remembering that the full rhythmic effect of any specific sentence will depend upon some combination of most or of all of these patterns.

SYLLABIC RHYTHM

The simplest to understand is syllabic rhythm, which consists of a more or less regular arrangement of stressed and unstressed syllables. The difference in stress is essentially a matter of how loudly the syllable is spoken. (Since loudness is regarded as a quality of sound, English syllabic rhythm is often described as "qualitative.") In pronouncing any disyllabic word in English we speak one syllable relatively more loudly; this is called the stressed syllable and is indicated by ′. The other syllable will be relatively soft (indicated by ˣ). The word "above" is an example. Because many polysyllabic words or phrases have a syllable that is spoken with a degree of loudness somewhere between ˣ and ′, there is a need for a mark of secondary stress (\`). The first syllable of "inability," for example, has secondary stress: "inability." Of course, limiting the degrees of syllabic stress to three is arbitrary; it is possible to distinguish more, and many linguists distinguish at least four. Three stress levels are enough for our purposes, however.

Syllabic rhythm occurs when a writer so selects and arranges his words and phrases that they form a relatively regular pattern of stressed and unstressed syllables. Suppose, for instance, that to the preposition "above" we add the article-noun combination "the house" and to this the prepositional phrase "upon the hill." We would now have a group of words that scanned like this (the process of assigning the stresses and non-stresses to the syllables of a sentence or clause and arranging them into groups is called "scanning" or "scansion"):

ˣ ′ ˣ ′ ˣ ′ ˣ ′
above the house upon the hill.

If we were to complete the thought by adding "a cloud had formed," we should have a regular iambic sentence (an iamb consists of an unstressed syllable followed by a stressed syllable):

ˣ ′ ˣ ′ ˣ ′ ˣ ′ ˣ ′ ˣ ′
Above the house upon the hill a cloud had formed.

When, as in this example, each stressed syllable is preceded or followed by the same number of unstressed, the syllabic rhythm becomes highly regular and is called "meter." Meter is characteristic of poetry. In prose, however, it is felt to be out of place, and while some sentences do contain runs of meter, such runs are usually confined either to short sentences or to brief parts of longer ones. Generally syllabic rhythm in prose is less regular, that is, the stressed syllables are separated by varying numbers of non-stresses. Instead of there regularly being, say, one non-stress between each pair of stresses, there will be now one, now two, now four, now none at all, and so on. But of course a limit exists to such variety. Rhythm depends upon our responding to some degree of regularity; if the separation of stresses and non-stresses grows unpredictable, we lose all sense of rhythm. In bad prose this sometimes happens. In good prose at least a minimal degree of regularity will be preserved in the alternation of stressed and unstressed syllables. It is important in this regard to remember that the difference between the syllabic stress pattern of poetry and that of prose is not that the first is regular while the second is irregular. Rather the distinction lies in the degree of regularity: the syllabic rhythm of poetry is relatively more regular, that of prose relatively less.

For purposes of analyzing syllabic rhythm it is customary to regard the stresses and non-stresses in a sentence as forming certain patterns. There are two types of such patterns — one called "feet" and the other called "cadences." The kinds of feet into which English poetry and prose are scanned derive from Greek and still have their ancient names. There are dozens of varieties, but seven or eight are enough to handle most English prose. Feet are classified according to how many syllables they contain. Disyllabic feet include the *iamb*, the *trochee*, the *pyrrhic*, and the *spondee*. Iambs, as we have already seen, place the stress after the non-stress, as in "beyond"; trochees reverse this, placing the stress first, as in "lonely"; pyrrhics consist of two non-stresses (the pyrrhic does not normally occur except in a context of other syllables; the words "in a" might serve as an instance); while spondees have two stresses, as in "stone wall." Trisyllabic feet include the *anapest*, the *dactyl*, the *amphibrach*, and the *cretic*. The anapest consists of two non-stresses followed by a stress: "unadorned"; the dactyl is just the opposite: "seemingly"; the amphibrach places the stress between two non-stresses: "delightful"; and the cretic reverses the pattern of the amphibrach: "badly done." Of the tetrasyllabic feet we need mention only the *paeon,* which has three non-stresses and one stress. There are four varieties of paeon, depending upon whether the stress comes first ("early in May"), second ("the sky above"), third ("in the morning"), or fourth ("upon the door").

Cadences, like feet, consist of a collection of stressed and unstressed syllables. They differ from feet in being somewhat longer, in always beginning with a stress, and in having at least two stresses (the cretic and a few other classical feet also contain two stresses, but these are relatively rare). Prose cadences are in effect a flow of sound that is heard as a unit and that rises and falls between two and sometimes three points of syllabic stress. Some scholars distinguish two kinds of cadence. The first, the so-called cursus, derives from Latin and Greek, where it was used as a rhythmic signal that the speaker was coming to the end of a period (that is, to the end of what we should call a sentence). The various kinds of cursus were copied by early stylists in English, who adapted them to our language, where they have remained. They still are effective ways of rounding off a sentence or even of ending an essay, as we saw in the chapter on closings. The second type of cadence in English is simply called native cadence since, unlike the cursus, it has no specific analogues in Latin or Greek. It differs from the cursus, by often ending on a stressed syllable (cursus never do); but like cursus the many varieties of native cadence are used for emphasis and for closing. The two following sentences illustrate cursus and native cadence:

> The child, staring with round eyes, at this instance of liberality, wholly unprecedented in his large experience, took the man of gingerbread, and quitted the premises. NATHANIEL HAWTHORNE.

(The last three words — "quitted the premises" — are an instance of a classical cursus.)

> They could be seen on the roads, she tramping stolidly in her finery — gray dress, black feather, stout boots, prominent white cotton gloves that caught your eye a hundred yards away; and he, his coat slung picturesquely over one shoulder, pacing by her side, gallant of bearing and casting tender glances upon the girl with the golden hair. JOSEPH CONRAD.

("Girl with the golden hair" is a type of native cadence.)

In summary, then, syllabic rhythm may involve both the metrical foot and cadence. It is possible to detect both at once. In the final six words of Conrad's sentence one can hear beneath the cadence the metrical beat of iamb, anapest, iamb. It is true that prose sentences which scan neatly into perfect syllabic feet are rare and that rhythm consists of more than the beat of the syllables. Yet it is also true that syllabic rhythm is a part, and an important part, of the rhythm of prose. It is a kind of rhythmic base.

Occasionally syllabic rhythm may become quite regular without losing the feeling of prose. This sentence by F. L. Lucas is an example:

> A pretty dance *that* was to lead our world, and blood enough it cost.

As is this one by Logan Pearsall Smith:

> I love to lie in bed and read the lives of the Popes of Rome.

In both these cases the syllabic rhythm is metrical. Of the eight feet in Mr. Lucas's sentence, seven are iambs while the other, a trochee, is also a disyllabic foot; of the seven feet in Smith's sentence, six are iambs and the other is an anapest, which, like the iamb, is a rising foot. (A rising foot places the stress at the end, a falling foot at the beginning.)

Usually, however, the syllabic rhythm in a prose sentence, even when it is clearly felt, is less regular than in our examples. The following sentences are more typical:

> Spring, summer, autumn, each in turn, have brought their gifts and done their utmost.
>
> CARDINAL NEWMAN

> We hear the hum of life in the fields; a horse champs his bit; a butterfly circles and settles.
>
> VIRGINIA WOOLF

> There was a magic, and a spell, and a curse; but the magic has been waved away, and the spell broken, and the curse was a curse of sleep and not of pain.
>
> R. L. DUFFUS

STRESS GROUPS

Despite its basic importance, the syllabic beat is only part of what creates the full effect of prose rhythm. We do not really read prose as a series of syllables (we do not even read poetry this way, except for poetry of the simplest sort). Rather we tend to break the sentence into stress groups, that is, groups of words which make up syntactic wholes and which convey a unit of sense. Generally a stress group will include several words, but it may consist of only one or it may include all of a short, simple sentence. Whether they are large or small, all stress groups seem to have two essential features. The first is that while they may contain several stressed syllables, only one of these is paramount. Thus each stress group will have one and only one major stress, which may be called the "centroid" — the center of its mass. The second feature (and there is some doubt about it) is that the stress groups composing any given sentence will use up about the same amount of time. That is, they occupy roughly equal time intervals; to use a technical term, they are isochronic. In order to be isochronic, however, it is not necessary that they have the same number of syllables. In fact, the stress groups composing any sentence will probably have different numbers of syllables. But within the same sentence a group of six or seven syllables will be spoken somewhat more rapidly than a group of three or four, so preserving the relatively equal time units.

Thus the audible sentence, in addition to being a series of stressed syllables, is also a series of stress groups. One or two of the sentences we scanned can also be analyzed to show their stress groups. We shall mark only the centroidal stress within each group (using the symbol ″) and shall fix the boundaries between successive groups with a bracket (]). So that you may see how stress groups enclose the syllabic rhythm, we shall indicate both, placing the stress group analysis in line (b) above the foot scansion in line (a). So analyzed, here is the sentence by F. L. Lucas:

(b) ″] ″]
(a) x ′ x ′ ′ x x ′ x ′
A pretty dance *that* was to lead our world,

(b) ″]
(a) x ′ x ′ x ′
and blood enough it cost.

In terms of stress groups the sentence divides into three units, each with one major stress — upon "*that*" in the first group, upon "lead" in the second, and upon "blood" in the third. The sentence by Logan Pearsall Smith reveals this pattern:

(b)] ″ ″]
(a) x ′ x ′ x ′ x ′ x ′
I love to lie in bed and read the lives

(b) ″]
(a) x x ′ x ′
of the Popes of Rome.

The examples suggest that the stress groups and the metrical feet are generally different. Occasionally they may correspond, but more likely the stress group will encompass several feet. The stress of only one of those feet, however, is given maximum emphasis within the group and becomes its centroid, though any other syllabic stresses the group may include will be heard as a kind of secondary stress.

In analyzing sentences into their stress groups, an element of subjectivity is inescapable. Equally sensitive and skilled readers may make slightly different decisions. In Mr. Lucas's sentence, for example, it would certainly be possible to place the centroid in the second group upon "world," though the earlier importance of "dance" and "*that*" seems to us to make "lead" a more reasonable choice. But assuming equally well-trained readers, we may say that the differences are slight and would not invalidate the main outlines of any analysis. Analyzing a sentence into stress groups is essential when one reads aloud. In fact, acquiring skill at reading aloud is in essence acquiring the ability to intuit how the sentence must be broken into stress groups.

It is the writer's business to give his readers enough cues to enable them to analyze the sentence properly. The principal way to do this is to keep the syntactic units clear. Very broadly, stress groups correspond with syntactic units. The correspondence is far from exact. Not every syntactic unit is necessarily felt to be a stress group; not every prepositional phrase, for example, is read as a separate unit. But while a stress group may include several syntactic units, it will never cut across a syntactic grouping, splitting a preposition, say, from its object. Stress groups divide at lines of normal grammatical cleavage within the sentence. For instance, in reading the sentence "The man in the house shouted in alarm," we would probably divide it into two stress groups, the first composed of the subject plus all its modifiers (all of which constitutes a natural syntactic unit), the second including the verb plus the prepositional phrase (which together make up the predicate). The centroids would go on "man" and "shouted":

″] ″]
The man in the house shouted in alarm.

Only poor readers would divide this sentence into stress groups that cut across the syntax; it would be a very bad reading to say:

″] ″] ″]
The man in the house shouted in alarm.

As a sentence grows longer and more complicated, it will be necessary to split it into more than two stress groups. But no matter how many groups the sentence may contain, the breaks between them will occur at natural dividing lines.

In part, then, the writer depends upon his reader's knowing enough about English syntax to hear the audible sentence correctly. Often, however, a writer will need to indicate more specifically how he wants his sentence to be read. There are several cues he can employ. Stops, especially commas, are often used for this purpose. For instance, most people would read the sentence "He went home mad" as a single stress group. But if the adjective is preceded by a comma, the sentence must be read as having two parts:

″] ″]
He went home, mad.

Inversions, both primary and secondary, also suggest — in fact they demand — that the audible sentence be analyzed in a certain way. Even without a comma after "morning" few of us would read "In the morning he left town" as a single stress group; rather we would say:

″] ″]
In the morning he left town.

Interrupters also break the audible sentence into specific stress groups. For example, the sentence "The owner, who was a very nice man, decided not to press charges" must be read:

″] ″] ″]
The owner, who was a very nice man, decided not to press charges.

There is room for disagreement about how "decided not to press charges" may be stressed, but the three-part analysis of this sentence is pre-determined by the interrupted movement. Notice that it is the word order that is essential here, not the commas. In this case the commas simply make clear a pattern already established. Even if this sentence had no commas at all, an experienced reader would figure out, after one or two trials, how to analyze it. The commas merely save him the one or two trials.

INTONATIONAL PATTERN

So far we have seen that the rhythm of a sentence consists both of a series of stressed and unstressed syllables, and of a succession of two or more stress groups (though a short sentence may contain only one such group), each having one major stress and occupying roughly the same amount of time. There remains one further element of prose rhythm. This is the intonational pattern. Intonation involves two things: (1) what is happening to the voice at the end of the sentence or clause, and (2) the succession of pitches the voice goes through in speaking the sentence or clause.

By the first we simply mean whether the voice is falling, rising, or remaining level at the end of the sentence. The second consideration, pitch, requires a little more explanation. Pitch means the frequency of sound, whether it consists of 450 vibrations per second or 700 or whatever number. As the number of vibrations increases, the pitch goes up; as the number of vibrations decreases, the pitch goes down. As an aspect of speech, pitch is a difficult thing for many English speaking people to understand, especially if they are untrained in music. There are several reasons for the difficulty. One is that pitch is not a very obvious element in English speech, as obvious, for instance, as stress. Another is that the range of pitch differences in normal speech is quite small. Most of us recognize the difference in pitch between a shriek and a growl; but in conversation we rarely do either, and we are hardly aware of the much smaller variations in pitch that do exist. Still a third reason is that these variations are exceedingly relative. For example, there is an obvious difference between a man's shriek and a woman's, between a boy's growl and his sister's. Nor is there any arithmetic ratio of differences that remains standard for all voices, as there is for musical instruments. The range between one woman's throaty whisper and her scream will be quite different from the same range for another woman.

Yet despite all these reasons why it is difficult for most of us to grasp the idea of pitch in speech, it is a reality to which we are very responsive. By using crude lines to represent the rise and fall of pitch in the voice, we may suggest visually several ways in which "yes" may be spoken:

yes yes yes.

The first might suggest incredulity, uncertainty, or inquisitiveness; the second, agreement; the third, emphatic assertion. A more subtle analysis would reveal other meanings conveyed by the intonations with which we say "yes." To take another example, most of us recognize that

a working man

is a man who happens to be working, but that

a working man

is someone who makes his living with his hands. (If you do not mind sounding like a tipsy parrot, try whistling these various forms of "yes" and "a working man," along with the other examples cited in the following paragraphs. You should hear the intonational patterns quite clearly.)

Intonation, then, is not an insignificant element in speech. In order to discuss it, linguists distinguish two things: first, four levels of pitch designated by the numbers 1,2,3,4 — 4 being the highest and 1 the lowest; and second, terminal contours. Terminal contours are the ways in which voice pitch acts at the end of the sentence or clause; there are three possibilities, all symbolized by arrows: a falling contour (↓), rising (↑), or level (→). Certain intonational patterns have become standard in English. For instance, the usual pattern for statements is 2 3 1 ↓. Whether the statement consists of a single word or an entire sentence, the voice begins on the next to lowest pitch, rises to the next to highest, and then toward the end falls to the lowest, continuing to fall as the statement concludes. In a lineal representation, that pattern looks like this:

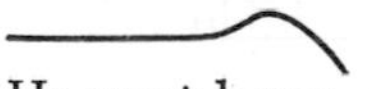

He went home.

(These lines are merely schematic; they do not purport to show exactly where the rise or fall in pitch begins or ends, or how long it occurs, or the relative difference in the frequencies involved. They simply suggest, in a crude way, what the pitch pattern is.) The intonation for a question to which the probable answer would be "yes," "no," or "maybe" is 2 3 3 ↑:

Are you going home?

While that for a question which requires a statement in answer is much like the pattern of the statement:

Why are you going home?

There are, of course, other conventional patterns of intonation in English, those expressing polite disagreement, irony, strong determination, and so on. That people are aware of these is suggested by the frequency with which they complain, "It's not *what* he said; it's how he *said* it." Our interest here, however, is less in the varieties of intonation than in what intonation has to do with prose rhythm. In sentences of two or more clauses, intonation may have a great deal to do with rhythm. In such sentences it is possible to discern a rhythm that comes from repeating the same pattern of intonation two or three times. In the sentence by Virginia Woolf, for example, the same 2 3 1 ↓ pattern occurs in each of the three clauses:

> We hear the hum of life in the fields;
>
> a horse champs his bit; a butterfly circles and settles.

Since rhythm is the repetition of similar patterns, there can exist, as that sentence demonstrates, a rhythm of intonation. The same effect sometimes is found in poetry, as in these lines by Tennyson:

> The long day wanes, the slow moon climbs;
>
> the deep / Moans round with many voices.

This intonational rhythm, which binds together the clauses in the sentences by Mrs. Woolf and Tennyson, may also give a rhythmic unity to successive sentences within the paragraph. A series of rhetorical questions, for instance, or of relatively short, straightforward sentences, is, in effect, a series of similar intonational patterns. Too closely or too long pursued, this kind of rhythm easily becomes a fault. When readers complain that prose is monotonous they often mean that the intonations are too much the same sentence after sentence.

It is important to realize that intonational rhythm does not occur in every sentence, and that when it does occur it is not a substitute for the other kinds of prose rhythm. Rather it is an addition to them. Just as the stress groups overlie and enclose the syllabic feet, so the intonational rhythm overlies and encloses the stress groups. Thus the rhythm of the audible sentence will be the complex product of at least two and, if the sentence is of any length, of all three kinds of rhythm we have considered.

Such a three-level analysis is admittedly complicated (though even at that it oversimplifies the reality), yet the rhythm it reveals is important; for properly employed, rhythm can increase the range and effectiveness of the sentence. We can feel, for example, in the strong beat of Frederick Lewis Allen's statement about the collapse of the stock market ("The Big Bull Market was dead") a sense of certainty and finality that is less apparent in the following statement, even though there is no substantial difference in the meanings of the words:

> The rising stock market of the 1920's had come to an end.

Rhythm may even serve a more specific function in communication than this kind of general appropriateness. We have already seen in Miss Carson's description of the tidal flow that prose rhythm may imitate physical movement. Here are two other examples, sentences similar to Miss Carson's, although somewhat longer:

> On the edge of disaster the river seems to gather herself, to pause, to lift a head noble in ruin, and then, with a slow grandeur, to plunge into the eternal thunder and white chaos below.
> (The sentence describes Niagara Falls.) RUPERT BROOKE

> A wave of movement passed through the crowd from end to end, passed along the heads, swayed the bodies, ran along the jetty like a ripple on the water, like a breath of wind on a field — and all was still again. JOSEPH CONRAD

> (He is describing a sudden movement in a crowd watching the arrival of a boatload of shipwrecked sailors.)

Rhythm may even imitate an abstract idea as well as a physical movement. Study, for instance, this sentence by John Ruskin:

> Bláck bréad, rúde róof, dárk níght, laborious day, weary arm at sunset; and life ebbs away.

The six unrelieved stresses at the beginning suggest the dreary monotony of existence for the Savoyard peasant, whose life Ruskin is describing. Then in the middle, non-stressed syllables are introduced and the sentence picks up speed and runs rapidly to a close, just as life slips away from the peasant before, Ruskin implies, he has had time to hold and enjoy it.

In making such practical applications of prose rhythm, writers are more often guided by intuition than by a highly conscious attention to stresses and intonations. Few writers, as they compose, count syllables, or deliberately arrange and rearrange stress groups, or balance intonational patterns. Mostly this work is done by ear. Yet the ear is ultimately directed by the mind, and its ability to discriminate the elements of rhythm and to arrange them to best advantage, will be increased if at some time one has consciously thought about how prose rhythm works.

By way of summary we shall suggest three or four general principles that may help you in trying to attain a better rhythm in your own prose. The first principle is that rhythm is built into language; it is not something artificial forced onto prose (or poetry) from outside. Whenever you compose a sentence, the words on the paper possess a latent rhythm ready to be released when the sentence is read. Your task is to see that this rhythm works for you and not against you.

Secondly, rhythm always involves the repetition of similar units. For language the basic rhythmic units are syllables. But the syllables may be grouped in different ways: (1) into the more or less regularly alternating patterns of stress and non-stress called metrical feet; (2) into the somewhat longer patterns called cadences; (3) into stress groups, which correspond to what the ear feels constitutes a basic syntactic unit and which have one major stress (the centroid); and (4) into clauses, which are characterized by having an intonational pattern. In most sentences several or all of these arrangements will occur. But in any case, effective rhythm requires that the sounds be grouped into units similar enough to enable the reader to discern the likeness, yet not so exactly alike that the prose approaches the metrical quality of poetry.

A third consideration is that prose rhythm may be faulty in either of two ways. The first is failing to construct the sentence so that its rhythmic units — whether feet, cadences, phrases, or clauses — are clear; or else arranging it into units which, although clear, are so dissimilar that the ear cannot perceive them as comparable. The second fault is making the units too much the same.

As an example of the first mistake, consider this sentence:

> Each party promises to make the city bigger and better before the election but what happens after the election?

One problem here is that the first clause does not break into clear-cut stress groups. This can be corrected by changing the position of the phrase "before the election" (which will have the secondary advantages of removing an ambiguity and of breaking up the alliteration of "bigger . . . better . . . before"). For example, the phrase could be placed first, in which case most readers would hear the first clause something like this:

> Before the election], each party promises to make the city] bigger and better] . . .

A slightly different effect could be obtained by using the phrase as an interrupter:

> Each party promises], before the election], to make the city bigger and better] . . .

A further problem in this sentence is the awkward mixing of the quite different intonational patterns of the two clauses. The first clause, whereever we place the prepositional phrase, follows the intonation 2 3 1 ↓. The second follows the pattern 2 3 3 ↑. It would sound better to separate these two clauses into two sentences. So revised the passage would read:

> Before the election, each party promises to make the city bigger and better. But what happens after the election?

Other improvements might be made; the close repetition of "election" seems monotonous, for example. Rhythmically, however, the revision is an improvement because the rhythmic units are more clearly indicated.

An instance of the second mistake of maintaining the rhythm too regularly is this sentence:

> The man was standing on the stairs and far below we saw the boy, who wore an old, unpressed and ragged suit.

The iambic meter is too perfect. The regularity blunts the emphasis of the sentence and obscures the larger rhythmic units. It drives the reader on, making it less likely that he will pause between stress groups and clauses. By breaking up the iambs and joining the clauses with a semicolon instead of by "and," we arrive at a sentence whose rhythm is still interesting and effective, yet not overly regular:

> The man stood on the stairs; down below we saw the boy, dressed in an old, unpressed, ragged suit.

Now it is possible to hear the rhythm of the stress groups and of the clauses:

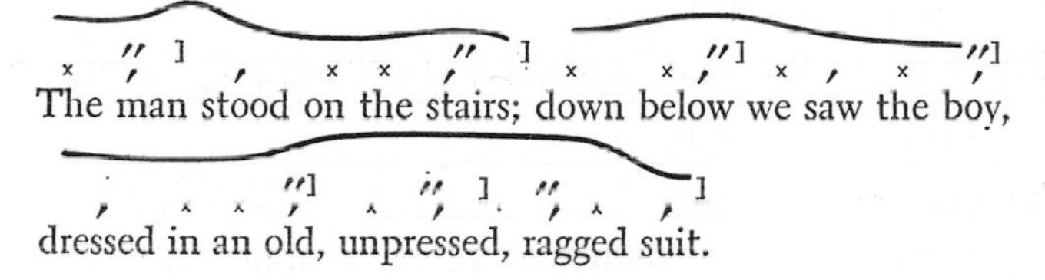

The fourth and last principle is that rhythm is not an insignificant element in communication, a mere surface "prettiness" that makes the sentence sound "nice." No one would deny that it is what the words mean that is chiefly important in prose, and that the rhythmic quality of language is an adjunct to its symbolic function. But it is an adjunct that may mark the difference between a sentence that succeeds in communicating and one that fails. At the very least, good sentence rhythms are a concession to the reader that helps maintain his interest. At their best they are an integral part of communication, not only reinforcing what the words say, but on occasion suggesting moods and attitudes too subtle to be conveyed easily in any other way.

Shape and Balance in the Sentence

Before leaving the audible sentence, we must consider one or two other points, intimately related to rhythm, yet slightly different. One of these is sentence shape. Shape means that the sentence possesses a clearly discernible focus, that one part of it is the most important and the most strongly stressed. Not all sentences are shaped in this sense, but the good ones are. Consider the sentence "We call them savages." As these four words stand, there is no indication of how they ought to be read, that is, a reader could not be sure which one he ought to stress the most. Four possibilities are open to him:

1. WE call them savages.
2. We CALL them savages.
3. We call THEM savages.
4. We call them SAVAGES.

In the absence of a context or of any clues within the sentence itself, all four choices are equally possible; and since they are, we may say that the sentence is shapeless. As these words were actually employed by Benjamin Franklin to begin his essay "Remarks Concerning the Savages of North America" (where, to be honest, they constitute only the first clause and are not a separate sentence), they were arranged in this order:

Savages we call them.

Immediately we realize that maximum stress must go on the first word:

SAVAGES we call them.

Now, the sentence has shape.

In simple, relatively brief sentences, there are four basic shapes, depending upon where the point of maximum stress falls. It may come at or near the beginning, at or close to the end, at or near the middle, or there may be two main stresses, one at either end. A few examples will make the difference clear:

1. Suddenly, a cloud of dust appeared.
(The stress is upon "suddenly.")
2. He was tired, very tired.
(The stress is upon "tired, very tired.")

3. A magnificent death had come like a grace, like a gift, like a reward to that old ship at the end of her laborious days. JOSEPH CONRAD

   (The stress is in the middle, upon "like a grace, like a gift, like a reward.")

4. Into that field, as I watched it, rose the sun. HILAIRE BELLOC

   (There are two points of maximum stress here, one toward the beginning upon "field," the other at the end upon "sun.")

It is not necessary, of course, that the "point" of maximum stress be literally a point, that is, a single word or syllable. It may be, as in the sentence by Conrad, a kind of plateau spread over several words. Whether it falls upon one word or upon an entire phrase, however, it is the focal point of the sentence. That focus is established not by chance, but by very specific devices. One important determining factor is context. What comes before and after a sentence often gives the reader clues about how he should read it. For instance, the words "John was tired" contain no indication of a point of maximum stress; if, however, they were followed by "but Henry wasn't," the obvious reading would be:

JOHN was tired, but HENRY wasn't.

If, on the other hand, the same three words were followed by "he was exhausted," the emphasis would change:

John was TIRED; he was EXHAUSTED.

But a writer cannot depend exclusively upon context to establsh the shape of his sentence; there would be no place to begin and it would be logically impossible ever to discern shape at all. At least a few sentences in any context must carry cues within themselves. In fact, in well written prose, most sentences have cues. They are the same devices we studied in connection with emphasis: subordination, isolation, interruption, restatement, the use of intensives, and so on. They tell the reader: "This is the important point." And when he hears the sentence (and we have argued that people do hear sentences, even when reading silently), he hears a shape that depends upon where that point occurs.

The examples so far have all been relatively short, uncomplicated sentences, containing only one clause. Yet even when a sentence gets quite long and complicated, it is still possible to discern in it one of the basic shapes we have mentioned. The intricate opening sentence of Poe's "The Fall of the House of Usher," for example, places its important point last:

> During the whole of a dull, dark, and soundless day in the autumn of the year, when the clouds hung oppressively low in the heavens, I had been passing alone, on horseback, through a singularly dreary tract of country, and at length found myself, as the shades of evening drew on, within view of the melancholy House of Usher.

It is possible, also, for two or more shaped clauses to be set side by side as parts of the same sentence. Often two such clauses will form a mirror symmetry, the second reversing the shape of the first:

> Fear was not uncommon, but there was no panic.
>
> The revolt had begun suddenly, and suddenly it ended.
>
> Talent, Mr. Micawber has; capital, Mr. Micawber has not.
>
> CHARLES DICKENS
>
> (Here there is no reversal of shape, each clause being stressed on both its ends, the stresses falling on "Talent" and "has" in the first clause and on "capital" and "has not" in the second.

Or the symmetry may be less antithetical, involving simply the repetition of the same shape:

> Ability we don't expect in a Government office, but honesty one might hope for. ANTHONY HOPE
>
> He seemed discouraged, he seemed very discouraged indeed.

Such sentences are simple instances of what is called the balanced sentence, that is, the sentence that breaks into two roughly equal halves about a pause somewhere in the middle. The two parts may be two main clauses, or a main clause and a subordinate clause, or even a main clause and a participial or prepositional construction. The two units do not have to be of equal syntactic order, but they do have to be of more or less the same auditory weight.

The balanced sentence is capable of almost infinite variations. At its simplest it consists of the two-part sentence, which like those we have just seen, splits into two units: ——— ———. But either or both of these halves may again be split, in one or in two places, resulting in a variety of patterns. Here are a few examples:

1. I stood today watching harvesters at work, and a foolish envy took hold of me. GEORGE GISSING

   (A simple balanced sentence with the pattern: ——— ———.)

2. The works of a writer past the prime of life are apt to display certain

excesses or extravagance: what was once his strength has now become his weakness, and his virtue has changed into his vice.

LIONEL JOHNSON

(——— —|—)

3. The irremovable boundaries of knowledge are the same for every age; human sense is feeble, human reason whimsical and vain, human life short and troubled. WALTER RALEIGH

(——— —|—|—)

4. It is the living, and not the dead, that are to be accommodated.

THOMAS PAINE

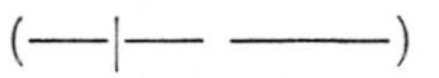

5. In the beginning of each war, England has to seek in blood for the knowledge to ensure success, and like the fiend's progress towards Eden, her conquering course is through chaos followed by death.

SIR WILLIAM F. P. NAPIER

(—|— —|—)

6. The place might have been a convent in some Tuscan *vicolo,* so blind a look it had; but in our country, when a little house faces the sun, it has no use for windows to the north. MAURICE HEWLETT

(—|— —|—|—)

7. I stood like one thunderstruck, or as if I had seen an apparition: I listened, I looked round me, but I could hear nothing, nor see anything. DANIEL DEFOE

(—|— -|—|—|-)

Many more variations of balance are possible, but these are examples enough. Such patterns of balance do not take the place of the prose rhythm we discussed earlier. They provide, as it were, a kind of framework for the rhythm, an over-all design within which the rhythmic effects are carried out. Balance is merely one way of structuring the mass of the sentence. Within that mass, in the dispositions of its parts, the writer works out certain repetitions which constitute the rhythm.

Aside from providing a frame for rhythm, the balanced sentence, while hardly the best style for all occasions, has certain advantages. For one thing, balance in itself implies an attitude toward experience, a stance, so to speak, of reasoned restraint. Whether or not one shares the philosophical skepticism expressed in the sentence by Walter Raleigh, he feels that the skepticism *is* philosophical; the balanced structure suggests that the writer has accepted the limitations of which he speaks and has adjusted his expectations to them. Balance is effective in a slightly different way in this sentence by Samuel Johnson; it occurs in the preface to his dictionary:

> I have protracted my work till most of those whom I wished to please have sunk into the grave, and success and miscarriage are empty sounds: I therefore dismiss it with frigid tranquillity, having little to fear or hope from censure or from praise.

Perhaps there is a trace of self-pity here, yet the balanced construction (the general pattern is—|— —|—) disciplines the sentiment and keeps it from seeming mawkish. It may even be argued that the elaborate balance gives a finer edge to the emotion.

The sense of objectivity and control implicit in the balanced style is advantageous in other ways. In the following estimate of Lord Chesterfield by F. L. Lucas, one is half convinced by the reasonableness of the style, a reasonableness that reinforces the lack of dogmatism suggested by such phrases as "seem to me" and "I think":

> In fine, there are things about Chesterfield that seem to me rather repellent; things that it is an offence in critics to defend. He is typical of one side of the eighteenth century — of what still seems to many its most typical side. But it does not seem to me the really good side of that century; and Chesterfield remains, I think, less an example of things to pursue in life than of things to avoid.
>
> THE SEARCH FOR GOOD SENSE

Because the balanced sentence tends to keep a distance between the writer and his subject, it is often useful for mild satire and comedy. Consider this sentence in which the novelist Anthony Trollope expresses his disapproval of a domineering female character:

> It is not my intention to breathe a word against Mrs. Proudie, but still I cannot think that with all her virtues she adds much to her husband's happiness.

The balanced construction, implying the reasonableness of the author, slyly increases the credibility of his criticism, while at the same time it comically reveals that the novelist is indulging in the second clause in the very gossip he foreswears in the first. Similarly comic is the following sentence from the autobiography of Edward Gibbon, describing an unhappy love affair of his youth that was broken upon his father's command:

> After a painful struggle I yielded to my fate: I sighed as a lover, I obeyed as a son; my wound was insensibly healed by time, absence, and the habits of a new life.

Writing from the calmer waters of age, when the tempests of twenty are dim in recollection, Gibbon seems to be smiling at himself. The very balance of this sentence, as nimbly formal as a minuet, is an ironic commentary upon the headlong passions of his youth.

Finally, the balanced style may be comically effective by being violated. Voltaire sometimes uses this trick; here, for instance, is the first part of a sentence from *Candide*, Part II:

> It was reported that there had been, at Constantinople, a kind of free-thinker, who had insinuated, that it was proper to inquire into the truth of the Alcoran's having been actually written with a quill taken from the angel Gabriel . . .

Against this long, elaborate first clause, with its hesitations and careful qualifications, Voltaire sets this simple construction to complete the sentence:

> but he was stoned.

The very imbalance makes us laugh — if somewhat cynically — at the contrast between the scholarly intellectual, timid, learned, diffidently choosing his words, and the man in the street, rock in hand.

We would not have you suppose that in Voltaire's sentence, or in any of the others we have seen, the balance conveys meaning by itself. The primary symbols of meaning are, of course, the words. The balanced construction simply reinforces and enriches the meaning. Or, to be more exact, it reinforces and enriches certain kinds of meaning, for not every sentence can be, or should be, cast in this pattern. Like every device of style, balance has the vices of its virtues. If it suggests reason and restraint, this makes it a poor style for conveying strong emotion, or suggesting the immediacy of raw experience, or communicating the urgency of passionate conviction. Even where it is appropriate, the balanced style easily becomes a mannerism, and needs to be relieved now and again by the short, direct sentence.

Sound Quality and Rhyme

The last aspect of the audible sentence that we shall consider is its tonal quality, that is, the character of the sounds that compose it. Aside from affecting the rhythm of the sentence, sounds may function in two possible ways: as communicative elements and as aesthetic elements. Let us consider first the communicative aspect of sounds.

The question of whether sounds in themselves can convey meaning quite apart from the words which they compose, is not easily answered. Psychologists who have investigated the problem of sound symbolism, as it is called, have concluded that there is no evidence to suggest that meanings inhere in sounds. We may think that the long *e* in "eeny," "meeny," "teeny," "weeny" is a "small sound," but the chances are that this feeling is the result of cultural conditioning and that, in another language, a different chance will have conditioned people to think some other vowel a "tiny sound." Even in onomatopoetic words (those which, like "slurp," directly imitate a sound) there is much difference from culture to culture. The Frenchman's word for a rooster's crowing looks and sounds different from an American's, though presumably roosters sound the same in Brittany and in Connecticut.

But if there is no evidence that certain sounds contain innate meanings that are the same for all peoples, it is true that within a particular culture, certain sounds tend to evoke certain attitudes. Even here, however, one must be very careful in talking about the "meaning" of speech sounds. Such "meanings" are very broad and resist precise interpretation. Probably in the following sentence the frequent use of the *l* sounds, of the *s*'s, and perhaps of the *m*'s and *n*'s contributes to the sense of peace and quiet which the passage describes. Words like "lull," "lullaby," "loll," "slow," "silent," "sh," "shush," "hush," "mute," "moo," have conditioned us to associate these sounds with quietness; but that is about all we can say:

> After all these years I can picture that old time to myself now, just as it was then: the white town drowsing in the sunshine of a summer's morning; the streets empty, or pretty nearly so; one or two clerks sitting in front of the Water Street stores, with their splint-bottomed chairs tilted back against the walls, chins on breasts, hats slouched over their faces, asleep — with shingle shavings enough around to show what broke them down; a sow and a litter of pigs loafing along the sidewalk, doing a good business in watermelon rinds and seeds; two or three lonely little freight piles scattered about the "levee"; a pile of "skids" on the slope of the stone-paved wharf, and the fragrant town drunkard asleep in the shadow of them; two or three wood flats at the head of the wharf, but nobody to listen to the peaceful lapping of the wavelets against them; the great Mississippi, the majestic, the magnificent Mississippi, rolling its mile-wide tide along, shining in the sun; the dense forests away on the other side; the "point" above the town, and the "point" below, bounding the river-glimpse and turning it into a sort of sea, and withal a very still and brilliant and lonely one.
>
> MARK TWAIN, *Life on the Mississippi*

If we do not insist upon interpreting their "meaning" too closely, then, it is fair to say that sounds can convey various moods, or at least reinforce those moods as they are conveyed by the meanings of the words. Sounds may also contribute to meaning in another, less direct, way. By rhyming key words, a writer may draw attention to them, thus indicating to his readers what is important. In prose, rhyme often takes the form of alliteration, the repetition of initial sounds in successive or near successive words. In the following sentence, for instance, Lafcadio Hearn stresses the idea of "wilderness" by repeating the *w* sounds and of "decay" by repeating the *d*'s:

> Otherwise the place is bleakly uninteresting: a wilderness of wind-swept grasses and sinewy weeds waving away from a thin beach ever speckled with drift and decaying things, — worm-riddled timbers, dead porpoises.

Alliteration, however, can be risky. Hearn succeeds, or so it seems to us; but G. K. Chesterton rides alliteration a little too far in this sentence:

> Thus a creed which set out to create conquerors would only corrupt soldiers; corrupt them with a craven and unsoldierly worship of success: and that which began as a philosophy of courage ends as the philosophy of cowardice.

Excesses like this have led some teachers to damn and blast all alliteration — and, in fact, all other varieties of rhyme — in prose. There is no doubt that for prose an extreme use of rhyme is a fault. The trick is to keep the rhyme unobstrusive, subordinate to the sense. Prose suffers when rhyme comes to the surface, a fault to which poets are sometimes given when they write artistic prose:

> Her eyes were full of proud and passionless lust after gold and blood; her hair, close and curled, seems ready to shudder in sunder and divide into snakes.
>
> SWINBURNE

> His boots are tight, the sun is hot, and he may be shot . . .
>
> AMY LOWELL

These contain too much rhyme for most tastes. Miss Lowell's sentence, an example of the so-called polyphonic prose she developed, seems especially awkward, employing in "hot . . . shot" the kind of vowel-consonant rhyme that poets use at the ends of lines. It is interesting, too, that the unrelieved meter of her sentence contributes to the awkwardness:

x / x / x / x / x x / x /
His boots are tight, the sun is hot, and he may be shot . . .

Still, even when such abuses have been acknowledged, it is a little extreme to deny rhyme any place at all in prose. It seems more reasonable to admit that sound qualities, including rhyme, can serve a function, both communicative and aesthetic, within the sentence. Negatively, there are certain things to be avoided: obvious and jingling rhyme or combinations of awkwardly dissimilar sounds. Positively, sounds can create a tonal harmony which delights the ear, as in this sentence by John Donne:

> One dieth at his full strength, being wholly at ease, and in quiet, and another dies in the bitterness of his soul, and never eats with pleasure; but they lie down alike in the dust, and the worm covers them.

Or sounds can enhance the effect of an image, as in the following passage by Virginia Woolf:

> Dust swirls down the avenue, hies and hurries like erected cobras round the corners.

Thus sound is — or can be — a positive element in prose. It is less significant than rhythm, but it is not negligible. Too great a concern with sound, too much "tone painting," is a fault in prose (it is in poetry too). Controlled by a sensitive ear, however, the sound quality of a sentence can enrich and widen its meaning: it can underscore the important point, and it can enhance the aesthetic value of the audible sentence.

For the audible sentence does have an aesthetic quality. Not only can prose be beautiful to the ear; good prose must be beautiful to the ear. Joseph Conrad once wrote:

> . . . it is only through an unremitting never-discouraged care for the shape and ring of sentences that an approach can be made to plasticity, to colour, and that the light of magic suggestiveness may be brought to play for an evanescent instant over the commonplace surface of words: of the old, old words, worn thin, defaced by ages of careless usage.

Conrad was a novelist, a creative writer, and yet that "never-discouraged care for the shape and ring of sentences" is equally unremitting for anyone who seeks to express himself in prose. No writer can neglect the shape, the sound, and the rhythm of his sentences.

Summary

Rhythm in prose derives essentially from the syllables of words and depends upon those syllables being arranged in relatively similar patterns that reoccur with some degree of regularity. These patterns include metrical feet, cadences, stress groups, and intonational units (usually, but not necessarily, clauses). The actual rhythm of any sentence is a complex function of several such groupings which exist simultaneously. Prose rhythm ought not to approach the relatively strict regularity of poetry, although it may do so for brief and infrequent runs. Rhythm, finally, is a legitimate and an important element in the meaning of a sentence, and a good writer makes use of it.

Sentence shape means, roughly, that the audible sentence has been organized around a center (or centers) of primary importance. To put it another way, a shaped sentence is one which is so clearly cued that a sensitive reader knows how he must stress it when reading aloud. A balanced sentence is one that splits into two parts, more or less of the same auditory weight.

The sound qualities of a sentence are less important communicatively than its rhythm. Moreover, the integrity of prose can easily be violated by rhyme. Still, sound can be a positive element in prose. It can be appropriate to the subject and reinforce meaning; and it can underscore key terms and enhance a vital image or figure of speech.

Exercises

1. The following sentences are all examples of the skillful use of rhythm. Scan each one to determine the stressed and the unstressed syllables. Mark off the stress groups into which you think the sentence would be broken by a sensitive reader and indicate where the centroid falls in each group. Do any words seem to be thrown into special prominence by the rhythm?

1. Perhaps she too would see the sunset and pause for a moment, turning, remembering, before he faded with her sleep into the past.
F. SCOTT FITZGERALD

2. Then, tucking his paper under his pillow, he popped out the guttering candle, and turning round upon his side with a smile of exceeding sweetness, settled himself to sleep. AUSTIN DOBSON

3. Sad is the day, and worse must follow, when we hear the blackbird in the garden, and do not throb with joy. W. S. LANDOR

4. For, though I speak to you, I think the king is but a man, as I am: the violet smells to him as it doth to me; the element shows to him as it doth to me; all his sense have but human conditions: his ceremonies laid by, in his nakedness he appears but a man; and though his affections are higher mounted than ours, yet, when they stoop, they stoop with the like wing. SHAKESPEARE

5. When all is done, human life is at the greatest and the best but like a froward child, that must be played with and humoured a little to keep it quiet till it falls asleep, and then the care is over.
SIR WILLIAM TEMPLE

6. The hard road goes on and on — and the wind sings through your helmet-plume — past altars to Legions and Generals forgotten, and broken statues of Gods and Heroes, and thousands of graves where the mountain foxes and hares peep at you. RUDYARD KIPLING

7. Below me was the ship, a leaping mad thing, with little silly figures, all heads and shoulders, pulling silly strings along the deck. There was the sea, sheer under me, and it looked grey and grim and streaked with the white of our smother. JOHN MASEFIELD

8. The rain still fell on thirsty ground; the sun still pursued his daily, and the moon her nightly journey across the sky: the silent procession of the seasons still moved in light and shadow, in cloud and sunshine across the earth: men were still born to labour and sorrow, and still, after a brief sojourn here, were gathered to their fathers in the long home hereafter. SIR JAMES G. FRAZER

9. The world of Goldsmith's poetry is, of course, a flat and eyeless world; swains sport with nymphs, and the deep is finny.
VIRGINIA WOOLF

10. She became a beautiful old saint, in whose character my mother could find only one flaw, if flaw indeed it could be called.
LOGAN PEARSALL SMITH

11. There was a stiff, dry, west wind blowing, and a blue haze in the air. HERBERT QUICK

12. One of the more remote has turned a marvellous tone, — a seemingly diaphonous color, the very ghost of gold. LAFCADIO HEARN

13. They glittered and shone and sparkled, they strutted, and puffed, and posed. BEVERLEY NICHOLS

14. Before it, far out on the soft Turkish-rugged waters, went the glistening white shadow from his broad, milky forehead, a musical rippling playfully accompanying the shade; and behind, the blue waters interchangeably flowed over into the moving valley of his steady wake; and on either hand bright bubbles arose and danced by his side. HERMAN MELVILLE

15. Bitter are the waters of old age, and tears fall inward on the heart.
D. H. LAWRENCE

2. In these sentences, the rhythm seems especially appropriate to the sense. In each case explain why.

1. The city so sound asleep one minute past, was now awake and alive in every fibre. Bugles sounded there; arms and armour rang, and fierce voices in a strange tongue shouted passionate commands. Dogs bayed, horses neighed, women wailed, and children wept; and all the time the noise of trampling feet sounded like low thunder, a bass accompaniment to all that treble. STANDISH O'GRADY

2. [Of a beech tree seen from a fast-moving automobile] It grew bigger and bigger with blinding rapidity. It charged me like a tilting knight, seemed to hack at my head, and pass by. G. K. CHESTERTON

3. Everything was alive about them, flashing, splashing, and passing, ships moving, tugs panting, hawsers taut, barges going down with men toiling at the sweeps, the water all a-swirl with the wash of the shipping, scaling into millions of little wavelets, curling and frothing under the whip of the unceasing wind. H. G. WELLS

4. [Of a whaleboat approaching a whale] Like noiseless nautilus shells, their light prows sped through the sea; but only slowly they neared the foe. HERMAN MELVILLE

5. All is hubble-bubble, swarm and chaos. VIRGINIA WOOLF

6. The traffic jam reaches its highest peak, tapers off, and slowly disappears, all within forty-five minutes. STUDENT

7. Suddenly, as if the movement of his hand had released it, the load of her accumulated impressions of him tilted up, and down poured in a ponderous avalanche all she felt about him. VIRGINIA WOOLF

3. Modeling your work upon the sentences in exercise 2, compose six sentences on similar topics. In each case use the movement of the sentence to reinforce the sense, as Melville, for example, slows down his sentence to suggest the caution with which the boat approaches the whale.

4. The following sentences are all instances of balanced construction. Some exhibit a simple 1-1 balance; others are more complicated. Identify the general pattern of each, whether ——— ———, —|— —|—, and so on. Do you find any where the balanced construction seems especially appropriate to the subject?

1. Publishers, I am told, are worried about their business, and I, as a writer, am therefore worried too. JOSEPH WOOD KRUTCH

2. As for me, I am no more yours, nor you mine, Death hath cut us asunder; and God hath divided me from the world, and you from me. SIR WALTER RALEIGH

3. Religion is not a diseased self-introspection, and agonizing inquiry: their duties are clear to them, the way of supreme good plain, indisputable, and they are traveling on it. THOMAS CARLYLE

4. [Of Joan of Arc] Her dexterity in managing her steed, though acquired in her former occupation, was regarded as fresh proof of her mission; and she was received with the loudest acclamations by the spectators. DAVID HUME

5. This was not an altogether healthy condition of mind, and it met with its due punishment. GEORGE SAINTSBURY

6. We live in an ascending scale when we live happily, one thing leading to another in an endless series. ROBERT LOUIS STEVENSON

7. To treat life in the spirit of art, is to make life a thing in which means and ends are identified; to encourage such treatment, the true moral significance of art and poetry. WALTER PATER

8. I have done various bold things in my life: this is the boldest: and, were I not sure that I should after all succeed in my object, it would be madness to set about it. CARDINAL NEWMAN

9. Then she shrieked shrilly, and fell down in a swoon; and then women bare her into her chamber, and there she made overmuch sorrow. SIR THOMAS MALORY

10. The poem will please, if it is lively; if it is stupid, it will fail; but I will have none of your damned cutting and slashing. LORD BYRON

11. True, you were born under a Kingly Government; and so was I as well as you; but I was not born under Six Acts; nor was I born under a state of things like this. I was not born under it, and I do not wish to live under it; and, with God's help, I will change it if I can. WILLIAM COBBETT

12. Bodily labor is of two kinds, either that which a man submits to for his livlihood, or that which he undergoes for his pleasure. JOSEPH ADDISON

13. Let me come to the point boldly; what governs the Englishman is his inner atmosphere, the weather in his soul. GEORGE SANTAYANA

14. Man has no property in man; neither has any generation a property in the generations which are to follow. THOMAS PAINE

15. The notice which you have been pleased to take of my labours, had it been early, had been kind; but it has been delayed till I am indifferent and cannot enjoy it, till I am solitary and cannot impart it; till I am known and do not want it. SAMUEL JOHNSON

16. Building ceases, births diminish, deaths multiply; the nights lengthen, and days grow shorter. MAURICE MAETERLINCK

17. He may be ill-bred, stupid, uneducated; no matter. LYTTON STRACHEY

18. I show your lordship what I would do, and what I ought: I commit my desires to the imitation of the weak; my actions to the censures of the wise and holy; my weakness, to the pardon and redress of my merciful God. JOSEPH HALL

5. Try your hand at a few balanced sentences. Compose six or eight, each imitating a different one of the patterns exemplified on pages 392–393.

6. Indicate the rhyme in the following sentences. Do you think it is effective? Why? (Or why not?)

1. And I see a bay, a wide bay, smooth as glass and polished like ice, shimmering in the dark. JOSEPH CONRAD

2. The day is fresh-washed and fair, and there is a smell of narcissus in the air. AMY LOWELL

3. So we lurch and lumber through the most famous novels in the world. VIRGINIA WOOLF

4. Green field, and glowing rock, and glancing streamlet, all slope together in the sunshine towards the brows of ravines, where the pines take up their own dominion of saddened shade; and with everlasting roar in the twilight, the stronger torrents thunder down, pale from the glaciers, filling all their chasms with enchanted cold, beating themselves to pieces against the great rocks that they have themselves cast down, and forcing fierce way beneath their ghastly poise. JOHN RUSKIN

5. Ruskin's sentence branches into brackets and relative clauses as a straight strong tree branches into boughs and bifurcations . . . G. K. CHESTERTON

6. Walking one day into a field that I had watched yellowing beyond the trees, I found myself dazzled by the glow and great expanse of gold. LOGAN PEARSALL SMITH

20
SOME POINTS OF GRAMMAR

Introduction

So far we have been concerned with the rhetoric of the sentence, with those techniques of style which make the sentence an emphatic and clear unit of expression capable of achieving the purpose the writer intended. Before leaving it altogether, we must say something about the sentence as a grammatical unit. When subjects and verbs and objects and modifiers are put together to form sentences, they must be combined in accordance with certain principles, or rules, of grammar. Unless writers observe these rules communication cannot proceed. It is important, then, to understand, even in a superficial way, the problems of sentence grammar that most often prove troublesome to students.

Before we look at these problems, we should make clear in what sense we are using the expression "rules of grammar." These rules are not absolute laws that determine now and forever how the language is to be used. Rather they signify a general description of how people actually do use the language at this particular point in time. Of course, some patterns of usage are so fundamental that to violate them is in a sense to break the law. Someone who writes "The saw man boat the" instead of "The man saw the boat," for instance, has ignored conventions of word order so essential to English that he has violated the "natural law" of our language. Although mistakes as fundamental as this are unlikely in native speakers of sound mind, writers can and do commit grammatical errors serious enough to muddle the meanings of their sentences. When, for example, someone writes "He asked after Julia and that he was worried about her health," the mistake of co-ordinating a noun clause with the proper noun "Julia" after "ask" makes the sentence difficult to understand. We may assume that the writer meant: "He asked after Julia and said that he was worried about her health"; but we must assume it because the writer has not actually said this in the grammar of his sentence.

When the violation of a principle of grammar results in ambiguous or nonsensical constructions, there can be no dispute about the rightness of applying the appropriate rule and correcting the mistake. There are, however, situations in which the errors are more matters of usage or style than errors of sense. Here the rules are less absolute, and one needs to remember that if a rule of grammar is a general statement of how people use the language, there are all sorts of people, some very ignorant about language, others very learned; some extremely conservative in their speech habits, others very liberal. Accordingly, some "rules" will be appropriate for all Americans (no adult, for instance, would say "I are going to town"), while others will be true for some kinds of speakers or writers but not for all. By tradition the uncompromising purist says "It is I"; most of the rest of us prefer "It is me."

Such distinctions are often referred to as "levels of usage." Where there is a distinction of this sort to be made about the applicability of the rules we are going to discuss, we shall note it. Generally, in regard to the matter of usage level, you should keep in mind that you are — or hope to be — educated Americans living in the latter half of the twentieth century, and that if you aspire to the careers and professions open to educated people you should cultivate the language habits appropriate to such people. There is nothing "wrong" with saying "I ain't goin' noplace"; and there is no reason why you shouldn't say it — so long as you are sufficiently independent not to care that some people who hear you say it will conclude that you are ill-educated and will, on the basis of that conclusion, deny you opportunities. In this respect language is like dress. Within the demands of decency and safety you may dress as you please; but if what pleases you deviates too far from what is conventional, you must be willing to pay the price for being different.

Rules of Agreement

Rules, then, are conventions of usage; the ones we shall discuss are (1) rules of agreement, (2) rules of case in nouns and pronouns, (3) rules of co-ordination and subordination, and (4) rules of tense sequence and consistency. Agreement means essentially that the form of one word determines that of another, as when a plural subject requires a plural verb. Words may be required to agree in number, person, gender, or case. In one or another of these categories agreement must be observed in English between subjects and verbs, complements and subjects, pronouns and antecedents, and to some degree between nouns and adjectives.

Agreement

BETWEEN SUBJECT AND VERB

The most troublesome area of agreement is that between subject and verb. The rule itself is simple: singular subjects take singular verbs and plural subjects take plural verbs. The difficulty comes in determining whether some subjects are singular or plural. One problem concerns the COLLECTIVE NOUN, which is a word signifying a single entity composed of discrete units. *Team* is an example. Some collective nouns are always regarded as plural and hence create no problem — *police*, for instance. Other collective nouns, however, may be treated as either singular or plural, depending upon whether the writer wishes to stress their oneness or their plurality. Emphasizing its unity, he would select a singular verb and say "The team *is* playing well tonight"; but if he desired to emphasize that it is made up of several persons, he would say "The team *are* leaving for New York tomorrow." In short, the number of a collective noun of this kind must be determined by its intended meaning. Once a writer has decided how to treat a noun like *team*, it is best that he continue to handle it that way all the way through his text, writing consistently "The team plays . . . it is . . . the team tries . . ." If one shifts, in the same passage, from a singular treatment of a collective noun to a plural treatment, there must be a clear and justifiable reason for doing so.

A special group of collective nouns exists only in the plural form: for example, *news, measles, scissors*. Some of these are conventionally regarded as singular: "The news *is* good tonight." Others as plural: "The scissors *are* on the table."

A second problem in agreement between subject and verb is presented by certain PRONOUNS WHICH ARE GRAMMATICALLY SINGULAR BUT NOTIONALLY PLURAL. The most common of these are *everyone, everybody,* and *none*. In "Everybody in the room is going," for instance, the word "everybody" may designate thirty or forty people, and in that sense it is plural. But by the conventions of grammar all forms of *-one* and *-body* are construed as singular, and therefore the verb that follows them must also be in the singular. Such disparities between grammar and common sense occur in all languages. Generally, grammatical categories such as tense and number, correspond more or less closely to such aspects of the real world as time and oneness or more than oneness. There are, however, places where the fit between grammar and reality is imperfect. The problem of *everyone, everybody,* and *none* is such a case in English. In everyday speech the ambiguity is often resolved by following common sense rather than grammar and saying "Everyone are taking their seats." Even so, the rule in formal composition is that these words are treated as singular.

A third source of difficulty in subject-verb agreement is the COMPOUND SUBJECT. A compound subject is a construction in which two or more words (or phrases or clauses) are acting in conjunction as subjects of the same verb. "Jack and Jill were going up the hill," is an instance; "Jack and Jill" constitutes the compound subject of "were going." As a general rule compound subjects are plural and require a plural form of the verb. However, there are exceptions:

(1) When the compound subject is in effect a compound noun, as in "Corned beef and cabbage *is* my favorite dish."

(2) When the compound subject, while not a true compound word, consists of two or more synonyms for the same thing. Speaking of Abraham Lincoln, one would not say, "This great leader and great human being *were* dead." Although this sentence technically has two subjects, these refer to the same man and hence the verb is in the singular.

(3) When several compound subjects constituting a compound construction are regarded separately rather than collectively, a singular verb may be used: "A book, a glass of wine, a lovely day, *is* all I need to be content"; or "Each man and woman *has* to decide individually."

(4) When the disjunctive relationship implicit in (3) is openly expressed, a singular verb is required (assuming that each of the individual subjects is itself singular): "John or Sam *is* going"; "John but not Sam *has* come."

(5) If in such disjunctive compound subjects one member is singular and the other plural, usage is as follows. In *either . . . or* constructions the verb agrees with the closest member of the compound subject: "Either John or the boys *are* going," but "Either the boys or John *is* going." In *but . . . not* constructions the verb agrees with the positive member no matter whether it follows or precedes the negated member: "John but not the boys *is* going"; "The boys but not John *are* going." On the whole, however, disjunctive compound subjects that mix singular and plural mem-

bers are likely to prove awkward. Usually it is best to recast the sentence so as to avoid the compound subject altogether; for example: "Either John is going or the boys are"; "The boys are going but John isn't."

(6) When similar mixing of singular and plural members occurs in compound subjects joined by *not only . . . but* (*also*) and by *neither . . . nor,* the rule is the same: the member nearest the verb determines its number. Thus one would write: "Neither the pencils nor the book *has* arrived," but "Neither the book nor the pencils *have* arrived"; "Not only Harry but also all his friends *are* going," but "Not only all his friends but also Harry *is* going." Since subjects joined by *neither . . . nor* and *not only . . . but* (*also*) are really plural in idea, it is best to arrange the several subjects so that the plural one comes last, thus naturally forcing the verb form to be plural, which is what the idea requires. Even though it is grammatically correct, a sentence like "Not only all his friends but also Harry is going" is still awkward. If in such cases it is not possible to place the plural member last, the entire sentence is better recast.

Closely related to compound subjects are constructions which have the notional force of compounds but which are syntactically quite different. We may call these constructions FALSE COMPOUNDS; they are a fourth source of difficulty in subject-verb agreement. An example is "John, along with Sam, is going to town." Because such a construction means in effect that both John and Sam are going, it is sometimes confused with the true co-ordinate pattern of "John and Sam" and written "John, along with Sam, *are* going to town," which is clearly a grammatical error. The subject of the verb is "John." "Sam" is the object of the preposition "along with." The entire prepositional phrase modifies "John" and has nothing directly to do with the verb. Not only *along with* but also the prepositions *besides, plus, minus, with, like, in addition to, together with,* and *as well as,* are often used in such constructions. When you employ these words to introduce phrases modifying the subject, remember that the nouns they introduce do not affect the number of the verb, which is singular or plural depending solely upon the word which is its grammatical subject.

Still a fifth construction that may cause an error in subject-verb agreement is the ANTICIPATORY SENTENCE. This begins with a pronoun like *it, that, this, these, those,* or the adverb *there,* as in "It was surprising that he went alone." The initial subject (in this case the pronoun "it") anticipates the notional subject (here the noun clause "that he went alone"), which is delayed until after the verb. Grammarians usually treat such sentences as having two subjects — the pronoun (or adverb) — and, in delayed apposition, the clause, phrase, or word that the pronoun anticipates. When the anticipatory subject is one of the pronouns, there is generally no problem of agreement, since *it*, *this*, and *that* can anticipate only singular subjects, and *these* and *those* only plural ones. The adverb *there*, however, occasions more difficulty since it can anticipate, with no change in its own form, either singular or plural subjects. Thus one can write "There is the man" or "There are the men." In anticipatory constructions using *there* the number of the verb cannot be determined until it is clear what subject *there* anticipates. If that subject is plural, the verb must be plural; if it is singular, then so is the verb.

A sixth case of trouble in subject-verb agreement somtimes occurs in INVERSIONS. When a verb precedes two or more subjects, as in "Upon the platform sit an old man, three ladies, and a cat," there is a tendency to make the verb singular. If these subjects were in their normal order, probably there would be no trouble. When they follow the verb, however, it seems to some writers awkward to juxtapose a plural verb form and a singular subject (". . . sit an old man . . ."), resulting in the error. Such constructions, of course, must be treated like any other compound subject.

The same kind of awkward juxtaposition accounts for a seventh source of agreement difficulty often called ATTRACTION. Sometimes a sentence is so arranged that a singular subject is followed by a clausal or phrasal modifier that ends with a plural noun placed just before the main verb, as in "The old desk standing among the modern chairs seems out of place." The plural noun in the modifying construction (here "chairs") is liable to exert a pull upon the verb immediately following it, thus attracting the verb into the same number as itself: "The old desk standing among the modern chairs *seem* out of place." The same error can occur when a plural subject is followed by a modifier ending with a singular noun: "The old roll-top desks set in that shiny new room *seems* out of place." Errors in subject-verb agreement due to attraction are likely to be common in rapid writing and ought to be anticipated in revision.

In addition to those we have listed, there are some rather special problems in number agreement between subject and verb. Titles of books, newspapers, films, plays, and radio and television programs are usually regarded as singular even when they have a plural form. Thus one writes " 'The Defenders' *is* a good show" and "The London *Times has* denied the report." Similarly the proper noun *United States* is usually treated as singular: "The United States *has* decided to accept the proposal" (though there are those whose political opinions persuade them that "The United States have decided . . ." is the more appropriate form). Often, too, a subject in plural form is felt to have a collective sense. This is especially true of nouns signifying measure, as in "Thirty cents *is* all he found" or "Twelve feet *is* all the headroom we have." When the subject of a sentence is a phrase or clause, the entire construction has collective force and the verb is in the singular: "To work while you are going to school *is* never easy." If two or more parallel phrases or clauses compose the subject, they constitute a compound subject and require a plural verb.

So far our discussion of agreement between subject and verb has been concerned with agreement in number. Problems of subject-verb agreement also arise with reference to PERSON. These are, however, much less frequent, being confined to situations in which a compound subject consists of two or more pronouns of different persons. The rules, briefly put, are these:

(1) When one pronominal subject is positive and the other is negated, the verb agrees with the positive member. The rule remains the same no matter what the position of the pronouns relative to the verb may be. One would write: "He, not you, *is* responsible" and "Not you, but he *is* responsible"; but "You, not he, *are* responsible" and "Not he, but you *are* responsible."

(2) When pronouns of different persons are joined by *or* or *nor*, the verb agrees with the nearest pronoun: "Either you or he *is* going" but "Either he or you *are* going." Usually, however, such constructions are awkward and ought to be recast as compound sentences: "Either you are going or he is." The awkwardness is particularly acute when *I* is one of the pronouns. Such alternatives as "Either you or I *am* going" or "Either I or you *are* going" seem equally strained.

(3) When a pronoun in the first or second person is followed by an appositive noun — which is, of course, in the third person — the verb agrees with the pronoun because that is felt to be the real subject: "I, your friend, *tell* you not to do it," not "I, your friend, *tells* you not to do it."

The "simple" rules of agreement in number and in person between subjects and verbs, are not, as you see, so simple after all. Generalizations about how language is used rarely are. Most of the time, however, agreement between subject and verb is no great problem. When difficulties arise the chances are that the problem will be one of those we have listed in the preceding pages. It is well to remember that there are enough exceptions and complications to subject-verb agreement in English so that even experienced writers make mistakes when they are working rapidly. Accordingly, when you check and revise your work be alert for errors of this sort.

COMPLEMENTS AND SUBJECTS

Between the subject and the verb is not the only place in the sentence where agreement is a problem. Agreement also is involved between complements and subjects, pronouns and antecedents, and adjectives and nouns. With complements the rule is easy: predicate nouns must agree in number with the subject. "These men are my *friends,*" for example. The only exceptions are when the predicate noun has collective force or is the name of a material used metaphorically, in which cases it remains singular even though the subject is plural: "Those people are the *heart* of the enterprise"; "The funds are a *gift* from heaven." But there are even exceptions to the exceptions, and one would write: "These men are the *brains* of the plot."

When the complement is a pronoun, it is supposed, according to strict usage, to agree not only in number but in case with the subject. By this rule one should write: "The person who called you last night was I," not ". . . was me." However, few people continue to observe this principle of case agreement between pronominal complements and subjects. Be guided in your own writing by your preference and by that of your teacher.

PRONOUNS AND ANTECEDENTS

Pronouns agree with their antecedents in number, person, and gender. (An "antecedent" is the word for which the pronoun stands. As its name implies it generally precedes the pronoun, though now and then it may follow.) Agreement is a problem only for the personal pronouns and for the demonstrative pairs *this-these* and *that-those*. In the sentence "Harry lost his book," for example, "his" is the required form of the pronoun because its antecedent "Harry" is (1) masculine, (2) singular, and (3) third person. Notice, however, that the case of the pronoun is determined by its own function, not by that of the noun to which it refers.

If the general principles of pronominal reference are clear, there are a few special problems in applying these principles. One concerns those pronouns like *everyone, everybody,* and *none,* which, as we noted earlier, are notionally plural but grammatically singular. When these pronouns become antecedents themselves, they should be referred to by singular personal pronouns: "Everyone took *his* books and left the room." In everyday speech common sense tends to override grammar, and one is likely to hear "Everyone took *their* books and left the room." But in composition the singular pronoun is still preferred.

A second problem in pronominal agreement arises from the fact that English has no personal pronoun in the third person that applies equally well to males and females. In a sentence like "Each student must bring his paper to class," the writer faces a minor dilemma. By selecting "his" he seems to exclude all co-eds. If he writes "their" — not an uncommon solution — he has committed an error in number agreement. If he says "his or her paper" he has cobbled together a sentence that is grammatically correct and clear but painfully awkward. The conventional solution is to use the appropriate form of the third person masculine singular pronoun, allowing the context to make clear that the *he, his,* or *him* has in this case no gender significance.

The same problem occurs when one wishes to refer to singular impersonal pronouns such as *none* and the various compounds of *-one* and *-body* in a situation where these impersonal pronouns may signify women as well as men. If women are included in the group designated in the sentence "Everyone took his hat," the use of "his" is misleading. Here, too, the temptation is to fall back on "their." But "their" again violates number agreement and it is best to stay with "his," relying upon the context to make clear that it has no specifically masculine significance.

When the impersonal pronoun is *one,* another solution is possible. *One* may be used to refer to itself: "When one goes to college, one must learn to study," the "one" applying equally to boys and girls. But while acceptable in England, such repetitions of *one* strike most Americans as stilted, and consequently *one,* useful as it is, is not nearly so often employed in American English as it might be. Colloquially, Americans have developed a generic form of the second person pronoun as a workaday impersonal: "When *you* go to college, *you* must learn to study." This "you" does not mean the specific person addressed but any student of either sex. Thus *you* has acquired, in addition to its traditional meaning of "the person spoken to," a second meaning of "people in general." Its widespread use in speech indicates how convenient such a generic pronoun is. Even so, some teachers dislike the generic *you.* For one thing it is felt to be a little too colloquial. For another, it is easily abused. Some students fall into the habit of reducing every sentence to a pattern built around the generic *you:* "When *you* paint *your* house, the first thing *you* do is to go to *your* paint store and buy *yourself* a paintbrush. *You* take *your* paintbrush home and . . ." and on and on it goes. For these reasons beginning writers would be wise to avoid the generic *you* in composition unless their purpose requires a colloquial tone (and even then they must show that they can control the tendency of the pronoun to spread).

There is another problem of AMBIGUOUS REFERENCE involved in using *him* and *her*, a problem which, though it is not really a question of grammatical agreement, we shall discuss here. The difficulty is revealed in a sentence like this: "John gave Harry his book." Since there are two nouns to which "his" might refer, the sentence is ambiguous: does the book belong to Harry or to John? In some languages it is possible to change the pronoun to clarify the reference in such situations. English, however, has no way of "ranking" the third person pronoun. The old rule was that a sentence like this should always be constructed so that the true antecedent of the pronoun is the noun placed closest to it. According to this rule, then, "Harry" owned the book. But today few readers remember that rule and few writers observe it. Consequently such sentences are felt to be ambiguous, a feeling that is often revealed by the addition of an uneasy explanation, as in "John gave Harry his (i.e. Harry's) book." The parenthetical remark does remove the ambiguity, but it makes the sentence extremely awkward.

A better solution is often to change the verb so as to clarify the relationship. "John returned his book to Harry," for example, increases the probability that the reader will understand it was Harry's book. "John loaned his book to Harry," on the other hand, makes it clear that the book was John's.

Not infrequently this problem crops up in situations where there is no need to keep both nouns to which the pronoun might refer in the same number. Here another, much neater, solution is possible: make one noun singular and the other plural, thus removing ambiguity since the pronoun will point unmistakably to the noun with whose number it agrees. Suppose, for instance, that a student is writing about college. He might say: "The new freshman hesitates to ask his teacher for help. He is afraid that he will take up too much of his time." Probably the second sentence means that the student fears he will waste the teacher's time, but we cannot be sure because the pronouns are ambiguous. The ambiguity disappears if "teacher" is made plural: "The new freshman hesitates to ask his teachers for help. He is afraid that he will take up too much of their time." Now, the antecedents of "he" and "their" are perfectly clear. Since the writer is concerned with students and teachers in general, there is no reason he cannot make one or the other term plural so long as he is consistent about it. When it can be done without altering the substance of the thought, then, changing the number of one of the possible antecedents is the most graceful solution to this kind of ambiguous reference.

LOGICAL AGREEMENT

The types of agreement we have treated thus far have all involved grammatical relationships, situations in which the number (or gender or person) of one word is determined by that of another word to which it is syntactically tied. There is another kind of agreement, which we shall call logical. Logical agreement involves chiefly questions of number, and it occurs when there exists a notional, though not a syntactic, relationship between words so that the number of one logically demands the same number in the other. A common instance is the use of limiting adjectives. A word like *one* cannot be employed except to modify a singular noun; adjectives like *some, many, several,* or *few* except with plural nouns.

A second case of logical agreement involves nouns so closely associated in meaning in a specific context that the plurality of one requires the plurality of the others. This sentence, for example, violates logical agreement: "Many men take their wife to Chicago on a business trip." "Many men" take "trips," and in a monogamous and predominantly married society such as ours, "many men" have "wives." Thus to observe logical agreement the sentence should read: "Many men take their wives to Chicago on business trips." Lapses in logical agreement are less serious than errors in grammatical agreement, and in the less formal atmosphere of conversation may be quite acceptable. In composition, however, they are sloppy at best and at worst can cause ambiguity.

Although it is not strictly a question of number agreement, there is another rule governing adjectives and nouns that we can conveniently consider here. The rule involves the distinction between class nouns and mass nouns. A class noun signifies either a group composed of specific and separable units or the separate entities themselves — nouns like *automobile, book, horse* are examples. A mass, or material, noun refers to a mass of matter possessing common substance — *water, gold, nitrogen.* While some limiting adjectives may be applied equally well to either type of noun (*some,* for instance), other adjectives are restricted to one variety or the other. *Much* and *little* (in the sense of limited in quantity), for example, can be applied only to mass nouns. On the other hand, adjectives like *many, several, two* can be used only with class nouns. Thus one says "much water" and "little air," but "many automobiles" and "a few books." The same distinction applies to the nouns *amount* and *number,* which are restricted to mass and class words respectively: "a large amount of water," but "a great number of automobiles."

Case

Agreement, the first of our "rules" of grammar, concerns the relationships between subjects and verbs, subjects and complements, pronouns and antecedents, and in some cases adjectives and nouns. The second rule we must consider is usually called government or rection, though we shall use the simpler term "case." The rule deals with the relationships between (1) nouns and genitive modifiers, (2) verbs and objects, and (3) prepositions and objects. The principle of case is quite simple: nouns when they act as possessive modifiers must be placed in the genitive (or possessive), and verbs and prepositions require that their objects be placed in certain cases. In inflectional languages case can be a difficult problem. Those of you who have studied Latin may recall that certain prepositions demand an object in the accusative, others in the ablative, and so on. English, however, has largely dispensed with case endings; they linger on only in the genitive singular of nouns and in certain pronouns, namely the personal pronouns and the relative pronoun *who.* Thus case in English is relatively simple, involving only the possessive form of nouns and the possessive and objective forms of the personal pronouns and of *who.*

THE GENITIVE OF NOUNS

The English noun has two genitive forms: the inflectional genitive ("the *boy's* hat") and the periphrastic or *of* genitive ("the hat *of the boy*"). In writing, the inflectional genitive is formed in the singular by adding *-'s* to the noun and in the plural of nouns having the regular *-s* ending by affixing only the apostrophe (*boys'*). There are, however, a few special cases:

(1) If the singular form of the noun ends in *-s,* the modern tendency is to add the full genitive ending: *Thomas-Thomas's.* But the older custom of suppressing the genitive *-s* in such words lingers on. We say "for goodness' sake," for example, not "for goodness's sake"; and some writers still prefer to drop the second *-s* in proper names ending in *-s,* though when

they do they continue to use the apostrophe: *Dickens-Dickens'*. Still, most contemporary editors prefer "Dickens's novels" to "Dickens' novels."

(2) When both nouns in a co-ordinate construction are in the genitive, the *-'s* is added, in formal English, to each: "John's and Harry's friend is here," though in speech the group genitive is more common: "John and Harry's friend is here."

(3) As we have seen, only the apostrophe is added to plural nouns with the regular plural ending of *-s*: "the ladies' auxiliary," "the boys' books." But if the plural is irregular (that is, not marked by *-s*), the genitive is in the regular *-'s* form: *men's, oxen's, children's, the five sheep's.*

The periphrastic genitive presents no problems in form. It is regularly an *of* phrase. A question arises, however, about when to employ the periphrastic and when the inflectional genitive. Very broadly, the *-'s* is used with nouns signifying human beings and the *of* phrase with all others. More narrowly, there are exceptions and qualifications. With nouns signifying animals relatively familiar to man, the inflectional genitive is often preferred to the periphrastic. With animate objects relatively distant from man — plants and the lower animals — the *of* genitive is more likely. Yet even with nouns designating humans it may be better to use the periphrastic genitive if one wishes to achieve a particular shade of emphasis. "The coat of the boy," for instance, lays greater stress on "boy" than does "the boy's coat," and therefore might be preferable in such a sentence as: "The coat of the boy lay heaped on the chair, the coat of his little sister carefully folded beside it."

Similarly, there are exceptions to the rule that abstractions and inanimate nouns take the *of* genitive. In informal situations the *-'s* is often applied to such nouns: "The book's chances are good"; "The tree's trunk stood straight and tall." Here, too, a question of emphasis is involved. In these sentences the use of the *-'s* lays relatively more stress on the noun in the genitive than on the headword (the noun to which the genitive is attached). Moreover, some idioms require the inflectional genitive even though the headword is an abstract or inanimate noun; "a stone's throw" would seem ludicrous in the form "the throw of a stone." Other idioms also exist in which an inanimate noun takes an uninflected genitive; "the table top" and "the chair leg" are examples.

There is, finally, one construction in which the two kinds of genitive may be combined, the so-called double genitive, as in "a friend of my father's." The double genitive is quite an old idiom in English, though in their arguments against it some people appear to regard it as one more corruption of modern times. No doubt it is illogical, or at least repetitious. Still it is an established idiom and is, in fact, completely accepted with personal pronouns like *mine* and *hers,* as in "a friend of hers." There is no reason to avoid the double genitive in composition; in some cases one's purpose may make it preferable. If a writer desires, for instance, to stress the word "friend" and at the same time to make clear that the friend is not this or that specific person but an indefinite one of several possibilities, it may be better to write "a friend of my father's" rather than "my father's friend" or even "one of my father's friends." However, the double genitive ought to be restricted in composition to situations where established idiom or necessary emphasis require it and not extended beyond those occasions. "A car of my sister's," for example, sounds, and is, silly.

PRONOUNS

With nouns, then, the problem of case applies only to the genitive. With the personal pronouns and *who,* case usage is more complicated. Let us look at the personal pronouns first. In English the personal pronouns have three cases: the subjective (or nominative), the possessive (or genitive), and the objective (which combines the old dative and accusative). Generally there is little difficulty with the possessive pronouns, which have two forms, one used as an attributive adjective (*my, your, his, her, its* in the singular and *our, your, their* in the plural), and the other used in the predicative position after a linking verb or in the *of* genitive (*mine, yours, his, hers, its* in the singular and *ours, yours, theirs* in the plural).

The objective forms give writers a little more trouble. After prepositions the objective form of the pronoun should always be used. A few prepositional constructions give even native speakers difficulty. One such is the phrase "between you and me," which is frequently expressed as "between you and I." People who make this error may have been been misled by a false sense of elegance, or perhaps they desire emphasis and feel that *I* is somehow stronger than *me.* In any event, the proper form here is *me.*

After finite transitive verbs a pronominal direct object should be in the objective case: "The men recognized *me*"; "We took *him*"; "You saw *them.*" When the verb is a copula, however, the subjective form of the personal pronoun, as we have seen, is still regarded by precise speakers as the correct choice, at least on formal occasions: "It is *they.*"

Choosing the case of a pronoun that is acting as the subject of verbals (participles, infinitives, or gerunds) presents some special problems — especially with gerunds; the infinitive is simple enough. Subjects of infinitives are in the objective case: "They wanted *me* to go"; "We asked *them* to ride with us." The subject of a gerund is normally in the possessive case: "They appreciated *our* taking the children." But when the gerundial phrase is itself acting as the object of a verb or preposition its subject is sometimes placed in the objective case; and one may also write: "They appreciated *us* taking the children." The possessive form, however, is conventional here and preferable in composition unless there is a special reason — such as emphasis or idiomatic restriction — for employing the objective form.

When they act as the objects and complements of verbals, personal pronouns are treated much as they are after finite verbs. With participles and gerunds a pronominal object is normally in the objective case: "Ignoring *him*, we started off"; "The people objected to the state's taxing *them*." If the participle or gerund is a linking verb, however, a formal style again requires that a pronominal complement be in the subjective: "They were surprised at its being *she*," though the objective form would be common on any but formal occasions.

With infinitives the rules are much the same. If the infinitive is transitive, its pronominal object is in the objective case: "The family decided to visit *us*." If, however, the infinitive is a linking verb (*to be*, for example), a problem arises about the case of the following pronoun. The solution depends upon whether or not the linking infinitive has a subject of its own. If it does not, the pronoun acting as its complement is placed in the subjective case because it is understood to refer back to the main subject of the sentence, with which, of course, it must agree in case. In the sentence "The man was supposed to be *he*," the appropriate form of the pronoun is "he" because the infinitive has no subject and its complement thus refers to "man," which is in the subjective case. On the other hand, if the linking infinitive has a subject of its own, the application of the rule that a complement must agree in case with the subject leads to a different result. Consider the sentence "We suspected the man to be *him*." The linking infinitive now has a subject of its own ("man"). Since the subject of an infinitive is by definition in the objective case, the rule governing complements now forces the selection of the objective form, "him."

Before leaving the personal pronouns, we should say a word about the use of the reflexive forms *myself, yourself, himself, herself, itself, ourselves, yourselves,* and *themselves*. These compound personal pronouns may be used in two ways. The first is for emphasis, as in "I saw him myself" or "I myself saw him." The second is the true reflexive function of bending the action indicated by a transitive verb back upon the subject: "I hurt myself"; "We took ourselves home"; "Henry talked only about himself." Strict grammarians insist that when they are used as reflexive objects these pronouns cannot be employed except to refer to a noun or pronoun that clearly designates the same person as the reflexive. They would argue that the sentence "They sent invitations to Helen and myself" is incorrect since the sentence contains no word (in this case it would be "I") to which "myself" can refer. Despite such strictures, the loose employment of the *-self* pronouns is quite common, especially *myself*. A preference for *myself* may be due to modesty; *me* often seems more assertive than the diffident *myself*. In any case, precise users of the language frown on such loose employment of the reflexives, a fact that a careful writer will remember.

In addition to the personal pronouns, the *who-whose-whom* complex poses a few problems of case. *Whose* is employed to show genitive relationship. Like all forms of *who*, *whose* is usually confined to referring to nouns that signify human beings (or the higher animals). Good writers, however, not uncommonly use *whose* to relate to inanimate and abstract nouns in order to avoid a cumbersome "of which" genitive. For example, the construction "The decision, the wisdom of which we all agree to . . ." strikes some people as stilted, and they prefer the simpler pattern "The decision, whose wisdom we all agree to . . ." More conservative writers, however, feel that the "of which" construction is more suited to formal occasions. To us, either pattern is good English, but your teacher may prefer one or the other.

Whom is a thornier word. It is so easy, in fact, to stick oneself in using *whom* that in ordinary conversation the *who-whom* distinction has just about vanished for many contemporary Americans, *who* serving all occasions. But in composition a careful differentiation of *who* and *whom* is still regarded as a mark of cultivated usage. Whether it is used interrogatively (for example, "Who are you?") or relatively ("You are not who I thought you were"), the proper form of *who* must be determined by its use in the sentence or clause.

If it is the subject of the verb, *who* is correct: "*Who* sent you?"; "*Who* steals my purse steals trash." When *who* is the subject of a noun clause that is acting as the direct object of a verb, students sometimes get confused. They wonder whether the "who" in the sentence "He asked who went home" should not really be "whom" since it comes after the verb "asked." The answer, of course, is that in this case "who" is the subject of "went" and hence must be in the subjective; it is the entire clause ("who went home") that is the object of "asked," not simply the relative pronoun alone.

When the pronoun is the object of a preposition, the appropriate form in cultivated usage is *whom:* "About *whom* did you ask?"; "The people to *whom* you lent the boat have torn the sail." Notice that the form of the pronoun remains *whom* even when it precedes the preposition, as it may do in less formal patterns: "*Whom* did you ask about?"; "The people *whom* you lent the boat to have torn the sail." When the pronoun is the object of a verb, the form after transitive verbs is *whom:* "*Whom* did you see?"; "The man *whom* you invited is here." But after linking verbs the pronoun is in the subjective case: "He is *who?*"; "We know *who* they are."

Used with infinitives, *who* presents some special problems. As the subject of an infinitive it is, like the personal pronouns, cast in the objective form: "He is no longer the same man *whom* we had supposed to be a trustworthy leader." When the infinitive is a linking verb and the relative pronoun acts as the subjective complement, its case, again like that of the personal pronouns, will depend upon whether or not the linking infinitive has a subject of its own. If it does not have a subject, the relative pronoun will be in the subjective case, a pattern that sometimes occurs with the interrogative *who,* as in "He was thought to be *who?*" If, on the other hand, the infinitive does have its own subject, that subject must be construed as in the objective case, and consequently the subjective complement, which must agree with the subject, is also in the objective form. Thus in the sentence "She didn't turn out to be the person *whom* we had thought her to be," the form of the complement is "*whom*" since it must agree with "her," the subject of the linking infinitive.

All in all, the problem of when to use *who* and when to use *whom* is not really worth all the trouble it occasions, and probably it will be an improvement when the leveling of *whom* to *who,* which has already largely occurred in common speech, reaches the literary language. (This, we hasten to add, is a personal opinion with which some teachers will disagree.) In the meantime, *whom* is still very much with us in composition, and you should try to use it correctly. A careful attention to the proper employment of *who* and *whom* will not make you a good writer; but it will indicate to your readers that you are attempting to use English in a cultured way. This impression is often important to your success in communicating your ideas.

Co-ordination and Subordination

So far we have considered those rules of construction involving agreement and case, the areas that give beginning writers the most trouble. There are also rules about co-ordinating and subordinating the various parts of a sentence. Some of these are more conventions of style or aspects of logic than strict rules of grammar. There is nothing *grammatically* wrong with writing "I like summertime, and elephants have big, floppy ears"; the two clauses are of equal rank and so may be co-ordinated. But from the point of view of rhetoric such a sentence is nonsensical, an extreme instance of forced co-ordination.

This kind of error, however, will not concern us here; in this chapter we are interested only in problems of grammar. Grammatically, co-ordination means joining together two or more words, phrases, or clauses with one of the following conjunctions or pairs of conjunctions: *and, but, for, or, nor, yet, either . . . or, neither . . . nor, not only . . . but (also), both . . . and.* The grammatical rule governing co-ordination is quite simple: co-ordinated elements must be of the same grammatical order. Two nouns may be co-ordinated ("He bought *bread* and *cheese*"); two verbs ("He *went* home and *got* bread"); two adjectives ("a *tired* and *hungry* man"); two adverbs ("She talked *slowly* but *effectively*"); two prepositional phrases ("We sat *on Harry's right* and *on Sam's left*"); two participial phrases ("*Running down the street* and *crying after his mother,* the child disappeared from view"); two infinitive phrases ("*To prepare meals* and *to wash dishes* are among the duties of a housewife"); two gerundial constructions ("*Preparing meals* and *washing dishes* are . . ."); two dependent clauses ("It was a time *when no man was secure* and *when all men were afraid*"); and finally two independent clauses ("*It was very late,* and *we were very tired*").

Conversely, elements that are of different grammatical order may not be co-ordinated. The fault of doing so is called a SHIFTED CONSTRUCTION, and it is a serious solecism. The sentence "It was very late and because we were tired" is an example. The fault lies in co-ordinating unequal clauses, the first being independent and the second dependent. Similarly, these sentences are all instances of shifted constructions:

1. He left because it was a dull affair and because of the lateness of the hour. (This sentence co-ordinates a dependent clause and a prepositional phrase.)

2. To wash the dishes and preparing the meals are the duties of a housewife. (One phrase in the compound subject is an infinitive construction; the other, a gerundial.)

3. John went home and seeing his father. ("Went" is a finite verb form; "seeing" is non-finite.)

It would be easy to multiply examples, but there is little point in exploring all the possible shifted constructions a writer of English can commit. One rather frequent case, however, does merit a glance. Consider the following sentence: "He was a man of great character and who always did his duty." The difficulty is that the sentence contains no first *who*-clause with which the construction "who always did his duty" may be co-ordinated; hence the use of "and" is an error. It is an error easy to commit in rapid composition when one is adding further adjectival modification to a sentence. It is temptingly easy to tack on the extra idea in the form of a relative clause introduced by *who, that,* or *which.* But if the previous modification was not cast in the form of a relative clause, the sentence will be ungrammatical. There are several solutions. One is to recast the relative clause into an adjective construction of the same kind as the first one. Here that solution is not feasible since it is difficult to reduce the clause "who always did his duty" to a single adjective comparable to "character." An alternate solution is to turn the first modifier into a relative construction, thus making it parallel to the second: "He was a man who had great character and who always did his duty." The third solution is to do away with the co-ordinating conjunction: "He was a man of great character who always did his duty." If this revision seems to leave the relative clause floating a little loosely, it can be tied down by repeating the noun it modifies: "He was a man of great character, a man who always did his duty." And if two uses of "man" seem repetitious, another word, either a synonymous noun or an impersonal pronoun like *one,* may be substituted: "He was a man of great character, a true leader who always did his duty."

The rules of subordination are the obverse of those of co-ordination: constructions of unequal grammatical rank must be related by subordinating connectives. These include all prepositions and such conjunctions as the relative pronouns *who, that,* and *which;* the relative adverbs *when, where, why, how, whether;* and the so-called subordinating conjunctions like *since, because, although, though, if, as, than,* and so on. The list is far from complete; there are too many subordinating connectives in English for us to note them all. On the whole, native speakers are not likely to make serious grammatical errors in using subordinating constructions. Stylistic errors

—subordinating what should be the chief idea, for example—are not uncommon, as we have seen; but these do not concern us here.

There is, however, one special problem of subordination involving prepositional phrases. This is a tricky construction in which one word functions simultaneously as the object of two different prepositions, as in "They were aware of and concerned about the problem." "Problem" is the object of both the preposition "of" and the preposition "about." The syntax can be seen in this diagram:

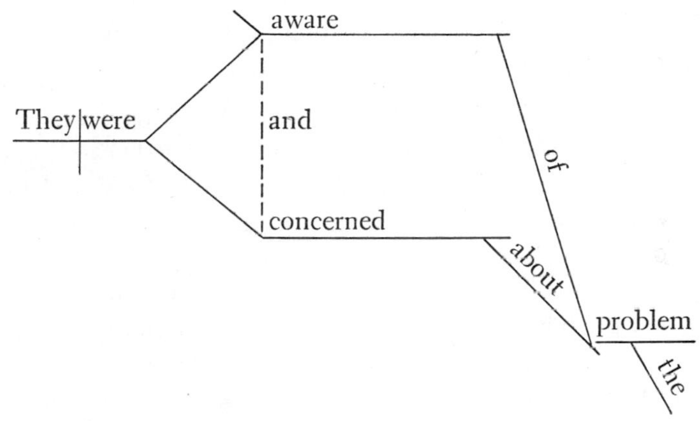

The danger is that a writer will omit one of the prepositions, as, for instance: "They were aware and concerned about the problem." The omission of the connective "of" is a fault because idiom will not allow the preposition "about" to be coupled with the adjective "aware." Since the words "aware" and "concerned" require different prepositions, each preposition must be stated. A syntactical pattern like this is known as a "suspended construction," because the first phrase is suspended after the preposition and not completed until a second prepositional phrase has been introduced. Suspended constructions usually are more trouble than they are worth. Their virtue is economy, but they are highly formal and artificial, and even when handled correctly are likely to confuse the reader. Our advice is to avoid them. Such sentences can be recast in a more natural, if somewhat wordier, form: "They were aware of the problem and concerned about it." If you feel in a specific case that a suspended construction is advantageous, be sure that you have supplied all the connectives idiom demands.

Tense Sequence and Consistency

Using tenses in composition is subject to certain conventions or rules, which, although they are really matters more of style than of grammar, we shall consider here. The first problem concerns what is called tense sequence; the second, tense consistency. Sequence involves the relationship between the tenses of verbs in main and subordinate clauses. The tense of the subordinate verb may be determined either by that of the main verb (which is called idomatic sequence) or, quite independently of the main verb, by the sense of the sentence (natural sequence). As examples of natural sequence, consider these two sentences:

> I was disappointed because I had hoped for better news.
> I was disappointed because I hoped for better news.

In each case the tense of the verb in the subordinate *because*-clause was chosen as a result of the meaning the writer wished to communicate and had nothing to do with the tense of the main verb. Thus in the first sentence the subordinate verb ("had hoped") was placed in the past perfect because the meaning is that the hope preceded the disappointment and now, the disappointment having occured, the hope is gone. In the second sentence placing "hope" in the past suggests that the hope and the disappointment were more or less simultaneous; this sentence does not imply so clearly that the hope is gone.

In idiomatic sequence, on the other hand, the tense of the subordinate verb is determined simply by that of the main verb, without much attention to the logic of ideas. Idiomatic sequence is often employed in indirect statement (though it doesn't have to be). For example, Sam says, "I am going." John, reporting Sam's remark, may say either: "Sam says that he is going" or "Sam said that he was going." In both cases he employs idiomatic sequence. Placing the main verb ("says") in the present tense in the first sentence requires, by the conventions of idiomatic sequence, that the subordinate verb ("is going") also be placed in the present. In the alternate sentence John used the past tense to report Sam's remark and consequently must set the subordinate verb ("was going") also in the past. Similarly, the verb of a statement originally in the future tense is transformed by idiomatic sequence from *will* to *would* when it is indirectly reported after a main clause whose verb is in the past. Thus Sam's remark "I will go" becomes "Sam said that he would go" when John reports it.

Idiomatic sequence is often used in handling clauses of purpose or intent, as in "He volunteered for the extra work so that he *would* get a promotion." In such constuctions *would* or *could* or *should* are more common than *will* or *can* or *shall* when the main verb is placed in the past. If one assumes that the purpose is likely to be realized (that is, that he *will* get the promotion), it would be more logical to say: ". . . so that he will get a promotion." But the logic of natural sequence is often overridden by the feeling of many speakers and writers that it is somehow unnatural to have two verbs in the same sentence in different tenses.

Both natural and idiomatic sequence are ways of solving the vexing problem of how to deal with several time intervals in the same sentence. Neither brings about a satisfactory solution, and each at times can lead to ambiguity. On the whole, it is better to use natural sequence in formal composition unless a consideration of tone or idiom suggests otherwise.

The second rule about the tenses concerns consistency. Consistency involves two related principles: (1) not using different tenses in the same passage to refer to the same time segment, and (2) shifting tenses properly when referring to different time segments. It is possible to violate consistency in a variety of ways; these, however, are the chief errors that writers make:

(1) Shifting needlessly from the past to the present tense, as in "Yesterday I *met* a friend and I *say* to him . . ." It is true that for special effect, short story writers and historians sometimes utilize the historical present. (The "historical present" is the use of the present tense to describe an event which took place in the past, for example: "General Lee sits on his horse, silently surveying the battlefield.") But these are unusual situations, rarely encountered when writing themes for English class.

(2) Shifting needlessly from the present to the past. This is a less common error, and a less defensible one. It is difficult to justify such sentences as "Today I am going to the store and I was buying a hat" or "I am taking the book and returned it to the library." When such errors occur, they are usually the result of extreme haste in writing or of careless revision.

(3) The obverse of (2), failing to shift from the present tense to the past, as in "I am going to see *Lawrence of Arabia* a second time because I enjoy it so much the first time."

(4) Failing to shift from the past to the past perfect. This is perhaps the most frequent of tense inconsistencies, probably because many people are uncertain about exactly what the past perfect does. Roughly, it designates a more remote past in reference to a less remote past; this sentence is an example:

> Yesterday I went downtown to see a movie, but I discovered when I got there that I had already seen all the movies that were being shown.

The writer begins with the simple past ("went," "discovered," "got") because his point of reference is today and the event he is describing (going downtown, arriving there, and discovering a fact about the films) is over in reference to today. But the event of his seeing the films being shown occurred in a more remote past and was over in reference, not to today, but *to yesterday*. Hence the need to shift to the past perfect.

More and more, however, writers are neglecting to make this change from the past to the past perfect. The tendency is so common, in fact, that sentences like "I tried to get in but they wouldn't let me since I forgot my ticket" have become idiomatic. Logically, "had forgotten" is preferable here, and a precise writer would have used it. On formal occasions, or on any occasion when clarity demands it, you should distinguish the past and the past perfect. However, in an informal situation when no ambiguity is likely to result, the past tense may be loosely employed to refer to both a more immediate and a less immediate past time.

Summary

The principal grammatical rules to consider when you write and when you revise sentences are those concerning agreement, case, co-ordination, subordination, and tense. Of agreement, be sure (1) that subjects and verbs agree in number and, when the subject is a personal pronoun, in person; (2) that complements agree with subjects; (3) that pronouns agree with their antecedents in number, person, and gender; (4) that in those few cases where it is a problem, adjectives agree in number with nouns; and (5) that logical agreement has been observed. Of case, be certain (1) that you have used the proper genitive form of nouns; (2) that a personal pronoun not only agrees with its antecedent but is in the proper case as determined by its function; and (3) that you have employed *who-whose-whom* correctly. Of co-ordination and subordination, be sure to co-ordinate *only* constructions of equal grammatical order and to subordinate constructions of unequal order. Finally, of tense, observe either natural or idiomatic sequence, depending upon the context, and do not move about from tense to tense inconsistently.

It is worth repeating here that observing these rules will not make you a good writer, or even keep you from being, in other and perhaps more important ways, a bad one. Still, a careful attention to the rules of grammar is a preliminary and necessary condition to writing well. In the final analysis, grammatical "correctness," in the broad and inclusive sense, is not simply a matter of fashion. It is rather the foundation upon which rhetorical effectiveness must be built, the base for the clear, efficient style so vital to communication. People who write grammatically may not yet have learned to write clearly; but people who insist upon writing ungrammatically never will learn.

Exercises

1. In the following sentences select the form most appropriate according to the conventions of formal English grammar.

1. Both Henry and Mary (is, are) going.
2. The idea that all men should have equal opportunities (is, are) a relatively recent one.
3. Neither the desk nor my books (have, has) arrived.
4. There (is, are) several causes of this condition.
5. I, not you, (are, am) to blame.
6. They asked George and (myself, me, I) to the party.
7. The man about (who, whom) we spoke called last night.
8. They were annoyed at its being (me, I).
9. He knew (who, whom) was responsible.
10. I remembered that I (intended, had intended) to bring my paper.
11. She was (who, whom)?
12. Harry, together with John, (have, has) left.
13. They suspected (who, whom) I was.
14. The victim was intended to be (he, him).
15. (Whoever, whomever) goes to the garage will have to shovel a path through the snow.
16. They asked (she, her) to work for them.
17. Not only my cousins but my uncle also (plans, plan) to go.
18. The woman at the door was (her, she).
19. *The New York Times* (is, are) on strike.
20. The library, along with the dorms, (are, is) going to be rebuilt.
21. My brothers, my sister, and my father (hopes, hope) to attend.
22. Either he or I (are, is) the one.
23. Of all the courses I am taking none (are, is) really difficult.
24. The books but not the desk (have, has) arrived.
25. Either this glass or that one (is, are) mine.
26. Susan, as well as her friends, (are, is) going.
27. They appreciated (him, he, his) minding the children.
28. (Who, whom) did he ask about?

29. We thought that the victim was intended to be (him, he).
30. They were not the men (who, whom) he had supposed them to be.

2. The grammar of these sentences is either wrong or awkward. Explain the error or the awkwardness and correct it.

1. Susan and Janet used her car.
2. Each student must do his or her own work.
3. Everyone was taking notes with their pencils.
4. Many students let their homework assignment go until the last minute.
5. That is a book of my brother's.
6. There were a large amount of automobiles in the lot.
7. There are many men of great wealth and who are bored with life.
8. It was late and because we were tired.
9. The other day I was going to class and I ran across an old friend. I stopped and we begin a conversation.
10. They were held responsible for and accused the crime.
11. It was a time of great stress and when no man was sure of his neighbors.
12. To study hard and doing his homework are the responsibilities of a college student.
13. Those are the womens' coats.
14. The orchestra have tuned up and is about ready to start.
15. Everybody are leaving and taking their coats with them.

21
PUNCTUATION
I. The Stops

Introduction

The first thing to realize about how punctuation marks are used in composition is that they are *not* used according to a set of hard and fast rules. This is a truth many people find hard to accept. They want, not unreasonably, to be told when to use a comma and when not to, when a semicolon is required and when a dash. Such certainty would be comforting, but it is no good making up rules about how punctuation *ought* to be handled. One must look instead at what competent, experienced modern writers really do. When one does look he finds that a great many questions about using punctuation marks must be prefaced by a conditional statement: "If you want emphasis on this word, use a comma; if you don't want emphasis, leave it out." In short, much of what we shall say about punctuation must be qualified by recognizing that "it all depends upon what you want to do." We cannot promise a neat set of rules; a mass of generalizations and qualifications and exceptions will be more like it.

There are several reasons for the confused state of punctuation. One is that punctuation, to some degree, is a matter of fashion and that fashions do not change uniformly. Fifty or seventy-five years ago, writers tended to employ more commas, semicolons, and colons in their sentences than they do today. This older fashion has been called "closed punctuation" and distinguished from the contemporary "open" fashion, which reduces sentence punctuation to a minimum. But the shift from the closed to the open style has been neither consistent nor complete. For example, some people still feel the need for a comma after an initial prepositional phrase. Many others do not.

Here another complication is revealed: temperament. Writers feel differently about punctuation; and, in fact, the same writer may feel differently about it from day to day, now adding a comma that last week he scrupulously erased. An extreme instance of the temperamental attitude toward punctuation is the well-known passage by Gertrude Stein in her essay "Poetry and Grammar":

> And what does a comma do, a comma does nothing but make easy a thing that if you like it enough is easy enough without the comma. A long complicated sentence should force itself upon you, make you know yourself knowing it and the comma, well at the most a comma is a poor period that it lets you stop and take a breath but if you want to take a breath you ought to know yourself that you want to take a breath. It is not like stopping altogether which is what a period does stopping altogether has something to do with going on, but taking a breath well you are always taking a breath and why emphasize one breath rather than another breath. Anyway that is the way I felt about it and I felt that about it very very strongly. And so I almost never used a comma. The longer, the more complicated the sentence the greater the number of the same kinds of words I had following one after another, the more the very many more I had of them the more I felt the passionate need of their taking care of themselves by themselves and not helping them, and thereby enfeebling them by putting in a comma.

One may, or may not, share Miss Stein's feelings about the comma; the important point is that a similar, if less intense, temperamental response to punctuation is not uncommon, and that it is one of the factors complicating any attempt to reduce punctuation usage to rule.

A third factor—and the most important—is that marks of punctuation have not one, but several functions, and that how necessary they are in any given instance will depend upon what the function is. A major distinction to be made here is between the compositional uses of punctuation and its noncompositional uses. The latter include how marks of punctuation are employed in correspondence (the salutations and closings of letters, for example), dates, footnotes and bibliographies, legal instruments, business inventories and orders, other languages such as mathematics and symbolic logic, and so on. In these areas the use of commas, colons, dashes, and what have you is relatively well defined. There may be different systems of punctuation in some cases (that is true of footnoting, for instance), but within any system everything is reducible to arbitrary rules. These noncompositional uses of punctuation marks, however, will not concern us, not because they are unimportant, but because they are outside the limits of our subject.

Our subject is composition, and our interest is in how punctuation is used within the English sentence. But even in this restricted area it is necessary to distinguish at least three different functions. In expository writing punctuation may be used to indicate the syntactic (and logical) structure of the sentence, to establish emphasis, and to alter the rhythm and movement of the sentence. The first function, much the most important, is illustrated in a sentence like "The wind shifted to the starboard quarter, and the sea began to show whitecaps," where the comma is syntactical, indicating the two-part co-ordinate structure. On the other hand, emphasis is the reason for the comma in a sentence like "They beat him, with a whip." Here the comma isolates the final phrase and so stresses it. And in the following passage by Virginia Woolf the numerous commas and the dash have primarily a rhythmic purpose; by chopping up the sentence they suggest the disorder in which the modern letter-writer takes care (or rather does not take care) of his correspondence:

> There then, pell-mell, with all their imperfections thick upon them, they are stuffed — today's post on top of yesterday's post and so on, undocketed, unsorted, as they came.

The problem is further complicated by the fact that a comma or colon or dash may serve not only one of these functions, but any two of them or all three simultaneously. Anytime a comma is set into a sentence, for instance, it affects the movement and rhythm. It may not have been the writer's primary intention to change the rhythm, but he has done it willy-nilly. Now all this means that before one can ask about any sentence, "Is a comma (or whatever) needed here?" he must first ask, "What function do I wish the comma to perform?" The question whether a comma is required before the phrase in the sentence "They beat him with a whip" is nonsensical because it has not been phrased in an answerable way. One must be specific: (1) "Is a comma needed here to show syntactic or logical relationship?" (The answer is no.) (2) "Is a comma an effective way of throwing strong emphasis upon 'with a whip'?" (Yes.) (3) "Is it required for rhythm?" (Probably not, unless this were a closing sentence and the writer wanted to slow it down.)

Each of these questions, moreover, must be formulated not abstractly but with reference to specific readers. Younger people, for example, need more help with the syntactic structure of sentences than do older, more experienced readers. The unsophisticated reader is likely to be frustrated and annoyed by sentences like Gertrude Stein's, while highly educated people may well be irritated by heavy-handed punctuation that labors the obvious. Ultimately, consideration for the reader must be the test of any specific use of a mark of punctuation: will it help the reader to understand? Rather than proceeding by inflexible rules, punctuation must be determined by what the reader needs and expects and by what the writer is trying to say and do.

For all these reasons, then, most questions about compositional punctuation have no clear and simple answer. That is not to say that punctuation is anarchic, that anyone may do as he pleases. There is a famous story of a writer who used no punctuation at all in the course of his book but instead gathered an appendix of several pages closely printed with commas, semicolons, dashes, periods, and so on, with instructions that his reader could distribute them as he pleased. Things are not so bad as this. There are "rules" of punctuation, but they are complex and far from absolute.

These rules will be easier to understand if we divide punctuation into two broad categories, which, while not absolutely distinct, are distinct enough for our purposes. The first, and compositionally the most important, includes the marks known as "stops." Stops, which correspond to a breath pause in speech, include the period, question mark, and exclamation point, and the colon, semicolon, comma, and dash. The marks in the other category are not known by any generic title and we shall call them simply "marks." These do not generally correspond to a breath pause. They include the apostrophe, quotation mark, hyphen, parenthesis and bracket, ellipsis, diacritics, and such related matters as underlining, capitalization, and superscripts.

End Stops

THE PERIOD

Stops divide, in turn, into two broad groups: end (or "full") stops and internal (or "partial") stops. The first occur at the end of the sentence, the latter within the sentence. Here, too, the classification is not perfect; for example, the question mark and exclamation point, classified as end stops, sometimes occur within the sentence. However the distinction is generally accurate and we shall keep it.

The most common of the end stops is the period (also called the "point"). It is used to close a declarative sentence, which in expository writing probably means about 98 per cent of all sentences. Occasionally a writer may omit a period in the haste of composing, but it does not pose any special difficulties as closing punctuation.

The period is also used after abbreviations such as "Mr.," "Mrs.," "Dr.," and so on. ABBREVIATIONS, incidentally, must be used with caution in composition. Conventional abbreviations like "Mr.," "M.," "Mrs.," "Dr.," are legitimate (though many teachers do not like "Prof."). Abbreviations like "etc.," "i.e.," and "e.g.," however, are not universally accepted. Some teachers (we include ourselves) prefer that students write "and so on," "that is," and "for example." Private abbreviations such as you may employ in taking notes and informal abbreviations like the slang that students use to name courses ("econ" for "economics," "phys ed" for "physical education," "bacti" for "bacteriology," and so on) are not generally permissible in composition. Nor do most teachers allow the ampersand ("&") for "and."

THE QUESTION MARK

The question mark (also known by the name of "query" and "interrogation point") offers more possibilities for error. For one thing it can be used only with a direct question, and ought not to close an indirect question. A direct question is one signaled by a special pattern of intonation, which may or may not be accompanied by the inversion of a verbal auxiliary. In writing, of course, intonation does not operate, so that a written question is usually signaled by inversion: "Are you going downtown?" But sometimes, especially in handling dialogue, a writer will follow the colloquial habit of asking a question without inverting the verb, a pattern which in speech is signaled solely by intonation. In that case he will close an apparently declarative sentence with a question mark, the query serving as a cue to the intonation: "You're going downtown?"

It should be remembered here that a rhetorical question is a variety of direct question and must be closed by a query, no matter whether the writer intends to answer it or not. (The conception of a rhetorical question as being one that does not require an answer is inaccurate. Rhetorical questions are often asked precisely so that the writer can compose the answer. And even when the writer himself does not state the answer, he expects his readers to supply it.)

An indirect question, like a direct one, demands a response, but it is expressed as a declaration without the formal characteristics of a question.

That is, it is neither inverted nor spoken with the intonational pattern of a genuine question. We can imagine a situation in which John says to Sam, "Are you going downtown?" Sam does not hear and a third person says, "John asked if you were going downtown." The bystander's statement is an indirect question. It fully demands that Sam make an answer, but it is a statement and so is closed by a period.

Question marks are occasionally used within the sentence. A novelist, for example, may place a query after a word or phrase to imply a rising intonation affecting only that part of the sentence: "Harry? he'd never agree." But in exposition one would rarely have occasion to do this. In exposition, however, an internal question mark is sometimes enclosed within parentheses to indicate uncertainty. If one is not sure of a spelling or the accuracy of a fact, he may admit his doubt with a parenthetical query after the potential inaccuracy. This can properly be done only when no reasonable way of checking the information is available. It is abusing a privilege to write: "In 1492 (?) when Columbus discovered America . . ." If one is not sure when Columbus discovered America, he is expected to find out.

There is, finally, a bit of a problem with how the query ought to be positioned relative to a closing quotation mark. But since this problem affects all the stops, we shall treat the whole matter when we discuss the quotation mark.

THE EXCLAMATION POINT

Exclamation points are used for emphasis. Most often they close a sentence and signal the importance of the total statement. Used after imperative sentences ("Come here!") they indicate the intonational pattern with which such a command would be spoken. Even more often than queries, exclamation points are set within the sentence in order to emphasize the preceding word or phrase. Interjections are usually followed by an exclamation point: "Bah! you expect me to believe that?"

As a device of emphasis exclamation points are of limited value. Restricted to occasional use they can be effective. But like most mechanical means of emphasis (see page 334) they are less satisfactory than techniques of syntax and diction. The practice of piling up exclamation points — a habit no sober writer should indulge — is an indication of the essential inadequacy of the exclamation mark.

Internal Stops

THE COLON

The internal stops occur within the sentence. They are sometimes called partial stops on the theory that the pause they induce is briefer than that of the end (full) stops, though this theory is difficult to prove.

The colon, supposedly the "strongest" of the internal stops, has three compositional functions. The first, the so-called "grouping" function, is relatively uncommon today. When very long, complicated sentences were fashionable, a colon was often used to mark the primary divisions of the sentence into the two (or several) groups of clauses that composed it. Occasionally today one finds a colon between the independent parts of a long compound or compound-complex sentence. It even occurs between paratactic independent clauses that are quite short when, for emphasis, the writer wants a long, pregnant pause. Often in such cases the second clause restates an important point, perhaps affirming more precisely or in more positive terms an idea hinted at or stated negatively in the preceding clause. An example is the following sentence by Lytton Strachey about the Prince-Consort Albert:

> For in addition to his intellectual and moral qualities, he enjoyed by virtue of his position, one supreme advantage which every other holder of high office in the country was without: he was permanent.

The grouping function of the colon, however, is no longer very common.

More frequently the colon acts as a mark of introduction. It may set up a list or series: "The plan failed for three reasons: insufficient money, inadequate preparation, and poor leadership." It may introduce a quotation: "There is much truth in the old proverb: 'He travels fastest who travels alone.'" Or it may introduce an example, as it has done so often in this book. As introductory punctuation the colon is quite formal, and in less formal styles is often replaced by a dash or comma.

Finally, the colon may be employed as an isolating stop to achieve strong emphasis. This is essentially what Strachey did in the sentence about Prince Albert. In the following cases the only difference is that the isolated element is not independent:

> There is only one wish realizable on earth; only one thing that can be perfectly attained: Death. ROBERT LOUIS STEVENSON

> The shouting had continued for so long that it had assumed the appearance of being a solid and unvarying thing: like life.
>
> FORD MADOX FORD

Used as an isolating mark, the colon is more common toward the end of the sentence than toward the beginning. An initial word or phrase may be isolated for emphasis by a dash or a comma, and so may a word or phrase in the middle of the sentence; but a colon would not often be employed in these places. And even to cut off the final portion of the sentence with a colon has come to seem rather formal; a contemporary writer would be as likely to use a dash or comma.

THE SEMICOLON

The semicolon bothers many students. But it is simple enough, having only two functions: (1) between independent clauses and (2) on occasion between the items in a list or series. The first is by far the more important. When they come together in the same sentence, independent clauses may be joined either by co-ordination (that is, linked by *and, but, for, or, nor, yet*) or by parataxis (that is, butted together with no co-ordinating term). Parataxis between independent clauses usually demands a semicolon; co-ordination does not require one (though, as we shall see, a semicolon may be used in this event).

Parataxis is a useful means of emphasis. By omitting the connective the writer forces his readers to discover the logic for themselves and so to see it more clearly. In both the sentences following, for example, the second clause is the reason for the first; but by omitting the *for* each writer achieves a stronger statement:

> Visit either you like; they're both mad. LEWIS CARROL
>
> I never read a book before reviewing it; it prejudices a man so.
>
> SYDNEY SMITH

When the paratactic independent clauses are not punctuated with a semicolon (or colon), the error is called a COMMA FAULT. In some instances of comma fault a comma is used in place of a semicolon ("It was late, therefore we went home"); in other cases no stop of any kind separates the two clauses ("It was late we went home"). The most frequent cause of comma faults is mistaking the function of conjunctive adverbs. When two clauses are joined by a word like *however,* inexperienced writers often treat the *however* as if it were a co-ordinating conjunction and place only a comma between the clauses. Probably this mistake is the result of a false analogy between *however* and *but*. Both words show contradiction and usually one can be substituted for the other with no substantial change of meaning. But syntactically the two connectives have quite different functions: *but* is a true conjunction; *however* is an adverb, capable of showing a relationship in idea but not of establishing a relationship in grammar. Consequently, when a conjunctive adverb (*therefore, thus, hence, still, nevertheless* are other examples) mediates between independent unco-ordinated clauses, the conventional punctuation is a semicolon: "The exam seemed easy; however, it was difficult"; "The library closed early; consequently I didn't finish my work."

When comma faults occur, whether because of a mistake about conjunctive adverbs or because of some other misconception, they may be corrected in several ways, though for any specific case one way will probably be best. The two independent constructions may be recast as separate sentences. Again, the clauses may be kept just as they are, only with a semicolon set between them. Or the clauses may be retained and joined by the appropriate co-ordinating conjunction (with or without a comma). One clause, finally, may be subordinated to the other. In the latter case a comma may be used to separate the two constructions (though it is not invariably required); a semicolon, however, should not be used. Precisely because it conventionally stands between independent constructions in the same sentence, the semicolon ought not to separate a dependent clause from the main construction. A sentence like "When the train arrives; I'll take care of the baggage" is unconventionally punctuated. If any stop at all is needed here, it should be a comma.

Now and again a comma fault may be allowable (then it is often called a "comma link"). If the paratactic clauses are very short and their notional relationship is perfectly clear and if the writer wants a rapid sentence, he may write: "I didn't like the book, it was too contrived." But such punctuation would be inappropriate in most college compositions.

The semicolon, then, is required punctuation between unco-ordinated independent clauses. It is also optional punctuation even when independent clauses are joined by a co-ordinating conjunction. The usual stop in that case is a comma, but a semicolon is permissible. It may even be preferable if the co-ordinated clauses are themselves long and complicated and contain commas of their own. A stronger stop is then needed to signal the break between the primary parts of the sentence. The Duke of Wellington, for instance, used the semicolon in that way in the following sentence. (He is commenting with pleasant cynicism upon the capacity of young ladies to endure the absence of their lovers gone to war.)

> They contrive, in some manner, to live, and look tolerably well, notwithstanding their despair and the continued absence of their lover; and some have even been known to recover so far as to be inclined to take another lover, if the absence of the first has lasted too long.

Even when the co-ordinated clauses are not very long, a semicolon may still replace the comma if the writer wants a longer pause either for emphasis or for rhythmic effect, as in these sentences:

> Children played about her; and she sang as she worked.
>
> RUPERT BROOKE

> So the silence appeared like Death; and now she had death in her heart.
>
> FORD MADOX FORD

In addition to its use between independent clauses, the semicolon has a second function of separating all the items in a list or series when any item contains a comma within itself. A typical list (punctuated in the usual manner) is: "He bought bread, butter, eggs, and cheese." (The comma before the "and" is optional.) Suppose, however, that the sentence read: "He bought bread, which, when he got home, he discovered to be moldy; butter; eggs; and cheese." A comma after "moldy" might well have seemed ambiguous. Since the first item now is the whole construction "bread, which, when he got home, he discovered to be moldy," a comma after "moldy" might be taken to signal not the end of the first item but merely the end of the "which" clause. Conceivably the writer could be going on to say more about the bread. To mark the end of the item a stronger stop is required. Since a semicolon is used between these two items, consistency requires semicolons to be employed between all items, even though none of the others contains a comma. In fairness, we should add that some modern writers do not follow this rule but simply continue to separate items in such a construction with commas, assuming that the context makes perfectly clear when the list is moving to a new item.

THE COMMA

Of all marks of punctuation the comma is the most widely used, the most troublesome, the most difficult to reduce to rule. It is difficult even to decide how to organize a discussion of the comma. From the point of view of the expository writer it seems most useful to distinguish four basic areas of comma usage: (1) with the main elements of the sentence, (2) with modifiers, (3) between clauses, and (4) in lists and series.

The comma with the main elements

With the main elements (that is, the subject, verb, and object) we may note first that a subject and verb are not separated by a comma unless the subject is quite long and complicated. In a formal style it sometimes happens that a long noun clause (or several such clauses) constitutes the subject, as in:

> That the Confederacy had little hope of winning the war which it had so confidently begun, was clear to many experienced Southerners.

Here the subject (everything from "That" to "begun") is so involved that the writer felt the need to signal the approach of the verb by a comma; in this case subject and verb are literally split. Even when a single subject word is followed by extensive restrictive modification, a comma is sometimes placed immediately before the verb:

> Men who have developed a sense of history and have acquired a wide experience of politics and government, are more aware than others of the uncertainties of even reasonable political decisions.

In both these cases the commas can be justified as aiding the reader, telling him in effect, "The subject is over; here comes the verb." In either case, too, the comma could have been omitted had the writer felt his readers did not need help. No one can say when the subject of a sentence grows long enough that a comma will be useful in indicating the structure of the sentence. The test can only be the likelihood of confusion. Few student sentences, however, would be so formal or so complicated to need a comma between subject and verb.

When two subjects are co-ordinated, they are not usually divided by a comma. One should write "Jack and Jill went up a hill" not "Jack, and Jill went . . ." But there are several exceptions:

(1) If the first of the two subjects is relatively long and heavily modified, a comma before the *and* may make the syntax clearer: "The books that are to be returned to the library, and those that belong to me are stacked together in the hall." (Often in such cases the judicious use of *both . . . and* will clarify the sentence even more effectively than a mere comma and may even render the comma superfluous: "Both the books that are to be returned to the library and those that belong to me are stacked in the hall.")

(2) If the conjunction joining two subjects is *but not,* a writer may feel a comma is necessary for clarity even though the subjects are single words: "John, but not Harry, is going." When the subjects joined by *but not* are phrases or clauses a comma is all the more needed.

(3) Two single word subjects co-ordinated by *either . . . or, neither . . . nor,* or *both . . . and* do not usually require a comma: "Either Harry or John will go"; "Both Harry and John are going." But here also a comma becomes more useful as the subjects increase in length and complexity: "Both the people who resisted the new law, and those who welcomed it have concluded that it has not worked well."

(4) When the correlative is *not only . . . but* (*also*), a comma is sometimes placed before the *but,* even when the subjects are short: "Not only these books, but all those in the next room must be sold."

(5) When two subjects are joined by *or,* their punctuation depends upon whether the *or* separates alternative choices or two names for the same thing. In the former case no comma is required; in the latter case a comma usually precedes the *or* and another comma follows the synonymous term or phrase. Thus one writes: "Coffee or tea will be fine," but "Hypotaxis, or subordination, is common in the expository style." The synonymous *or* construction is sometimes punctuated by dashes or enclosed in parentheses: "Hypotaxis — or subordination — is . . ."; "Hypotaxis (or subordination) is . . ." Commas, however, are more frequent.

In addition to these legitimate varieties of the compound subject, there is a construction very similar in meaning but quite different in syntax which requires different punctuation. The sentence "John, along with Sam, is going" is an example. Phrases like "along with Sam" (the prepositions *together with, plus, in addition to* are often used in this construction) are not true compounds but rather examples of the nonrestrictive modification which we shall discuss in a moment. They should be set off by commas.

When, finally, three or more subjects are joined together, they are punctuated as any other list or series, a matter treated further on in this chapter.

Between the verb of a sentence and its direct object (or subjective complement in the case of a linking verb) there is little problem. When interrupting constructions are set in this position (and they are not common in normal English idiom), they are set off by commas: "They seem convinced, quite without reason, that they have been cheated"; "He is determined, although I cannot see why, to go."

When two verbs or two objects are co-ordinated they are separated by a comma only under conditions essentially the same as those which we have listed for co-ordinated subjects. The punctuation of three or more verbs or objects set in series, like that of three or more subjects, will be treated with the discussion of lists and series.

The comma with adjectives

Comma usage with modifiers is far more complex. With adjectives an important consideration is the distinction between restrictive constructions (also called "limiting" and "defining") and nonrestrictive (or "nonlimiting," "nondefining"). Restrictive modifiers are those which so limit or change the meaning of the noun they modify that their removal affects the substantial meaning of the sentence. For example, the sentence "All men who wear beards will be shot," considered as a logical proposition, asserts that of the class of beings called "men," those wearing beards will be shot. If the adjective clause is removed, the sentence reads "All men will be shot," which asserts a very different proposition. The clause is therefore restrictive. On the other hand, the essential meaning of the sentence "General Grant, who wore a beard, became President" is not altered if the clause is removed; "General Grant became President" asserts the same central idea. Thus the clause in this case is nonrestrictive. Nonrestrictive modifiers supply information relevant, but not essential, to the primary idea.

While it is a fairly late development in English style, the punctuation of restrictive and nonrestrictive modifiers is firmly fixed. It is, in fact, one of the few cases in which a rule governing the comma can be laid down with confidence: restrictive modifiers are never set off by commas; nonrestrictive modifiers are almost always set off. (By "set off" we mean that if the modifier precedes its noun it is followed by a comma, or that if it follows the noun a comma is placed before it and a comma — or suitable end stop punctuation — is placed after.)

While it is occasionally possible to write an adjective clause that can be punctuated either as a restrictive or a nonrestrictive modifier, such cases are rare. Most often an adjective construction will be one or the other and must be punctuated according to rule.

That rule applies equally to all kinds of adjectives. No restrictive modifier can be set off from its noun, whether single words ("the tired man," "the hungry horse," "running water"); phrases ("the house on the hill," "the boy running down the street"); or clauses ("the gentleman who is to give the lecture," "the idea we spoke about").

With equal consistency nonrestrictive modifiers are always set off by commas. When the nonrestrictive construction is a participle or participial phrase it may vary in position. But whether it comes before the noun, after it, or is pushed to the end of the sentence, it is punctuated: "Running down the street, the boy fell"; "The boy, running down the street, fell"; "Tired, the man sat down"; "The man, tired, sat down"; "The man sat down, tired." Even simple adjectives, when they are nonrestrictive, may be varied in position, but they are still punctuated: "Hungry, the children headed straight for the refrigerator"; "The children, hungry, headed straight for the refrigerator." Adjective clauses, however, are fixed in position after the noun. When they are nonrestrictive a comma must precede them and a comma follow, unless, of course, the clause closes the sentence. (Now and then dashes may be employed to set off a nonrestrictive adjective clause in order to signal a longer pause for emphasis. But dashes ought to be utilized only rarely for this purpose.)

Although they are not modifiers, we shall consider appositives here since their punctuation depends upon whether they are regarded as essentially restrictive or nonrestrictive. In the case of a sentence like "My brother John has bought a new car" the appositive "John" is not punctuated because it is more precise (that is, more "restricted") than the expression "my brother." Even the fact that the speaker has only one brother does not change the restrictive quality of "John" in this case. On the other hand, in "John, my brother, bought a new car" the appositive ("my brother") is punctuated because it is less restricted than the noun it follows, that is, it is relatively nonrestricted. Similarly one would write "The novel *Gone with the Wind* was made into a movie" but "*Gone with the Wind*, a novel, was . . ."

A second problem involving adjectives is how they are punctuated in series. In a construction like "the ancient, decrepit house," "ancient" is separated from "decrepit" to indicate that both adjectives modify "house." Often, however, the adjective immediately before the noun is felt in effect to form a compound with that noun and thus any earlier adjective is regarded as modifying not the noun alone but the compound idea expressed by the noun-adjective combination. In that case the comma between the two adjectives is omitted: "He's a bright young chap," for instance. But this sentence could also be rendered: "He's a bright, young chap." How such a construction is punctuated depends upon whether one is talking about a "young chap" who is "bright" or a "chap" who is both "young" and "bright." The rule one sometimes hears "to separate with commas adjectives in a series" is a bit oversimple. But generally such constructions can be punctuated properly if the writer will ask himself exactly what it is he wishes to say.

The comma and adverbs

The use of commas with adverbs is even more complicated than with adjectives. For one thing adverbs are more variable in their positioning, and may be shifted about with considerable freedom. For another, adverbs show many kinds of meaning — there are adverbs of time, place, manner, transitional words like *however*, and so on. Both the kind of meaning the adverb conveys and its place in the sentence affect how it must be punctuated. And so, too, does the grammatical form of the adverb — whether it is a single word, a phrase, a clause, or an absolute. Because all these variables influence how an adverb is punctuated, it is excessively difficult to make any but rough generalizations about adverbs and commas.

In the initial position, single word adverbs of time, place, or manner are not usually followed by commas. In sentences like "Tomorrow we'll go to town"; "Earlier he had disagreed"; "Here we'll rest"; "Suddenly it began to rain" the initial adverb is not punctuated except for very strong stress (the device we called isolation in the chapter on emphasis). "Tomorrow, we'll go to town," for example, draws the reader's attention to "tomorrow."

Initial transitional adverbs, however, are more likely to be followed by commas: "However, we don't like it"; "Nonetheless, it is true"; "Consequently, the bank failed"; "Still, it is not too late"; "Therefore, the policy will have to be modified"; "Moreover, the idea is unworkable." There is a tendency among contemporary writers to drop the comma after some of these words (especially with *therefore*). Such open punctuation is all right so long as it does not lead to syntactic ambiguity, which it is likely to do with *however*. Since *however* is also employed as an adverb of manner (meaning "in whatever manner or way") omitting the comma from after an initial linking *however* can be confusing. For example, the words "However we plan to go" could be taken to mean "In whatever manner we plan to go" rather than "But we do plan to go." If the latter is the intended meaning, the comma should be retained.

In connection with initial transitional adverbs, remember that when coordinating conjunctions function in this way, they should not automatically be followed by commas. Do not place a comma after an initial *for, or, but, and,* or *nor* unless the following construction is an interrupter of some sort.

The proper punctuation is "But we'll stay," not "But, we'll stay"; "And the rains came," not "And, the rains came." (The old rule "Don't begin a sentence with *and* or *but*" is, incidentally, wrong. Many fine writers begin sentences this way. Like any device of style, initial *and's* and *but's* should not be overused, but judiciously employed they are very effective transitional words.)

Initial adverbial phrases are handled much like initial single word adverbs. Probably with phrases of time, place, and manner the tendency to use commas is more pronounced than it is after single word adverbs. Still, contemporary open punctuation does not usually employ a comma in constructions like these: "By tomorrow they'll have forgotten it"; "In Boston there are many good places to eat"; "With a terrific crash the car hurtled against the tree." For emphasis a comma can — and should — be set after an initial phrase. When the initial phrase is a transitional element, the comma is generally retained: "On the contrary, we did exactly as you said"; "On the other hand, the boat is very comfortable"; "Despite this fact, they continued with their scheme."

Initial adverbial clauses are usually followed by commas: "Because it was late, we went home"; "When the smoke had cleared, we could see the car wrapped around the tree"; "Since the poem is very difficult, you had better read it carefully." But in contemporary prose the comma is sometimes omitted when the opening clause is short and obviously related to the main idea. Our advice, however, is to punctuate after initial adverbial clauses.

There is less option with initial absolutes. Nominative absolutes in the opening position are invariably followed by commas: "The tide having turned, the crew weighed anchor." And the same is true of absolute participial and infinitive constructions: "Speaking of Herman, whatever became of his wife Dorothy?"; "To tell the truth, I haven't had the time to work on it."

Adverbs set in the middle of the sentence are subject to the same exceptions and qualifications as initial ones. Between the subject and verb single adverbs of time, place, or manner are not generally set off: "The men slowly settled into the routine of camp life"; "The bowman silently fitted an arrow to his string." Adverbial phrases set between subject and verb are usually set off by commas: "The women and children, in the meantime, had left"; "The army, at the end of two weeks, had advanced exactly one mile." If the interrupting adverbial phrase could possibly be read as an adjective phrase, the commas are obligatory: "The boat, with its sails up, was a handsome sight."

Adverbial clauses are not often placed between the subject and verb. When they are, they must be set off: "The truth, when it is revealed, will surprise a great many people"; "These walls, if they could only talk, would tell many secrets." Absolute constructions are similarly rare between subject and verb, and similarly punctuated when they do occur: "Lee's army, the war now over, dispersed to their homes"; "Harry, speaking of jobs, has a good position"; "The novel, to be honest about it, is not a good piece of work."

In addition to coming between subject and verb, adverbs may also be placed within a verb phrase, though such splitting of the verb can easily become awkward. So positioned, single word adverbs of time, place, and manner are not punctuated: "The family had quietly left town"; "The incident had later been exploited"; "We did not get to the party." But any of these, especially if it is intensified by its own modifier, may be set off for emphasis: "The family had, very quietly, left town," though such patterns are relatively rare. When a transitional adverb is placed within a verb phrase, it is conventionally punctuated: "The party had, however, decided on another candidate"; "We have, therefore, employed no people with that background." (Here, too, "therefore" might be unpunctuated.) It seems to us, however, that such splitting is awkward and that little is gained by placing a transitional word within the verb phrase. If interruption is desired it can be had by setting the transitional adverb some place else, between subject and verb, for instance: "The party, however, had decided on another candidate."

Prepositional phrases within the verb are even more likely to prove awkward and ought to be avoided. If they do occur, they should be set off: "The children have, after all, agreed to leave early." Adverbial constructions longer than a brief phrase ought not to interrupt the verb phrase at all. A sentence like "The children have, when all is said and done, agreed to leave early," is simply bad writing, no matter how it is punctuated.

When they come at the end of the sentence, single word adverbs are not preceded by commas except to be isolated for emphasis. "He completed his work easily" might be punctuated "He completed his work, easily," but only when the writer wants to throw a lot of weight upon "easily." Similarly with "He appeared suddenly" and "The people left quietly." Adverbial prepositional phrases in the final position are handled much as single word adverbs. The phrase in the sentence "The people responded with great willingness" would be preceded by a comma only for special stress. Nor are final adverbial clauses usually preceded by commas, especially when they are short and uncomplicated. Occasionally, however, when the preceding main clause has been long and intricate, a comma may signal the following adverbial clause.

A special problem is created when a *because* clause follows a negated main clause. A sentence like "The strategy did not succeed because of poor planning" may be a literal explanation of why the strategy failed, or it may be an emphatic, if somewhat informal, way of saying that "the strategy succeeded because the planning was good." While it might not remove all the ambiguity in such constructions, a comma before "because" would increase the chances of the first reading.

Absolute constructions in the final position are preceded by commas: "He clattered down the stairs, his robe trailing behind"; "It is not a pleasant prospect, to put it mildly."

Commas between clauses

In addition to being used with modifiers, commas are also the conventional stops to set between clauses. We have already touched upon some of the problems of punctuating dependent clauses, and need only summarize them: (1) Adverbial clauses, when first in the sentence, are usually followed by commas; are set off when they are in the middle of the sentence; and are not usually punctuated when they come at the end. (2) Adjective clauses, when nonrestrictive, are always set off by commas; when restrictive they are never set off, though a long restrictive clause set between subject and verb may be followed by a comma to indicate the approach of the verb. (3) When a noun clause acts as the subject of a sentence, it is not usually separated from the verb by a comma, unless the noun clause has been quite long, in which case a comma may signal its conclusion. When a noun clause acts as the direct object of a verb or as the object of a preposition, it is not preceded by a comma, no matter whether it is a *that* clause, a clause employing a relative word, or a contact clause: "He said that he would go"; "He asked where you were"; "He said he would go." (Direct quotations, of course, are preceded by commas, but this is another matter, which we shall treat in the following chapter.)

Commas are also used with co-ordinated independent clauses. Briefly, their use follows these conventions:

(1) When the co-ordinated clauses are short and the relationship between them is obvious, the comma may be omitted. In open punctuation the comma usually is dropped when the conjunction between such brief clauses is *and:* "It was cold and the sky was gray." If the conjunction is

but, the comma between short clauses may be retained since the contradictory relationship may require a pause for assimilation. The conjunction *for* presents a special problem. Since *for* is very common as a preposition, syntactic ambiguity may occur if its conjunctional use is not clearly marked. For example, the sentence "The woman went home for her children were tired" may momentarily throw a reader; it is clearer like this: "The woman went home, for her children were tired." Therefore many writers always set a comma before the conjunction *for,* no matter how short the clauses it joins.

(2) When the co-ordinated clauses are longer, when the sense requires a pause, or when the writer wants to accentuate the divisions of a balanced sentence, a comma is desirable between co-ordinated independent clauses.

(3) If the clauses are quite long and complicated or if the emphasis requires one, a semicolon, as we have seen, may be set between co-ordinated clauses instead of a comma.

(4) No matter which stop is used between co-ordinated clauses, the comma or semicolon *always* precedes the conjunction; it never comes after. The following usage is completely unconventional in English: "The house was very old and, it seemed uncared for."

(5) When independent clauses are joined paratactically (that is, without a conjunction), it will be recalled that the conventional mark is a semicolon. While it is normally a misuse to place a comma here, a comma link may be effective under these conditions: the clauses are short, the relationship between them is clear, and a speedy movement is desirable. Three brief independent paratactic clauses are frequently linked by commas in modern style: "The day dawned clear, the air was warm, the sea calm." But even here semicolons are more formal, and you ought not to punctuate any paratactic independent clauses with commas unless your teacher is willing to allow it.

The comma with lists and series

The fourth compositional use of the comma is in lists and series. Any group of syntactically parallel words (or phrases or clauses) can be grouped into a series. For convenience we shall use only nouns as examples, but the principles of punctuation apply similarly to all cases. The usual way of handling a series is to join all items paratactically except the last two, which are co-ordinated (commonly with *and,* occasionally with *or*); commas are set between the paratactic items, while before the conjunction the comma is optional. Conventionally, then, a series is punctuated like this: "The desk was cluttered with books, pencils, notepaper(,) and scribbled sheets of manuscript." (Remember that when any item in such a series contains a comma within itself, semicolons are usually placed between all items.)

But while this is the most common treatment, it is not the only way of handling a series. As we saw in the chapter on emphasis, a writer may prefer to use *and* between all the items: ". . . with books and pencils and notepaper and scribbled sheets of manuscript." In this case a comma may precede each *and*, but usually the series would not be punctuated at all. Conversely, a writer may use parataxis throughout, dropping even the single *and* of the conventional treatment: ". . . with books, pencils, notepaper, scribbled sheets of manuscript." Here, of course, commas (or, if necessary, semicolons) are required between the items. A third possibility is organizing the items into two or more groups, the items within each group being joined by *and*, while the groups themselves are separated only by commas: ". . . with books and pencils, notepaper and scribbled sheets of manuscript." In any specific case one of these ways of treating a series will be most appropriate to the exact shading of stress the writer had in mind. But all are possible, and each is punctuated as we have indicated.

The final use of the comma is to introduce quotations and dialogue. But since there are various ways of punctuating quotations and since the problem involves several punctuation marks in addition to the comma, we shall postpone discussion of the comma in this function until we come to the quotation mark, where the entire matter will be treated.

THE DASH

The dash has no function that is uniquely its own. Rather it is a stop that, under certain conditions, acts as a stronger equivalent to the comma, or, in other situations, as a less formal substitute for the colon. A common function of the dash is to set off interrupting constructions when the writer wants a longer, more significant pause than the conventional punctuation by commas would provide. Almost any construction that can be set off by commas can also be marked by dashes, a nonrestrictive adjective clause, for example: "This desk — which once belonged to my grandfather — is as strong today as when it was made"; or interrupting adverbs: "I cannot — in all honesty — agree to this"; "The townspeople — even when at long last they learned the truth — were strangely apathetic." But in this use dashes should be reserved for occasions when extraordinary emphasis is needed, or when the idea expressed in the interrupter is related only tenuously to the main clause. Such conditions do not often occur in exposition, and 90 per cent of the time commas are the appropriate stop to set off the usual kind of interrupting construction.

There is, however, an unusual kind of interruption that cannot be handled by commas. This is the intrusive construction that is not syntactically related to the main sentence, and which therefore must be enclosed in parentheses or, less formally, separated by dashes. An intrusive sentence is a good example: "In the morning — it was summer then and the mornings were warm — we would always go swimming." Here a new and independent sentence has simply been stuck into the middle of the containing sentence without being tied to it in any grammatical way. This is a syntactic pattern reminiscent of speech, where people often begin a sentence, think of something they need to say by way of explanation, and casually slip it in. A writer trying to suggest the tone and rhythms of conversation will occasionally use intrusive sentences. While they can be enclosed in parentheses, the very informality of the device makes dashes more appropriate.

The second function of the dash is to establish strong isolation for emphasis. If, for example, the comma in "Suddenly, it began to rain" is replaced by a dash ("Suddenly — it began to rain"), the pause is longer and the emphasis upon "Suddenly" is greater. Similarly the dash can be used rather than a comma to isolate a final or a medial construction: "They searched and searched — but in vain"; "They searched — long and diligently — but without finding a thing."

Finally the dash may replace the colon as a less formal mark of introduction before lists of various kinds: "The fleet had to do three things — maintain defensive patrols, guard merchant shipping, and seek out and destroy enemy naval forces." Now and then the colon and dash are combined as a mark of introduction: "The fleet had to do three things: — . . ." However, this usage is old-fashioned.

The dash, then, is a useful stop. Its very versatility, however, encourages some writers to overuse it. The dash is *not* simply a strong comma or an informal colon. It may *not* be freely substituted for these other stops, but rather may replace them only under very specific conditions. When the dash is extended beyond these conditions, it loses its special advantages. There is even a tendency, perhaps the result of a practice in personal letters, to employ the dash as end stop punctuation in place of the period. Such usage is not usually allowed in composition.

Summary

Stops are those marks of punctuation which correspond to a pause in speech. They include the period, question mark, and exclamation point (collectively called the end, or full, stops); and the colon, semicolon, comma, and dash (known as the internal, or partial, stops). Because of differences in fashion, temperament, and function, it is impossible to lay down iron-clad rules about how stops should be used in expository composition. Careful attention to how good modern writers employ them, however, will reveal the general pattern of contemporary usage. This pattern is what you should strive for in your own punctuation, always with the intent of employing stops so that they increase the chance of readers understanding what you want them to understand.

Exercises

1. The following sentences all exhibit faulty punctuation. Keeping to the exact word order, add, delete, or change the stops in each sentence in order to clarify it. Be able to explain why you did what you did.

    1. Not all tragic heroes are flawed for example Ethan Frome has no flaw.
    2. He asked if you were going downtown?
    3. George, and his friend are going.
    4. Although the book is very long; it is quite interesting.
    5. Not only the volunteer firemen but also the ladies' auxiliary will help out at the fair.
    6. Joe DiMaggio who was a great centerfielder for the New York Yankees still helps them in spring training.
    7. The book, on the table next to the flowers, is mine.
    8. My father together with his brother has gone into business.
    9. The children with great and solemn deliberation inspected the new arrival.
    10. Quickly he mounted the steps.
    11. Because the labs are only on Tuesday and Thursday I was unable to take chemistry this semester.
    12. However we shall leave at once.
    13. The children famished rushed to the table.
    14. He sat in the sagging dirty broken-back chair.
    15. Edward my friend has bought a new car.
    16. And, I loved her.
    17. It was a large, green, house.
    18. Speaking of books have you read the newest novel by Jones?

19. The day having begun so well we were surprised when things turned out badly.
20. Nobody has in fact denied the report.
21. It was I believe I can remember the exact date 3 Sept. 1939.
22. We need tables chairs desks and lamps.
23. The game was not won because of poor quarterbacking.
24. He asked, were you ready.
25. He saw Harry and Sue George and Mary and Bob and Evelyn.
26. The trial if the truth could be told was a farce.
27. The average American who has in general little sense of the horror of war cannot appreciate the greater caution of the European.
28. She likes all kinds of Italian food lasagne spaghetti pizza and so on.
29. The town will in that event seek another site.
30. A well-styled car the Mustang has had great success.
31. But; we didn't see him.
32. The walls were painted a lovely, old, rose.
33. TNT or trinitrotoluene is highly explosive.
34. The idea that great states can conduct their affairs according to the ethical principles by which decent men conduct their private affairs is fallacious.
35. George but not his friends is going.
36. Are you going downtown.
37. The day began very well trouble however was soon apparent.
38. Only one thing can explain his inaction cowardice.
39. Both my brother and, his wife, have agreed to the plan.
40. Three consequences flowed directly from the war inflation political unrest and far-reaching social change.
41. They have argued although with very little success for the proposal.
42. It was a weary business to settle all the accounts and pay off all the debtors and he received no help from any member of the family.
43. I would like to go; although I wasn't invited.

2. Did you find any sentences in exercise 1 which remained cloudy even after you had improved the punctuation? If so, revise them with the minimal changes in word order and diction required for clarity.

3. On a sheet of paper copy down the passage by Gertrude Stein quoted on page 430. Add appropriate stops where you think they will clarify her sentences. Can you think of any legitimate reason (that is, a reason related to the purpose of effective communication) which might have led Miss Stein to omit these stops?

4. Comment upon the use of stops in the following sentences. What purpose does each stop serve? Could any be omitted altogether? Ought any to be changed?

1. She had left him. She had left him — sick — helpless — thirsty.

JOSEPH CONRAD

2. Meanwhile, and behind all this activity, brute terror, like the scurrying of rats in a deserted attic, filled the more remote chambers of his brain with riot; the hand of the constable would fall heavy on his shoulder, and his nerves would jerk like a hooked fish; or he beheld, in galloping defile, the dock, the prison, the gallows, and the black coffin. ROBERT LOUIS STEVENSON

3. Over this little territory, thus bounded and designated, the great dome of St. Paul's, swelling above the intervening houses of Paternoster Row, Amen Corner, and Ave Maria Lane, looks down with an air of motherly protection. WASHINGTON IRVING

4. The bird, however hard the frost may be, flies briskly to his customary roosting place, and, with beak tucked into his wing, falls asleep. He has no apprehensions; only the hot blood grows colder and colder, the pulse feebler as he sleeps, and at midnight, or in the early morning, he drops from his perch — dead. W. H. HUDSON

5. Phocian took it aright, who, being applauded by the multitude, asked, What had he done amiss? W. S. LANDOR

6. The carter has tied his horse to a tree; the soldiers stroll in barefoot in their shoes; the many fez shine vividly against the straight white wall. The muezzins are waiting on the minarets; they lean over their balconies; then voice after voice, in the wailing Eastern tone, cries the salutation, one voice striking through another. They move round their balconies, crying to north and south and east and west. The men go in slowly at all the doors, pushing aside the heavy curtain. ARTHUR SYMONS

7. Here it rushes and pushes, the atoms triturate and grind, and, eagerly thrusting by, pursue their separate ends. RICHARD JEFFRIES

8. The Burong Islands may be boldly approached from the westward; large sailing vessels had better pass outside them, but smaller craft and steam vessels may often, with advantage, pass between them, taking care to avoid the charted dangers.
China Sea Pilot, 1st edition

9. In going on there was safety — and on they went. LEW WALLACE

22
PUNCTUATION
II. The Other Marks

Marks

APOSTROPHE

If the "rules" governing the stops are complicated, those dealing with the other marks are, fortunately, relatively simple. These marks include the apostrophe, the quotation mark, hyphen, ellipsis, parenthesis and bracket, diacritics, and such related matters as underlining, capitalization, and superscripts. The primary function of the apostrophe is to indicate the omission of sound. In poetry, for instance, a vowel or consonant is sometimes dropped to justify the meter: *e'er* (for *ever*), *th'end* (for *the end*), and so on. It would be difficult, however, to conceive of a legitimate use of such words in expository prose. But exposition, especially if it is informal, may use contractions in which part of a negative particle or verbal auxiliary has been omitted: *hasn't, won't, I'll, they're, he's.*

Even more common is the use of the apostrophe to mark possession. (This function was originally also an indication of an omitted sound.) There is no need to repeat the limitations on the employment of the *-'s* genitive (see page 415), but we should note again how the *-'s* is applied. With singular nouns ending in *-'s* the modern fashion is to add both the apostrophe and the genitive *-s*, though an apostrophe alone is pemissible: "Charles's coat" (usual), "Charles' coat" (less common). With regular plurals only the apostrophe is added: "the girls' books," "the horses' oats," "the bakers' equipment." Irregular plurals, however, add *-'s:* "the children's shoes," "the alumnae's dues," "the geese's feathers." The apostrophe is also used to mark the plural of symbols: "Mind your p's and q's"; "He makes his A's in a peculiar way."

Of all marks of punctuation the apostrophe seems to be the one most consistently omitted by students. It may very well be that they are ahead of their teachers in this matter. The apostrophe is rarely an absolutely necessary signal. We get along without any equivalent quite well in speech and only rarely would a written sentence be made ambiguous by omitting the apostrophe from a contraction or a possessive. Perhaps in another century or two students will have had their way and the apostrophe will be gone. But in the meantime it is still very much with us, and a competent writer should use it and use it properly. An apostrophe may not be, in the strictest sense, necessary; but it is sometimes convenient.

THE QUOTATION MARK

Quotation marks (which the British call "inverted commas") have two forms, single (' ') and double (" "). Which form one prefers is a matter of taste. Some people like single quotes because they blend more easily with the type and do not clutter up the page. To other writers, this very unobtrusiveness is a disadvantage, increasing the chances that a reader will fail to distinguish a quotation. In exposition, at least, we ourselves prefer the double quotes for the reason that clarity is more important than aesthetic pleasure. In any case you should follow your teacher's advice about which to use.

Whichever form a writer chooses as the primary quotation mark, he must use it consistently throughout his work. But if he has occasion to enclose a quotation within a quotation, he should shift to the other form. Thus in the following sentence, the title is set within single quotes because it occurs within a quotation enclosed by double marks:

> A critic has observed that "of all Hemingway's stories, 'The Killers' is the best known."

Had the primary mark been single quotes, the title would have been set within double marks.

In either form, quote marks are used (1) to signal dialogue, (2) to enclose written quotations, and (3) to indicate that a word or phrase is to be taken in a special sense. With dialogue, quote marks are used only with direct quotations, that is, only with words that are literally those said by the speaker. These must be distinguished from indirect quotations, which are reports of the substance of what someone has said. Indirect quotations show some change in wording, a shifting in pronouns and verb tenses, if nothing else. Of the following two sentences, the first contains a direct quote, the second an indirect:

Sam said, "I'll go."
Sam said that he would go.

The punctuation of direct quotations varies according to the position of the quoted speech in relation to the verb of address. Most commonly it follows the verb and the rule is: place a comma after the verb, then the opening quote mark, and capitalize the first word of the quotation:

The man said, "Everyone must leave."

If the quotation precedes the verb of address, the rule is: opening quotation mark, comma after the last word of the quote (on occasion the comma may be replaced with a question mark or exclamation point, according to a rule to be mentioned in a moment), closing quote mark, and then the verb:

"Everyone must leave," said the man.

Finally, the verb and noun of address may be intruded into the middle of the quoted remark:

"Everyone," said the man, "must leave."

Here the punctuation is: opening quote mark, first part of quotation, comma, first closing quote, noun and verb of address, comma (or semicolon if required), second opening quote mark, small letter for the first word of the continued quotation (unless, of course, it is "I" or a proper noun), and final closing quote. If the continuation of the quoted passage begins a new sentence, the punctuation is this:

"Everyone must leave," said the man. "No one at all will be allowed to stay."

Handling written quotations — a more frequent task than dialogue in college writing — is a little different. First of all, the modern tendency is to employ quote marks only with relatively brief passages, longer ones usually being indented. When a written passage is set within quote marks, it is usually introduced by a colon:

Professor Jones writes: "*Hamlet* is Shakespeare's greatest play."

More and more, however, academic writing is moving toward informality, and today scholarly quotations are often worked more neatly into the text without the use of a colon, avoiding the effect of a sentence split in two. Thus many people would consider it better style to write:

Professor Jones writes that "*Hamlet* is Shakespeare's greatest play."

The quoted passage may even be handled without a *that*, especially if the verb of address is put in an intruding position. The following sentence by Professor G. H. Vallins is an example:

> Addison's prose, says Dr. Johnson, "is the model of the middle style. . . . His sentences have neither studied amplitude, nor affected brevity; his periods, though not diligently rounded, are voluble and easy. Whoever wishes to attain an English style, familiar but not coarse, and elegant but not ostentatious, must give his days and nights to the volumes of Addison."

If more than a single paragraph is set within quotes, the opening quote mark must be repeated at the beginning of each new paragraph, though a closing quote is placed only at the end of the last paragraph of the passage. Generally, however, such extended passages would be handled by indentation. When a quoted passage is indented, quote marks are not necessary (though any that occur in the passage itself must be retained). The fact that the material is indented (and usually more closely spaced and often set in smaller type) constitutes an adequate visual signal of quotation.

In addition to enclosing quoted matter, quotation marks are also used to indicate that a word has a special or limited significance. Irony, for instance, is frequently signaled in writing by quotes. If one says of someone "He's a generous person," irony can be indicated in speech by the peculiar stress and intonation given the key word "generous." Graphically the irony can be conveyed like this:

> He's a "generous" person.

Often, too, it is necessary to use a word even though it has not been clearly or completely defined. In this book, for instance, we must talk about the meaning of words without dealing adequately with all the logical and metaphysical problems inherent in the idea of meaning. To indicate the rough nature of our usage we might write:

> In this sense, then, the "meaning" of a word involves both what it designates and what effect the writer intends it to have upon the man who reads it.

Still a third case of special signification is when a word is used as a word, that is, to designate itself rather than its usual referent: "The word 'table' is a noun." More commonly words used as words are set in italic type (or, in manuscript, underlined); but in some books you will find them enclosed in quotes. Another special use of quote marks is to indicate the conventional meaning of a word or phrase:

> The word *pride* often means "conceit, an unwarranted opinion of one's worth."

Some writers also employ quotation marks to enclose a word that seems a little inappropriate to its context. Usually this means apologizing for a word that they fear is too colloquial. Newspapers which, like *The New York Times*, are stylistically conservative do this. Our opinion is that quote marks ought not to be used for this purpose, that, indeed, the purpose itself is wrong. No word can be justified by an apology. If it says exactly what the writer wants, no apology is necessary. If it really is too informal for the context, no apology will help.

The final function of quote marks is to indicate titles. The old rule is that titles of brief works (short stories, most poems, radio and TV shows, movies — but not full-length plays) are set in quotes, while those of longer works (novels, epic poems, drama — three- and five-act plays, at least) are italicized (which in composition means underlined). The practice of contemporary writers, however, shows considerable variation. Some italicize almost all titles; others more or less keep to the old rule, though they may have different opinions about whether a specific work is long or short. If the work, long or short, has been published separately, its title will often be set in italic.

One last point to consider about the quotation mark is its relation with the stops. With opening quotes, the rule is simple: any stop set beside an opening quote is always before and outside it. One never writes "John said ',I'm going,' " but always "John said, 'I'm going.' " Closing quotes, however, have a more complicated relationship with stops. In American usage (British practice is quite different) commas and periods are always set inside the closing quote mark, regardless of whether or not they literally belong to the quotation:

> "I'm going," he said. *Not:* "I'm going", he said.
> He said, "I'm going." *Not:* He said, "I'm going".

Colons and semicolons, on the other hand, are set outside in American usage:

> He said, "I'm going"; but we didn't believe him. *Not:* He said, "I'm going;" but we didn't believe him.
>
> His exact words were, "I'll be there": he didn't make it. *Not:* His exact words were, "I'll be there:" he didn't make it.

The relationship between question marks and exclamation points and the closing quote depends upon whether the query or the exclamation applies only to the quotation, only to the containing sentence, or to both. We shall illustrate the possibilities only for the question mark, but the principles are the same for the exclamation point:

1. If the question applies only to the quotation, while the containing sentence is a statement of fact, the mark is set inside:

> He asked, "Are you ready?"

2. If the quotation is a statement of fact while the containing sentence is a question, the mark is set outside:

> Did he say, "Sam is here"?

3. If both the quotation and the containing sentence are questions, the mark is again placed inside. To be strictly logical, one should use two marks, the first inside the quote, the second outside. But such repetition would seem pedantic. One mark is enough:

> Did he ask, "Is Sam here?"

THE HYPHEN

The hyphen is a relatively simple mark to use. It indicates syllabic division of a word between two lines and also separates the elements of some compound words. In its first function the hyphen ought always to be placed at the end of the upper line, never at the beginning of the lower one. Thus a word like *supper* must be divided:

> sup- *not:* sup
> per -per.

Words can be divided only between syllables, and since many people — even well-read people — have only a hazy idea of the syllabication of many words, it is best to consult a dictionary when a word must be split between two lines.

In certain compounds the hyphen separates the individual words. English does not treat compounds with much consistency. Many are printed as separate words (*contact lens, drawing room, milk shake*); others as one word (*gunboat, footlights, midships*); still others are hyphenated (*gun-shy, photo-offset, teen-ager*). Some compounds are treated differently by various writers; *teen-ager,* for example, sometimes appears as *teenager.* Generally there is no way to tell how any particular compound is conventionally written except by looking in a reliable and recent dictionary or observing how publishers print it.

The examples in the preceding paragraph are all conventional compound words. Another kind of compound exists called the "nonce compound." This is a construction, usually a modifier, made up for a specific occasion but which does not have status in the language as a legitimate compound word. For instance, someone might write: "He had that don't-care-a-hang feeling." The elements of nonce compounds are always hyphenated.

Hyphens, finally, have several special applications. When a word is spelled out in composition, the pauses which in speech would separate the letters are often signaled by hyphens: "*Affect* is spelled a-f-f-e-c-t." When it is necessary to cite inflectional endings or affixes, they are preceded (or in the case of prefixes, followed) by hyphens: "*-s* is the regular sign of the plural in English"; "*Anti-* and *un-* are common prefixes, while *-ence* is a frequent suffix." When several different terms are understood to be commonly combined with the final element of a compound word, hyphens are placed after each of the initial elements: "He bought both eight- and ten-foot boards."

THE PARENTHESIS AND THE BRACKET

Parentheses are used primarily to enclose parenthetical matter, which is a construction (it may or may not be syntactically related to the containing sentence) sufficiently remote in relevancy to require a stronger pause than commas would give. The following sentence by G. K. Chesterton is a good example:

> Even for those who can do their work in bed (like journalists), still more for those whose work cannot be done in bed (as, for example, the professional harpooners of whales), it is obvious that the indulgence must be very occasional.

Parenthetical remarks of this sort — which may also be punctuated with dashes — can be a source of interest and variety as well as of necessary information. One smiles here at the extravagance of offering a harpooner as an example of someone whose work cannot be done in bed. Moreover, Chesterton's parenthetical intrusions loosen the rhythm of the sentence, suggesting the pattern of cultivated speech. The effectiveness of parenthetical remarks, however, depends directly upon their rarity. Parenthetical asides can easily become a bad habit. The full stop at the end of a parenthetical statement, by the way, is set inside the parentheses if that statement is a self-contained sentence; otherwise it is set outside:

> The army disappeared. (Its fate was never determined.)

But:

> He did not like her (perhaps because she had once made fun of him).

Parentheses are also employed in composition for the mechanical function of enclosing the numbers introducing items in a series:

> We must do three things: (1) study the route thoroughly, (2) purchase all supplies and equipment, and (3) hire a reliable guide.

Occasionally numbers like these are punctuated with only a following parenthesis, and sometimes with no parenthesis at all. The latter custom runs a risk of confusing the reader.

Brackets (which look like this: [ ]) are used in exposition primarily to enclose within a quotation any matter that is not part of the quotation. Sometimes, for example, a writer must slightly edit the grammar of a written quotation to fit it into the containing sentence of his own text; anything added for that purpose is set within brackets. In the following case we may imagine that the verb "is" had to be supplied:

> Professor Jones writes that "*Hamlet* . . . [is] Shakespeare's greatest play."

Such changes, we need hardly add, are dishonest if they alter the substantial meaning of the original passage. Now and then a writer may need to add a phrase of explanation to a quotation, and that too is placed in brackets. Taken from its context, for instance, the sentence by Chesterton quoted above is a little cryptic, and we might have made the last part clearer like this: ". . . it is obvious that the indulgence [of lying in bed] must be very occasional." Brackets are also used to enclose parenthetical matter set within a longer parenthetical comment (though such a labyrinthine style would be [with rare exception] both unusual and annoying).

THE ELLIPSIS

The ellipsis is a series of periods (less commonly asterisks or dashes may be used) which indicates (1) the omission of material within a quotation, or (2) in dialogue a falling tone expressive of doubt, uncertainty, weariness, and so on, as in:

> She sighed and answered, "I really don't know . . ."

In expository writing the first function is the more frequent. If the omitted matter is in the middle of the quoted sentence, three periods are necessary:

> Dante, someone has noted, is "the last . . . great Catholic poet."

If the omission occurs at the end of the sentence, four points are often used, the extra one being the end stop:

> Dante, someone has noted, "is the last great Catholic poet. . . ."

But even here some publishers prefer to use only three periods. If the quoted sentence is closed by a question mark or exclamation point, the proper punctuation is three points plus that closing stop:

> It has been asked, "Was Dante the last great Catholic poet . . . ?"

DIACRITICS

A diacritic is a mark placed above, below, or through a letter in order to indicate a special pronunciation. Diacritics are employed because the number of graphic symbols (that is, letters) in any language is usually fewer than the number of significantly different sounds. Diacritical marks thus supplement the alphabet, enabling one basic letter to do the work of two or three. English, while it certainly has more sounds than letters, has dispensed with all diacritic marks except an occasional diaeresis, as in *naïve* or *coöperate* (indicating that the marked vowel must be pronounced in a separate syllable). But diacritical marks are relatively common in many other languages (the accents grave and acute of French, for example; the umlaut of German; or the tilde of Spanish). When one uses a foreign word not yet assimilated into English, he should reproduce all the diacritics the word would normally have.

UNDERLINING AND CAPITALIZATION

Underlining is the compositional equivalent of italic type. There are several reasons for underlining a word or phrase. One is to indicate the name of a ship or the title of a newspaper, periodical, or relatively long literary work. With newspapers the title is what appears on the masthead, including the name of the city if that appears there, but not otherwise. Thus one writes *The New York Times,* but *The Times* of London or the London *Times.* As we noted earlier, there is no rule to decide when a literary work is short enough so that its title should be enclosed in quotation marks and when long enough that its title warrants underlining. Notice, however, that the length in question is that of the work itself, not of its title. Customarily, titles of short stories and brief poems are set in quotes, those of long poems and of novels in italic type; one-act plays are referred to in quotes, full length drama in italics; radio and TV titles are more often placed in quotation marks. But variations are common. Many newspapers, for instance, avoid italics because of the trouble and expense of changing type and put all titles within quotation marks.

In addition to titles, foreignisms are usually set in italics. Since English has always been quick to borrow words from other languages and equally quick to assimilate them, it is sometimes difficult to decide whether a foreign word is really foreign and requires to be underlined. Few people think of words like *delicatessen* or *perfume* or *chef* as being German or French. Any foreign expression, on the other hand, that has not been given currency in English idiom should be italicized (though one ought not to sprinkle his prose with foreignisms merely to demonstrate that he has passed freshman French). In between the fully assimilated word of foreign origin like *cavalier,* say, and the plainly foreign phrase like *de trop,* there exist in English many words recently arrived on our shores and still having an exotic air, yet very commonly used, at least by some groups, words like *schuss* (a skier's term) or *boutique* (a word becoming increasingly familiar to New York shoppers). Editors differ in how to treat these terms. If the word is not listed in a standard desk dictionary, the best bet is to underline it. If it is listed, one should follow the dictionary or a respected style sheet.

Words used as words are also underlined. When, for example, one writes "*Table* is a noun," he is using *table* to refer, not to a piece of furniture, but to itself as a word. Rather than underlining, however, some writers will enclose words used as words ("citation terms") in quotation marks.

Finally, underlining may be utilized for emphasis. Some writers are quite clever at stressing certain words in order to create the illusion of a voice talking. The following sentence by the philosopher J. L. Austin is an example:

> I should like to say, in concluding this section, that in the course of stressing that we must pay attention to the facts of *actual* language, what we can and cannot say, and *precisely* why, another and converse point takes shape.

While this sort of thing is difficult to do well (and very easy to do badly or too often), underlining, carefully and infrequently employed, is a legitimate way of achieving emphasis.

Capitalization in English is another subject about which generalizations are dangerous. We can, however, say the following. The singular of the first person pronoun is capitalized, as is the initial word of a sentence. In dialogue the first word of the opening quotation (though not necessarily of a continued quotation) is capitalized; but in quotations of written matter the first word is not capitalized unless it is in the source. In titles the first word and all subsequent important words require capitalization. All nouns, pronouns, verbs, and modifiers in titles are considered important. Most articles, conjunctions, and prepositions (excepting their occurrence in the first position) are not capitalized, though sometimes the longer prepositions (*together* or *beneath,* for example) begin with a capital letter, especially when in an emphatic position.

Proper nouns are generally capitalized. These include geographical and proper names, the names of political parties and official government agencies, months of the year and days of the week, registered trade-marks, personifications of abstract ideas such as "Peace," and so on.

But proper nouns and adjectives employed frequently often lose their special character and become common nouns no longer requiring capitalization. Thus one speaks of "a macintosh" (the apple or the coat), not "a Macintosh." Sometimes the same term is treated as a proper word in one expression and as a common term in another, as: "French horn" but "french fries." Verbs derived from proper nouns are usually not capitalized; one would write: "The original pronunciation of many French words has been anglicized," not ". . . Anglicized." In short, there are many variations in the capitalization of proper words; any reputable dictionary indicates the conventional treatment of specific cases.

SUPERSCRIPTS

Superscripts are marks printed slightly above the line of the text. Although their usage in technical writing is varied and complicated, in expository prose they are most frequently used to indicate footnotes. Asterisks, daggers, and other printer's marks are occasionally employed as superscripts; but more usual is the use of an arabic numeral, usually set in slightly smaller type than that of the text. If the superscript comes after a quotation, it is placed outside, slightly above, and immediately after the closing quote mark. A superscript not associated with a quotation is set after the word, phrase, or sentence that occasioned the note. When numerals are used to signal footnotes, the simplest plan is to number the notes consecutively throughout the paper, or, in longer manuscripts, throughout the chapter. The note itself may be placed on the bottom of the page (the most convenient place for the reader), or in a separate section at the end of the paper.

Footnotes serve two purposes — explanation and citation. In the first case the writer delegates to a footnote a tangential explanation, qualification, or further evidence in support of (or some disagreement about) the point in the text. While they have their value, explanatory footnotes often prove to be the last line of pedantry. Generally speaking, something important enough to tell the reader ought to be worked into the text; and conversely, anything not significant enough for the text can probably be dispensed with.

Citation footnotes identify the source of something stated in the text — an actual quotation, a paraphrase, a fact or assertion originally made by someone else. A citation is always in order if a writer has used any specific information or ideas originating in another source, and it makes no difference whether he has literally quoted from that source or not. Between them, the text and the note should include the following information: full name of the writer, full title of the book or article (and in the case of an article the title and volume number of the journal or magazine in which it appeared), place and date of publication, and pertinent page numbers. Any of this information already available in the text of the paper or in earlier footnotes does not have to be repeated in the note itself.

The typographical form of footnotes and all the various abbreviations they involve and the numerous problems connected with them constitute a subject in themselves. We shall not attempt to treat this complex matter. Several fine handbooks are available for writers of term papers and dissertations, and in these the art of writing footnotes and bibliographies is explained with great thoroughness. Anyone confronted with the task of composing a scholarly paper should realize that footnote and bibliographical procedures vary a good deal from one academic discipline to another, and he should consult an appropriate manual.

Summary

The second class of punctuation marks does not generally correspond to breath pauses. It includes the apostrophe, quotation marks, hyphen, parenthesis and bracket, ellipsis, diacritics, underlining and capitalization, and the superscript. While they play a less important part in determining the structure and movement of the sentence, these marks remain important adjuncts to communication. Their usage is more settled, less subject to the whim of the writer. One must simply learn the conventions governing the hyphen, apostrophe, parenthesis, and so on, and having learned those conventions, observe them in his own writing.

Exercises

1. The following sentences reveal misuse of the marks of punctuation we have studied in this chapter. Correct them and be ready to justify your corrections.

1. The mens gear was left on the beach, but the womens had been carefully put away.
2. The girls hats and coats hadnt been picked up.
3. Dont forget to dot your i s.
4. He said I dont care what you think Ill do it my way.
5. I dont care what you think he said Ill do it my way.
6. I dont care what you think Ill do it my way he said.
7. The famous critic R. L. Smith has said Donne is my favorite poet.
8. Book is a germanic word.
9. A farewell to arms is a very good novel and the killers an equally good short story.
10. Ill see you on monday John said though I wont get there until late afternoon.
11. He said look at me no one did.
12. We asked are you prepared to obey us?
13. I like catching pan fish.
14. Not all teen agers drive recklessly, though thats the general impression.
15. I have that end of the world feeling.
16. Hes learned three things 1 not to believe whatever he reads 2 to think about the consequences of his actions and 3 not to boast so much.
17. Were in the market for a twenty or thirty-foot boat.
18. I see where the russians wouldnt you know it claim to have invented baseball.
19. Prof. McIntyre writes that "the greatness of Rome has not been . . . . as widely appreciated as it should be'.
20. The suffix en is an old plural ending and is still seen in words like children and oxen.
21. Hes meeting with governor Rockefeller in Albany next week.
22. It has been claimed that the play Hamlet is an "artistic failure [1]".

2. The following passage is the first paragraph of Chapter 2 of Charles Dickens's *American Notes,* with all of its punctuation and capitals removed. Without looking at a copy of Dickens's book, divide this passage into sentences and

punctuate them. When you have finished, compare your version with what Dickens actually wrote.

> we all dined together that day and a rather formidable party we were no fewer than eighty six strong the vessel being pretty deep in the water with all her coals on board and so many passengers and the weather being calm and quiet there was but little motion so that before the dinner was half over even those passengers who were most distrustful of themselves plucked up amazingly and those who in the morning had returned to the universal question are you a good sailor a very decided negative now either parried the inquiry with the evasive reply oh i suppose im no worse than anybody else or reckless of all moral obligations answered boldly yes and with some irritation too as though they would add i should like to know what you see in me sir particularly to justify suspicion

3. Write a brief expository or descriptive paragraph on a topic of your own choice. When you have checked it carefully, placing in all the marks of punctuation you think it requires, copy it on a separate sheet of paper, omitting *all* capitals, stops, and other marks. The result should be one long string of words like the paragraph from Dickens in the preceding exercise. Give it to a classmate and ask him to punctuate it as he thinks it should be. You do the same with a similar paragraph that he will give to you.

V
DICTION

Introduction

A good prose style, says Jonathan Swift, is a matter of "proper words in proper places." So far we have considered the "proper places"; we have talked about the effective shaping of words into paragraphs, into whole essays, and we have discussed the effective arrangement of words within sentences. We turn now to the study of "proper words." Word choice, or diction, is interesting, complex, and exceedingly important. It is interesting because the study of words brings us inevitably to the study of thought and human behavior. Much of what we know we know indirectly through words rather than directly through immediate experience. The study of diction is complex because words are not simply counters that stand for things, and because our understanding of how words operate must depend upon knowledge from disciplines like linguistics, semantics, philosophy, and psychology. Furthermore, diction, even more directly than grammar and syntax, affects clarity. Errors in grammar and usage may irritate the reader and so distract him, but they are less likely seriously to mislead him than errors in diction. Poor syntax may weaken the effectiveness with which an idea is presented, but poor diction may mean it is not presented at all. The study of words, then, is of the utmost significance to the student of composition. We shall treat diction in four chapters beginning with definitions of important characteristics of words. A second chapter will consider figurative language, and a third chapter will describe the qualities of good diction. Finally, a fourth chapter will discuss dictionaries and how to use them.

23

DEFINITIONS OF VERBAL PROPERTIES

Definitions

CONTEXTS

Most words have more than one meaning. Which of several definite meanings a word may convey becomes clear only when it is used with other words in a sentence. The other words surrounding a specific word in a meaningful sentence, its linguistic environment, so to speak, form what is called its verbal context. The following sentence will illustrate this point:

> If civilisation has been the curse of *man*, it might seem that the logical course for Rousseau to recommend was its destruction.
>
> J. B. BURY

The words before and after *man* in this sentence lead us to understand that the writer is referring to mankind as an entity, not to an individual male of the human species. In fact, "man" as the word is used here means all women as well as all men. That the meaning "mankind" is intended becomes clearer and more certain if we examine the paragraph set in the context of other paragraphs of the chapter, and so on. The idea of context is relative and, as we shall see, can be meaningfully expanded to embrace the writer's complete work, the writer himself, his intentions, his audience, and even all Western culture and experience. For the moment, however, let us look at *man* in still different contexts:

1. If a *man* will begin with certainties, he will end in doubts; but if he will be content to begin with doubts, he will end in certainties.
   FRANCIS BACON

2. If we can imagine an unrepressed *man* — a man strong enough to live and therefore strong enough to die, and therefore what no man has ever been, an individual — such a man, having overcome guilt and anxiety, could have no money complex. NORMAN O. BROWN

3. MACBETH: Prithee peace.
I dare do all that may become a *man*.
Who dares do more is none.

LADY MAC.: What beast was't then
That made you break this enterprise to me?
When you durst do it, then you were a *man*.

SHAKESPEARE

4. Frankie went down to the barroom
To get a bottle of beer,
She went and asked the bartender,
"Has my lovin' *man* been here?
He was my *man*, but he done me wrong."

"FRANKIE AND JOHNNIE"

5. MAN: to put the proper number of men on a detail so that the work can be done. "GLOSSARY OF NAVY TERMS AND PHRASES"

In the first example Francis Bacon is using *man* to designate not all mankind, but merely a person, whether man or woman; *man* is roughly synonymous to *anyone*. *Man*, therefore, may refer to a plural idea (all men) or to a singular idea (one man); it may refer to someone masculine or to women as well as men. In the second sentence the italicized *man* refers not to anyone at all, but to a particular kind of man, a man furthermore ideally conceived and nonexistent. The third example conveys still different ideas. Defending his decision to spare Duncan's life, Macbeth uses *man* to signify human beings in relation to God, to refer to human beings as inferior to God and subject to divine law. Lady Macbeth, on the other hand, in heaping scorn upon what she considers her husband's cowardice, uses *man* as synonymous with courage, strength, and resolution. In the fifth example *man* signifies husband or lover, and in the last *man* is a verb equivalent to *work* or *operate*. These contexts, as different as they are, by no means exhaust the possible meanings of *man*. *Man* may refer to a valet or servant, to an employee or agent, and to many other things that will occur to the reader. But if we have not illustrated all the common meanings of *man*, we have seen enough to make an exceedingly important generalization about words: a given word may have, potentially, many definite meanings. It is true that often these multiple meanings have, so to speak, a common denominator: all the various meanings we have illustrated rest upon the identification of *man* with the adult male of the human species. Nevertheless we cannot know precisely what a word means until we can see it in its context.

Now the context of a word, narrowly defined, consists of the other words in the sentence in which it appears. But the more widely we interpret the notion of context the more exactly we can understand what a writer intends. In the following sentence, for example, the meaning of "Wit" becomes clear only if we know its temporal context, the time or date when it was used. The whole utterance becomes completely understandable only if we know something about its social and historical context:

> I hope no Reader imagines me so weak to stand up in the Defence of real Christianity, such as used in primitive Times (if we may believe the Authors of those Ages) to have an Influence upon Men's Belief and actions: To offer at the restoring of that, would indeed be a wild Project, it would be to dig up Foundations; to destroy at one Blow all the Wit, and half the Learning of the Kingdom; to break the entire Frame and Constitution of Things; to ruin Trade, extinguish Arts and Sciences, with the Professors of them; in short, to turn our Courts, Exchanges, and Shops into Desarts; and would be full as absurd as the Proposal of Horace, where he advises the Romans, all in a Body, to leave their City and seek a new Seat in some remote Part of the World, by way of a Cure for the Corruption of their Manners.

The naïve reader might suppose that "Wit" in this sentence refers to the ability to make cleverly humorous remarks and that the whole passage is an attack upon Christianity. Yet setting the word and the sentence in a wider context will reveal the high probability of a different interpretation. To determine what that context is, we may well ask about this, as about any sentence or passage:

> Who said it?
> When did he say it?
> Upon what occasion did he say it?
> To whom did he say it?
> Why did he say it?
> How did he say it?

The extract quoted above was written by Jonathan Swift in 1708 as part of an essay called "An Argument Against Abolishing Christianity." On the surface Swift appears to consider judiciously the reasons why it might be a great advantage to abolish Christianity, although he concludes that, as doubtful as the whole matter is, it might be well to retain Christianity (of the polite and harmless sort, of course, not the real thing) at least for the time being. In the conclusion of the essay Swift gives this final reason for his stand:

> . . . I do very much apprehend, that in six Months Time after the Act is past for the Extirpation of the Gospel, the Bank and East India Stock, may fall at least One per Cent. And since that is fifty Times more than ever the Wisdom of our Age thought fit to venture for the Preservation of Christianity, there is no Reason we should be at so great a Loss, merely for the sake of destroying it.

Swift, as we know from historical evidence, was a devout and loyal Christian, a clergyman, in fact. From evidence outside this essay we can establish that Swift was not likely to entertain seriously any reason for abolishing Christianity. But, indeed, we need do no more than read the piece attentively to see that Swift's literal statement is so extreme, his premises (that no one takes Christianity seriously) are so at variance with the avowed belief of his day that we conclude that, if he is not mad, he means the opposite of what he says. In fact, his purpose in this piece of sustained irony is to attack those who use Christianity for social and political ends without caring a staw for its principles. Swift's audience in 1708 was composed of educated and sophisticated men who were more likely to be moved by his amusing but powerful irony than by a straightforward sermon. Thus Swift uses irony to defend "real Christianity" in spite of the fact that to practice it would destroy "all the Wit and half the Learning of the Kingdom."

We have seen now what in general the whole passage means. But what does Swift mean by "Wit"? The word means more than clever word play as we can see from its being yoked with the idea Learning. No doubt the notion of cleverness is lurking within the word, but the context of time (1708) reveals that "Wit" here means "reasoning power, intellect, intelligence, intellectual notions." Thus Swift is saying, ironically of course, that restoring true Christianity would destroy contemporary learning and intellectualism.

We see then that the meanings of words vary, often, not only from sentence to sentence but also from age to age. As we shall point out in more detail later on, words change in time: they come into existence, they suffer transformations, they may decay and die. The meaning of a word, therefore, is always relative, never absolute: its precise meaning depends upon a broad context of many considerations. In this sense no word means exactly the same thing twice. Once we have understood this important fact we shall cease to be misled by the superstition that for each word there is a single "correct" meaning or "real" meaning which we can find by looking in the dictionary. To be sure, we can scarcely overstress the importance of a dictionary as the record of the way in which a word has been used, or is being used. A dictionary, furthermore, supplies us with indispensable linguistic information about words, but the dictionary definition almost never tells us *all* we need to know about a given word. Words are best studied in their relationship to the writer, his readers, and the purpose and occasion of his writing.

Just as important to the writer as a knowledge of contexts and multiple meanings of words is an understanding of the complex relationship between words and meanings. Again we are likely to encounter dangerous superstitions concerning how words mean. First of all, we are liable to believe that a word is merely a sign or a symbol that stands for a thing. Everything, we might suppose, has one and only one "correct word" to name it; every word, we mistakenly assume, must refer to some tangible thing. Unfortunately, as even a moment's reflection will show, this simple account of meaning is far from being the whole story: one word, for example, may have several potential meanings; the same word may mean different things to different people; words denote much more than tangible things; words may change their meanings gradually over the years or at times quite suddenly. In order to explore further the complexities of words and their meanings we should observe that words mean in different ways and can be conveniently grouped into different classifications.

CONCRETE AND ABSTRACT WORDS

It is frequently useful to classify all words under the headings "abstract" and "concrete." Oversimplifying somewhat, we may define concrete words as those whose referents may be perceived by one or more of the five senses. Concrete words denote whatever has physical existence or whatever can be brought within the range of sensory experience; usually we can measure the referents of concrete words, we can make some kind of record of them — by photography or by sound-recording apparatus — and, thus, we can come to agreement about them. To define or to identify the referent of a concrete word we may often stand in its presence and quite literally point to it. Clearly, then, many proper nouns (though not all) are concrete, as are the most frequently occurring words in workaday speech — *New York City, dormitory, tree, garden, horse, lake, valley, blue, stumble, kneel.* These words can usually be said to evoke a sensory image.

In contrast, abstract words do not have individual, perceivable referents; they import, instead, a single quality, characteristic, or attribute shared by a number of concrete entities. Words like *excellence, liberality, truth, exis-*

tentialism, infinitude, goodness, beauty, nature, love suggest no clear picture or sensory impression of the sort evoked by *The Eiffel Tower* or *sailboat.* It is, of course, possible to picture to oneself a beautiful woman or a beautiful home or a beautiful boat, but if *beauty* itself has a referent, it belongs to a different order of reality from the referent of *woman.*

Closely related to the terms *abstract* and *concrete* (and equally useful) are the classifications *general* and *particular.* A classification of all words into general and particular, of course, is a relative matter and requires a point of reference. It may help to think of all words as falling somewhere along a continuum whose ends are labeled *general* and *particular.* The more nearly a word denotes a restricted class of entities the more particular it is; the larger the class of things that can be denoted by a word the more general it is, as the following scheme will perhaps make clear:

PARTICULAR GENERAL
The *Mona Lisa* – painting – work of art – creation – object – being

The *Mona Lisa* is the most particular of these terms, for it denotes a class of one member, something unique. If we make the *Mona Lisa* our point of reference, then *painting* is general. But in comparison with *work of art,* a term that includes sculpture, music, literature, and all other major and minor art forms, *painting* is particular. These terms, then, are relative and whether we label a word *general* or *particular* depends upon its relationship to other words. The more particular a word is the more likely it is to be also concrete. As a general rule, writing is clear, lively, and interesting in proportion to the number of concrete and particular words it contains. While a discussion involving ideas and relationships will often demand abstractions and general terms, these ought to be anchored in concrete illustrations and simple concrete diction whenever possible. Classifications like abstract and concrete, general and particular remind us once more that words have many different properties.

DENOTATION AND CONNOTATION

To explore these differences further we must mention the distinction between the denotations and the connotations of words. In rhetoric the denotation of a word is the thing or entity to which a word refers considered apart from any feelings or attitudes or associations that thing might arouse. Some words have only a denotative dimension, that is, they awaken no associations and supply no clues as to how their referents are to be evaluated or experienced emotionally; they merely name, point to, or identify the subject of a discourse. Such words constitute the language of science, of all impersonal informing and reporting. Listen, for example, to I. E. S. Edwards as he describes the passage leading from the Grand Gallery to the King's Chamber in the Great Pyramid:

> A high step at the upper end of the Grand Gallery gives access to a low and narrow passage leading to the King's Chamber. About a third of the distance along its length, the passage is heightened and enlarged into a kind of antechamber, the south, east, and west walls of which are composed of red granite. Four wide slots have been cut in both the east and west walls of the antechamber, three extending to the floor and one — the northernmost —stopping at the same level as the roof of the passage. The long slots were intended for three portcullises, no traces of which have survived. Stretching across the antechamber and fitting into the short slot, there still remain two blocks of granite, one resting on the other; a third block may originally have filled the space between the upper block and the ceiling. *The Pyramids of Egypt*

This diction is concrete, straightforward, and impersonal. The writer, quite properly, remains in the background. Whether or not he finds the Great Pyramid dull or fascinating, good architecture or bad is irrelevant to his purpose, which is to present the verifiable facts about his subject. These facts, however, need not always concern themselves with concrete objects; it is possible to use a combination of abstract and denotative language as in the following extract:

> But there are two ways of finding a truth by means of thought. In one of these, what we think of an object is simply that which is implicit in the concept of the object. In other words, the predicate by which we define the object in our mind cannot be omitted without thereby nullifying the concept of the object. For example, the knowledge that two is an even number or that one must not violate one's duty is of this kind. For the number two is defined as the double of one, and an even number is one that is double any whole number; therefore, it is a contradiction to think of two as not even. Nor can one, without annulling the concept of duty itself, think that it is permissible to violate one's duty.
> LEONARD NELSON, *Socratic Method and Critical Philosophy*

Again, as in the example about the Great Pyramid, the writer remains unemotional and aloof, using his words only as a means of pointing to his ideas; he is concerned only with the denotative aspect of language.

But many words do more than merely designate; they bring with them an atmosphere composed of attitudes, associations, and feelings. These emotive suggestions aroused by a word are called its connotations. The word *nightingale*, for example, denotes a European bird of the thrush family, but it connotes a great many things — night, mystery, sadness, beauty, romance. To some the word will evoke the legend of Philomela, the unfortunate girl who, changed into a nightingale, forever sings her sad story. Some will think of Keats's "Ode to a Nightingale," and of other appearances of the bird in English poetry. Some — not all, for, of course, different individuals will respond differently to the connotations of a word. Most Americans, for example, have never seen or heard a nightingale, and many may be unfamiliar with the myth and poetry of the Western tradition. Moreover, a particular context will limit the number and kind of associations evoked by a word. But the chances are good that most of us have in the past come across *nightingale* in contexts associated with poetry, song, melancholy, and beauty.

The connotations of *nightingale*, we say, are rather literary, pleasant, and favorable. Words may evoke, however, any kind of emotional and evaluative response ranging from the very favorable to the very unfavorable, from respect and love to disgust and horror. Consider, for instance, the word *Fascism*. It denotes a political philosophy which is rather difficult to define with precision. But its connotations — for most of us, at least — are definite enough: we think of Mussolini, Hitler, dictatorship, racism, the concentration camps, and World War II.

In contrast to words like *nightingale* and *Fascism*, which both denote and connote, some words (adjectives are frequently of this sort) scarcely denote at all. Such words are almost purely emotive and tell us little beyond the fact of the writer's approval or disapproval. Examples are *good, beautiful, wonderful, nice, cute, splendid, magnificent, horrible*. Used by themselves, words like these do not tell the reader enough. We don't much care whether a writer likes or dislikes something unless we are given the reasons why. It is not sufficient to write "It is a bad novel; the characters are poor" unless the writer immediately begins to explain in detail what makes the characters poor and the novel a failure. Purely emotive words often appear in advertisements where they weave a kind of spell. Products are called *elegant, fabulous, exquisite, exciting, exclusive, modern, distinctive, new, luxurious, ultra-smart, brilliant, exuberant, reliable, full-bodied, superb*, and *choicest*. In the context of an advertisement these are words with connotations but with little, if any, denotation. For this reason, most of them can be, and are, applied indifferently to automobiles, tooth paste, and soap flakes.

At one extreme, then, words have reference mostly to the emotional response of their users, and although most words denote as well as connote, words are often used primarily for their emotive effects. Like any instrument, highly connotative words may be used for legitimate or for questionable ends. Quite properly, words with strong connotations appear in description, narration, and exposition in which the writer is clearly concerned with his own feelings or with the feelings of characters he has created. In its concern with feeling, prose can approach poetry in its choice of words. In the following passage H. M. Tomlinson describes a November morning in a London suburb:

> That day was but a thin solution of night. You know those November mornings with a low, corpse-white east where the sunrise should be, as though the day were still-born. Looking to the dayspring, there is what we have waited for, there the end of our hope, prone and shrouded. This morning of mine was such a morning. The world was very quiet, as though it were exhausted after tears. Beneath a broken gutterspout the rain (all night I had listened to its monody) had discovered a nest of pebbles in the path of my garden in a London suburb. *The Sea and the Jungle*

This feeling of utterly depressing deadness is created by the connotations of words and phrases like "a thin solution of night," "corpse-white," "still-born," "prone and shrouded," "exhausted after tears," "broken," and "monody." Except perhaps for "a thin solution of night" and "corpse-white" these words contribute nothing to the physical description of the scene, but they do establish clearly the writer's feeling and tone.

A different use of emotive language appears in the following extract from H. L. Mencken's essay "Journalism in America":

> Thus there is something to be said for the new newspaper Babbitts, as reluctant as every self-respecting journalist must be to say it. And in what is commonly said against them there is not infrequently a certain palpable exaggeration and injustice. Are they responsible for the imbecile editorial policies of their papers, for the grotesque lathering of such mountebanks as Coolidge and Mellon, for the general smugness and lack of intellectual enterprise that pervades American journalism? Perhaps they are. But do they issue orders that their papers shall be printed in blowsy, clumsy English? That they shall stand against every decent thing, and in favor of everything that is meretricious and ignoble? That they shall wallow in trivialities, and manhandle important news? That their view of learning shall be that of a bartender? Has any newspaper proprietor ever issued orders that the funeral orgies of a Harding should be

> described in the language of a Tennessee revival? Or that helpless men, with the mob against them, should be pursued without fairness, decency or sense? I doubt it. I doubt, even, that the Babbitts turned Greeleys are responsible, in the last analysis, for the political rubbish that fills their papers — the preposterous anointing of Coolidge, the craven yielding to such sinister forces as the Ku Klux Klan and the Anti-Saloon League, the incessant, humorless, degrading hymning of all sorts of rogues and charlatans.
>
> *Prejudices, Sixth Series*

It is revealing to contrast this extract with I. E. S. Edwards's description of the Grand Gallery in the Great Pyramid. Mr. Edwards is constantly pointing to concrete referents; how he feels about these referents is irrelevant to his purpose. Mencken, on the other hand, designates very few objective facts about American journalism; instead he is telling us how he *feels* about the subject. Highly connotative words and phrases like "grotesque lathering," "mountebanks," "wallow in trivialities," "funeral orgies," "political rubbish," "degrading hymning" are not words describing American journalism as much as they are words describing H. L. Mencken. In more neutral and more denotative language we might express Mencken's idea like this:

> There is something to be said in favor of the newspaper proprietors. They are not responsible for the poor English of journalism or for its lack of taste, learning, and moral courage.

In this kind of translation all the color, pungency, and force of the original has disappeared. There can be no doubt that emotive, connotative language adds liveliness and interest to persuasive writing. But strongly connotative words easily become name-calling. To call someone a mountebank does not necessarily make him a mountebank; and strong phrases like "funeral orgies" may exemplify the very meretriciousness that Mencken deplores. Too many emotionally charged words, furthermore, may produce the effect of a man shouting too loudly for too long. To persuade those not committed already often requires more than highly emotive language.

Words, as we have demonstrated, can be primarily denotative or primarily connotative, and they can, at other times, be both. It is impossible to write very much without using some words denotatively and others connotatively. As a general rule, impersonal, scientific prose tends to use words without strong connotations. Personal writing, which is often concerned with what one likes and dislikes, will communicate by means of both denotation and connotation. But in reading or in writing argument and persuasion it is well to remember that some words are purely emotive and cannot be used in place of evidence or proof.

TONE

Abstraction and concreteness, denotation and connotation are properties of single words. But just as important is the effect of words in combination. Except in theoretical discussions we seldom react to a word in isolation. As we have suggested in our definition of contexts, words become fully operative only in relation to other words: verbal combinations also have characteristics. One of these is tone. Although the notion of tone, the emotional atmosphere generated by a piece of writing, is elusive, we can analyze it into three closely related attitudes expressed by the writer. These are:

1. The writer's attitude toward himself.
2. The writer's attitude toward his subject.
3. The writer's attitude toward his readers.

A writer's tone is something he can quite consciously strive for and control although, doubtless, it is partly unconscious. It is revealed in several ways: by the writer's choice of subject, by what he chooses to say about it, and by how he chooses to express his thought and feeling, that is, by his organization, his sentence structure, and his diction. But the writer's diction perhaps is the most effective vehicle of his tone. One's choice of words, especially through their connotations, projects an image of the writer and his values. To illustrate these points let us see how meaning can be conveyed indirectly through three quite different tones. First, Ernest Hooten is contemplating the plight of man in 1940, shortly after the beginning of World War II:

> Of course, we have been sowing the wind for the larger part of a century and we have now reaped the whirlwind. The democracies have drugged themselves with soporific platitudes, while demagogues and dictators have wrought havoc in a debauched and moronic society. I listened today to the chairman of a national political convention addressing his party in "an hour of great national danger." It was apparent that no help was forthcoming from his quarter, because he burbled about Lincoln and patriotism and the evils wrought by the administration of the rival party with the same resounding and witless verbosity which, I suppose, has characterized political orators ever since man became articulate.
>
> The world chaos of today is due to the debased intelligence of the mass of "civilized" men and to nothing else. "Shall I not take

> mine ease in mine inn?" has been the slogan of an animal, which, through knowledge handed down by his striving forebears, has gained control of natural resources that make subsistence well nigh effortless. The biological fiber of man has been rotted by indolence and inertia so that degenerative behavior has become the rule and not the exception. The cultural causes of human atrophy through idleness are machines and public charity. The human animal must work with his brain and with his hands in order to maintain his health and his evolutionary status. He must stand on his own feet and walk with his own legs in order to stay erect and to retain mobility. If he does not exercise his organs and his faculties both deteriorate.
>
> *Why Men Behave like Apes and Vice Versa*

This writer speaks with the authority and bitterness of an Old Testament prophet, an impression created in part by the Biblical allusion (Hosea 8,7) that begins this extract, by rather formal expressions like "have wrought havoc," and "the evils wrought by," and by Shakespeare's wording of a proverbial expression "Shall I not take mine ease in mine inn?" The prophet is foretelling the doom of mankind, a punishment for too much luxury and ease. Telling us that civilization is sick, the voice of the prophet becomes the voice of the doctor diagnosing our ills: we are suffering from "degenerative behavior," "human atrophy," a potential deterioration in our "faculties"; our democracies "have drugged themselves with soporific platitudes." The writer expresses contempt for his subject: our "debauched and moronic society." Social and political solutions to our problems are impossible owing to our "debased intelligence." Politicians only "burble" or speak with "witless verbosity." Toward his readers, the writer is exhortatory and stern. To be saved we must give up "indolence and inertia" in favor of struggle, hard physical work, and simple, lean living.

Contrast the angry, scornful, and hortatory voice of Ernest Hooten with the different tone of Harold Nicolson, who is writing about himself and the subject of men's clothes:

> It is well enough for the fashionable and the slim. Their bodies fall naturally into the shape of their clothes, their waistcoats sit lightly, concavely, upon their adolescent frames. Couth and gainly they rise in the morning, couth and gainly they don their silken pajamas for the night. Buttons for them are mere finishing touches to a lineal design, mere points of break in what would otherwise appear too rigidly perpendicular. A button more, a button less, what matters it to those whose bodies are encased *in* but not *by* their clothes? It is only for those whom buttons are things which are apt to bulge and burst that this clothes question assumes the

> proportions of deep human drama. It is for such people that I write these words of encouragement. I write for men. I do not write for boys and maidens. I write for men who, though still young in conscience, are yet not slim in shape. I do not write for women. It is not necessary, it would in fact be a mistake, to give women any gratuitous encouragement about their clothes.
>
> It is for convex males that I write, and above all for those among them who are not exuberantly young. "MEN'S CLOTHES"

The writer's subject is far from being the decadence of a society about to be plunged into war. His subject is essentially himself, or, one might almost say, his subject is his tone. His diction at times suggests a formality and dignity — "adolescent frames," "too rigidly perpendicular," "gratuitous encouragement," yet this effect is qualified by words suggesting an air of relaxed informality; he talks to his readers as a genial host might talk to his guests. He wins our liking by his urbanity and by his ability to laugh at himself. If he is addressing primarily those who, like himself, are "convex males," "not exuberantly young," he is conscious of the other members of his audience, treating them all — men and women, the old and the young — with charm and courtesy. His intention is to entertain.

To entertain is also the purpose of Mark Twain in an essay called "A Cure for the Blues," but Twain's tone is different from that of Harold Nicolson or Ernest Hooten. He is enjoying himself at the expense of an obscure American writer, whom he calls G. Ragsdale McClintock. First, a sample of McClintockian prose. In the pages of McClintock, Major Elfonzo on a walking tour has just met a young man sitting by a brook. They introduce themselves:

> "My name is Roswell. I have been recently admitted to the bar, and can only give a faint outline of my future success in that honorable profession; but I trust, sir, like the Eagle, I shall look down from lofty rocks upon the dwellings of man, and shall ever be ready to give you any assistance in my official capacity, and whatever this muscular arm of mine can do, whenever it shall be called from its buried greatness." The major grasped him by the hand, and exclaimed: "O! thou exalted spirit of inspiration — thou flame of burning prosperity, may the Heaven-directed blaze be the glare of thy soul, and battle down every rampart that seems to impede your progress!"

About McClintock's prose Twain has this observation:

> There is a strange sort of originality about McClintock; he imitates other people's styles, but nobody can imitate his, not even

an idiot. Other people can be windy, but McClintock blows a gale; other people can blubber sentiment, but McClintock spews it; other people can mishandle metaphors, but only McClintock knows how to make a business of it. McClintock is always McClintock, he is always consistent, his style is always his own style. He does not make the mistake of being relevant on one page and irrelevant on another; he is irrelevant on all of them. He does not make the mistake of being lucid in one place and obscure in another; he is obscure all the time. He does not make the mistake of slipping in a name here and there that is out of character with his work; he always uses names that exactly and fantastically fit his lunatics. In the matter of undeviating consistency he stands alone in authorship. It is this that makes his style unique, and entitles it to a name of its own — McClintockian. It is this that protects it from being mistaken for anybody else's. Uncredited quotations from other writers often leave a reader in doubt as to their authorship, but McClintock is safe from that accident; an uncredited quotation from him would always be recognizable. When a boy nineteen years old, who had just been admitted to the bar, says, "I trust, sir, like the Eagle, I shall look down from lofty rocks upon the dwellings of man," we know who is speaking through that boy; we should recognize that note anywhere. There be myriads of instruments in this world's literary orchestra, and a multitudinous confusion of sounds that they make, wherein fiddles are drowned, and guitars smothered, and one sort of drum mistaken for another sort; but whensoever the brazen note of the McClintockian trombone breaks through that fog of music, that note is recognizable, and about it there can be no blur of doubt.

Twain, who expects only a little sanity and common sense from writers, has found these traits not so common as one might suppose. He invites his reader, as his equal, to share his exasperation, his outrage, and also his huge amusement at the lunatic prose of G. Ragsdale McClintock. Toward that prose he expresses mock seriousness conveyed in part by patterned syntax and in part by clichés of literary criticism. Often Twain's tone is heavily ironical; his words mean the opposite of what they seem to say. McClintock has "a strange sort of originality"; "he is always consistent"; "an uncredited quotation from him would always be recognizable"; his style is unique. But words like "idiots" and expressions like "exactly and fantastically fit his lunatics" make a comic discord, and repetitions suggest a combination of mounting exasperation and hilarity: "He does not make the mistake of being relevant on one page and irrelevant on another; he is irrelevant on all of them." The elaborate orchestral metaphor of the last sentence would be normally appropriate to literary praise; here it mocks and burlesques by means of words like "drowned," "smothered," "McClintockian trombone," and "breaks through that fog." In Twain's critical judgment McClintock makes himself, unintentionally, one of the great comic writers.

As we see from the contrasting tones of these extracts, writers can, if they wish, convey something like the sound of a speaking voice and a personality. Some writers speak with assurance and dogmatic authority; others are much more aware of their limitations and failings. Writers may delight in their subject, they may despise it, or express almost any feeling in between. Their purpose may be only to inform or to please or it may be to move the reader to action. Writers may exalt or degrade or enrage or soothe. But an atmosphere of feeling and evaluation appears in all but the driest kind of formal writing. This atmosphere arises from the connotations of the writer's words and their cumulative effect. It is sometimes referred to as what we read between the lines. We shall call it the writer's tone.

WORD CHANGE

The subtle, elusive quality of meaning is one reason that meanings are never stable but always in a state of change, always becoming, as a Platonist would say, and never being. Words have never possessed simple, fixed meanings: they have continuously undergone changes of meaning in the past, are changing now, and will continue to change their meanings as long as they are used. In the case of a word like *road* the changes may be slight and gradual, depending upon changes in what we call roads and upon changes in our relationship to them, or in the case of a word like *atom* (which is over two thousand years old) the changes may be sudden and dramatic under the impact of intellectual and historical events. In their capacity to grow, develop, change, age, and die words are like living beings; we naturally think of languages as either living or dead, and only in dead languages like Latin or Sanskrit can we say that words have ceased to change.

BROADENING

The first type of change we shall discuss is called *broadening*. Sometimes a word begins by referring to a limited area of experience, as *layman* did at first, applying only to one not in holy orders; today the word has so broadened that it can designate any person outside almost any profession. Most of us, including clergymen, are laymen with respect to the medical profession, while doctors of medicine are laymen with reference to archaeology and archaeologists. Another example of broadening is *cavalier,* which referred in the Middle Ages to a horseman. Since most horsemen were also noblemen the word broadened to designate one of noble birth. Later *cavalier* broadened still more to include an adjectival form describing the characteristics of noblemen — hauteur, dash, elaborate courtesy, lack of concern with workaday matters, and irresponsibility. A still further broadening permits the application of this word to anyone — no matter how baseborn — who exhibits these qualities.

The process of broadening may be carried so far that a word really degenerates, becoming almost meaningless. *Wonderful,* for example, meant at first that which inspires wonder. But it has broadened so much by this time that it is applied to the least surprising and wondrous things. We hear of "a wonderful play" or "a wonderful evening," where *wonderful* is merely a mild all-purpose word of approval. For this reason *wonderful* has all but disappeared from the written language, and similar words of general blame or praise like *appalling, astounding, dreadful, ghastly, tremendous, awful, fabulous,* if not completely ruined, need to be used with care. In writing, at least, one does well to dispense with adjectives like these. In the same class are intensive modifiers like *very, extremely,* and *absolutely.* So many things have been said to be *very* which simply aren't *very* that this word has lost much of its force; in most contexts such overly broadened words are deadwood. On the other hand, it must be stressed that broadening is a normal and inescapable process. If it results in the degeneration and loss of some words, it increases the usefulness of others.

NARROWING

A second kind of linguistic change is called narrowing or specialization. Words that denote a large class of things may later refer only to a smaller, more restricted class. The word *silly,* for example, meant "happy" in Old English. During the later Middle Ages and Renaissance (1150–1500) the word acquired the meaning of "innocent." Perhaps because simple shepherds and other rustic folk were regarded as happy and innocent, the word was applied to things rustic, lowly, plain; along the way, however, the word picked up additional meanings of "pitiable," "feeble," and "foolish." In short, the word broadened. But today *silly* has narrowed. The unpleasant or unfavorable meanings of "foolish," "not reasonable," "absurd" have driven out the other meanings.

The word *virtue* has had a similar development. The English word can be traced to Latin *virtus,* which in turn derives from Latin *vir,* man. To the Romans *virtus* meant, first, "manliness," and then, by a slight broadening, "courage and prowess in battle." After the word entered English by way of French during the Middle Ages, it began to broaden even more, so that by Shakespeare's time *virtue* meant any sort of excellence, whether mental, moral, or physical. But since the seventeenth century the word has narrowed to mean almost exclusively moral excellence. Today we would never call the ability to sing well a virtue, as Shakespeare might have done.

PEJORATION

In addition to broadening and narrowing a third form of word change is pejoration. Derived from Latin *peior,* meaning "worse," pejoration refers to a worsening in both the denotations and connotations of a word. Some words begin with neutral or favorable meanings but develop into expressions of disapproval. *Lewd* is typical. In its Old English form *lǣwede* meant "the laity," "the ignorant," "the unlearned," as distinct from the clergy. Perhaps because the bias of educated speakers and writers attributed baseness and vileness to the uneducated classes, the word has become synonymous with words like *salacious* and *obscene.* The word *villain,* which designated originally a medieval farm-tenant or serf, has had a similar history. Another example of pejoration is the word *crafty,* meaning at first simply skilled, especially in some handicraft. It has been suggested that words having to do with knowledge, wisdom, skill, and cleverness have a tendency to pejorate in English, as if there were a resentment against intelligence and competence. The word *wise* may be undergoing a pejoration in our time if we can judge by expressions like *wise guy, wisenheimer, wiseacre,* and *wisecrack.* Words sometimes pejorate because of the adjectives modifying them. For example, *wench* meant in earlier usage "child," "daughter," "pupil," "orphan," being derived from Old English *wencel,* meaning "weak," "in need of protection." The word first narrowed to apply only to a girl or young woman; then during the Renaissance and later *wench* was so often accompanied by adjectives like *saucy, impertinent, ill-favored,* and *light* that the word pejorated into a term of contempt.

AMELIORATION

Some words take the opposite course from pejoration and change in a direction called amelioration, from Latin *melior*, meaning "better." Beginning as unpleasant words they develop into neutral or even favorable expressions. *Pluck* will illustrate this kind of change. The word is derived from the phrase "a pluck of lights," meaning the entrails — heart, liver, and lungs — that can be drawn forth from a dead animal or bird. Since the heart is often associated with courage, this word used to name offal became synonymous with courage and heroism, being used even by Victorian ladies in their drawing rooms. It is interesting to note that since *pluck* has become respectable it has lost some of its force. Our more emphatic and informal equivalent — one that employs the same metaphor — is *guts*.

Another instance of amelioration is *pioneer*. In Shakespeare's day a pioneer was one of the soldiers of lowest rank whose job was to clear a path for an advancing army by cutting down trees, digging ditches, building roads and bridges, and performing menial tasks of every kind. When the comparison was made between these military pioneers and the settlers of the American West, the word began to take on a much more favorable meaning, now being associated with strength, determination, resourcefulness, courage, and independence. The development of this word illustrates the fact that history may intervene at any time to pejorate or ameliorate any of our words.

Words, however, do not move in only one direction or in only one dimension. They may exhibit narrowing and pejoration at the same time; words can broaden and ameliorate, or they can specialize and ameliorate. So, too, they can have their ups and downs by pejorating for a time and then regaining their lost status. *Enthusiasm* has an interesting history in this respect. Judging by its etymology, we should suppose that *enthusiasm* is a word of entirely favorable connotations, for it is made from Greek *entheos*, meaning "a god from within," from *en*, "in" + *theos*, "god." Consequently, an early meaning of enthusiasm is "inspiration, divine assistance," But to writers of the eighteenth century *enthusiasm* had become strongly pejorative. In defining *enthusiasm* in his dictionary, Dr. Samuel Johnson employs a quotation from Locke: "*Enthusiasm* is founded neither on reason nor divine revelation, but rises from the conceits of a warmed or overweening brain." Thus, *enthusiasm* meant to the men of the

Age of Reason something similar to what *fanaticism* means to us. Possibly owing to the influence of the Romantic Movement, which highly valued emotion and intuition, the word has since ameliorated. Today the word, at the very least, has no unfavorable connotations, and enthusiasm to many is a desirable quality.

Summary

The single most important fact about words is that they have only potential meanings apart from their contexts. In our discussion we have considered two kinds of contexts: (1) the verbal context, which consists of the words and sentences immediately surrounding a given term; and (2) what we have called the total context of a term, consisting of the writer, his temperament, knowledge, and past experience; his position in time and space, his occasion for writing or speaking, his audience, his purpose, his techniques of expression, and, of course, what he communicates — his essay, novel, or unit of writing. While in any particular situation not all of these will be equally important to the full understanding of a word or passage, any one of them or any combination of them, can be of the utmost significance.

Meaning is further complicated by the fact that a word may have a wide range of reference. Some words, which we call concrete, designate physical entities; others refer to qualities shared by a number of concrete objects and so are called abstract words. Abstractions have no reality apart from the concrete objects from which they are abstracted.

Words also have denotative and connotative properties. A word denotes when it merely points to a referent without making any comment about it. Denotation describes the ability of a word to designate something. The connotation of a word stirs the emotions of the reader or listener and causes him to evaluate the thing named. Most writing contains both denotative and connotative words, but scientific writing and objective reporting contain a much larger percentage of denotative terms than of connotative. As writing grows more subjective and becomes more a matter of personal judgments, more connotative terms begin to appear. The connotations of words are largely responsible for the writer's tone, which indirectly expresses his attitude toward himself, his subject, and his readers. Formal, scientific writing conveys almost no tone beyond objectivity and detachment; but informal or personal writing usually has a decided tone, which is one dimension of the writer's meaning. Finally, words change their meaning. These changes may go on slowly for many years or they may occur quite suddenly under the influence of historical events.

Exercises

1. What is the meaning of each of the italicized words in the following contexts? You may wish to consult an unabridged dictionary. For brief descriptions of such dictionaries see pages 547–8.

1. In language one should be *nice* but not difficult.
   JAMES RUSSELL LOWELL

2. The flowers appear on the earth; the time of the singing of birds is come, and the voice of the *turtle* is heard in our land.
   The Song of Solomon

3. All day long, a stream of porters from the wharves beside the river, each bearing on his back a bursting chest of oranges, poured slowly through the narrow passages; while underneath the archway by the public-house, the *knots* of those who rested and regaled within, were piled from morning until night. CHARLES DICKENS

4. If such minds [those of Galileo, Shakespeare, Beethoven, etc.] have been rare, and spread thinly over three thousand years, after all they still represent the *sports* that indicate the high possibilities of fortunate genetic combinations. HANS ZINSSER

5. The mess cooks seized their *black-jacks* and hurried to the tub where the grog was served out. JOHN MASEFIELD

6. In *fine*, the man who seems trying to deceive others has often first deceived himself. F. L. LUCAS

7. O Romeo, Romeo! *wherefore* art thou Romeo?
   SHAKESPEARE, *Romeo and Juliet*, II, i, 33

8. The offerings of the sea in the ebb of *springs* were always more momentous than those of ordinary tides. MARY ELLEN CHASE

9. With empty hands no tassels you can lure,/ But *fulsome* love for gain we can endure . . . ALEXANDER POPE

10. If you want to understand anything, make it yourself, is a sound rule. Your *faculties* will be alive, your thoughts gain vividness by an immediate translation into acts. ALFRED NORTH WHITEHEAD

2. Analyze the broad context of the following passage by answering the kind of questions listed on page 471. Describe how the writer's diction helps him to achieve his purpose:

It was a crisp and spicy morning in early October. The lilacs and laburnums, lit with the glory-fires of autumn, hung burning and flashing in the upper air, a fairy bridge provided by kind Nature for the wingless wild things that have their home in the tree-tops and would visit together; the larch and the pomegranate flung their purple and yellow flames in brilliant broad splashes along the slanting sweep of the woodland; the sensuous fragrance of innumerable deciduous flowers rose upon the swooning atmosphere; far in the empty sky a solitary oesophagus slept upon motionless wing; everywhere brooded stillness, serenity, and the peace of God.

MARK TWAIN, "A DOUBLE-BARRELED DETECTIVE STORY"

3. Point to examples of concrete words and abstract words in the following passages. What are the most particular words? the most general? Which is the easier to read? Why? Can you suggest any way to improve the clarity of the more difficult passage? Or is it as clear as its subject matter permits?

1. Let me again emphasize that the process of deployment is related to the evolutionary opportunities available and is conditioned by them. A striking example of this is provided by the ground finches of the Galápagos Islands, the *Geospizidae,* which more than anything else persuaded Darwin of the fact of evolution. They are a small group of songbirds, undoubtedly derived from some species of New World finch which got blown out from the mainland and succeeded in establishing itself on this remote oceanic archipelago. The group now consists of four distinct genera and fourteen separate species, adapted for many distinct modes of life. Some are seed eaters, others omnivorous ground feeders, others insectivorous, others leaf and bud eaters, while one has gone in for a woodpecker type of life. All have evolved beaks adapted to dealing with their particular type of food, with the exception of the woodpecker type, which has developed the unique instinct of using a twig instead of its beak to pry for insects in crevices. David Lack has summarized our knowledge of this group in his book *Darwin's Finches.*

JULIAN HUXLEY, *Evolution in Action*

2. There is first one point which should be obvious, but which seems often forgotten. In asking whether goodness can, in the end, be self-consistent and be real, we are not concerned merely with the relation between virtue and selfishness. For suppose that there is no difference between these two, except merely for our blindness, yet, possessing this first crown of our wishes, we have still not solved the main problem. It will certainly now be worth my while to seek the good of my neighbour, since by no other course can I do any better for myself, and since what is called self-sacrifice, or benevolent action, is in fact the only possible way to secure my advantage. But then, upon the other hand, a mere balance of advantage, how-

ever satisfactory the means by which I come to possess it, is most assuredly *not* the fulfilment of my desire. For the desire of human beings (this is surely a commonplace) has no limit. Goodness, in other words, must imply an attempt to reach perfection, and it is the nature of the finite to seek for that which nothing finite can satisfy. But if so, with a mere balance of advantage I have *not* realized my good. And, however much virtue may be nothing in the world but a refined form of self-seeking, yet, with this, virtue is not one whit the less a pursuit of what is inconsistent and therefore impossible. And goodness, or the attainment of such an impossible end, is still self-contradictory. F. H. BRADLEY, *Appearance and Reality*

4. Analyze the tone of the following excerpts. Identify words that are largely denotative. Describe the feelings and associations clinging to the connotative words. Compare your associations with those of someone else.

1. Bewildered or sullen or defiant, the young who are wise enough to conclude that meetings are no substitute for careers, nor publicity for power, gravitate toward the last institution that promises rest from evil and uncertainty — the self-centered family. Having started an exclusive courtship in childhood, John marries Jane as soon as practicable, for only she means peace, goodness, and truth — that is, until little Jonathans come to share the exclusive virtue and interest of John and Jane. The self-centered family competes with study, politics, and social life, and makes them show cause why they should interfere with individualism *à deux*. To put it another way, this latest substitute for status and privilege gains strength by domesticating everything — love, study, pleasure, ambition, liberality, and the broken remnants of intellectual curiosity and conversation. By reducing all these to its appetite, the self-centered family is a small fortress against the monsters outside — the huge institutions, the anonymous mass, the agitated world. The self-centered family is not an institution, it is a cocoon. Warm and small, it matches the other reductions in size and scope we are witnessing: the tiny house, the tiny car, the tiny stature of humanity on the bluish window through which cozily, in the dark, the family views some of the strange events outside. JACQUES BARZUN, *The House of Intellect*

2. Indeed, it is a memorable subject for consideration, with what unconcern and gaiety mankind pricks on along the Valley of the Shadow of Death. The whole way is one wilderness of snares, and the end of it, for those who fear the last pinch, is irrevocable ruin. And yet we go spinning through it all, like a party for the Derby. Perhaps the reader remembers one of the humourous devices of the deified Caligula: how he encouraged a vast concourse of holiday-makers on to his bridge over Baiae bay; and when they were in the

height of their enjoyment, turned loose the Praetorian guards among the company, and had them tossed into the sea. This is no bad miniature of the dealings of nature with the transitory race of man. Only, what a chequered picnic we have of it, even while it lasts! and into what great waters, not to be crossed by any swimmer, God's pale Praetorian throws us over in the end! We live the time that a match flickers; we pop the cork of a gingerbeer bottle, and the earthquake swallows us on the instant. Is it not odd, is it not incongruous, is it not, in the highest sense of human speech, incredible, that we should think so highly of the gingerbeer, and regard so little the devouring earthquake? The love of Life and the fear of Death are two famous phrases that grow harder to understand the more we think about them. It is a well-known fact that an immense proportion of boat accidents would never happen if people held the sheet in their hands instead of making it fast; and yet, unless it be some martinet of a professional mariner or some landsman with shattered nerves, every one of God's creatures makes it fast. A strange instance of man's unconcern and brazen boldness in the face of death! ROBERT LOUIS STEVENSON, "AES TRIPLEX"

3. From the standpoint of both politics and urbanism, Rome remains a significant lesson of what to avoid: its history presents a series of classic danger signals to warn one when life is moving in the wrong direction. Wherever crowds gather in suffocating numbers, wherever rents rise steeply and housing conditions deteriorate, wherever a one-sided exploitation of distant territories removes the pressure to achieve balance and harmony nearer at hand, there the precedents of Roman building almost automatically revive, as they have come back today: the arena, the tall tenement, the mass contests and exhibitions, the football matches, the international beauty contests, the strip-tease made ubiquitous by advertisement, the constant titillation of the senses by sex, liquor, and violence — all in true Roman style. So, too, the multiplication of bathrooms and the over-expenditure on broadly paved motor roads, and above all, the massive collective concentration on glib ephemeralities of all kinds, performed with supreme technical audacity. These are symptoms of the end: magnifications of demoralized power, minifications of life. When these signs multiply, Necropolis is near, though not a stone has yet crumbled. For the barbarian has already captured the city from within. Come, hangman! Come, vulture!

LEWIS MUMFORD, *The City in History*

5. Rewrite one of the passages in (4), changing its tone. Retain the writer's ideas but change the diction as much as your new tone requires.

6. Using an unabridged dictionary or *The Oxford English Dictionary,* discover what kind of word change is exemplified by each of the following words. Write a history of one of these words.

admire	egregious	luxury	pompous
boor	giddy	meat	promoter
buxom	grocer	naughty	quaint
cunning	hound	nice	specious
disease	humor	ordeal	starve
divan	insane	peculiar	undertaker

24
FIGURATIVE LANGUAGE

Introduction

Whenever language is simple, plain, and direct, whenever it employs words to mean what most users conventionally mean by them, we say it is literal, a term derived from Latin *litera,* letter: what is literal is according to the letter. To put it another way, literal meanings are those recorded in a dictionary. Consider, for example, this literal statement: "A writer's style should be purposive, not merely decorative." These words are plain, direct, and straightforward. Figuratively, the same thought has been expressed like this: "Style is the feather in the arrow, not the feather in the cap." Figurative statements differ from literal statements by using words or phrases that normally designate one thing to designate another. The writer can make this kind of transfer because of some likeness (or other relationship) between two different things that is clearly apparent from his verbal context. In the example just given the *literal* referent of "feather in the arrow" is a weapon propelled by a bow; the *figurative* referent is style as effective communication. In addition to designating a referent in a surprising and therefore striking way, figurative language intentionally transfers connotations of the literal referent to the figurative referent: associations surrounding "feather in the arrow," such as swiftness, directness, sureness, and strength, now become attached to the idea of functional style. Thus at least three general effects of figurative language, properly used, are greater clarity, greater emphasis, and a more decided tone. These characteristics we shall see illustrated in more detail as we list and discuss some of the more common figures of speech.

METAPHOR AND SIMILE

By far the largest and most important class of figurative language draws a comparison between two unlike things. If the comparison is explicit, employing such terms as *like, as, as . . . as, comparable to,* and so on, the figure is called a simile. The following passages contain examples:

1. It was senseless, it was utterly foolish, but all that was best and richest in Mr. Polly's nature broke like a wave and foamed up at that girl's feet, and died, and never touched her.
   H. G. WELLS, *The History of Mr. Polly*

2. It is possible, occasionally, to get something completely right — a scene, or a pattern of larceny, or a man's mind. These are the reporter's victories, as rare as a pitcher's home runs.
   A. J. LIEBLING, *The Press*

3. Or again the summer sea may glitter with a thousand thousand moving pinpricks of light, like an immense swarm of fireflies moving through a dark wood. RACHEL CARSON, *The Sea Around Us*

4. [Barbara Tuchman quotes and comments upon Kitchener's order to the British Expeditionary Force in 1914:] "The special motive of the Force under your control," he wrote, "is to support and cooperate with the French Army . . . and to assist the French in preventing or repelling the invasion by Germany of French or Belgian territory." With a certain optimism, he added, "And eventually to restore the neutrality of Belgium" — a project comparable to restoring virginity. *The Guns of August*

If in order to compare two different things a statement asserts an identity between them or otherwise implies a comparison between them the figure is called a metaphor. Following are several examples of these implicit comparisons:

1. Censure is the Tax a Man pays to the Publick for being eminent.
   JONATHAN SWIFT, "THOUGHTS ON VARIOUS SUBJECTS"

2. Cape Cod is the bared and bended arm of Massachusetts . . .
   HENRY DAVID THOREAU, *Cape Cod*

3. How does chlorophyll, green old alchemist that it is, transmute the dross of earth into living tissue?
   DONALD CULROSS PEATTIE, *Flowering Earth*

4. World War II seemed really so extensively predetermined; it developed and rolled its course with the relentless logic of the last act of a classical tragedy. GEORGE F. KENNAN, *American Diplomacy*

Clearly, similes and metaphors may be used to make comparisons between unlike things. But what is the significant difference between them? Rhetoricians are not agreed about the answer. To some, metaphor and simile differ only in the degree of closeness they establish between the things compared. To others, simile and metaphor do essentially different things. This disagreement, however, is more a matter of theory than of practice, and for our purposes we shall assume that metaphor and simile are more alike than different. As a matter of convenience we shall henceforth use *metaphor* to designate similes as well as implicit comparisons.

Of more immediate concern to the practical writer are the questions, why use metaphors at all? cannot any idea be expressed as well in plain, literal language, if not better? The answers to these questions are not simple or easy. It is true that some great English prose writers, like Jonathan Swift, are sparing in their use of figurative language. It is also true that unless metaphors and other figures are used properly they had better not be used at all. But metaphors form so vital a part of both our spoken and our written language that no doubt many writers use them as naturally as they use literal statements, for metaphors serve writers in at least four important ways:

(1) One important function of metaphor is to explain or clarify. It may do so by comparing the remote and unfamiliar to something homely and commonplace, or it may condense abstractions into concrete and vivid images. The following quotation achieves at least the first of these purposes:

> An expression of this repulsion [of an electron for an electron] is today likewise given in terms of exchange forces: a photon is tossed from electron to interacting electron. In general circumstances those photons, like cheques passed backwards and forwards between two firms to constitute their relation to one another, do not come into circulation, but in other circumstances, in the presence of nuclear forces in one case and the presence of market forces, let us say, in the other case, the photons or the cash do come into circulation.
>
> E. N. DA C. ANDRADE, *An Approach to Modern Physics*

Using metaphor, William James both makes the unfamiliar easier to grasp and also transforms abstraction into a more understandable concreteness:

> Your mind in such processes is strained, and sometimes painfully so, between its older beliefs and the novelties which experience brings along.
>
> Our minds thus grow in spots; and like grease-spots, the spots spread. But we let them spread as little as possible: we keep unaltered as much of our old knowledge, as many of our old prejudices and

> beliefs, as we can. We patch and tinker more than we renew. The novelty soaks in; it stains the ancient mass; but it is also tinged by what absorbs it. *Pragmatism*

Metaphors of this type help the expository writer to explain abstruse or elusive subjects. Though they are especially common in popularizations of science and philosophy, they are useful in any kind of expository discussion, for they are an expression of the writer's courtesy to his readers; such metaphors help them to comprehend his idea quickly and clearly.

(2) Secondly, metaphors may both clarify a point and drive it home with unusual emphasis. Listen, for example, to George Bernard Shaw, who is a master of the emphatic metaphor:

> But if you venture to wonder how Christ would have looked had he shaved and had his hair cut, or what size in shoes he took, or whether he swore when he stood on a nail in the carpenter's shop, or could not button his robe when he was in a hurry, or whether he laughed over the repartees by which he baffled the priests when they tried to trap him into sedition and blasphemy, or even if you tell any part of his story in the vivid terms of modern colloquial slang, you will produce an extraordinary dismay and horror among the iconolaters. You will have made the picture come out of its frame, the statue descend from its pedestal, the story become real, with all the incalculable consequences that may flow from this terrifying miracle. It is at such moments that you realize that iconolaters have never for a moment conceived of Christ as a real person who meant what he said, as a fact, as a force like electricity, only needing the invention of suitable political machinery to be applied to the affairs of mankind with revolutionary effect.
>
> "PREFACE" TO *Androcles and the Lion*

This is indeed emphatic language. Its vigor results from several causes: Shaw's deep emotional commitment to his subject; his skillful use of parallelism; his vivid, concrete diction; his brilliant and paradoxical word *iconolater*. But equally important sources of Shaw's strength are his emphatic metaphors, especially the last: Christ is a force like electricity — a startling comparison, outrageous, yet apt; it lingers in the mind. Writers who believe fiercely in their causes, writers whose chief concern is to persuade by shock and frontal assault are likely to use emphatic metaphors.

(3) Metaphors serve a third purpose in creating, or helping to create, the writer's tone. Tone, we recall, is a combination of the writer's attitude toward himself, toward his subject, and toward his readers. It is expressed in many ways — through the writer's handling of his "point of view,"

through his syntax, and through his diction. In his tone a writer may be entirely aloof and objective, depending upon his subject and purpose, or he may wish to react personally to his subject and evalute it more or less vigorously. In writing with a personal tone metaphors are well-nigh indispensable, for one term of the comparative figure is usually concrete and familiar. No matter how abstract or colorless the subject might seem in itself, it is always possible by using figurative language to inject into the discussion every range of feeling between the extremes of love and hate. In the next example the metaphor is primarily tonal in its purpose; its subject is pedagogy — or more accurately the subject is pedagogy and H. L. Mencken:

> There are fanatics who love and venerate spelling as a tom-cat loves and venerates catnip. There are grammatomaniacs; schoolmarms who would rather parse than eat; specialists in the objective case that doesn't exist in English; strange beings, otherwise sane and even intelligent and comely, who suffer under a split infinitive as you and I would suffer under gastro-enteritis. *Prejudices: Third Series*

The writer is paying a backhanded compliment to the old-fashioned English teacher, whom he regards as vastly superior to the modern "scientific" pedagogue. But Mencken's tone is complex and deeply ambivalent.

A different tone appears in the following description of German artillery at Liège in 1914:

> Liège was cut off from the outside world; when the great black weapons [the German seige guns] reached the outskirts within range of the forts, only the local inhabitants saw the advent of the monsters that to one observer looked like "overfed slugs." Their squat barrels, doubled by the recoil cylinders that grew on their backs like tumors, pointed cavernous mouths upward at the sky.
> BARBARA TUCHMAN, *The Guns of August*

The metaphors in this description are partly explanatory, giving us a more focused and vivid picture of the German guns than we should have had otherwise. But the metaphoric terms have been chosen to create an atmosphere of mounting fear and horror. The guns are alive, whether they are giant slugs or deformed, diseased monsters. By means of these tonal metaphors the writer ranges herself and her readers on the side of the Allies.

The writer's tone, however, need not involve extremes of praise and blame, respect or contempt. Tonal metaphors can create any kind of attitude, feeling, or mood, including hilarity. A passage by S. J. Perelman will illustrate this point. In his youth the writer had helped to write a revue called *Sherry Flip* — a disaster. This is his description of one of the dance numbers:

> In the dance division, there was a similar lack of co-ordination. The production numbers, two portentous ballets of the type informally known in dance circles as "Fire in a Whorehouse," had got way out of hand. Muscle-bound youths stamped about bearing dryads who whinnied in ecstasy, shoals of coryphees fled helter-skelter across the stage, and the choreographer, wild-eyed with exhaustion, sat slumped in the apron, dreaming up new flights of symbolism. It was a holocaust. "THE SWIRLING CAPE AND THE LOW BOW"

We join Mr. Perelman's laughter at the wild mindlessness of the scene and we can appreciate the humorist's laughter at himself; but most of all we enjoy Mr. Perelman's verbal performance — effective metaphors mixed with his satiric manipulation of trite metaphors to underscore the triteness of the ballet and its creators. And this fact brings us to the fourth purpose of metaphor—which is simply to give the reader pleasure. Most of us will never have the wit and charm of the great humorists or the power to compel of the great writer engrossed in his subject. But we can admire and applaud the writer's ability to please wherever we find it. The desire to please a specific reader—as much as the subject, the writer's purpose, and his verbal skill permits—ought to be the aim of every writer.

Now it is obvious that the four purposes of metaphor—explanation, emphasis, tone, and pleasure—are interdependent rather than separate. Quite clearly, all four purposes are to be found in this highly figurative passage by Donald Culross Peattie:

> Animal life lives always in the red; the favorable balance is written on the other side of life's page, and it is written in chlorophyll. All else obeys the thermodynamic law that energy forever runs down hill, is lost and degraded. In economic language, this is the law of diminishing returns, and is obeyed by the cooling stars as by man and all the animals. They float down its Lethe stream. Only chlorophyll fights up against the current. It is the stuff in life that rebels at death, that has never surrendered to entropy, final icy stagnation. It is the mere cobweb on which we are all suspended over the abyss.
>
> *Flowering Earth*

This is the voice of a man who is fascinated by his subject and completely devoted to it, and a part of his purpose is to share this enthusiasm and interest with his readers. But the passage is also a clear and forceful statement of his point. And although the metaphors are not great or perfect (and they are not intended to be), they are serviceable and give pleasure to most readers.

Some, however, may object that the passage contains too many figures and may point out that in a short space chlorophyll is compared to green ink, a man swimming upstream against a stiff current, a rebel, and a cobweb. That there should be this possible disagreement reminds us that metaphors and similes are judged partly by standards of fashion and taste and partly by common-sense rules to which the writer should pay close attention. Let us consider four of the most important rules governng successful metaphors.

(1) *Metaphors should be fresh and original.* Within the limits of appropriateness, this ought to be the writer's aim. One should usually avoid banalities of the order *busy as a bee, happy as a lark, the staff of life, a tower of strength, the game of life* — to list only a few out of hundreds of such expressions. Although humorists, personal essayists, and others have managed at times to make stereotyped similes and metaphors work for them, most of us are better off avoiding such exhausted figures of speech.

(2) *Metaphors should not be mixed or faulty.* One term of the metaphor or simile is almost always concrete, producing an image that many readers, if not all, perceive clearly. For this reason, and in the interests of logic and consistency, the picture created by a metaphor, or a cluster of metaphors, ought to be natural, normal, and believable, not something like a surrealistic painting or a nightmare, not an expression that will unintentionally make the reader gasp or snicker. Sometimes a writer produces this unhappy result by beginning to express one metaphor, leaving off in the middle, and concluding with part of a different metaphor, as did the writer who declared: "The time has come to grab the bull by the tail and look it squarely in the face." This unfortunate image is actually a mixture of three metaphoric expressions: *to grab the bull by the horns, to have a tiger by the tail,* and *to look someone squarely in the face.* They have been telescoped into absurdity.

When several metaphors appear in the same sentence they should harmonize with one another to produce a consistent and logical sequence of ideas and pictures. Failure to remember this principle leads to passages like this: "The moon, a silver coin hung in the draperies of the enchanted night, let fall her glance which gilded the roof tops with a joyful phosphorescence." Perhaps this *sounds* inpressive. But how can silver be used for gilding? Do coins ever hang in draperies, whether clothing or window decorations? The moon is in the same breath a coin and a person. "Phosphorescence" has a connotation that is at cross purposes with "joyful."

One must not mix even dead metaphors. These are metaphors that long ago actually became the name of the thing designated: *the eye of a needle, the leg of a table, the housing of an engine,* a *bottleneck.* These expressions are now conventional and ordinarily have no metaphoric quality at all. But used close together they come to life. The dead metaphors *leg of a journey* and *mouth of a river,* for instance, work very well alone, but it would be clumsy indeed to write: "The last leg of our journey began at the mouth of the river."

(3) *Metaphors should not be piled one upon the other, especially in expository writing.* If they are, the result will be a kind of prose poem too emotive and too theatrical for most purposes. Horace calls this kind of overwriting a "purple patch," and as Virginia Woolf has pointed out the trouble with a purple patch is not that it is purple but that it is a patch; it seldom seems appropriate to the writing as a whole. In exposition, figurative language should communicate swiftly and clearly, calling attention more to the thought than to the cleverness of language.

(4) *Metaphors should be appropriate to the context.* A metaphor should contribute to, not shatter, the general atmosphere and tone. Metaphors have their own connotations and their own levels of formality and informality. Except for burlesque and other humorous effects, the same principles governing diction in general govern the diction of metaphors.

We have treated metaphors at some length because they appear more frequently than any other figures and because in their various forms and guises they create a wider variety of effects than any other figure of speech. This emphasis is justified, furthermore, because more often than other figures they are liable to abuse and mismanagement. Understanding metaphor is therefore important to all writers. Not everyone can produce brilliant metaphors, but every writer can avoid creating bad ones.

PERSONIFICATION

Personification is a special kind of metaphor which consists of giving to nonhuman things human characteristics and attributes. Some rhetoricians define this figure more narrowly and apply it only to the personification of abstractions like Vice, Virtue, Rumor, Justice, Truth—terms often capitalized as a sign of their personification. Seventeenth- and eighteenth-century writers are fond of personifying abstractions of this kind, which often turn into shadowy figures performing one or two commonplace actions. More usual and more effective in the prose of nineteenth- and twentieth-century writers is the personificaton of inanimate objects. Dickens, for instance, often employs such a figure:

> The poulterer's shops were still half open, and the fruiterer's were radiant in their glory. There were great round, pot-bellied baskets of chestnuts, shaped like waistcoats of jolly old gentlemen, lolling at the doors, and tumbling out into the street in their apoplectic opulence. There were ruddy, brown-faced, broad-girthed Spanish onions, shining in the fatness of their growth like Spanish Friars, and winking from their shelves in wanton slyness at the girls as they went by, and glanced demurely at the hung-up mistletoe.
>
> *A Christmas Carol*

Dickens turns masses of piled-up food into a lolling, tumbling, winking crowd of jolly Christmas celebrators; his delight in the sights and sounds of London streets warms and animates everything he sees.

Like Dickens, James Thurber finds personification useful in description, but the personality that Thurber sees in the city has both a comic and a slightly mad streak:

> Behind the pigeon I am looking at, a blank wall of tired gray bricks is stolidly trying to sleep off oblivion; underneath the pigeon the cloistered windows of the Harvard Club are staring in horrified bewilderment at something they have seen across the street . . . It is only with an effort that I am conscious of the pigeon, but I am acutely aware of a great sulky red iron pipe that is creeping up the side of the building intent on sneaking up on a slightly tipsy chimney which is shouting its head off.
>
> "THERE'S AN OWL IN MY ROOM"

Prose may personify both inanimate things and abstractions. In doing so it often makes them vivid by employing several concrete details. This passage by Bruce Catton illustrates how vivid personification can serve expository writing:

> There is a rowdy strain in American life, living close to the surface but running very deep. Like an ape behind a mask it can display itself suddenly with terrifying effect. It is slack-jawed, with leering eyes and loose wet lips, with heavy feet and ponderous cunning hands; now and then when something tickles it, it guffaws, and when it is angry it snarls; and it can be aroused more easily than it can be quieted. Mike Fink and Yankee Doodle helped to father it, and Judge Lynch is one of its creations; and when it comes lumbering forth it can make the whole country step in time to its own irregular pulse-beat.
>
> *This Hallowed Ground*

In this personification the writer both evaluates his subject and makes his point with extraordinary emphasis. Thus, the effects of personification are roughly those of metaphor, yet personification has the additional advantage of bringing the writer's subject into a human and social relationship to the reader. Dickens's poulterer's shops radiate human warmth and a genial sensuality; things, says Thurber, have a life of their own; beware. Irrational violence, Bruce Catton reminds us, is nothing imaginary but a real and personal threat in American life. Skillfully employed, personification is one of the most dramatic of the figures of speech.

OVERSTATEMENT AND UNDERSTATEMENT

Not all figures, like metaphor and personification, are figures of comparison. Some depend upon various kinds of contrast: the difference between what is and what ought to be or might be, the difference between what is said and what is meant, the difference between apparent contradiction and real contradiction, to name some of the most important. Overstatement and understatement are figures of contrast. In either case the writer depends for his effect upon the difference between reality and what is said about it. A writer may choose to argue and persuade by simply presenting the facts as precisely and as unemotionally as possible; often facts, statistics, evidence, and the inescapable inferences to be drawn from them are the most eloquent means of convincing a reader. Yet not all subjects can be treated by marshaling factual evidence, and not all writers wish to do so, for emotion is also a powerful persuader. One way of speaking emphatically and persuasively about a subject is to magnify it in every dimension. The rhetorical name for this device is hyperbole, from Greek *hyperbole,* excess, or — to give it a simpler name — overstatement. Loosely speaking, we can identify two varieties of overstatement — the comic and the serious — both of which are common in English prose.

Comic overstatement is used in humor and satire for the purpose of ridiculing and burlesquing. It is like a caricature, which exaggerates features and proportions until they become monstrous, until we laugh at the disparity between the deformity produced and some ideal standard in the back of our minds. We laugh, too, at the difference between the exaggeration, which we know is false, and the reality. The reality may be bad, defective — we think to ourselves — but it can't be *that* bad. But all those who have struggled with German verbs and word order will understand the point of this combination of parody and overstatement by Mark Twain:

> An average sentence in a German newspaper, is a sublime and impressive curiosity; it occupies a quarter of a column; it contains all

> the ten parts of speech — not in regular order, but mixed; it is built mainly of compound words constructed by the writer on the spot, and not to be found in any dictionary — six or seven words compacted into one, without joint or seam — that is, without hyphens; it treats of fourteen or fifteen different subjects, each inclosed in a parenthesis of its own, with here and there extra parentheses which reinclose three or four of the minor parentheses, making pens within pens: finally, all the parentheses and reparentheses are massed together between a couple of king-parentheses, one of which is placed in the first line of the majestic sentence and the other in the middle of the last line of it — *after which comes the* VERB, and you find out for the first time what the man has been talking about; and after the verb — merely by way of ornament, as far as I can make out — the writer shovels in "*haben sind gewesen gehabt haben geworden sein,*" or words to that effect, and the monument is finished. *A Tramp Abroad*

Comic overstatement, for whatever the reason, has deep roots in American culture, appearing, for example, in the tall tales about Davy Crockett and Mike Fink. Frontier humor, which is largely overstatement, may have been the safety-valve of men whose lives were normally full of hardship, strange encounters, and sudden disasters. Mark Twain was doubtless influenced by this backwoods humor, as many others have been.

Serious overstatement, which stems in part from this tradition, appears more often perhaps in American prose than in English prose, being common in satire and polemics. H. L. Mencken, who owes much to Twain, uses overstatement as he cudgels American venality, stupidity, and smugness in the 'twenties:

> It is . . . one of my firmest and most sacred beliefs, reached after an enquiry extending over a score of years and supported by incessant prayer and meditation, that the government of the United States, in both its legislative arm and its executive arm, is ignorant, incompetent, corrupt, and disgusting — and from this judgment I except no more than twenty living lawmakers and no more than twenty executioners of their laws. It is a belief no less piously cherished that the administration of justice in the Republic is stupid, dishonest, and against all reason and equity — and from this judgment I except no more than thirty judges, including two upon the bench of the Supreme Court of the United States. It is another that the foreign policy of the United States — its habitual manner of dealing with other nations, whether friend or foe, is hypocritical, disingenuous, knavish, and dishonorable — and from this judgment I consent to no exceptions whatever, either recent or long past. And it is my fourth (and, to avoid too depressing a bill, final) conviction

> that the American people, taking one with another, constitute the most timorous, sniveling, poltroonish, ignominious mob of serfs and goose-steppers ever gathered under one flag in Christendom since the end of the Middle Ages, and that they grow more timorous, more sniveling, more poltroonish, more ignominious every day.
>
> "ON BEING AN AMERICAN"

Quoted out of context, this sounds even more extreme than it is. Mencken appears a bit less outrageous as later in his essay he begins to explain why he prefers to live in the United States rather than elsewhere, but it is undoubtedly an example of extreme overstatement, in spite of the fact that if asked about their intentions writers like Twain and Mencken would probably deny any exaggeration, swearing they were telling only the sober, unvarnished truth.

Overstatement is the result of several devices. For one thing, overstatement employs superlative adjectives referring to long time spans, large numbers, and extremes of all sorts. It prefers the sweeping generalization with frequent use of words like *all, always, never, none.* There is generally either an absence of qualification or else disclaimers that amount to nothing. Mencken's use of qualification in the passage above is typical of overstatement. The syntax of overstatement is usually emphatic as a result of frequent parallel constructions, very long and very short sentences side by side, periodic constructions, the use of anaphora and other forms of repetition. Overstatement often has a strong rhythm and emphatic rhythmic variations. The diction employs strongly connotative words like "sniveling," "poltroonish," "ignominious," and "knavish." In short, overstatement calls upon all the devices of emphasis that a language provides.

The advantage of overstatement, therefore, is its power. In its extreme form it shocks or smites and it may hugely amuse or severely irritate. Its disadvantages are equally obvious. Overstatement is hard to take in large quantities or for any length of time. And more important, overstatement is liable to abuse: emotion and name-calling may be substituted for fact and reasoned argument, as in the case of the newspaper columnists who have imitated Mencken's techniques. Used often, overstatement, furthermore, causes the reader to distrust the writer's judgment and motives. Yet in spite of its disadvantages overstatement will continue to thrive in prose; every writer should understand its use and misuse.

Overstatement implies a contrast between an exaggeration (which we are usually conscious of) and the theoretical "true" state of affairs. Overstatement depicts things as many times larger or worse or better than we suppose they are. Understatement — or litotes, to give the device its classical name — deliberately and for conscious effect plays down the magnitude or intensity of the subject. It achieves emphasis by seeming to avoid emphasis. Like overstatement, it can be either comic or serious, for all contrasts between what is ideal and what is actual are potentially either a source of amusement or a source of indignation. Writers, therefore, often use both overstatement and understatement for satire and humor. "I have been strictly reared," says Mark Twain, "but if it had not been so dark and solemn and awful there in that vast, lonely room, I do believe I should have said something then which could not be put into a Sunday-school book without injuring the sale of it." Or we might instance the grim humor of Jonathan Swift's remark: "Last week I saw a woman flayed, and you will hardly believe how much it altered her appearance for the worse."

Serious understatement has for its subject usually a situation of great sorrow, fear, pain, or destruction. In Hemingway's *A Farewell to Arms* Lieutenant Henry meditates on death in a hospital as his mistress is dying from childbirth:

> Now Catherine would die. That was what you did. You died. You did not know what it was about. You never had time to learn. They threw you in and told you the rules and the first time they caught you off base they killed you. Or they killed you gratuitously like Aymo. Or gave you the syphilis like Rinaldo. But they killed you in the end. You could count on that. Stay around and they would kill you.

This is less emotion than the situation seems to warrant. The reader unconsciously contrasts the reticence of Lieutenant Henry with the more expressive grief of most literary characters and persons in a similar plight. The effect — for many readers, at least — is great emphasis. By not saying very much, the writer forces the reader to supply the feeling the scene calls for.

When words cannot do full justice to the subject, understatement is good strategy. Alexander H. Leighton describes the atomic bombing of Hiroshima like this:

> In the heart of the city near the buildings of the Prefectural Government and at the intersection of the busiest streets, everybody had stopped and stood in a crowd gazing up at three parachutes floating down through the blue air.
>
> The bomb exploded several hundred feet above their heads.
>
> The people for miles around Hiroshima, in the fields, in the mountains, and on the bay, saw a light that was brilliant even in the sun, and felt heat. "THAT DAY AT HIROSHIMA"

Mr. Leighton's description is even less emotional and more matter-of-fact than Hemingway's. Its very simplicity is the source of its power. In this instance the horrors of the facts speak for themselves; any attempt to embellish them would merely enervate and cheapen. Understatement usually avoids the very emphatic devices of diction and syntax found in overstatement. Understatement tends to express an idea negatively rather than positively, preferring, for example, a phrase "not spacious" to an adjective like "cramped." It works indirectly and always seems to be holding something back. The very strength of understatement, on the other hand, is also its weakness, for to the naïve or inexperienced reader understatement may seem like callousness or tepidity. But used with the right subject and the right audience understatement can deliver more punch than overstatement.

IRONY

There is a subtle similarity between understatement and the figure of speech called irony. While irony sometimes accompanies overstatement, it seems more at home with the restrained and indirect device of understatement. Irony is any utterance which says one thing and means another. Consider for a moment this passage from Voltaire's story of Candide:

> After the earthquake which destroyed three-quarters of Lisbon, the wise men of that country could discover no more efficacious way of preventing total ruin than by giving the people a splendid auto-da-fé. It was decided by the university of Coimbre that the sight of several persons being slowly burned in great ceremony is an infallible secret for preventing earthquakes. Consequently they had arrested a Biscayan convicted of having married his fellow godmother, and two Portuguese who, when eating a chicken, had thrown away the bacon; after dinner they came and bound Dr. Pangloss and his disciple Candide, one because he had spoken and the other because he had listened with an air of approbation; they were both carried to extremely cool apartments, where there was never any discomfort from the sun; a week afterwards each was dressed in a sanbenito and their heads were ornamented with paper mitres . . . Dressed in this manner they marched in procession and listened to a most pathetic sermon, followed by lovely plain-song music. Candide was flogged in time to the music, while the singing went on; the Biscayan and the two men who had not wanted to eat bacon were burned, and Pangloss was hanged, although this is not the custom.

On the surface Voltaire seems to be describing ordinary events which he views with detached approval. The even-flowing, unemphatic syntax is suitable more for the description of a Sunday afternoon walk than for executions. Note, for example, that Candide's flogging and Pangloss's hanging are followed by dependent constructions that make the sentence loose and unemphatic. If the tone of this passage is one of serenity and detachment, how do we know that Voltaire means the opposite of what he seems to mean? How does the writer provide us with clues to his real intention and meaning? Sometimes he encloses an ironic word in quotation marks. But often the only clue is that what the writer seems to say is so extreme, so fantastic, outrageous, and contrary to elementary common sense that he must mean the reverse of what he says. In this instance there are also two other indications of irony. One is the extreme disparity between the smoothness of the writer's syntax and the violence and horror of his subject, a mistake an experienced writer would never make, using this disparity only for some special or ironic purpose; the other clue to the irony of this passage is knowledge about the writer and his views. The slightest acquaintance with Voltaire's convictions would tell the reader that in this passage Voltaire is fighting hard against superstition and religious intolerance, not condoning it.

At times diction provides the necessary hint of irony, if any is needed. In the following quotation the removal of three or four words might prevent us from seeing the writer's intention:

> Charles Henry Twain lived during the latter part of the seventeenth century and was a zealous and distinguished missionary. He converted sixteen thousand South Sea Islanders, and taught them that a dog tooth necklace and a pair of spectacles was not enough clothing to come to divine service in. His poor flock loved him very, very dearly; and when his funeral was over, they got up in a body (and came out of the restaurant) with tears in their eyes, and saying to one another that he was a good tender missionary, and they wished they had some more of him.
>
> MARK TWAIN, "A BURLESQUE BIOGRAPHY"

This is comic irony combined with understatement. Its point is at first obscure and then it flashes out suddenly. Not all forms of irony work in this way. Some depend upon a subtle tone of mockery that the inexperienced reader might overlook. Listen to Anthony Trollope's observation about elderly lovers:

> It is we believe, common with young men of five and twenty to look on their seniors — on men of, say, double their own age — as so many stocks and stones, — stocks and stones, that is, in regard to feminine beauty. There never was a greater mistake. Women, indeed, generally know better; but on this subject men of one age are thor-

> oughly ignorant of what is the very nature of mankind of other ages. No experience of what goes on in the world, no reading of history, no observation of life, has any effect in teaching the truth. Men of fifty don't dance mazurkas, being generally too fat and wheezy; nor do they sit for the hour together on river banks at their mistresses' feet, being somewhat afraid of rheumatism. But for real true love, love at first sight, love to devotion, love that robs a man of his sleep, love that 'will gaze an eagle blind,' love that 'will hear the lowest sound when the suspicious tread of theft is stopped,' love that is 'like a Hercules, still climbing trees in the Hesperides,' — we believe the best age is from forty-five to seventy; up to that, men are generally given to mere flirting. *Barchester Towers*

Stout, wheezy, rheumatic old men "gazing an eagle blind" and climbing trees like Hercules — we realize that Trollope cannot be anything but ironic. Trollope *says* that old men are the greatest lovers of all. What he means is that some old men think they are the greatest of lovers, old fools that they are. Again, a combination of surface absurdity and diction indicates the writer's ironic purpose.

If much irony is comic, comedy is not its essence. Its essence lies in making us see a surface falseness in contrast with an underlying reality. The surface meaning always says, "This is how things appear to be, or, in some instances, how they are." The underlying meaning says, "This is how things actually are, or how they ought to be." The underlying meaning is revealed by one or more of these three means: the context (including what we know about the author, his beliefs, his other work), the patent absurdity of the surface meaning, and the writer's diction. Because of the way it works, irony is essentially a device of persuasion, satire, and criticism, whether its aim is the reform of manners or of grave social and political evils. Its advantage lies in its appeal to the thoughtful, experienced reader, who enjoys seeing the irony as irony. Its disadvantage is that it may be misunderstood. Some readers thought Swift wrote *Gulliver's Travels* in order to deceive the English public with sensational travel yarns. And after Swift wrote "A Modest Proposal" — the finest example of sustained irony in English — there were those who regarded him as a monster. It is this risk, however, that makes irony the aristocrat of rhetorical figures and provides the pleasure of those who enjoy writing it and those who enjoy reading it.

PUNS AND WORD PLAY

Irony depends upon a contrast between what seems to be said and what is actually said. Puns and most kinds of word play are also figures of contrast.

A full account of the many kinds of puns and their verbal operations are beyond the small scope of this chapter, but we can identify three common varieties of punning. Probably the most common, at least in writing, uses the same word with deliberately different meanings. Speaking about the demise of the New York *Sun* in 1950, A. J. Liebling writes: "But the *Sun* had its good spots during its last, coverlet picking days, such as the series on water-front rackets by Malcolm John . . ." Harlow Shapley on the problem of aging has this observation: "With the mind senile, a virile body is rudderless; the centenarian's closing days should be bright, but not balmy!" "Even as a schoolboy," said Mark Twain, "poultry-raising was a study with me, and I may say without egotism that as early as the age of seventeen I was acquainted with all the best and speediest methods of raising chickens, from raising them off a roost by burning lucifer matches under their noses, down to lifting them off a fence on a frosty night by insinuating a warm board under their feet."

Another kind of pun plays upon two different words that are identical in sound: "The last time I gazed at the scene I realized I had lost interest in that particular strip of beach (and if the surf hath lost its savor, wherewith shall we be surfeited?)" (E. B. White, *Points of My Compass*). In a different variety of pun, the two different words, rather than being identical in sound, are simply similar. In good puns of this sort, there should be a witty resemblance of meaning. For example, S. J. Perelman entitles a collection of essays *The Road to Miltown, or Under the Spreading Atrophy*. The pun is effective not simply because "atrophy" sounds like "a tree" but because atrophy may very well be spreading. Perelman often uses punning titles: "Nesselrode to Jeopardy," "De Gustibus Ain't What Dey Used to Be," "The Saucier's Apprentice," "Long Time No Sheepskin."

Most punning today is comic in intention, but it is by no means confined to humorous essays like those of Twain or S. J. Perelman. The examples quoted above from A. J. Liebling, Harlow Shapley, and E. B. White appear in writing whose primary intention is not satire or comedy. Indeed, the essay by Harlow Shapley is a listing of the major social problems with which science urgently needs to deal. The puns we have quoted thus far, however, all represent the light touch. The writers of Renaissance England, on the other hand, employed puns for both comic and serious occasions. Shakespeare often uses serious puns:

> Golden lads and girls all must,
> As chimney-sweepers, come to dust.

In the following lines of Cassius in *Julius Caesar* the pun becomes apparent if we realize that in Elizabethan English *Rome* was pronounced almost exactly like *room:*

> Now it is Rome indeed and room enough,
> When there is in it but one only man.

Serious punning is rare in twentieth-century prose, but the comic pun is more frequent than we might imagine and will no doubt be always with us. Quintilian, the great Roman rhetorician, deplored it; eighteenth-century critics — perhaps appalled at the excessive punning of the earlier two centuries — legislated against it. Today we are likely to remember such catch phrases as "the pun is the lowest form of humor" and "He who would make a pun would pick a pocket." But writers of informal English will continue to make an occasional pun in spite of any pronouncements by rhetoricians. The pun can help to create an atmosphere of informal geniality even in writing that is not intended as humor. The trouble is, of course, that a clumsy or inappropriate pun is ten times worse than no pun at all. The best advice for the beginning writer, consequently, is to pun rarely and then only in light, informal, and personal writing.

SYLLEPSIS

Another figure used for verbal humor is syllepsis, which comes from a Greek work meaning "yoking together." Syllepsis occurs when one word syntactically governs two or more other words in some unusual fashion. Often the result is a parallel construction in which two or more words of different weight or kind are yoked together for comic effect: "He entered the room with dignity and Mrs. Parkes-Fenton." A combination of punning and syllepsis was used by Mark Twain to berate the German language for its unreasonable difficulties:

> Now there are more adjectives in this language than there are black cats in Switzerland, and they must all be as elaborately declined as the examples above suggested. Difficult? — troublesome? — these words cannot describe it. I heard a California student in Heidelberg say, in one of his calmest moods, that he would rather decline two drinks than one German adjective. *A Tramp Abroad*

ALLUSIONS

The last of the verbal figures of speech we shall treat in this chapter is allusion, a common and important figure that consists of referring to specific persons, places, and things, whether real or imaginary. The writer obtains most of his allusions from classical mythology, the Bible, literature — especially the plays of Shakespeare — history, and geography. Quotations from famous works can likewise count as allusions. The writer who is fond of allusions is likely to draw from several of these sources in a single paragraph as F. L. Lucas does in an observation about cleanliness and health in the eighteenth century:

> The Renaissance, though it returned to the springs of Helicon, did not return to Roman baths. Even the Age of Reason was slow to apply reason to its health. Our eighteenth century largely over-ate and over-drank, and paid for it yelling with the gout. Even Swift, whom one tends to picture lean as Cassius, was really, as Thackeray reminds us, fat. 'His happy constitution,' writes Lady Mary Wortley Montagu of Fielding, '(even when he had, with great pains, half demolished it) made him forget everything when he was before a venison-pasty, or over a flask of champagne.' Similarly Horace Walpole, of the gentlemen of Norfolk: 'I here every day see men who are mountains of roast beef, and only seem just roughly hewn out into the outlines of the human form, like the giant-rock at Pratolino.' And indeed it is enough to recall the menus in Parson Woodforde's journal, or Boswell's alcoholic confessions. *The Greatest Problem*

In this paragraph we see most of the common purposes of allusion. Most important of these, perhaps, is the use of allusion as a method of paragraph development: the writer turns to history or literature or to a combination of sources for examples to support his topic sentence. In addition, allusions are often the basis of other figures, particularly metaphor and simile. Here "the springs of Helicon" is a metaphor; Cassius and "the giant-rock at Pratolino" form similes. A more general purpose, like that of all figurative language, is emphasis. This paragraph gains in force because the writer gives us two eye-witness accounts of the overindulgence he is describing; instead of generalities we have the much more interesting specific references to Swift, Fielding, Parson Woodforde, and Boswell. Allusions also help the writer to establish and maintain a definite tone, for allusions usually have strong connotations which define a writer's attitude toward his subject and his readers.

Allusions, moreover, have two general advantages. First, they are economical, being capable of saying a maximum amount in a minimum of space. Anyone who has read Boswell's *Journals*, for example, will understand what a world of implication there is in the phrase "Boswell's alcoholic confessions." A second advantage is that allusions give pleasure to both writer and reader: the writer enjoys being able to recall and use the knowledge he has gained from reading; for the reader there is the pleasure of recognition, realizing, for example, that the writer is alluding not so much to the Cassius of history in general as to the Cassius of Shakespeare, about whom Shakespeare's Caesar said:

> Let me have men about me that are fat;
> Sleek-headed men and such as sleep o' nights;
> Yond' Cassius has a lean and hungry look;
> He thinks too much: such men are dangerous.

Some readers, too, may recall that Thackeray was often unsympathetic to Swift in his essay on the English humorists of the eighteenth century. But, on the other hand, some readers may not know anything about "the springs of Helicon" or Henry Fielding or James Boswell, and to them the passage will seem mysterious. The disadvantage of using allusions is that one must be reasonably sure they give one's readers pleasure instead of pain; used inappropriately or upon the wrong occasion they become a severe liability.

Summary

Prose as well as poetry uses figures of speech for the purposes of clarity, emphasis, tone, and pleasure. But figurative language in prose should always speed comprehension. It is not decoration but a means of communicating. Most figures are either figures of comparison or figures of contrast. The most frequent and most useful figures are metaphors — figures of comparison. In general they help the writer to relate unfamiliar ideas and experiences to things familiar and easy to grasp. Because they can be blended into a discussion in various and subtle, yet striking forms, metaphors are the most useful of all figures. Metaphors, however, require careful handling if they are to succeed. They should be fresh and original; they should not be faulty or mixed; they must be appropriate to the writer's level of usage and his context; they must not be used by the dozen in a small space.

A second major class of verbal figures depends upon some kind of contrast either in grammatical structure or in sense. Because most comedy depends upon contrasts between things as they are and things as they ought to be, the figures of contrast are often employed in humor and satire. Of the figures of contrast the most important are overstatement, understatement, and irony. Overstatement and understatement are both powerful devices of emphasis, but which one a writer prefers depends upon his temperament, his subject, and his audience. Many rhetoricians regard understatement as the more forceful of the two, and so it is, provided the writer's audience is fairly well educated; otherwise, as a general rule, overstatement is probably more effective. Like understatement, irony is an entertaining and subtle form of emphasis. It is a favorite device of Voltaire, Swift, and other great satirists. It can be gentle and good-natured or it can be as harsh and corrosive as any kind of utterance in English — but only for the right audience. Allusions, also, should be adapted to a particular audience. Properly used, they are forceful, economical, and pleasing.

Looking back at our brief account, we can now hazard one or two broad observations about figurative language. The first concerns the answer to the question beginning writers sometimes ask, "Can you learn how to create good figures of speech, especially metaphors?" The answer, as, alas, it sometimes must be, is "Yes and no." Yes, because the student who becomes aware of the varieties of figurative language, who begins to notice them in his reading, who collects and studies examples will doubtless be able to learn something through imitation. And the student can learn also from trying, failing, and correcting his mistakes, for in the beginning he must expect failures just as one takes spills in learning to ski or makes noises in learning to play a musical instrument. Study, practice, failure, and correction will generally improve the writer's ability to use figurative language in the service of most workaday prose. But in another sense the answer is "No." The ability to use a high order of figurative language is an endowment which is not equally distributed. The power to see connections and relationships where none are apparent is a function of the imagination in its highest sense — the instrument of the great artist and scientist. This thought, however, leads us to a second and more comforting observation, which is that figurative language is not the essential characteristic of good prose, even prose in the first rank. Clarity of diction, forceful and economical sentence structure, a distinct pattern of organization — these are the fundamentals of rhetoric.

Exercises

1. Evaluate the figurative language in the following examples. Explain why you think each one is successful or unsuccessful. Decide whether each metaphor is primarily explanatory, emphatic, or tonal.

    1. Well, then, if books are pouring out at this rate, the first and main principle of selection is not to meddle with them at all if you can help it. Keep out of their way. Blow your horn vigorously and thread

your way through the flock till you can get a clear road on the far side, and then buzz off. HILAIRE BELLOC

2. In Edward Ponderevo, he [H. G. Wells] drew the portrait of a small man boosted up to the heavens by tremendous accidental opportunities, who flames there like an exploding rocket, then hurtles down to earth again as a charred and extinguished stick. PETER QUENNELL

3. President Roosevelt took the helm and with rapier-like strokes slew the monster of depression that had our economy on the ropes. STUDENT

4. My object is not to describe Burke's style, but to examine its texture and to discover, if I can, the methods he employed by means of words to produce his effects. Hazlitt has set forth the rich succulence of the dish; my aim is to ferret out the ingredients that give it savour. W. SOMERSET MAUGHAM

5. Simple style is like white light. It is complex but its complexity is not obvious. ANATOLE FRANCE

6. [About New Yorkers and New York] Hard-mouthed, hard-eyed, and strident-tongued, with their million hard gray faces, they streamed past upon the streets forever, like a single animal, with the sinuous and baleful convolutions of an enormous reptile. And the magical and shining air — the strange, subtle and enchanted weather, was above them, and the buried men were strewn through the earth on which they trod, and a bracelet of great tides was flashing round them, and the enfabled rock on which they swarmed swung eastward in the marches of the sun into eternity, and was masted like a ship with its terrific towers, and was flung with a lion's port between its tides into the very maw of the infinite, all-taking ocean. THOMAS WOLFE

7. [About Lake Ontario] Its glint was inexplicably sinister and dead, like the glint on glasses worn by a blind man. RUPERT BROOKE

8. The driveway twisted up to the big white house like a snake in the grass. STUDENT

9. Gleason's character was formed in a poverty-run boyhood . . . and an affection-starved adolescence. . . . Out of that flesh grew benign tumors of driving energy and unsatisfied appetite that stuck to his psyche and swelled into a galloping disease that at once blights and regenerates him. *TV Guide*

10. The style is not, as philosophic style should be, so transparent a medium that one looks straight through it at the object, forgetting

that it is there; it is too much like a window of stained glass which, because of its very richness, diverts attention to itself.

BRAND BLANSHARD

2. Identify the figures of speech in the following:

1. Newspeak, indeed, differed from almost all other languages in that its vocabulary grew smaller instead of larger every year. Each reduction was a gain, since the smaller the area of choice, the smaller the temptation to take thought. Ultimately it was hoped to make articulate speech issue from the larynx without involving the higher brain centers at all. This aim was frankly admitted in the Newspeak word *duckspeak,* meaning "to quack like a duck." Like various other words in the B vocabulary, *duckspeak* was ambivalent in meaning. Provided that the opinions which were quacked out were orthodox ones, it implied nothing but praise, and when the *Times* referred to one of the orators of the Party as a *doubleplusgood duckspeaker* it was paying a warm and valued compliment.

GEORGE ORWELL

2. Man is born broken. He lives by mending. The grace of God is glue!

EUGENE O'NEILL

3. For prose is so humble that it can go anywhere; no place is too low, too sordid, or too mean for it to enter. It is infinitely patient, too, humbly acquisitive. It can lick up with its long glutinous tongue the most minute fragments of fact and mass them into the most subtle labyrinths, and listen silently at doors behind which only a murmur, only a whisper, is to be heard. With all the suppleness of a tool which is in constant use it can follow the windings and record the changes which are typical of the modern mind.

VIRGINIA WOOLF

4. Nearly all our professional historians are poor men holding college posts, and they are ten times more cruelly beset by the ruling politico-plutocratic-social oligarchy than ever the Prussian professors were by the Hohenzollerns. Let them diverge in the slightest from what is the current official doctrine, and they are turned out of their chairs with a ceremony suitable for the expulsion of a drunken valet.

H. L. MENCKEN

5. Famagusta reminded me irresistibly of Metro-Goldwyn-Mayer's back lot at Culver City. There, under the high fog of the Pacific, one used to wander between the façades of Romeo and Juliet's Verona into Tarzan's jungle, and out again, through Bret Harte, into Harun al-Rashid and *Pride and Prejudice.* Here in Cyprus, the mingling of styles and epochs is no less extravagant, and the sets are not merely realistic — they are real. At Salamis, in the suburbs of Famagusta, one can shoot *Quo Vadis* against a background of solid masonry

and genuine marble. And downtown, overlooking the harbor, stands the Tower of Othello (screen play by William Shakespeare, additional dialogue by Louella Katz); and the Tower of Othello is not the cardboard gazebo to which the theater has accustomed us, but a huge High Renaissance gun emplacement that forms part of a defense system as massive, elaborate and scientific as the Maginot Line. ALDOUS HUXLEY

6. As a result, academic institutions are not gentle civilized retreats, high, high above the dark jungle of business. Alas, at precisely the time that business has become somewhat less feral, academia now dances to the beat of the tom-tom. DAVID BOROFF

7. The fact of having been born is a bad augury for immortality. GEORGE SANTAYANA

25
PRINCIPLES OF GOOD DICTION

Introduction

With some notion of just how complex language can be, both in its literal and in its figurative use, we are ready to ask, what "rules" or principles govern the choice of words? Generalizations applying to all kinds of language are difficult to formulate. Language has so many purposes and so many different users, its resources are so vast that general pronouncements about good diction must be hedged with qualifications and exceptions. We shall simplify the problem a little by excluding the diction of poetry and of prose fiction and drama. At times what we say will also apply to them, but chiefly we shall treat of exposition, the workaday writing people do in their business or professional capacity. Yet even here the principles of good diction are often relative, and therefore the basic tenent of good diction must be this: what constitutes good diction depends upon the temperament of the writer, the occasion on which he writes, his purpose, and his readers. At any time these considerations may justify a writer's qualifying or setting aside any rhetorical rule. Whatever most exactly conveys the writer's thought and feeling to his readers is good diction for his purpose; whatever interferes with this conveyance is poor diction. Understanding this, we can begin to identify the qualities of effective diction.

The Qualities of Good Diction

CLARITY

In talking about sentences we said that clarity means not simply that a sentence makes sense to the reader, but that it makes the sense the writer intended. The same definition applies to diction: a word is clear if the reader understands it in the sense in which the writer used it. Clarity in diction is of fundamental importance in composition, for words are the primary mediators between the mind of the writer and that of the reader. But, as someone has said, the most absolute break in all nature is between one human mind and another. At best communication is only approximate. In spite of the wonders it can work, language contains a significant amount of built-in imprecision; there are more things to be named and more shades of thought to be expressed than we have words for. Consequently, a word may name or express more than one thing and so open the door to ambiguity. In addition, a writer often has to choose among a number of words that designate very roughly the same thing, and readers, even when they agree about the designation of a word, will probably have quite different associations with it. If added to limitations like these, the speaker or writer uses words carelessly or inappropriately, the confusion is serious indeed. Keeping potential confusion to a minimum is the first job of every writer. His success depends upon a careful choice of words so that they designate only what he intends to designate, and upon his skill in making his readers feel what he wants them to feel. All this sounds simple and commonsensical enough, yet unnecessary OBSCURITY is all too frequent, especially in the prose of inexperienced writers. What are the causes of this needless confusion and what can the writer do about it?

One of the most common and most serious is ignorance about how words behave. A writer must know, for example, that there are no *exact* synonyms in English. Although several words may point in the same direction, no two words convey precisely the same thing. Consider for a moment the following list of related words and phrases:

destitute	unmoneyed	financial difficulties
indigent	penniless	strapped
impoverished	bankrupt	hard up
necessitous	beggared	broke
insolvent	poor	down on one's uppers
impecunious	needy	tapped out
poverty-stricken	straitened	

This is the sort of collection found in a thesaurus or a dictionary of synonyms, but it would be a mistake to suppose that these words and phrases are interchangeable. Some, like "destitute" and "indigent," are almost twins; but others, "needy" and "insolvent," for instance, are distant cousins. Each word has a slightly different denotation and connotation from the others. To be "destitute" is to be without the means of supporting life;

to be "impoverished" is to be poor after having enjoyed wealth; to be "impecunious" is, often, to become poor as the result of folly or extravagance. Each word or phrase, furthermore, expresses a different attitude or tone. "To be down on one's uppers" is mildly humorous in contrast to the more blunt and serious "poverty-striken." In any sentence, then, one of these words ought to indicate the writer's meaning more accurately than any of its synonyms. Awareness that related words aften designate important distinctions and express different nuances is one trait of a careful writer. Insensitivity to this fact, failure to take advantage of the precision in words results in prose that, like a bad photograph, is slightly out of focus. One cause of obscurity, then, is ignoring the fact that words can mean the "same thing" only in a very rough sense.

Another form of obscurity is the MALAPROPISM, named after Mrs. Malaprop, a character in Sheridan's play *The Rivals*, an ignorant, pretentious woman, who constantly confuses words with similar pronunciations but different meanings. These are examples from college themes:

1. From the street music and revelry were *emulating*.
2. Russia started to *transcend* from one epoch to another during the twentieth century.
3. The leisure class tends to be *immobile* to change.
4. The hero's actions *promote* the gods to wrath.
5. Geoffrey Chaucer was the first important *figurehead* in English literature.

Each of these sentences says something different from what the writer intended, if, in fact, it is not absolute nonsense. While one can sometimes guess at what word the writer had in mind, the malapropism is distracting, if not downright misleading. Though it is not the most common error in diction, the malapropism is one of the more serious.

A third cause of obscurity is a fondness for GENERAL TERMS and abstractions. If a writer tells his reader, "In high school we read a number of literary works" and says no more, then the reader is left to guess what "number" and "literary works" mean. *King Lear*? *Paradise Lost*? *Moby Dick*? *Ethan Frome*? *Rebecca of Sunnybrook Farm*? In this context the abstract phrase "literary works" conceals a high degree of ambiguity and potential misunderstanding. The writer should have offered examples or, preferably, have avoided the abstraction altogether: "In my senior year of high school we read *Hamlet* and Arnold Bennett's novel *The Old Wives' Tale*." A more serious example is the following passage from a piece of art criticism; it is obscure to most readers because of its many undefined abstract terms:

> Nothing demonstrates the subjective determination of the object more clearly than the fact that even its most matter-of-fact representations seem mined by our attitudes toward it. Reality, exposed to the sharp catalyst of modern doubt, has separated into a number of irreducible components, each of which has given rise to a realist school. Traditional realist figuration has shriveled up, struck by the chlorotic exhaustion typical of a *fin de race*. The great merit of Gruber was to have achieved the fusion between the "wan" look of realism and the data of our time — in short, to have made the extenuated signs meaningful again.
>
> PIERRE SCHNEIDER, "FACETS OF REALISM"

Any reader who has puzzled over this sort of thing can see why abstractions, especially when they are key terms, need to be defined and illustrated as soon as they are used. There are hundreds of such terms that crop up in modern exposition. The following list is typical (you should be able to add others):

realism	progress	socialized medicine
liberty	idealism	the common man
democracy	Romanticism	the American way of life
beauty	spiritual values	the finer things of life

The point about such words is not that they are meaningless and ought at all costs to be avoided; it would be difficult to write about modern political systems if the words "democracy" and "liberty" were ruled off the course. Rather the point is that such words will be useless the writer is careful to make very clear what he is using them to mean.

A failure to select the exact word among a number of so-called synonyms, the use of malapropisms, and a reliance upon undefined generalizations all lead to obscurity. But these errors are only the immediate causes of obscurity. Behind them lie certain habits of mind. One such habit is not showing consideration for readers. Unless a writer constantly looks at his words through the eyes of his readers, he may find that he is talking to himself. Good diction, like other aspects of good style, is a matter of good manners and of making a reasonable estimate of what a reader may be expected to know and what he must be told. Another mental trait that leads to obscurity is laziness. Very few people can say exactly what they mean the first time they put pen to paper. Perhaps the most important aspect of revising is sharpening diction, for many times the first word that comes to mind is not the most precise word. But the habit most certain to produce obscurity is pretentiousness. The pretentious writer assumes that the bigger the word, the grander and more impressive its meaning. The result is often something like this:

> Society today exists in a dynamic, never-ending civilization of progressive mores. "Progressive" in this sense does not comply a rate of betterment, rather a constant change of industry and general concepts. This thought can most clearly be explained by social and political changes and their individual action.

These three sentences contain almost all the characteristics of bad diction and several kinds of obscurity. But most of the errors reflect the attempt to make a simple idea — that we live in times of social and political change — seem difficult and impressive.

Clarity, then, depends upon knowing how words work and upon being honest with oneself and considering one's reader. To write clearly every writer must learn as much as he can about the behavior of words and acquire respect for their potential accuracy and subtlety. He needs to use his dictionary often, both when he reads and when he writes. He should use concrete language as much as his subject permits, and if he must employ abstractions he ought to define and illustrate them. Above all, he must be intellectually honest. The effective writer impresses his readers with the clarity of his thought, not with the sound of polysyllables.

APPROPRIATENESS

There can be little question that in expository writing the chief virtue of diction is clarity. About ranking the other desirable qualities of diction there may be some legitimate disagreement, but nearly as important as clarity is appropriateness. Appropriateness means that the overtones of a word — the associations it commonly suggests to us — are in keeping with the context in which the word has been set and with the writer's purpose. To say that something "stinks" may be clear enough; but it is easy to imagine occasions when "stink," while wonderfully accurate, would be woefully inappropriate. Not all words, obviously, fit all occasions; for words, like people, are known by the company they keep. Words may appear frequently in one context and seldom in another. *Indigent* has one kind of linguistic companionship and *broke* a completely different one. It is useful to think of language as divided roughly into "levels of usage" (or better, perhaps, into "divisions of usage"). One of these is formal English, whose purpose is to communicate precise, often technical, information as clearly and as efficiently as possible. Formal English is the language of encyclopedia articles, most textbooks, college term papers, most scholarly and professional writing (especially that in learned journals), and the language of law and government. It draws upon a large vocabulary of technical terms and words derived directly or indirectly from Latin and Greek. A good example of formal English is the following passage by Charlton Hinman, who is discussing how damaged printing type is a clue to understanding how the First Folio of Shakespeare was printed:

> We cannot possibly hope to identify every imperfect type in the Folio, to recognize infallibly every occurrence of every such type throughout the book. Some types, although imperfect, are not really distinctive. And others may be too much so; for the most grossly damaged types do not necessarily provide the best evidence. Easy though they may be to recognize, they are not likely to appear often enough to be very useful, since any especially striking abnormality is, as a rule, soon noticed by the printers themselves, who at once cull the peccant type. On the other hand a type with a relatively small but nevertheless well-defined peculiarity may continue in use, and remain easily recognizable, for surprising lengths of time. Particularly valuable are such types, which are numerous; and also types with small but multiple defects — a type showing both a nick and a bend, say, being especially easy to identify. It should be appreciated, however, that some highly distinctive types gradually become more or less unrecognizable, and hence unreliable as evidence, as wear or further injury blurs the impressions they give.
>
> *The Printing and Proof-Reading of the First Folio of Shakespeare*

The vocabulary of this passage — unlike the technical vocabulary of some formal writing — is not difficult to follow. There are only a few technical terms ("neck," "bend"), and while the diction is quite Latinate most of these words ("peccant" is an exception) are familiar enough. But the frequency of the Latinate words, which are certainly appropriate to the subject, helps to make the passage formal. The writer makes no effort to suggest conversation; there are no contractions or colloquialisms. This is the voice of a specialist addressing a special audience. Sentence structure, as well as diction, contributes to the formal tone. Since the subject matter of formal exposition is often complicated and technical, the writer will employ more dependent constructions than appear in an informal style. This means more punctuation, a slower movement, and longer sentences. In short, of all levels of usage, formal English least resembles conversation; and its vocabulary is often technical and Latinate.

But the purpose of formal English is not to give the writer an opportunity to display his collection of big words; its aims are clarity, precision, and efficiency. If the writer of formal English chooses a word like *destitute*, he does so because, for his purpose, *destitute* is more precise than the general term *poor*. Longer sentences appear in formal writing, not because the writer wants to display his ingenuity, but because the subject demands them. It is true, of course, that clarity and efficiency are characteristics of all good prose, but the subject and purpose of formal writing require that they be achieved, at times, in special ways.

At the opposite end of the scale of usage is VULGATE, the language of uneducated speakers. Vulgate often includes slang, dialect words, and unconventional grammar. It may include also the technical slang of shops and trades, and the special, restricted argot of groups like tramps and convicts. Vulgate is almost always a spoken language, except in the work of novelists and playwrights whose characters speak vulgate English. In comparison with formal English, the vocabulary of vulgate is limited, but the words of vulgate are usually concrete, and at their best they are colorful and forceful. Mark Twain's Huckleberry Finn speaks one form of vulgate:

> Next, for about a half an hour, I whoops now and then; at last I hears the answer a long ways off, and tries to follow it, but I couldn't do it, and directly I judged I'd got into a nest of towheads, for I had little dim glimpses of them on both sides of me — sometimes just a narrow channel between them, and some that I couldn't see I knowed was there because I'd hear the wash of current against the old dead brush and trash that hung over the banks. Well, I warn't long losing the whoops down amongst the towheads; and I only tried to chase them a little while, anyway, because it was worse than chasing a Jack-o-lantern. You never knowed a sound dodge around so, and swap places so quick and so much.
>
> *Huckleberry Finn*

This is vivid description and skillful characterization. The language, furthermore, is interesting in itself and pleasing in its rhythm. Like all good vulgate this is clear, but it is clear only to a restricted audience. Probably its unconventional grammar will seem obscure only to foreigners, but the dialect words will be obscure to many American readers. More than one reader will be put off by "towhead" and "Jack-o-lantern," dialect terms that may not even be listed in the dictionary. The vocabulary of vulgate, then, has the disadvantage of often being obscure to all but a relatively small audience. But there is no denying the concreteness of that vocabulary, its potential eloquence, and the beauty of its rhythm when it is properly handled. There is both eloquence and beauty in these passages from John M. Synge's *The Playboy of the Western World,* passages modeled on the natural speech of Irish country people:

> It's well you know what call I have. It's well you know it's a lonesome thing to be passing small towns with the lights shining sideways when the night is down, or going in strange places with a dog noising before you and a dog noising behind, or drawn to the cities where you'd hear a voice kissing and talking deep love in every shadow of the ditch, and you passing on with an empty, hungry stomach failing from your heart.

> There was not, but a story filled half a page of the hanging of a man. Ah, that should be a fearful end, young fellow, and it worst of all for a man who destroyed his da, for the like of him would get small mercies, and when it's dead he is, they'd put him in a narrow grave, with cheap sacking wrapping him round, and pour down quicklime on his head, the way you'd see a woman pouring any frish-frash from a cup.

These passages by Twain and Synge illustrate vulgate at its best, purged of repetition, irrelevancy, and ambiguity. But even in its finest, most expressive form vulgate is not appropriate for expository writing. Its vocabulary is limited and obscure and smacks too much of the attitudes and opinions of ignorant people.

In between vulgate and highly formal English lies the informal style. Most of the written prose we encounter in the course of an ordinary day is informal English. It is the language of the better magazines and newspapers, of familiar essays and works of general nonfiction such as travel books and popularizations of technical subjects. Most freshman compositions will be written in informal rather than in formal English. Informal prose employs shorter and simpler sentences than formal. It may, from time to time, use contractions and colloquialisms, and even slang if the writer can be reasonably sure that his audience will understand him and if his prose serves a limited audience for a limited purpose. Informal prose suggests, though it does not reproduce, the conversation of an educated man. E. B. White is a master of informal prose:

> My own house is about a hundred and forty years old — three times my age — yet I, a mere upstart, approached it as though it didn't know its business and weren't quite fit for me the way it was, when the truth, as I now see it, was that I was not quite fit for *it.*

> Quite aside from the expense and inconvenience of razing one's newly acquired home, there is a subtle insult in the maneuver, the unmistakable implication that the former inhabitants lived either in squalor or in innocence, and that one's neighbors, in houses of similar design and appointments, are also living in squalor or innocence. Neither is true. But the demolition goes right ahead. The place of a newly arriving city man always looks more like a battleground than a home: earthworks are thrown up around the foundation wall, chimneys are reduced to rubble, and on the front lawn a cement mixer appears, with its little wheels and big round abdomen. It would be a comical sight if it were not so dispiriting.
>
> *One Man's Meat*

Much of the diction in this passage — "unmistakable implication," "maneuver," "appointments," "demolition," for example — is also appropriate to formal English. But the subject, the personal tone, the contractions, and expressions like "goes right ahead," "didn't know its business," and "as I now see it" all indicate the essential informality of the prose.

As this illustration suggests, any classification of prose into a mere three kinds is bound to be crude; there will be instances when informal prose shades off into formal writing on the one hand and into vulgate, or near-vulgate, on the other. Moreover, all levels, especially that of informal prose, include variations of sentence style and diction. Still, these classifications are useful, a reminder once more that rather than appealing to some absolute standard of "correctness," we are wiser to think of appropriateness in deciding what words and patterns are effective for a particular subject and purpose.

Not only must diction be appropriate, but it must be consistent as well. It is difficult to mix levels of usage effectively. Gifted comic writers can manage such mixtures, and often, indeed, attain some of their funniest effects that way; S. J. Perelman and P. G. Wodehouse are notable examples. Less gifted writers, however, and especially expository writers, are well advised not to mix vulgate and formal diction. Observe, for instance, the unhappy result of INCONSISTENT DICTION in the following discussion of art criticism (the writer's argument is that all judgments about art are relative):

> . . . let's return now to the previous subject, namely, the real motive in these "puny mannikins' " hate of relativism. It's that relativism thwarts their ambition to grow up and be the same size as other fellows. You can't four-flush under relativism. You can't cover your own inadequacies in tall talk, whereas under Absolutism you can — and do. Under Absolutism you step up onto the rostrum

> and deliver your world-shattering decisions (based on nothing) about any subject you think you can get the biggest kick out of. What can they do to you? Not a thing. It's exhilarating. And that's not all. You can also bawl out celebrities — big international ones; call them "fourth rate hacks," "nine-day wonders," "juvenile bunglers," "pathological screw-balls"; anything that bolsters your ego. It's more fun than getting up in a high tree and shooting lions, tigers and elephants, as the beaters drive them by.
>
> And the way the big dopes react! They cringe. They take you seriously. THEODORE L. SHAW, *Precious Rubbish*

The problem of whether judgments about art are hopelessly relative or can claim some objective validity is a philosophical issue that requires a calm, reasonable frame of mind. The highly charged, emotional diction of this passage is plainly inappropriate and reveals that the writer is hardly arguing with the detachment and open-mindedness his subject warrants. Colloquialisms like "four-flush," "tall talk," and "bawl out" are simply bad diction here.

But if it is usually good practice to avoid mixing extremely different levels of usage in exposition, it must be pointed out that twentieth-century prose shows a growing tendency to treat formal subjects more informally than was common in the past. Even scholarly writers are tending to be casual and to seem no more artificial in their diction or patterned in their sentence structure than is absolutely necessary. The following passage from a critical discussion of Shakespeare is an example:

> Shakespeare's mature conception of tragedy had not, at this time, taken shape. He was still working to the mediaeval idea of tragedy as a cautionary tale, illustrating that man is never out of range of the side-swipes of fate. This is the view we find in Chaucer. 'Tragedie is to seyn a dite of a prosperitie or a time, that endeth in wretchednesse.' High-born persons were the natural protagonists of tragedy, because tragic misfortune strikes at people who are conspicuously getting away with it, and thus open to the temptations of pride and forgetfulness of God's power. Mediaeval tragedy did not site the tragic element within man's nature, except in so far as that nature was corrupted by the Fall. It was content to point out the inescapable presence of calamity. The lesson it taught was one of piety and resignation; man was to look for mercies from the hand of God and nowhere else.
>
> JOHN WAIN, *The Living World of Shakespeare*

Colloquialisms like "the side-swipes of fate" and "getting away with it," while not to everyone's taste, do not jar the reader as does slang like "big dopes" in the passage on art criticism. It is even arguable that such idioms add interest and that their very contemporaneity enables the writer to leap across time and bring to life an older way of looking at tragedy. But slipping so neatly from one level of usage to another requires a good deal of taste and experience. A beginner ought to try it only very cautiously.

SIMPLICITY

It would be manifestly untrue to say that all good writing is easy to read, that simplicity is the same thing as simpleness. Simplicity means ease of comprehension relative to subject and purpose, and by that standard simple prose may not be easy to read in any absolute sense. Philosophical prose, even good philosophical prose, usually demands a good deal of hard thought, and so does much writing about scientific subjects. When a subject is subtle or technical, it will need a subtle or technical vocabularly. Yet it is true that no good writer employs complicated diction merely because it *is* complicated. A good writer uses words as simple as his subject, tone, and purpose allow. Understood in this way, simplicity is a virtue of all good prose, however learned or commonplace its subject matter. At one end of the scale is this uncomplicated but appropriately worded paragraph by Hal Borland:

> We have found that in the Spring or Fall all kinds of fish, even sunfish, can be caught in either sun or shade. In the summer most fish except sunnies seem to prefer shaded water. Early morning and late afternoon are the best times for Summer fishing, though we have struck a school of hungry yellow perch in sunny water at 2 o'clock on a hot July afternoon. Perch, by the way, run in schools. Catch one and you probably can catch more in the same place. We sometimes drift down the river, slow-trolling with a small spoon ahead of a big worm until a perch strikes. Then we anchor and fish, usually with luck. We have found some of our choice perch holes that way, places that looked so unpromising we would have passed them by. *Beyond Your Doorstep*

Mr. Borland's diction is clear, concrete, lean, and easy on the reader, partly because most of the words are short and familiar. Many of these words derive from the original Anglo-Saxon foundation of our language: *spring, fall, fish, sun, shade, water, early, late, morning, hot, catch, spoon, way.* Long words, abstract words, and technical terms, on the other hand, are likely to stem from Latin or Greek. But it would be a mistake to conclude that simple Saxon words are necessarily preferable to Latinate ones. Often they are. But sometimes they are not. For one thing, many Latinate words in English are just as short and forceful as the Saxon ones. In Mr. Borland's paragraph, for instance, *place, river, anchor,* and *passed* all come ultimately from Latin in addition to the more obvious cases of *except, prefer,* and *unpromising.* For another thing, a Latinism may be more precise for a given context than a Saxon word of approximately the same meaning. There are occasions, for instance, when *torrid* is preferable to the more general term *hot.* Moreover, it is not always easy to tell by looking if a word is Latin or Saxon. The best thing is to use plain and unpretentious words no matter what their origin. All other things being equal, short, concrete words are better than long, abstract, unfamiliar ones.

The subject, then, largely dictates how "simple" diction can be. The diction of the following passage, for example is vastly different from that of the paragraph about fishing. Yet given its technical nature — the method of reasoning used by Socrates — it is as simple as it well can be:

> This account of what may almost be called the 'conversion' of Socrates implies two things. It implies a peculiar method; and implies a peculiar doctrine. The method is the method of dialectic. In place of the Ionic method of adumbration, in cryptic prose or riddling verse, of results already obtained; in place, again, of the sophistic method of ordered arrangement of topics according to a set scheme in an eloquent discourse, Socrates pursued the method of question and answer, and he pursued it everywhere and among all sorts of men. It was a definite method, as much (we may almost say) as the scholastic method of the Middle Ages: there were rules for the adoption of the theme of discussion, and rules for the relevant answering of questions. It was a method unpleasant for the victim, and a method which might become merely eristic, turning to argument in any direction for the sake of argument; but was, all the same, in the hands of Socrates a genuine organ of truth. ERNEST BARKER, *Greek Political Theory*

This paragraph contains as high a proportion of Latinate words as the preceding extract about fishing contains words of Saxon origin. Yet expressions like *dialectic, eloquent discourse, scholastic method, relevant,* and *eristic* have no simpler equivalents. To express an idea such as *scholastic method* in *plain* language would require half a dozen words, if not half a dozen sentences. The long, abstract, technical terms of philosophy are appropriate in this passage, which is as clear and as simple as its subject permits. Simplicity, then, does not imply naïveté or the avoidance of "hard" words. It is as much a virtue of difficult as of easy prose, provided the writer employs diction no more technical than his purpose requires.

All too often, however, writers use big words to express simple ideas. The result is a pompous, usually flabby, kind of prose, called jargon or, more colorfully, GOBBLEDEGOOK. The following quotation from Thorstein Veblen's *Theory of the Leisure Class* (1899) is not the worst example of gobbledegook one could find, but it will serve; Veblen is discussing American attitudes toward sports:

> There is a feeling — usually vague and not commonly avowed in so many words by the apologist himself, but ordinarily perceptible in the manner of his discourse — that these sports, as well as the general range of predaceous impulses and habits of thought which underlie the sporting character, do not altogether commend themselves to common sense. "As to the majority of murderers, they are very incorrect characters." This aphorism offers a valuation of the predaceous temperament, and of the disciplinary effects of its overt expression and exercise, as seen from the moralist's point of view. As such it affords an indication of what is the deliverance of the sober sense of mature men as to the degree of availability of the predatory habit of mind for the purposes of the collective life. It is felt that the presumption is against any activity which involves habituation to the predatory attitude, and that the burden of proof lies with those who speak for the rehabilitation of the predaceous temper and for the practices which strengthen it. There is a strong body of popular sentiment in favor of diversions and enterprise of the kind in question; but there is at the same time present in the community a pervading sense that this ground of sentiment wants legitimation. The required legitimation is ordinarily sought by showing that although sports are substantially of a predatory, socially disintegrating effect; although their proximate effect runs in the direction of reversion to propensities that are industrially disserviceable; yet indirectly and remotely — by some not readily comprehensible process of polar induction or counter-irritation perhaps — sports are conceived to foster a habit of mind that is serviceable for the social or industrial purpose. That is to say, although sports are essentially of the nature of invidious exploit, it is presumed that by some remote and obscure effect they result in the growth of a temperament conducive to non-invidious work.

Veblen's point here is not really so difficult. Why does he, or any writer of gobbledegook, take such pains to obfuscate a simple idea? Perhaps it is love of elaboration for its own sake. Perhaps it is to conceal the fact that an idea is so obvious it hardly needs to be said. Or perhaps it is an attempt to impress readers with the writer's profundity and learning. If so, it is ironical that gobbledegook impresses no one but the ill-educated reader, who, of course, doesn't really understand it at all. Experienced readers will be irritated at having to work so hard to get so little and will regard the writer as either a charlatan or a very bad workman. Reading gobbledegook is like hacking one's way through dense jungle, whereas ideally the reader should move easily along a wide and straight path laid out by the writer. In simpler language Veblen's point seems to be (one cannot be certain):

> Apologists for sports often betray an uneasiness about their moral value. Mature men plainly condemn sports, and since sports foster aggression and violence it is up to their defenders to prove their social usefulness. Even many who favor sports have doubts of their social value, but they argue that while sports may sometimes be harmful, they are, in some mysterious way, ultimately beneficial.

This revision, of course, does not say exactly what Veblen says. The tone is much less formal; the subject no longer seems so remote and difficult, capable of being treated only by someone possessing esoteric knowledge. But the revision is clear and simple. It neither bestows upon the subject a dignity it scarcely deserves nor unduly burdens the reader with purely verbal difficulties.

Gobbledegook is especially common in business correspondence and in government documents. Nor is it unknown in academic writing. Professors have been guilty of dressing up simple ideas in elaborate verbal costume, striving to seem "learned" or "scientific." The result is usually something like this passage from a journal of educational psychology:

> A second consideration is the extent to which the present findings are generalizable to classroom instructional procedures other than programming. Systematic evaluation of the effects of spaced review under a variety of instructional conditions may indicate that retention is optimized not so much by instructional procedure per se as by temporal conditions employed in their presentation.

To distinguish between legitimate, useful technical language and gobbledegook is occasionally difficult. There are borderline cases. But most gobbledegook is unmistakable. Legitimate technical language is clear and concise; gobbledegook is obscure and wordy. (If you doubt the obscurity, try to translate into clear English the last sentence of the passage just quoted.)

If it is easy to see that simplicity is desirable, it is less easy to see how to achieve it. Essentially, simplicity is the result partly of intelligence, the ability to concentrate on what is important and set aside trivialities, and partly of honesty with oneself and consideration for one's reader. The honest writer, dealing with a simple and obvious point will leave it so, without trying to make it seem complicated. He will not deceive himself or others by his diction. More specifically, we can list these few principles that will help a writer keep his diction simple:

(1) Use as many short, concrete words as the subject allows. Although informal expository prose is not exactly the same as educated speech, it ought never to stray too far from such speech. "It is a remarkable thing," says G. H. Vallins, "that our spoken language even if halting and 'ungrammatical' is at least direct and forceful. We call a spade a spade. But immediately we begin to write or prepare a speech or lecture the language seems to formalise, to become abstract, to fall into set patterns. . . . Most of us, when we write, have a fear of dropping into colloquialisms and will go to almost any lengths of stilted periphrasis to avoid it." One might add that of the polysyllables which "formalise" written prose long nouns ending in *-tion* and *-sion* and adjectives ending in *-ible* and *-able* are especially frequent offenders.

(2) A large vocabulary of transitive verbs in the active voice contribute to a simple and forceful style. While the verb *to be* is the workhorse of English prose, the skillful writer does not use it when a more expressive verb is available. Veblen's sentence "There is a strong body of popular sentiment in favor of diversions and enterprise of the kind in question" might read in simpler form: "Popular sentiment strongly favors these sports."

(3) There is such a thing as being overly precise, of being more accurate than occasion and purpose require. Such pedantry is one form of gobbledegook. For example, a writer who is beginning to acquire the technical vocabulary of psychology or anatomy or economics is often tempted to display his new learning in a theme about a nontechnical subject. Simplicity is often a matter of appropriateness, and we may repeat the principle we stated at the beginning of this discussion: good diction is as plain, as simple, as easy as subject and purpose allow. Ernest Barker's discussion of Socrates is "simple" in this sense; Thorstein Veblen's discussion of sports is not.

ECONOMY

Our samples of gobbledegook are not only vague and pretentious, they are also verbose. Writers of gobbledegook like lots of sound and little sense, and simplifying their diction generally results in drastically shortening their sentences. Veblen, for example, often sacrifices economy and emphasis to his fondness for heavy, abstract nouns. What would be more forcefully expressed in a transitive verb, he turns into a noun ending in *-tion*. Instead of utilizing the subject-verb-object nexus to convey key ideas, he places key words in a series of prepositional phrases. Thus to express the simple thought "It shows that sober, mature men often condemn sports," Veblen writes:

> As such it affords an indication of what is the deliverance of the sober sense of mature men as to the degree of availability of the predatory habit of mind for the purposes of the collective life.

This kind of verbosity saps whatever strength and liveliness this prose might have. The best diction, on the other hand, does its job economically. This does not mean that good prose must read like a telegram; but it does mean that pruning whatever can be removed without damaging the subject and purpose will improve clarity, grace, and vigor. While there is no need to study economy in detail a second time (see Chapter 16), we can scarcely fail to note that economy is one of the most important characteristics of good diction.

EUPHONY

Diction is a matter of sound as well as of sense. As we saw in Chapter 19, words play a subtle melody of their own and their qualities of sound and rhythm contribute to tone. Some writers — James Joyce, for example — use sound as an important dimension of prose. Most expository writers, however, give little thought to sound effects. If they succeed in saying what they mean, this neglect does no real harm; for as someone has said, take care of the sense and the sound will take care of itself. Still, it is worth knowing what not to do; no writer ought to irritate and distract his readers with unpleasant sounds. One thing to avoid is EXCESSIVE ALLITERATION, which is clumsy because it calls attention to the writer's manner and so distracts the reader's attention from his matter. It is certainly true that a restrained use of alliteration can create prose of real beauty, especially when combined with the subtle varieties of rhyme called assonance and consonance:

> The rough sea near the beach glittered like gold; the deep green water, flecked with foam, was mingled with fire; the one boat that remained on it, tossing up and down near the beach, was like a boat of ebony in a glittering fiery sea.
>
> W. H. HUDSON, *Afoot in England*

Alliteration is not excessive here, though it is easy enough to find. Less readily apparent is the assonance — "deep green," "boat of ebony" — and the repetition of *-er* in "glittering fiery sea." The positive use of sound is not as likely to appear in sober exposition as it is in description and various kinds of emotive writing. But sound is one of the resources with which a writer works, and every student of composition should be aware of its power and of its limitations. And the limitations are real, as the first of the two following sentences reveals:

1. In addition, it was his initiation into desperation.

2. Somewhere, far away, our friends and relatives were humming and bustling, shaping and contriving, planning, disputing, getting, spending; but we were as gods, solidly occupied in doing nothing, our minds immaculate vacancies.

J. B. PRIESTLEY, "ON DOING NOTHING"

The first sentence is unpleasant because of ACCIDENTAL RHYME between words that are not grammatically parallel. In the second sentence, on the other hand, the *-ing* repetitions occur in a series of past progressive verbs; here the rhyme contributes to emphasis. Remember that when words are rhymed attention is drawn to them, and that if they cannot stand being thrown together, the rhyme is awkward and should be broken up.

EMPHASIS

A final and important characteristic of good diction is strength or emphasis. Vigorousness in diction often has its source in a large, wide-ranging, and lively vocabulary. Emphasis is a complex rather than a simple characteristic, not easy to separate from clarity, concreteness, simplicity, and economy. Any diction possessing all these qualities is almost sure to be vigorous as well. Still, diction that strikes us because of its forcefulness has something more. It is fresh and original. The vigorous writer has the happy talent of turning a phrase, of creating his own metaphors which say something new, or at least something old in a new and remarkable way:

1. None of the three [Diogenes, Socrates, and Solon] ever occupied his hours in tingeing or curling the tarnished plumes of prostitute *Philosophy*. WALTER SAVAGE LANDOR, *Imaginary Conversations*

2. A yawn may be defined as a silent yell.

G. K. CHESTERTON, *George Bernard Shaw*

3. I have come to distrust higgledy-piggledy reading. But at twenty-two it may have been right. One has to find one's tastes, like a dog casting about for a scent, before one can follow them.

F. L. LUCAS, "OF BOOKS"

4. Such a gentleman [as Plato] may exist, spinning an intricate spider web of dialectic, along whose tenuous gossamers the daring intellect darts insecurely outwards towards its elusive prey, a conclusion. VIDA D. SCUDDER, "PLATO AS NOVELIST"

If forcefulness of diction derives from originality, wit, and freshness, it disappears from prose laden with triteness. The CLICHÉ is the enemy of vigor. Clichés — expressions, once bright and shiny, that have been circulated so long that they have been worn smooth — are an insidious habit of style. Expressions like the following enable one to write without having first to think:

last but not least
the more the merrier
the moment of truth
history tells us
in the arms of Morpheus
an agonizing reappraisal
up to the hilt
the finer things of life
cool, calm, and collected
by leaps and bounds
an unconfirmed rumor

Many clichés are trite similes and metaphors:

happy as a lark
gentle as a lamb
old as Methuselah
cool as a cucumber
as pleased as Punch
as white as snow
as sober as a judge
as light as a feather
the patience of Job
the pinnacle of success
the pink of condition

Famous quotations quoted once too often are another mine of triteness: "To damn with faint praise" has become a cliché and so have "To be or not to be" and "Something is rotten in the state of Denmark."

Still another kind of cliché is the EUPHEMISM (those expressions designed to soften or conceal an improper or unpleasant reality). Euphemisms for death include "to pass away," "to pass over," "to depart this life," "to pass into one's eternal reward," all equally trite. Phrases like "to be in want" and "to be in financial difficulties" are euphemisms for *poor*. An airline stewardess may speak euphemistically of a "precautionary landing" when an airplane is in serious difficulties, and a general "strategically withdraws" when his troops are in headlong retreat. Sexual matters are frequently veiled in euphemisms; a pregnant woman, for example, may be described as "expecting" or "in an interesting condition" or "in a family way." While there is a time and place for euphemisms, expecially in conversation, they are likely to enervate an expository style.

Another characteristic of vigorous diction is that its movement is rapid and lively, largely because of active verbs. Such verbs are simple, concrete, and economical, thrusting a sentence on with great power. A good example is the series of active verbs in the following passage by Charles Dickens, describing a revolutionary mob dancing the Carmagnole:

> They advanced, retreated, struck at one another's hands, clutched at one another's heads, spun round alone, caught one another and spun round in pairs, until many of them dropped. While those were down, the rest linked hand in hand, and all spun round together: then the ring broke, and in separate rings of two and four they turned and turned until they all stopped at once, began again, struck, clutched, and tore, and then reversed the spin, and all spun round another way. Suddenly they stopped again, paused, struck out the time afresh, formed into lines the width of the public way, and, with their heads low down and their hands high up, swooped screaming off. No fight could have been half so terrible as this dance.
>
> *A Tale of Two Cities*

The same kind of emphasis appears in this passage by Rachel Carson:

> Strontium 90, released through nuclear explosions into the air, comes to earth in rain or drifts down as fallout, lodges in soil, enters into the grass or corn or wheat grown there, and in time takes up its abode in the bones of a human being, there to remain until his death. Similarly, chemicals sprayed on croplands or forests or gardens lie long in soil, entering into living organisms, passing from one to another in a chain of poisoning and death. Or they pass mysteriously by underground streams until they emerge and, through the alchemy of air and sunlight, combine into new forms that kill vegetation, sicken cattle, and work unknown harm on those who drink from once-pure wells. *The Silent Spring*

Finally, vigor is helped by the unusual or rare word, provided it is used accurately and reserved for a specially appropriate place. Each of the following sentences is sparked by the sudden intrusion of a strange term:

1. And we ran down the garden, with snowballs in our arms, toward the house; and smoke, indeed, was pouring out of the dining-room, and the gong was bombilating, and Mrs. Prothero was announcing ruin like a town crier in Pompeii.
   DYLAN THOMAS, *A Child's Christmas in Wales*

2. It [science] pronounces only on whatever, at the time, appears to have been scientifically ascertained, which is a small island in an ocean of nescience. BERTRAND RUSSELL

3. Not long ago, examining the network of laughter lines around my eyes in the mirror, it occurred to me that I was in peril of becoming a slippered popinjay. S. J. PERELMAN, "I'M SORRY I MADE ME CRY"

Even everyday words, used in an odd and startling way, can enliven prose. Dylan Thomas is adept at this, creating surprise and vigor by slipping familiar, commonplace words into strange contexts; in the following sentence he is describing how adults on a beach appear to a child:

> Lolling or larriking that unsoiled, boiling beauty of a common day, great gods with their braces over their vests sang, spat pips, puffed smoke at wasps, gulped and ogled, forgot the rent, embraced, posed for the dicky-bird, were coarse, had rainbow-coloured armpits, winked, belched, blamed the radishes, looked at Ilfracombe, played hymns on paper and comb, peeled bananas, scratched, found seaweed in their panamas, blew up paper-bags and banged them, wished for nothing. "HOLIDAY MEMORY"

Thomas's diction delights us because it is clear, apt, and frequently surprising. It is the work of a man who has a rare sensitivity for all the potentialities that hide in words, even in the ordinary, undistinguished words of our everyday talk.

Summary

A writer's diction is governed by his subject, his purpose, and his audience. In no small part, good diction results from the writer's courtesy toward his readers. By being careful in his choice of words, the writer can communicate swiftly and easily, using his words as conveyers of thought, not as impediments to its passage. Above all the good writer is honest. He does not inflate the obvious or the trivial to make it seem like oracular wisdom. And he remembers that good diction is:

1. Clear and concrete
2. Appropriate
3. Simple
4. Economical
5. Euphonious
6. Emphatic.

Exercises

1. Each of the following illustrates one or more sources of obscurity: undefined abstractions, the wrong word, the nearly-right word, malapropisms. Explain why each example is obscure and suggest a revision.

    1. The large coves are surrounded by old structures and are full of activity; the smaller coves, on the other hand, are a definite contrast.
    2. The moral ideals of people change; they become increasingly introspective and money orientated.
    3. I was enthralled by the amount of freedom given to college students.

4. I had the usual kind of childhood that everyone has who grows up in a small town.
5. When it came to repairing his car, my father had no use for theory; he was very practicable.
6. I imply from his words that he is disinterested in the student tour.
7. Her dark violet eyes added to her beauty; her figure was perfect and fulsome.
8. My uncle never did anything to get his name in history books, but even though he was infamous everyone respected him.
9. No one can be expected to accept an incredulous tale of that kind.
10. We adduce from this fact one inescapable conclusion.
11. I like existentialism because it is the most realistic philosophy for modern man, allowing him to be idealistic as well as unsentimental. No philosophy is any good unless it faces the unpleasant facts of existence.
12. It was an ingenuous solution to a complex industrial problem.

2. Rank the following according to level of usage. Which is the most formal, the least formal? Which informal passage seems most nearly to approach formality?

1. As a Detroit designer, you go on and on, putting curlicue on curlicue, adding dream to dream, adding the fragment of one illusion to the fragment of another and you spend enough money to operate a state university to imitate the sound of a slammed door. When you're all through, you discover that you've transformed a rolling shoebox into a combination of the Blue Grotto and the Crystal Palace, wherein is placed a psychiatrist's couch that has enough Procrustean potential to suit any psyche, no matter how warped.

   JOHN KEATS, *The Insolent Chariots*

2. It all happened one Monday morning. I was busy dishing dinner up for all my gang, and I just happened to say how fed up I was. It was washday and I'd rather be at the seaside than washing over the dolly-tub. And father said to me, "What's wrong with you taking a day off and going down to the coast with your youngest boy?" That properly put the cat among the pigeons because everybody wanted to come as well. MRS. LILIAN BALCH, "HOLIDAY AT THE SEASIDE"

3. The scullery was a mine of all the minerals of living. Here I discovered water — a very different element from the green crawling scum that stank in the garden tub. You could pump it in pure blue gulps out of the ground; you could swing on the pump handle and it came out sparkling like liquid sky. And it broke and ran and shone on the tiled floor, or quivered in a jug, or weighted your clothes with cold. LAURIE LEE, *The Edge of Day*

4. If the hearer makes an incorrect objective reference the utterance will in many cases not make sense; the mistake is then quickly

detected and rectified. This, I think, is the most important censoring factor. However, mistakes due to misunderstandings and equivocation are deplorably common, even in scientific discussions. The speaker not seldom, although mostly unintentionally, makes use of ambiguous terms; for his own part, he intends one of the possible meanings, and he neglects to provide against the hearer's apprehending another. GUSTAF STERN, *Meaning and Change of Meaning*

5. Probably the most common and in some ways the most accomplished of American dilettantes is the baseball fan, though the national pastime is being crowded out of its position as top banana of entertainment these days by serious music. The baseball fan knows his subject with something very close to genuine scholarship. He is an expert in the minutiae of its history and understands the nuances and subtleties of its performance. RUSSELL LYNES, "TIME ON OUR HANDS"

3. Explain what is inappropriate about the diction in the following passages.

    1. Neither did he choose serious topics of conversation nor uninteresting ones but ones suitable for jesting. Such a topic involved the fairer sex. Willy employed waiting tactics: he believed the aggressiveness of the male was more a liability than an asset when it came to the winning of feminine hearts.
    2. It is easy to see that *King Lear* is a play about fools and all kinds of folly. The intricate pattern of parallels and contrasts relating to folly is truly impressive. But King Lear himself is hard to figure.
    3. Since our home is in the country we are able to enjoy an unusually rich biota. Between the first appearance of *Galanthus nivalis* to the last of the *Chrysanthemum* hybrids we see almost every kind of local flora.
    4. Just at even-tide we began to prepare for our long journey.

4. Translate the following examples of gobbledegook into simple, clear English.

    1. A child belonging to a constantly mobile family is deprived of the opportunity of establishing solid academic and interpersonal relationships to a given educational environment. With each environmental transplantation he must experience the process of readjustment to unfamiliar academic surroundings and new societal and personal relationships with instructional personnel and attempt to establish new acquaintanceship patterns in his own academic peer group.
    2. It has been empirically and theoretically established that some pupil personnel in institutions of primary and secondary academic and vocational instruction have been shown to be qualitatively differentiated in regard to their learning and retention quotient indices and that furthermore this qualitative differentiation is nonenvironmental in its genesis.
    3. The upper strata of the socio-economic socialization categories are

characterized by a higher per capita possession of wealth and upper-status identifications than are those who are generally to be found in the lower socio-economic echelons.

4. Experiments are described which demonstrate that in normal individuals the lowest concentration in which sucrose can be detected by means of gustation differs from the lowest concentration in which sucrose (in the amount employed) has to be ingested in order to produce a demonstrable decrease in olfactory acuity and a noteworthy conversion of sensations interpreted as a desire for food into sensations interpreted as a satiety association with ingestion of food. FROM THE *Lancet;* quoted by SIR ERNEST GOWERS in *The Complete Plain Words*

5. Make a list of ten or twenty clichés you find especially offensive.

6. Each profession, trade, sport, and activity has its own clichés. Write a short paper on the clichés of baseball, newscasting, college life, or some similar subject.

7. Write an essay about the kinds of diction that weaken good prose. Use copious examples.

8. Study the prose of two or three good twentieth-century writers; then write a theme in which you show what makes their diction vigorous and effective. Use frequent short quotations.

26
DICTIONARIES

Introduction

Every serious reader and writer works with at least a good desk dictionary within easy reach. The vocabulary of English is growing and changing so rapidly that everyone whose job is communication needs constantly to find and check information about words — their spellings, their grammatical forms, their often numerous meanings, the ways in which their meanings are changing, and their appropriateness to a particular subject, occasion, purpose, and audience. Fortunately, in the past forty or fifty years there have been giant strides in the scientific study of language and word behavior. Utilizing the solid achievements of linguistic scholarship, dictionary-makers today can give writers a better understanding of the nature and operation of language than ever before. If the influences of social change and rapid technological advancement are altering our language, we are at the same time better equipped to understand and use the facts of linguistic change.

Dictionaries

DEFINITION

To derive the maximum benefit from his dictionary, however, the writer should understand what a dictionary is and what it is not, for mistaken notions about the nature and purpose of dictionaries are common, even among well-educated persons. Two of the most serious make their appearance when someone says, "That's the correct way to pronounce it; I know because I looked it up in the dictionary." This speaker apparently supposes

(1) that there exists "the dictionary," a single work which everyone can identify, and (2) that "the dictionary" is an infallible authority that dictates how language must be used. The falseness of the first of these two assumptions is so obvious as to require little comment. There are many dictionaries in use today, differing in price and size from a paperback dictionary on sale in a supermarket for less than a dollar to multivolumed dictionaries that cost hundreds of dollars. Some dictionaries are highly specialized; others are quite general. Some dictionaries are long out-of-date; others reflect recent usage and linguistic change. Some dictionaries are inadequately revised editions of older dictionaries; others are monuments of linguistic scholarship. But even equally reputable and recent dictionaries do not always list the same words or provide the same kind of linguistic information or express agreement on every point. As we shall see in more detail later on, it makes a considerable difference which dictionary one consults.

The second assumption in our hypothetical, but typical, statement about the dictionary is not quite so obviously false, but it is, at best, misleading. It is true that preparing a dictionary may cost millions of dollars and years of work by a large staff of the best scholars and lexicographers, yet no dictionaries pretend to be infallible or to record every word and every usage in the English vocabulary. Nor do they claim to prescribe how language *must* be used or *ought* to be used. Because a word or a usage does not appear in a good unabridged dictionary, one does not have to discard it altogether. While one cannot coin words at will and expect to be understood, new words and new usages are constantly appearing in our language. One comes across them in newspapers and magazines; one hears them in radio or television newscasts. As long as our language remains living, no dictionary, no matter how large or how well edited, can possibly keep pace with its growth and development. In one sense, then, every dictionary is out-of-date the day it is published. On the other hand, because a word is listed in a dictionary it is not therefore permissible to use it in any and every context. Good dictionaries (including desk dictionaries) often include archaic words, dialect words, slang, argot, and substandard words that the writer will use sparingly, if at all. For example, *irregardless* appears in most unabridged and desk dictionaries, but, while all of them do not label it in the same way, all agree that it is seldom used by careful writers in any but the most informal contexts and suggest that many, or most, avoid it altogether as substandard or nonstandard English.

This fact, doubtless, may prompt someone to object, "But isn't this another way of saying that according to 'the dictionary' *irregardless* is incorrect?" The answer is no, it isn't quite the same thing. To see why no is the right answer brings us to the subject of what a dictionary is and what purpose it intends to achieve.

Simply defined, a dictionary describes or records how words have been used and how they are being used up to the date of publication. A dictionary, then, is authoritative to the degree it has accurately determined past and present usage. To reach this goal the editors and staff preparing *Webster's Third New International Dictionary* (1961), for instance, collected more than 10,000,000 examples of usage (called citations) upon which they based the information given in the more than 450,000 entries of this unabridged dictionary. The result was one of the most detailed descriptions of the English language ever recorded and probably the most complete description we possess of recent developments in our language. This description, of course, included *irregardless,* which it labeled "*nonstand,*" meaning "not conforming to the usage generally characteristic of educated native speakers of the language." But the point is that *irregardless* is nonstandard, not because *Webster's Third New International* says so or its editors think it ought to be, but because at present educated native speakers seldom use it, a fact the dictionary records. Dictionaries, then, are primarily descriptions of how we use our language. Speaking about the aim of *The American College Dictionary,* Clarence L. Barnhart, the editor, has written a memorable definition of dictionaries in general:

> This dictionary records the usage of the speakers and writers of our language; no dictionary founded on the methods of modern scholarship can prescribe as to usage; it can only inform on the basis of the facts of usage. A good dictionary is a guide to usage much as a good map tells you the nature of the terrain over which you may want to travel. It is not the function of the dictionary-maker to tell you how to speak, any more than it is the function of the mapmaker to move rivers or re-arrange mountains or fill in lakes. A dictionary should tell you what is commonly accepted usage and wherein different classes of speakers or regions differ in their use of the language.
>
> "GENERAL INTRODUCTION" TO *The American College Dictionary,* P. XIX

We should notice that this editor speaks of "a dictionary" and "this dictionary," not of "the dictionary," for "the dictionary" is a misleading abstraction that may cause us to forget that dictionaries are made by men at a particular point in time and that dictionaries differ widely in their aims and scopes. Partly to dispel a belief in "*the* dictionary" and partly to suggest the astonishing variety of good dictionaries, we might profitably classify and exemplify some of the more useful dictionaries available to the writer.

SPECIAL DICTIONARIES

First, a large class of dictionaries presents only technical or special words related either to a particular discipline or to some special or restricted aspect of language. A small sample of the former — which usually define technical terms — appears in the following list:

Dictionary of Scientific Terms, New York, 1960
Dictionary of Geology, New York, 1962
Dictionary of World Literature, New York, 1953
The Dictionary of Sports, New York, 1959
Funk and Wagnalls Standard Dictionary of Folklore, Mythology and Legend, 2 vols., New York, 1949–50
The Harvard Dictionary of Music, Cambridge, Mass., 1961
The Oxford Classical Dictionary, Oxford, 1949
Psychiatric Dictionary, New York, 1960

Dictionaries of this kind usually give more detailed information about the thing defined than does even a large unabridged dictionary. Users of special dictionaries are likely to turn to such works more for knowledge about a particular subject than for linguistic information; thus dictionaries of technical terms often resemble an encyclopedia more than a general dictionary. For a full bibliographical listing of technical dictionaries one should consult a reference work like *Guide to Reference Books* (7th ed., ed. Constance M. Winchell, Chicago, 1951, with supplements).

Words having a restricted use or illustrating some particular aspect of language are also likely to form the basis of special dictionaries. For the specialist or the student of language there are dictionaries of slang, dialects, pronunciations, etymologies, and synonyms. The following are examples of this kind of special dictionary:

American Dialect Dictionary, New York, 1944
A Dictionary of Slang and Unconventional English from the Fifteenth Century to the Present Day, New York, 1961
An Etymological Dictionary of the English Language, ed. Walter W. Skeat, 1879–1882; new ed. rev. and enlarged New York, 1956
Roget's Thesaurus of English Words and Phrases, rev. ed., New York, 1964
Webster's Dictionary of Synonyms: A Dictionary of Discriminated

Synonyms, with Antonyms and Analogous and Contrasted Words, Springfield, Mass., 1951

Of these special dictionaries the expository writer is likely to find the last two most useful. Strictly speaking, *Roget's Thesaurus* is not a dictionary but a classified listing of words of varying usage levels and connoations grouped according to broad categories of meaning. In *Roget's Thesaurus* synonyms of the word *dialect*, for example, are given as follows:

> *dialect*, idiom, lingo, patois, brogue, vernacular, 557n. *language;* cockney, Doric, broad Scots, Lallans; broken English, pidgin E., pidgin, Chinook; Koine, lingua franca, hybrid language; Briticism, Anglicism, Americanism, Scoticism, Hibernicism, Gallicism, Teutonism, Sinicism; chi-chi, babuism; provincialism, localism, vernacularism; sigmatism, iotacism 580n. *speech defect;* neologist, word-coiner, neoterist; dialectology, 557n. linguistics.

It should be noticed there is no attempt to define these terms or to discriminate among them, and most often the listed words are analagous not synonymous. While *Roget's Thesaurus* helps to jog one's memory if one already has a large vocabulary, the book needs to be used with caution by the inexperienced writer, who should consult it only in conjunction with a good desk dictionary. The writer who wishes to understand the distinctions among similar words will turn with profit to a work like *Webster's Dictionary of Synonyms,* which stresses differences as well as similarities. The following is the first part of the entry under DIALECT:

> **dialect,** *n.* **1 Dialect, vernacular, patois, lingo, jargon, cant, argot, patter, slang** are here compared as denoting a form of language or a style of speech which varies from that accepted as the literary standard. **Dialect,** as here compared (see also LANGUAGE, 1), is applied ordinarily to a form of a language that is confined to a locality or to a group, that differs from the standard form of the same language in peculiarities of vocabulary, pronunciation, usage, morphology, and the like, and that persists for generations or even centuries. It may represent an independent development from the same origin as the standard form (as, the Sussex *dialect*) or a survival (as, the *dialect* of the Kentucky mountaineers). The term is often, in spite of some philological opposition, applied to a corruption of the standard language (as, the Gullah *dialect,* a corrupted English used by descendants of African Negroes living chiefly along the coast of South Carolina and Georgia). "A Babylonish *dialect* Which learned pedants much affect" (*Butler*). **Vernacular** (usually *the vernacular*) has several applications, though it always denotes the form of language spoken by the people in contrast with that employed by learned or

literary men. In the Middle Ages, when the language of the church, of the universities, and of learned writings was Latin, the vernacular was the native language of the people, whatever it might be in the locality in question; as, to translate the Bible into the *vernacular*. "Freeman ...laments...that the first Christian missionaries from Rome did not teach their converts to pray and give praise in the *vernacular*" (*Quiller-Couch*). When a contrast with the literary language rather than with Latin is implied, *the vernacular* is an underogatory designation for the spoken language, that is, for the language that represents the speech of the people as a whole, that is colloquial but not necessarily vulgar, and is marked chiefly by the spontaneous choice of familiar, often native (as opposed to exotic), words and phrases. "Pope... is absolute master of the raciest, most familiar, most cogent and telling elements of the *vernacular*" (*Lowes*). In current use, *vernacular* often implies a contrast with scientific nomenclature; as, the botanical and the *vernacular* names for flowers. **Patois,** a French word adopted in English, is often used as if it were the equivalent of *dialect*. It tends, however, to be restricted, especially in North America, to designating a form of speech used by the uneducated people in a bilingual section or country; the word often specifically refers to the hybrid language (English, and French Canadian) spoken in some parts of Canada. **Lingo** is a term of contempt applied to any language that is not easily or readily understood. It is applicable to a strange foreign language, a dialect, a patois, or to the peculiar speech of any class, cult, or the like. "I have often warned you not to talk the court gibberish to me. I tell you, I don't understand the *lingo*" (*Fielding*).

The remainder of this entry just as carefully and thoroughly defines and distinguishes the other synonyms given at the beginning of the entry.

HISTORICAL DICTIONARIES

One kind of special dictionary is so important to the writer and the student of language that it deserves to be treated in a separate section. This is the historical dictionary, which, in addition to the kind of linguistic information found in general dictionaries, traces the history of each word from some early appearance in written records to some terminal point usually close to the date of the dictionary's publication. Of these the most monumental is *The Oxford English Dictionary* (often abbreviated *OED*). Bound in twelve volumes and a supplement, the *OED* consists of some 15,000 large quarto pages and contains the histories of nearly 500,000 words. Begun in 1858 and not completed until 1933, the *OED* aims to "present in alphabetical series the words that have formed the English vocabulary from the time of earliest records [about A.D. 1000] down to the present day [1933], with all the relevant facts concerning their form, sense-history, pronunciation, and etymology." The *OED* not only records the standard language of literature and conversation present and past, it also includes the main technical vocabulary of our language and a "large measure of dialectal usage and slang." From an entry in the *OED* it is possible to trace the sense-history of a word quite easily, for this dictionary presents within a given entry, first, the oldest known usage of a word in written records. This usage is defined and illustrated by one or more dated examples of the word in a sentence or some clear context. If the word has undergone sense-changes of any kind since its first discoverable appearance in English, the *OED* records, illustrates, and dates these changes. When the *OED* was finally completed, it clearly was, and so far remains, the greatest dictionary ever made in any language. Its influence has been far-reaching. Because of its extraordinary wealth of linguistic information, the *OED* has helped to give the science of linguistics a more firm foundation than it might otherwise have had. While the ordinary expository writer engaged in an ordinary task is not likely to consult the *OED*, no student of language can work for very long without using it. Better than any other single work the *OED* permits us to see that language behaves according to laws and principles that can be described objectively and scientifically. What someone thinks language ought to be must today be judged in the light of the history of English usage as reflected in the *OED*. Since the *OED* was published, it is no longer as easy as it once was to be arbitrary and dogmatic about matters of usage.

Similar to the *OED* in purpose but much smaller is *A Dictionary of American English on Historical Principles* (abbreviated *DAE*), edited by William A. Craigie and James Hulbert. The purpose of this four-volume dictionary (1936–44) is specifically to present linguistic information, including sense-histories, for those words which distinguish the speech of the American Colonies and the United States from that of England and that of other English-speaking peoples. The *DAE*, the editors say, includes "not only words and phrases which are clearly of American origin, or have greater currency here than elsewhere, but also every word denoting something which has real connection with the development of the country and the history of its people." In the *DAE* the terminal point for new words is the end of the nineteenth century, but illustrations of those common before that time are often carried into the first quarter of the twentieth century. The *DAE* restricts the inclusion of slang and dialect words to those "of early date and special prominence." Though more restricted in scope, the *DAE* does for the distinguishing features of American English what the *OED* does for English in general.

UNABRIDGED DICTIONARIES

The most notable characteristic of both the *OED* and the *DAE* is their historical treatment of words. But strictly speaking, we can also call them examples of unabridged dictionaries, that is, neither is a shortened form of some larger dictionary; each one was intended to be the size it is. Applying this definition consistently, we should have also to label some desk dictionaries as unabridged. *The American College Dictionary,* for instance, is not an abridgment of some larger work. Still, in common usage, the term *unabridged dictionary* is likely to evoke thoughts of a work containing three or four times as many entries as most desk dictionaries and presenting a general vocabulary without stressing the historical development of language in the same way as the *OED* or the *DAE.* Two widely used unabridged dictionaries published by the G. & C. Merriam Company are *Webster's New International Dictionary,* second edition, 1934 (hereafter referred to as *Webster II*) and the more recent *Webster's Third New International Dictionary of the English Language, Unabridged,* 1961 (hereafter referred to as *Webster III*).

Webster II lists some 550,000 main entries, "the largest number ever included in a dictionary of any language." In addition to these are some 36,000 names of geographical places in the Gazeteer, 13,000 biographical entries, and 5,000 abbreviations, making a total of some 600,000 entries, so far (1965) the largest number of entries ever included in a single dictionary. Many of the words in *Webster II,* however, belong to older forms of English. The whole vocabulary of Chaucer, for example, has been retained. But the more literary, technical, and conversational vocabulary of the twentieth century is also included, and without doubt *Webster II* is one of the most remarkable of unabridged dictionaries. It will continue to be useful for some time, especially as an aid in reading our older literature. But no dictionary published in 1934 is adequate for present-day needs. Since 1934 our language has changed, and under the influence of history and technological progress, our vocabulary has grown at an extraordinary rate. World War II, the Cold War, growing populations, and advancing technology have combined to create new social problems and patterns, all of which influence our attitudes toward language.

In order to record our modern vocabulary and to reflect our less formal approach to the use of language, the G. & C. Merriam Company in 1961 published a new unabridged dictionary, *Webster III*. Begun almost immediately after the publication of *Webster II* in 1934, *Webster III* is based upon some 10,000,000 citations or usage examples, many of which are taken from modern or recent publications. *Webster III*, furthermore, is the work of experts who have applied the recent findings of linguistic science to the making of a dictionary that will accurately and objectively reveal our language as it is presently written and spoken. In size, *Webster III* is somewhat smaller than *Webster II*, having 450,000 entries in the main vocabulary section as against 550,000 in *Webster II*. But of these 450,000 there are more than 100,000 new words or new meanings not included in *Webster II*. Unquestionably, *Webster III* is the most up-to-date of the large unabridged dictionaries. Because it has faithfully recorded linguistic change, *Webster III* has surprised some and irritated others. At its appearance in 1961 there occurred a furious debate as to its merit and the validity of its method and philosophy. But as the smoke from this battle begins to drift away, most agree that a living language cannot be fixed by arbitrary rules or some preconceived notion of "correctness." *Webster III* is a monumental achievement because it has faithfully mirrored modern usage. It is the work to which most writers will want to turn when a desk dictionary proves inadequate.

ABRIDGED DICTIONARIES AND DESK DICTIONARIES

The kind of dictionary most people use is smaller than the unabridged *Webster II* and *Webster III* and includes typically between 75,000 and 150,000 entries. Some of the dictionaries of this smaller size are abridged (by our strict definition) and some are not. For example, *The Shorter Oxford English Dictionary on Historical Principles* is a two-volume abridgment of the twelve-volume *OED*. *The Shorter Oxford English Dictionary* aims to keep the historical orientation of the larger work, presenting in miniature all the important characteristics of the parent dictionary. The one-volume *Concise Oxford Dictionary of Current English* is a still more radical abridgment, intended to serve as a desk dictionary and designed to emphasize the modern English vocabulary. Others, as we shall see, are short in comparison with *Webster II* or *Webster III*, and yet they are not abridgments of some larger work. Except, possibly, for *The Shorter Oxford English Dictionary*, all the dictionaries in this class are frequently used as desk books and the college student as well as writers of all kinds will need to consult one frequently. Four of these desk dictionaries (often called collegiate dictionaries) deserve special mention:

The American College Dictionary, New York, Random House, 1947 (hereafter abbreviated *ACD*)
Funk & Wagnalls Standard College Dictionary, New York, Funk & Wagnalls Company, 1963 (hereafter abbreviated *SCD*)
Webster's New World Dictionary of the American Language, College Edition, Cleveland, Ohio, World Publishing Company, 1953 (hereafter abbreviated *NWD*)
Webster's Seventh New Collegiate Dictionary, Springfield, Mass., G. & C. Merriam Company, 1963 (hereafter abbreviated *Webster 7*)

Each of these desk dictionaries is suitable for college work and for most tasks of the expository writer. They differ in particular ways, but each is well edited and each has its strong points. While almost everyone uses desk dictionaries like these, not everyone has taken the trouble to discover just how much a dictionary can tell us about language. Expository writers, in particular, should know how to extract all the linguistic information contained in a dictionary entry.

Using a Dictionary

FRONT MATTER

Upon first acquiring a desk dictionary, one should read at least once all the material appearing before the alphabetized entries. This material differs from dictionary to dictionary; the front matter may include essays on language and linguistics as well as information on punctuation and mechanics, on letter writing and forms of address, and on the preparation of manuscript for the press. But somewhere in the front matter all dictionaries state their aims, reveal something about their linguistic philosophy, and explain in detail what they contain and how they are to be used.

THE MAIN ENTRY

Printed in heavy black type at the beginning of each alphabetized entry is the word to be described and defined, called the main entry. This main entry is useful to the writer for at least three reasons. First, the main entry is divided into syllables by means of centered dots. These tell the writer where to divide a word at the end of a line in his manuscript. Thus, the word *knowledge* is conventionally divided *knowl·edge* rather than *know·ledge*. It is easy, of course, to see that *knowledge* is a word of two syllables; not so easy to decide, however, is the point where one syllable ends and another begins. As yet, linguistic science has provided writers and printers with no easy rules for dividing words into syllables. For this reason, dictionaries still follow the conventions established by eighteenth-century printers, the purpose of which is to create an arbitrary kind of consistency and to improve the appearance of a page. In preparing a typewritten manuscript, for instance, the writer will have to know how words are conventionally divided, or whether a compound is hyphenated, written as one word, or written as two. Does one conventionally write *crossexamine, cross examine,* or *cross-examine?* Do most users of English write *highschool* or *high school?* The main entry of a good dictionary will supply the answer.

Not infrequently a word has one or more variant spellings. A second purpose of the main entry is to record these and to suggest whether variants are equally common or if one is more frequently used than the other(s). Thus, *theatre* is a variant of *theater*. The *ACD*, the *NWD*, and the *SCD* give *theatre* as a secondary variant. *Webster 7*, however, believes that *theatre* occurs as commonly as *theater*, evidence that well-edited dictionaries sometimes differ in their judgments.

A third purpose of the main entry is to show how words are conventionally spelled. Since English SPELLING and pronunciation are often quite divergent, learning to spell conventionally is difficult for everyone. Writers and editors of all kinds must constantly refer to a dictionary, especially at the time of revising a first draft. But if frequent misspellings are liable to occur in the first draft of a manuscript, there is no excuse for more than an occasional misspelling in a completed essay if the writer has a good dictionary at hand. Several classes of words deserve attention in any manuscript.

(1) The writer ought to check the spelling of any words he is using for the first time or has used only rarely in the past. If the writer misspells technical words like *phthalocyanine* or *paleontology,* for example, his readers are likely to suspect he is incompetent to discuss his subject or is only superficially acquainted with it. Should he misspell rare formal terms like *ineluctable* or *eleemosynary,* his readers may suspect him of merely trying to display a learning he does not properly possess.

(2) Certain words in English are more commonly misspelled than others. The writer should know which these are and make an effort to master them, checking their spelling in a dictionary if he has any doubt about them. A few of these spelling demons are the following:

accommodate	embarrass	misspelled	sophomore
all right	environment	noticeable	succeed
amateur	etc.	occurred	temperament
athlete	existence	pertain	tragedy
benefited	hypocrisy	psychology	vacuum
conscientious	intramural	receive	vengeance
disastrous	lightning	rhythm	villain
divine	maintenance	shepherd	writing

(3) Some words in English are pronounced alike but have different derivations, meanings, and spellings. Such words, called homophones, are often misspelled. The most common examples are these:

to, two, too   its, it's   there, they're, their.

Misspelling such simple, familiar words generally correlates with haste, carelessness, or a lack of consideration for the reader.

(4) Many English words employ an unstressed mid-central vowel sound called schwa (symbolized in phonetic notation as ə), which appears in the first and last syllables of the word *America*. This common sound is sometimes spelled *a*, sometimes *i*, sometimes *u*, sometimes by other letters or combinations of letters. There seems to be no consistent rule determining which letter of the alphabet is likely to represent the schwa sound in a given word. The spelling of words containing this unstressed vowel sound — especially words ending in *-ible, able, -ence, ance* — simply have to be memorized or looked up. Typical of the words in the class are *incredible, noticeable, desirable, enviable, tractable, inextensible, providence, maintenance, provenance,* and *independence.*

(5) Many words have pronunciations that seem to be poorly reflected in their spellings. In addition to common words like *through, bough,* and *cough* are words like these:

sergeant	boatswain	comptroller	phthisis
colonel	forecastle	chthonic	brougham
lieutenant	leeward	psychology	yacht

(6) Sometimes words have similar spellings but different pronunciations. *Loose,* for example, is often a misspelling for *lose.* The first syllables in *woman* and *women* are pronounced differently although spelled the same. The second syllables are spelled differently but pronounced much the same. Inconsistencies between spelling and pronunciation like these require a frequent use of the main entry in the dictionary. Some dictionaries include a section on spelling rules. Often, however, these are complex and

difficult for poor spellers to follow. One best learns to spell, perhaps, by wide reading, by mastering a particular subject and its vocabulary, and by learning to take pains. Poor spellers ought to keep a notebook in which they write down — spelled conventionally — words they have misspelled.

PRONUNCIATION

Following the main entry in most dictionaries is an indication in phonetic symbols of the common pronunciation(s) of the word. Unfortunately, each dictionary employs its own system of phonetic notation so that one must carefully study the pronunciation symbols of each dictionary one uses. These symbols, of course, only approximate the pronunciation of a word in actual speech, for words pronounced in isolation differ from words as they occur in running speech, where they are modified by the other sounds near them, the emotional state of the speaker, and so on. At best, the pronunciations recorded in dictionaries are approximate and general; they cannot, and should not, be more. Still, they are important. Since our culture depends more and more upon oral communication, we should know how words are most commonly pronounced and what variants exist. To make a newly learned word his own, the writer should learn a conventional pronunciation of it as well as its spelling and its range of meanings.

By what means do makers of dictionaries determine the prounuciation or pronunciations of words? Almost all agree that pronunciations are determined by the usage of cultivated and influential speakers during the years the dictionary is being compiled. But the problem of applying this hypothetical standard is complicated in a number of ways. Can one obtain representative samples of the speech of all cultivated and influential speakers? Precisely who are cultivated speakers and where do they live? What if two such speakers pronounce words differently? About this problem *Webster 7* has this to say:

> The standard of English pronunciation, so far as a standard may be said to exist, is the usage that now prevails among the educated and cultured people to whom the language is vernacular; but since somewhat different pronunciations are used by the cultivated in different regions too large to be ignored, we must admit the fact that uniformity of pronunciation is not to be found throughout the English-speaking world, though there is a very large percentage of practical uniformity.

About the problem of "correct" pronunciation the editors remind us that

> **The function of a pronouncing dictionary is to record as far as possible the pronunciations prevailing in the best present usage rather than to attempt to dictate what that usage should be. Insofar as a dictionary may be known and acknowledged as a faithful recorder and interpreter of such usage, so far and no farther may it be appealed to as an authority.**
>
> **By permission. From *Webster's Seventh New Collegiate Dictionary,* copyright 1965 by G. & C. Merriam Company, Publishers of the Merriam-Webster Dictionaries.**

To illustrate that all dictionaries do not always agree about matters of pronunciation we might consult each of the four collegiate dictionaries we have mentioned earlier to see how they have recorded pronunciations of the simple words *often* and *again.* As we might expect they do not entirely agree in their judgments. For example, *Webster 7* and the *NWD* record the variant pronunciation "of-tən"; the *ACD* and the *SCD* do not. The *ACD,* the *NWD,* and the *SCD* record as a variant pronunciation "ə-gān′." *Webster 7* does not. Instead of speaking of the "correct" pronunciation of *again* or *often* as given in "the dictionary," it is more meaningful to speak of the pronunciation(s) recorded as most common by the *ACD,* or whatever work has been consulted.

GRAMMATICAL INFORMATION

After the phonetic notation pronouncing the main entry, desk dictionaries classify the main entry according to its function as one or more of the traditional eight parts of speech. Should a verb be both transitive and intransitive this fact is indicated by appropriate labels (usually abbreviated). Sometimes abbreviations for such other labels as *noun suffix, prefix,* or *combining form* stand in the same position as the part of speech label. Irregular plurals are usually given after the part of speech label, thus: **spoonful** (spo͞on′·fo͝ol′) n. pl. ·FULS (*SCD*). If there are two or more plurals in common usage, these by some arbitrary convention are usually designated as equal or secondary variants: [1]FOX \ ′fäks \ n, pl FOXES *or* FOX (*Webster 7*) (in this dictionary *or* introduces equal variants and *also,* a secondary variant). In addition to noun inflections, most dictionaries give the principal parts (past, past participle, and present participle) of irregular verbs and irregular comparative and superlative forms of adjectives. Thus, the dictionary is an important reference work if the writer is uncertain about conventional inflections or which variant form is most suitable for his subject, purpose, and audience.

ETYMOLOGIES

All collegiate dictionaries indicate the etymology of their vocabulary entry, some presenting the etymology after the part-of-speech label, others placing it at or near the end, after the definition(s). Briefly and simply defined, the etymology of a word identifies its origin in an older form of English or in some foreign language or otherwise explains the facts of its origin and development. Etymologies can be of practical use in at least three ways. First, they can help a writer see the relationship among seemingly quite different meanings of a word. For instance, we speak of a *radical* change in procedure, a *radical* political party, of a *radical* quantity in mathematics, and of *radical* leaves in botanical studies. What these uses of *radical* have in common becomes clear if we know the word is derived from Latin *radix, radicis,* meaning *root.* A radical change is one that affects the very roots of things, as does a radical political philosophy; in mathematics a radical has to do with the roots of a number; and in botany radical refers to the roots of plants. Knowing the etymology in this case will help writers to use the word more precisely and will help readers when they encounter a phrase like *radical image* in a context that seems to rule out meanings of *extreme* or *exaggerated.*

Some etymologies perform a second practical service to the writer by showing him how native words are related to words of similar meaning derived from other languages. The etymology of *light* taken from the *NWD* will illustrate this point (abbreviations have been changed to words): [Middle English *liht;* Anglo-Saxon *leoht;* akin to German *licht;* Indo-European base **leuq-*, to shine, bright, seen also in Latin *lucere,* to shine, *lux, lumen,* light (compare LUCID, LUMINOUS), *luna,* moon (compare LUNAR), etc.].

Third, etymologies can help the writer to learn and remember the meaning of an unfamiliar word. One is likely to remember the meaning of *patriarch,* say, if one knows that it is derived indirectly from Greek *patēr,* father + *archēs,* ruler.

The word *etymology* itself has its origin in Greek *etymon,* the literal or true sense of a word + *-logia,* doctrine, theory, science. Thus, etymology might seem to be the study of the root meaning, and therefore the true or "correct" meaning of a word. In the case of some words, especially scientific and technical words, the etymology is indeed almost a definition. But as we saw in Chapter 23, words may undergo several kinds of change as they continue to be used. Merely because the etymology of *dilapidated,* for example, includes Latin *lapidare,* to throw stones, we need not restrict the word only to a paraphrase of the original Latin meaning, *to throw stones. Dilapidated* clearly means something else today. It has undergone a normal and common variety of word change. Etymologies, then, may or may not be of immediate practical concern to the writer. But if not regarded as necessarily synonymous with the "true" meaning of a word, etymologies can help a writer to remember what a word means and how to use it accurately.

STATUS LABELS AND SUBJECT LABELS

Among the many kinds of information a dictionary supplies about words may be a judgment about the kind of context in which they usually appear. Most words are not restricted to special contexts and require no special labels, but a significant number of words in a dictionary are usually employed only in special situations, and users of language need to know what they are. One important class of restricted words is that which has either grown antiquated or fallen almost completely into disuse. Words no longer used are labeled "obsolete" by most dictionary-makers. Only a few of these are likely to appear in most desk dictionaries. Typical obsolete words are *cockshut* (meaning twilight), *witting* (knowledge or information), *quillet* (quibble). Older words that are still used but only in some special context like prayers or ceremonial language are labeled "archaic," for example, *thine, ye, yea, eke, whilom, haply.* Except for special purposes and rare occasions one should avoid all obsolete and archaic words, for most of which there are contemporary equivalents. Another class of labeled words consists of localisms and expressions peculiar to a region. Thus, *selectman* is usually labeled as belonging to New England speech; *levee* in reference to an embankment is sometimes labeled "Southern U.S." Of greater importance to most writers, however, are those words whose status in the language is shifting and uncertain. About these the writer may need advice. Words and expressions used by only uneducated speakers may be variously labeled "illiterate," "dialect," or "substandard." *Ain't,* for example, is given one or another of these labels in the four desk dictionaries we have mentioned. Other words usually labeled "substandard" or "chiefly dialect" are *reckon* (meaning judge, suppose), *no-how* (not at all), *drownded* (for *drowned*). Most dictionaries include, but label "slang," comparatively recent and colorful words like the following:

windbag	crackpot	corny	pass the buck
scram	hep	goon	schmo
flapdoodle	egghead	goop	junkie
hokum	double cross	to goof	schnozzle

There are words which appear in the speech of cultivated persons, in their letters, and even in their informal writing, but which are rarely found in the most formal prose. Such words may be labeled "colloquial" or "informal." Typical are expressions like the following:

miff	top notch	splurge	cold shoulder
fizzle	poppycock	groggy	ruckus
bunco	shoo-in	to needle (prod)	tie-up
fetching	spoof	bigwig	blues

Colloquial words are difficult to differentiate from slang on the one hand and unrestricted words on the other. If we recognize, furthermore, that usage is constantly changing and that presently it is tending to grow more informal, we should expect dictionaries to differ in their usage labels. For instance, *crackpot* is called slang in the *ACD* and the *SCD*. The *NWD* labels it colloquial, and *Webster 7* leaves it unrestricted. This fact should occasion neither surprise nor dismay if we recall that we are dealing with the judgment of dictionary-makers, not with some absolute standard of correct or incorrect.

In addition to status labels dictionaries often indicate the trade, profession, activity, or special subject with which one or more meanings of a word may be associated. A word like *jib* may have one meaning in general use and a different meaning applied to things nautical; hence, the nautical sense may be indicated by *Naut.*; *scherzo, andante,* and *pizzicato* are often labeled *Music,* and so on.

DEFINITIONS

Each dictionary has its own way of presenting the definitions of a word. To understand fully how a dictionary handles an entry the user should read carefully the explanatory notes on definitions which usually appear in the front matter. Whenever words have more than one meaning, some dictionaries give the oldest meaning first and, wherever practical, the other meanings in order of historical development. This procedure allows the reader to see the semantic evolution of a word and often the relationship among its various senses. Other dictionaries, however, prefer to give the central meaning or the most frequently used meaning first, following with figurative meanings, special meanings, and so on, leaving obsolete, archaic, and rare meanings until last. Some dictionaries include closely related definitions as well. Some also indicate the grammatical forms customarily used with certain words. In defining *different*, for example, the *ACD* observes "unless used absolutely fol. by *from*, often *to*, sometimes *than*; use of *to* and *than* considered improper by many; but the use of *to* is especially common in England." A few minutes spent learning in what order a dictionary lists the various definitions of a word will greatly increase its usefulness to the writer.

SYNONYMS

All collegiate dictionaries help the writer to use words more precisely by listing and discriminating among the synonyms of many words. These synonymies are usually presented at the end or near the end of the entry and are often followed by lists of antonyms. If a writer recognizes, for example, that *old, ancient, venerable, antique, antiquated, antediluvian, archaic,* and *obsolete* are not always interchangeable, he can find how to distinguish them by looking up the synonyms given usually (though not always) after the simplest word in the group. Cross references, however, will generally guide him to the entry where the synonyms are given, but it must be remembered that no two dictionaries are exactly alike. They may not all list the same synonyms for a particular word, and they may present them differently. Still, all collegiate dictionaries list synonyms, recognizing the writer's need to make precise distinctions. For a fuller treatment of synonyms, however, the writer may need to turn to a special dictionary like *Webster's Dictionary of Synonyms,* which we discussed earlier on page 544.

Summary

Dictionaries are indispensable to all kinds of writers. If writers are to communicate with different kinds of readers and achieve varying purposes they must know how their language is being currently used at differing levels of formality. A good dictionary, if it is reasonably up-to-date and well edited, will supply this important information. It is more accurate and more linguistically sophisticated, therefore, to speak of a particular dictionary made at a particular time and place for a particular purpose than to suppose there exists "the dictionary" to which one can appeal as an infallible authority giving judgments of right and wrong, correct and incorrect.

Dictionaries vary widely in cost, size, date, purpose, and editorial quality. Some present only technical terms peculiar to a particular subject or discipline; some present only facts about some restricted area like slang or dialect; some dictionaries stress the historical development of words; some aim to give general information designed more for the ordinary reader and writer than for the scholar or specialist. General dictionaries may be large, containing as many as 400,000 to 500,000 words; or they may be smaller works often called desk dictionaries or collegiate dictionaries, ranging from 75,000 to 150,000 entries.

Although they do not always include the same words or interpret usage in exactly the same way, all general dictionaries give information about spelling and spelling variants, pronunciation, grammatical forms and inflections, etymology, the status of certain words, the various meanings of a word, and its synonyms and antonyms. For this reason the writer will consult a general dictionary more often perhaps than any other work. In doing so he will benefit most from his dictionary if he apreciates both its tremendous value and its limitations.

Exercises

1. All the following compounds have been written as one word. Which are conventionally written as one word and which as two? Which are hyphenated?

allright	grandopera	mailorder
daybed	grandparent	softspoken
daynursery	hitormiss	stagefright
fullback	mailbag	stagestruck

2. How are the following words conventionally divided?

parliament	sportscast	tragedy
melodrama	surgeon	windowsill

3. How does your dictionary give the pronunciation of the following? Note variants.

abdomen	chameleon	foreign	pecan
address	chassis	forehead	pique
Arkansas	coupon	gaol	pumpkin
almond	despicable	gnomic	quay
apogee	desuetude	herb	respite
bouquet	disparate	iodine	Roosevelt
bauxite	economics	issue	schedule
breeches	envelope	jejune	Thames
cacao	extraordinary	ogre	tryst
cacique	falcon	ordure	vagary

4. What grammatical information does your dictionary give about the following?

1. *due to* introducing an adverbial phrase
2. *It's me.*
3. *Drive slow.*
4. *like, as, as if*
5. *different from, different than*
6. *ain't I, aren't I*
7. the plural of *shrimp, attorney general, scissors, gladiolus, measles, hippopotamus*
8. the past tense of *swim, dive*
9. the present tense of *wrought*

5. Find the etymologies of each of the following:

agnostic	butcher	equinox	kaleidoscope
amateur	candidate	error	libertine
amuck	cardinal	finite	mosquito
amu	caricature	flagrant	oligarchy
anemia	carol	goodbye	orchid
August	caterpillar	gnomic	rhetoric
bedlam	civil	gospel	schizophrenia
Bible	dextrous	gymnasium	sophomore
blank	domestic	hippopotamus	tornado
bloomers	dope	idiot	undulate
bowdlerize	dumb	incarnate	uxoricide
bunk	duplicate	jurisdiction	vital

6. Many words used in science begin with the following prefixes. What is the meaning of each one? These, of course, are only a small sample; the general reader as well as the student of science will need to know many others.

a-	co-	hypo-	radio-
auto-	con-	micro-	super-
bi-	dia-	mono-	syn-
bio-	endo-	neo-	tetra-
chloro-	eu-	oxy-	tri-
chromo-	extra-	paleo-	ultra-
chrono-	geo-	peri-	xero-
circum-	hyper-	pyro-	xylo-

7. What status label does your dictionary give the following?

(the) brush-off	double talk	jive	O.K.
chucklehead	fathead	kickback	skid row
cinch	fink	know-how	skulduggery
civvies	henpeck	letdown	socialize
corker	highfalutin	lowbrow	sockdolager
crummy	jerk	neat	yak

8. Discriminate among the meanings of the words in the following groups:

1. flag, ensign, standard, banner, color, pennant
2. healthful, healthy, wholesome, salubrious, hygenic, sanitary
3. impassive, stoic, phlegmatic, apathetic, stolid
4. myth, legend, saga
5. fate, destiny, lot, portion, doom
6. ornate, rococo, baroque, flamboyant, florid
7. brave, courageous, bold, audacious, dauntless, undaunted, intrepid, valiant, valorous, doughty
8. kill, slay, murder, assassinate, dispatch, execute
9. caprice, freak, whim, whimsey, vagary, crotchet
10. show, exhibit, display, expose, parade, flaunt

9. In newspapers, magazines, and recent books find ten or twenty words not appearing in the most recent dictionary. For two or three of these words take down on separate slips or cards examples of the word being used in a sentence. When you have collected several of these citations on separate slips, write a definition of the word. Imitating the format of your dictionary, compose entries for these words, giving as much linguistic information about them as you can.

INDEX

INDEX

CORRECTION SYMBOLS

To identify your mistakes your teacher will use the symbols listed below. Except for those few which are self-evident, a brief statement of meaning follows each symbol, and this statement in turn is followed by a page number referring you to that section of the text where the problem is discussed.

Symbols marked by an asterisk are further analyzed in a second list immediately following this one. Although there is no necessity for his doing so, your teacher may occasionally wish to refer you to this special list in order to indicate more precisely the nature of a mistake. If on your paper you find one of these symbols followed by an abbreviation in parentheses — "CASE (PRON.)" would be an example — turn to this second list. There you will find a more exact explanation of the error along with a reference to the appropriate page. In our example, "CASE (PRON.)" means an error in the case of a pronoun, a matter which is treated on page 417.

GENERAL LIST

AB.	Inappropriate ABBREVIATION, 433
ABST.	ABSTRACT diction; use more specific, concrete diction, 519
AGR. PRON.	PRONOUN does not AGREE with antecedent, 411
*AGR. S./V.	Error in AGREEMENT BETWEEN SUBJECT AND VERB, 406
AMBIG.	Passage is AMBIGUOUS, 342
APOS.	APOSTROPHE, 453
BARB.	BARBARISM; no such word exists in English
*BEGIN.	Poor BEGINNING; study Chapter 6, 73
BRACK.	BRACKET, 459
C.	CARELESS error
CAP.	CAPITALIZE letter(s) indicated, 463
*CASE	Wrong CASE of noun or pronoun, 415
CF.	COMMA FAULT, 436
*CL.	Passage is not CLEAR, 341
CLICHE	534
*CLOS.	CLOSING is inadequate; study Chapter 8, 117
COL.	COLON, 435
*COMMA	438
CONTRAD.	Awkward treatment of CONTRADICTION, 364
CONTRACT.	Inappropriate CONTRACTION; write out full form
CO-ORD.	CO-ORDINATE constructions indicated
CO-ORD. AWK.	AWKWARD CO-ORDINATION, 360
*D.	DICTION; word has wrong or inappropriate meaning
DASH	448
*DEAD.	DEADWOOD; study Chapter 16, 282

DNG.	DANGLING MODIFIER, 345
DOUB. NEG.	DOUBLE NEGATIVE, 370
ELL.	ELLIPSIS, 460
EMPH.	Inadequate EMPHASIS in sentence; study Chapter 17, 312
EX. PT.	EXCLAMATION POINT, 434
FIG.	Inappropriate FIGURE OF SPEECH, 500
*FRAG.	Unallowable FRAGMENT, 366
FRAM. WDS.	Use FRAMING WORDS here, 102
GOB.	GOBBLEDEGOOK; use simpler diction, 529
HY.	HYPHEN, 458
INTER.	Awkward INTERRUPTION, 350
*INVEN.	Inadequate INVENTION; study Chapter 3, 32
INVER.	Awkward INVERSION, 355
L. C.	Set letter(s) indicated in LOWER CASE, 463
LEG.	Writing is not LEGIBLE
LOG. AGR.	Violation of LOGICAL AGREEMENT, 414
MAL.	MALAPROPISM, 519
MEAN.	Passage is without MEANING, 343
MIS. MOD.	MISPLACED MODIFIER, 346
MIX. MET.	MIXED METAPHOR, 499
NEG.	Awkward NEGATION, 369
*OUTLINE	Inadequate OUTLINE; study Chapter 4, 47
OVERSUB.	OVERSUBORDINATION, 362
¶	Begin a new PARAGRAPH
NO ¶	NO PARAGRAPH; run this material into preceding paragraph
*¶ COH.	PARAGRAPH COHERENCE is poor, 141
*¶ DEV.	PARAGRAPH needs more DEVELOPMENT; study Chapters 10–12, 156
*¶ FLOW	There is a gap between the sentences indicated, 144
¶ U.	Lack of PARAGRAPH UNITY, 141
PARAL.	Constructions indicated should be grammatically PARALLEL, 262
PAREN.	PARENTHESES, 459
PER.	PERIOD, 432
PU.	PUNCTUATION is unconventional; study Chapters 21 and 22, 429
PURP.	PURPOSE seems confused; study Chapter 2, 19
P. V.	POINT OF VIEW is inappropriate or inconsistent, 81
Q. M.	QUESTION MARK, 433
QUOT.	QUOTATION MARK, 454
READER	Consider READER more carefully, 8

REF.	REFERENCE of pronoun is not clear
REV.	Work requires more careful REVISION, 64
SEMICOL.	SEMICOLON, 436
SENT. ANAL.	SENTENCE ANALYSIS; sentences do not adequately analyze topic, 357
SENT. OVER.	SENTENCE is OVERLOADED, 359
SENT. RHY.	SENTENCE RHYTHM is inappropriate; study Chapter 19, 375
SHIFT. CON.	SHIFTED CONSTRUCTION, 421
SIGN.	Passage requires more SIGNPOSTS, 98
SP.	SPELLING error, 550
SUB.	SUBORDINATE passage indicated, 363
SUB. IMP.	IMPROPER SUBORDINATION; key idea has wrongly been subordinated, 363
TENSE CON.	Error in TENSE CONSISTENCY, 425
TENSE SEQ.	Inappropriate TENSE SEQUENCE, 424
*TRANS.	Inadequate TRANSITION between paragraphs, 105
TRITE	307
TYPO.	TYPOGRAPHICAL ERROR
UNDERLINE	461
VAGUE	VAGUE diction; choose more precise word, 518
VULG.	VULGATE; use more formal diction, 523

SPECIAL LIST

AGR. S./V. Error in AGREEMENT BETWEEN SUBJECT AND VERB
(ANTIC.) Error due to ANTICIPATORY CONSTRUCTION, 408
(ATTRACT.) Error due to ATTRACTION, 409
(COLL. N.) Error due to COLLECTIVE NOUN, 406
(COMP. S.) Error due to COMPOUND SUBJECT, 407
(FALSE COMP.) Error due to FALSE COMPOUND, 408
(INV.) Error due to INVERSION, 409
(PRON.) Error due to PRONOUN that is grammatically singular, 406

BEGIN. Poor BEGINNING
(ANNOUNCE.) Poor ANNOUNCEMENT OF TOPIC, 74
(INTEREST) Beginning lacks INTEREST, 84
(LIMIT.) Topic inadequately LIMITED, 79
(PLAN) Need to indicate PLAN of essay, 83

CASE Wrong CASE of noun or pronoun
(GEN.) Error involving GENITIVE CASE of noun, 415
(PRON.) Error in CASE of PRONOUN, 417

CL. Passage is not CLEAR
(C./E.) Vague treatment of CAUSE AND EFFECT, 364
(INT.) Clarity obscured by INTERRUPTING CONSTRUCTION, 350
(INV.) Awkward INVERSION, 355
(PARAL.) Ambiguous PARALLELISM, 356

CLOS. CLOSING is inadequate
(CYC. RET.) Use CYCLIC RETURN, 122
(JUDG.) Final JUDGMENT called for, 119

(RHYTHM)	Vary RHYTHM for better closing, 123
(SUM.)	SUMMARY needed, 118
(TERM. WDS.)	Use TERMINAL WORDS, 121

COMMA

(ADJ.)	COMMA misused with ADJECTIVE, 441
(ADV.)	COMMA misused with ADVERB, 443
(CLAUSE)	COMMA misused between CLAUSES, 446
(L./S.)	COMMA misused with LIST or SERIES, 447
(M. E.)	COMMA misused with MAIN ELEMENTS, 439

DEAD. DEADWOOD

(ADJ.)	Use ADJECTIVE as noun, 305
(ADV.)	Use ADVERB, 294
(ADV. CL.)	Awkward ADVERBIAL CLAUSE, 293
(ANT. CST.)	Wordy ANTICIPATORY CONSTRUCTION, 292
(BIG WORD)	WORD TOO BIG, requires too much modification, 301
(COLON)	Use COLON (or DASH) for concision, 299
(CONN.)	Overlong CONNECTIVE, 305
(D. A.)	Unnecessary DEFINITE ARTICLE, 305
(D. W. D.)	DISTINCTION WITHOUT DIFFERENCE, 287
(ELLIP.)	Use ELLIPSIS for economy, 298
(GER.)	Use GERUND for economy, 306
(IND. MOD.)	INDIRECT MODIFICATION, 294
(M. E.)	Inefficient use of MAIN ELEMENTS, 292
(O. E.)	OVEREXPLICITNESS, 288
(O. Q.)	OVERQUALIFICATION, 291
(PARAL.)	Use PARALLELISM for concision, 298
(PART.)	PARTICIPLE would be more economical, 296
(PASS.)	Wordy use of the PASSIVE, 303
(PIL. VBS.)	PILING UP VERBS, 304
(PRET. D.)	PRETENTIOUS DICTION, 307
(PRON.)	Use PRONOUN as substantive, 304
(RED.)	REDUNDANCY, 290
(STATE.)	Unnecessary STATEMENT, 290
(SUB.)	SUBORDINATE for economy, 297
(U. I.)	UNDEVELOPED IDEA, 287
(UN. DEF.)	UNNECESSARY DEFINITION, 288
(VERB)	VERB not used communicatively, 302
(W. S.)	WRONG SUBJECT, 287

DICTION	
(ALLIT.)	Excessive ALLITERATION, 532
(EUPH.)	EUPHEMISM; use straightforward diction, 534
(INCONST.)	INCONSISTENT DICTION, 525
(INFORM.)	DICTION too INFORMAL, 521
(FORM.)	DICTION too FORMAL, 521
(RHYME)	Accidental or unpleasant RHYME, 533
FRAG.	Unallowable FRAGMENT
(ADV. CL.)	Detached ADVERBIAL CLAUSE, 367
(MOD. N.)	Detached MODIFIED NOUN, 368
(PART.)	Detached PARTICIPIAL CONSTRUCTION, 368
INVEN.	Inadequate INVENTION
(AD./DIS.)	Develop topics of ADVANTAGE and/or DISADVANTAGE, 36
(C./E.)	Develop topics of CAUSE and/or EFFECT, 35
(DEF.)	Develop topics of DEFINITION, 34
OUTLINE	Inadequate OUTLINE
(ANAL.)	Violation of rules of ANALYSIS, 50
(FORM.)	Violation of rules of FORMAT, 48
¶ COH.	PARAGRAPH COHERENCE
(ORDER)	Idea indicated out of proper ORDER in paragraph, 142
(REL.)	Idea indicated not RELEVANT to topic, 142
¶ DEV.	PARAGRAPH DEVELOPMENT
(ANALOGY)	Use ANALOGY, 175
(ANALYSIS)	Make closer ANALYSIS, 159
(C./E.)	Develop CAUSES and/or EFFECTS, 181
(COMPAR.)	Work out a COMPARISON (or CONTRAST), 168
(DEF.)	Develop DEFINITION, 188
(ILLUS.)	ILLUSTRATION needed, 157
(NEG.)	Use NEGATIVE DEVELOPMENT, 199
(QUAL.)	Topic requires QUALIFICATION, 196
(RESTATE.)	Point deserves RESTATEMENT, 161
¶ FLOW	
(CONN.)	Add CONNECTIVE word or phrase, 147
(ORG. ELEM.)	Use ORGANIZING ELEMENT and FRAMING WORDS, 151
(REPEAT)	REPEAT key term, 145
(SYN. PAT.)	Unify sentences by SYNTACTIC PATTERNING, 149

TRANS. Inadequate TRANSITION between paragraphs
(ADD.) ADDITIVE TRANSITION needed, 109
(ADV.) ADVERSATIVE TRANSITION needed, 106
(C./E.) CAUSE/EFFECT TRANSITION needed, 108